6208

Dictionary of Literary Biography • Volume Forty-three

American Newspaper Journalists, 1690-1872

Dictionary of Literary Biography

Documentary Series

Yearbooks

Dictionary of Literary Biography • Volume Forty-three

American Newspaper Journalists, 1690-1872

6208

Edited by
Perry J. Ashley
University of South Carolina

A Bruccoli Clark Book
Gale Research Company • Book Tower • Detroit, Michigan 48226

Manufactured by Edwards Brothers, Inc.
Ann Arbor, Michigan
Printed in the United States of America

Library of Congress Cataloging-in-Publication Data
Main entry under title:

American newspaper journalists, 1690-1872.

   (Dictionary of literary biography; v. 43)
   "A Bruccoli Clark book."
   Includes index.
   1. Journalists—United States—Biography.
I. Ashley, Perry J.   II. Series.
PN4871.A48 1985   070'.92'2 [B]   85-20575
ISBN 0-8103-1721-4

For "Grandmother" Ashley

Who Inspired Four Generations

Contents

Plan of the Series

. . . Almost the most prodigious asset of a country, and perhaps its most precious possession, is its native literary product—when that product is fine and noble and enduring.

Mark Twain*

The advisory board, the editors, and the publisher of the *Dictionary of Literary Biography* are joined in endorsing Mark Twain's declaration. The literature of a nation provides an inexhaustible resource of permanent worth. It is our expectation that this endeavor will make literature and its creators better understood and more accessible to students and the literate public, while satisfying the standards of teachers and scholars.

To meet these requirements, *literary biography* has been construed in terms of the author's achievement. The most important thing about a writer is his writing. Accordingly, the entries in *DLB* are career biographies, tracing the development of the author's canon and the evolution of his reputation.

The publication plan for *DLB* resulted from two years of preparation. The project was proposed to Bruccoli Clark by Frederick G. Ruffner, president of the Gale Research Company, in November 1975. After specimen entries were prepared and typeset, an advisory board was formed to refine the entry format and develop the series rationale. In meetings held during 1976, the publisher, series editors, and advisory board approved the scheme for a comprehensive biographical dictionary of persons who contributed to North American literature. Editorial work on the first volume began in January 1977, and it was published in 1978.

In order to make *DLB* more than a reference tool and to compile volumes that individually have claim to status as literary history, it was decided to organize volumes by topic or period or genre. Each of these freestanding volumes provides a biographical-bibliographical guide and overview for a particular area of literature. We are convinced that this organization—as opposed to a single alphabet method—constitutes a valuable innovation in the presentation of reference material. The volume plan necessarily requires many decisions for the placement and treatment of authors who might properly be included in two or three volumes. In some instances a major figure will be included in separate volumes, but with different entries emphasizing the aspect of his career appropriate to each volume. Ernest Hemingway, for example, is represented in *American Writers in Paris, 1920-1939* by an entry focusing on his expatriate apprenticeship; he is also in *American Novelists, 1910-1945* with an entry surveying his entire career. Each volume includes a cumulative index of subject authors. The final *DLB* volume will be a comprehensive index to the entire series.

With volume ten in 1982 it was decided to enlarge the scope of *DLB* beyond the literature of the United States. By the end of 1984 fourteen volumes treating British literature had been published, and volumes for Commonwealth and Modern European literature were in progress. The series has been further augmented by the *DLB Yearbooks* (since 1981) which update published entries and add new entries to keep the *DLB* current with contemporary activity. There have also been occasional *DLB Documentary Series* volumes which provide biographical and critical background source materials for figures whose work is judged to have particular interest for students. One of these companion volumes is entirely devoted to Tennessee Williams.

The purpose of *DLB* is not only to provide reliable information in a convenient format but also to place the figures in the larger perspective of literary history and to offer appraisals of their accomplishments by qualified scholars.

We define literature as the *intellectual commerce of a nation:* not merely as belles lettres, but as that ample and complex process by which ideas are generated, shaped, and transmitted. *DLB* entries are not limited to "creative writers" but extend to other figures who in this time and in this way influenced the mind of a people. Thus the series encompasses historians, journalists, publishers, and screenwriters. By this means readers of *DLB* may be aided to perceive literature not as cult scripture in the keeping of cultural high priests, but as at the center of a nation's life.

DLB includes the major writers appropriate to each volume and those standing in the ranks immediately behind them. Scholarly and critical counsel has been sought in deciding which minor figures to include and how full their entries should be. Wherever possible, useful references will be made to figures who do not warrant separate entries.

Each *DLB* volume has a volume editor responsible for planning the volume, selecting the figures for inclusion, and assigning the entries. Volume editors are also responsible for preparing, where appropriate, appendices surveying the major periodicals and literary and intellectual movements for their volumes, as well as lists of further readings. Work on the series as a whole is coordinated at the Bruccoli Clark editorial center in Columbia, South Carolina, where the editorial staff is responsible for the accuracy of the published volumes.

One feature that distinguishes *DLB* is the illustration policy—its concern with the iconography of literature. Just as an author is influenced by his surroundings, so is the reader's understanding of the author enhanced by a knowledge of his environment. Therefore *DLB* volumes include not only drawings, paintings, and photographs of authors, often depicting them at various stages in their careers, but also illustrations of their families and places where they lived. Title pages are regularly reproduced in facsimile along with dust jackets for modern authors. The dust jackets are a special feature of *DLB* because they often document better than anything else the way in which an author's

work was launched in its own time. Specimens of the writers' manuscripts are included when feasible.

A supplement to *DLB*—tentatively titled *A Guide, Chronology, and Glossary for American Literature*—will outline the history of literature in North America and trace the influences that shaped it. This volume will provide a framework for the study of American literature by means of chronological tables, literary affiliation charts, glossarial entries, and concise surveys of the major movements. It has been planned to stand on its own as a vade mecum, providing a ready-reference guide to the study of American literature as well as a companion to the *DLB* volumes for American literature.

Samuel Johnson rightly decreed that "The chief glory of every people arises from its authors." The purpose of the *Dictionary of Literary Biography* is to compile literary history in the surest way available to us—by accurate and comprehensive treatment of the lives and work of those who contributed to it.

The *DLB* Advisory Board

*From an unpublished section of Mark Twain's autobiography, copyright © by the Mark Twain Company.

Foreword

This volume contains the stories of those great pioneers who created the American press and nurtured it from a position of complete subjection to authority in the late seventeenth and early eighteenth centuries to the political and economic independence of the "penny press," which catered to the newly enfranchised working class of the nineteenth century.

In 1690 the first American newspaper—Benjamin Harris's *Publick Occurrences*—was banned after one issue because Harris had not submitted to the colonial licensing laws. The years between that event and the American Revolution represented constant struggles by newspaper publishers to exercise their right as "free born British citizens" to print without prior restraint the social, political, and economic debates of the day. Writers such as "Father of Candor" argued that ideas and opinions which do not lead to destruction of life or property should be of no concern to the "civil authority" and that only those expressions which led to civil disorder should be tried in the courts. Lawyers argued, as Andrew Hamilton did in the case of John Peter Zenger, that printer/editors had the right to express their opinions and to defend them on the basis of their truth.

Even as these debates continued, colonial printers were laying the foundations of modern American journalism: John Campbell started the *Boston News-Letter*, the first continuous American newspaper; James Franklin tweaked the noses of the establishment with his lively *New-England Courant;* Andrew Bradford founded the first newspaper outside of Boston, the *American Weekly Mercury* in Philadelphia; and William Parks started the first newspapers in both Maryland and Virginia. Such entrepreneurs as Benjamin Franklin and James Parker established, through various partnerships and copublishing arrangements, rudimentary newspaper "chains."

As the American Revolution approached, newspaper publishers were aligning themselves with the opposing factions in the debate over separation from British authority. On one side, Patriot editors such as William Bradford III, Benjamin Edes, John Holt, and Isaiah Thomas risked imprisonment and confiscation of their property for their support of independence and their pub-

lication of the fiery writings of men like Samuel Adams and Thomas Paine; on the other side, Loyalist editors such as James Rivington faced the threat of mob violence for their opposition to breaking away from the mother country. There were those, such as Hugh Gaine and Benjamin Towne, who switched sides according to which army was currently dominant in their areas; and those, such as William Goddard, who courageously resisted pressure from both sides and allowed both points of view a forum for expression.

In the post-Revolutionary years, when the attention of the nation was being turned to debates over the adoption of the Constitution, alliance with France, the relative strength of the new states compared to the national government, and political party control over the central government, the nation's press once again was divided as editors chose sides with political parties and, in return, received financial support and political patronage from the dominant parties. The issues were battled out, sometimes with vitriolic and scurrilous invective, by such Federalist editors as William Cobbett, Joseph Dennie, John Fenno, Benjamin Russell, Noah Webster, and Republican (or Democratic) editors including Benjamin Franklin Bache, William Duane, Philip Freneau, Samuel Harrison Smith, William Winston Seaton, and Thomas Ritchie. In spite of the First Amendment guarantee of freedom of the press, there were still attempts to use government power to silence editorial opponents—mainly through libel suits and the short-lived Alien and Sedition Acts of 1798. Meanwhile, far from the hotbed of political partisanship in the successive national capitals of New York, Philadelphia, and Washington, D.C., journalism was moving westward with the frontier through the efforts of editors such as John Bradford in Kentucky.

As the nineteenth century opened, all of the new states and most of the older ones began to incorporate universal manhood suffrage into their constitutions and a new age of egalitarianism was inaugurated. Journalism historian Michael Schudson observes that America underwent "a democratic revolution. It did so beginning in the years after 1815 and reaching a height in the 1830s and 1840s. In these decades the country was transformed from a liberal mercantilist republic, still cradled in aristocratic values, family and deference, to an egalitarian market democracy, where money had new power, the individual new standing, and the pursuit of self-interest new honor." Such a reform demanded public education and the means by which the newly franchised voter could be an informed, participating citizen.

The penny press, a press for the masses, began with Benjamin Day's *New York Sun* in 1833 and grew in response to the need for political, economic, and social information; the *Sun* was joined over the next two decades by other one-cent papers, including Arunah Abell's *Philadelphia Public Ledger* and *Baltimore Sun,* James Gordon Bennett's *New York Herald,* Horace Greeley's *New-York Tribune,* and Henry Raymond's *New-York Times.*

Changes in news content and writing style to meet the needs of a barely literate readership enabled the press for the masses to grow to unprecedented levels in only a few years. The number of daily newspapers increased from 42 in 1820 to 574 by 1870, while the number of weeklies rose from 512 to 5,091 in the same half-century. While the population increased about 400 percent, the circulation of the daily press bounded forward at the astronomical rate of 7,700 percent, from about 33,000 in 1820 to 2,601,000 in 1870.

Mechanical innovations were also essential to the rise of the mass-circulated, "populist" press. The introduction of the steam-powered cylinder press during the first decade of the nineteenth century increased daily production rates to almost 10,000 "perfected" newspapers per hour by 1870. The telegraph, introduced in 1844, expanded the potential of the daily newspapers by providing instantaneous news. By 1879 there were over 100,000 miles of lines bringing fresh intelligence on a continuous basis. Distribution of newspapers was enhanced by the advent of the railroad in the 1830s; by 1870 over 52,000 miles of rails carried news across the nation.

In addition to the mass-circulation penny press, smaller papers sprang up in the first half of the nineteenth century to promote various radical social and economic views. Among these were George Henry Evans's several labor-movement newspapers and Anne Royall's early muckraking sheets, *Paul Pry* and the *Huntress.* More important in the context of the growing sectional conflicts were abolitionist papers, such as those of Henry Ward Beecher, Cassius Marcellus Clay, Frederick Douglass, William Lloyd Garrison, and Jane Grey Swisshelm. Extremist Southern editors such as Duff Green and Robert Barnwell Rhett replied to aboli-

tionist agitation with defenses of states' rights and calls for nullification and even secession, while more moderate ones—notably George D. Prentice in Louisville—opposed abolitionism but sought to preserve the Union.

Adding to the tension between the sections of the nation was the influence of the still-dominant partisan political press. Important Democratic editors included Francis P. Blair of the *Washington* (D.C.) *Globe* and William Cullen Bryant of the *New York Evening Post;* the Whig party was represented by James Watson Webb's *Morning Courier and New-York Enquirer* and Samuel Bowles III's *Springfield* (Mass.) *Republican,* along with Greeley's *Tribune* and Raymond's *Times.* Joseph Medill and his *Chicago Tribune* were influential in securing the replacement of the Whigs by the Republicans and the nomination of Abraham Lincoln for president by the new party. The partisanship of the press during this period sometimes degenerated into street brawls and duels between editors of opposed convictions.

The petty feuds of the party journalists were swallowed up in the vastly greater conflict that began in April 1861. Several hundred correspondents and illustrators covered all fronts in the Civil War for an anxious American audience. B. S. Osbon was a leading correspondent for the North, as was Felix Gregory de Fontaine for the South. *Frank Leslie's Illustrated Newspaper* brought the look of war to its readers with woodcuts based on sketches by its artists in the field. Editors on both sides were quick to criticize war policies of their respective governments of which they disapproved; Bennett of the *New York Herald* and John M. Daniel of the *Richmond Examiner* were prominent in this regard. The disputes continued into the Reconstruction period, with the Democratic papers generally favoring a moderate policy toward the South and the Republican papers—with the notable exception of Raymond's *New-York Times*—advocating a hard line.

The American press has grown in response to the demand for news on the part of its readers. In the first half of the eighteenth century, for example, the early newspapers provided mercantile "intelligence," literary materials, and news from "back home" in England. But as the debate over independence began to take shape, the newspapers became intimately involved and divided over the issues.

By the second decade of the nineteenth century, as the focus and strength of the nation were turned to westward expansion, economic growth and development, political equalitarianism, and "market democracy," emphasis within the press once again shifted to reflect these needs. Newspapers either changed their content to meet the needs of their readers or were forced to yield to the new penny papers.

Walter Lippmann once observed that the American press has passed through four distinct stages of development: control by government, control by political parties, control by the public, and, finally, control by professional managers.

American journalism had substantially passed through the first two stages and was well into the third stage by the last quarter of the nineteenth century. The transition to the final stage, which has only been completed in our own time, is covered in three earlier volumes in the *Dictionary of Literary Biography* series.

—Perry J. Ashley

Acknowledgments

This book was produced by BC Research Karen L. Rood is senior editor for the *Dictionary of Literary Biography* series. Philip B. Dematteis was the in-house editor.

Art supervisor is Patricia M. Flanagan. Copyediting supervisor is Patricia Coate. Production coordinator is Kimberly Casey. Typesetting supervisor is Laura Ingram. The production staff includes Rowena Betts, Tara P. Deal, Kathleen M. Flanagan, Joyce Fowler, Pamela Haynes, Judith K. Ingle, Victoria Jakes, Vickie Lowers, Beatrice McClain, Judith McCray, George Stone Saussy, and Joycelyn R. Smith. Jean W. Ross is permissions editor. Joseph Caldwell, photography editor, and James Adam Sutton did photographic copy work for the volume.

Walter W. Ross and Jennifer Castillo did the library research with the assistance of the staff at the Thomas Cooper Library of the University of South Carolina: Lynn Barron, Daniel Boice, Connie Crider, Kathy Eckman, Michael Freeman, Gary Geer, David L. Haggard, Jens Holley, David Lincove, Marcia Martin, Dana Rabon, Jean Rhyne, Jan Squire, Paula Swope, and Ellen Tillett.

Professor Frederic B. Farrar of Temple University provided valuable assistance in securing illustrations for this volume.

Dictionary of Literary Biography • Volume Forty-three

American Newspaper Journalists, 1690-1872

Dictionary of Literary Biography

Arunah S. Abell

(10 August 1806-19 April 1888)

Jon A. Roosenraad
University of Florida

MAJOR POSITIONS HELD: Founder and co-owner, *Philadelphia Public Ledger* (1836-1864); founder, owner, and editor, *Baltimore Sun* (1837-1888).

In the *Baltimore Sun,* Arunah S. Abell created the prototype of the impersonal, institutional newspaper that today dominates American journalism. As an advocate of the "penny press" he helped push the newspaper from a medium for the elite to a carrier of information to the common citizen. He developed the modern newspaper in its management style, physical plant, and institutional strength. Abell's *Sun* was the national leader in finding new methods to gain news from its start in 1837 until the Civil War.

Arunah Shepherdson Abell was born in East Providence, Rhode Island, on 10 August 1806 to Caleb and Elona Shepherdson Abell. His great-grandfather Sir Robert Abell had come to America from England about 1630; Abell's grandfather and father were officers in the military, his father in the War of 1812.

Abell attended school in East Providence until the age of fourteen, when he started working for a dealer in West Indian goods. Two years later, in 1822, his father gained him a printer's apprenticeship at the *Providence Patriot.* In 1827 he moved to Boston, where he became foreman of a large print shop. He left Boston in 1828 for New York because of the demand for journeyman printers there. Abell, who was qualified as a master printer, went to work for the *Mercantile Advertiser,* where he met Benjamin Day, William Swain, and Azariah Simmons.

Day started his own print shop in 1831 but

Arunah S. Abell

cherished a dream of owning a paper aimed at the increasingly literate "common man." Day discussed this idea for a one-cent, more reader-oriented paper with Abell and Swain, who thought poorly of the idea and warned Day against trying it. Unconvinced, Day put his idea into practice on 4 September 1833 with the first edition of the *New York Sun;* Swain became the paper's foreman. The *Sun* quickly became successful and a model for other

Abell (center) and his partners in the Philadelphia Public
Ledger: *William M. Swain (left) and
Azariah H. Simmons*

papers: it was cheap; its philosophy and content
were aimed at the working and common man; it
was filled with stories of crime, pathos, and humor;
and it editorially attacked the six-cent papers as
conservative and elitist.

Finally convinced of the merits of Day's idea,
Abell entered into a partnership with Swain and
Simmons in 1836 to start a penny paper in Philadelphia that would follow the *Sun*'s formula for content and that would be politically neutral. The first
issue of the *Public Ledger* appeared on 25 March.
While it was not the first penny press in Philadelphia, it was the first successful one.

Abell saw possibilities for a similar penny paper in Baltimore, ninety miles from Philadelphia.
A major manufacturing and trade center, Baltimore already had six dailies—the *American, Federal
Gazette, Republican, Chronicle, Patriot,* and *Transcript*—all appealing to the higher commercial and
financial classes and with small circulations. Abell's
partners were at first opposed to this move but
relented and agreed to back the venture only on

the condition that Abell personally take charge of
the new paper.

The *Baltimore Sun,* a not-so-vague copy in content and name of the *New York Sun,* began publishing on 17 May 1837 by giving away copies to
all 15,000 houses in the city. In format and policy
it was another *Public Ledger,* with facetious police
and court reporting and great attention to local
happenings. The lead story in the first edition concerned a local banking crisis. The banks' insistence
on redeeming personal checks in their own paper
money instead of in gold or silver greatly affected
the common man in Baltimore and other cities and
became the first "popular cause" the *Sun* would
adopt. Its coverage of this issue and its editorial
attacks on the banks were immensely popular and
helped establish the success of the *Sun,* with a first-
year circulation of 12,000.

From the beginning Abell voiced many of the
trivial and personal features common in penny papers and developed an "impersonal" style of reporting that became a forerunner of modern
journalism. The paper was editorially independent, free from partisan political controversy. In
May 1837 the paper editorialized that "we do not
attach ourselves to the chariot wheels of any political party . . . we go for the good of the whole American people if we know how to do so."

On 23 December 1838 Abell and Mary Fox
of Peekskill, New York, were married in Philadelphia. The couple had twelve children, nine of
whom reached maturity.

With the death of Simmons in 1855, Swain
and Abell formed a new partnership controlling
the Philadelphia and Baltimore papers, although
each paper remained editorially independent of
the other. Abell remained a partner with Swain in
Philadelphia until 1864, when he sold his interest
to George Childs. In 1868, with the death of Swain,
Abell became sole proprietor of the *Sun.*

Swain and Abell became extremely rich from
ownership of the two papers; according to one estimate, the thirty-year partnership netted each man
three million dollars. While that figure is disputed,
one indication of the size of the profits was the
purchase of Guilford, an estate near Baltimore, by
Abell in 1837 for $475,000 cash. On the fortieth
anniversary of the *Sun* in 1877, the *Maryland Journal,* a Baltimore weekly, called Abell the wealthiest
newspaper publisher in the world, except for the
proprietor of the *Times* of London.

One reason for the financial success of the
Sun was Abell's management skills, which led the
paper to pioneer in three major areas in the de-

THE  SUN.

VOL. I.—NO. 1.]   BALTIMORE, WEDNESDAY, MAY 17, 1837.   [PRICE ONE CENT.

Front page of the first issue of Abell's Baltimore Sun

The Sun Iron Building, the prototype of modern skyscrapers because the weight of the building rested on interior columns and not on the exterior walls. The building was erected in 1850 and destroyed in the great Baltimore fire of 1904. This picture was taken in 1886.

velopment of the modern newspaper: where the paper was printed, how it was printed, and how it was distributed.

The *Sun* had moved from its original location on Light Street in February 1838 and remained in its second location at Gay and Baltimore Streets. When it was time to move again, Abell, intent on having the finest newspaper building in the nation, contracted James Bogardus of New York to build such a structure at Baltimore and South Streets. Bogardus had erected in 1847 a factory constructed on the new principle which he had urged in vain on other New York builders—a building with a cast iron frame supporting the weight on interior columns and not exterior walls, as was then common. While the *Sun* building rose only five stories, it was the prototype of the modern urban skyscraper. Known as the "Sun Iron Building," it would house the paper until it was destroyed in the great Baltimore fire of 1904.

Into this new building, Abell in 1853 placed large new rotary presses which made the *Sun* the most efficiently printed paper in the nation. When Richard Hoe was unable to convince any New York papers to use his new presses, he turned to his friends Abell and Swain. While the *Public Ledger* in Philadelphia was the first paper to be printed on a rotary press, it lacked the space for large enough presses to print its entire run. The *Sun,* with its new building, became the first major paper to permanently convert to the presses which were to revolutionize newspaper printing.

Abell's third major innovation was in using individual carriers for home deliveries. The carriers were independent merchants who got the papers in bulk from the *Sun* and resold them to individuals along a certain route.

Abell's real mark in American journalism, however, came in devising innovative ways to get news to the *Sun* hours and even days before other leading national papers could get it. Abell was a pioneer in systematic news gathering, constantly striving for speed in obtaining and printing news.

His first news "wire" in 1837 utilized carrier pigeons to carry news back and forth to the *Sun*'s sister paper in Philadelphia. For the next ten years, until the telegraph network was developed, Abell kept between 400 and 500 trained birds to transport news to Philadelphia, New York, and Washington.

The nation's first "hot line" to the capital started on 6 September 1837, when Abell had a reporter in Washington run a copy of President Martin Van Buren's address to Congress to the Baltimore and Ohio train station for delivery to Baltimore in less than two hours. Abell published the address in its entirety, filling most of pages two and three and bumping most of the day's advertising from the paper. Until then, papers outside the capital waited until they received copies of Washington papers and reprinted their accounts of government action or speeches.

In 1838, Abell added his own pony express system from Washington to relay presidential messages and Congressional votes. Because Baltimore was a major seaport, news from other American ports was of great interest. To gain such news, Abell established a pony express service to Boston. In 1840 he chartered a train to rush President Benjamin Harrison's inaugural address to Baltimore and on to Philadelphia. A staff of forty-nine printers had the *Baltimore Sun* on the streets with the complete text less than two hours after it was delivered at the Capitol.

The *Sun,* as was the custom then as now, exchanged editions with other major papers throughout the nation. The constant speed with which the *Sun* and *Public Ledger* published news made those papers—especially the *Sun*—major sources of Washington and Southern news for papers in New York and Boston. Papers in those cities, in turn, made sure the *Sun* received their news on Northern commerce and shipping.

Besides exchanging individual news accounts, Abell and the *Sun* pioneered in cooperative news gathering with papers sharing their resources, starting with the *Public Ledger* in 1841. In 1847 the *Sun* and *Ledger* joined with the *New York Herald* in the first cooperative telegraph news service, a forerunner of the Associated Press wire service.

The telegraph thus became an almost "immediate" way for Abell to transport news. Swain was one of the incorporators of the company formed to promote Samuel Morse's invention; and Abell used the columns of his paper, which was well read in Washington, to demand Congressional help in subsidizing Morse's work. After Congress granted $30,000 dollars in 1842 to construct an experimental line from Washington to Baltimore, Abell and Swain pooled their own money to extend it to Philadelphia.

The *Sun* carried the first published account of Morse's initial message, sent on 25 May 1844 from the Supreme Court room in Washington to the Baltimore and Ohio station in Baltimore, and consisting of the words "What hath God wrought?" Despite Abell's personal and financial interest in the telegraph, this historic moment was not given great play, running on page two under the heading "Local News" and consisting of only eleven lines. The *Sun* used the new service at first to gain the tallies of important Congressional votes, but proved its merit in copy transmission on 11 May 1846 when the *Sun* and *Ledger* published exclusively the complete text of a speech to Congress by President James Polk sent entirely over the telegraph. This was considered such an important breakthrough that the Academy of Sciences in Paris later published the *Sun*'s telegraphic copy of the message side by side with a copy of the president's remarks as delivered in Washington.

The telegraph provided the final link in what would become Abell's most famous news transportation accomplishment—his network of wire, railroads, steamboats, stagecoaches, and "sixty blooded horses" to bring news of the Mexican War back to the *Sun* and the Northern papers it fed faster than mail delivery—often by thirty hours— and in one case, faster than the government's own official delivery system. With the outbreak of fight-

ing in 1846, national attention shifted southward, and Abell's *Sun* was looked to for leadership in providing news. New Orleans became the key point for receiving news of the war because it was the army's base for troop and supply movement. The *Sun* entered into a cooperative venture with the *Picayune* in New Orleans to gather news, as it had earlier with the *New York Herald.* The most successful use of this private news service came on 10 April 1847 when the *Sun* received a report of the fall of Vera Cruz twelve days previously—thus assuring an American victory in the war—before the official army message reached Washington. When the news was received in Baltimore, Abell telegraphed Washington to inform President Polk of the American victory!

Baltimore and the *Sun* suffered because of the Civil War. The city was tied economically to the South and it slipped in population and importance. Despite its reputation as the gateway to the South, the city was not involved politically or in battles. The paper had generally ignored the national slavery issue and the history-making election of 1860. Since Maryland was a border state, Abell and other Baltimore editors were threatened by citizens from both sides and were suspected by the army of Southern sympathies. During the war the paper even lost its claim to be a "penny paper" as the price went to two cents in 1864.

After the war, Baltimore grew old in a hurry—the prostration of the South swept away its only market. The city was passed in national importance by New York and Philadelphia and the new midwestern cities of Chicago, Detroit, and St. Louis. What had been a vibrant and aggressive city became a slow, dull town, and the *Sun* became conservative, stodgy, and dull, too. Safety seemed to be its motto—sober and dignified, it ignored the vulgarities of politics. Even as local Baltimore politics in the 1870s became very corrupt, the *Sun* remained apathetic.

The *Sun*'s only real editorial battle, fought mainly because of the growing editorial leadership of Abell's son George, came in the early 1880s when the paper attacked the failure of judges to rotate from one court to another as prescribed by law. The *Sun* supported an independent slate for the judiciary in 1882; the independents won and the courts were cleaned up. But instead of following this victory with other campaigns, the *Sun* returned to its previous apathy and the *Evening News* became the chief critic of local government and politics.

On 17 May 1887, the *Sun*'s fiftieth anniversary, Abell made his sons Edwin, George, and

Walter partners. The paper grew editorially, and by the end of the century it had built a strong reputation for honesty and integrity and had won fame as a fighter against corrupt local and state political machines.

Abell died at 3:05 A.M. on 19 April 1888, less than a year after giving up sole control of the paper. The *New York Times* obituary said that he died of old age, the "general failure of vital powers," and continued: "Mr. Abell exhibited enterprise, sound judgment and a tenacity of purpose which helped him carry projects to a successful issue in spite of discouragements."

Abell had made the *Sun* noteworthy for impartial enterprise; for fair, orderly business and editorial methods; and for moderation and trustworthiness in presenting the news. The paper never carried the obvious personal imprint of Abell; his theory from the beginning was that a newspaper is the composite product of many minds and should not be associated with any single personality. For almost fifty years the paper did not run by-lines, even from its Washington columnists. The *Sun*, as a composite personality, was Abell's ideal. The paper's success would rest on something more permanent than the genius of one man. Abell's conception of the newspaper as an independent institution, devoted to the publication of news, was his greatest contribution to journalism.

Reference:

Gerald Johnson, Frank Kent, H. L. Mencken, and Hamilton Owens, *The Sunpapers of Baltimore* (New York: Knopf, 1937).

Samuel Adams
(27 September 1722-2 October 1803)

Rosemarian V. Staudacher
Marquette University

See also the Adams entry in *DLB 31, American Colonial Writers, 1735-1781.*

MAJOR POSITION HELD: Founder and editor, *Boston Independent Advertiser* (1748).

BOOKS: *An Appeal to the World; or, A Vindication of the Town of Boston . . .* (Boston: Printed & sold by Edes & Gill, 1769);
The Writings of Samuel Adams, edited by Harry A. Cushing, 4 volumes (New York: Putnam's, 1904-1908).

Strictly speaking, Samuel Adams was not a journalist. That is, his principal occupation was not that of a reporter, editor, or publisher of newspapers. He was a prominent statesman in the era of the American Revolution who wrote prolifically and effectively, using the press to express his political beliefs and agitate for the cause of the colonies' separation from the British crown. Francis Bernard, British governor of Massachusetts in 1760, once said of him: "Every dip of his pen stung like a horned snake."

Samuel Adams was born on 16 September 1722 in Boston. His father, Samuel, a deacon in the Congregational church, owned a small malt house and a few slaves. His mother was Mary Fifield Adams.

Young Sam attended the Boston Latin School and Harvard College, from which he received his bachelor's degree in 1740. He received a master's degree in 1743 at the age of twenty-one. The subject of his master's thesis, "Whether it be lawful to resist the Supreme Magistrate, if the commonwealth cannot be otherwise preserved," was prophetic of his future thinking and of events to come.

Upon graduation from Harvard, Adams was apprenticed to a merchant, Thomas Cushing. Adams's interest in politics rather than in business caused him to perform so poorly in the counting-house that Cushing soon returned the lad to his father. The elder Adams finally gave Sam £1,000 and put him on his own. Through unwise business ventures Adams lost the money. In 1748 Deacon

Adams died, leaving the malt business and a house to his son.

Meanwhile, Adams and some friends had formed a political club to write and debate about public affairs. They established a newspaper, the *Independent Advertiser*, in 1748 and took turns supplying articles for it. Apparently there was no formal editorial staff.

In 1749 Adams married Elizabeth Checkley, daughter of the Rev. Samuel Checkley, his friend and pastor. She bore him five children, only two of whom still survived when she died eight years later. Adams spent much time and energy supervising the education of Samuel and Hannah.

In 1763 he held his first significant political office when he became a tax collector for the town of Boston. In carrying out his duties, he met and talked with people in all walks of life about public affairs and politics. His opinions became widely disseminated, and he earned from scornful Royalists the title "Sam the Publican." Other townspeople

revered him for his wisdom and knowledge and often sought his advice.

His career as tax collector was beset with difficulties because his humane nature would not allow him to press those who were delinquent in payments. The financial condition of the province was precarious. There was an alarming spread of smallpox in 1764, which caused many merchants to move their establishments into the country, thus paralyzing business. Adams, like other tax collectors, was in arrears, unable to balance his account.

Although reelected by a large majority in 1764, Adams at first declined to serve but was finally persuaded to continue. In the term that followed, he attempted to collect the back taxes without success and at last resorted to a published notice urging citizens to discharge their duties or be subjected to penalty of law. At the next election, Adams and his companion collectors were unanimously reelected but all refused to serve. Several finally capitulated and returned to office, but Adams declined.

For a few years afterwards, attempts were made to hold Adams and his colleagues liable for the uncollected public funds. A group of Tories, apparently out to get Adams, brought up the matter at a town meeting in 1768 but were voted down by a crushing majority. At a later town meeting Adams was relieved of all liability by a vote of the townspeople.

Between 1750 and 1764 Adams was a regular contributor to the Boston newspapers, warning his fellow citizens of the increasing usurpation of colonial power by England and consistently bringing before his readers the issue of colonial rights. A year before Patrick Henry in Virginia made his famous stand against Parliamentary schemes of taxation in the colonies, Samuel Adams warned his compatriots against them in Boston.

Chosen in 1764 to draft instructions for the newly elected representatives to the General Court from Boston, Adams outlined his expectations that the representatives would "constantly use your power and influence in maintaining valuable rights and privileges of the Province, of which this town is so great a part, as well as those rights which are derived to use by royal charter, as those which, being prior to, and independent of it, we hold essentially as free-born subjects of Great Britain. . . . If taxes are laid upon us in any shape without our having a legal representative where they are laid, are we not reduced from the character of subjects to the miserable state of tributary slaves?"

Adams's instructions were published and circulated through the colonies as the opinions of Boston and Massachusetts citizens. They soon became the foundation for provincial policy after the documents were acted upon by the legislature in June 1764. The colonial agent in London was sent a letter pledging the loyalty of the colonists to just and necessary trade regulations and instructing him to uphold the rights and privileges guaranteed the people by charter or by birth.

Boston patriots took the lead in asking their sister colonial assemblies to unite in efforts to protect their basic rights. It was the first concerted effort of the colonies to oppose oppression from Parliament, and the originator of the move was Sam Adams.

From that time on, Adams had a hand in the drafting of many important state papers and barely managed to conduct his malt business because of the press of public duty. However, income from the business provided sufficient money for his children to be educated and to attain a respectable rank in Boston society, where social status depended upon wealth. Adams married for the second time on 6 December 1764. The bride was Elizabeth Wells, twenty-four-year-old daughter of Francis Wells, an English merchant who had been a close friend of Adams's father. It was said that Elizabeth was amiable, educated, thrifty, and well qualified to support Adams in all his patriotic endeavors.

Passage of the Stamp Act in 1765 by the British Parliament was met with resistance by every colony. In the Virginia House of Burgesses, Patrick Henry lead the opposition with ringing denunciation of taxation without representation. In Boston, tension mounted. On 14 May mobs hanged in effigy the appointed distributor of stamps, Andrew Oliver, who resigned. Within the year, societies dedicated to the nullification of the act sprang up everywhere under the name "Sons of Liberty." Adams belonged to such a group, and it was with their aid that he inspired the mobs that terrorized Boston. Once again he was called upon to write the instruction to be carried out by colonial representatives to General Court. They were printed in the *Boston Gazette* in October 1765. Again they stressed the rights of the colonies.

On 27 September 1765 Adams was elected to replace Oxenbridge Thacher in the Massachusetts legislature, a position he held until 1774. Before long he was serving on every important committee in the legislature and had a hand in drafting all important papers.

Adams and the Sons of Liberty perceived themselves as defenders of the British constitution rather than as enemies of the British Empire. In historian Cass Canfield's words, they said that the Stamp Act was "an encroachment by the House of Commons upon George III's 'crown and dignity.' While the Sons of Liberty were toasting the King as they were threatening to annihilate royal troops, the British government repealed the Stamp Act."

While he carried on his legislative duties, Adams continued to attend town meetings and contributed numerous articles to the *Boston Gazette*. As early as 1768 Adams decided that the British Parliament had no right to legislate for the colonies, but he wisely refrained from airing his views because of lack of public support at that time.

In 1770 British troops occupied Boston Common. They were a rough lot; many had been impressed into service or had enlisted to avoid jail terms. As the occupation dragged on, the troops grew more and more at odds with the Boston citizenry, and eventually an incident occurred in which five citizens were killed. The event quickly became known as the Boston Massacre, and the people demanded satisfaction. The British captain and six of his men stood trial; the court released five and branded the hands of two. Adams, irate at what he considered an extraordinarily light sentence, wrote a scorching series of articles for the *Boston Gazette* under the by-line "Vindex the Avenger."

In 1772 Adams was instrumental in organizing a committee of correspondence to disseminate ideas and promote unity among the colonists and persons of like sympathies in England. In the *Boston Gazette*, he wrote: "Let it [colonial rights] be the subject of conversation in every social club. Let every town assemble. Let Associations and Combinations be everywhere set up to consult and recover our just Rights." Some of the Boston patriots, among them Thomas Cushing, Samuel Phillips, and John Hancock, were at first markedly indifferent. But Adams quickly found support in other towns, and eventually a committee of twenty-one persons under the chairmanship of James Otis was appointed to define the rights of the colonists, to declare violations of those rights, and to disseminate such information. Within two years, Adams's idea had spread as far as Charleston, South Carolina, despite the fact that Massachusetts governor Hutchinson called it ridiculous. Nonetheless, Hutchinson charged the legislature to either endorse or disavow the proceedings of the committee. It did neither.

Two months before the Boston Tea Party, Adams wrote in the *Boston Gazette:* "I beg leave to

Letter of 18 June 1777 from Adams to James Warren, Speaker of the House in the Continental Congress, discussing events in the Revolutionary War (Massachusetts Historical Society)

offer a proposal to my countrymen, namely that a Congress of American States be assembled as soon as possible; to draw up a Bill of Rights and publish it to the world; choose an Ambassador to dwell at the British Court to act for the united Colonies. . . ." This was his plea for an American commonwealth. Adams was treading upon dangerous ground; yet the British did not arrest him, perhaps because they were fearful of consequences in the colonies. He was always behind the scenes at significant events, an organizer, an instigator, a mover. He knew how to enlist the talents and aid of others, such as Hancock, Josiah Quincy, Jr., and Joseph Warren. Meanwhile, Boston was fast becoming a hotbed of rebellion.

In 1773 British merchant ships sailed for Charleston, Philadelphia, New York, and Boston loaded with tea, which was then a staple in the diet of the colonists. Colonial officials in every port except Boston convinced the consignees of the taxed tea to resign. Adams, meanwhile, organized a mass meeting at Old South Meeting House, where the colonists voted to send the tea back to England. Since the ships had already entered the customs limits, the resolution was illegal; but the incensed citizenry stood its ground. On 16 December, a mob boarded the ships and dumped 342 chests of tea into the harbor. Adams was not part of the mob, but he supported its action.

In April 1774 Governor Hutchinson was replaced by General Gage and his troops, and the British attempt to starve the colonists into submission began. England demanded satisfaction for the destroyed tea; the demand merely solidified the defiance of the colonists. Never again would they recognize the sovereignty of England.

The Sons of Liberty, with Adams's inspiration, proposed a congress. The measure was supported by the Virginia House of Burgesses, which invited Massachusetts to arrange a meeting. A conglomerate meeting of the committee of correspondence from Massachusetts gathered to lay plans. Adams locked the door of the meeting room and pocketed the key, lest any fainthearted members attempt to leave. One, feigning illness, did leave and went straight to General Gage, who attempted unsuccessfully to dissolve the meeting. When the proposals were passed, Adams was elected one of the five delegates from Massachusetts to the First Continental Congress, which met in Philadelphia on 5 September 1774 with representatives from all colonies except Georgia.

Meanwhile, relations were steadily worsening between the colonists and the mother country.

Fearing war, many families began to move from Boston into the countryside. British authorities laid plans to capture Adams and Hancock, either to hold them as hostages or to execute them in Boston or England. General Gage expressed strong misgivings because of the immediate retaliation he knew would occur. When Paul Revere rode into Lexington to warn the citizenry that the Redcoats were advancing, he found a guard of eight men posted around the house in which Adams and Hancock lodged. Soon after, the revolution began.

The Second Continental Congress opened on 10 May 1775 in Philadelphia with Adams in attendance. Five days later, upon the nominations of Adams and his cousin John Adams, George Washington was elected commander in chief of the Continental army. Adams was impatient for a declaration of independence but discerned that the congress was not yet prepared for it. However, he never ceased publishing letters, treatises in papers, and pamphlets urging resistance to British proposals of reconciliation. For him, nothing short of complete independence would do. On 4 July 1776 the Declaration of Independence was signed by Hancock; in August, it was signed by Adams and others. Canfield states that when Adams "signed the Declaration of Independence, with that great stroke of the pen he signed away his real vocation; it was the great culminating point in his career, but this success ended his leadership. America no longer needed an agitator. His important work was done between 1765 and 1776."

Adams remained active in politics and served as secretary of state for Massachusetts in 1779 and 1780. In 1779 he was Boston representative to the state constitutional convention and in 1782 became a Massachusetts state senator, holding the position until 1786. He was a member of the convention to ratify the federal Constitution in 1788. From 1789 to 1792 he was lieutenant governor of Massachusetts and assumed the governorship upon the death of Hancock in 1793. He was elected governor of Massachusetts in 1794 and held the post until 1797, when he retired from public life.

During the entire period in which he served in the Massachusetts Assembly and Senate, Adams used his writing talents and powers of persuasion in the preparation of official addresses, state papers, and messages sent within the colonies and abroad, and he corresponded prolifically with other statesmen and with friends. Between 1797 and 1803 he corresponded on state matters with Thomas Jefferson, who greatly admired Adams, and with Thomas Paine, whose *Common Sense*

(1776) and *American Crisis* (1776-1783) Adams praised. Some of these letters were printed as circulars and pamphlets. In the last few months of his life, Adams was seldom seen in public because of failing health. He died quietly on Sunday, 2 October 1803.

In his day, Adams's enemies denounced him vehemently. Governor Hutchinson declared in 1770 that he thought there was "not a greater incendiary in the King's dominion or a man of greater malignity of heart [or one] who less scruples any measure however criminal to accomplish his purpose." In his defense, Adams's cousin John wrote in 1819: "A systematic course has been pursued for thirty years to run him down. His merits and services and sufferings are beyond all calculation." Canfield writes in *Samuel Adams's Revolution:* "It is apparent to me that it was primarily Adams who fanned the flame of rebellion and that he did so more effectively than any other American leader. Without him . . . American independence could not have been declared in 1776."

Biographies:
William V. Wells, *The Life and Public Services of Samuel Adams*, 3 volumes (Boston: Little, Brown, 1865);

James K. Hosmer, *Samuel Adams* (Boston: Houghton Mifflin, 1891);

John C. Miller, *Sam Adams: Pioneer in Propaganda* (Boston: Little, Brown, 1936);

Stewart Beach, *Samuel Adams* (New York: Dodd, Mead, 1965);

Cass Canfield, *Samuel Adams's Revolution, 1765-1776* (New York: Harper & Row, 1976).

References:
P. L. Franklin, "Father of the Revolution," *National Republic,* 18 (February 1931): 18-30;

John R. Galvin, *Three Men of Boston* (New York: Crowell, 1976);

Wesley S. Griswold, *The Night the Revolution Began: The Boston Tea Party, 1773* (Brattleboro, Vt.: Stephen Greene Press, 1972);

Ralph Volney Harlow, *Samuel Adams, Promoter of the American Revolution: A Study in Psychology and Politics* (New York: Holt, 1923);

S. H. Holbrook, "Sam Adams; Our First Agitator," *American Mercury,* 59 (December 1944): 741-748;

E. D. Mead, "Editor's Table: Relations of John and Samuel Adams," *New England Magazine,* 16 (April 1897): 252-256;

John C. Miller, *Origins of the American Revolution* (Stanford, Cal.: Stanford University Press, 1943);

Kenneth Umbreit, *Founding Fathers: Men Who Shaped Our Tradition* (Port Washington, N.Y.: Kennikat Press, 1941);

Alexander Winston, "Firebrand of the Revolution," *American Heritage,* 18 (April 1967): 60-64, 105-108.

Papers:
Collections of Samuel Adams's papers are held by the New York Public Library, the *Boston Gazette,* the *Boston Evening News,* and the Boston Public Library. Because Adams desired anonymity, he seldom wrote under his own name. He burned nearly all of his own correspondence; other papers have been scattered or destroyed by thoughtless descendants or by autograph and souvenir seekers.

Benjamin Franklin Bache

(12 August 1769-11 September 1798)

Margaret A. Blanchard
University of North Carolina at Chapel Hill

MAJOR POSITION HELD: Owner and editor, *Philadelphia General Advertiser, and Political, Commercial, Agricultural and Literary Journal*, renamed *General Advertiser and Aurora* in 1794 (1790-1798).

BOOKS: *A Specimen of Printing Types Belonging to Benjamin Franklin Bache's Printing Office, Philadelphia* (Philadelphia: B. F. Bache, 1790?);
The Probationary Odes of Jonathan Pindar Esq., a Cousin of Peter's and Candidate for the Post of Poet Laureat to the C. U. S. (Philadelphia, 1796);
Remarks Occasioned by the Late Conduct of Mr. Washington, as President of the United States (Philadelphia: Printed for Benjamin Franklin Bache, 1797);
Truth Will Out! The Foul Charges of the Tories against the Editor of the Aurora Repelled by Positive Proof and Plain Truth, and His Base Calumniators Put to Shame . . . (Philadelphia, 1798).

TRANSLATIONS: *Important State Paper, A Report Made in the National Convention, in the Name of the Committee of Public Safety. By Citizen Roberspierre [sic] a Member of That Committee, on the Political Situation of the Republic. The 27th Brumaire, the 2D. Year of the Republic. Translated from the French, for the Information of the American Republic* (Boston: Reprinted by T. Fleet, jun. for William T. Clap, 1794);
Jean Antoine Joseph Fauchet, *A Sketch of the Present State of Our Political Relations with the United States of North-America. By Joseph Fauchet, Ex-Minister of the French Republic at Philadelphia. Translated by the Editor of the Aurora* (Philadelphia: Printed by Benj. Franklin Bache, 1797).

Benjamin Franklin Bache, grandson of Benjamin Franklin, is best known for his virulent attacks on Federalism in support of Jeffersonian principles and revolutionary France during the early days of the Republic. Historians credit Bache with being a primary force in driving George Washington from office and with being the primary target of the Federalist-backed Sedition Act of 1798;

he escaped being charged under the law, however, due to his death during the yellow fever epidemic in Philadelphia that year. Although he is less known for his efforts to open up Congressional sessions to journalists, this was one of his major crusades, and he did achieve some success in it.

The eldest son of Franklin's daughter Sarah and her English merchant husband, Richard Bache, Benjamin Franklin Bache, known as Benny, was just under six years old when he met his famous grandfather for the first time. Franklin had served in England for years as the colonial agent for Pennsylvania. As the rupture between the colonies and the mother country grew, Franklin returned home to Philadelphia; soon, he was a member of every important revolutionary committee in the colonies. Since Franklin made his home with his daughter, he soon became the most important influence in his young grandson's life; from the beginning of their relationship, he filled the child's mind with political and philosophical ideas on what Franklin considered to be the best way to establish a new government. As the great and near-great of the era met in the family home to relax and to plan strategy, Benny soaked up their conversation and their beliefs. He would later use those ideas as the basis for criticizing the way in which the Federalists were shaping the new nation.

By October 1776, Franklin's work in America was finished, and he was dispatched to France to serve as the new nation's ambassador to the court of Louis XVI. His assignment was to secure French aid for the revolutionary cause. Accompanying him was his grandson, now age seven. The boy was enrolled in a French boarding school; Benny took to his new school so successfully that, according to his biographer Bernard Faÿ, his grandfather began to wonder whether the child was more French than American. To compensate for the French influence, Franklin packed Benny off to a Geneva boarding school, declaring: "I intend for him [to be] a Presbyterian as well as a Republican." These early experiences, however, conditioned Benny to prefer things French, ultimately leading him to support the French position politically in later years. He never lost his ability to speak, write, or translate French, and he was one of the few journalists who could do his own translations from foreign-language newspapers.

While Benny was with his grandfather in France, he met the distinguished colony of Americans in that country, for, sooner or later, they all wound up at Franklin's table. The child also was exposed to leading French intellectuals who visited his grandfather. When he attended school in Geneva, his kinship to the distinguished Dr. Franklin moved young Benny into exclusive circles in the Swiss community as well. After his Geneva years, Franklin planned to send Benny to England to learn about English ideas of liberty, but he enjoyed the child's company so much that he kept Benny with him in Passy.

In his early teens, Benny picked up his grandfather's dislike of some developments in America after the war. Franklin's distaste for the Society of the Cincinnati, a fraternal organization of Revolutionary War officers headed by George Washington, for instance, formed young Benny's opinions about such associations, feelings that would emerge in the columns of Bache's newspaper in another ten years. During these years, Franklin was being increasingly criticized at home. Some leaders of the new Congress felt that Franklin had been abroad too long, and they raised questions about some of Franklin's actions and friends. Franklin, however, was protected by the king of France, who would not allow his recall. The Congress was able to attack Franklin's family, however. His son-in-law—Benny's father, Richard Bache—was fired from his position as postmaster general. William Temple Franklin, the son of Franklin's illegitimate son and Benny's cousin, was unable to obtain a diplomatic post and was even fired as secretary to the Paris mission, being replaced by a friend of George Washington. A youthful Bache was slowly building a list of persons to distrust and upon whom to take revenge. That list would grow.

Franklin, determined to give his grandson a nonpolitical way to support himself, began teaching Bache typefounding and printing. For a while, Bache was instructed by a printer brought to Passy. During his last few months in France, Bache studied under a master printer during the week and returned to his grandfather's home for weekends and holidays. In May 1785, Franklin was recalled, leaving the French court in the capable hands of Thomas Jefferson. Grandfather and grandson went home. During the next few years, Benjamin

Franklin would help to shape a new form of government, and Benjamin Franklin Bache would never be far from his side.

Bache, however, was far more of a European than an American and had difficulty adapting to life as an American teenager. Although he finished his education at the University of Pennsylvania, he preferred to stay close to his grandfather, at whose knee he learned to love the common man and to distrust those with aristocratic tastes. He also abandoned typefounding and devoted himself to mastering the printing trade. Franklin set his grandson up in business, and Bache attempted to build the business by printing and selling children's books and Greek and Latin grammars. There were few buyers for such products, especially since Franklin was, as Faÿ says, "publishing everywhere vehement condemnations of all classical studies."

The new government, which Franklin had helped form, was now in power, and Franklin's clan attempted to win its share of the patronage. All efforts were rebuffed; even Franklin himself was refused reimbursement for bills incurred in the service of the government. Franklin spent his last days as a "fallen politician," Faÿ says, as Bache watched. Franklin died in 1790; Bache's family took the inheritance Franklin had provided and moved to the country, leaving the twenty-one-year-old Bache alone in Philadelphia. All he had left were a failing publishing house, rich memories of his grandfather, and an increasing hatred of all those Americans in power for the way in which they had treated his grandfather and for the way in which they were perverting the government his grandfather had helped to establish.

Benjamin Franklin soon became anathema to the Federalists because of his democratic ideas. Many of these politicians took it upon themselves to sully Franklin's name; they wanted no part of his grandson. Consequently, Bache, preparing to launch his newspaper, could find no patron among the ranks of the Federalists; there would be no government printing contracts to ease his way. Jefferson, a longtime family friend, was able to give Bache copies of the *Leyden Gazette* as a source of foreign news, but Jefferson had other plans for establishing a newspaper to serve as his voice. Jefferson wanted to build his own image, not stand in Franklin's shadow.

In 1790, Bache's *General Advertiser, and Political, Commercial, Agricultural and Literary Journal* appeared for the first time. James D. Tagg finds these early issues of Bache's newspaper calm in comparison with the later editions, and he hypothesizes

First and second pages of Bache's Aurora. *As with most eighteenth-century newspapers, the first page consisted of advertisements, with the "hard news"—frequently items from Europe obtained from incoming ships—on the inside pages.*

Lailson's Circus,

SOUTH FIFTH STREET.

Le Tableau Parlant;

OR,

THE SPEAKING PICTURE.

The Philadelphia Lyceum

FOR FREE DEBATE,

AT CELLERS' GREAT ROOM,

SATURDAY EVENING, May 13

Miniature Painting.

Type-Founders.

Notice.

AURORA

LATEST FOREIGN INTELLIGENCE.

From LONDON PAPERS to MARCH 18, received by the KELICE, HEAVEY, arrived at New-York, from London.

PARIS, MARCH 6.

LONDON, MARCH 16

MARCH 17.

MARCH 18.

PARIS, MARCH 11.

MADRID, FEB. 20.

LONDON MARCH 18.

LETTER

From Major General Eustace, of the United States, to the Editor of the Morning Post.

Gravesend, March 14, 1797.

SIR,

FROM PARIS.

MARCH 14

that Bache had not yet gained enough confidence in himself to carry on any sustained campaigns against anyone. The newspaper's name was soon shortened to *General Advertiser,* and its contents were aimed at winning an audience among the intellectual opponents of Federalism. Bache put in eighteen-hour days in an attempt to make his newspaper a success in the crowded Philadelphia market. Setting Bache's newspaper apart from his competition, however, was his ability to relate to the man on the street in his everyday life. Bache had excellent connections with French, German, and Irish residents of the city. He capitalized on this relationship when news of the French Revolution arrived, for his connections with the French exile community in America and with persons in France gave him excellent sources of news. Bache's newspaper, says Faÿ, "served as a rallying center" for all those with grievances in Pennsylvania. Before long, some mild criticisms of George Washington began to appear. These early commentaries touched on the way in which Washington celebrated his birthday, the president's love of formality, his aristocratic manners, and so on. Bache was developing a fear that Washington was being elevated to the position of a demigod, that the people would soon come to think that the president could do no wrong, and that republican government would be doomed to failure if this happened.

Bache married Margaret Hartman Markoe, of Danish descent, on 17 November 1791. Their son, Franklin, became a prominent chemist and physician.

While he was establishing his position on Washington, Bache's pro-French tendencies made him the likely target of French diplomats assigned the task of gaining American support for revolutionary France. Edmond Charles Genêt was the first of these diplomats to seek Bache's help. Bache was delighted about the prospects of such a relationship, and soon the pages of the *General Advertiser* were filled with columns, letters, and stories aimed at winning the American common folk over to the French cause. The Federalists dominating the new national government despised the developments in France, denigrating the excesses of the French Revolution and fearing that similar impulses, if ever unleashed in America, might topple the Federalist hierarchy.

By 1793, however, the political scene was significantly altered. The rulers of revolutionary France had changed again, and Genêt fell from favor. About the same time, Jefferson resigned his post as secretary of state, returning to the quiet life

of a Virginia gentleman. The *National Gazette,* the Republican voice edited by Philip Freneau, went out of business. Almost simultaneously, Alexander Hamilton, Jefferson's archenemy, momentarily departed the national scene. The departures left Washington, who basically opposed political factions, as the leading Federalist and Bache's *General Advertiser* as the only real defender of the Republican cause. By 1794, Bache had added *Aurora* to his newspaper's name, and, known primarily by that name alone, the paper began exciting the emotions of both Federalists and Republicans.

Washington and Bache would have numerous encounters over the years, but the first major dispute involved Jay's Treaty. Washington had sent John Jay to England to win a treaty that would settle several problems left outstanding at the end of the American Revolution. The treaty Jay returned with stopped just short of making additional concessions to the British and represented few, if any, gains for the United States. So distasteful were the terms of the treaty that Washington refused for several weeks to send it to the Senate for ratification. When he finally did submit it, Washington demanded a pledge of secrecy from the senators. The treaty was ratified on 24 June 1795; on 28 June, extracts from the treaty were delivered to Bache for publication in the next day's *Aurora.* By 2 July, Bache had a pamphlet containing the entire treaty text available for sale, and he hopped aboard the fastest stagecoach North with hundreds of copies of the pamphlet, selling them as the coach made its way from Philadelphia to Boston. The new French ambassador, Pierre Auguste Adet, apparently had been able to convince Senator Stevens Thomas Mason of Virginia to leak the document to Bache.

The French and their supporters in America were particularly distressed about Jay's Treaty because it was seen as abrogating the treaty of friendship signed between the United States and France at the conclusion of the American Revolution. In this time of political turmoil, the last thing the French wanted was an America allied in some way with the British. Although, as Faÿ says, "General Washington found against him a hostile public opinion which even his popularity could not shake," he signed the treaty. The only voice in the capital to maintain opposition to Washington and his increasingly anti-French postures was Benjamin Franklin Bache, and Bache kept the pressure on the president. So successful was Bache in accomplishing this task that historian James E. Pollard terms the journalist "a sharp thorn in Washington's side," a persistent annoyance recognized by the

Page from the notebook in which Bache recorded speeches in Congress for the Aurora. *A sketch of Bache's grandfather Benjamin Franklin can be seen among the doodles at the bottom of the page (courtesy of Franklin Bache).*

president in his correspondence when he wrote that "the continual attacks which have been made . . . on the administration, in Bache's and other papers of that complexion, [are as] indecent as they are void of truth and fairness." Realizing that it was impossible to convert Washington to the Republican cause, Bache decided that there was only one other alternative—drive the president from office. He set about doing just that, and, because of his position as the sole Republican voice still heard from the capital, his influence was magnified. Most other Republican newspapers throughout the country republished his articles critical of Washington. The *Aurora* was widely distributed; the federal government even included copies of it in pouches going to diplomatic posts abroad. As the criticism of Washington increased, however, the *Aurora* was cut from the list of papers sent to the embassies. Bache responded by sending diplomats copies on his own. He also made sure that copies were delivered to Washington so that the president would not miss anything.

This was the most partisan period in American history. The struggle was over how to shape the new nation; each side believed that only it knew the correct direction for the development of the country. Bache was convinced that Washington was wrong for the new nation, and he set about trying to prove it. As one of Bache's correspondents put it in the *Aurora* (23 December 1796): "If ever a nation was debauched by a man, the American nation has been debauched by WASHINGTON. If ever a nation was deceived by a man, the American nation has been deceived by WASHINGTON. Let his conduct then be an example to future ages. Let it serve to be a warning that no man may be an idol, and that a people may confide in themselves rather than in an individual. Let the history of the federal government instruct mankind, that the masque of patriotism may be worn to conceal the foulest designs against the liberties of a people."

Bache's newspaper articles carried forth that theme. For instance, he published articles from a contributor correctly charging that Washington had overdrawn his salary, and he resurrected and printed discredited letters allegedly written by Washington during the Revolutionary War that purportedly showed the president as a lukewarm patriot. As the struggle continued unabated, the Federalists decided that John Fenno's *Gazette of the United States* was unable to combat Bache on his own level. Thus, they set up a new editor and newspaper, William Cobbett and his *Porcupine's Gazette*, with the assignment to defeat Bache.

As Washington left office, Bache allowed himself a few parting shots at the president. His goal, as he said in a pamphlet published as the administrations changed, was to "*destroy undue impressions in favor of Mr. Washington.*" One of his most famous anti-Washington essays appeared in the *Aurora* on 6 March 1797, just as the president was leaving office. Terming Washington "the source of all the misfortunes of our country," Bache proclaimed his delight in the fact that Washington now was "no longer possessed of power to multiply evils upon the United States." This event was just cause for "a period for rejoicing." For now, "every heart in unison with the freedom and happiness of the people ought to beat high with exultation that the name of Washington ceases from this day to give currency to political insults, and to legalize corruption. A new era is now opening upon us, an era which promises much to the people, for public measures must now stand upon their own merits, and nefarious projects can no longer be supported by a name." Bache predicted that when Americans looked back upon the Washington administration they would be astonished to find "that a single individual should have cankered the principles of republicanism in an enlighted people just emerged from the gulf of despotism, and should have carried his designs against the public liberty so far as to have put in jeopardy its very existence. Such, however, are the facts. . . ." Bache concluded by noting that the day that America was finally freed of Washington's influence was so marvelous that it should be celebrated as "a JUBILEE in the United States."

Even while Bache was pursuing his dream of hounding Washington from office, he was making at least one significant contribution to the future of American journalism: he was reporting on the proceedings in the House of Representatives—the only house of Congress open to the press—and, as historian Donald H. Stewart said, he had "publicly pledged his accounts to be as correct as was humanly possible." Bache also campaigned for open government, apologizing once for an error that crept into a story by explaining that "mistakes of this kind would not so often happen, were the doors of the Senate kept open." Bache's antiadministration views, however, ultimately led to his being barred even from the floor of the House of Representatives. When Republican members of the House tried to set up uniform rules for the stenographers and reporters who wished to cover House sessions, they were told that admittance of reporters was at the discretion of the Speaker. What the

Speaker could give, the Speaker could take away, as he did in the case of Bache.

The partisan battle abated briefly as Jefferson came out of retirement to become vice-president under John Adams. The Republicans, Bache included, hoped that Adams would be different from Washington, that there was a greater chance to lure him away from friendliness toward Great Britain, from monarchical tendencies, and from other faults they saw in Washington. Hoping to increase the potential for such a policy shift, Bache had several complimentary things to say about the new Adams administration. Such support quickly melted away, however, when France refused to accept a new American ambassador. The pro-French bias of Jefferson and the pro-British bias of Adams came to the fore. Bache was back in the business of criticizing the president, calling him "President by three votes," "His Rotundity," "His Serene Highness," or "Bonny Johnny Adams." Such comments were not appreciated by Abigail Adams, the president's wife, as revealed in her correspondence when she referred to "this lying wretch of a Bache."

Bache was in fine fettle. His hero Jefferson was in high office, and by 1798 Bache's newspaper was the leading voice of Republicanism. Abruptly, though, his promising future disappeared. President Adams had sent a trio of negotiators to France, and the French authorities had refused to meet with them unless the Americans offered a substantial bribe. The sordid mess became known as the XYZ Affair, and when the American public heard about this occurrence, support of France on any issue became very dangerous indeed. Jefferson and his friends assumed a low profile, hoping for the storm to abate; but Bache remained a visible target for anti-French hatred. His advertising fell off, as did his list of subscribers; he was beaten twice, and his shop was the target of rock throwers. Through it all, he remained true to his principles.

Although Jefferson remained out of the limelight, he was concerned about Bache's ability to stay in business. He urged other Republicans to subscribe to Bache's publication and to the *New York Time Piece*, another newspaper hated by the Federalists and a target of their wrath. "If these papers fail," he wrote James Madison, "republicanism will be entirely brow beaten." Whether Bache agreed that his publication was in danger is not entirely clear; more likely he thought that he would be able to ride out this storm as he had so many others. Cobbett did his part in keeping Bache's political affiliations before the people, writing in one issue of *Porcupine's Gazette,* "The most famous of the Jac-

obins is BACHE [.] Editor of the *Aurora,* Printer to the French Directory, Distributor General of the principles of Insurrection, Anarchy and Confusion, the greatest of fools, and the most stubborn sans-culotte in the United States."

The current wave of anti-Republican feeling aimed at the press was different from previous ones, however. So strongly did the Federalists feel that Republican publications ought to be silenced that the Federalist lawmakers sought a legal way to shut down such papers as Bache's *Aurora.* The chosen vehicle was the Alien and Sedition Acts. The Federalists were impatient, however; thus, when they moved against Bache, they did so without the Sedition Act, for it had not yet been enacted. The Federalists charged Bache not with sedition, therefore, but with treason.

Precipitating the charge was Bache's publication of a long letter in which the French minister, Talleyrand, tried to put the best possible face on recent French behavior. According to the Federalists, the only way Bache could have obtained a copy of the Talleyrand letter was if he were an agent of France; if that was the case, then Bache was guilty of treason. The letter had just arrived in the United States, and the secretary of state had not even shown it to the president. After considerable effort, Bache was able to convince the authorities that he had received the letter from a resident of Philadelphia, and the Federalists' case evaporated. But the Federalists were not to be dissuaded from their goal of quieting Bache.

On the very day that the sedition statute was introduced into the Senate, 26 June 1798, the Federalists, using as a pretext comments Bache had made in defending himself from the treason charges, had him arrested on the common-law charge of seditious libel for "libelling the President & the Executive Government, in a manner tending to excite sedition, and opposition to the laws." The *Aurora* was smaller than usual the next day; Bache apologized to his readers for this, promising that "prosecution no more than persecution, shall cause him to abandon what he considers the cause of truth and republicanism; which he will support to the best of his abilities, while life remains." When Bache was brought into court on 29 June 1798, the best his lawyers could do was to obtain his release on $4,000 bond to await trial during the October term of court. He continued his attacks on the government while he awaited trial, telling his readers about the rights of the people under the Constitution: "One of the first rights of a human is to speak or to publish his sentiments; if any government founded upon the will of the people passes any ordinance to abridge this right, it is as much a crime as if the people were, in an unconstitutional way, to curtail the government of one of the powers delegated to it."

Whether Bache could have been convicted under the common-law indictment is questionable; only a few months earlier, U.S. Supreme Court Justice Samuel Chase had ruled that actions without a base in statutory law could not be upheld. The soundness of the indictment soon became a moot point, however, as a yellow fever epidemic swept through Philadelphia. Although it was the worst such epidemic in years, Bache refused to leave his post, reasoning that if he discontinued his publication he might not be able to obtain the necessary support to start it up again. He contracted the fever on 5 September 1798 and died on 11 September. The *Aurora* suspended publication for a few weeks; on 1 November, the paper resumed publication with Bache's widow, Margaret, as publisher, and his assistant, William Duane, as editor. Duane and Mrs. Bache were married in 1800.

Bache's widow wrote one of his most fitting epitaphs: "In these times . . . men who see, and think, and feel for their country and posterity can alone appreciate the loss; the loss of a man inflexible in virtue, unappalled by power or persecution, and, who, in dying knew no anxieties but what were excited by his apprehensions for his country—and for his young family." The Federalists, needless to say, were delighted to find Bache removed from the scene. Some Federalists, says historian John C. Miller, thought that Bache's death in the midst of the yellow fever epidemic was an indication of the pleasure of divine providence shining down upon them. This line of thought, however, was abandoned when Fenno, publisher of the *Gazette of the United States*, the Federalist voice, died in the same epidemic.

To evaluate Benjamin Franklin Bache's career is almost as difficult today as it was in his own time. Opinions of him are always colored by how the critic views the rightness of Bache's political stand. A Jeffersonian will find Bache's activities justified and will label him a true democrat. A proponent of Federalism will find Bache to be the most scurrilous editor of all time. Neither view is abso-

lutely correct. Bache's behavior was not unusual for the period in which he lived. He used the press well to put forth his opinions, and he did help to open up the legislative process on the federal level to the press. Even more important, however, is the fact that he showed, very early in the history of the United States, how far freedom of the press could be extended and how fragile that freedom could be.

Biography:
Bernard Faÿ, *The Two Franklins* (Boston: Little, Brown, 1933).

References:
Everette E. Dennis, "Stolen Peace Treaties and the Press: Two Case Studies," *Journalism History*, 2 (Spring 1975): 6-14;

Bernard Faÿ, "Benjamin Franklin Bache, A Democratic Leader of the Eighteenth Century," *Proceedings of the American Antiquarian Society*, 40 (October 1930): 277-304;

Eugenia W. Herbert, "A Note on Richard Bache (1731-1811)," *Pennsylvania Magazine of History and Biography*, 100 (January 1976): 97-103;

Claude-Anne Lopez, "A Story of Grandfathers, Fathers, and Sons," *Yale University Library Gazette*, 53 (April 1979): 177-195;

John C. Miller, *Crisis in Freedom* (Boston: Little, Brown, 1951);

James E. Pollard, *The Presidents and the Press* (New York: Macmillan, 1947);

James Morton Smith, *Freedom's Fetters* (Ithaca, N.Y.: Cornell Paperbacks, 1956);

Donald H. Stewart, *The Opposition Press of the Federalist Period* (Albany, N.Y.: State University of New York Press, 1969);

James D. Tagg, "Benjamin Franklin Bache and the Philadelphia *Aurora*," Ph.D. dissertation, Wayne State University, 1973;

Tagg, "Benjamin Franklin Bache's Attack on George Washington," *Pennsylvania Magazine of History and Biography*, 100 (April 1976): 191-230.

Papers:
Benjamin Franklin Bache's papers are at the American Philosophical Society Library, Philadelphia.

Henry Ward Beecher

(24 June 1813-8 March 1887)

James S. Featherston
Louisiana State University

See also the Beecher entry in *DLB 3, American Writers in New York and the South.*

MAJOR POSITIONS HELD: Editor, *Cincinnati Journal* (1836), *Western Farmer and Gardener* (1844-1847), *New York Independent* (1861-1864), *Christian Union* (1870-1881).

SELECTED BOOKS: *An Address, Delivrred [sic] before the Platonean Society of the Indiana Asbury University, September 15, 1840* (Indianapolis: Printed by W. Stacy, 1840);

Seven Lectures to Young Men, on Various Important Subjects (Indianapolis: T. B. Cutler/Cincinnati: H. W. Moore, 1844); expanded as *Twelve Lectures to Young Men on Various Important Subjects* (New York: G. H. Doran, 1870);

The Means of Securing Good Rulers: A Sermon Delivered on the Occasion of the Death of Noah Noble, Late Governor of Indiana (Indianapolis: Printed by E. Chamberlain, 1844);

A Dissuasive from Moral Intolerance, Delivered at Bloomington, Ind., before the Philomathean Society of the Indiana University (Indianapolis: S.V.B. Noel, 1845);

A Discourse Delivered at the Plymouth Church, Brooklyn, N.Y., upon Thanksgiving Day, November 25th, 1847 (New York: Cady & Burgess, 1848);

Great Speech, Delivered in New York City, by Henry Ward Beecher, on the Conflict of Northern and Southern Theories of Man and Society, Jan. 14, 1855 (Rochester, N.Y.: Steam Press of A. Strong, 1855);

Star Papers; or, Experiences of Art and Nature (New York: J. C. Derby/Boston: Phillips, Sampson/Cincinnati: H. W. Derby, 1855; revised, New York: J. B. Ford, 1873);

Defence of Kansas (Washington, D.C.: Buell & Blanchard, printers, 1856);

Man and His Institutions. An Address before the Society for the Promotion of Collegiate and Theological Education at the West, Delivered in Tremont Temple, Boston, Mass., May 28, 1856 (New York: Calkins & Stiles, 1856);

How to Become a Christian (Boston: American Tract Society, 1858);

Life Thoughts, Gathered from the Extemporaneous Discourses of Henry Ward Beecher. By One of His Congregation, edited by Edna Dean Proctor and A. Moore (Boston: Phillips, Sampson, 1858; Glasgow: Collins, N.d.);

Plain and Pleasant Talk about Fruits, Flowers and Farming (New York: Derby & Jackson, 1859);

Summer in the Soul; or, Views and Experiences (Edinburgh: A. Strahan, 1859);

New Star Papers; or, Views and Experiences of Religious

Photograph by Mathew Brady

23

Subjects (New York: Derby & Jackson, 1859);

Addresses on Mental Culture for Women, by Beecher and James T. Brady (New York: E. D. Barker, 1859);

Woman's Influence in Politics: An Address Delivered by Henry Ward Beecher, at the Cooper Institute, New York . . . Feb. 2d, 1860 (Boston: R. F. Wallcut, 1860);

War and Emancipation. A Thanksgiving Sermon, Preached in the Plymouth Church, Brooklyn, N.Y., on Thursday, November 21, 1861 (Philadelphia: T. B. Peterson, 1861);

Civil War: Its Causes, Its Consequences, Its Crimes, and Its Compromises, by Beecher and John Hughes (New York: R. Vose, 1861);

Royal Truths (Edinburgh: A. Strahan, 1862; Boston: Ticknor & Fields, 1866);

Eyes and Ears (Boston: Ticknor & Fields, 1862);

Freedom and War (Boston: Ticknor & Fields, 1863);

American Rebellion. Speech of the Rev. Henry Ward Beecher, Delivered in the Free Trade Hall, Manchester, 9th October, 1863 (Manchester, U.K.: Union and Emancipation Society, 1863); republished as *The American Cause in England!* (New York: Coutant & Baker, 1863);

Universal Suffrage (New York: Published by Wm. E. Whiting, 1865);

Oration at Raising the Old Flag over Fort Sumter, April 14, 1865 (New York: Schermerhorn, Bancroft, 1865); republished with *Sermon on the Death of Abraham Lincoln, President of the United States* (Manchester, U.K.: A. Ireland, 1865);

Woman's Duty to Vote (New York: American Equal Rights Convention, 1867);

Norwood; or, Village Life in New England (3 volumes, London: Sampson Low, Son & Marston, 1867; 1 volume, New York: Fords, Howard & Hulbert, 1867);

Prayers From Plymouth Pulpit (New York: Scribners, 1867);

Sermons, 2 volumes (New York: Harper, 1868; London: S. Low, 1870);

Plymouth Pulpit, 19 volumes (New York: Fords, Howard & Hulbert, 1868-1884);

Lecture-Room Talks (New York: Ford, 1870); republished as *Familiar Talks on Themes of General Christian Experience* (London: Nelson, 1870);

Common Sense for Young Men on the Subject of Temperance (New York: National Temperance Society & Publication House, 1871);

The Life of Jesus, The Christ (New York: Ford, 1871); volume 2 edited from Beecher's notes by S. Scoville and W. C. Beecher (New York: Bromfield/London: R. D. Dickinson, 1891);

Liberty and Love: An Appeal to the Conscience to Banish the Wine-Cup (New York: National Temperance Society & Publication House, 1872);

Should the Public Libraries Be Opened on Sunday? (New York: J. B. Ford, 1872);

Yale Lectures on Preaching, 3 volumes (New York: Ford, 1872-1874); republished as *Lectures on Preaching,* 2 volumes (London: T. Nelson, 1872-1874);

The Discipline of Trouble: A Sermon (New York, 1873);

The Discipline of Sorrow (New York, 1874);

A Summer Parish (New York: J. B. Ford, 1875);

Oratory (Philadelphia: Culbertson & Bache, printers, 1876);

The Background of Mystery: A Sermon (Boston: Pilgrim Press, 1877);

Jew and Gentile: A Sermon (New York: "Christian Union," 1877);

Christianity Unchanged by Changes. Two Addresses on the "Signs of the Times" (New York: Christian Union Print, 1878);

The Army of the Republic, Its Services and Destiny (New York: Christian Union Print, 1878);

Why the Republican Party Should Be Trusted (Brooklyn, N.Y.: Union-Argus Book & Job-Printing Establishment, 1880);

Henry Ward Beecher's Statement before the Congregational Association of New York and Brooklyn, in which He Resigns His Membership in the Association and Gives a Full Statement of His Doctrinal Beliefs and Unbeliefs (New York: Funk & Wagnalls, 1882);

A Circuit of the Continent: Account of a Tour through the West and South (New York: Fords, Howard & Hulbert, 1884);

Evolution and Religion (New York: Fords, Howard & Hulbert, 1885);

Eulogy on General Grant (New York: Jenkins & McCowan, 1885);

Why I Am a Free-Trader (New York, 1886);

Christian Self-Denial (London: J. Clark, 1886?);

Patriotic Addresses in America and England, from 1850 to 1885, on Slavery, the Civil War, and the Development of Civil Liberty in the United States, edited by John R. Howard (New York: Fords, Howard & Hulbert, 1887);

Heaven-Sent Words (Boston: Cassino, 1887);

I Am Resolved What to Do: Last Sermon Preached by Rev. Henry Ward Beecher at Plymouth Church, Sunday Evening, February 27, 1887 (New York: Gallagher & Hoffer, 1887);

Proverbs from Plymouth Pulpit; Selected from the Writings and Sayings of Henry Ward Beecher by Wil-

liam Drysdale. Revised in Part by Mr. Beecher, and under Revision by Him at the Time of His Death (New York: D. Appleton, 1887; London: Burnet, 1887);

A Summer in England with Henry Ward Beecher, edited by James B. Pond (New York: Fords, Howard & Hulbert, 1887);

Book of Prayer from His Public Ministrations; Compiled from Unpublished Reports by T. J. Ellinwood (New York: Fords, 1890);

"Faith": Last Morning Sermon Preached in Plymouth Church, Brooklyn, Sunday, Feb. 27, 1887 (Brooklyn, N.Y.: T. J. Ellinwood, 1891);

Bible Studies. Readings in the Early Books of the Old Testament, with Familiar Comment, Given in 1878-9. Edited from Stenographic Notes of T. J. Ellinwood by John R. Howard (New York: Fords, 1892);

Autobiographical Reminiscences of Henry Ward Beecher, edited by T. J. Ellinwood (New York: Stokes, 1898).

OTHER: *Plymouth Collection of Hymns and Tunes; for the Use of Christian Congregations,* edited by Beecher (New York: A. S. Barnes, 1855);

Illustrated Bible Biography; or, The Lives and Characters of the Principal Personages Recorded in the Sacred Scriptures, introduction by Beecher (Boston: Published by Lee & Shepard for W. L. Gross & Co., 1868).

Henry Ward Beecher, clergyman, orator, editor, and author, was considered the greatest preacher of his time. The famous son of a famous father, he also was the brother of a famous sister, Harriet Beecher Stowe, who wrote *Uncle Tom's Cabin* (1852). Beecher, a flamboyant, magnetic personality, was for many years pastor of the fashionable Plymouth Church in Brooklyn Heights, New York, which boasted a membership of about 2,500. He was at various times also a newspaper editor and writer. He wrote several books, including a novel; collections of his sermons and orations also appeared in book form. However, Beecher is sometimes best remembered for his involvement in one of the most widely publicized sex scandals in American history.

Beecher was born 24 June 1813 in Litchfield, Connecticut, the eighth of thirteen children. His father, Lyman Beecher, a widely known and sometimes controversial minister, was then pastor of a church in Litchfield and considered a leader among New England theologians. The elder Beecher was a highly emotional man who would sometimes work

himself into a frenzy while preaching. He was also virulently anti-Catholic. Henry Ward Beecher's mother, born Roxanna Foote, was a hardworking housewife who also taught and took in boarders but still found time to paint, sew, and play the guitar. She died after bearing nine children, and her husband soon remarried a woman named Harriet Porter.

Henry Ward Beecher developed into a healthy, vigorous boy, but as a younger child in a large family, he did not receive much attention or affection. He loved the outdoors and spent much time by himself in the fields and woods. Consequently, he was a shy lad who spoke haltingly and was considered somewhat backward. He also was reared around much adult talk about heaven and hell, and this led young Beecher to fret over his unsaved soul. He was never given a toy, and he was thirty years old before he ever attached any joyous significance to Christmas. His early life was austere. In addition to attending school, he awakened before daybreak to build the kitchen fire before sunrise prayers. In the winter he shoveled snow and cut and split firewood. In the warmer months he did farm and house chores and took care of a cow and a horse.

At the age of ten, he was sent to a school in Bethlehem, Connecticut, but he neglected his studies and roamed the wooded hills. He was then sent to Hartford to attend a female seminary his sister Catharine had opened. Beecher was the only boy among forty or more girls, but his sister was a demanding teacher and he learned his lessons. Catharine taught him drawing and Latin and tried to correct his scholastic shortcomings as much as possible. Beecher attended his sister's school for only six months, then left for Boston when his father became pastor of the Hanover Church there in 1826. He was approaching adolescence and was plagued with self-doubts and a longing for adventure. He fell in love with the sea and spent countless hours on the waterfront. He longed to go to sea, but his father would have none of that; Lyman Beecher intended for all of his sons to become ministers, and they eventually did. Beecher was sent to the Mount Pleasant Classical Institute, a remarkable school in the Berkshire foothills at Amherst, Massachusetts, where for the first time he was associated with boys from throughout the nation and much of the world. Among his 200 or more schoolmates were about a score of boys from the South as well as six Greeks, four Colombians, two English boys, two Canadians, a Brazilian, and a Cuban. Beecher then was fourteen and knew a little Latin and some English grammar but little else. He also spoke "as if he had pudding in his mouth" and had no conception of how to study. Beecher, however, soon blossomed under the tutelage of two fine teachers: William P. N. Fitzgerald taught him mathematics, drawing, natural philosophy, and good study habits; John E. Lovell made an orator out of Beecher by teaching him not only the mechanics of elocution but self-confidence. Beecher was given words to pronounce over and over again until the precise inflection and intonation had become ineradicable habit. Beecher became popular among his schoolmates and a leader in sports activities. By the time he left Mount Pleasant at the age of seventeen, he was a gifted speaker, an accomplishment that would serve him well in future years.

Lyman Beecher decided to send his son to Amherst College rather than to Yale, his own alma mater, because the classes at Amherst were smaller. Beecher enrolled at Amherst in 1830. Although his academic standing was low, he read voraciously and was particularly fond of the English classics. He was a popular and active student, noted for his humor, wit, and playfulness. He wrote for one of the college newspapers and blossomed as a public speaker. During vacations, he taught school and sometimes lectured and preached.

By the time Beecher graduated from college in 1834 his father had become head of the Lane Theological Seminary in Cincinnati, and Beecher entered this institution although he had not as yet felt called to the ministry. While at the seminary, he wrote for the *Cincinnati Daily Evening Post* and briefly served as editor of the Presbyterian weekly *Cincinnati Journal*. He also armed himself and volunteered his services as a special constable after a proslavery mob destroyed James G. Birney's abolitionist newspaper, the *Philanthropist*. Although opposed to slavery, Beecher had yet to take a stand against it. He also still had doubts about stern Calvinism and the type of Christianity he could preach. Gradually, however, he "came to see in Christianity something besides the iron face of God." He later recalled, "There rose before me a vision of Jesus as the savior of sinners—not of saints but of sinners unconverted, before they were any better—because they were so bad and needed so much; and that view has never grown from me."

In 1837 Beecher accepted a call to preach at a struggling Presbyterian church in Lawrenceburg, Indiana, that had only twenty members. He also borrowed $300 and hurried back to Massachusetts, where on 3 August 1837 he married Eunice White

Bullard, whom he had met while attending Amherst and to whom he had been engaged for seven years. In Lawrenceburg, Beecher's pay was low; the young couple lived in rooms above a warehouse, and Beecher wore hand-me-down clothes. It was during these hard times that the first of the couple's ten children was born. Beecher once called Lawrenceburg a "town with two distilleries and twenty devils in it," but he remained there until he moved to Indianapolis to become pastor of the Second Presbyterian Church in July 1839.

Beecher's preaching skills were constantly improving, and his popularity was continually growing. He genuinely liked people, and they liked him. He seemed neither pompous nor particularly pious. He went about with his trousers tucked into his boots, and he would be preaching one day and pitching manure the next. He painted his house and helped fight fires. He was unconventional both in and out of the pulpit. His magnetism drew people to his sermons, and soon his congregation was able to build a new church building. Beecher also became a popular lecturer outside the church. One series of his lectures was so widely admired that it was published in 1844 under the title *Seven Lectures to Young Men, on Various Important Subjects*. The Indiana State Synod lavishly praised the book and said, "Every father should place it in the hands of his sons; it should be in every Sabbath School Library, in every steamboat, hotel and public resort."

The wide acclaim the book received led to a part-time job offer for Beecher. The *Indiana State Journal* planned to launch a farm journal and Beecher, an amateur gardener, was named editor. Beecher increased his knowledge of agriculture by studying books on the subject. His articles, written with both humor and imagination, were not confined to agriculture but also urged cleanliness, temperance, better public schools, and better education for farmers. Beecher also discussed such weighty problems as prostitution but was strangely silent about slavery. Within a year, the journal, named *Western Farmer and Gardener*, had about 1,200 subscribers and an exchange list that took it, with Beecher's name as editor, into nearly every newspaper office in the nation. Even Horace Greeley's *New York Tribune* quoted from Beecher's articles.

As Beecher's popularity grew, so did criticism for his silence on the burning issue of the day— slavery. The Indiana State Synod finally adopted a resolution aimed directly at Beecher. It called upon every Presbyterian minister in the state "to preach on the sin of oppression, on the evils of slavery, and on the doctrine and laws of the Bible in reference to servitude." Beecher finally began preaching against slavery.

Meanwhile, Beecher's fame was increasing. His congregation had grown from 33 to 275 members. A new church building had been erected and a splendid organ installed. A choir had been organized, along with a club for young men and a Bible class for girls. He was the editor of a prosperous farm journal, president of the state horticulture society, and a trustee for the Deaf and Dumb Institute. He was in demand statewide as a lecturer and was a leader in crusades against drunkenness, gambling, and other vices. Indiana State Senator Oliver H. Smith, a member of his congregation, praised him in these words: "As a preacher he is a landscape painter of Christianity. Mr. Beecher had no model. He is the original of himself. He is always new. He imitates no man and no man can imitate him. The great power of Mr. Beecher over his congregation consists mainly in the clearness of his mental vision, the range of his thoughts, the deep interest he imparts to whatever he touches."

In 1847 Beecher declined pastorates at two Boston churches but accepted a call to take over

Beecher with his wife, Eunice Bullard Beecher, and two of their children, shortly after their move to Brooklyn

the new Congregationalist Plymouth Church in Brooklyn, New York. He became a Congregationalist because of the independence the denomination offered. On 10 October 1847 he began his spectacular career at Plymouth Church, where he was to spend the rest of his life. His salary started at $1,500 a year, a handsome sum then, but grew to $20,000 within a few years. His dramatic flair, wit, vivid vocabulary, fervor, and friendliness attracted larger and larger audiences. When the original church building burned on 30 January 1849, Beecher raised funds to build a much larger one, and soon his congregation averaged about 2,500. Visitors from throughout the country and the world came to hear him. He also became one of the nation's most popular speakers on the lecture circuit.

Beecher became a contributor to the *New York Independent,* a religious weekly which had been established in December 1848, and he served as its editor from 1861 to 1864. Once he decided to speak out against slavery, Beecher became an uncompromising foe of the "peculiar institution." From both his church and the lecture platform he lambasted slavery, and he became a recognized leader of the antislavery forces. He also used the columns of the *Independent* to call for an end to slavery. He advocated disobedience of the Fugitive Slave Law and urged Northerners to settle in Kansas and, if necessary, to use force to make it a free territory. He campaigned in 1860 for Abraham Lincoln. When the Civil War erupted, he preached and wrote in support of the Union cause. "Since war is upon us, let us have the courage to make war," he proclaimed as he addressed recruiting meetings and blessed flags. He criticized Lincoln for his delay in issuing an emancipation proclamation. In 1863 Beecher visited England and lectured in an effort to swing public opinion to the side of the North. After the war, however, he urged reconciliation with the Southern states.

During the postwar years, Beecher's remarkable popularity continued unabated, and there were some who suspected that he harbored presidential ambitions. He never sought political office, however, but continued to preach, lecture, and write. He not only contributed to the *Independent* but also began writing for the *New York Ledger,* a mass circulation paper published by Robert Bonner. Bonner also paid Beecher $30,000 to write a novel, *Norwood,* which was serialized in the *Ledger* before appearing in book form in 1867. Beecher, in addition, wrote the first of a projected two volumes of his *The Life of Jesus, The Christ,* which ap-

The interior of Beecher's Plymouth Church, Brooklyn, which was criticized for its resemblance to a theater. Beecher's congregation averaged about twenty-five hundred (American Antiquarian Society, Worcester, Massachusetts).

peared in 1871. Beecher was also editor of the *Christian Union*, a religious weekly, from 1870 to 1881. During this time he was praised for writing some of the "strongest editorials in the American press."

The latter part of Beecher's career was marred by a scandal that "rocked Victorian America to its very foundations." Beecher was accused of seducing Elizabeth Tilton, the wife of Theodore Tilton, who had succeeded Beecher as editor of the *Independent*. Tilton and his wife were both active in the woman suffrage movement, in which Beecher also became involved. They were also members of Plymouth Church, and Beecher frequently visited their home. Tilton, a tall, handsome journalist who had begun his career under Horace Greeley, was a great admirer of Beecher. It was through Beecher that Tilton had become assistant editor and later editor of the *Independent*. Henry Bowen, owner of the *Independent*, became unhappy with Tilton because he refused to back the Grant administration and ousted him as editor of the *Independent*. Bowen, however, then made Tilton editor of the *Brooklyn Union*, another of his newspapers. Later, Tilton was

fired from this position, and he filed a breach of contract lawsuit against Bowen.

Beecher, at the time of the sex scandal, was well into his fifties, and his flowing, gray-streaked hair would turn white before the controversy abated. A portly man of average height with blue gray eyes and ruddy complexion, Beecher was not conventionally handsome, but women had always found him attractive. Physically powerful and thick-necked, he was a striking figure with a great cape draped across his shoulders and a slouch hat perched jauntily on his head. Rumors of sexual indiscretions had circulated about Beecher for many years. Tilton, who had unorthodox views about love and marriage, also had been suspected of immoral conduct, and Beecher once had advised Elizabeth Tilton to leave her husband. Then on a July night in 1870, Mrs. Tilton in a written confession told her husband that she had been seduced by Beecher on 10 October 1868 at his residence, where she had gone for counseling, "being then in a tender state of mind, owing to the recent death and burial of a young child." She also told others, including the suffrage leader Susan B. Anthony, of her unfaithfulness. On 30 December 1870 Tilton

Theodore Tilton, who succeeded Beecher as editor of the New York Independent, *and his wife, Elizabeth. The greatest sex scandal of nineteenth-century America occurred when Tilton accused Beecher of seducing his wife.*

confronted Beecher and accused him of committing adultery with his wife. News of the incident did not become public knowledge, however, until the irrepressible and free-thinking sisters Victoria Woodhull and Tennessee Claflin devoted almost the entire 2 November 1872 issue of *Woodhull & Claflin's Weekly* to an article headlined "The Beecher-Tilton Case." Woodhull wrote, "I intend that this article shall burst like a bomb-shell into the moralistic social camp." Single copies of that issue soon sold for as much as forty dollars. Beecher waited until the following June to deny the story, whereupon Tilton publicly accused Beecher of committing an unspecified offense against him.

Beecher then formed a six-member committee from Plymouth Church to investigate the incident, and this group, after hearing thirty-six witnesses, including Tilton, exonerated the pastor. Over a year later, in August 1874, Tilton filed a $100,000 damage suit charging Beecher with adultery with his wife. The trial began in Brooklyn City Court on 11 January 1875 and ended with a hung jury on 2 July 1875, after 112 days of testimony

and arguments. For six months, the trial was the biggest story in America, and many of the newspapers that had earlier supported Beecher now turned against him. The *New York Times* said the facts "tell heavily against Mr. Beecher," and Henry Watterson in the *Louisville Courier-Journal* labeled the pastor "a dunghill covered with flowers." The furor spread to England, and the *Times* of London and the *Spectator* censured Beecher, while the *London Daily Telegraph* asserted that Beecher had "acted with an imbecility that would have disgraced an uneducated girl."

The congregation of Plymouth Church considered the failure of the jury to reach an agreement on acquittal for Beecher and raised $100,000 to help pay the pastor's legal expenses. Beecher also went on a lecture tour to raise money and was surprised to discover that he had an even greater drawing power than before. His lecture trip was sensationally successful. He also crusaded for civil service reform and urged that the condition of the working class be improved. A longtime Republican, he repudiated the party's candidate, James G. Blaine, and campaigned for the Democratic can-

Beecher near the end of his life

didate, Grover Cleveland, in 1884. He preached against belief in a literal hell and espoused evolution, for which he was greatly criticized, causing him to resign from the Association of Congregational Ministers. At the age of sixty-five he became a regimental chaplain of the New York National Guard and once paraded the streets on horseback and in full uniform. His book *Evolution and Religion* was published in 1885, and during the following year he lectured and preached in England for several months. He was working on the second volume of his *The Life of Jesus, The Christ* when he suffered a stroke and died two days later on 8 March 1887 at the age of seventy-three. An estimated 40,000 persons, most of them women, filed by to view his body as it lay in state at Plymouth Church amid a profusion of flowers. The National Guard provided an honor guard. Peddlers sold souvenirs on the sidewalks. He was buried in Greenwood Cemetery.

References:

William C. Beecher and the Rev. Samuel Scoville, assisted by Mrs. Henry Ward Beecher, *A Biography of Henry Ward Beecher* (New York: Webster, 1888);

Clifford E. Clark, *Henry Ward Beecher: Spokesman for a Middle-Class America* (Urbana: University of Illinois Press, 1978);

J. E. P. Doyle, *Plymouth Church and Its Pastor; or, Henry Ward Beecher and His Accusers* (Hartford, Conn.: Park Publishing, 1874);

Thomas W. Handford, *Beecher: Christian Philosopher, Pulpit Orator, Patriot and Philanthropist* (Chicago: Donohue, Henneberry, 1887);

Paxton Hibben, *Henry Ward Beecher: An American Portrait* (New York: The Press of the Readers Club, 1942);

Thomas W. Knox, *The Life and Work of Henry Ward Beecher* (Hartford, Conn.: Park Publishing, 1887);

J. T. Lloyd, *Henry Ward Beecher: His Life and Work* (London: Walter Scott, 1887);

Robert Shaplen, *Free Love and Heavenly Sinners* (New York: Knopf, 1954).

James Gordon Bennett

Warren Francke
University of Nebraska at Omaha

BIRTH: New Mill, Keith, Banffshire, Scotland, 1 September 1795; parents' names unknown.

EDUCATION: Blair College, Aberdeen, Scotland, 1810-1814.

MARRIAGE: 6 June 1840 to Henrietta Agnes Crean; children: James Gordon, Jr.; Jeanette; Cosmo; a daughter who died in infancy.

MAJOR POSITIONS HELD: Assistant editor, *Charleston* (S.C.) *Courier* (1823); reporter, *New York National Advocate* (1824, 1826); publisher, *New York Courier* (1825); Washington correspondent, *New York Morning Enquirer* (1827, 1829); *New York Courier and Enquirer* (1829-1832); editor-publisher, *New York Globe* (1832); editor-publisher, *Philadelphia Pennsylvanian* (1833); editor-publisher, *New York Herald* (1835-1867).

DEATH: New York City, 1 June 1872.

Rival publishers grudgingly recognized James Gordon Bennett as the most successful of the revolutionaries who created modern journalism in the mid-nineteenth century. The news-gathering enterprise of the *New York Herald* and its attention-getting style attracted circulation and advertising that compelled Bennett's legion of critics to acknowledge his accomplishments. But contemporaries could not agree on what caused the *Herald* to become the leading newspaper. Was it, they debated, because it was so good or because it was so bad? In 1866, thirty-one years after Bennett founded the *Herald*, a conclusion forced itself on James Parton, the biographer of Horace Greeley: "It is impossible any longer to deny that the chief newspaper of [this city] is the *New York Herald*. No matter how much we may regret this fact, or be ashamed of it, no journalist can deny it." In an essay unmatched by subsequent analysis, Parton explained why neither the great Greeley he so admired nor Henry Raymond of the *New York Times* could equal Bennett's accomplishment—despite Parton's declaration that in Bennett, "that region

of the mind where conviction, the sense of truth and honor, public spirit, and patriotism have their sphere, is ... mere vacancy." This very defect numbed Bennett to the noble distractions—Greeley's editorial devotions and Raymond's political concerns—that reduced his rivals to also-rans on the crucial point of competition: news gathering. "That daily newspaper which has the best corps of reporters," Parton announced as the Civil War ended, "and handles them best, necessarily takes the lead of all competitors."

Harper's Weekly had offered the same conclusion in 1858: "No American journal at the present

Gale International Portrait Gallery

31

time can compare with it in point of circulation, advertising, or influence. Its most bitter assailants concede to it unrivaled sagacity and enterprise in the collection of news." Raymond once mused that it would be worth a million dollars "if the Devil would come and tell me every evening, as he does Bennett, what the people of New York would like to read about next morning." Greeley, on his rival's death, reviewed those notorious defects but allowed, "It was as a collector of news that Bennett shone conspicuously. . . . He had an unerring judgment of the pecuniary value of news. He knew how to pick out of the events of the day the subject which engrossed the interest of the greatest number of people, and to give them about that subject all that they could read."

Bennett may have been both the most acclaimed and the most criticized journalist of his time, if not of all time. The sharply contrasting praise and criticism suggest that the story of this man becomes a microcosm of the larger story of journalism from the first day that editors reached out for the full audience. If so, it is the story of a lonely profession. Bennett lived a life in which accomplishment was shadowed by conflict and alienation.

The rural north Scotland of Bennett's birth in 1795 was more than an ocean apart from New York City. The 136 inhabitants of New Mill, where his father farmed, dwelled a mile down from Keith, population about 800, and Keith was fifty-five miles and a few days distant from the 40,000 residents of Aberdeen. Claiming descent from Benoits of Normandy, the Bennetts shared the common occupation of the community. But as Catholics they were in a small minority among their Protestant neighbors. Bennett's earliest biographer, Isaac Pray, claimed in 1855 without evidence that the name James Gordon came from a Protestant clergyman, but ample evidence portrays an upbringing pervaded by Catholic beliefs and practices. Bennett was steeped in Scriptures before learning the Greek and Roman classics and, like his younger brother Cosmo, was raised for the priesthood. The law, however, required that they attend public school. Bennett later recalled floggings as a regular feature of his early education.

At fifteen, he left Cosmo, his parents, and two sisters, Margaret and Anne, to attend Blair College, a Catholic seminary in Aberdeen. By the time he abandoned his religious vocation four years later, his doubts about organized religion in general and Catholicism in particular had long been persistent. Eventually, he left the faith and, as an editor,

harshly criticized the Catholic church. He actually threatened revenge on the church when he learned much later that Cosmo's death at twenty-three could be blamed on the hardships of his priestly training at the College of the Angelites.

But his own departure from Blair involved no apparent bitterness. He seemed more the traditional teenager who had bitten into the apple of new ideas: he had reveled in Lord Byron, the idol of his school literary club, and Robert Burns; he read Smollett, Scott, Rousseau, and Thomas Paine. While little is recorded of the five years between seminary and his voyage to America in 1819, he apparently wandered to Scotland's literary and historical shrines, published an article in an Aberdeen periodical, and continued his avid reading, which included Ben Franklin's *Autobiography*. When he discovered that a friend named William was going to America, Bennett said that he would join in the journey so he might "see the place where Franklin was born."

He arrived in Halifax, Nova Scotia, in the spring of 1819, and taught bookkeeping for little reward before heading down to Portland, Maine, and then, in January 1820, to Boston. Just as he had, with romantic reverence, toured the shrines of Scotland, he now worshipped at the sites of Revolutionary War battles. "I lounged whole afternoons," he recalled, at Bunker Hill, and "passed a whole moonlit night within the old ruined fort on Dorchester Heights, which Washington formerly occupied." His enthusiasm burst into Byronic poetry which gushed with such sentiments as "These are thy blessings, blue-eyed Liberty." These emotions did not aid his search for employment, however, and he went days without eating before he found a position as a proofreader in the printing house of Wells and Lillie. His duties later varied as he stayed with the firm for three years, and he resumed his reading, attended the theater, and wrote poetry of Bostonian inspiration until he moved to New York in 1822.

Bennett apparently held no salaried position in the winter of 1822-1823 but managed to acquire some income from miscellaneous writing. More important, he met Aaron Willington, the proprietor of the *Charleston* (S.C.) *Courier*. For five dollars a week and Willington's assurance that the whole town would soon be talking about his journalistic work, Bennett headed south to Charleston. The *Courier* received Spanish newspapers from Havana, and Bennett translated items. He also wrote poetry, mingled with the talented literary contributors to the newspaper, and observed Willington's pioneering use of harbor boats to rush news from ocean-going ships. Bennett also observed and approved of the institution of slavery. He would retain his anti-Negro bigotry, and what Parton termed his "true Celtic sympathy" for the aristocratic South, up to and beyond the Civil War.

After ten months in Charleston, he returned to New York City in search of employment more rewarding than low-paying journalism. He lectured on political economy and announced that "J. Gordon Bennett" would open a "permanent commercial school" for young gentlemen. Neither pursuit was successful, so he settled again for the bare subsistence of a newspaper paragraphist, scissorer, and all-around editorial assistant. In 1824, he worked for Thomas Snowden, who ran the *National Advocate* for the state's Republicans, and contributed to the *Mercantile Advertiser*. In 1825 he was first an employee of John Tryon's *New York Courier*, and then for a few weeks, after signing promissory notes, its owner. Failing as publisher, he returned the *Courier* to Tryon and wrote for several papers, primarily the *Advocate* again, until late 1826 when he joined Mordecai Noah on the *Morning Enquirer*. Noah, the self-proclaimed King of the Jews and would-be founder of a Jewish island-nation off Canada, had been a victim of Bennett's editorial barbs, but they shared pro-Jackson sentiments. Bennett would soon travel to Washington as Noah's correspondent, but the style that later made the *Herald* a success first attracted attention, and increased sales for the *Enquirer*, in entertaining essays on such mundane subjects as the custom of shaking hands.

The writing style and reporting methods which led the *New York Times* to name Bennett in 1871 "more truly a man of genius than any other" journalist blossomed even more amid the parties and politics of the nation's capital. On 8 January 1828, the *Enquirer* carried Bennett's letter describing President Adams's New Year's party: White House guests grabbed refreshments "scudding round on the heads of the servants" and the poor president "most pathetically shook hands the whole time." After commenting freely on costumes and conduct, Bennett asked, "Don't you think that both sexes return to a state of nature at large parties?"

Frederic Hudson, his managing editor at the *Herald*, later claimed that Bennett had introduced into American journalism a new style of writing: the French style, characterized by a dash and vigor that contrasted with the heavy, argumentative English style. One of Bennett's editorial reminiscences placed the roots of his Washington correspondence

in an episode that found him browsing in the Congressional Library in the spring of 1828 and discovering an edition of Horace Walpole's letters. In this version of the birth of his successful style, Bennett adopted the Walpole letters as his model. Walpole was probably a fresh influence that spring, but the "French" style had already been present for the most part that January and before. So were his well-read Bible—the source of his literary "force, brevity, spirit," Bennett claimed—those Greek and Roman classics of his school days, and his romance with Sir Walter Scott, Lord Byron, and the rest. The Bennett who flushed with emotion at the sites of Scott's Waverley novels, and who lounged and rhymed away the hours on Boston's Bunker Hill—not the Bennett declared vacant in the nobler qualities—is present in this purple passage on the inauguration of Jackson in 1829: "The Chief Justice of the United States then administered the oath of office; and thus, in the sight of Heaven and the surrounding multitude, was Andrew Jackson declared the chief of the only free and pure republic upon the earth. The welkin rang with music and the feeling plaudits of the populace; beauty smiled and waved her kerchief—the first spring birds carolled their notes of joy, and nature poured her various offerings to the giver of all good. The very marble of the pediment seemed to glow with life—justice, with a firmer grasp, secured her scales—'Hope, enchanted, smiled,' and the Genius of our country breathed a living defiance to the world." Bennett summarized the event as "the simple and sublime spectacle of twelve millions of freemen, imparting this Executive Trust to the MAN OF THEIR CHOICE."

As Washington correspondent for the newspaper which, in May 1829, merged with the paper Bennett had briefly owned to form the *Courier and Enquirer*, he ranged widely; he was not only both irreverent and worshipful in tone but diverse in topics and treatment. He wrote not only his long letters from Washington but also paragraphs and poems. When he left those parties and politics, however, for a murder trial in Salem, Massachusetts, the style showed the same dash and vigor. When the state's attorney general, Perez Morton, imposed rules for covering the trial, Bennett displayed the same eagerness to exploit conflict that would characterize his first attention-getting years at the *Herald*. "It is an old, worm-eaten, Gothic dogma of the Courts, to consider the publicity given to every event by the Press, as destructive to the interests of law and justice," Bennett lectured Morton. Rather, "The Press is the living Jury of the Nation." When the court then threatened to banish anyone "detected" taking notes, he sneered at *detected,* exclaiming, "Shade of Franklin! What a word to make use of relative to reports of a public trial." His defense of the right to report can be viewed as early artillery in a perpetual war, but it reveals more about Bennett's entertaining brand of adversary journalism.

Thanks primarily to his work, the *Courier and Enquirer,* with its solid circulation of 3,500, was acclaimed the outstanding newspaper of the day. But in 1832 the paper was controlled by James Watson Webb, who abandoned Jackson. By switching to Nicholas Biddle, the U.S. Bank, and Henry Clay, Webb lost Bennett and eventually the *Courier and Enquirer*'s status among New York dailies. Bennett's loyalty to Jackson and Martin Van Buren was not repaid, however, as two more of his publishing ventures failed. Two months after leaving Webb, he issued the *New York Globe* on 29 October 1832; he closed it exactly one month later on a note of hollow optimism. Jackson and Van Buren were firmly seated in office, the editor had met his obligations to party, principle, and men, and "I now retire from the political field," signed, "J. Gordon Bennett." More to the point, he was broke and unbacked by the Democrats he had intended to serve.

So he turned to Philadelphia and spent most of 1833, that landmark year when Benjamin Day's *Sun* gave New York its first successful penny paper, struggling to keep his new daily, the *Pennsylvanian,* afloat. While Biddle, the Bank, and Wall Street have been blamed for denying the credit needed to keep the paper going, Bennett blamed Van Buren and his political allies. His loan-seeking correspondence with Jesse Hoyt, a Jacksonian leader, lasted all summer, with Bennett pleading, then complaining, and Hoyt denying a $2,500 loan. Reading over their shoulders, one understands why Van Buren might consider the editor a risky investment. Opening with oblique references to ingratitude, Bennett ends by accusing Hoyt of "deadly hostility" and calling Van Buren "cold, heartless, careless, and God knows what not." His independence, based less in political disloyalty than in greater loyalty to the news, cost him support in 1833. But the episode encouraged his complete independence in the future and cemented his conviction that the support of the public could free him from politicians.

Ben Day nearly hired him when he returned to New York in the summer of 1834, but Day's partner and police reporter, George Wisner, argued that the fast-growing *Sun* was already pleasing its readers without adding another salary. Meanwhile, the literary journals accepted Bennett's offerings, and he discussed his next venture with two printers named Anderson and Smith, who had established a shop that served the *Transcript* and the *Sun.* With $500 and a risk-sharing agreement with the printers, Bennett brought out the first issue of the *New York Herald* on 6 May 1835. The four column, four-page sheet joined eighteen newspapers, with circulations from 500 to 6,000, including an average of 1,700 for the dominant six-penny papers. This announcement greeted the city of 270,000 residents:

> James Gordon Bennett & Co. commence this morning the publication of the MORNING HERALD, a new daily paper, price $3 per year, or six cents per week, advertising at the ordinary rates. It is issued from the publishing office, No. 20 Wall Street, and also from the printing office, No. 34 Ann Street, 3d story, at both of which places orders will be thankfully received.
>
> . . . .
>
> We shall support no party—be the organ of no faction or COTERIE, and care nothing for any election or any candidate from president down to a constable. We shall endeavor to record facts on every public and proper subject, stripped of verbiage and coloring, with comments when suitable, just, independent, fearless, and good-tempered.

The *Herald,* Bennett explained, was intended for "the great masses of the community," for both worker and employer, and he hoped to "pick up at least twenty or thirty thousand for the Herald" among the 150,000 readers then buying 42,000 daily papers. The prospectus continued, "By furnishing a daily morning paper at the low price of $3 a year, which may be taken for any shorter period (for a week) at the same rate, and making it at the same time equal to any of the high-priced papers for intelligence, good taste, sagacity, and industry, there is not a person in the city, male or female, that may not be able to say, 'Well, I have got a paper of my own which will tell me all about what's doing in the world.'" In the 11 May issue, the editor promised to "give a correct picture of the world—in Wall Street—in the Exchange—in the Police office—at the Theater—in the Opera— in short, wherever human nature and real life best displays [*sic*] their freaks and vagaries."

This new penny paper would compete with the *Sun* and three lesser one-cent sheets. The publisher would one day be credited with freeing daily newspapers from both political and financial bondage, and he was already the ablest journalist engaged in the new press for the masses, but his prospects and talent were not matched by his initial resources. The first *Herald* office was an oblong underground room where a plank on two flour barrels supplied both business counter and editing desk. For five months, Bennett toiled alone, reporting, writing, editing, clerking, billing, and keeping the books. His day began at 5:00 A.M. and ended at presstime, 11:00 P.M. He worked at home and then in the office from 8:00 to 1:00 before hitting Wall Street, the police court, and other news sites in the afternoon. Back in the office for editing between 4:00 and 6:00, he attended theaters and concert halls in the evening before returning to the office once more for final proofreading.

At age forty, Bennett's assets obviously included high energy and good health, credited in part to the absence of vices. His spare diet left him lean and hard; his hair already showed some gray, but his most striking feature was a cross-eyed stare. His ample experience helped, of course, and he possessed what Parton defined as "a little Scotch sense" and "an almost inexhaustible fund of French vivacity." Thus armed, he created that newspaper which succeeded either because it was so bad or so good. Perhaps it was *both* so bad *and* so good. From the start, the *Herald* carried the "money articles," soon recognized internationally as the most reliable independent news of Wall Street and the stock exchange. The first money piece appeared on 11 May, and they ran daily from 13 June. But also from the start, Bennett titillated readers by attacking his rivals, especially the *Sun*, and then exploiting their reactions. When the 15 May *Sun* made fun of his efforts to win attention at its expense, Bennett's reply the next day signaled the rowdy brand of personal journalism he would practice. The *Sun*, he declared, "is too indecent, too immoral for any respectable person to touch," with its "brace of blockheads for editors and lead of dirty and indecent police reporters." They were "the garbage of society," he mock-fumed. The counterfire raged on, with Day suggesting that Bennett's best hope for dying an upright citizen would be to hang "perpendicularly from a rope."

In December 1835 Bennett's graphic, detailed narratives of the great Wall Street fire were so thorough and unconventional that Parton proclaimed that "American journalism was born amid the roaring flames." If so, it had almost died four months before, when the Ann Street fire destroyed the *Her-*

ald plant and suspended the paper for nineteen days. Both the journalistic innovations and the excesses which dichotomized Bennett's reputation were glaringly visible in his most famous early episode as a reporter, his accounts of the hatchet murder of Helen Jewett, whose fire-charred body was found in the sporting house of Madame Rosina Townsend. New Yorkers were startled in April 1836 when Bennett guided his readers up the stairs of a brothel and introduced the corpse of a prostitute. It was unique reporting on the first day when Bennett condemned one Richard Robinson as "the cold-blooded villain" who committed the crime against Helen, "a finely formed and most beautiful girl." (Later, Bennett came to believe in the innocence of Robinson, who was eventually acquitted.) But it was shocking reporting on the second day when a police guard said, "Mr. B., you can enter." The crowd outside the brothel complained when Bennett was permitted entry, but the policeman explained, according to the *Herald* account, "He is an editor—he is on public duty." The guided tour did not stop with the furnishings in the madam's parlor or the cataloguing of books, paintings, and other items in the prostitute's room but lingered morbidly over the body itself. When the policeman said, "Here is the poor creature," Bennett reported: "He half uncovered the ghastly corpse. I could scarcely look at it for a second or two. Slowly I began to discover the lineaments of the corpse as one would the beauties of a statue of marble. . . . Not a vein was to be seen. The body looked as white, as full, as polished as the purest Parian marble. The perfect figure, the exquisite limbs, the fine face, the full arms, the beautiful bust, all, all surpassed in every respect the Venus De Medici according to the casts generally given of her." Where the fire had charred the body, it "was bronzed like an antique statue." And so the metaphor went on, until "I was recalled to her horrid destiny by seeing the bloody gashes on the right temple, which must have caused instantaneous dissolution." One critic compared Bennett to a vampire and a vulture, but the general public reaction was indicated by a note in the *Herald* which apologized for some printing problems and claimed that single copies were selling at scalper prices: "We could have sold 30,000 copies yesterday if we could have got them worked."

Yet the same incident saw Bennett conduct the interview which came to be credited as the first formal use of this basic reporting technique. The technique that produced the famous first was more an interrogation, modeled on the familiar police

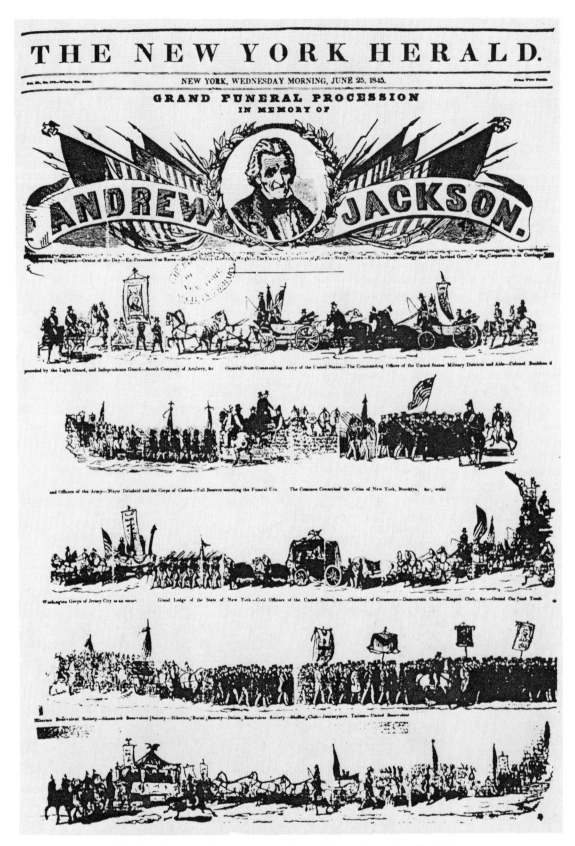

The first illustrated front page, from Bennett's New York Herald, *1845*

courts where stories were elicited as testimony, than the conscious invention of a journalistic method. Madame Townsend described the murder scene on that fateful night, depicting Helen in her loose dress and a man lying on her bed.

Question:	What was he doing?
Answer:	He was lying on his left side, with his head resting on his arm in the bed, the sheet thrown over him, and something in his other hand.
Q:	What was that?
A:	I can't say.
Q:	Was it a book?

And so went the first interrogation-interview, with another nine questions and answers, followed by Bennett's interpretation of the responses from "Mrs. T." The other papers insisted that no such conversation ever took place and that "Mr. B" visited the house for the conventional reasons. Bennett denied flirting with the girls and made the most of the criticism by reporting that his only prior visit to "a house of that kind" was in Halifax, and then the girls had said, "You are too ugly a rascal to come among us; . . . you can talk; we doesn't them things; . . . we be Demoston's scholars, all action."

Both before and after the Jewett murder sensation, Bennett entertained readers with detailed accounts of assaults on his person by indignant rival editors. After he was attacked for the second time by Webb, Bennett on 9 May tallied the damages to both parties, listing his scratched finger and missing vest buttons against Webb's torn coat "and a blow in the face. . . . Balance in my favor, $39.94."

The *Herald*'s second year, 1836, also saw the paper initiate its precedent-setting policy of cash in advance for advertising. On 17 August the price per issue was doubled to two cents. In 1839 the price climbed to three cents, or triple the charge that has named this revolution the "Penny Press" era. The first increase came with an accounting that claimed 20,000 circulation and estimated that the two-cent *Herald* would "clear" $1,000 per week. The circulation figure was highly exaggerated; Bennett once boasted of 100,000 daily issues in this period, but no convincing numbers appear until 1847, when an impartial committee settled a wager by comparing sales of the *Herald* and Greeley's *Tribune;* they credited 16,711 to the *Herald*, 11,455 to the *Tribune*.

Bennett expanded in December 1836, when he launched the *Weekly Herald*. Featuring news summaries, it was a forerunner of the more pop-

ular *Weekly Tribune*, as well as of such descendants as *Leslie's* and *Harper's* weeklies and the twentieth-century news magazines. On 22 May 1837 Bennett announced the *Evening Chronicle*, designed to carry "a great deal of local and amusing matter" pushed from the *Herald*'s pages by its burgeoning business news. While Bennett's alleged upgrading of the *Herald* should not be taken too seriously, this plan might be viewed as its route to respectability. However, the venture lasted less than two months as the *Chronicle*, and less than two years when renamed the *Evening Herald*.

Borrowing from his Charleston experience with harbor craft, Bennett used his growing income in 1837 to buy pilot boats to battle his six-penny rivals for earliest publication of news from ocean ships. When Arunah S. Abell of Baltimore and Daniel H. Craig of Boston developed the pigeon express in 1838, Bennett joined the enterprise, and a coop on the *Herald* roof became the New York haven for their birds. The race for news, whether by water, rail, pigeon, or pony express, found Bennett an early and aggressive entry. He was to cheer the new telegraph in 1844 as an opportunity for organized news gathering that would "make journalism a more potent force than ever before." Similar enthusiasm prompted his passage in May 1838 on the first transatlantic steamer, the *Sirius*. He took time from visiting his family in Scotland to hire a half-dozen correspondents to represent the *Herald* from Glasgow to Rome. Later in the year, he hired others linking the paper to Canada, Mexico, and the Texas Republic led by his friend Sam Houston. Innovations soon to follow were the exchange of the *Herald*'s advance "news-slips" for items from inland papers, a Washington bureau, and a primitive precursor of the Associated Press.

Enterprise in the transportation and gathering of news was matched by advances in its illustration. The paper's first pictures were woodcuts of the burnt district and the Merchants' Exchange after the great fire in 1835; only one engraving, a map locating advertisers' places of business, appeared in 1836. Six woodcuts were used in 1838, but their frequency accelerated in late 1839 when fourteen ran between August and December. Maps, crimes, camp meetings, dancing girls, and a giraffe decorated the *Herald* in 1840; cuts ranged from the gravity of President Harrison's funeral to the frivolity of fancy dress balls.

News stories ran the gamut, too, from elections to murders to church meetings. On his return from Europe in 1838, Bennett revived the society reporting that had won notice during his first days in Washington. His "letters" on European social events were soon followed by similar accounts from his trips to Washington, Niagara Falls, and Saratoga Springs. William Attree, a *Herald* man, showed up at a costume ball in 1839 dressed in a knight's armor; an irate guest seethed at this "unblushing impudence" and sneered, "They find that the more personalities they have in their papers, the more papers they sell." Annual meetings of religious organizations were also covered, and the innovation, though at first criticized, became so accepted that it led to regular coverage of Sunday sermons by 1844. It was only a short hop from society "letters" to the more socially prominent sporting events, such as yachting and horse races. When Bennett wrote about an October 1840 meeting of the New York Jockey Club, he stressed the comings and goings of the crowd more fully than the actual races. In politics, the old ingratitude of Van Buren was repaid in 1840 when Bennett not only endorsed Harrison but spun dramatic narratives of Tippecanoe's triumphs as a soldier. The *Herald*'s story of the siege of Fort Meigs, Hudson suggests, "produced considerable effect on the public mind." In subsequent campaigns, Bennett backed Polk, Taylor, and Pierce.

Bennett's news enterprise and his excesses may be inseparable as causes of the *Herald*'s success. And its success, as much as his excesses, may have prompted the "Great Moral War," as Hudson called it, waged against the paper in 1840. Led by his old employers, Noah and Webb, along with Park Benjamin of the *Evening Signal*, the "war" featured a boycott by advertisers, vendors, and subscribers, and an acceleration of the name-calling long aimed at Bennett. Webb called the *Herald* "disgusting, vile, ribald, disreputable and vulgar" and Bennett a "moral pestilence," among other things; Noah's string of epithets included "turkey-buzzard" and "depraved appetite"; Benjamin mentioned the "ghoul-like propensity" of this "infamous blasphemer" and "venomous reptile"— a sampling of dozens of insults compiled by managing editor Hudson in his friendly history.

Dubbing his opponents the "Wall Street Holy Allies," Bennett declared himself the victor by quoting circulation figures to his advantage. But the boycott campaign, extending from spring through summer of 1840, apparently caused a temporary drop in his daily circulation from 17,000 to less than 15,000. The Moral War, from Pray's 1855 perspective, stemmed from economic envy and from Bennett's practice of writing *leg* instead of *limb* and *petticoats* rather than *inexpressibles*. Unfor-

tunately for the reputation of this influential journalist, the "Allies," including many churchmen, were responding to aggravations greater than these mild improprieties.

For example, his old complaints against the Catholic church erupted repeatedly, as in this early instance: "As a Catholic, we call upon the Catholic Bishop and clergy of New York to come forth from the darkness, folly, and superstition of the tenth century." He condescended that "we do not wish them to discard their greatest absurdities at the first breath. . . . We may for a while indulge ourselves in the delicious luxury of creating and eating our Divinity. A peculiar taste of this kind, like smoking tobacco or drinking whiskey, cannot be given up all at once." "If we must have a Pope," he advised, make him an American pope, "not such a decrepit, licentious, stupid, Italian blockhead" as the Roman cardinals provide. Bennett's only evident sympathy for priests arose when Protestants exposed Catholic indiscretions. He viewed this as hypocrisy and used it as an excuse to report Protestant misbehavior. In March 1836, one Friday's account of an Episcopal clergyman "making love too suddenly" to the widow Griffin, who "owns a pair of fine eyes, and a bust unmatchable in Broadway in its sunniest day," was followed the next Monday by a lengthy rehash of the same alleged seduction. "He could stand it no longer, but started up and * * * * ecstasy * * * * soft cheek * * * * clasped * * * * bust * * * * arms * * * * screamed," and so on, with Bennett inserting the modest stars before noting that "this was kept up for several minutes." In an aside, Bennett winked: "If it had been a Catholic clergyman, and the widow had been at her confession, it would have been altogether another story. We could have believed then without evidence. As the matter stands, it must be ripped up to the bottom." But one passionate Episcopalian did not satisfy his cynical crusade against hypocrisy. The next day he advertised: "Five hundred dollars reward will be given to any handsome woman, either lovely widow or single seamstress, who will set a trap for a Presbyterian parson, and catch one of them flagrante delicito, [*sic*] and a la Griffin."

The *Herald* editorial "Shocking Depravity of the Age" in 1838 treated the same subject in broader strokes. Bennett mocked the *Journal of Commerce* for grumbling about "much adultery, fornication, seduction and concubinage, existing amongst actors and actresses," and then sniffing, "Of the correctness or incorrectness of these rumors we know nothing." A gleeful Bennett wrote, "Now then, we have some extraordinary instances of adultery, seduction and depravity to state amongst the clergy! Of the truth or falsehood of these we know something." Then he recited "the horrible seduction . . . the seduction upon seduction . . . the lamentable seduction" of one woman after another, all victims of one or another reverend or Sunday school teacher. The editorial went into detail on a Presbyterian preacher who "became apparently attached to a dozen different females, all of whom, it is believed, he abused." It was this sort of entertainment, not just bold references to petticoats, that armed the moral warriors and embarrassed the historians who blushed to confess his remarkable success. Fortunately, the accomplishments flowed as swiftly as the stream of sensationalism and titillation.

The money articles attracted middle-class readers and gave them a more acceptable reason for buying the *Herald*. Such coups as his early prediction of the stock market crash of 1837 were an added bonus. This financial reporting—"the true Baconian path in commercial science," Bennett called it—exemplified his advantage over two groups of competitors. The penny papers lacked strong interest in financial news, and the six-penny papers lacked the *Herald*'s independence, the detachment that gave its Wall Street coverage such credibility that a Hamburg banker paid a premium for all the back issues.

When Bennett married Henrietta Agnes Crean on 6 June 1840, however, he had not entirely abandoned personal journalism for the pursuit of more substantial news. In what can only be regarded as a display of amazing vulgarity, Bennett delineated Miss Crean with the same anatomical ogling once reserved for the remains of Miss Jewett. In fact, he publicized the young piano teacher, composer, and descendant of two Irish families— the Warrens and the Crean Lynchs—on several occasions. "Her figure is most magnificent—her head, neck and bust, of the purest classical contour," he rhapsodized on first setting eyes on her. Five days before the wedding, he headlined the event, "Declaration of Love—Caught at Last— Going to be Married," and so on. "In purity and uprightness," he boasted, "she is worth half a million of pure coin." He then added, in passing, that the *Herald* paid him "nearly $25,000 per annum, almost equal to the President's salary." After the ceremony at St. Peter's Catholic Church, his editorial rhapsodies soared on, and his critics reciprocated by abusing the couple both in print and in society. The birth of James Gordon Bennett, Jr., on 10 May 1841 climaxed his father's year-long

public prancing about the marriage and impending paternity and spurred the countering parade of rumors and innuendo from his rivals. When the *Sun* openly jeered that Senior had not fathered Junior, Bennett sued for libel and won a demeaning $250. The sympathetic Pray directly blamed such editorial malevolence for the fact that Mrs. Bennett chose to reside chiefly in Europe for the rest of her life. Their children—James Gordon, Jr., and a daughter, Jeanette—were educated there; another son, Cosmo, died at the age of five, and another daughter did not survive infancy. Through the 1840s and 1850s, Bennett journeyed often to the Continent, both on business and for reunions with his wife, but generally lived alone in New York.

Still known for his long hours and close attention to all phases of the operation, Bennett expanded the news enterprise again in 1841. Robert Sutton was employed to head what Bennett identified as his "corps of reporters" in Washington. Less than a month after his son's birth, he complained to Henry Clay that his corps, "organized at an expense of nearly $200 per week," was excluded from the Senate gallery. The letter assured the senator that the *Herald* would, without charge, fully report proceedings then printed at great cost to the government. Clay sympathized, and the rule favoring the District of Columbia press was soon dropped. The same year saw his nemesis, Horace Greeley, introduce the *New York Tribune* and supply Bennett with a new personal target. Like Day and others before and after, Greeley was labeled an "unmitigated blockhead." But Greeley alone was a "pumpkin": "Galvanize a large New England squash, and it would make as capable an editor as Horace."

When the *Herald* moved to a new building at Fulton and Nassau Streets in May 1842, its presses could spin out some 60,000 copies a day. Bennett broke, but only briefly, his rule of remaining independent of all other business interests when he published the short-lived *New York Lancet*, a medical journal. Hudson had managed the *Herald* as early as 1838, when his publisher first steamed to Europe, and was now trusted to preside whenever Bennett was occupied elsewhere. However, despite two more European voyages in 1843 (a trip that was marred when the Irish Repeal leader, Daniel O'Connell, attacked Bennett on obscure grounds) and 1846, Bennett directly supervised even greater growth of news-gathering capacity. Anticipating the Mexican War, he arranged overland express runs, with the *New Orleans Crescent City* in charge of the Southern end. By January 1845, their system shuttled news to New York from one to four days ahead of the U. S. Mail. Postal authorities proclaimed such victories illegal and arrested the *Crescent City* partner, but when war erupted in 1846 the expresses ran both efficiently and more frequently through cooperation with the *Baltimore Sun* and *Philadelphia Ledger*. Such far-flung enterprise paid well in 1848 when Thomas O. Larkin, the *Herald* correspondent on the West Coast of Mexico, mailed a gold dust sample from newly discovered mines in California. Succeeding letters grew more enthusiastic about the find until Bennett consulted an assayer that December and confirmed "one of the most extraordinary events of the age."

The gold rush of 1849 seemed more ordinary when the events of the next decade culminated in the Civil War. The Bennett position on slavery and

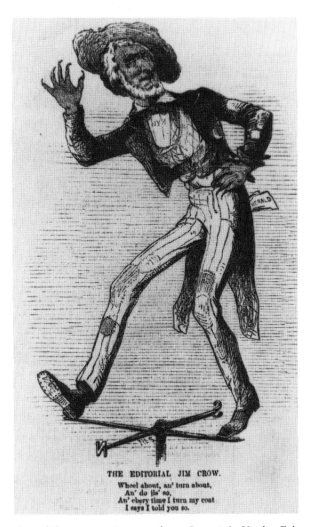

THE EDITORIAL JIM CROW.

Wheel about, an' turn about,
An' do jis' so,
An' ebery time I turn my coat
I says I told you so.

One of the many cartoon attacks on Bennett in Vanity Fair *(27 April 1861)*

union had been enunciated before, but the Compromise of 1850 and the Fugitive Slave Act provided new opportunities for firm stands. His "uniform course from the first," Pray wrote in 1855, was to throw "the whole weight of his influence against the agitation of the slavery question in the North." The racial slurs of his earlier rhetoric succumbed to "save the Union" slogans from a Bennett cloaked in the Constitution. The *Herald* still headlined sensational stories—exposure of the One-Eyed Thompson gang, the Drury Trials, the Forrest divorce—in 1850, and Bennett still worked long hours when not wintering in Europe. A newcomer to the cheap paper ranks in 1851, Henry Raymond's *New York Times* added to the challenge.

Bennett met it, at age fifty-six, with an office day that started at 7:30 in the morning and ended past 10:00 in the evening. Once his private correspondence and letters for publication were read, he scanned articles, particularly on finances and the theater, marked for his attention amid an array of exchange newspapers. Comments were scribbled in margins, and memos accumulated as he flipped pages. "Every now and then," an employee said, "dot, dot, goes down a mysterious little word." Then, until noon, a sequence of assistants entered his office—first a stenographer, taking dictation while Bennett recited one item after another; then an editor who took less specific notes on editorial ideas; and, finally, a specialist or two, men from the money department or the courts, to be quizzed about current developments on their beats. The early afternoon permitted close reading of pieces completed for the next issue, plus their marking for layout placement. From 2:00 to 3:00 P.M., he wandered from desk to desk chatting with reporters, pausing longest to ask about the theater in both its business and aesthetic aspects. After huddling briefly with Hudson, Bennett would retire for a few hours to his apartment, only to return between 8:00 and 9:00 after stops at the opera or theater. If urgent news required it, he would scribble a few lines of comment before heading home at 10:00 P.M. Only if winter found him in New York rather than vacationing in Europe was this pattern broken. Then, plagued by chronic bronchial problems, he conducted most of these duties while confined to his home.

Bennett was sixty years old in 1855, but his age scarcely shielded him from criticism. Raymond joined the traditional name-calling, gibing at the "Satanic Brother Bennett" on one occasion. A theatrical manager won $6,000 in one of several successful libel suits against the publisher; the *Herald*

Bennett (seated, center) and the editorial staff of the Herald *(James Melvin Lee, Department of Journalism, New York University)*

had described his opera house as a common resort of prostitutes and gamblers. Yet, whether the change was attributable to age, wealth, success, or experience, Bennett began to show signs of editorial moderation to match his always moderate personal habits. He supported General Frémont, the presidential candidate of the new Republican party in 1856, rather than accept the Democratic party's extension of slavery. (The ensuing Buchanan victory marked his first losing endorsement.) Now he was more likely to charge the Abolitionists with hypocrisy than with racial treason. For example, "The African Slave Trade" article filling most of page two on 15 August 1859 described the illegal activity in full detail after a lead paragraph blaming the Black Republicans. "It is now a well-established fact," the *Herald* reported, "that nearly the whole of the slave fleet is fitted out in Boston, Portland, New Bedford and other Eastern ports, which may be regarded as the very strongholds of that party."

Bennett had long since swung back to the Buchanan administration, and when John Brown

raided Harper's Ferry in October, the *Herald* editorial blamed "that demogogue, William H. Seward," and his doctrine of the "irrepressible conflict." But the *Herald*'s leading news coverage gave Brown a voice of dignity in the "verbatim report" of his replies to jailhouse interrogation. And, while Bennett applauded the candidacy of Stephen Douglas in 1860, he allowed Henry Villard to write full and friendly accounts of Abe Lincoln's campaign.

In the year that Lincoln entered the White House, the *Herald* claimed circulation ranging from 105,000 to 135,000 a day. Raymond scoffed, calling Bennett a "First-Class Wind-Bag," and wagered that the daily issue was under 75,000. One estimate had it as 77,000 daily and 82,000 Sunday. Whatever the exact figures may have been, the *Herald* was rich enough to outspend its rivals in coverage of the Rebellion. But first Bennett had to retreat from his language, just days before the attack on Fort Sumter, which characterized the Lincoln administration as "vicious, imbecile, demoralized," and which advised its "over-throw" as the last hope against war. On 14 April a mob threatened the

Herald building until Bennett displayed a hastily-obtained American flag, but the presses kept rolling until that vaunted 135,000-issue run was complete. On the 15th the *Herald* proclaimed its support for the Union cause, and on the 16th Bennett called Villard to New York and began lining up the staff that would grow to sixty-three war correspondents.

Six reporters, already placed in the South, sent graphic stories of narrow escapes from crowds angered over the firing at Fort Sumter. In Hudson's enthusiastic version, "with every division marched a young representative" of the *Herald:* "At every fight one of its correspondents was an eyewitness. There was a *Herald* tent and a *Herald* wagon with each Army corps." From 1861 through 1865, Bennett lavished more than a half-million dollars on this ultimate enterprise. The *Herald*'s contribution to the "Bohemian Brigade" of war reporters included B. S. Osbon, the scandalous Henry Wikoff, and George Alfred Townsend. Young George, then with the *Philadelphia Press,* was wide-eyed at his first glimpse of a well-outfitted *Herald* reporter, with the best cushioned saddle, the plumpest saddle bags, and the most money to buy news items. Townsend resolved "to seize the first opportunity of changing establishments." It became widely known that Bennett not only paid more for news, but more for expenses, particularly the gifts of whiskey and watermelons that procured cooperation from sources. "No rigid or grudging scrutiny" greeted expense accounts at the *Herald,* Parton explained, "no minute and insulting inquiries respecting the last moments of a horse ridden to death in the service." Historians debate whether the *Herald* or the *Tribune* best reported the war, but a Greeley editor complained, "The *Herald* is constantly ahead. We are obliged to copy from it." Clearly, Bennett was better organized at the outset. If getting the news first and in greatest detail is the measure, the *Herald* was the leader. Oddly, the full, fast account of a major battle was not its most talked-about reportage: the most startling exclusive came in 1862 when the paper published the roster of the entire Rebel army.

Lincoln received Bennett's endorsement for reelection in 1864, and the *Herald* received even-handed or better cooperation from the president. When Lincoln was shot, Andrew Johnson inherited Bennett's approval. After resisting emancipation, then accepting it as inevitable, Bennett favored a generous policy of reconstruction.

The war had ended and seventy years had passed since his birth in Scotland when the senior Bennett arranged in 1866 for his twenty-five-year-old son to take command of the *Herald.* Circulation stood at 90,000, and yearly profits had risen to $400,000. Managing editor Hudson retired when James Gordon, Jr., took over and Bennett tried to reduce his own involvement over the next three years, until his visits totaled a few half-days each week. Journalist Junius Browne noticed in 1869 that the nation's leading dailies were still delivered to Bennett's door—either his country residence at Washington Heights or the town house at Fifth Avenue and Thirty-eighth Street—and he continued to mark them and make other suggestions. He wrote rousing editorials as late as 2 June 1871, when he ridiculed the opulent wedding of the daughter of Boss Tweed.

His health failing in the winter of 1871-1872, Bennett moved from the country to his Fifth Avenue mansion. He planned to join his family in Europe that spring, but on 21 May he summoned the Catholic archbishop, received the last sacrament, and rejoined his natal church. A stroke on 25 May brought Hudson to his bedside, but no family members attended his death on 1 June 1872. While old enemies—Greeley, George Jones of the *Times,* and Charles Dana—served as pallbearers, only James Gordon Bennett, Jr., returned from Europe for the funeral. There were eulogies, but the praise was still muted with qualifications. Greeley said, "He developed the capacities of journalism in a most wonderful manner, but he did it by degrading its character. He made the newspaper powerful, but he made it odious." On the other hand, as *Harper's Weekly* had pointed out in 1858: "No one can seriously deny the merit of the *Herald* without impugning the judgment or the morals of the community" which supported it. Some, of course, would so impugn, and would argue that Bennett's great gifts to modern journalism were badly encumbered with debts, and that his descendants inherited the entire estate.

Biographies:

Isaac Pray, *Memoirs of James Gordon Bennett and His Times* (New York: Stringer & Townsend, 1855);

Don Seitz, *The James Gordon Bennetts* (Indianapolis: Bobbs-Merrill, 1928);

Oliver Carlson, *The Man Who Made News* (New York: Duell, Sloan & Pearce, 1942).

References:

Anonymous, *Life of James Gordon Bennett* (New York, 1844);

James L. Crouthamel, "James Gordon Bennett, the

New York Herald, and the Development of Newspaper Sensationalism," *New York History*, 54 (July 1973): 294-316;

Warren T. Francke, "Sensational Roots: The Police Court Heritage and the Investigative Mr. B," in his "Investigative Exposure in the Nineteenth Century," Ph.D. dissertation, University of Minnesota, 1974, pp. 22-54;

Frederic Hudson, *Journalism in the United States from 1690 to 1872* (New York: Harper, 1873), pp. 408-456;

"James Gordon Bennett, Esq.," *Harper's Weekly*, 2 (10 July 1858): 433-434;

James Parton, "The New York Herald," *North American Review*, 102 (April 1866): 373-419;

Michael Schudson, "Egalitarianism: The Penny Press," in his *Discovering the News: A Social History of American Newspapers* (New York: Basic Books, 1978), pp. 12-60.

Francis Preston Blair
(12 April 1791-18 October 1876)

Hazel Dicken-Garcia
University of Minnesota

MAJOR POSITIONS HELD: Contributor, *Frankfort* (Ky.) *Argus of Western America* (1817-1830); editor, *Washington* (D.C.) *Globe* (1830-1845).

BOOKS: *Answer of F. P. Blair, to the Orders of Messrs. Boyle, Ousley and Mills* (Frankfort, Ky., 1825?);

Republican Documents. Gen. Jackson and James Buchanan. Letter from Francis P. Blair. To the Public (Silver Spring, Md., 1836);

The Life and Public Services of Gen. William O. Butler, by Francis P. Blair, with His Letters and Speeches on Various Subjects (Baltimore: N. Hickman, 1848);

Letter of Francis P. Blair, Esq., to the Republican Association of Washington, D.C. (Washington, D.C.: The Republican Association, 1855);

A Voice from the Grave of Jackson! Letter from Francis P. Blair, Esq., to a Public Meeting in New York, Held April 29, 1856 (Washington, D.C.: Buell & Blanchard, printers, 1856);

Origin of Modern Nullification. Letter from F. P. Blair, to the New York Republicans (Silver Spring, Md., 1856);

Shall the Usurpation of the Government, by the Fragment of a Congress, Be Perpetuated by Negro Suffrage? Speech of Gen. Frank P. Blair, Delivered at Memphis, Tennessee . . . September 20, 1866 (Washington, D.C.: Intelligencer Printing House, 1867);

Relief without Repudiation. Apply to Public Use the Cred- *it and Money of the Government Now Enriching Banking Corporations: Letter to the Workingmen* (Silver Spring, Md., 1869);

Letter from Francis P. Blair. To My Neighbors (New York: Evening Post, n.d.).

Francis Preston Blair's life spanned the administrations of the first eighteen United States presidents; Blair played political roles of varying degrees of importance in the last twelve of those administrations. The most significant position Blair ever actually held was editorship of the *Washington* (D.C.) *Globe* during the Jackson-Van Buren-Harrison-Tyler administrations. But his position in his contemporaries' minds was more important, if less tangible. Indeed, Blair's political acumen and involvement were such that he has been called the most influential journalist of his time. During Andrew Jackson's two terms as president, Blair used his newspaper to advance Jackson's policies, to give the cue to other Jacksonian editors on positions they should take, to "whip into line" any recalcitrant party members, and to provide copy to the nation's Jacksonian press as a means of "reflecting" and cementing grass roots support for the administration. At a time in American history when the party press achieved its zenith, Blair was in the nation's highest party-editor position. His contribution to raising the party press to its unmatched level during the Jackson years was surely unsur-

Francis Preston Blair

passed and probably unequaled. He, with Amos Kendall, deserves credit for making the press an important force in national elections.

Historians suggest, though with little hard evidence, that Blair was the architect of many Jackson administration policies. Even without the evidence, the idea that Blair played such a role is believable. A leader in Jackson's "kitchen cabinet," he met first thing in the morning with the president almost daily. He vacationed with Jackson and on at least one occasion when Jackson vacationed without him, the Blair family moved into the White House as caretakers until Jackson returned. Jackson trusted and confided in Blair above all others. During years critical to the nation's development, Blair was closer to the president than anyone else—and perhaps no other, except immediate family members, has ever been so close to an American president. After his career as an editor had ended, Blair became an elder statesman of American politics. He was one of the founders of the Republican party and a confidant of Abraham Lincoln.

Blair's heritage, familial ties, and early environment make his highly political life unsurprising. He was raised on a tradition of politics. His Scotch-

Irish ancestry, traced as far back as 1625, boasts peerages, titles, and rebels. The Blairs, for example, held Derry against James II until King William afforded relief in 1689.

Blair's grandfather and five great-uncles and great-aunts came to the American colonies in the early eighteenth century and settled in Pennsylvania, from where descendants moved into the Shenandoah Valley of Virginia. Blair's grandfather John and great-uncle Samuel were Presbyterian ministers; John held the first chair of theology at Princeton University, and Samuel was a leader in the first Great Awakening that swept the colonies from 1735 to 1745. Blair's father, James, was a lawyer and a member of the Virginia legislature when Francis Preston, the second of seven children, was born on 12 April 1791 at the family's Abingdon, Virginia, home. Blair's mother, Elizabeth Smith Blair, was a granddaughter of Virginia planter and patriarch John Preston, and Blair's relatives, primarily on his mother's side, included several prominent Virginia and Kentucky families: Marshalls, Browns, Madisons, Breckinridges, Harts, and McDowells. Further, among his forebears were a Princeton University president, a Union College president, and David Rice, the "father of Presbyterianism in Kentucky," who was associated with the development of Transylvania University in Lexington, Kentucky.

Soon after Blair's birth, James Blair, seeking better financial opportunities, moved to Frankfort, Kentucky; by 1796 he was state attorney general, a position he held for more than twenty years.

Transylvania University was the natural choice for Blair's education: his father was a trustee; the institution, suiting the liberal Blair family tradition, inculcated in its students a spirit of Jeffersonianism; and it was headed by Presbyterian James Blythe. At age nineteen, Blair rode horseback from Frankfort to Lexington to enroll; a year later, in 1811, he graduated with honors, after having studied moral philosophy, criticism, logic, belles lettres, and law.

Also in 1811, Blair assisted his father in writing a pamphlet defending states' rights to tax the Bank of the United States and opposing recharter. Thus, Blair's 1811 published views were precursors of those that would characterize the Jackson administration more than twenty years later. Blair entered the War of 1812 as an aide to his uncle, George Madison, who was then governor of Kentucky. However, he became seriously ill on the campaign, nearly dying of a hemorrhage of the lungs

ARGUS OF WESTERN AMERICA.

[Number 39.]　　　FRANKFORT, KENTUCKY, WEDNESDAY, NOVEMBER 17, 1824　　　[Volume XVII.]

Front page of Amos Kendall's Argus of Western America, *the Frankfort, Kentucky, newspaper to which Blair contributed and which he helped edit before he took over the* Washington (D.C) Globe *in 1830*

at Vincennes, Indiana, and returned home, ending his military "career."

Blair, the eldest of four surviving children, was, in fact, a sickly young man and may have had tuberculosis. Although he seems to have recovered from the illness, he was never robust and he feared a recurrence. His health concerned his prospective father-in-law, General Charles Scott, who warned his stepdaughter that marriage to Blair would make her a widow within six months; she replied that she would rather be Francis Preston Blair's widow than any other man's wife. On 21 July 1812, the twenty-one-year-old Blair married eighteen-year-old Eliza Violet Gist, the granddaughter of explorer Christopher Gist, who guided George Washington on his first trip across the Allegheny Mountains. Blair's great wish, as his young family grew, was to live to be at least forty and see his sons and daughter comfortably established.

Blair was admitted to the Kentucky bar in 1817 but never practiced, because his lung condition had left him with a voice too weak for the sustained oral argument necessary in the courtroom. With farming as an avocation, he became clerk of the circuit court in Franklin County at an annual salary of $40, with the promise of an additional $2,000 in annual fees. But Blair, often able to collect less than half the fees, faced financial struggles during the eighteen years he remained in the post.

By 1817, Blair may have already tried journalism sufficiently to feel he had found his niche. A trained lawyer skilled with words, his voice inhibited his performing in courtrooms but he would have no such problems with the written word. Other than the political tract he had assisted his father in writing in 1811, it is difficult to pinpoint when his journalistic efforts or his association with Amos Kendall and the *Argus of Western America* began. Some sources note his association with the *Georgetown* (Ky.) *Patriot*, a newspaper edited by Kendall from 1816 until at least 1820; but it was Blair's writing in the *Argus* after 1817 that brought him national attention. Kendall, a recently transplanted Massachusetts schoolteacher, had bought part ownership in the *Argus* with a loan from Kentucky statesman Henry Clay in 1816. Both Blair and Kendall were close to Clay at the time, and this, plus the fact that the *Argus* was published in Blair's hometown of Frankfort, makes it plausible that Blair's association with Kendall stems from at least 1816.

Blair's political views ripened in the Kentucky War on the Bank (also called the Relief War) that erupted after 1817. During that struggle, Blair came to hate the United States Bank as a danger to democracy, and his journalistic career was made as he fought the bank through the *Argus* and a "flood of pamphlets."

The Second Bank of the United States, chartered in 1816, refused in the 1817 economic crisis to do business with banks that had suspended specie payments. Kentucky, where money was scarce, speculation rife, and the typical frontier debtor economy prevailed, was hit hard. Forty newly chartered independent banks were ruined, and debtors—among them Blair—suffered. In the ensuing panic, Blair was sued thirteen times for his own debts and six times for debts he had endorsed for friends. He owed $20,744 to the bank, plus another $17,488.60 in judgments against him.

Blair and others saw the bank as the source of the problem and intensified opposition to it. A Relief party (so named because it sought relief for debtors) was formed and the struggle, marked by periods of violence, lasted nearly ten years. The Relief party legislature incorporated the Bank of the Commonwealth (a paper money "machine" without capital) to inflate currency and raise prices until debtors could pay off their debts—and then passed laws forcing acceptance of its notes as payment of debts. When Kentucky courts declared the laws invalid, the legislature repealed laws establishing the court of appeals and created a new court. Blair was named clerk of the new court and sent to seize the records of the old court, whose members refused to disband or to give up the records. Finding the office locked, Blair broke in and took the records. When the old court judges protested, Blair answered them in a series of published letters: "Gentlemen: you are engaged in a fearful contest. Your attempt to hold and exercise a portion of the judicial power of this Commonwealth is considered a direct and gross usurpation. . . ." He argued that people had merely exercised their right to correct wrongs in government by removing the old court from power and accused the judges of deepening their wrongs by not resigning: "You do not resign but set the public voice at defiance. You rallied around you the power and influence of the state and national banks, of most of the lawyers, of the merchants, of the rich, of the non-residents and idle chatterers who infest our towns. You determined you commanded always more than one-third of the legislature and thus would conquer the people or sink the state. . . . It is my design . . . to unmask you; to strip you of the gauze of sophistry which you have flung around you; to exhibit you

Silver Spring, the Maryland estate where Blair held court as an elder statesman after retiring from journalism

in your true attitude as bold usurpers unsupported by a single argument drawn from the constitution or the principles of our government."

During the 1825 sessions, Kentucky had two courts of appeals; but a more conservative legislature was elected in 1826 and returned the old court to power. Blair then refused to give up the court records, saying he would resist with blood until the act establishing the new court was repealed. A mob on the way to seize the records from Blair was diverted, and Blair ultimately bowed to the inevitable—but only after the law setting up the new court had been repealed. He, of course, lost his clerkship of the court of appeals; but he remained circuit court clerk in Franklin County, he had become president of the Bank of the Commonwealth, and he was well ensconced at the *Argus of Western America*—all of which positions he kept until he departed for Washington, D.C., in 1830.

The Relief War hastened that departure by diverting Blair's political support from United States Bank supporter Clay to Jackson. Because Clay was of the old court party, the Blair-Clay relationship was strained; and when Kendall broke with Clay, Blair went along. Clay had loaned Ken-

dall money to buy the *Argus* partnership and advanced another loan in 1825. Kendall, probably due chiefly to Clay's efforts, had been public printer in Kentucky almost from the beginning of his *Argus* ties. But as the Relief War wore on, Kendall lost that patronage and the *Argus* fell on financial hard times. He and Blair ardently supported Clay for the presidency in 1824. But Clay, the loser in that election, voted for John Adams, despite his constituents' instructions to vote for Jackson. After Adams named Clay secretary of state, Kendall published a series of letters to Clay charging that he had made a bargain with Adams for position and had sold out the interests of the West. Kendall said that proof of his charges were in Clay letters to Blair. Embarrassed, Blair assured Clay he had never shown his correspondence to Kendall. The Kentucky Senate ordered an investigation, but Blair refused to testify, saying that his personal correspondence was private. Because the investigators were Clay friends hoping to clear his name, the opposition press called the inquiry a whitewash. Clay, hoping to end the matter, pressed Blair, who finally turned over the correspondence to Clay with permission to publish it. At that point,

Clay also pleaded privacy and refused to make the letters public—an action that added to Kendall's arsenal and deepened suspicion that hung over Clay for the rest of his life.

Blair had already turned to the Jackson camp. He identified Clay with Adams, who, to Blair, was a Federalist in disguise and meant only anti-Jeffersonian policies. Blair now believed hope of completing the work of Jeffersonian democracy in America lay with Jackson. After all, Jackson had received the "people's" vote in 1824—only a House of Representatives vote had denied him the presidency—and the popular will was a mark of Jeffersonian politics. So, by late 1826, Blair and Kendall were leaders of the Jackson campaign in Kentucky. The two journalists filled *Argus* columns with denunciations of the Adams administration and support for Jackson. Pro-Jackson meetings, probably instigated by Blair and Kendall, were reported thoroughly; Jackson's life was reviewed in weekly segments; and Jackson's wife, Rachel, was staunchly defended against charges by the Adams-Clay press that she had deserted her first husband, Lewis Robards, and had lived in adultery with, and later bigamously married, Jackson. It was a newspaper campaign without precedent or equal at the time.

The campaign brought Blair more editorial responsibility. He conducted the *Argus*, with no letup in the Jackson campaign, when Kendall left Frankfort on a tour that took him back to his New England roots, and he faithfully published Kendall letters telling of Jackson support in every quarter visited on his trip. Blair was soon left to run the *Argus* again when Kendall hurried to Washington after the election to await a hoped-for appointment and to offer suggestions on the selection of Jackson advisers.

Thomas Hart Benton, in *Thirty Years' View*, credits *Argus* editorials and articles during this interim with catching Jackson's attention and prompting the invitation to Blair to become a Washington newspaper editor. But Jackson surely knew of Blair and his views long before 1829; he must have read the *Argus* at least since it had become his leading newspaper supporter. Furthermore, he must have been aware of Blair's tireless work on behalf of Jackson candidates for the 1828 election in Kentucky. Finally, Kendall proposed Blair as a Washington editor as early as 3 February 1829. That suggestion, in a letter from Kendall to Blair, was followed up in several 1830 letters that made clear the dissatisfaction with Duff Green as administration editor and the intention of dis-

creetly edging him out after Blair was established in Washington.

In October 1830, Kendall made a full-fledged proposition that Blair come by mid-November to edit a Washington newspaper that should be in print by 1 December. That proposition, in a letter to Blair, spelled out what should be the paper's thrust, Blair's political position, the financial means for the paper, and the prospects such an enterprise offered Blair. The new newspaper must support government reform, payment of the national debt, a "judicious" tariff, and reduced duties on imports; it must call for "leaving the States to manage their own affairs without other interference than the safety of the whole imperiously requires"; and it should oppose the Bank of the United States and the South Carolina nullifiers. Blair, as editor, should be the "friend of General Jackson and the administration, having no further political views other than the support of his principles," and should be obligated to no one else, including Martin Van Buren (who had interceded to pay Kendall's debt to Clay with Jackson funds). Blair could depend on $2,000 to $3,000 of Postmaster General W. T. Barry's $4,000 to $6,000 annual patronage, Kendall said, plus Van Buren's influence and most of his patronage. Further patronage would come from the departments of war, navy, register, second comptroller, and second and fourth auditors. In sum, Blair could expect at least $4,000 a year in government printing—an amount that could increase to $10,000 to $15,000. Jackson friends would provide the printer for the newspaper, while members of the administration would ensure circulation.

On 6 November 1830, Blair, with his wife and daughter, boarded a stage departing for Washington after depositing his sons with Lexington relatives and taking leave of the posts that provided his $3,000 annual income. One month later, on 7 December, the first issue of the *Globe* appeared, under the motto "The world is governed too much."

The *Globe* was successful from the beginning; Blair biographer Elbert B. Smith summarizes Blair's influence: "Blair was everything his supporters had hoped for, and soon his firey editorials were being read all over America. By 1835, [the Globe] had 17,000 subscribers, and its influence went far beyond its numbers. Democrats bought it for the benefit of state legislatures. People unable to subscribe as individuals took it as partners and in groups. As the Jacksonians used the patronage to build up their grass-roots organizations, subscriptions . . . became the responsibility of local politicians everywhere. It was the authentic voice of Andrew Jackson—first to know his views on any subject and first to communicate and justify them to the faithful. Ultimately, more than 400 newspapers around the country drew information, arguments, and inspiration from its columns. They regularly exchanged news and editorials with it, and promptly wheeled into line with each change in official policy."

Blair and the *Globe* were unsurpassed in Jackson's esteem, and the president used pressure to obtain printing contracts for Blair from government agencies. Still, Blair remained burdened with debts, and he struggled before realizing financial security. Fierce competition for printing contracts and a divided Congress meant congressional patronage during only four of the *Globe*'s fifteen years of existence, and Blair never received more than half of the government monies for printing in any year. Meanwhile, Joseph Gales and William Winston Seaton, editors of the *National Intelligencer*, received in one year alone half the sum Blair received in the *Globe*'s first eleven years—and one third of Blair's total came in 1840-1841, long after Jackson had left office. Nevertheless, within six years of his arrival in Washington, Blair had discharged his debts and bought a comfortable home on Pennsylvania Avenue, across the street from the White House.

The *Globe*, while under Blair's constant direction, benefited from the efforts of at least three other significant individuals. During its first few months, Kendall proposed a profitable arrangement that would give him a toehold at the *Globe* and assure him a half-interest if he left public office within six years. Whether Blair accepted this arrangement is unknown, but in December 1831, Kendall asked Jackson's permission to write occasional *Globe* articles for pay—saying that he had previously done so without pay. Jackson objected to formal involvement by government officials in any business holding government contracts. Kendall promised that he would have no formal tie to the newspaper. With Blair's endorsement, Jackson approved.

In March 1832, John C. Rives resigned his Treasury Department clerkship to become *Globe* business manager. Two years later, he became a full partner and shared the *Globe* office for another fifteen years. In 1834, Blair and Rives began publishing the *Congressional Globe*, an indexed record of proceedings of Congress that Blair regarded as his chief contribution to history. This publication competed with the *Register of Debates*, which was published by Gales and Seaton until it was discontinued in 1837. Blair and Rives published the *Congressional Globe* until 1849, after which Rives and his son continued it until 1874.

The third person important to the *Globe* was Eliza Blair. She became editor of foreign news, human interest items, and special features such as fiction, poetry, reviews, anecdotes, and letters from travelers and diplomats abroad. Blair had confidence that Eliza's work would make *Globe* contents palatable to his political adversaries, some of whom he sent copies with a note saying that he hoped they would "find Eliza's page as interesting as they were certain to find his obnoxious."

The *Globe*, though conceived and used for partisan purposes, filled the role of a *news*paper, with items about marriages, deaths, robberies, accidents, trials, lawsuits, and so forth. But its function as a partisan organ was paramount. In the first issue, Blair asserted: "It is the purpose of the Editor to dedicate this paper to discussion and maintenance of the principles which brought General Jackson into office, and which he brought with him into office," and to advocate his reelection "as a means of giving permanent effect to those principles, which are considered essential to the preservation, peace, and prosperity of the union."

Blair, who was learned and bright with a mind of piercing logic and a gift for sarcasm and satire, ran the *Globe* with a policy he called "shooting the deserters." He would first try to cajole and persuade errant party members back into the fold; then he would warn those who persisted in their willful ways; if all else failed, he would destroy them politically by omitting their names from the pages of the *Globe*.

The issues receiving most *Globe* attention were the bank and nullification. The administration position on the bank was clear from the first *Globe* issue, and the paper's attacks reached crescendos at various times until Jackson finally crushed the bank. That process began with the 1832 election campaign. Clay, nominated to oppose Jackson in 1832, called for early renewal of the bank's charter, hoping to make it a campaign issue. Knowing that Jackson would oppose recharter, he believed forcing Jackson's hand, at a time when a majority of Congress supported the bank, would doom Jackson's chances for reelection. The bill for recharter passed, and Jackson, ill at the time, vetoed it. Some historians believe that Blair wrote the veto message, the major points of which had already appeared in the *Globe*. Among other charges against the bank,

Blair called it a monopoly, saddled with foreign influence, that created inequality and catered to the rich. Of Clay's efforts he wrote, "It is not for the benefit of the Country that the 'New Coalition' has been formed; nor is any improvement in the public prosperity expected from its success. The struggle is for power, for place, for the public treasure. Men who want foreign missions, judgeships and other valuable offices, unable to swerve the stern integrity of Andrew Jackson and sell to him their influence and support, have united with other aspirants to the Presidency in all sorts of combinations to destroy his popularity and defeat his re-election, that his place may be occupied by one with whom they may bargain for promotion." Of course, the *Globe* applauded the veto. Jackson won reelection by a landslide, but the campaign against the bank continued as Jackson moved toward removal of the deposits—an idea some say came from Blair—and ultimate destruction of the bank. When Blair published details of debts owed by probank congressmen and newspaper editors, support for the Jackson position was secured.

Blair believed that states should have authority over their own affairs—especially slavery—so long as the Union was not threatened; but he could not tolerate nullification and attacked that movement as vehemently and as repeatedly as he attacked the bank. In 1832, after Congress passed reduced tariff rates, most of the South, where opposition to the tariff was strongest, was mollified. But South Carolina continued nullification threats. In 1832, a nullification legislature in South Carolina called the tariff unconstitutional and passed laws ordering resistance to its collection. In an action Blair would admire until his death—and would urge on Lincoln during the Civil War—Jackson sent warships to Charleston. He also issued a proclamation condemning South Carolina's action, a document Blair helped prepare.

Blair argued against nullification while trying to maintain a states' rights view, pointing out that Jackson had said that "the reserved rights of the States are *Not Less Sacred*, than those which are delegated to the General Government." Going further, Blair wrote that Jackson believed "we live under two *distinct, separate, independent,* and *limited* governments. . . . Each of these Governments has its powers, which, without usurpation on the one side or the other, can never come in conflict."

Blair saw abolitionists as being equally threatening to the Union as nullificationists and called them all Whigs. "There is not a single political friend of Martin Van Buren and democracy who

is an abolitionist or WHOEVER CAN BE AN ABOLITIONIST," he wrote during Van Buren's election campaign, "because abolition is as much in opposition to the principle of democracy as Nullification, Federalism, Monarchy or Bankism." When Congress passed the "gag rule," thereby refusing to consider petitions to abolish slavery, Blair wrote, "We congratulate the country upon the final overthrow of the joint plot of these malcontents to unsettle the Government and disturb the union, by agitating the slave question in Congress."

After Jackson left office in 1837, Blair remained his closest confidant and served as conduit of his ideas and wishes to the party and, through the *Globe*, to the nation and world. The *Globe* supported Van Buren as Jackson's chosen successor and served as steadfastly through the complex issues that beset his term as it had for Jackson. Blair blamed the bank for the depression which plagued Van Buren's term and used the *Globe* to keep alive the image of Jackson. But some of the luster drained from the *Globe* with Jackson's departure from Washington.

During the campaign and short term of Whig President William Henry Harrison and the term of his successor, John Tyler, the *Globe* played the role of a caustic opposition press, but after Van Buren's term, Blair increasingly showed signs of deviating from the party. The Democrats needed the Tyler and Calhoun factions to defeat Clay and elect James K. Polk in 1844, but, despite pleas from party members, including Jackson, Blair would not relent in attacks on Tyler. Then, when Texas annexation became a crucial issue in the Polk campaign, he took too long to come around to the party position. Blair, an adherent of Manifest Destiny, wanted Texas annexed, but not as a slave state and not without negotiation with Mexico. The former would alienate the North and the latter would bring war with Mexico—both of which would rend the Union, in Blair's opinion. On 12 March 1843, Jackson wrote a letter for publication supporting immediate annexation; Blair held it for a year without publishing it. Frustated party members tried to fathom his actions and ultimately reclaimed the letter after eleven months. A month later, on 20 March 1844, Blair published the letter from a copy he had made; but it was too late. Democratic leaders had lost confidence in Blair's party loyalty.

Although Blair ardently supported Polk, after the election party members urged a change in the administration editor. Despite Jackson's protests, Blair was asked to sell the *Globe* to Thomas Ritchie, who had long been Jacksonian editor of the *Rich-*

mond (Va.) *Enquirer.* Polk offered Blair a diplomatic post in Spain, but he refused. Though he had run the *Globe* successfully without patronage for four years and could have continued, Blair believed it best for the party that he step down. He and Rives continued publishing the *Congressional Globe* and carried on job printing until 1849, but his days as a newspaper editor ended with the last *Globe* issue on 30 April 1845.

Unassociated with a newspaper for the first time in at least a quarter century, Blair "retired" to a Maryland estate he had bought in 1842 and named Silver Spring and took on the role of a dean of politics. To Silver Spring the great, near-great, and political hopefuls trekked to get his views and advice; from there he wrote letters, memos, and pamphlets dispensing advice to presidents, cabinet members, and legislators—advice that was more often sought than not and was always valued.

Biographer William E. Smith, comparing Blair to other political editors, called him "more vitriolic" than Edwin Croswell of the *Albany* (N. Y.) *Argus,* "less learned, calm and sedate than Gales, broader visioned and keener than Ritchie, more truthful and loyal than Green, less original than Horace Greeley, and not a nice political editor like Thurlow Weed." Smith says that Blair was "an experienced . . . journalist clothed with granted and assumed powers" and had "far more influence with Jackson and Van Buren than is generally credited to him."

More than this, however, Blair's opinions had an impact on virtually all those explosive, divisive issues that threatened a young country groping to find direction, cohesion, stability, and a firm footing amid almost unwieldy expansion. This was as true—if not more so—after the Jackson presidency as during it. But despite the years of beating the editorial drums for Jackson—and although Blair's devotion to Jackson never wavered—Blair had by the 1840s philosophically parted company with "Old Hickory" in some respects, and his actions thereafter appear to have sprung from genuine concern for the nation's welfare above party and all else. One biographer says that he had become a "responsible" journalist just at the time he was removed as editor of the *Globe.*

Many instances attest to his changing views, but perhaps on no issue was it more apparent than slavery. With Jackson, Blair had opposed the abolitionists; but as the years passed, he increasingly sought the end of slavery, though not from the most noble moral position. He believed blacks were inferior, but he advocated emancipation for the

Blair and his wife, Eliza, in later years

sake of the Union. In the 1840s, he joined the Free Soilers and supported Van Buren in 1848; he supported Franklin Pierce in 1852, but as he saw Pierce failing to adopt Jacksonian democratic methods, he began to withdraw from the party. He denounced the 1854 Kansas-Nebraska Act as a violation of the 1820 Missouri Compromise that barred slavery in new Northern states. He became a chief organizer of the Republican party, presided over the 1856 Pittsburgh convention, and was active in the 1860 Chicago convention. He contributed tirelessly to getting Abraham Lincoln elected after the nomination and then was, in some respects—though without a newspaper—as instrumental in Lincoln's administration as he had been in Jackson's thirty years earlier. In 1864, Blair came up with his own solution to the Civil War and traveled to the Confederate capital to confer with Jefferson Davis. His efforts resulted in the Hampton Roads Conference in 1865.

When post-Civil War Republican leaders deviated from Lincoln policies, Blair became disenchanted with the political party he had helped bring into being and returned to the one he had helped make so strong. He supported Horace

Greeley and Samuel Tilden in the 1872 and 1876 elections, respectively. He died in 1876 at Silver Spring, still hoping that the country would become the nation idealized by Jacksonian visionaries.

One cannot be certain which of the views published in the *Argus* and the *Globe* were Blair's sincere beliefs and which were expressed for the sake of party and the convenient manipulation of opinion. Most of Blair's other writings are pamphlets, among which are *Gen. Jackson and James Buchanan* (1836); *A Voice from the Grave of Jackson!* (1856); and *Relief without Repudiation* (1869). A more extended work, incorrectly attributed to his youngest son, Francis Preston Blair, Jr., is *The Life and Public Services of Gen. William O. Butler* (1848). Blair long intended to write an extensive biography of Andrew Jackson, and Jackson gave him all his papers for this purpose, but Blair never produced the work.

Belying his youthful fears of an early death, Blair enjoyed eighty-five active years, outliving four of his six children. Two of his sons achieved political prominence rivaling that of their father; the third showed equal promise but died in his early thirties. Francis and Eliza Blair were intensely devoted to each other, and their secure, sixty-four-year marriage seems to have rested on a concept of equal partnership that surely ran counter to contemporary customs. Eliza died within a year after Blair's death, and such is their legacy that their descendants have occupied public office ever since.

Though some may question his motives, Blair devoted himself to what he believed best for the nation. He was a dedicated party man, but he saw the function of the political party to be the fulfilling of the popular will. Besides his arguments against the United States Bank, nullification, and abolitionism, he argued for elimination of imprisonment for debt, legislative control over judicial decisions, cheap lands for settlers, and direct election of the president. In the process, he spent part of his life making the *Globe* a monument to Andrew Jackson. He also assured the nation other monuments to Jackson: he named the Washington print-

ing plant he built Jackson Hall; he raised the money for, and oversaw the sculpting of, the bronze equestrian Jackson statue in Lafayette Square; and he protected Jackson's home, the Hermitage, on which he and John Rives held a lien, from the squandering tendencies of Jackson's adopted son until Blair arranged for its sale to the state of Tennessee in 1855. Although there are no similar memorials to Francis P. Blair, the Washington family home, Blair House—bought by the United States government in 1942 to serve as the nation's guest house—and the town of Silver Spring, Maryland, serve as reminders of his dynamic life.

Biographies:
William Ernest Smith, *The Francis Preston Blair Family in Politics*, 2 volumes (New York: Macmillan, 1933);

Elbert B. Smith, *Francis Preston Blair* (New York: Free Press, 1980).

References:
George Baber, "Blairs of Kentucky," *Register of the Kentucky Historical Society*, 14 (1916): 47;

Thomas Hart Benton, *Thirty Years' View*, 2 volumes (New York: D. Appleton, 1854), I: 129;

Michael W. Singletary, "The New Editorial Voice for Andrew Jackson: Happenstance or Plan?," *Journalism Quarterly*, 53 (Winter 1976): 672;

William E. Smith, "Francis Preston Blair, Pen-Executive of Andrew Jackson," in *Highlights in the History of the American Press*, edited by Edwin H. Ford and Edwin Emery (Minneapolis: University of Minnesota Press, 1954), pp. 138-149.

Papers:
Francis Preston Blair's papers are held in the Blair Papers and the Blair-Rives Collection in the Library of Congress, and the Blair-Lee Papers in the Princeton University Library.

Samuel Bowles III
(9 February 1826-16 January 1878)

James Glen Stovall
University of Alabama

MAJOR POSITIONS HELD: Editor and publisher, *Springfield Daily Republican* (1844-1878); editor, *Boston Traveller* (1857).

BOOKS: *Across the Continent: A Summer's Journey to the Rocky Mountains, the Mormons, and the Pacific States with Speaker Colfax* (Springfield, Mass.: S. Bowles/New York: Hurd & Houghton, 1865);
The Switzerland of America: A Summer Vacation in the Parks and Mountains of Colorado (Springfield, Mass.: S. Bowles, 1869);
Our New West: Records of Travel Between the Mississippi River and the Pacific Ocean (Hartford, Conn.: Hartford Publishing Co./New York: J. D. Dennison, 1869).

In 1856, the *New York Tribune* called the *Springfield* (Mass.) *Republican* the "best and ablest country journal ever published on this continent." It was a tribute given as much to the paper's editor, Samuel Bowles III, as to the paper itself. Bowles, his father, and his son—all of whom carried the name Samuel Bowles—all had distinguished newspaper careers, but it was Samuel Bowles III who stood out. Building on the strong foundation his father had established in founding the *Republican,* Bowles pioneered many of the tenets of modern journalism—emphasis on local news; strong, concise writing; and, in later years, independence from party politics—and in doing so showed how a small town editor could wield national influence. It was hard work, rather than an abundance of education or wealth, that made him one of the nineteenth century's most prominent journalists.

One of Bowles's great strengths as an editor was the ability to attract young men with potential as journalists and to encourage them—sometimes by praise and often by badgering—to become better reporters and writers. Bowles cared deeply about journalism and its future. The *Republican* gained a reputation not only of being a first-class newspaper but of training some of the nation's best writers and editors. Among them were Dr. Josiah

G. Holland, cofounder of *Scribner's* magazine; Francis A. Walker, later president of Massachusetts Institute of Technology; Frank B. Sanborn; and Charles Whiting. Bowles hired men with college educations because, as he once said, he wanted journalism to be a "profession not a stepping stone."

Samuel Bowles III was born on 9 February 1826, seventeen months after his father founded the *Republican*. Bowles's parents were of sturdy New England stock. His mother, the former Huldah Deming of Wethersfield, Connecticut, was a direct descendant of the Puritan leader Miles Standish. Bowles's grandfather was a Boston pewterer whose business had been ruined during the American Revolution; he had moved his family to Hartford, Connecticut, where he kept a grocery store and where Samuel Bowles II was born in 1797. When the father died in 1813, Samuel Bowles II received only a watch and a family Bible as his inheritance. He was apprenticed to a printer and during his apprenticeship tried to satisfy his intellectual interests by forming a literary and debating club. Toward the end of his life, the elder Bowles wrote that this action was one of the most important of his life because it gave him "a sort of redeeming season, saving me from dangerous tendencies. It gave a good direction to my habits, strengthening my mind to resist temptation and led me to prefer mental to sensual pleasure."

When his apprenticeship was finished, Samuel Bowles II got a job as a printer with the *New Haven Register,* and in 1819 he formed a partnership to found the *Hartford Times,* a weekly newspaper. This venture was unsuccessful, partly because of his ill health and the incompetence of his partner. In 1824, he loaded his wife, baby daughter, some household goods, and a printing press on a flatboat and steered up the Connecticut River to Springfield, Massachusetts. His purpose was to start a weekly newspaper at the invitation of some Anti-Federalists who wanted a strong editorial voice for their party in western Massachusetts.

The first issue of the *Springfield Republican* appeared on 8 September 1824, with Samuel Bowles II as proprietor, publisher, reporter, editor, compositor, pressman, and business manager. It had about 250 subscribers, each paying two dollars a year. From the very beginning Bowles showed some independent streaks. He supported William H. Crawford for president and opposed Massachusetts native son John Quincy Adams; four years later, however, he endorsed Adams's reelection efforts against Andrew Jackson because he distrusted Jackson's autocratic temper. Bowles and the *Republican* became thoroughly identified with the Whig party by opposing Jackson during his administration and by endorsing the election of Henry Clay in 1832. The paper was against slavery and its spread, but it had little to do with the abolitionist movement. It also opposed the annexation of Texas and the Mexican War.

Locally, the *Republican* was beset by a number of rival newspapers, but it outlasted all of them. One of the most distinguished graduates of Bowles's print shop was Benjamin H. Day, later the famous editor of the *New York Sun,* who received his first newspaper training at the *Republican.* By the early 1840s, the paper's subscription list had grown to 1,200 and Bowles was printing fourteen to fifteen columns of news every week. The *Republican* gained a reputation for thorough coverage of local news through a system of correspondents, and it soon became indispensable to those who wanted to know what was happening in western Massachusetts.

Springfield was growing; the opening of the Boston and Albany Railroad in 1839 had made it an industrial city and a railroad center, and Bowles felt that the city could support a daily newspaper. He announced plans for one in 1842 but was dissuaded by local business friends who thought the venture too risky. There were no daily newspapers in Massachusetts outside of Boston and there was only one daily in Connecticut, they argued. Bowles was on the verge of abandoning the plan completely, only to have his mind changed again by his son, who promised to assume the responsibility for the paper.

Samuel Bowles III was seventeen years old when he began work on his father's newspaper. He had been a studious lad, voraciously devouring books, newspapers, and magazines in his father's office and at home. He had wanted to go to college, but his family lacked the means, and he had to begin learning his father's business as a teenager. The younger Bowles was convinced that a daily edition of the paper could survive and prosper, and with his father's assent he started the *Springfield Daily Republican* on 27 March 1844. The paper began with no advertising, and Bowles announced that he would try daily publication for a year and a half to see if it worked. From the very beginning, he showed the same proclivity for hard work that was to characterize his entire career. In fact, he worked himself into such exhaustion during those first months that he had to spend the winter of 1844-1845 in Louisiana to recover his health. From there, he could do little for the paper but contribute a series of letters describing the South and his travels. By the spring, however, he was back in Springfield, working furiously. The paper turned the corner in December 1845 when it switched from an afternoon to a morning edition, and in April 1846, the owners announced that the *Daily Republican* would be published on a permanent basis.

From that point, Bowles took over more and more of the editorial responsibilities while his father handled the financial aspects of the business. He drove himself and his staff hard, often working until two or three o'clock in the morning. Much of his time was spent in improving the writing quality of the news stories and editorials. Bowles himself was not a great writer, but he valued good writing and could bring it out of others.

His first challenge, after putting the paper on a sound financial footing, came from the *Springfield Gazette,* founded in 1846. This newspaper had openly declared that it wanted to become the leading paper of the city, and it began trying to run the *Republican* out of business. Bowles responded to this challenge with vigor, and in 1848, the *Republican* absorbed the *Gazette* and was considered the leading newspaper of the area. The reputation and influence of the paper and its editor were growing. Bowles had a small, hardworking staff that was joined by Josiah Holland in 1849. Holland became associate editor and part owner of the paper and stayed there until 1856.

Politically, this was an exciting time to own a newspaper. The country was struggling with the vexing question of slavery, and newspapers contributed in a major way to the public debates. Like his father, Bowles did not approve of slavery and in 1848 declared firm opposition to its expansion. Yet he was unwilling to side with the abolitionists, urging his readers to avoid their meetings, and in 1850 he supported Henry Clay's compromise plan.

In the middle of these turbulent times, on 8 September 1851, Bowles's father died. The elder Bowles's hard work and conservative management had put the paper in a position in which it could grow with its surroundings. At his father's death, Bowles assumed the full management responsibilities for the paper. He was also drawn more deeply into the political debates that were engulfing the nation—debates that grew increasingly hostile and less susceptible to compromise. Bowles's position evolved into a hard-line antislavery stance. While he once argued that the Fugitive Slave Act should be enforced in Northern courts, he now declared the Kansas-Nebraska Act, another concession to the slaveholding states, a "monstrous proposition." He became a chief supporter of the Emigrant Aid Company formed to assist antislavery settlers in moving to Kansas.

In June 1855 Bowles performed an important piece of investigative journalism. The Know-Nothing party had become a political force by attracting a wide constituency of pro- and antislavery elements. Bowles had few kind words to say about the Know-Nothings. He considered the party merely a collection of opportunists and wrote, "Every hour's experience here increases the conviction of the utter folly and wickedness of this effort to patch up an organization that shall satisfy the nation and

shirk the only vital question of the time." The party met in Philadelphia in closed session, but Bowles managed, through contacts with Massachusetts delegates, to find out what was happening in the sessions and was able to send full reports on the party's activities to the *Republican,* the *New York Tribune,* and the *Boston Atlas.* He denounced the party as "weak tools of political gamblers and slavery propagandists," and even though the party enjoyed a brief period of power, his reports helped put an end to the movement.

Recognizing that the Whig party was dead, Bowles called for the formation of a new antislavery party. In August 1855 Bowles, Charles Francis Adams, Richard Henry Dana, Jr., George Boutwell, and Henry L. Dawes tried to merge the Know-Nothings, Free-Soilers, and independent Whigs with the newly formed Republican party. This effort failed, but Bowles had helped to lay the basis for the Republican party in Massachusetts.

Bowles was not yet thirty years old, but his reputation was national and his influence was widespread. He had taken a small country newspaper and had built it into an influential journal whose daily circulation was more than 5,000 and whose weekly edition had a national circulation of more than 10,000. New Englanders who had emigrated west looked forward to the weekly edition not only for news from home but also for the strong antislavery opinion pieces that it furnished. Physically, Bowles was an impressive figure. He had a substantial beard and shaggy eyebrows which masked his piercing eyes. He was tall, had a penetrating gaze, and was known as a good listener. Bowles maintained a large capacity for hard work, but illness plagued him even in these early years. He had periodic bouts with intestinal illness and later suffered from headaches and sleeplessness. These maladies caused him to be moody and severe, often dealing with his staff more harshly than was necessary. He later wrote that "my will has carried me for years beyond my mental and physical power; that has been the offending rock." Yet he could also be charming and congenial. His praise was, when it came, generous, and it was much sought after because his staff respected his obvious abilities. He was well known and well liked in Washington and New York, and his friend Dawes once wrote of him, "I never knew a man who knew him who wouldn't rather have him at his table than any other man in the world." Bowles enjoyed the company of women and loved to gossip, and even his friends saw him as a man who could not keep a confidence well. His opinions were strongly held, his criticisms were sharp and biting, and he made substantial enemies as well as friends.

Bowles had married Mary S. D. Schermerhorn of Geneva, New York, on 6 September 1848, and from all accounts the marriage was a happy one. The couple had ten children; three died at birth but the rest survived into adulthood. The most notable was their first son, Samuel Bowles IV, born on 15 October 1851, who would one day take charge of the *Republican*. The Bowleses' home life was quiet; at home, Bowles was said to be gracious and kindly.

Bowles needed such a retreat because of the frantic life he was leading in his office and on the road. The positions he had taken, and the influence he had gained, inevitably placed him in the vanguard of the newly formed Republican party, and he became an enthusiastic supporter of John C. Frémont, the party's first presidential candidate, in 1856. He attended the Republican convention in Philadelphia at which Frémont was chosen, and he was also at the Democratic convention in Cincinnati when that party renominated James Buchanan. Bowles worked hard for the success of the Republican party, going without sleep for two successive nights during election week, and even though the party was not successful nationally, it made a strong showing in the *Republican*'s circulation area. The paper's alliance with a popular political movement increased its circulation and reputation.

The *Republican* was among the first newspapers to advocate universal suffrage without regard to race or color. It was also among the first to advocate woman suffrage. Bowles felt strongly that voting was a right that should not be denied to any citizen.

His newspaper career, at this point, took an odd turn. He had refused offers to join the *New York Tribune* as an editorial writer and head of the Washington bureau, and he had not encouraged Charles Dana in his plans for a new daily newspaper in Philadelphia with Bowles as the editor. Yet, Bowles did succumb briefly to the temptation of editing a newspaper in a larger city. Early in 1857, he resigned his editorship of the *Republican*, left his family in Springfield, and invested $10,000 in the *Boston Traveller*, a combination of several weak and dying journals. The *Traveller* was to be a voice of Republicanism and progressivism but was to retain its independence. Unfortunately for Bowles, it lacked sufficient capital, and it also lacked a commonly agreed upon policy among its investors. Bowles found himself thwarted in many of his efforts, and he resigned after four months. After

a vacation trip to the West, he returned to Springfield, where he had kept a controlling interest in the *Republican*, and resumed his duties with that paper. This brief foray into big city journalism confirmed in his own mind his proper place as a small town editor.

The election of Buchanan settled little about the more far-reaching debates on slavery and the right of states to defy the wishes of the federal government. An adequate compromise still eluded the antislavery and states' rights factions, and events carried the country toward a violent split. Bowles criticized the hanging of John Brown, writing, "We can conceive of no event that could so deepen the moral hostility of the people of the free states to slavery as this execution. This is not because the acts of Brown are generally approved for they are not. It is because the nature and spirit of the man are seen to be great and noble. . . ."

Bowles's support of Lincoln was tempered but consistent during Lincoln's first term. Bowles called for the "defense of the Union and the enforcement of the laws" when states began seceding; he backed Lincoln's slow pace for emancipation and defended Lincoln against opposition factions at the 1862 Massachusetts Republican convention. During Lincoln's famous disputes with his generals, the *Republican* urged the president to take personal command of the army, praising him as a strategist equal to any general on the scene. On the other hand, Bowles did speak up against Lincoln's infringements of civil liberties. He had high praise for the Gettysburg Address: "His little speech is a perfect gem; deep in feeling, compact in thought and expression, and tasteful and elegant in every word and comma." He supported Lincoln's reelection, saying, "Every man, loose from the bondage of political ambition, loose from the greed of power and the love of slavery, thinks well of Abraham Lincoln and casts in his lot with him. Thousands of Democrats, converted to freedom by the war, have, from the moment of their conversion, become his friends. His way of saving the country is recognized as the only way. A conquered peace is the only peace deemed possible." Despite some disagreements with the president, the *Springfield Republican* and the *New York Times* were the only two newspapers of national stature that Lincoln could count on for loyal and consistent support. After the president's assassination, Bowles refused to join the radicals and advocated the conciliatory policies toward the South that Lincoln had initiated. However, despite the fact that Andrew Johnson was following these policies, Bowles advocated his impeachment, believing that the president had exceeded his authority in dealing with the War Office.

These turbulent times took their toll on Bowles. He increasingly sustained bouts of sleeplessness, dyspepsia, and sciatica. Holland, who had left the *Republican* but who continued to write for it during the war, said later that Bowles's hard work drained his life away. "The sparkle, the vivacity, the drive, and the power of the *Republican* cost life. We did not know when we tasted it and found it so charged with zest that we were tasting heart's blood, but that was the priceless element that commended it to our appetites. A pale man, weary and nervous, crept home at midnight, or one, two, or three o'clock in the morning, and while all nature was fresh and the birds were singing and thousands of eyes were bending eagerly over the results of his night's labor, he was tossing and trying to sleep."

In 1865, partly as a journalist in search of a story and partly as a sick man seeking relief from his daily pressures, Bowles traveled to the Pacific Coast with a number of political leaders, including Schuyler Colfax, speaker of the U.S. House of Representatives, and sent back a series of letters to the *Republican*. These were compiled in a book, *Across the Continent: A Summer's Journey to the Rocky Mountains, the Mormons, and the Pacific States with Speaker Colfax* (1865). Bowles's letters were full of interesting descriptions and prophetic statements. At Atchison, Kansas, the group had to leave the railroad and board a stagecoach, and the journey across the plains was tiresome and hazardous. They were accompanied by an army guard much of the way, but the danger of Indian attack was always present. In Utah, Bowles was fascinated with the Mormons and their marital customs; he said that there was "much to admire, many to respect" in this religious sect. In California, Bowles found the treatment of the Chinese to be a disgrace, saying that they were "victims of all sorts of prejudice and injustice." The group returned by ship through the Isthmus of Panama.

The post-Civil War era ushered in a time of great industrial expansion, immigration, and big city political bossism. Bowles was one of several editors of the time to defy the bosses. He railed so strongly against railroad baron James Fisk and the political corruption he provoked that Fisk filed a $50,000 libel suit against him. Nothing came of the suit, but when Bowles visited New York in December 1868, he was arrested by Fisk's Tammany allies and kept overnight in the Ludlow Street jail. Bowles's courage and independence were undiminished. He campaigned against the policies of the Erie Railroad and exposed a railroad lobby at the Massachusetts state capitol which was gaining contracts through corruption of legislators.

Bowles's opposition to the scandal-ridden Grant administration carried him to the 1872 Liberal Republican ("mugwump") convention in Cincinnati. There he and fellow editors Horace White, Murat Halstead, and Carl Schurz tried unsuccessfully to have Charles Francis Adams nominated for president but Horace Greeley was chosen instead. For the first time since its inception, he broke with the mainstream Republican party and backed Greeley, who later also received the Democratic nomination. Bowles saw some good coming out of the Greeley nomination, particularly his endorsement by Southern delegates, but he remained unenthusiastic and told the *Republican* editors to support Greeley's candidacy but "not to gush." The Greeley endorsement was confirmation that the *Republican* had become a truly independent newspaper.

Bowles's ill health was always a problem during this time, and he had taken to traveling frequently for relief. He made another trip to the West in 1868 which resulted in a second book, *The Switzerland of America: A Summer Vacation in the Parks and Mountains of Colorado*, published in 1869. Also in that year, material from both of his books about the West was gathered under one cover as *Our New West: Records of Travel Between the Mississippi River and the Pacific Ocean*. Bowles had taken a trip to Europe in 1862, and he returned for another tour in the summer of 1870. He went back again in 1871 and for the fourth time in 1874. He also made another trip to California in 1873.

Despite his absences, he remained an active editor and manager of the *Republican*. That activity decreased somewhat when Samuel Bowles IV was added to the staff in 1873. The younger Bowles had attended Yale for a time, but like his father's, his health was delicate, and he had remained at the university for only two years; he had traveled and lived in Europe for most of the time between 1869 and 1871. He worked as a reporter and editorial writer when he first came to the paper, but when a rift occurred between his father and his uncle, Benjamin Franklin Bowles, the paper's business manager, the younger Bowles took over the financial side of the paper. As his father's health grew worse during the next three years, he assumed more and more of the responsibilities for the paper and its company.

By 1876 the elder Bowles had suffered an attack that left him partially paralyzed. He still had his wits, however, and directed an active editorial campaign for Rutherford B. Hayes, the Republican presidential candidate. Despite his support for Hayes, he thought that Samuel Tilden, Hayes's Democratic opponent, had been fairly elected and that the election had been stolen from him in the electoral college. Still, he was enthusiastic about Hayes's policies of reform and of reconciliation with the South, both of which Bowles had advocated since the Civil War had ended. The next year Bowles suffered a series of strokes that debilitated him completely, and he died on 16 January 1878. He was three weeks short of his fifty-second birthday.

Samuel Bowles IV carried on the management of the newspaper in the tradition of his father, but he shunned the limelight, saying, "I realize I came after a great man; I have never expected personal fame." He ran the *Republican* quietly, traveling little, rarely mingling in political circles, and signing few articles. He saw himself as an editor rather than a writer. His one major journalistic innovation was the development of the *Sunday Republican*, which began on 15 September 1878. He remained fiercely independent of political factions, but he never hesitated to take stands on issues. He supported Grover Cleveland in 1884, 1888, and 1892, but he opposed the Free Silver movement and William Jennings Bryan, the next Democratic presidential nominee, in 1896. He denounced jingoism, particularly that of Massachusetts senator Henry Cabot Lodge. Like his father, Bowles shunned all attempts to get him to run for public office, but he was active in the community and the journalism profession. He was a member of the advisory board of the Pulitzer School of Journalism at Columbia University and in 1913 became a director of the Associated Press. He and his wife, Elizabeth Hoar of Concord, Massachusetts, whom he married on 12 June 1884, had two sons. He died on 14 March 1915.

He was succeeded by one of his sons, Sherman Hoar Bowles, but the *Republican* was beset by competition and falling on hard times. In 1926 Sherman Bowles bought out his three competitors, the *Union*, the *Evening Union*, and the *News*. He continued to maintain the editorial identity of each paper until 1947, when a printer's strike shut down all of the papers for six months. At the end of the strike, Bowles continued the *Union* as the morning paper and the *News* as the evening paper, but the *Republican* was only published on Sundays. The three papers today are part of the Newhouse Newspapers group.

These three generations of the Bowles family performed a valuable service for nineteenth-century American journalism. They originated, developed, and maintained a newspaper concern that served as a model for other small town journalistic enterprises across the country. The *Springfield Republican* defied its own circulation size and location to become one of the most influential newspapers in the country. The Bowleses held up high standards of journalistic practice, and their office served as one of the most productive "schools of journalism" of the century. The people trained there went on to exercise great influence on the profession. The Bowleses were also quick to embrace innovations that would improve the journalism they practiced.

Samuel Bowles III, particularly, anticipated many of the modern trends in journalism. He placed heavy emphasis on local news, and the *Republican* covered the western Massachusetts area thoroughly with a battery of local correspondents. In an age of flowery prose, Bowles was far ahead of his time in demanding accuracy, precision, and conciseness in writing. "Put it all in the first sentence," he would tell his news writers. "Don't suppose that anyone will read through six lines of bad rhetoric to get a crumb of news at the end." Bowles spent much of his time as an editor making sure that his paper's readers were not burdened with unnecessary words.

Bowles was a man of strong opinions who was unafraid to express them. He has been frequently criticized for inconsistency, but he lived in an age in which public issues were so vexing that few could claim complete consistency in their views. The charge of inconsistency did not faze Bowles; he often changed the course of his thinking and was not ashamed of doing so in public. He once wrote that he could not "live to be as old as Methuselah, and brood in silence over a thing till, just before I die, I think I have it right." Bowles was part of a school of newspaper editors who felt not just the right but the duty to speak out on the issues of the day; the editor who did not do so, they believed, was not doing his job.

In building his newspaper, and in speaking out fearlessly on the fearsome issues that his nation faced, Samuel Bowles III is ranked with Horace Greeley and William Cullen Bryant as the most important and influential editors of their time. Historian Allan Nevins, in *Ordeal of the Union* (1947), calls Greeley, Bryant, and Bowles the era's journalistic "triumvirate": "These three men were in very different fashion masters of controversial

journalism, Greeley excelling in forcible, hard hitting prose such as Cobbett wrote, Bryant in swelling
eloquence and Bowles in logical power and slashing
wit. They scattered their weekly and semi-weekly
editions all over the North and West, and every
page was a fragment from an incendiary bomb."

Biographies:
Samuel Bowles II, *General and Historical Notes of the
    Bowles Family* (Springfield?, 1851);
George S. Merriam, *The Life and Times of Samuel
    Bowles*, 2 volumes (New York: Century, 1885);
Thomas M. Farquhar, *History of the Bowles Family*
    (Philadelphia, 1907).

References:
Gamaliel Bradford, "Samuel Bowles," in *Union Por-
    traits* (Boston & New York: Houghton Mifflin,
    1916), pp. 263-294;
Solomon Griffin, *People and Politics Observed by a
    Massachusetts Editor* (Boston: Little, Brown,
    1923), pp. 9-43;
Richard Hooker, *The Story of an Independent News-
    paper: One Hundred Years of the Springfield Re-
    publican* (New York: Macmillan, 1924);
Allan Nevins, *Ordeal of the Union*, 2 volumes (New
    York: Scribners, 1947), II: 132.

Andrew Bradford
(1686-24 November 1742)

Elsie S. Hebert
Louisiana State University

MAJOR POSITION HELD: Founder and editor,
American Weekly Mercury (1719-1742).

For 140 years the Bradford family played a
significant role in the printing and publishing history of early America, particularly in Philadelphia.
Here Andrew Bradford, pioneer printer and
founder of the first newspaper outside Boston, contributed to the wealth, political growth, and enlightenment of the Quaker colony. He was printer
to the commonwealth of Pennsylvania from 1712
to 1730, established the *American Weekly Mercury* in
1719, and launched the first magazine in America,
the *American Magazine*, in 1741.

Bradford was born in Philadelphia in 1686,
the first of two sons of William and Elizabeth Sowle
Bradford. His brother, William Bradford II, was
born in 1688. The boys inherited from both sides

of their family the tradition of the press, their
grandfathers being printers in England. The elder
Bradford had met Elizabeth Sowle when he was
apprenticed to her father, Andrew Sowle, a well-
known printer and publisher in London during the
period of the Commonwealth and the Restoration,
whose press turned out most of the early Quaker
literature. Sowle was a man of distinction in Quaker
circles, a friend of both George Fox and William
Penn, and one of the witnesses to the original
charter of Pennsylvania.

It was through Sowle that Bradford met Penn
and became interested in Pennsylvania. Penn arranged for Bradford to move to Pennsylvania so
that the colony might have the benefit of a printing
press. In 1685 Bradford arrived in Philadelphia
with a new bride, a printing press and materials,
and letters of introduction (including one from
Fox) which stated that he was coming to be a printer
of Quaker books and laws for the people, and asking the Quakers of the colony to patronize him.
Moreover, he had the personal sanction of the
great and wealthy proprietor, whose own taste in
literature and attitude toward the press were those
of intelligence and liberality.

In spite of the understanding with Penn that
his was to be a free press, William Bradford from

the outset incurred the ire of the Provincial Council for small infractions. The most serious occurred in 1692 when Bradford published a broadside entitled *An Appeal from the Twenty-eight Judges to the Spirit of Truth* for Quaker apostate George Keith, which the Provincial Council considered seditious. Bradford was taken into custody and his printing materials were seized. After his acquittal and the return of his equipment in 1693, Bradford moved his family to New York, where he had been appointed official printer to the colony.

Andrew Bradford was seven years old when his family moved to New York. He received his printing training under his father's tutelage and on 22 February 1708/1709 was made a freeman of the City of New York, listing himself as a printer. About this time he declined a position as printer for the Rhode Island colony. Biographer John W. Wallace wrote that William Bradford was keeping a paternal eye over young Andrew's career and, having some reason to be dissatisfied with the terms of the offer, encouraged his son to turn it down.

At any rate, Andrew was in partnership with his father in 1710-1711. During this period they printed at least three books jointly: Daniel Leeds's *American Almanack for . . . 1711* (1710); the second edition of *The Young Man's Companion* (1710); and *A Plat-form of Church-Discipline, Gathered out of the Word of God, and Agreed upon by the Elders and Messengers of the Churches Assembled in the Synod at Cambridge in N.E.* (1711).

Conditions in Pennsylvania about this time perhaps caused the Bradfords to look once again toward Philadelphia as a particularly promising place for Andrew to establish a new printing business. From the time of William Bradford's departure, the Friends in Pennsylvania had had difficulty in setting up a satisfactory printing arrangement. They had even imported a press and other equipment and installed them on the upper floor of the schoolhouse in 1704, but still the Quakers were without a regular printer.

After Andrew Bradford became a freeman, he brought himself to the attention of the Pennsylvania Assembly and won the good will of both the government and the Quakers. Joseph Morgan's *Gospel Ordinances,* which bears the imprint of both William and Andrew Bradford, was published in Philadelphia in 1712. Although William never returned to Philadelphia as a place of residence, there is little doubt that he supported his son's venture.

There is no record in the votes and proceedings of the Pennsylvania General Assembly of Andrew Bradford's employment by the colony, but in 1713 he issued from his press in Philadelphia the *Acts and Laws of the Province of Pennsylvania, October 14th, 1712 to March 27, 1713.* This publication established him, unofficially, as the provincial printer. The government did not officially recognize him as "Printer of the Province" until 1720.

In 1716 Bradford took as his office the printing room of the Friends' school, with its press and other equipment, for which he paid the Yearly Meeting an annual rent of ten pounds. He maintained these quarters until 1724, when he moved to a house on Second Street owned by Richard Hill, a prominent Quaker with whom he had business dealings. This location, which became widely known as "The Sign of the Bible," was the site for successive generations of Bradford printing operations for the next hundred years.

During his first ten years in Philadelphia Bradford was the only printer in the colony. Between 1713 and 1723 he printed approximately seventy-five items, three of these jointly with his father. His major publications were almanacs, the mainstay of the early eighteenth-century printers. He published annually the Jacob Taylor almanac, the Titan Leeds almanac (beginning in 1715), and the John Jerman almanac (beginning in 1720).

His other important publications were for the government. In 1714 he published the first printed collection of the laws of the colony, *The Laws of the Province of Pennsilvania.* He regularly printed the acts of the General Assembly, Indian treaties, letters and proclamations of Governor Keith, and other official actions. He also printed at least two items for other colonies: *The Laws of the Province of Maryland* in 1718 and Governor Burnet's speech to the Assembly of New Jersey in 1723. About a third of Bradford's printing work consisted of books and pamphlets on social, political, and religious matters.

Bradford made his most important contribution to American and journalism history when he began publication of the *American Weekly Mercury* on 22 December 1719. It was one of the longest-lived of early colonial papers, continuing without interruption for more than twenty-six years. This was the first newspaper to be published outside Boston and missed by one day being the second successful newspaper to be published in the British colonies. It had been preceded by John Campbell's *Boston News-Letter,* which was started in 1704, and William Brooker's *Boston Gazette,* which published its first issue on 21 December 1719. Although Pennsylvania was one of the younger colonies, it was the second to support a continuous newspaper:

Flags from the first issue (top) and a later issue of Bradford's American Weekly Mercury *(Library Company of Philadelphia)*

Massachusetts had waited sixty-four years for the *News-Letter*, and a hundred years transpired between the establishment of New York in 1625 and the founding of William Bradford's *Gazette*; but Pennsylvania was only thirty-eight years old when the *Mercury* was started.

Beginning with its issue of 9 June 1720, the *Mercury*'s imprint was expanded with the statement that the paper might also be obtained from "William Bradford in New York, where Advertisements are taken in." Once again evidence is given of the business association between the Bradfords. This arrangement between father and son continued until 21 December 1725, when William started his *New York Gazette*, the first newspaper in the New York colony.

For its day, the *Mercury* carried a moderate amount of advertising and appears to have had a wide readership, although none of Bradford's account books are extant to help determine the exact circulation. The paper enjoyed popularity in places far from Philadelphia and was an important source of news for editors in other colonies. Its handling of news, both colonial and foreign, was considered generally dependable. In addition to the news, the weekly also carried entertainment items typical of the period, such as literary essays and philosophical treatises.

Although Bradford managed to avoid conflict with the government during his first eight years in Philadelphia, the nature of his printing and publishing made it unlikely that he would stay clear of difficulty indefinitely. In 1721 a pamphlet appeared entitled *Some Remedies Proposed, for the Restoring the Sunk Credit of the Province of Pennsylvania; with Some Remarks of Its Trade. Humbly Offer'd to the Consideration of the Worthy Representatives in the General Assembly of this Province, By a Lover of This Country*. Neither the name of the author, Francis Rawls, nor Philadelphia, nor the printer's name appeared on the publication, but since Bradford's press was the only one in the colony, the pamphlet could hardly have emanated from any other source. In the *Mercury* for 2 January 1721/1722 Bradford carried a news item on the content of the tract and closed with this editorial observation: "Our General Assembly are now sitting, and we have great Expectations for them at this Juncture, that they will find some effectual Remedy, to revive the dying Credit of this Province, and restore us to our former happy Circumstances."

Public officials were extremely sensitive to printed criticism, which they regarded as a new form of protest. In their opinion, Bradford had in his own name assumed a position on the problem of public credit and the disordered condition of trade and finance by publicizing these issues in the columns of his paper. He was ordered to appear before a board of the Provincial Council, reprimanded by the governor, and ordered not to publish anything concerning the Pennsylvania government or the government of any other colony without the permission of the governor or secretary of Pennsylvania.

This order did not cause Bradford to change his practices noticeably. This experience with the provincial authorities of Pennsylvania probably moved him to sympathize with and give editorial support to James Franklin in 1723, when the latter found himself in a confrontation with the government of the Massachusetts Bay colony. Not only did the *Mercury* of 26 February carry a full report of the "Proceedings of the General Assembly at Boston against Mr. Franklin," reprinted from Franklin's *New England Courant* of 21 January, but Bradford also penned a lengthy commentary in which he lamented the severity of the penalty inflicted on his fellow publisher and stated that the "Assembly of the Province of the Massachusetts Bay are made up of Oppressors and Bigots, who make Religion the only Engine of Destruction to the People. . . ." In spite of his making these and ensuing remarks in defiance of the council's admonition not to publish anything relating to the government of any other English colony, Bradford did not receive any censure from local authorities. Besides going on record as opposing censorship of the press, he had other reasons for publishing this story in the *Mercury*. The incident was news in itself; the account of it made good reading for his patrons; and moreover, its publication might bring Bradford recognition and prestige in Boston.

That the Bradford family was widely known in colonial America there can be no doubt. It was to William Bradford in New York that young Benjamin Franklin applied for work in 1723 when he ran away from Boston and his brother James, to whom he was apprenticed. The elder Bradford could not employ him but recommended that he apply to Andrew in Philadelphia. The story goes that when Franklin, after traveling by ship to Philadelphia, called at Andrew's house, William Bradford had arrived in Philadelphia before him, having traveled on horseback. He introduced Franklin to his son, who received him "civilly" and gave him breakfast. At the time Andrew had no need for a new employee either but referred Franklin to a new printer in town, Samuel Keimer.

If Keimer would not employ him, Andrew told Franklin, he would be welcome to lodge at the Bradford house, and a little work would be found for him to do now and then until the situation improved. William Bradford took Franklin to see Keimer. Although Franklin became a journeyman in the rival printing house of Keimer, he boarded for some time with Bradford.

During the next few years a rivalry developed between Keimer and Franklin, with the latter secretly making plans to bring out a new paper. Meanwhile, Bradford published a number of political pamphlets with some provocative ideas concerning the election of assembly members, but apparently none of them incurred the wrath of the council. Then, on 28 January 1729, the *Mercury* began publication of the famous series of "Busy-Body" papers, six of which were written by Franklin denouncing Keimer and his new weekly *Universal Instructor in all Arts and Sciences; and Pennsylvania Gazette*, which he had brought out on 24 December 1728 to preempt Franklin's publication plans. (The others were penned chiefly by Joseph Breintnall under Franklin's guidance.) The Busy-Body series was published in the *Mercury* until 25 September 1729, one week before Franklin bought out the *Universal Instructor* from Keimer. Franklin then allowed the essays to come to an end.

It was number thirty-one of the thirty-two Busy-Body papers, published on 18 September 1729, which got the *Mercury* and Bradford into trouble with the authorities. It insisted that those in authority should be inspired with a public spirit and with a love of country, stressed the danger of power which was not subservient to the public good, and emphasized the tendency of power to perpetuate itself. It then suggested a measure to prevent undue extension of political influence: rotation of office. Had the essay not appeared just before an election, it might have been allowed to pass unnoticed; but its timing and forcefulness disturbed the council. Bradford was arrested, sent to jail, and later bound over to the court. In colonial days editors did not seem to mind going to jail; editing a paper from prison was always sure to increase circulation. Bradford's *Mercury* never occupied as important a place in Philadelphia before he had been put in prison as it did afterward. After he was released, Bradford apparently went steadily on his way without making any real concession to the threats of the government, and in the 1730s the *Mercury* became bolder than ever.

Bradford amassed considerable wealth and was a respected and moderately influential citizen of Philadelphia. He was involved in a number of business ventures in addition to printing and newspaper publishing. Customarily, to boost income a colonial printer sold a wide variety of goods, and Bradford was no exception. His merchandise ranged from barrels of molasses, Barbados rum, chocolate, and tea to "live goose feathers," Spanish snuff, beaver hats, and a variety of patent medicines. The newspaper office also naturally became a kind of bureau of inquiry, where lost and found items might be claimed or left, and where one might obtain information about runaway servants or about buying and selling Negro slaves, real estate, or lottery tickets. As Bradford grew more prosperous, his store increased the range of its stock, including imported items that appealed to the Philadelphia gentry—for example, English red leather, English cherry brandy, looking glasses, "Women's black Velvet fit for Scharves and Hoods," black and colored "Taffeties and Persians," sewing and stitching silk, and from time to time a harpsichord or a virginal. After reviewing the items which Bradford advertised in the *Mercury* through the years, one writer observed that if Bradford's shop could be reconstructed, it would pass as the American eighteenth-century collection of a well-stocked museum.

In addition to operating a kind of "general store," Bradford also built up a sizable business as a stationer and bookseller. Bradford's aunt in London, Tacy Sowle Raylton, the daughter of Andrew Sowle, was a bookseller and printer. The Philadelphia Friends had business dealings with her, and books were shipped through the Bradford shop. Both Bradford and Franklin have been praised for the books they imported, but they have been censured for not printing more books in their own shops; doubtless it was more economical to import the books from Europe. By 1725, the *Mercury* was advertising a large stock of books from London, including Bibles, concordances, grammars, spellers, and dictionaries. In the 1730s, more books relating to history, literature, science, pseudoscience, and philosophy were being advertised. Even though the output of his own press was limited, the volumes Bradford imported showed considerable variety and worth. It is believed that his English aunt played a great role in the selection of the titles that were sent to her nephew's shop. Even though Bradford did not have an interest in literary works to the same degree as Franklin or Keimer, he nevertheless contributed significantly to the intellectual and cultural development of colonial Philadelphia by helping to make its citizens

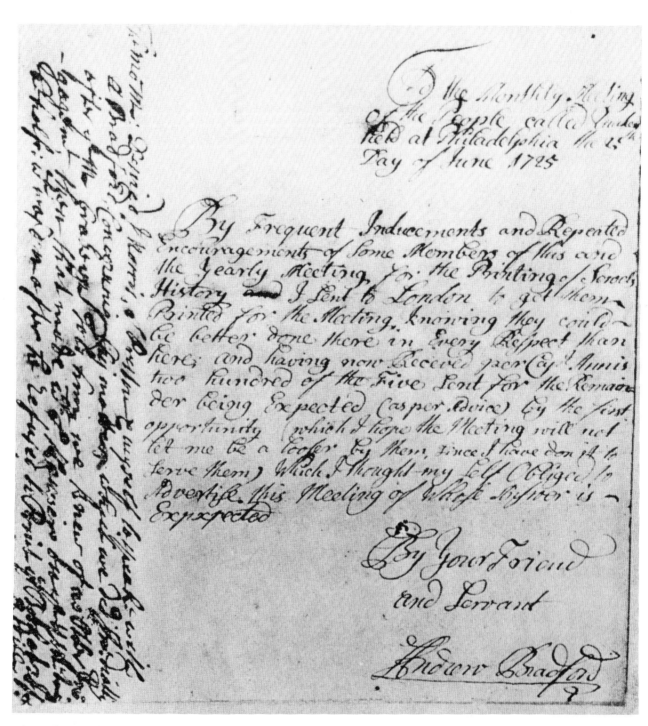

Letter from Bradford to the Monthly Meeting of the Quakers in June 1725, informing them that he has received 200 copies of William Sewel's History of the Quakers *from his aunt, Tacy Sowle Raylton, in London. Bradford expresses the hope that the Quakers will take these books, and the 300 more he has ordered, off his hands. In the left-hand margin of Bradford's note is a reply from "R. Hill" indicating that the Quakers have decided to subscribe to an American edition of the history to be published by Bradford's rival, Samuel Keimer. Keimer's edition was not completed until 1728 (Historical Society of Pennsylvania).*

aware of books and by opening the way to a regular and systematic book trade with Europe.

Bradford's press was less prolific than those of his leading rivals, Keimer and Franklin. Nevertheless, he retained his position as the colony's official printer until 1730, when Franklin printed the proceedings of the assembly for the first time. Bradford continued to print the votes and proceedings of the New Jersey Assembly; additionally, he retained the patronage of the Friends after he moved his printing office from their schoolhouse, and he did almost all of the printing of the Society of Friends until his death in 1742. The Quakers were responsible for his publishing some of the first foreign language books in America: in 1721 he printed the first book in Welsh published in the colonies. He also published the first German books in America, beginning as early as 1728.

Although Bradford built his career and reputation in printing and newspaper publishing, he was active in other business and civic affairs. He was made a freeman of Philadelphia on 20 May 1717, and on 3 October 1721 he was elected a member of the city council, a position to which he was reelected annually for the remainder of his life. In 1738 he became a charter member of the Fellowship Fire Company formed by Philadelphia citizens. Although Bradford enjoyed the patronage of the Friends and was sympathetic to the tastes and habits of the society, he himself was a member of the Anglican church. In 1726 he was appointed to the vestry of Christ Church, and he served as a vestryman at least until 1737. In 1739 he was one of the contributors to the fund for the completion of the interior of the church.

In 1728 Bradford was appointed postmaster of the colony, a position which worked to his advantage as a newspaper publisher because the post brought him into contact with people who received both official and personal correspondence. Frequently, his patrons were willing to share their news with the postmaster-publisher and the readers of the *Mercury*. As a postmaster, he could send his own mail free, and he was able to maintain regular contact with other colonial postmasters, some of whom were also newspaper publishers—for instance, Campbell of the *Boston News-Letter* and Brooker of the *Boston Gazette*. He was able to establish and maintain a wide reputation for himself and the *Mercury*, and the paper doubtless profited substantially from his tenure as postmaster until 1737, when he lost the post to Franklin. The latter wrote in his autobiography that because Bradford kept the post office, he was thought to have had better opportunities for obtaining the news. Moreover, Franklin said, the *Mercury* was thought to be a better distributor of advertisements than his own *Pennsylvania Gazette* and, therefore, carried many more of them.

Bradford's other business ventures helped him to acquire considerable wealth. In 1726 he joined with eleven other Philadelphia businessmen in forming the Dunham Iron Company to erect a blast furnace and other works on 6,000 acres near the Delaware River. The partnership agreement continued until 1773, by which time his share was in the possession of Cornelia Smith, his widow's niece.

Bradford had considerable real estate investments. His father had long favored speculation in land; when Andrew was only three years old, William had bought land along the Philadelphia riverfront upon which to build houses and a wharf "for the better improvement of the place as well as for his own particular profit." William continued to hold the land after he left the city, and between 1717 and 1729 he bought considerable acreage in eastern New Jersey. Andrew took up the tradition and in 1723 purchased two whole squares in the city between Spruce and Pine Streets, one between Twelfth and Thirteenth Streets, and the other between Sixteenth and Seventeenth Streets. He and his brother William II inherited a thousand acres from their aunt, Tacy Sowle Raylton, land which had been given to Andrew Sowle by William Penn. Andrew purchased his brother's half on 7 December 1732 for £160. In 1738 he moved his shop from "The Sign of the Bible" on Second Street to a more imposing and strategic location on Front Street near Market Street. However, Andrew retained possession of the old place, and it was there that his nephew, William Bradford III, would install himself in the summer of 1742.

Several of his father's other business investments redounded to Andrew's advantage. In 1690 the senior Bradford had joined with Klaas and William Rittenhouse in establishing the first papermaking business in Pennsylvania. The very first issue of the *American Weekly Mercury* was printed on a half sheet of pot paper from the Rittenhouse mill. The *Mercury* was unusually consistent among colonial journals in the size and shape of the sheets on which it was printed. Throughout its history its pages measured 7 1/2 to 7 3/4 by 11 3/4 to 12 1/4 inches. Through 1728 the paper usually consisted of two pages, occasionally being enlarged to four pages; thereafter, a four-page paper became the rule. Beginning in 1733, the *Mercury* sometimes expanded to six pages. The proximity of the mill aided Andrew greatly, both for general printing and for the publication of the newspaper. The fact that most of the paper on which the *Mercury* was printed bears one of the several Rittenhouse watermarks indicates that Bradford depended primarily on the Rittenhouse mill, which is said to have made paper solely for the Bradfords. In 1728 William Bradford purchased another large paper factory in Elizabethtown, New Jersey, in order to make both his own and Andrew's newspapers completely independent of British manufacturers.

On 13 February 1741 Andrew Bradford brought out the first magazine in America, the *American Magazine or a Monthly View of the Political State of the British Colonies.* Bradford was prompted to undertake this novel form of journalism by his long-standing rivalry with Benjamin Franklin, who brought out his *General Magazine and Historical Chronicle* three days later. The central figure in this magazine "race" was John Webbe, Franklin's editorial assistant, who became dissatisfied with the arrangement struck with Franklin for publication of the *General Magazine* and took Franklin's plan to Bradford. According to Webbe, he was to "compose" the magazine; Franklin was to print it and take three-quarters of the profits. Bradford presumably made more equitable arrangements with Webbe for his editorial services.

Bradford announced his proposed magazine in the 7 November 1740 issue of the *Mercury* in the longest advertisement in the history of the paper—two and three-quarters pages. It was to be patterned after the English magazines of the period, notably the *Gentleman's Magazine* and the *London Magazine.* The time was not right, however, for this ambitious and expensive journalistic undertaking to succeed in Philadelphia. Neither Bradford nor Franklin was able to sustain publication of his magazine for any significant period: the *American Magazine* lasted for three issues, the *General Magazine* for six. Webbe was not a versatile enough writer to build good readership for the *American Magazine.* Franklin's *General Magazine* had more variety, was more entertaining and less weighty, but it contained mostly borrowings from other sources. Bradford's magazine undertaking was hastily contrived and lacked the financial security of a subscription list. Moreover, no time had been taken to prepare for its proper distribution in other colonies, which Bradford in initiating the *Mercury* had arranged with great care. Possibly the feud between Franklin's *Gazette* and Bradford's *Mercury* damaged both magazines. Nevertheless, Bradford deserves

Title page for the first magazine published in America, Bradford's American Magazine *(New York Historical Society)*

recognition for his initiative and courage in interrupting a comfortable middle-age life and financial ease to pioneer another journalistic field and to assume once again the responsibility for publication of controversial political and religious opinion. Articles by Webbe, the magazine's editor, centered on the people's right to judge the government and its officials. Claiming much attention were controversies challenging English authorities which were raging in the Pennsylvania, New Jersey, and Maryland assemblies. The magazine also supported the eighteenth-century view of Christianity as "only the Religion of Nature in its original Purity and Perfection," discussing the religion of the American Indians and reprinting a diatribe against Roman Catholicism from the *South Carolina Gazette* of 16 October 1740.

Encouraging Andrew Bradford to undertake the magazine publishing venture was his energetic and enterprising young nephew and adopted son, William Bradford III, who was his business partner from December 1739 to December 1740. Even though family problems caused William to leave the firm before the project was announced, he is considered partly responsible for the original plan of the undertaking. The year 1740 had been a banner year for the Bradford printing firm, with the press having its largest output since 1738, thanks to the assistance and contributions of the former apprentice.

Bradford was married twice. His first wife, Dorcas Boels Bradford, died about 1740, and he married Cornelia Smith of New York City, a relative of his father's second wife. Bradford died on 24 November 1742 at the age of fifty-six and was buried in Christ Churchyard at Fifth and Arch Streets. The *Mercury* missed one issue—the week after his death. On 2 December Cornelia Bradford assumed the duties of publisher and brought out the *Mercury* heavily lined in mourning columns and containing the notice of her intention to continue both the printing shop and the newspaper to the satisfaction of her husband's customers. She continued publication until 1747, thereby becoming one of the first woman newspaper editors in America.

During his twenty-three years of publishing Andrew Bradford made a significant contribution to American journalism history and to the economic and cultural progress of the colony of Pennsylvania. He showed initiative, enterprise, and pioneer courage in establishing the first newspaper in the Middle Colonies and the first magazine in America. But unlike most colonial printers and publishers who barely eked out a living, Bradford became a prosperous businessman. He enjoyed a respected position in the Philadelphia community and served the colony of Pennsylvania in political, economic, and social matters. Throughout his newspaper publishing career he fought and won small battles for freedom of the press, especially freedom to discuss local problems. Noteworthy in this area was his long-running criticism of Andrew Hamilton, a prominent Pennsylvania political figure and lawyer who, ironically, successfully defended John Peter Zenger in 1735 in journalism's most celebrated freedom of the press trial. The controversy over Hamilton's various political activities filled the columns of the *Mercury* from 1733, when Bradford was instrumental in keeping Hamilton from being reelected to the Pennsylvania As-

sembly, until Hamilton's death in 1741.

Although Bradford did not have the literary prowess or the intellectual interests of his rival, Benjamin Franklin, neither was he "very illiterate," as Franklin once accused him of being. Samples of his written work show order and clarity of expression. In the books he imported from England, in the ones he printed in his own shop in a number of languages, and in the information carried in the columns of his newspaper, he helped to form the tastes and opinions of the citizens of Pennsylvania and other American colonies in the early decades of the eighteenth century.

Biographies:

John William Wallace, *An Address Delivered at the Celebration by the New York Historical Society, May 20, 1863, of the Two Hundredth Birth Day of Mr. William Bradford, Who Introduced the Art of Printing into the Middle Colonies of British America* (Albany, N.Y.: J. Munsell, 1863);

Horatio G. Jones, *Andrew Bradford, Founder of the Newspaper Press in the Middle States of America* (Philadelphia: King & Baird, Printers, 1869; New York: Arno, 1970);

Henry Darrach, *Bradford Family, 1660-1906* (Philadelphia, 1906);

Anna J. De Armond, *Andrew Bradford: Colonial Journalist* (Newark, Del., 1949).

References:

Henry L. Bullen, "The Bradford Family of Printers," *Americana Collector*, 1 (February 1926): 164-170;

John T. Faris, "The Story of Three Bradfords, Colonial Publishers and Printers," in his *The Romance of Forgotten Men* (New York & London: Harper, 1928), pp. 34-62;

Charles R. Hildeburn, *A Century of Printing: The Issues of the Press in Pennsylvania, 1685-1784*, 2 volumes (Philadelphia: Press of Matlack & Harvey, 1885-1886), I: 9, 47, 294; II: 88, 92;

James M. Lee, *History of American Journalism* (Boston & New York: Houghton Mifflin, 1917), pp. 31-33;

Douglas C. McMurtrie, *A History of Printing in the United States*, 2 volumes (New York: Bowker, 1936), II: 7-9, 14-16;

Isaiah Thomas, *The History of Printing in America*, 2nd edition, 2 volumes (Albany, N.Y.: Joel Munsell, printer, 1874), I: 208-229;

Lawrence C. Wroth, *The Colonial Printer* (Charlottesville, Va.: University Press of Virginia, 1964).

Papers:
The Bradford Manuscripts and Papers are held by the Historical Society of Pennsylvania, Philadelphia.

John Bradford
(6 June 1749-21 March 1830)

Hazel Dicken-Garcia
University of Minnesota

MAJOR POSITION HELD: Editor, *Kentucky Gazette* (1787-1802; 1825-1827).

BOOKS: *The General Instructor; or, The Office, Duty, and Authority of Justices of the Peace, Sheriffs, Coroners and Constables, in the State of Kentucky. With Precedents Suited to Every Case That Can Possibly Arise in Either of Those Offices, under the Laws Now in Force, with References to the Laws Out of Which They Do Arise. The Whole Alphabetically Digested under the Several Titles; with an Index for the Ready Finding of any Matter Sought* (Lexington, Ky.: Printed by John Bradford, 1800);
John Bradford's Historical &c. Notes on Kentucky, from the Western Miscellany Compiled by G. W. Stipp, in 1827, introduction by John Wilson Townsend (San Francisco: Grabhorn Press, 1932).

OTHER: *The New Clerk's Magazine and Farmer's Safe Guide, Containing Precedents, or Forms of Writing, Suited to All Kinds of Business, by which Every Farmer, as Well as Others, May Execute Any Writing That May Be Needed, without the Assistance of a Lawyer*, compiled by Bradford (Lexington, Ky.: Public Advertiser, 1821).

John Bradford's place in history rests on his establishing the *Kentucky Gazette*, the first newspaper in Kentucky and second west of the Allegheny Mountains; his "Notes on Kentucky" (1826-1829); and his leadership in municipal and state development. Though he was not a trained printer, Bradford's efforts led to a strong, leading western newspaper that lasted more than half a century. His "Notes on Kentucky," published in that newspaper from 1826 to 1829, reveal keen abilities as a scholar and historian and remain important sources of information about early Kentucky. Bradford was closely associated with the newspaper he founded for only seventeen of its sixty-one years, but throughout his life, he was a leading citizen in his community and state.

Though no extensive biography of Bradford exists, he and the *Kentucky Gazette* have been the subjects of much study, with the result that conflicting information appears—especially in earlier sources. Douglas McMurtrie and others, for example, say that Bradford was a printer who came from a family tradition of printers, but more recent sources show that he probably knew nothing about the printing trade when he agreed to establish a newspaper in "the Kentucke Country" in 1785—seven years before the area became a state. Up to that time, Bradford had been a surveyor whose activities demonstrated his keen interest in acquiring Western land.

Bradford was the second of eleven children—and the oldest son—born to Daniel and Alice Morgan Bradford in Prince William County, Virginia. Little is known about his youth or education. His father was county surveyor, and John himself settled as a surveyor in Fauquier County after his marriage to Eliza James in 1771. Bradford served in the Revolutionary War and may have gone to Kentucky as a soldier as early as 1776. More certain evidence shows that he went to Kentucky in 1779 as a surveyor, probably serving under George May, chief surveyor of Kentucky County. During 1779 and 1780, he completed several Kentucky land surveys. In 1780 he was appointed deputy surveyor to May and assigned to the district north of the Kentucky River, where he bought for himself and a brother more than 6,000 acres in the present Fayette and Scott counties.

In the summer of 1780, Bradford served under George Rogers Clark and Benjamin Logan in the expedition against the Indian towns of Chillicothe and Piqua, Ohio. Records show him back in Fauquier County on 23 July 1781, when he was sworn in as an ensign in the county militia there.

Bradford was in Kentucky again in 1782, serving as deputy surveyor to Col. Thomas Marshall, surveyor for Fayette County, where Bradford purchased another 1,900 acres. He lost an election for county representative to the Virginia Assembly in 1783. In the spring of 1785, Bradford moved his family from Fauquier County and settled them on land he had bought about five miles northeast of Lexington. That summer, he filed a lawsuit in which he claimed ownership of the site of Lexington, and he persisted in litigating numerous claims to Kentucky land in ensuing years.

During that same summer of 1785, circumstances propelled him toward his position as editor of the first Kentucky newspaper. By the mid-1780s, the Bradfords and thousands of others who had settled in the Kentucky District of Virginia had grown increasingly disgruntled at the inconveniences of trying to maintain a relationship with a state government located five weeks' travel away in Richmond. So, in late 1784, Kentuckians met at Danville in the first of ten conventions called for the purposes of applying and preparing for statehood. In May 1785, members attending the second statehood convention resolved "that, to insure unanimity in the opinion of the people respecting the propriety of separating the district of Kentucky from Virginia, and forming a separate State Government, and to give publicity to the proceedings of the Convention [,] it is deemed essential to have a printing Press."

After the committee charged with procuring a printer failed to find one from the East willing to locate on the frontier, Bradford agreed to set up a press if he was guaranteed public patronage. The September 1786 convention unanimously accepted the committee's recommendation that Bradford establish a press.

That summer, John Scull had established the first newspaper west of the Allegheny Mountains— the *Gazette* in Pittsburgh, Pennsylvania, some 500 miles from Lexington. In March 1787, Bradford sent his brother Fielding to learn printing from Scull and to secure any available supplies in Pittsburgh; other equipment was procured in Philadelphia and transported overland to Pittsburgh. Fielding left Pittsburgh on 1 June, transporting the cargo by water to Limestone (the present Maysville, Kentucky). On 28 July, the Lexington Trustees re-

solved "that a part of In Lot No. 43 . . . be granted to Mr. [John] Bradford on condition that the printing press be established in . . . Lexington." While waiting at Limestone for overland transportation, Fielding Bradford set type for the first issue of the newspaper. Travel via packhorses over rough roads from Limestone to Lexington upset the types, and Bradford apologized in the first issue of the *Kentucke Gazette* (as the name was then spelled) on 11 August 1787: "My customers will excuse this, my first publication, as I am much hurried to get an impression by the time appointed. A great part of the types fell into pi in the carriage of them from Limestone . . . and my partner, which is the only assistant I have, through an indisposition of the body, has been incapable of rendering the smallest assistance for ten days past."

A printing office had not yet been built on the donated lot, so this first issue was printed in a makeshift shop in the back room of Lexington's two-story log courthouse at the corner of Main and Broadway Streets. No originals of the first issue can be located now, but in 1872 George Ranck described it as "a quaint little brown thing, about the size of a half sheet common letter paper . . . without a heading, and contains one advertisement, two short original articles, and . . . apology from the editor."

In the second issue, Bradford enumerated the advantages of having a newspaper in the district. He promised to report on "our neighbouring enemies" and on the proceedings of the Virginia Assembly, in order to "prevent us from undergoing Various evils by being unacquainted with the laws . . . some of which have been in force sometime before they reached the district." Further, he would report on Congress, "teach us to prepare for foreign wars," report on other nations, "lay open all the Republic of Letters," and enable Kentuckians to better understand each other and to agree "for the common good." Finally, Bradford said that the newspaper would "bring the latent sparks of Genius to light," and give the world a respectable view of those "who have come so many leagues to cultivate a deserted land." This, he assured readers, would lure others and strengthen "our hands."

Bradford kept clearly in view the convention's reason for seeking a newspaper: publicity for the statehood issue. "A Farmer," in an essay in the second issue, expected the newspaper to "be employed at first in discussing political subjects," and supposed separation from Virginia to be the "most interesting." The writer hoped "our politicians" would give sentiments on both sides of the question and he directed queries to proponents and opponents of separation. The same writer, a few months later, criticized "the leading men" for too little discussion of the statehood issue.

Still, the separation question dominated most early *Gazette* issues, with Bradford giving it more attention than developments in the rest of the new nation. Extant 1787 issues carry long essays, often taking up three of the newspaper's four pages. Extant 1788 issues show nineteen lengthy articles about separation and statehood-convention proceedings. After 1788 the newspaper carried more diverse offerings: news from abroad, other newspapers' items, Virginia Assembly and Congressional news; poetry, anecdotes, and essays on varied topics; and an ever-expanding volume of advertising. The spelling in the title changed to *Kentucky* in 1789, when the Virginia Assembly ordered some information printed in the "Kentucky" *Gazette*.

The *Kentucky Gazette* was clearly Jeffersonian. Bradford supported France, and some articles attacked England. Nevertheless, under Bradford's control, the *Gazette* never manifested the fierce, personal attacks characteristic of the party press that developed and intensified during the paper's early years. Bradford refrained from the kind of journalism that indulged in "personalities," and Dwight Mikkelson concludes that he was a party follower rather than a leader. He seldom publicized his own stand on political issues, though he advocated educational and cultural developments and institutions. Although operating a newspaper at a time when the editorial emerged as a journalistic feature, Bradford refrained from writing editorials.

Bradford's brother Fielding served as his partner at the *Gazette* until 1788; thereafter, John Bradford ran the newspaper alone, except for journeymen assistants. The newspaper's first fifteen years, while Bradford edited it, coincided with stirring events in Kentucky, the United States, and the world: Kentucky's threat to secede from the United States over rights to use the Mississippi River, and to join Spain, which controlled access to the river; Indian battles of the early 1790s; formation of state government and a state constitution; the creation of the United States Constitution, including debate over its ratification and the Bill of Rights; and the French Revolution. Bradford reported on all, but with little comment. The columns contained diverse, often opposing viewpoints, and criticism even of subjects dear to Bradford. The newspaper reflected an editor who ran it with a spirit of fairness. While columns contained occasional fiery political essays and the newspaper was far from dull, the *Kentucky Gazette* remained calm, steady, forthright, informative, and financially sound while under Bradford's control.

Bradford enjoyed patronage without competition until 1795, when Lexington's second newspaper, the *Kentucky Herald*, began. He retained patronage until 1798, except for 1796, when the *Herald* (also known as *Stewart's Kentucky Herald*) won it from him briefly. Frankfort was made the capital when Kentucky achieved statehood in 1792, and Bradford and his son James established the *Guardian of Freedom* there in 1798 in an effort to retain patronage. They lost when the 1799 contract for printing was awarded to William Hunter, editor of the *Palladium,* and his partner, William H. Beaumont; but the *Guardian* continued as a kind of Frankfort branch of the *Kentucky Gazette*. Bradford dropped out of the *Guardian* partnership in 1801, turning the paper over to his son. The *Guardian* ceased publication in 1806.

In the meantime, Bradford acquired the *Kentucky Herald* in 1802 and merged it with the *Gazette*. That year, he relinquished editorship of the *Gazette* to his son Daniel, and for the next nineteen years remained outside the newspaper business. Daniel sold the *Kentucky Gazette* in 1809 to Thomas Smith, who kept it through a couple of partnerships before selling it to another of Bradford's sons, Fielding, in 1814. Fielding, beset with economic problems, suffered substantial losses in 1817 in lawsuits brought by his creditors; as a result, the newspaper was reorganized as John Norvell and Company, with Fielding as a partner. Several months later, in February 1818, unable to meet his financial obligations, Fielding relinquished all claim to the *Gazette*. Norvell, through successive partnerships, kept it until 1820, when it was sold to I. T. Cavins.

In 1821 Bradford became editor of the *Lexington Public Advertiser,* which his son Daniel had established in 1820, and remained in that position until the newspaper ceased in 1825. At that point, Bradford returned to the *Kentucky Gazette,* the newspaper he had founded nearly forty years earlier and had been away from for twenty-three years. Then in his late seventies, Bradford continued editorship of the *Gazette* for two years, until 1827—three years before his death.

Soon after returning to the *Kentucky Gazette* as editor, he produced the work for which, besides the founding of the newspaper, he is best known. The series of sixty-two articles called "Notes on Kentucky," which began on 25 August 1826 and continued through 9 January 1829, recorded for the first time accounts of numerous early Kentucky events—many of which Bradford participated in. The series, a work of literary excellence and enduring importance as a historical source, attests to Bradford's scholarly skills. He introduced it by lamenting that notes taken by the "first adventurers in Kentucky" had not been collected and turned over to someone "capable of arranging them in such order as to form a connected History of the country." Explaining that he had "come into possession of notes taken" by many such adventurers, including Daniel Boone and George Rogers Clark, he said he intended to publish them. He requested that participants in any of the events who were still living would point out any errors so that he could "correct them immediately upon being informed they exist."

Bradford wrote in the introduction to the "Notes" that "there were scenes presented to . . . the early adventurers to Kentucky, of so affecting a nature that to pourtray [*sic*] them in appropriate language, requires the aid of the tragic muse, and from which both the poet and painter could have copied the brightest colourings exhibited in the variety of the human passions, and presented also to the philanthropist, an ample field on which to exercise all the tender and sympathetic feelings of his nature." Although often relying on his own memory and on the memories of those providing information—who had usually made notes years after the events recorded—Bradford verified his material in other sources whenever he could. The series has the ring of truth and, because he had the vision to publish it, it remains a tribute to him.

As Kentucky's first printer, Bradford published the first books in the state, beginning before statehood with the first *Kentucky Almanac* in 1788 and continuing annually. In 1789 he published the first volume of literature in Kentucky—Thomas Johnson's *Kentucky Miscellany*, a book of poetry that went through four editions and was so well read that no copies remain. Other books and pamphlets he published included James Smith's *Life and Travels of Col. James Smith, of Bourbon County* (1799); *Voyages, Adventures and Situation of the French Emigrants, from the Year '89 to '99* (1800), attributed to a Mme Montelle; and John Robert Shaw's *Narrative of the Life and Travels of John Robert Shaw, the Well-Digger.*

Bradford used his press especially to keep people informed of laws. He published the Kentucky Constitution in 1792 and 1799 and the annual acts of the state legislature; he compiled the latter into the *Laws of Kentucky*, publishing volume one in 1799 and volume two in 1807. In 1799 he published laws passed by Congress in the *Kentucky Gazette* in a manner allowing them to be removed, folded, and assembled into booklets as the *Laws of the United States*. In 1800 he compiled and published *The General Instructor*, dealing with duties of local and state officials.

Bradford's leadership in city and state development ranged across diverse aspects of Kentucky life, but perhaps his greatest contribution was in education. His concern with educational development in the state led him to encourage and promote scholarly excellence. In the 1780s, he was one of the group that bought Lexington land and offered it free to Transylvania Seminary to induce the school to move from Danville—a feat accomplished in 1788. He was a trustee of Transylvania from 1790 to 1828, often chairman of the board of trustees, and helped organize it as a university in 1799. To him, scholarship was the most important aspect of the institution and Transylvania became an outstanding Western university during his lifetime.

A significant contribution to city and state development lay in the postal service Bradford provided before a post office was officially established in the state in 1792. The post riders he hired to carry his newspaper throughout the state also carried mail on their routes. Bradford received and dispensed mail from his office, and beginning in 1790, he printed a monthly list of people for whom mail was waiting in his office.

As a businessman, he was always involved in real estate. In addition, he and other Lexington merchants formed the Kentucky Insurance Company, which served as Kentucky's first "bank," with Bradford as its director. He operated a Frankfort tavern for several years, was a partner in a hemp and flax spinning company, operated a flour mill, advertised a bakery in 1815, and ran a bookstore and stationery shop in Lexington. In 1810 he led a movement to organize Lexington mechanics and manufacturers.

A man of respected integrity, often called "Old Wisdom," Bradford was Lexington's representative at Frankfort in June 1792, when the first governor arrived to take office. He was instrumental in founding Lexington's city library in 1795, often serving thereafter as trustee, and in establishing in Lexington the first hospital west of the Allegheny Mountains. He also served often as chairman of the Lexington Board of Trustees. He was named secretary of the Emigration Society of Lexington, which attempted to attract settlers to the area. He was also secretary of the Lexington Fire Department. Active politically, he founded the Democratic Society of Kentucky, modeled on the liberalism of the French Revolution, in 1793; served as representative of Fayette County in the state legislature in 1797 and 1802; and was county representative in the 1799 constitutional convention. In 1812 he lost a bid for lieutenant governor. He was high sheriff of Fayette County when he died at the age of eighty on 21 March 1830.

Bradford was not a brilliant editor, but he was exceptional in the newspaper business at the time. Beginning a newspaper in a town that in 1790 had only 834 residents, he served exceedingly well a state and community through the transition from pioneering uncertainty to stability.

Some sources associate John Bradford with the Philadelphia and New York Bradfords—William Bradford III and Andrew Bradford being the most famous among them—who were printers and newspaper publishers. But John Bradford's family, traced back to 1680, reveals no other printers, and no solid evidence has been found of a relationship to the other Bradfords. Although apparently not from a printing family, Bradford established one, and his life—whether he was editing a newspaper or not—reflects commitment to journalism. All of his five sons became printers, and three established and edited newspapers in other states: James became public printer in New Orleans, where he established the *Orleans Gazette* in 1804; Benjamin edited the *Tennessee Gazette*, the *Clarion*, and the *Nashville Banner* before his death in 1814; and Fielding established the *Asylum and Feliciapa Advertiser* in St. Francisville, Louisiana, in 1820. In 1805, John Bradford organized a kind of press association of Western printers and booksellers and was elected president at the group's first—and possibly only—meeting. The effort, even if unsuccessful, showed a journalistic vision ahead of its time.

Biographies:

Douglas C. McMurtrie, *John Bradford, Pioneer Printer of Kentucky* (Springfield, Ill.: Privately printed, 1931);

Nelle R. White, *The Bradfords of Virginia in the Revolutionary War and Their Kin* (Richmond, Va.: Whittet & Shepperson, 1932);

J. Winston Coleman, Jr., *John Bradford, Esq.: Pioneer Kentucky Printer and Historian* (Lexington, Ky.: Winburn Press, 1950).

References:

"Bradford's 'Kentucke' Gazette Became Leader in Public Minds," *Kentucky Press*, 8 (March 1937): 2-5;

Leland A. Brown, "Family of John Bradford," *Kentucky Press*, 9 (September 1937): 2-5;

Elizabeth G. Davies, "John Bradford's Contribution to Printing and Libraries in Lexington, Kentucky, 1787-1800," Master's thesis, University of Kentucky, 1951;

Richard Miller Hadsell, "John Bradford and His Contributions to the Culture and the Life of Early Lexington and Kentucky," *Register of the Kentucky Historical Society*, 62 (October 1964): 265-277;

Willard R. Jillson, *First Printing in Kentucky* (Louisville: C. T. Dearing, 1936);

Charles Kerr, "John Bradford: Address Before the Bradford Club in Advocacy of a Tablet to His Memory," *Register of the Kentucky Historical Society*, 17 (September 1919): 83-85;

Dwight Mikkelson, " 'Kentucky Gazette,' 1787-1848: The Herald of a Noisy World," Ph.D. dissertation, University of Kentucky, 1963;

William H. Perrin, *Pioneer Press of Kentucky: From the Printing of the First Paper West of the Alleghenies, August 11, 1787, to the Establishment of the Daily Press in 1830* (Louisville, Ky.: J. P. Morton, 1888);

George W. Ranck, *History of Lexington* (Cincinnati: R. Clarke, 1872);

Charles R. Staples, "John Bradford and the 'Kentucke' Gazette—First Newspaper," *Kentucky Press*, 8 (February 1937): 2-3;

Samuel M. Wilson, "John Bradford, Kentucky's First Printer: A Wide Open Letter," *Filson Club History Quarterly*, 11 (October 1937): 260-269;

Wilson, "John Bradford, Not Thomas Parvin, First Printer in Kentucky: An Open Letter," *Filson Club History Quarterly*, 11 (April 1937): 145-151;

Wilson, "The 'Kentucke Gazette' and John Bradford its Founder," *Papers of the Bibliographical Society of America*, 31, Part 2 (1937): 102-132;

Daniel A. Yanchisin, "John Bradford, Public Servant," *Register of the Kentucky Historical Society*, 68 (January 1970): 60-69.

Papers:

The most complete files of the *Kentucky Gazette* are in the Lexington Public Library. The John Bradford Papers are in the Samuel M. Wilson Collection in the University of Kentucky Library, Lexington.

William Bradford III

(19 January 1719-25 September 1791)

Elsie S. Hebert
Louisiana State University

MAJOR POSITION HELD: Editor, *Weekly Advertiser or Philadelphia Journal*, renamed *Pennsylvania Journal and Weekly Advertiser* in 1742 (1742-1791).

BOOKS: *Books Just Imported from London, and to Be Sold by William Bradford, at His Shop, Adjoining the London Coffee-House in Market Street* (Philadelphia: Printed by William Bradford, 1755);
Catalogue of Books Just Imported from London, and to Be Sold by William Bradford, at the London Coffee-House, Philadelphia. Wholesale and Retaile. With Good Allowance to Those That Take a Quantity (Philadelphia: Printed by William Bradford, 1760?);
Imported in the Last Vessels from London, and to Be Sold by William and Thomas Bradford, Printers, Booksellers, and Stationers, at Their Bookstore in Market-Street, Adjoining the London Coffee-House; or by Thomas Bradford, at His House in Second-Street, One Door from Arch-Street, . . . A Large and Neat Assortment of Books and Stationary [sic] (Philadelphia: Printed by W. & T. Bradford, 1769);
Catalogue of Books Just Imported from London, and to Be Sold by W. Bradford (Philadelphia: Printed by William Bradford, 1788).

No newspaper of the American Revolutionary period is better known, or played a more significant role in support of the Patriot cause, than the *Pennsylvania Journal and Weekly Advertiser*, founded in Philadelphia on 2 December 1742 by William Bradford III, a third-generation member of the Bradford printing family which brought printing and the first newspapers to the middle colonies. Every student who has studied America's Stamp Tax controversy with the British is familiar with the famous "tombstone" front page of the *Pennsylvania Journal*, which was published the day before the tax went into effect as a sign of mourning of the death of a free press. The *Journal* was an early advocate of independence and was the first newspaper to print Thomas Paine's original "Crisis" essay in 1776. For his support of the revolu-tionary cause, Bradford earned his place in American history as the "Patriot Printer."

William Bradford III was born on 19 January 1719 in Hanover Square, New York City, to William Bradford II and Sytje Santvoort Bradford. His father, who had received training in the printing trade in his earlier years, had become a successful merchant and pewterer. His grandfather, William Bradford I, had brought the first printing press to the colony of Pennsylvania in 1685, under the sponsorship of its proprietor, William Penn. After a quarrel with the Quakers, the senior Bradford moved to New York in 1693, where he was appointed official printer. In 1725 he established that colony's first newspaper, the *New York Gazette*.

William III learned the printing trade in the Philadelphia shop of his uncle, Andrew Bradford, to whom he was apprenticed at the age of fourteen. Andrew had founded the first newspaper in the middle colonies, the *American Weekly Mercury*, on 22 December 1719 and was a prosperous publisher and businessman. Having no children, he adopted and educated his nephew as his son and heir and took the twenty-year-old William into partnership in December 1739. But the partnership lasted only one year because a family problem arose which drove William to England.

When William was about nineteen, his devoted foster mother had died, and a short time afterward Andrew Bradford had married Cornelia Smith of New York City. According to Isaiah Thomas in his *The History of Printing in America*, Cornelia had an adopted niece, whom she wished to see inherit the Bradford fortune and whom she was desirous that young William should marry when he came of age. The plan was frustrated because William had settled his affections on another young lady. Thereafter, Cornelia treated him unkindly, and he was finally obliged to leave. Cornelia prevailed on her husband to revoke the will which he had made in favor of William and to make one in her favor.

In 1741 William sailed for England to visit his great-aunt, Tacy Sowle Raylton, who had inherited the famous Sowle publishing house in London from her father, Andrew Sowle, and was engaged in printing and bookselling. William was the first of the Bradfords to return to England since his grandfather and grandmother had left for Pennsylvania in 1685. Raylton introduced Bradford to the major printers and publishers in London and to a typefounder; she also gave him money. When Bradford returned to Philadelphia in 1742, he brought with him the greatest stock of books, stationery, and pictures ever seen in America; some new printing equipment; and a variety of mercantile items. In the summer of 1742 he leased or purchased the Second Street location where his uncle Andrew had formerly lived and operated his printing business at "The Sign of the Bible." William adopted this famous designation for his new shop.

On 15 August 1742 Bradford married Rachel Budd, daughter of the politically prominent Thomas Budd of Northampton Township, Burlington County, New Jersey. The Budd-Bradford relationship had been a long one, for William's grandfather had published Thomas Budd's *Good Order Established in Pennsylvania and New Jersey* in 1689, and the two had been imprisoned by the provincial authorities for supporting the controversial Quaker apostate George Keith in 1692.

Bradford did not waste any time in setting up a newspaper in competition with his aunt Cornelia, who took over the editorship of the *American Weekly Mercury* after her husband died on 24 November 1742. He had announced in Benjamin Franklin's *Pennsylvania Gazette* on 8 July that he was planning to initiate "very soon" the *Weekly Advertiser or Philadelphia Journal*, "in which paper, gentlemen may have extracts of their letters published, containing matter fit to be communicated to the Public." On 2 December 1742 he began publication of the paper, but the title was changed with the third issue to the *Pennsylvania Journal and Weekly Advertiser*. This weekly acquired extensive circulation throughout the colonies and is considered one of the best-printed papers of the period. The *Journal* was published for the next fifty-one years, with only two interruptions. These came during the Revolutionary War: for two months in 1776 while Bradford was with Washington in the Trenton-Princeton campaign, and in 1777-1778 when the British occupied Philadelphia. The last extant issue of the *Journal* is dated 18 September 1793.

The *Journal* was a bold Whig paper, devoted to the interests of the colonists. With its new types just imported from England, larger page size, and careful editing, it eclipsed all other papers of the time, including Franklin's *Pennsylvania Gazette*. As a result, Franklin spruced up his paper typographically and enlarged its size. Bradford's *Journal* was one of the first papers to publish "postscripts"— extra sheets added to the regular newspaper whenever a ship arrived with "the latest advices" after the paper had been made up.

In 1744 Bradford was appointed "Printer to the King's Most Excellent Majesty for the Province of New Jersey," an assignment which helped to establish him as one of the best printers in America. Between 1748 and 1753 Bradford printed several works by Gilbert Tennent and the two volumes of James Hervey's *Meditations and Contemplations* (1750).

The patriot printer first became active in military affairs during 1747-1748, when England, France, and Spain were at war and Philadelphia was in danger from French and Spanish warships and privateers. The Society of Friends was in control of the Pennsylvania government, and true to their principles of nonresistance, the Quakers denied the petition of the non-Quaker citizens for military protection. The citizens formed a defense association, called "The Associators," which Bradford strongly supported in the *Journal*. The organization raised money, acquired muskets and cannons, and erected a fort on the Delaware River. Eleven companies were formed, and Bradford was elected lieutenant of one of them.

A few years later in 1752, the colonies found themselves involved in another war with an invasion of French and Indians into Pennsylvania and Virginia. "The Associators" once again became active. By this time Bradford was a captain.

In spite of these disruptive conflicts, Bradford proceeded to expand his enterprises. In 1754 he opened the London Coffee-House for Merchants and Traders at the corner of Front and Market Streets, which became the commercial and civic center of town. Letters were addressed to the London Coffee-House in preference to the post office; it was the place where the newspapers were filed, ships were chartered, sailing dates were posted, and auctions of ships' cargoes and real estate were held. Leading citizens gathered there to discuss public affairs. During the days before 1760 the London Coffee-House was the "place of resort" for those who were loyal to the king, but after the Stamp Act crisis, it became a rallying spot for Patriots. During the revolution the coffeehouse was used as the meeting place for the town's various citizens' committees.

A new dimension was added to Bradford's publishing business in October 1757, when he established the *American Magazine and Monthly Chronicle for the British Colonies.* He had long been interested in the publication of a magazine, a relatively new form of periodical literature which had begun with the publication of the *Gentleman's Magazine* in London in 1731. He had been instrumental in getting his uncle Andrew to establish the first magazine in America in 1741. It too had been called the *American Magazine* but had lasted for only three issues. Bradford's new magazine was a literary vehicle which supported the British government, "the Church of England and the Proprietary side of things." The original subscription book records four annual subscriptions entered by George Washington in his own handwriting. The magazine was published for just one year. But Bradford persistently held onto his magazine idea, and in January 1769 he and his son Thomas began printing the *American Magazine, or General Repository*, edited by Lewis Nichola. However, this periodical lasted for only nine months.

In a five-year period, 1760 to 1765, more than a score of volumes, primarily on politics, religion, and literature, poured from the Bradford press, in addition to the *Pennsylvania Journal*. The largest work published by Bradford during the mid-eighteenth century was Aaron Leaming and Jacob Spicer's 763-page compilation of the laws of New Jersey, completed in 1758.

Like other members of the Bradford family before him, William became an eminently successful businessman. He consolidated some of his holdings in 1764 by moving his bookstore next to his coffeehouse. This gave him control of a group of businesses in adjoining buildings at the southwest corner of Market and Second Streets, including "The Sign of the Bible." He founded the successful Philadelphia Insurance Company and became its principal manager in 1762, in partnership with John Kidd.

From the time of the establishment of his printing business in 1742, Bradford was active in public affairs. His grandfather, after his quarrel with the Quakers, had reverted to the Church of England in 1698, and all of the Bradfords belonged to the established church. The non-Quakers in Pennsylvania were divided into a popular party, of which Franklin was the leader, and a "more select" party led by Bradford. In general, the *Journal* supported the Quaker-Penn interests against the Franklin party, which sought to revoke the proprietary rights of the Penn family.

But first and foremost, Bradford was an ardent and staunch patriot who put country before party, and in all matters which served to unite the various colonies for mutual protection he and Franklin usually found themselves in agreement. In fact, at the outset of opposition to the oppressive measures being instituted and enforced by the British government against the American colonies, Bradford was more outspoken than the *Gazette* publisher.

After the 1740s the articulate Franklin, Bradford's major rival, became more and more involved in public life and spent long periods in England and Europe representing the dissatisfied colonies. Franklin sold out all of his interests in his printing house in 1765, although his name and influence remained associated with the *Pennsylvania Gazette*. Thus, Bradford became the foremost editorial voice and leader in Pennsylvania in the movement for independence, from the early outset to the final victory.

One of the first intercolony open protests against offensive and hateful acts of the British ministry was made against the Stamp Act in 1765. Bradford, one of the first in Philadelphia to oppose the act, took an uncompromising stand and made the most striking protest. On the day before the act took effect, he published his 31 October issue "in mourning," with the front page black-bordered to create a tombstone effect. At the top was a skull and crossbones, flanked by a pair of pickaxes and shovels—tools of the grave digger. Under the nameplate was the announcement: "EXPIRING: In Hopes of a Resurrection to Life again." In the lower right-hand corner of the first page was another skull and crossbones, designed to create a stamp effect, with the legend "An Emblem of the Effects of the Stamp. O! the fatal Stamp." Other newspapers in the colonies employed the skull and crossbones in a similar manner, and these strong newspaper reactions to the unpopular tax helped to stimulate popular opposition.

At the time of the Stamp Tax controversy, Bradford, as the elected leader in Philadelphia of the Sons of Liberty continental society, was staunchly opposed to the measure, while Franklin's opposition was lukewarm; however, this "taxation without representation" served to unite all factions except the Friends. The *Journal* editor, in writing to leaders of the Sons of Liberty in New York and Boston on 15 February 1766, stated: "Our body in this city is not declared numerous, as unfortunate dissensions in Provincial politics keep us rather a divided people. But when the grand cause calls on

Front page of the famous "tombstone" edition of Bradford's Pennsylvania Journal, *published to protest the Stamp Act*

us, you may be assured we shall universally stand forth, and appear what we really are—Sons of Liberty in Philadelphia." As a member of the Sons of Liberty, Bradford campaigned for the act's repeal, and he was a signer of the Non-Importation Resolutions of 1765. His quick editorial and graphic response in the interests of self-determination and an unfettered press was only the beginning for the revolution's "Patriot Printer."

The *Journal* was an early proponent of a continental congress, and in the issue of 27 July 1774 Bradford used an old Franklin woodcut of a dissected snake, captioned "Unite or Die," to carry his point. Franklin had first used the woodcut in the *Pennsylvania Gazette* in 1754, but during 1774 it was used by a number of papers in the move to unite the colonies. The *Journal* carried the cartoon in its heading until 18 October 1775. When the First Continental Congress met in Philadelphia in September 1774, Bradford and his son Thomas were made its official printers. On the title page of the *Journal of the Proceedings of the Congress held at Philadelphia September 5th, 1774* was a vignette of twelve hands grasping a column based on the Magna Charta and surmounted by a Cap of Liberty. The next year the title page of the *Journal of Proceedings* showed a vignette of Patriot soldiers swearing upon the altar of their country.

Perhaps realizing that war was inevitable, Bradford literally complied with the resolve of those early patriots to risk life and fortune for the preservation of the rights and liberties of their country. He took an active role in the Convention of Pennsylvania in January 1775 and in May returned to duty as captain of a company of the Associators, making some of his own funds available for military use.

Ably assisting the patriot printer in his support of the revolutionary cause was Thomas Paine, who undoubtedly did the most effective journalistic work during the struggle for independence. Paine's first newspaper contribution, published in the *Pennsylvania Journal* on 4 January 1775, was a brief, imaginary "Dialogue between General Wolfe and General Gage in a Wood near Boston," in which Wolfe rebukes Gage for leading the British against the Americans. On 18 October Paine contributed another letter to the *Journal*, signed "Humanus," in which he came out not only for independence for the colonies but for the abolition of slavery.

In June 1776 President John Hancock of the Continental Congress dispatched Bradford with wagons and six boxes of money for delivery to General Washington in New York. Although he was fifty-seven years old and past the age required by law for military service, and notwithstanding that he had a family and substantial business interests useful to his country, he joined the Patriot army at Amboy. He was promoted to major of the second battalion of the Pennsylvania militia in July 1776 in the brigade of Gen. John Cadwalader. He braved the fatigue of the winter at Trenton and was severely wounded at the battle of Princeton. For his distinguished service he was promoted to colonel of the regiment in 1777.

It was at this time that Paine's journalistic ability was strikingly displayed in the famous "Crisis" essay, which was first published in the *Pennsylvania Journal* on 19 December 1776. It was read to Washington's disheartened soldiers on the eve of their attack on Trenton, opening with the familiar lines: "These are the times that try men's souls. The summer soldier and the sunshine patriot will, in this crisis, shrink from the service of their country; but he that stands it *now*, deserves the love and thanks of man and woman. . . ." The *Journal* was suspended for two months during this campaign but afterward continued publication until the British occupied Philadelphia.

Several days before the British troops marched into Philadelphia on 26 September 1777, Bradford was entrusted by Governor Wharton with the command of the city and was put in charge of removing the stores. When he had completed his work, he left the city as the British were entering it and went to Fort Mifflin. In this same year Bradford was appointed chairman of the Pennsylvania Navy Board, and he set about gathering an armed flotilla and fortifying and obstructing the Delaware River. On 20 October 1777 six British men-of-war were repulsed at Fort Mifflin, thanks largely to a marine cheveaux-de-frise which Bradford had constructed. This defeat destroyed for the moment the plan of the British campaign, and Washington congratulated the patriot printer by letter on his check of the enemy. A reinforced British fleet returned on 10 November and this time penetrated the defenses, but only after a six-day battle. Bradford destroyed that part of his flotilla which was in danger of being captured and retreated up the Delaware, sinking his remaining galleys in creeks and carrying the armaments inland for hiding. That winter Bradford suffered with his men at Valley Forge. The British sent an expedition to destroy Bradford's flotilla in the spring but could not find it. After the British fleet retired, Bradford refloated his boats. He retained his position on the Navy Board until the end of the war, cooperating with

Washington at times when some of the other officers were not as supportive of the commander in chief as they might have been.

When the British army left Philadelphia in June 1778, Bradford returned to the city and reopened his print shop and coffeehouse. But the patriot printer perceived that the customs and manners of the citizens had changed during the war years and that business had found new channels. When publication of the *Journal* resumed in December, son Thomas was listed as the sole publisher. In 1779 Bradford performed his last duty for the army: on 12 May he was appointed president of the court of inquiry concerning military officers. With his health broken, his fortune shattered, and his personal affairs in disarray because of the war, Bradford retired from active service in 1780. Ten years later, the Supreme Council of the State of Pennsylvania repaid him for several large sums he had personally advanced during the war.

Isaiah Thomas wrote in *The History of Printing in America:* "After peace was established, he consoled himself under his misfortune; and in his most solitary hours, reflected with pleasure, that he had done all in his power to secure for his country a name among independent nations; and he frequently said to his children, 'though I bequeath you no estate, I leave you in the enjoyment of liberty.' "

Bradford died on 25 September 1791 at the age of seventy-two, leaving a credible record as a prominent printer, a publisher, a bookseller, a businessman, and a citizen-soldier. His eldest son, Thomas, continued to publish the *Journal* until 1793.

Col. William Bradford was far from being a "sunshine patriot." He gave his talent, his press, his fortune, and his physical capabilities to the revolutionary cause of the American colonies. As an early leader of the Sons of Liberty, he was an ardent champion of the rights of a free people and a free press. In the most famous issue of the *Pennsylvania Journal*, the one that carried the "tombstone" front page, he published a fiery piece on liberty, declaring: "Liberty is one of the greatest blessings which human beings can possibly enjoy. . . . The *Liberty of the Press* has very justly been esteemed one of the main Pillars of the Liberty of the people. While this is maintained, the first Steps to Oppression are detected, and the Attention of the People seasonably awakened. . . . So essential is this to Freedom, Property, and Happiness, that the most plausible Attempts to curtail it, even in the smallest Degree, have always been strenuously opposed by the virtuous, free, and unbiased Patriot."

The *Pennsylvania Journal* is valued as a record of the French wars, the Indian war, the period of the Stamp Act, the revolution, the Constitution, and the administration of Washington. In an address to the New York Historical Society on 20 May 1863, John William Wallace said that "from 1764, when the Stamp Act was proposed, till the occupation of Philadelphia by the British, when the *Journal* was temporarily suspended, it is probably the most valuable of the American journals." In 1852 the *Germantown Telegraph* said that one of the reasons for the *Journal*'s great value was that there breathed throughout it a sentiment of patriotism, a detestation of oppression, a hostility to tyranny, and a love of liberty and freedom of the press as deep and fervid as exists anywhere.

During the thirty-eight years from the first issue of the *Journal* to his retirement in 1780, Bradford printed numerous books and two magazines in addition to his widely read newspaper. Citizens of Pennsylvania and the other colonies respected Bradford's publications because of his willingness to reflect in them the kaleidoscopic changes which were taking place in America in the latter half of the eighteenth century.

The Bradford printing house continued in operation after the death of the "Patriot Printer" and after the *Journal* ceased publication. After furnishing six generations of prominent and successful printers to early America, the 140-year-old Bradford printing dynasty appropriately closed out with the publication of the greatest typographical work attempted in America up to that time: *The Cyclopedia or Universal Dictionary of Arts, Science and Literature, by Abraham Rees, with the Assistance of Eminent Professional Gentlemen. First American Edition, Revised, Corrected, Enlarged and Adapted to This Country.* The first volume of this forty-one-volume work was issued in 1810, and publication was completed in 1825. The publisher was Samuel F. Bradford, the grandson of William Bradford III.

Biographies:

John William Wallace, *An Address Delivered at the Celebration by the New York Historical Society, May 20, 1863, of the Two Hundredth Birth Day of Mr. William Bradford, Who Introduced the Art of Printing into the Middle Colonies of British America* (Albany, N.Y.: J. Munsell, 1863);

Wallace, *An Old Philadelphian. Colonel William Bradford, the Patriot Printer of 1776. Sketches of his life* (Philadelphia: Sherman, 1884);

Henry Darrach, *Bradford Family, 1660-1906* (Philadelphia, 1906).

References:

Clarence S. Brigham, *History and Bibliography of American Newspapers, 1690-1820,* 2 volumes (Worcester, Mass.: American Antiquarian Society, 1947), II: 937-938;

Henry L. Bullen, "The Bradford Family of Printers," *Americana Collector,* 1 (February 1926): 164-170;

Anna J. De Armond, *Andrew Bradford: Colonial Journalist* (Newark, Del., 1949);

John T. Faris, "The Story of Three Bradfords, Colonial Publishers and Printers," in his *The Romance of Forgotten Men* (New York & London: Harper, 1928), pp. 34-62;

Charles R. Hildeburn, *A Century of Printing. The Issues of the Press in Pennsylvania, 1685-1784,* 2 volumes (Philadelphia: Matlack & Harvey, 1885-1886);

Douglas C. McMurtrie, *A History of Printing in the United States,* 2 volumes (New York: Bowker, 1936), II: 56-57;

Isaiah Thomas, *The History of Printing in America,* second edition, 2 volumes (Albany, N.Y.: Joel Munsell, 1874), I: 241-244;

Lawrence C. Wroth, *The Colonial Printer* (Charlottesville: University Press of Virginia, 1964), p. 34.

Papers:

The Bradford Manuscripts and Papers are held by the Historical Society of Pennsylvania, Philadelphia.

William Cullen Bryant

James Boylan
University of Massachusetts-Amherst

See also the Bryant entry in *DLB 3, Antebellum Writers in New York and the South.*

BIRTH: Cummington, Massachusetts, 3 November 1794, to Dr. Peter and Sarah Snell Bryant.

EDUCATION: Williams College, Williamstown, Massachusetts, 1810-1811.

MARRIAGE: 11 January 1821 to Frances Fairchild; children: Frances, Julia Sands.

MAJOR POSITIONS HELD: Editor, *New-York Review and Atheneum Magazine* (1825-1826), *United States Review* (1826-1827); editorial assistant, editor, coproprietor, *New-York Evening Post* (1826-1878).

DEATH: New York, 12 June 1878.

BOOKS: *The Embargo; or, Sketches of the Times; A Satire; by a Youth of Thirteen,* anonymous (Boston: Printed for the purchasers, 1808); second edition, corrected and enlarged, as Bryant (Boston: Printed for the author by E. G. House, 1809);

An Oration, Delivered at Stockbridge. July 4th, 1820 (Stockbridge, Mass.: Printed by Charles Webster, 1820);

Poems (Cambridge: Printed by Hilliard & Metcalf, 1821);

The American Landscape, No. 1 (New York: E. Bliss, 1830);

Poems (New York: E. Bliss, 1832; edited by Washington Irving, London: J. Andrews, 1832); second edition, expanded (Boston: Russell, Odiorne & Metcalf/Philadelphia: Marshall, Clark, 1834);

The Fountain and Other Poems (New York: Wiley & Putnam, 1842);

An Address to the People of the United States in Behalf of the American Copyright Club (New York, 1843);

The White-Footed Deer and Other Poems (New York: I. S. Platt, 1844);

A Funeral Oration, Occasioned by the Death of Thomas Cole, Delivered before the National Academy of Design, New-York, May 4, 1848 (New York & Philadelphia: Appleton, 1848);

Letters of a Traveller; or, Notes of Things Seen in Europe and America (New York: George P. Putnam, 1850);

Reminiscences of the Evening Post: Extracted from the Evening Post of November 15, 1851. With Additions and Corrections by the Writer (New York: William C. Bryant & Co., 1851);

Letters of a Traveller. Second Series (New York: D. Appleton, 1859);

A Discourse on the Life, Character and Genius of Washington Irving, Delivered before the New York Historical Society . . . 3rd of April, 1860 (New York: G. P. Putnam, 1860);

Thirty Poems (New York: D. Appleton, 1864);

Voices of Nature (New York: D. Appleton, 1865);

Letters from the East (New York: George P. Putnam, 1869);

A Discourse on the Life, Character and Writings of Gulian Crommelin Verplanck, Delivered before the New-York Historical Society, May 17th, 1870 (New York: The Society, 1870);

The Song of the Sower (New York: D. Appleton, 1871);

Orations and Addresses by William Cullen Bryant (New York: Putnam's, 1873);

Thanatopsis. (A Poem.) (New York: D. Appleton, 1874);

Among the Trees, by William Cullen Bryant, Illustrated from Designs by Jervis McEntee, Engraved by Harley (New York: Putnam's, 1874);

The Poetical Works of William Cullen Bryant, edited by Parke Godwin, 2 volumes (New York: D. Appleton, 1883);

The Prose Writings of William Cullen Bryant, edited by Godwin, 2 volumes (New York: D. Appleton, 1884);

Tremaine McDowell, ed., *William Cullen Bryant: Representative Selections, with Introduction, Bibliography, and Notes* (New York & Cincinnati: American Book Company, 1935).

OTHER: *Tales of Glauber-Spa,* edited with contributions by Bryant (New York: Harper, 1832);

The Iliad of Homer. Translated into English Blank Verse, translated by Bryant, 2 volumes (Boston: Fields, Osgood, 1870);

A Library of Poetry and Song: Being Choice Selections from the Best Poets, edited by Bryant (New York: J. B. Ford, 1871);

The Odyssey of Homer, translated by Bryant, 2 volumes (Boston: James R. Osgood, 1871-1872);

Sidney Howard Gay, *A Popular History of the United States, from the First Discovery of the Western Hemisphere by the Northmen, to the End of the First Century of the Union of States,* introduction by Bryant, 4 volumes (New York: Scribner, Armstrong, 1876-1881).

William Cullen Bryant brought to American newspaper journalism not only the argumentative and rhetorical skills of the lawyer but the sensibility of the poet. His reputation as one of the few major poets of the early republic has gradually overshadowed, since his death, his career as a newspaper editor, editorialist, and proprietor, to which he gave more than fifty of his eighty-three years. As editor in chief of the *New-York Evening Post,* he left his imprint, that of a classical liberal and humanitarian, on nearly every major national issue from the fight over the Second Bank of the United States through Reconstruction. To nineteenth-century journalism, he lent a civility and literary quality generally lacking in his contemporaries. By the time he concluded his career, he was hailed as New York's first citizen and elder statesman.

Bryant's long life began in 1794 in what was then a fringe of civilization, the town of Cummington in the western hills of Massachusetts. He was born—the second of seven children—into a literate family, which encouraged him in his precocious ability to speak and write. His father, Dr. Peter Bryant, was a well-read physician with an active interest in public affairs. His mother, Sarah Snell Bryant, was a daughter of one of Cumming-

William Cullen Bryant at age thirty, portrait by Samuel F. B. Morse (Permanent Collection, National Academy of Design)

Bryant's parents, Dr. Peter Bryant and Sarah Snell Bryant (New York Historical Society)

ton's first settlers; as Bryant wrote of her years later, she had little tolerance of injustice even when it was tolerated by society.

Bryant's education started early. He mastered the alphabet as little more than an infant and started at the community school when he was only four. At the age of nine he began to compose verses and the following year wrote a poem for his school's annual exercises; its publication three years later in the *Hampshire Gazette* of Northampton was his first newspaper appearance.

His first political commentary was similarly presented in verse. With his father, who was serving in the state legislature, footing the printer's bill, Bryant offered to the public *The Embargo; or, Sketches of the Times; a Satire; by a Youth of Thirteen.* It attacked President Thomas Jefferson on behalf of the New England Federalists; specifically, it deplored the administration's effort to coerce England and France by withholding American goods from trade. Its anonymous publication in 1808 raised doubts about its authenticity as a juvenile production, and Bryant's name appeared on it

when it was reissued a year later with other youthful verses.

Bryant's precocity was viewed by his family not as a forecast of a life to be spent as a poet but as an indication of his fitness for an intellectual profession. In 1808 he exchanged the community school for tutors charged with preparing him for college: first his uncle, the Reverend Dr. Thomas Snell of North Brookfield, then the Reverend Moses Hallock of Plainfield. These studies enabled him to enter Williams College as a fifteen-year-old sophomore in the fall of 1810. He did not stay the year, but withdrew the following July to prepare for Yale.

For reasons unknown, but probably financial, he did not go to Yale. Instead, in December 1811 he began to study law under Samuel Howe in Worthington and remained with him until mid-1814. In this period he wrote what has remained his best-known poem, "Thanatopsis," but it was not published until 1817, when it appeared in the *North American Review.* He received his final legal training under William Baylies, a member of Congress from

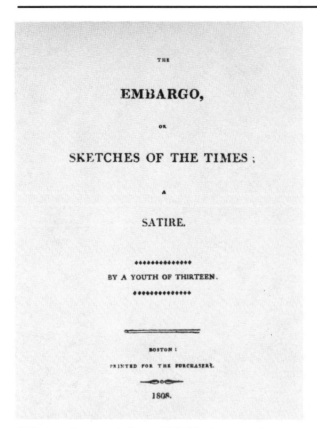

Title page for Bryant's first published book, an attack in verse on the trade policies of Thomas Jefferson

fore while she was living with a sister in Great Barrington. On 2 January 1822 their first child, Frances (Fanny), was born.

In the meantime a literary undercurrent continued to flow through Bryant's life. A collection of his poems was published in 1821. Starting in 1817 he contributed, more or less regularly, poems and reviews to the *North American Review* of Boston and other periodicals, and he was tapped in 1821 to write and deliver the Phi Beta Kappa poem at Harvard.

As early as 1818 he had made a brief visit to the nation's literary capital, New York City, and in April 1824 he made another visit there that proved to be a turning point in his life. As a newly recognized poet, he found himself welcomed into the community of letters by such eminences as James Fenimore Cooper, Fitz-Greene Halleck, and Robert C. Sands; and he began to glimpse the possibility of leaving the law. Later in 1824 he suffered a bitter professional disappointment when a slander case his client had won was reversed on a technicality. On 21 December 1824 he wrote to a friend: "I am fixed in my determination to leave this beggarly profession."

West Bridgewater, across the state from Cummington. After a little more than a year of study with Baylies, Bryant was admitted to practice and hung out his shingle in Plainfield, a hamlet a few miles north of Cummington.

Bryant thus began nearly a decade of trying to come to terms with a profession that he never liked, while at the same time being inexorably drawn toward a life of letters. He practiced only eight months in Plainfield before entering a partnership in the more substantial town of Great Barrington, in the southwest corner of the state. His partner remained only long enough to introduce Bryant to the community and to bequeath the practice to him.

For a time Bryant gave evidence of settling down to the career of a small town lawyer. In 1820 he became not only town clerk but a county justice of the peace, and he held other minor offices later. He was called on for such civic occasions as, for example, the Fourth of July oration at nearby Stockbridge in 1820. On 11 January 1821 he married Frances Fairchild of East Bloomfield, New York, an orphan whom he had met four years be-

Miniature portrait on ivory of Bryant's wife, Frances Fairchild Bryant (New York Historical Society)

Within six months Bryant had changed course. In May 1825 he moved to New York and in June became coeditor, with Henry J. Anderson, of a new periodical, the *New-York Review and Atheneum Magazine*. In August he sent for his family. Yet, even having symbolically left the law, he recognized that the magazine work hardly provided a living; as a precaution he obtained a license to practice law in New York and even handled one case.

But he was saved from returning to the law by an accident—a runaway in June 1826 in which the editor of the *New-York Evening Post*, William Coleman, was injured. Coleman had been editor of the newspaper since its founding in November 1801 as a Federalist organ under the sponsorship of Alexander Hamilton. It had shed its original political character in the realignment of parties after the War of 1812. When Coleman was disabled, the *Evening Post* needed immediate assistance. Perhaps attracted to a fellow native of western Massachusetts, Coleman hired Bryant as an editorial assistant.

For a time, Bryant split his working time between the newspaper and his magazine interests. The failing *New-York Review* was succeeded by the *United States Review*, cumbersomely coedited by Bryant in New York and Charles Folsom in Boston. "I drudge for the Evening Post," wrote Bryant in mid-1827, "and labour for the *Review,* and thus have a pretty busy life of it. I would give up one if I could earn my bread by the other, but that I cannot do." Before long, the balance tilted toward the newspaper; in 1828 Bryant was able to buy, with borrowed funds, a one-eighth proprietorship worth $1,000 a year, or double what he had been making as a hill-town lawyer. His old friend Richard Henry Dana asked how he, as a poet, could bear the world of politics into which the newspaper had thrust him; Bryant replied: "I do not like politics any better than you do—but . . . you know politics and a bellyfull are better than poetry and starvation."

Bryant turned out to have a lively talent for political analysis and argument. Influenced by the classical British political economists, he took a strong free-trade position, which at that time meant opposition to Whig-sponsored tariffs. Thus aligned with the Democrats, Bryant and the *Evening Post* in 1828 supported the winning candidate, Andrew Jackson, and later backed Jackson, in defiance of most of the rest of the city's press, in his struggle with the Bank of the United States.

Before long, Bryant was placed in charge of the destiny of the *Evening Post*. In December 1827

the enfeebled Coleman had promoted him to joint editor. A year and a half later, on 13 July 1829—one day before the founder's death—Bryant became editor in chief, a title he did not relinquish until his own death, just short of forty-nine years later.

When Bryant succeeded Coleman, newspapers were still relatively simple in organization. No corps of reporters or system of local news gathering had yet developed, and an editorial staff generally comprised only an editor and one or two assistants. Thus Bryant's initial choice of a lieutenant was of major importance. Within days after Coleman's death, he selected William Leggett, six years his junior. Leggett's choleric, impulsive temperament (he had left the navy after a court-martial for dueling) was in contrast with what many contemporaries found to be Bryant's chilly demeanor. Yet curiously, it was Bryant who, in this period, had his only angry physical confrontation with an editorial adversary; on 20 April 1831 he publicly horsewhipped Col. William L. Stone of the *Commercial Advertiser* for calling him a liar in print. Bryant was immediately remorseful and wrote in the *Evening Post* the next day: "I feel that I owe an apology to society for having, in this instance, taken the law into my own hands. The outrage was one for which the law affords no redress." Nor did Bryant, though he was challenged on occasion, ever permit himself to be drawn into another such incident.

Despite their differences in temperament, Bryant and Leggett produced a successful newspaper. In 1834 Bryant, who by then had purchased a one-third interest in the *Evening Post*, was rewarded with a year's share of profits worth $4,646.20. At this point he placed such confidence in Leggett that he all but decided to give up the paper to him, for Bryant had not yet banished the chimera of being a gentleman of letters. On 24 June 1834 he sailed with his wife and children (their second daughter, Julia Sands, had been born on 29 June 1831) for Europe, and there they remained for more than a year.

Their pilgrimage was interrupted by word, late in 1835, that Leggett had been taken seriously ill and that the *Evening Post* was rudderless. Still a proprietor and still holding the title of editor, Bryant could not shun responsibility. Once he was convinced of the seriousness of the situation, he left his family in Europe and hastened back to New York. On 26 March 1836 he resumed command of the newspaper. He found the *Evening Post* in dubious financial condition, partly because of what he

Part of the front page of the New-York Evening Post *in 1826, the year in which Bryant went to work for the paper as an editor's assistant*

called Leggett's "imprudences," partly because the books, kept by a drunken clerk, were in disarray. To his wife, Bryant wrote three months after his return that the newspaper had been "a sad dull thing during the winter . . . and people were getting tired of it." He added that it had "needed my attention very much—I fear that it would have been a gone case with it if I had passed another six months abroad." He set about rehabilitation with characteristic vigor: "I work harder than I ever did before, but I was never so well able to work hard." Although Bryant apparently never reproved Leggett, the younger man returned only briefly to the *Evening Post* before moving on to a new publication of his own.

Bryant's purpose at this point was simply to refurbish the *Evening Post* sufficiently to make it attractive to a purchaser. He wrote to his brother: "I have been employed long enough with the management of a daily newspaper, and desire leisure for literary occupations that I love better." Specifically, he became fixed on the notion of abandoning

the city for the Illinois prairie, to which his brother had already emigrated. But his goal always receded before him; the newspaper's profits were driven down further in the 1837 recession and Bryant could neither find a purchaser nor make further payments on the money due for his interest in the paper. He grumbled that he was merely a "draft horse harnessed to the wain of a daily paper."

Gradually, perhaps without conceding as much to himself, Bryant gave up the idea of leaving New York and daily journalism. Little as he said he liked the work, he succeeded nonetheless in righting the *Evening Post* and steering it through its financial crisis. As Allan Nevins noted in his history of the newspaper, this perilous passage marked the start of Bryant's "real editorial career," his commitment to the creation of an institution and a voice that would carry weight in the affairs of city, state, and nation.

The obstacles that Bryant faced in nurturing such an institution had grown in the years since he entered the field. By the mid-1830s New York journalism was in the throes of what has since been dubbed the "penny press revolution." The old six-cent "blanket sheets"—the *Evening Post* was one—suddenly faced the fierce competition of newspapers not only selling for one cent but offering more extensive and livelier news than the older newspapers.

The most formidable of these new papers were started by the only nineteenth-century New York editors whose eminence and longevity rivaled Bryant's: James Gordon Bennett, who started the *Herald* in 1835, and Horace Greeley, founder in 1841 of the *Tribune*. Bryant regarded both contemporaries with more than a little scorn and refused to reshape the *Evening Post* in the image of the penny press—although, like most of the other older newspapers, the *Evening Post* was eventually spurred to more energetic news coverage. But Bryant clung to an older conception of journalism. As John Bigelow, who was a colleague and later a biographer, wrote: "Mr. Bryant was not a journalist in the modern sense of the word: he had . . . but an imperfect appreciation of the financial importance of news for a newspaper. He had always been a leader-writer."

Thus the *Evening Post* continued to function much as it had in the era before the arrival of the penny press, with most of the editorial burden falling on Bryant and his assistants. In October 1839 Parke Godwin, whom the Bryants had met socially three years before, began his long, complex relationship with Bryant, his family, and the *Evening Post*. Godwin was a Fourierist socialist, twelve years younger than Bryant. Although his work at the *Evening Post* was competent enough, he found Bryant a distant superior, and the more so when he courted the Bryants' older daughter. Godwin married Frances on 12 May 1842 and a month later left the *Evening Post* to start a *Morning Post*, financed by the parent company. It failed, with a loss of $6,000; a subsequent publication that he attempted, the *Pathfinder*, also failed. Godwin then returned to the *Evening Post*, created a minor crisis over who was in command when Bryant at last dared to go again to Europe in 1845, and again left the newspaper (but not forever) at the end of 1846 for a customs job.

Even under the self-imposed handicap of forswearing sensational news and mass circulation, Bryant built the *Evening Post* into a paper to which the leaders of the nation paid close attention for decades, and which was profitable enough to confer on Bryant modest wealth. He never permitted the *Evening Post* to become so closely associated with a

Parke Godwin, Bryant's son-in-law, who repeatedly left and returned to the Evening Post *(Picture Collection, the New York Public Library)*

political party—through subsidies, for example—that it lost its air of independence; nor, on the other hand, did he permit it to drift so far outside the political mainstream that it forfeited its audience.

Bryant's gradually deepening personal commitment to the *Evening Post* after 1836 also brought the emergence of his mature editorial voice—the formal yet vigorous and outspoken style that created for him a reputation as the nation's most distinguished newspaper essayist. His mother's son, Bryant did not hesitate to defy conventional or majority opinion when his moral sense was challenged. One such instance occurred in 1836, when Bryant wrote a scathing series of editorials defending twenty-one tailors convicted of a conspiracy for their refusal to work at low wages. "If this is not SLAVERY," he thundered in the famous editorial of 13 June, "we have forgotten its definition. Strike the right of associating for the sale of labour from the privileges of a freeman, and you may as well at once bind him to a master, or ascribe him to the soil." So inflexible, on occasion, was this sense of justice that it did not relent even at the grave;

Bryant created widespread outrage when, on the death in 1844 of Nicholas Biddle of the United States Bank, he wrote: "If he had met with his deserts, he would have passed [the close of his life] in the penitentiary."

Bryant's political development in the 1840s and 1850s came to hinge, as did national politics, on the overriding issue of slavery. The evolution of the *Evening Post*'s position can be said to parallel that of advanced Northern opinion from tacit coexistence with slavery to, ultimately, the realization that it had to be extinguished. In the 1830s, although he was outraged by the slaying of the abolitionist editor Elijah P. Lovejoy as an assault on freedom of the press, Bryant was himself far from supporting abolition; in general, he agreed with the South's position that the slavery system should be left alone. But by 1846 he was prepared to resist the annexation of Texas because it expanded slaveholding territory; he supported the Wilmot Proviso, which would have barred expansion of slavery into territory won in the Mexican War; and as the Democratic party began to splinter, he joined the Free-Soil or Barnburner faction and emblazoned across the masthead of the *Evening Post* in 1848 the Barnburner slogan: "Free Soil, Free Labor, Free Trade, and Free Speech."

Still, it took years more for him to break definitively with the Democrats. In 1852 the *Evening Post* initially supported the Democratic candidate, Franklin Pierce, then all but withdrew its support before the end of the campaign. In 1854 Bryant rebelled over the Kansas-Nebraska bill, created by Senator Stephen Douglas of Illinois and backed by President Pierce and other Northern Democrats; the bill, permitting local sovereignty on the slavery question in the new territories, opened the door to guerrilla war between slavery and antislavery forces in Kansas. When Congress approved the bill in March 1854, Bryant's editorial despaired: "The Democratic Party has lost its moral strength in the free states; it is stripped of the respect of the people by the misconduct of those who claim to be its leaders. . . ."

In September 1855 Bryant signaled his change of allegiance by supporting the ticket of the new Republican party in the state elections. He declined, for personal reasons, to go to the convention in Pittsburgh in February 1856 that created the national Republican party: "I do not like public meetings. I do not like consultations. I am surfeited with politics in my vocation." But later in 1856 the *Evening Post* vigorously plumped for the first Re-

John Bigelow, Bryant's partner and associate editor at the Evening Post *from 1848 until 1860 (Brown Brothers)*

publican candidate for president, John C. Frémont, who lost to James Buchanan.

As the sectional crisis deepened, Bryant's position on slavery grew ever firmer. He was deeply distressed by the recapture of a slave in Boston under the federal Fugitive Slave Act (adopted as part of the Compromise of 1850), which he called "the most ruffianly act ever authorized by a deliberative assembly." He helped raise funds to send arms to embattled antislavery settlers in Kansas. The Dred Scott decision in March 1857, which ruled that slaves could not enjoy the rights of citizens anywhere in the United States, brought forth eight straight days of editorials. "Hereafter," he wrote, "wherever our flag floats it is the flag of slavery . . . ; it should be dyed black, and its device should be the whip and the fetter." Even while he deplored John Brown's raid on the armory at Harper's Ferry in October 1859, he wrote that history "will record his name among those of its martyrs and heroes."

As the election of 1860 approached, Bryant looked to a new political eminence, Abraham Lincoln of Illinois. Lincoln had caught Bryant's attention during the political campaign of 1856, even before the Lincoln-Douglas debates of 1858. It was Bryant who presided at Cooper Institute in New York when Lincoln delivered the great speech of 27 February 1860 on the extension of slavery which thrust him into the national arena. When the Republicans nominated Lincoln later in the year, the *Evening Post* was his most enthusiastic supporter in the East; and it exulted in his election, despite the threat the victory carried of providing the pretext for secession.

As a member of the circle of Lincoln's early supporters, Bryant offered the president-elect plentiful advice on the formation of his cabinet. In particular, Bryant advised against the appointment of Simon Cameron, who became a corrupt secretary of war, and in favor of Salmon P. Chase, who performed brilliantly as secretary of the treasury. Later, Bryant attempted to intercede at the White House in favor of the *Evening Post*'s business manager, Isaac Henderson, who had been dismissed as an agent by the Department of the Navy for accepting illegal commissions. Lincoln wisely declined to help Henderson.

The *Evening Post* was an important actor in a war in which the metropolitan press and its editors played a major role. The spectrum of the New York press, from the *Evening Post,* Greeley's *Tribune,* and Henry J. Raymond's *Times* on the one side to Bennett's *Herald* on the other, represented the range of Northern opinion. Like the other editorialists, Bryant constantly advised the president on how to handle secession, military strategy, diplomacy, financial policy, administrative details, and schemes to end the war. Robert S. Harper, in his *Lincoln and the Press,* has observed: "Bryant was one of the Republican radicals whose faultfinding with Lincoln's administrative policies did him more damage than even the Democrats were able to muster."

From the start of the secession crisis, Bryant took an aggressive line. The *Evening Post* urged the use of military power to keep the South in the Union and sprang to Lincoln's support when the first shots were fired at Fort Sumter. Once hope for a short conflict had faded, the *Evening Post* aligned itself with the radical position—that is, it supported total war against the South and speedy emancipation. Even after the Emancipation Proclamation of 1862, which freed slaves in former Confederate territory, Bryant pressed for universal emancipation. Like much of the rest of the press, the *Evening Post* was impatient with the military progress of the war. By 1864 Bryant was asking in private communications whether Lincoln ought to

be renominated. But the pages of the *Evening Post* never reflected these doubts; and during Lincoln's successful election campaign, it vouched for his conduct of the war.

In contrast with its war policies, the *Evening Post*'s approach to Reconstruction was moderate, in the spirit of the assassinated Lincoln. It pushed hard for the completion of the antislavery agenda—that is, the constitutional abolition of slavery and the assumption of civil rights by former slaves—but at the same time urged prompt restoration of the South. Indeed, Bryant saw the chief hope for a new, prosperous South to lie among blacks, because of what he viewed as their stable temperament, eagerness for learning, and ability to work, rather than among Southern whites, whom he regarded as an irretrievably damaged class. On the critical issue of the radical Republicans' effort to remove Andrew Johnson from the presidency for his mild Reconstruction policies, the *Evening Post* withheld its support, despite its harsh criticism of his executive actions. James Russell Lowell praised Bryant for the *Evening Post*'s conduct during Reconstruction: "Firmness equally tempered with good feeling is what we want—not generosity tempered with twitches of firmness now and then."

Bryant had entered the years of national crisis in early middle age; he emerged from them an old man. With pauses only for travel, he had remained in active charge of his newspaper for more than three decades. And even when traveling he wrote long descriptive articles for the newspaper, which were republished in his two volumes of *Letters of a Traveller* (1850, 1859). The *Evening Post* had remained a vital institution in part because Bryant had been able to recruit talented, independent associates. The most troublesome among these remained his son-in-law, Godwin, who repeatedly left and returned to the paper, the last departure of Bryant's lifetime taking place in 1868, when Godwin sold his one-third interest for $200,000.

Bryant's editorial mainstay during much of the period was John Bigelow. Like Bryant a lawyer by training, Bigelow came to the *Evening Post* in 1848, at the age of thirty-seven, as associate editor and partner. He applied himself vigorously both to writing and the management of the newspaper for a dozen years but left after the 1860 election to become a diplomat in Paris during the war.

Bigelow's able replacement was Charles Nordhoff, a Prussian-born orphan who had been a seafarer until he turned to writing and journalism. Unlike Bryant, he was intensely interested in news and wrote an 8,000-word account of the July 1863 draft riots in New York City. Nordhoff, the first man at the *Evening Post* to bear the title of managing editor, stayed for a decade but left after a bitter quarrel with the business manager, Henderson, over tampering with the news department.

Bryant himself inevitably began to ease his grip on the newspaper and to shed his identity as editor for that of public figure. The warm celebration offered for his seventieth birthday in 1864 by his literary colleagues marked a symbolic transition. In 1865 he took another symbolic step toward releasing himself from day-to-day duties with his purchase of the old Bryant family homestead in Cummington, much farther from the office than his longtime retreat at Roslyn, Long Island. His withdrawal was hastened when, after a long, painful illness, his wife died on 27 July 1866. Although still enjoying his own scrupulously preserved good health, he absented himself from daily operations of the *Evening Post* to devote his time to a translation of Homer. Even so, his editorial voice continued to intervene in local and national politics. For example, in 1872 he wrote a scathing editorial on the candidacy, on an offshoot Republican ticket, of his old rival Horace Greeley; but when Greeley died a few weeks after the election, Bryant was generous in his remembrance. In 1874 the observance of Bryant's eightieth birthday was a greater event still than the celebration of a decade before, being noted by literary societies and in newspaper columns across the country. For his part, Bryant observed the birthday by first working in the office until noon.

Bryant's final years were clouded by the machinations of the infamous Isaac Henderson, the *Evening Post*'s business manager. Gradually, as Bryant withdrew, Henderson's influence over the news and editorial columns grew, at the expense of the *Evening Post*'s integrity. In 1876 the newspaper's support in the presidential campaign of Rutherford B. Hayes over Bryant's old friend Samuel J. Tilden was read as a sign of Henderson's dominance.

For years Godwin had urged Bryant to investigate Henderson's handling of the *Evening Post*'s finances. Early in 1878 Bryant finally permitted the investigation and Godwin's charges were upheld. Henderson had overextended himself by underwriting a new building for the newspaper and had suffered losses as well in the panic of 1873; he had tried to recoup by raiding the newspaper's accounts and, indeed, had taken $200,000 directly from Bryant's earnings. Henderson was called to

Bryant during the Civil War (William Cullen Bryant II)

account and pledged his *Post* stock for repayment, with the result that Godwin again was awarded a share of the newspaper and became its editor for three years after Bryant's death.

That death came abruptly. Bryant had systematically maintained his health through exercise and diet and was vigorous and active in civic affairs up to the end. On 29 May 1878 he delivered a speech in Central Park—the creation of which he had originally conceived and had long advocated—and collapsed afterwards. For a time he rallied but eventually fell into a coma and died on 12 June at the age of eighty-three.

The first historical impressions of Bryant, once the eulogies had been spoken, were supplied by two biographers who had worked with him. Only five years after his death, Godwin produced a two-volume memoir that relied heavily on extracts from editorials and family correspondence. Godwin avoided sweeping interpretation, partly, he said, because the life of an editor is so difficult to capture: "His labors consist of a series of incessant and innumerable blows, of the real influences of which it is hard to judge, except in a general way. It can only be told of him what he endeavored to do, not what he actually did."

John Bigelow, writing seven years after Godwin, appraised Bryant as the exemplar of a superseded mode of journalism. He noted Bryant's jealousy of his literary reputation and the care with which he prepared copy, "commonly so disfigured by corrections as to be read with difficulty even by those familiar with his script." He found Bryant equally jealous of his disinterest: "I do not believe any man ever sat down to the discharge of a professional duty with a more resolute determination to exclude the influence of personal or selfish considerations." The most comprehensive recent biographical treatment, that by Charles H. Brown (1971), also emphasized Bryant's scrupulousness, particularly in matters of language.

The most acute biographical evaluation came in a history of the *Evening Post* completed by Allan Nevins, himself a journalist, in 1922. Nevins sought to explain Bryant's greatness as an editor and placed at the top of his assessment "mere industry," Bryant's ability to write his best every day and to attend to many details of the newspaper's operation. Nevins also credited Bryant with elevating the dignity of his profession, both personally and through the cultural gravity of what he wrote. Nevins concluded that "the foundation of Bryant's power as an editor lay simply in his soundness of judgment, and his unwavering courage in maintaining it.... And the number of instances in which his view of public questions became the view taken by history is remarkable."

Historians of American journalism may have slighted Bryant because he did not fit readily into their chronicles of the growth of the news-oriented press. Frederic Hudson was a contemporary and a competitor and wasted little praise on Bryant in his *Journalism in the United States* (1873). Similarly, Willard Grosvenor Bleyer buried Bryant in a chapter on the political press in his *Main Currents in American Journalism* (1927). The treatment by Frank Luther Mott in the third edition of *American Journalism* (1962) was more extended and appreciative, but with the fourth edition of Edwin and Michael Emery's *The Press and America* (1978) Bryant's stock fell again relative to his contemporaries Greeley and Bennett. By contrast, Vernon Louis Parrington devoted a major section of *Main Currents in American Thought* (1927) to him and credited Bryant with being a "power for sanity in a scurrilous generation." It may be that the generation of historians currently reassessing the political press of the nine-

teenth century will join Parrington in giving him a major place.

In the meantime, the newspaper institution that Bryant built survives, at least in name, after passing through many hands in the century after his death. Godwin sold it to the Villard family in 1881, and it enjoyed a period of reputability under the editorship of Edwin Lawrence Godkin. After the Villard ownership ended during World War I, it passed through the hands of other magnates and eventually, in 1942, into the control of Dorothy Schiff. Under her guidance, it became again a Democratic newspaper; but its tabloid format and tone were in the line of descent from the penny press that Bryant had so abhorred, and it became even more sensationalistic under the Australian Rupert Murdoch, who acquired it in the 1970s. Hardly memorialized in his newspaper, Bryant at least has a permanent tribute from New York City, for the midtown park adjacent to the New York Public Library bears his name.

Letters:

The Letters of William Cullen Bryant, edited by William Cullen Bryant II and Thomas G. Voss, 4 volumes (New York: Fordham University Press, 1975-1984).

Bibliography:

Henry C. Sturges, *Chronologies of the Life and Writings of William Cullen Bryant* (New York: Appleton, 1903).

Biographies:

George W. Curtis, *The Life, Character, and Writings of William Cullen Bryant* (New York: Scribners, 1879);

Parke Godwin, *A Biography of William Cullen Bryant, with Extracts from His Private Correspondence*, 2 volumes (New York: Appleton, 1883);

James Grant Wilson, *Bryant and His Friends: Some Reminiscences of Knickerbocker Writers* (New York: Fords, Howard & Halbert, 1886);

John Bigelow, *William Cullen Bryant* (Boston & New York: Houghton Mifflin, 1890);

William A. Bradley, *William Cullen Bryant* (New York: Macmillan, 1905);

Allan Nevins, *The Evening Post: A Century of Journalism* (New York: Boni & Liveright, 1922);

Henry Houston Peckham, *Gotham Yankee* (New York: Vantage Press, 1950);

Curtiss S. Johnson, *Politics and a Belly-Full: The Journalistic Career of William Cullen Bryant* (New York: Vantage Press, 1962);

Charles H. Brown, *William Cullen Bryant* (New York: Scribners, 1971).

References:

Gay W. Allen, "William Cullen Bryant," in his *American Prosody* (New York & Cincinnati: American Book Company, 1935), pp. 27-55;

Van Wyck Brooks, "New York: Bryant," in his *The World of Washington Irving* (New York: Dutton, 1944), pp. 234-261;

Kenneth W. Cameron, "Bryant's Correspondence: A Checklist," *American Transcendental Quarterly*, 13 (Winter 1972): 37-45;

James L. Crouthamel, "The Newspaper Revolution in New York, 1830-1860," *New York History*, 45 (April 1964): 91-113;

Michael D'Innocenzo, "William Cullen Bryant and the Newspapers of New York," in *William Cullen Bryant and His America, Centennial Conference Proceedings 1878-1978* (New York: AMS Press, 1983), pp. 39-50;

Howard R. Floan, "The New York *Evening Post* and the Ante-bellum South," *American Quarterly*, 8 (Fall 1956): 243-253;

Charles I. Glicksberg, "Bryant and the *United States Review*," *New England Quarterly*, 7 (December 1934): 687-701;

Glicksberg, "Letters by William Cullen Bryant, 1826-1827," *Americana*, 33 (January 1939): 346-355;

Glicksberg, "William Cullen Bryant and Fanny Wright," *American Literature*, 6 (January 1935): 427-432;

Glicksberg, "William Cullen Bryant and the American Press," *Journalism Quarterly*, 16 (December 1939): 356-365;

Max L. Griffin, "Bryant and the South," *Tulane Studies in English*, 1 (1949): 53-80;

Tremaine McDowell, "Bryant and the *North American Review*," *American Literature*, 1 (March 1929): 14-26;

Alfred F. McLean, Jr., *William Cullen Bryant* (New York: Twayne, 1964);

Vernon Louis Parrington, "William Cullen Bryant: Puritan Liberal," in his *Main Currents in American Thought, Volume II: The Romantic Revolution in America* (New York: Harcourt, Brace, 1927), pp. 238-246;

Judith Turner Phair, *A Bibliography of William Cullen Bryant and His Critics: 1808-1972* (Troy, N.Y.: Whitston, 1975);

Israel Shenker, "Bryant, Luminary of Old New York, Shines Again in Memory," *New York Times*, 12 October 1975;

Benjamin T. Spencer, "Bryant: The Melancholy Progressive," *Emerson Society Quarterly*, 43 (II Quarter 1966): 99-103;

Herman Spivey, "Manuscript Resources for the Study of William Cullen Bryant," *Papers of the Bibliographical Society of America*, 44 (III Quarter 1950): 254-268;

Bernard Weinstein, "Bryant, Annexation, and the Mexican War," *Emerson Society Quarterly*, 63 (Spring 1971): 19-24.

Papers:

The major collections of William Cullen Bryant's papers are the Henry W. and Albert A. Berg Collection, New York Public Library; the Bryant Family Papers, Manuscript Division, New York Public Library; the Bryant Family Association Papers, Bureau County Historical Society, Princeton, Illinois; the Bryant-Godwin Collection, Manuscript Division, New York Public Library; the Bryant Miscellaneous Papers, Manuscript Division, New York Public Library; the Flagg Collection, Manuscript Division, New York Public Library; and the Goddard-Roslyn Collection, including financial records of the *Evening Post*, Manuscript Division, New York Public Library.

John Campbell

(1653-4 March 1728)

Jo Anne Smith
University of Florida

MAJOR POSITION HELD: Editor, *Boston News-Letter* (1704-1721).

John Campbell gave America its first continuous newspaper, the *Boston News-Letter*. A cautious editor operating in an era of suppression, Campbell took pains to stay in the good graces of colonial authorities; and once he had found comfortable editorial ruts, he entertained few thoughts of change. If not exciting, Campbell was persistent. Without enthusiastic response to spur him on, he nevertheless maintained publication of the *News-Letter* for seventeen years, faithfully recording domestic and foreign events. Lacking competition for its first fifteen years, the *News-Letter* contained a jumble of items dominated by old news culled from foreign newspapers and shipping news picked up from incoming sea captains. Though both paper and editor might be described as "faithful but drab," the *News-Letter* scored many "firsts" in American journalism by dint of its pioneering role.

Comparatively little is known of editor Campbell's personal life. He is believed to have emigrated to the colonies from Scotland "before 1698 and probably before 1695." The family name appears to have been "Campbel"; Campbell used that spelling until 1711, when he added a second *l*. Isaiah Thomas's *The History of Printing in America* (1874) identifies a Duncan Campbell, who operated a bookshop "at the Dock Head over against the Conduit" in Boston, as "probably" John's father. Other sources refer to a brother named Duncan who helped Campbell with the tedious job of copying the manuscript letters that were the *News-Letter*'s predecessors. Other sources note no familial relationship between John and Duncan, describing John merely as Duncan's "successor" in the postmastership upon the latter's death in 1702. One account calls Duncan a "brisk young fellow" in 1686, when John would have been thirty-three; this would appear to rule out the notion that Duncan was John's father. Whether or not the two men were related or toiled over handwritten newsletters together, they both earned reputations of being "very industrious." Duncan is described as a man who dressed "a la mode" and won the heart of a "young Lady of Great Fortune."

John became postmaster with "approbation of" Governor Joseph Dudley in 1702. The postmaster's job had existed in Boston since 1639, when a Richard Fairbanks was designated as the man to whose house all incoming letters were to be delivered. In 1692 an intercolonial postal service was established under a patent granted to Thomas Neale; Duncan Campbell became postmaster in 1693. By the time of John Campbell's appointment, the mail coming into Boston included London's first dailies as well as other newspapers from abroad. The postmastership traditionally had been a low-paying job, and one way Campbell chose to augment his meager income was by providing handwritten news reports to the governors of other New England colonies. In one such letter to Governor Fitz John Winthrop of Connecticut, Campbell referred to his reports as "journals of Publick Occurances," a phrase remindful of Benjamin Harris's ill-fated Boston newspaper, the unlicensed *Public Occurrences Both Foreign and Domestick*, suppressed after a single 1690 issue. Typical letters from Campbell to the governors repeated information from incoming sea captains, who brought news from foreign ports, reported on activities of privateers, and detailed incoming and outgoing cargo. A 1703 letter to Governor Winthrop quotes "Talk from Jamaica of the Spaniards sueing for a peace" and tells of the capture of "a Spanish ship of 8 guns, Loaden with Canary and Brandy, and other goods, bound for the Havanne. . . ." Campbell also used the letters to seek financial aid for the post office. In another letter to Winthrop he said: "I must represent to your ho' and Assembly the state of the post office as I have done to this Gov''' and New Hampshire; in order to have some encouragement for the support of it, as they have done; else of necessity it must drop." The plea for support later would become a sad refrain of Campbell's journalistic efforts, frequently repeated throughout his editorship of the *News-Letter*.

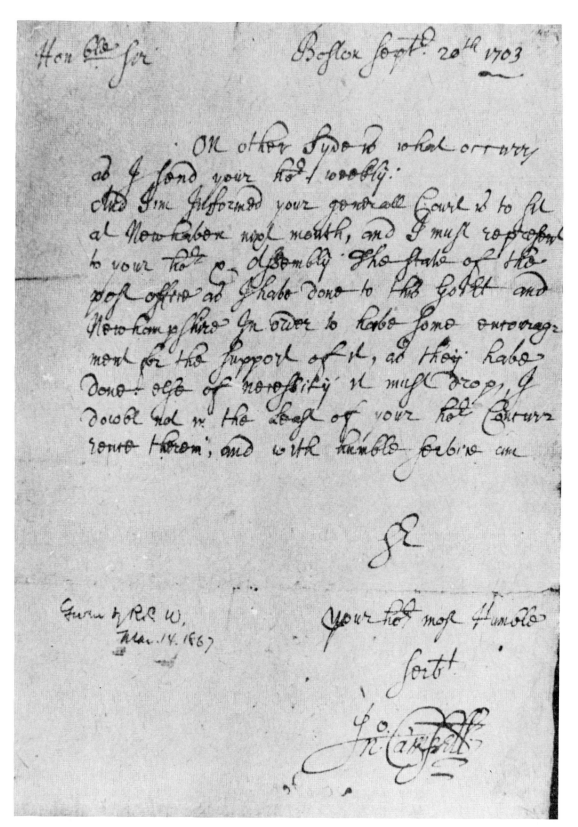

A 1703 letter from Campbell to Governor Winthrop of Connecticut, seeking financial aid for his post office (Massachusetts Historical Society)

The laborious job of hand copying the letters to the governors and merchants who subscribed kept Campbell bent over his pen for hours. Mindful both of Harris's earlier abortive effort at colonial newspapering and of the growth in the number and popularity of overseas newspapers, Campbell sought permission to produce his newsletters in printed form. With permission from and under the supervision of colonial authorities, who regarded the diligent fifty-one-year-old postmaster as politically "safe," Campbell began the weekly *Boston News-Letter* on 24 April 1704. Journalism historian Frederic Hudson noted that public tastes had "ripened" enough for authority to "tolerate and authorize the enterprise" but that Campbell operated "under great restrictions . . . such as prevailed in England a century before." The *News-Letter* prominently displayed the line "Printed by Authority." Chief Justice Samuel Sewall stood by the press at Bartholomew Green's print shop awaiting the first 1704 copy to take "damp from the press" to Samuel Willard, minister of the Old South Church and vice-president of Harvard University. Sewall's diary took note of the event: "I gave Mr. Willard the first *News-Letter* ever was carried over the River. He shew'd it the Fellows."

The initial copies of the *News-Letter*—on a half sheet, 6 1/2 by 10 1/2 inches, printed on both sides—were viewed as a "wonderful curiosity." But items in Campbell's pedestrian style trailed by journalistic leaps the diet of Addison, Swift, and Steele being feasted upon across the sea. In Campbell's first issue, foreign news many months old came from the London *Flying Post* and the London *Gazette* and was supplemented mainly by local shipping notices. The premier issue also featured America's first newspaper advertisement—for the *News-Letter* itself, informing readers of Campbell's intent to publish weekly and soliciting, at the "Reasonable Rate" of "Twelve Pence to Five Shillings," advertisements for goods for sale, property for rent, or "Servants Run-away." The ad also let readers know that they could arrange with Campbell to receive the *News-Letter* "every Week, yearly upon reasonable terms," apparently subject to bargaining.

Except for occasional ornamental initial letters, early issues of the *News-Letter* contained no display devices, and its items were arranged without particular order or emphasis. Brief obituaries might be tucked between a shipping notice and a line about a meeting of the General Assembly. Campbell recounted most items dryly and without comment, though he sometimes tacked on a moralizing sentence or indulged in safe praise of "an Excellent Sermon" or of the "brisk young men" who, as military "Voluntiers," protected the "Safety of Her Majesties good subjects." The capture and execution of a group of pirates clearly was the top local story covered by the *News-Letter* in its first year. The issue of 12-19 June devoted much space under five area datelines to stories of the capture of seven pirates and "45 ounces and Seven Penny weight of Gold" and the later surrender to townspeople of two more pirates who initially had escaped. The captured men "were sent to Salem Prison," and, after trial, six were sentenced to die. America's first on-the-spot news reporting came on 30 June 1704, when Campbell joined scores of other spectators in witnessing the hangings. The scaffolds had been erected on the banks of the Charles River, where the Reverend Cotton Mather stood to give a prayer ("Faithful Warnings to Prevent Fearful Judgments") immediately prior to the executions. The *News-Letter* gave comparatively little description of the event or its victims but did piously (and obediently to the wishes of authorities) devote nearly half the issue to Mather's prayer, with reporter Campbell adding the observation that it was very difficult to take down the churchman's words in the midst of the "great crowd." Sewall's diary, recounting the capture of the pirates, adds, "See the *News-Letter*." On the day of the hangings, Sewall, too, emphasized the "moral" of the occasion when recording the event in his diary; but unlike Campbell, he also noted the human reactions—that when the traps were sprung, such a "screech" went up from those in attendance that his wife heard it at their home nearly a mile away.

Early issues of the *News-Letter* told readers that they could buy single copies of the paper as well as advertising space at the bookshop of Nicholas Boone, called by Isaiah Thomas both an "eminent bookseller" and the first publisher of the *News-Letter* (with Green as printer and Campbell as "proprietor"). In issue number four Campbell listed himself as the one from whom to buy advertising, and issue number five dropped reference to Boone and substituted the line "Sold at the Post Office." In truth, not much advertising was sold by either Boone or Campbell; few issues carried more than one or two ads. At first, Campbell received help from the General Court, which subsidized the paper until 1706. After that, Campbell's petitions to the government to continue its support apparently failed. Subscribers, too, became lax in making payment. Before long, entreaties from Campbell to delinquent subscribers became a regular feature

Front page of the 16 January 1707 issue of Campbell's Boston News-Letter, *with the first newspaper illustration in America: a woodcut of the redesigned British flag* of the *News-Letter*. Unless he received support, Campbell wrote, he could no longer continue "this Publick Print of Intelligence."

Campbell spruced up a January 1707 issue with the first newspaper illustration in America, a woodcut of the new flag of the United Kingdom of England and Scotland. Still, the paper had scant liveliness, and Campbell complained that year that "there has not as yet a competent number appeared to take it annually so as to enable the Undertaker to carry it on effectually. . . ." A bit wanly, he pronounced himself "still willing to proceed with it" if more support could be acquired. Some writers suggest that the *News-Letter*'s drabness reflected the bleak life of colonial Boston, but that appraisal seems not entirely fair. To be sure, contemporary writings place great emphasis on disease, death, and disaster, but such events stand out from the more comfortable routine of every era and command attention. Sewall's diary contains its share of such references—to homes damaged by wind, fire, and lightning; to young women dying after "lying in"; to infants failing to survive their first months of life. At the same time, his account of colonial life mentions many neighborly visits, dinners with friends, celebrations of weddings and anniversaries, and other evidences of simple pleasures. Religious convictions and restrictions greatly tempered social life, and the *News-Letter* and other documents of the day amply attest to the stern influence of Puritanism in general and the Mather family in particular. Campbell apparently was conscientious in his duties as both citizen and churchman. His name frequently appears among those who served as pallbearers, worked on church committees, or met to discuss community problems. Certainly he was diligent in his role as recorder of the news; he met incoming vessels and attended local events and kept a running chronology of foreign occurrences, getting as much as he could in each issue. But the weekly half-page simply could not hold all he wished to relay. The *News-Letter*, as time passed, lagged farther and farther behind the news.

Whether out of worry over the widening time lag or out of an occasional need to be just a little defiant, Campbell sometimes put his editorial foot down and declined contributions, even those brought to him by the authorities under whose sufferance he operated. Sewall several times noted that Campbell had "refused" copy, although in most instances he would later add that Campbell had, in the end, agreed to "insert it." The relationship of Sewall and Campbell appears to have fallen somewhere between "strictly business" and friendship. Campbell is mentioned among dinner guests of the Sewalls even before he became postmaster or editor, and one of Sewall's diary entries tells of dropping by the Campbells' and giving Mrs. Campbell an invitation "to my House." Sewall obviously greatly valued his copies of the *News-Letter*: he kept a bound file, made careful marginal notes on the papers, and frequently made cross references to the *News-Letter* in his diary. He often sent copies of the paper to friends and relatives and even presented them as "hostess" gifts. His diary mentions giving copies to "Madam Winthrop," whom he courted (unsuccessfully) in 1720 after the death of Hannah, his wife of forty-one years.

Not enough of Campbell's readers showed Sewall's level of involvement, however, and "for want of any Tollerable encouragement," Campbell suspended publication in March 1709. Eight months later, with New Year's optimism, he decided to try again, resuming publication on 1 January 1710. From late 1707 to late 1711, John Allen, who had a print shop near the post office, handled the printing of the *News-Letter*. But on 2 October 1711, fire swept that section of the city, destroying many buildings, including the post office and Allen's shop. The next week the *News-Letter* (in issue number 391) reported on the "great fire." Once again, the paper was issued from the shop of Bartholomew Green. The postfire issues carried the new line "Boston: Printed in Newbury Street, for *John Campbell* Post Master," but not much else about the *News-Letter* was new. In its first seven years, the paper showed little change in style, format, or content, and Campbell only occasionally enlivened its columns with bits of human interest or colorful reportorial detail. The paper's primary audience consisted of the community's influential men of means, and there simply were not enough of them to make the *News-Letter* a viable means of support for its patient but plodding editor. Even some of those who could afford the luxury of delivered news failed to pay promptly or regularly the twelve shillings a year Campbell charged.

The dunning notice became a regular feature of the *News-Letter*, and Campbell's repeated humorless complaints took on an increasingly querulous tone. Perhaps this "nagging," added to Campbell's dreary and awkward writing style and the staleness of his product, militated against more enthusiastic response. At one point, the *News-Letter* lagged thirteen months behind on foreign news, thanks to Campbell's practice of including as much in each issue as he had room for and then picking up where he left off in the next issue without regard to freshness. In 1717, in an effort to make "the News Newer and more acceptable," Campbell began issuing supplementary full sheets of news every other week. Eventually he narrowed the news gap to less than five months, quite respectable for his time. His circulation *had* grown; the number of issues he complained that he "could not vend at an impression," once set at 250, grew to 300 in a later reference. But the *News-Letter* still left its editor struggling financially. In an August 1719 issue, Campbell addressed a long appeal to his readers. He began by noting his efforts in printing additional issues in order to make up the time deficiency on news from abroad, saying, "We have retrieved about 8 Months since January last, and any One that has the News-Letter since that time, to January next (life permitted) will be accommodated with all the News of Europe &c., contained in the Publick Prints of London that are needful for to be known in these parts. And in regard the Undertaker had not suitable encouragement, even to Print half a Sheet Weekly, seeing that he cannot vend 300 at an Impression, tho' some ignorantly concludes he Sells upwards of a Thousand: far less is he able to Print a Sheet every other Week, without an addition of 4, 6 or 8 Shillings a Year, as everyone thinks fit to give payable Quarterly, which will only help to pay for Press and Paper, giving his Labour for nothing." There was more in the same vein, ending with a request to those who had not "already paid for the half Year past the last Monday of June" to bring or send payment to Campbell at his house in Cornhill.

The 1718-1719 year had been an unhappy one occupationally for Campbell. Not only did he suffer a financial pinch incurred from the extra issues but he also left his longtime job as postmaster. Stubborn and proud, Campbell took issue with his successor William Brooker's report that he had been "removed" from the postmastership. Historians differ in accounts of Campbell's departure from the post office, some saying that he retired and others that he was fired. Brooker's version of the changeover was that the deputy postmaster general of North America, John Hamilton, had received "many complaints" about Campbell and therefore "thought fit to remove him." At any rate, when Campbell left, the *News-Letter* left with him. At first he refused to circulate the *News-Letter* through the post office, trying instead to distribute it on his own. Brooker, meanwhile, apparently had believed the *News-Letter* to be part of the postmastership. So when Campbell refused to relinquish

the paper, Brooker began one of his own on 21 December 1719. Also a half-sheet weekly, the *Boston Gazette* gave the *News-Letter* its first competition.

The whole sequence of events stung Campbell to more colorful expression than had been his pattern in the past. In response to Brooker's first editorial efforts, Campbell sniffed, "I pity the readers of the new paper. Its sheets smell stronger of beer than of midnight oil. It is not reading fit for people!" Soon Campbell and Brooker were locked in America's first "editorial war." Campbell disputed Brooker's version of the changeover at the post office; Brooker replied that his use of the word *removed* was a "softer epithet" than "*turned out*" and that Campbell had either been "*removed, turned out, displaced or superseded.*" The exchange was brief. Brooker, having fully aired his views on the matter in a January 1720 issue of the *Gazette*, concluded that he had "neither capacity nor inclination" to answer any more of Campbell's statements. Campbell, in turn, reminded his readers in 1720 that the *News-Letter* had been the "first and only intelligence on the Continent of America, till about a Year past" and left it to readers to determine how well his rival had met the "People's great Expectation."

Competition spurred Campbell to innovation. In 1721 he offered his subscribers an option. They could, if they chose, get a whole-sheet *News-Letter* instead of the regular half-sheet size. This would allow use of the blank half-sheet by the recipient to write his own letter and then mail both for the cost of a single mailing. But 1721 brought additional competition and annoyance for Campbell. James Franklin launched the *New England Courant* in August of that year and promptly branded Campbell's *News-Letter* a "dull vehicle of intelligence." For a time, Campbell lashed back, at one point calling Franklin "Jack of All Trades, and it would seem, Good at None." But Campbell soon wearied of the exchange. He had put much of his time into the *News-Letter* for seventeen years, and despite his many pleas for support he remained, in his own view, undercompensated and underappreciated.

Campbell was sixty-eight when he left journalism and became a justice of the peace in 1721. The *News-Letter* survived under a succession of editors until 1776. Campbell lived to the age of seventy-five; he died in March 1728. His widow was Mary Clark Pemberton Campbell, whom he had married in 1723 when he was seventy and she was forty-two. Boston birth and baptism records show daughters Elizabeth (born 6 February 1695) and Mary (born 23 July 1704) from an earlier wife, also named Mary. Sewall's diary noted in December 1713 that he had attended the funeral of Campbell's "eldest daughter," twenty-six-year-old Sarah, a "vertuous woman and the wife of a Boston merchant" (James Bowdoin). Campbell's will makes no mention of a daughter Mary but makes bequests to his grandchildren William and Mary Bowdoin and to his daughter Elizabeth Foye.

Of Campbell's death, Sewall recorded in his diary: "*Monday night, March 4th.* Mr. John Campbell dies, who writ the first *News-Letter*. Was inter'd Saturday March 9th. Bearers, Sewall, Byfield; Belcher, Oliver; Judge Menzies, Capt. Steel." The *News-Letter* carried a brief obituary notice: "On Monday last, the 4th inst, died here, at the age of seventy five years, John Campbell, Esquire, formerly director of the post in this town, many years editor of the Boston News-Letter, and one of her Majesty's justices of the peace for the County of Suffolk." Hudson, in his history, remarked on the brevity of the *News-Letter*'s account and its failure to take typographical note of the passing of its founder by turning the column rules. "So passed away the glory of John Campbell," Hudson concluded. Perhaps the best epitaph had been written by Campbell himself a few years earlier. After aiming a volley at Franklin for his "very, very frothy fulsom Account of himself," Campbell concluded: "I speak for the Publisher of this Intelligence, whose endeavours has always been to give no offence, not meddling with things out of his Province."

Indeed, Campbell's editorial career might be summed up as one that gave "no offence." Only once did colonial authorities find need to mildly rebuke the cautious Scotsman. And whereas Campbell's writings were graceless and dull, they gave colonial Boston a faithful record of local events and filled colonists' hunger for news, however stale, from abroad. The *News-Letter*, by nobody's measure a great paper, at least earned the respect due those who blaze new trails. It pioneered on-the-spot reporting and newspaper illustration, and its mere existence, acceptance, and long life provided a climate in which braver and livelier journals could thrive at a later time.

References:

Elizabeth Christine Cook, *Literary Influences in Colonial Newspapers 1704-1750* (New York: Columbia University Press, 1912), pp. 9, 10, 14-15, 28;

The Diary of Samuel Sewall, 2 volumes (New York: Farrar, Straus & Giroux, 1973), I: 419, 501, 527, 537, 607; II: 617, 723, 736, 788, 806, 812, 875, 879, 1007, 1043, 1045, 1051, 1060;

Benjamin Franklin IV, ed., *Boston Printers, Publishers and Booksellers: 1640-1800* (Boston: Hall, 1980), pp. 13, 46, 69, 70, 109, 114, 218;

Frederic Hudson, *Journalism in the United States from 1690 to 1872* (New York: Harper, 1873), pp. 52, 64;

Sidney Kobre, *The Development of the Colonial Newspaper* (Gloucester, Mass.: Peter Smith, 1960), pp. 17-27;

George Emery Littlefield, *Early Boston Booksellers 1642-1711* (New York: Burt Franklin, 1969), pp. 133, 135, 154, 193, 194;

Isaiah Thomas, *The History of Printing in America* (Albany, N.Y.: Joel Munsell, 1874), pp. 85, 87, 88, 188, 194, 215-225, 227, 231, 253, 293.

Papers:

Several libraries have collections of copies of the *Boston News-Letter*. Among the more sizable collections are those of the Massachusetts Historical Society, American Antiquarian Society, Boston Public Library, and Library of Congress. More than a score of libraries have the photostat reproductions made by the Massachusetts Historical Society. One volume of Samuel Sewall's file of *News-Letter*s, with Sewall's marginal notes in ink, is held by the New York Historical Society; another volume is held by the Boston Athenaeum.

Cassius Marcellus Clay
(19 October 1810-22 July 1903)

Ronald Truman Farrar
University of Kentucky

MAJOR POSITION HELD: Editor and publisher, *Lexington* (Ky.) *True American*, renamed *Louisville Examiner* in 1846 (1845-1846).

BOOKS: *Speech of C. M. Clay, of Fayette, in the House of Representatives of Kentucky, January 1841, upon the Bill to Repeal the Law of 1835, "to Prohibit the Importation of Slaves into This State"* (Washington, D.C.?, 1841);

Cassius M. Clay, and Gerrit Smith. A Letter of Cassius M. Clay, of Lexington, Ky., to the Mayor of Dayton, O., with a Review of It by Gerrit Smith, of Peterboro, N.Y. (Utica, N.Y.: Jackson & Chaplin, 1844);

Speech of Cassius M. Clay, against the Annexation of Texas to the United States of America, in Reply to Col. R. M. Johnson and Others, in a Mass Meeting of Citizens of the Eighth Congressional District, at the White Sulphur Springs, Scott County, Ky., on Saturday, Dec. 30, 1843 (Lexington, Ky.: Printed at the Observer and Reporter office, 1844);

Appeal of Cassius M. Clay to Kentucky and the World (Boston: J. M. Macomber & E. L. Pratt, 1845);

The Writings of Cassius Marcellus Clay: Including Speeches and Addresses, edited by Horace Greeley (New York: Harper, 1848);

Speech of C. M. Clay, at Lexington, Ky. Delivered August 1, 1851 (N.p., 1851);

Speech of C. M. Clay before the Young Men's Republican Central Union of New York in the Tabernacle, October 24th, 1856 (New York?, 1856?);

Speech of Cassius M. Clay, before the Law Department of the University of Albany, N.Y., February 3, 1863 (New York: Wynkoop, Hallenbeck & Thomas, printers, 1863);

The Life of Cassius Marcellus Clay. Memoirs, Writings, and Speeches, Showing His Conduct on the Overthrow of American Slavery, the Salvation of the Union, and the Restoration of the Autonomy of the States (Cincinnati: J. F. Brennan, 1886);

Two Papers, by Cassius Marcellus Clay (Louisville?, Ky., 1890);

Oration of Cassius Marcellus Clay before the Maumee

Photograph by Mathew Brady

Valley Historical and Monumental Association, of Toledo, Ohio, at Put-in-Bay Island, Lake Erie, on the 10th of September, 1891. The Anniversary of the Capture of the British Fleet by Oliver Hazard Perry (Philadelphia: Printed by J. B. Lippincott, 1891);

The Railway Issue, Labor, Money, Etc. (Philadelphia: Printed by J. B. Lippincott, 1891);

Oration of Cassius Marcellus Clay before Students and Historical Class of Berea College, Berea, Ky. October 16, 1895 (Richmond, Ky.: Pantagraph Job Works, 1896).

Though he is known primarily for his abolitionism, his military and diplomatic exploits, and his flamboyant personal life and political career, Cassius Marcellus Clay also served briefly—and turbulently—as a journalist. His crusading antislavery newspaper, the *True American*, touched off strong reactions in pre-Civil War Kentucky—and through his newspaper Clay struck a blow not only for civil rights but also for freedom of the press.

Clay was born at White Hall, the family estate near the Kentucky River, in the bluegrass region not far from Lexington. His mother was Sally Lewis Clay and his father was Green Clay, then the largest slave owner in the state and proprietor of one of the wealthiest plantations in Kentucky. Blessed with outstanding educational opportunities for that time, young Clay was sent to study at the home of Joshua Fry, a celebrated teacher, on the banks of the Dix River in nearby Garrard County, then to Danville Academy (now Centre College). Later he was dispatched to St. Joseph, a Jesuit college at Bardstown, Kentucky, to study French. Upon the death of his father, he returned briefly to White Hall, then enrolled at Transylvania University at Lexington, where he compiled an excellent academic record. In 1831 he took a leisurely tour East—during which he met President Andrew Jackson and a host of other notables who had been friends of his father—before enrolling as a junior at Yale. It was at Yale that he was inspired by William Lloyd Garrison, the fiery editor who had dedicated his life to the emancipation of the American Negro. The following year, his degree in hand, Clay returned to Kentucky determined to launch his own crusade to abolish the institution of slavery. He married Mary Jane Warfield of Lexington and enrolled again at Transylvania, this time for the study of law, and in 1835—he was then only twenty-five—he was elected to the state legislature from Madison County. He lost his bid for reelection in 1836, having ruffled the feathers of some powerful political figures with his proposals to reorganize the legislature, but mended his fences and won back his seat in 1837. His eye on a larger constituency, Clay moved to Lexington in 1840 and was elected representative from Fayette County. His increasingly strident opposition to slavery alienated him from many of Lexington's political leaders, however, and he was defeated after serving just one term. Ignoring the moderating counsel of friends and community leaders—including that of his distant cousin, Henry Clay—Clay intensified his antislavery crusade, speaking out vehemently against the "peculiar institution" at every opportunity. To

Clay's first wife, Mary Jane Warfield Clay, portrait by G. P. A. Healey (Courtesy of Miss Esther Bennett)

consolidate and extend his position, he decided in 1845 to establish an abolitionist newspaper, the *True American.*

Clay's fortune, mostly intact in spite of his political ventures, was sufficient to sustain the *True American* through its inevitable financial losses. A more serious problem was in finding trained staff members willing to associate themselves with so unpopular a cause. Clay's original choice as editor, T. B. Stevenson, was quickly intimidated by proslavery forces before he could move to Lexington from his home in Frankfort and never appeared on the scene. There were other desertions as well. "The present generation can know nothing of the terror which the slavepower inspired," Clay wrote in his memoirs (1886). "But it may be faintly conceived, when a professed minister of the Christian religion in South Carolina said that it were better for him, rather than denounce slavery, 'to murder his own mother, and lose his soul in hell.' " Undaunted, Clay lined the outside doors of his office with sheet iron, then "purchased two brass four-pounder cannon at Cincinnati and placed them, loaded with shot and nails, on a table breast high; had folding doors secured with a chain, which could open upon the move and give play to my cannon. I furnished my office with Mexican lances, and a limited number of guns. There were six or eight persons who stood ready to defend me. If defeated, they were to escape by a trap-door in the roof; and I had placed a keg of powder, with a match, which I could set off and blow up the office and all my invaders; and this I should most certainly have done. . . ."

The first issue of the *True American* appeared on 3 June 1845. Subtitled "Devoted to Universal Liberty; Gradual Emancipation of Kentucky; Literature; Agriculture; the Elevation of Labor, Morally and Politically; Commercial Intelligence, etc., etc.," the paper was a four-page broadsheet. In addition to Clay's passionate editorials, written under various pseudonyms, the *True American* contained a compilation of abolitionist news and commentary from throughout the country. No precise figures are available, but Clay claimed that the paper's circulation grew rapidly, and that the subscription list included political leaders in many states. Locally, however, opposition to the *True American* continued to mount. The Committee of Sixty, a secret group composed of powerful Lexington proslavery leaders, refused to confront Clay directly; the extent of his fortifications—and his willingness to defend his property—were well known. However, during the summer of 1845 Clay contracted typhoid fever; while he was recovering, members of the Committee of Sixty broke into his newspaper office, packed up his type, presses, and other equipment and shipped everything to Cincinnati. Clay stubbornly continued the *True American*—editing it in Lexington and having it published in Cincinnati—and he claimed that the paper's circulation continued to increase. His effectiveness was greatly diminished, however; eventually moved to Louisville and renamed the *Examiner,* the paper died a few months later when Clay went off to fight in the Mexican War.

Clay, meanwhile, learned the names of some members of the Committee of Sixty; he filed suit against them and collected damages in the amount of $2,500. In real as well as symbolic terms, the judgment helped reaffirm in Kentucky the right to publish. "I exposed in *The True American*," he wrote, "a vulnerable part of the State Constitution, by showing that the prohibition of the emancipation of slaves, without compensation, admitted the

power to liberate with compensation; and the right to act, therefore, implied the right to discuss." An eloquent orator, Clay took to the stump, accepting virtually all speaking invitations—even those before hostile audiences where his life was at risk. On one such occasion where an assassination threat had been made against him, Clay appeared on schedule before the tense crowd, then calmly placed a pistol on the rostrum and a Bible beside it. "For those who obey the rules of right and the sacred truths of the Christian religion, I appeal to this Book; and to those who only recognize the law of force," he said, laying his hand on the pistol, "here is my defense."

"Cash" Clay stood six feet three inches tall, weighed more than 200 pounds, and was well known for his pugnacious spirit. He fought at least one duel—this with Robert Wickliffe, Jr., in 1841, after Wickliffe mentioned Clay's wife in a speech—and numerous fist and knife fights. In one bloody skirmish, which began when Sam N. Brown of New Orleans charged into Clay at a political rally in 1845, Clay dodged a bullet from Brown, proceeded to gouge out one of Brown's eyes, then cut off an ear and split Brown's face with his ever-present bowie knife. In later years he stabbed another man to death in self-defense and after he was ninety he shot and killed a man who had broken into his house.

In 1846 Clay enlisted to fight in the Mexican War. He joined a Kentucky volunteer militia company which had been commanded by his father during the War of 1812, was commissioned a captain, and led the troops into Mexico. His combative nature and leadership qualities made him an outstanding field commander. He fought with valor, but was captured near Encarnacion on 23 January 1847, about a month before the Battle of Buena Vista, wherein outnumbered U.S. forces under General Zachary Taylor established their hold on northeastern Mexico. After a captivity during which his life frequently was in danger, Clay was liberated by forces of General Winfield Scott as part of a prisoner exchange. He returned to a tumultuous welcome, honored in Lexington and throughout Kentucky—ironically, by many who had vehemently opposed him on the slavery issue.

Clay resumed his abolitionist crusade, however, and once again put distance between himself and many fellow Kentuckians—notably Henry Clay and other moderates. Failing to attract support within the established political structure, Clay organized an Emancipation party in 1849 and ran for governor on that ticket. He was defeated but received 3,621 votes—enough to cause the defeat of the Whig candidate—and attracted national attention in the process. He joined the new Republican party in 1856, became friends with Abraham Lincoln, and was widely mentioned as a possible candidate for vice-president on the ticket with Lincoln in 1860. Meanwhile, back in Madison County, he donated lands and money to establish a racially integrated college for disadvantaged children of the Appalachian region. Berea College remains highly successful today; only students from low-income families are eligible for admission, no tuition is charged, and each Berea student must earn a portion of his or her expenses while on the campus.

Lincoln's election in 1860 led Clay to expect appointment to a key cabinet position. However, he was offered instead the ambassadorship to Spain, a post he refused. Somewhat embarrassed, Lincoln offered Clay a choice of other diplomatic assignments; Clay chose Russia, "a great and young nation that must much influence this great crisis," the Civil War. While moving his family East, Clay found the city of Washington virtually surrounded by Confederate forces and poorly defended; he hastily recruited 300 men, organized them into the "Clay Battalion," and deployed them into a defense perimeter for the capital. Impressed, high-level military authorities urged Clay to remain with the Federal army—with the rank of major general— but he chose instead to take up his post in Russia. He stayed in Russia a year but was summoned back to the U.S., commissioned a major general, and placed in command of volunteer units. Regarding the war as futile so long as slavery remained in effect, he used his influence with Lincoln in behalf of the Emancipation Proclamations and claimed in his memoirs that he had been at least partly responsible for Lincoln's having finally signed them.

He asked to be reassigned to Russia in 1863 and returned to St. Petersburg. His wife, who had borne his nine children (two of whom died in infancy), left him when he decided to go back to Russia. His zest for life and gracious manner ingratiated him with the court, and he became a popular favorite with the Russian nobility. He also took a mistress, Anna Jean Petrov, prima ballerina of the Russian Imperial Ballet. She is believed to be the mother of his illegitimate son, born in Russia, whom he named Launey Clay.

Returning to the U.S. in 1869, Clay found himself at odds with the Grant administration and threw his support to the Liberal Democrats and Horace Greeley in the election of 1872. Without a

Clay after his promotion to major general (Lincoln Memorial University)

national following and with little political base remaining, Clay retired to the family plantation, where he was known as "the Lion of White Hall." He and his wife, separated since 1863, were finally divorced in 1878. Now an old man, his fortune long since dissipated, Cash Clay still determined to live life to the fullest. At the age of eighty-four he married Dora Richardson, a girl of fifteen who lived nearby. Distraught neighbors protested to the county judge, who ordered the sheriff to remove the girl from White Hall. William F. Reed described the scene:

> When the posse rode up to White Hall on that day in 1894, Clay was ready. His rifle was in his hands, his bowie knife was strapped across his chest, and his cannon was loaded with scrap metal—pieces of trace chain, horseshoes, and nails. When the deputies moved forward, Clay fired his cannon, emptied his rifle, then charged down the steps with pistol in one hand, bowie knife in

Clay on the day of his second marriage—to a fifteen-year-old girl—in 1894. A sheriff's posse tried unsuccessfully to prevent the wedding (Photograph by Isaac Jenks, courtesy of Winston Coleman, Jr.).

another. The officers did the only intelligent thing—they turned and galloped off, stunned and bleeding from the ferocious assault.

In a subsequent report to the county judge, the sheriff recommended that the only way to overcome Clay was to send a couple of companies of state militia. Wrote the sheriff, "Judge, it was a mistake to go there with only seven men."

Clay's second marriage, however, ended in a divorce after three years. In 1897, Clay—now virtually bankrupt—applied for and received a pension of fifty dollars per month for his military service during the Mexican War. His emotional outbursts became increasingly more frequent, and shortly before his death a local court judge declared him incompetent. He died during a violent thunderstorm the night of 22 July 1903. The historian William Townsend wrote: "And then the storm was over. The stars came out. . . . The old general was asleep, his last sleep. Lying on his back with the favorite bowie knife peeking out from under the big pillow, the restless, violent, stormy spirit of the old lion of White Hall had gone to meet his Maker in the mightiest tempest that Central Kentucky had known. . . ."

Letters:

Letters of Cassius M. Clay (New York: Greeley & McElrath, 1844?).

References:

Thomas D. Clark, *A History of Kentucky* (Lexington: John Bradford Press, 1960), pp. 204-210, 298-300;

William F. Reed, *Famous Kentuckians: A Collection of Bicentennial Columns from the* Courier-Journal (Louisville: The *Courier-Journal*, 1977), pp. 46-47;

William H. Townsend, *The Lion of White Hall* (Dunwoody, Ga.: Norman S. Berg, 1967), p. 47.

William Cobbett

(9 March 1762-18 June 1835)

S. M. W. Bass

University of Kansas

MAJOR POSITION HELD: Editor, *Porcupine's Gazette and Daily Advertiser* (Philadelphia) (1797-1800).

SELECTED BOOKS: *The Soldier's Friend; or, Considerations on the Late Pretended Augmentation of the Subsistence of the Private Soldiers* (London: J. Ridgway, 1792);

Observations on the Emigration of Dr. Joseph Priestley, and on the Several Addresses Delivered to Him on His Arrival at New York (Philadelphia: Printed by Tho. Bradford, 1794; London: Reprinted & sold by W. Richardson, G. Kearsley & J. Debrett, 1794);

A Kick for a Bite; or, Review upon Review; with a Critical Essay, on the Works of Mrs. S. Rowson; in a Letter to the Editor, or Editors, of the American Monthly Review, as Peter Porcupine (Philadelphia: Printed by T. Bradford, 1795);

A Little Plain English, Addressed to the People of the United States, on the Treaty, Negociated with His Britannic Majesty, and on the Conduct of the President Relative Thereto; in Answer to "The Letters of Franklin." With a Supplement, Containing an Account of the Turbulent and Factious Proceedings of the Opposers of the Treaty, as Porcupine (Philadelphia: T. Bradford, 1795; London: Reprinted for F. & C. Rivington, 1795);

A Bone to Gnaw, for the Democrats, as Porcupine (Philadelphia: Printed by T. Bradford, 1795; London: J. Wright, 1797);

A New Year's Gift to the Democrats; or, Observations on a Pamphlet, Entitled, "A Vindication of Mr. Randolph's Resignation," as Porcupine (Philadelphia: T. Bradford, 1796);

A Prospect from the Congress-Gallery, during the Session, Begun December 7, 1795. Containing, the President's Speech, the Addresses of Both Houses, Some of the Debates in the Senate, and All the Principal Debates in the House of Representatives . . . With Occasional Remarks, as Porcupine (Philadelphia: T. Bradford, 1796);

Tit for Tat; or, A Purge for a Pill: Being an Answer to a Scurrilous Pamphlet, Lately Published, Entitled "A Pill for Porcupine." To Which Is Added, A

Poetical Rhapsody on the Times. Describing the Disasters of an Emigrant, as Dick Retort (Philadelphia: Printed for the author, 1796);

The Scare-Crow; Being an Infamous Letter, Sent to Mr. John Oldden, Threatening Destruction to His House, and Violence to the Person of His Tenant, William Cobbett; with Remarks on the Same, as Porcupine (Philadelphia: Printed for & sold by William Cobbett, 1796);

The Life and Adventures of Peter Porcupine, with a Full and Fair Account of All His Authoring Transactions; Being a Sure and Infallible Guide for All Enterprising Young Men Who Wish to Make a Fortune by Writing Pamphlets. By Peter Porcupine Himself (Philadelphia: W. Cobbett, 1796; Glasgow: Printed by D. Niven, 1798);

View of the War with France (Philadelphia: Jachin & Boaz, 1796);

A Letter to the Infamous Tom Paine, in Answer to His Letter to General Washington, as Porcupine (Philadelphia: William Cobbett, 1796; London: Reprinted for David Ogilvy & Son, 1797);

The Bloody Buoy, Thrown Out as a Warning to the Political Pilots of America; or, A Faithful Relation of a Multitude of Acts of Horrid Barbarity, Such as the Eye Never Witnessed, the Tongue Never Expressed, or the Imagination Conceived, until the Commencement of the French Revolution. Illustrated with Four Striking Copper-Plates, as Porcupine (Philadelphia: Printed for & sold by Benjamin Davies, 1796; London: Reprinted & sold by J. Wright, 1797);

An Antidote for Tom Paine's Theological and Political Poison: Containing 1. Tom Paine's Life, Interspersed with Remarks and Reflections by P. Porcupine. 2. An Apology for the Bible, in a Series of Letters Addressed to Paine by the Bishop of Landaff. 3. An Apology for Christianity, by the Same Learned, Elegant Writer. 4. An Answer to Paine's Anarchical Nonsense, Commonly Called, the Rights of Man (Philadelphia: Printed for & sold by William Cobbett, 1796);

History of the American Jacobins, Commonly Denomi-

National Portrait Gallery, London

nated Democrats, as Porcupine (Philadelphia:
Printed for William Cobbett, 1796);

*Observations on the Debates of the American Congress
on the Addresses Presented to General Washington,
on His Resignation: with Remarks on the Timidity
of the Language Held towards France; the Seizures
of American Vessels by Great Britain and France;
and, on the Relative Situations of Those Countries
with America*, as Porcupine (London: D. Ogilvy
& Son, 1797);

*The Life of Thomas Paine, Interspersed with Remarks
and Reflections*, as Porcupine (London: Reprinted for J. Wright, 1797);

Democratic Principles Illustrated, as Porcupine (London: Printed for J. Wright, 1798);

*French Arrogance; or, "The Cat Let out of the Bag"; a
Poetical Dialogue between the Envoys of America,
and X. Y. Z. and the Lady* (Philadelphia: Published by Peter Porcupine, 1798);

*The Democratic Judge; or, The Equal Liberty of the Press,
as Exhibited, Explained, and Exposed, in the Prosecution of William Cobbett, for a Pretended Libel
against the King of Spain and His Embassador,*

*before Thomas M'Kean, Chief Justice of the State
of Pennsylvania*, as Porcupine (Philadelphia:
Published by William Cobbett, 1798); republished as *The Republican Judge; or, The American
Liberty of the Press, as Exhibited, Explained, and
Exposed, in the Base and Partial Prosecution of
William Cobbett, for a Pretended Libel against the
King of Spain and His Embassador, before the Supreme Court of Pennsylvania. With an Address to
the People of England* (London: J. Wright,
1798);

*Detection of a Conspiracy Formed by the United Irishmen,
with the Evident Intention of Aiding the Tyrants
of France in Subverting the Government of the
United States of America*, as Porcupine (London: Printed for J. Wright, 1799);

*Remarks on the Explanation, Lately Published by Dr.
Priestley, Respecting the Intercepted Letters of His
Friend and Disciple, John H. Stone. To Which Is
Added, a Certificate of Civiam for Joseph Priestley,
Jun.*, as Porcupine (London: Printed for J.
Wright, 1799);

*Proposals for Publishing by Subscription, a New, Entire,
and Neat Edition of Porcupine's Works* (Philadelphia, 1799; London, 1799);

An Address to the People of England (N.p., 1800; Philadelphia: Printed by John Binns, 1812);

*The American Rush-light; by the Help of Which, Way-
ward and Disaffected Britons May See a Complete
Specimen of the Baseness, Dishonesty, Ingratitude,
and Perfidy of Republicans, and of the Profligacy,
Injustice, and Tyranny of Republican Governments*, as Porcupine (London: Published for
the author by J. Wright, 1800);

*The Trial of Republicanism; or, A Series of Political
Papers, Proving the Injurious and Debasing Con-
sequences of Republican Government, and Written
Constitutions. With an Introductory Address to the
Hon. Thomas Erskine, Esq.*, as Porcupine (Lon-
don: Printed for Cobbett & Morgan, 1801);

*A Collection of Facts and Observations, Relative to the
Peace with Bonaparte, Chiefly Extracted from the
Porcupine, and Including Mr. Cobbett's Letters to
Lord Hawkesbury. To Which Is Added, an Appen-
dix, Containing the Divers Conventions, Treaties,
State Papers, and Dispatches, Connected with the
Subject; Together with Extracts from the Speeches
of Mr. Pitt, Mr. Fox, and Lord Hawkesbury, Re-
specting Bonaparte, and a Peace with France*
(London: Cobbett & Morgan, 1801; Phila-
delphia: Printed for John Morgan & sold by
Benjamin Davies, 1802);

*Porcupine's Works; Containing Various Writings and
Selections, Exhibiting a Faithful Picture of the*

United States of America; of Their Government, Laws, Politics, and Resources; of the Characters of Their Presidents, Governors, Legislators, Magistrates, and Military Men; and of the Customs, Manners, Morals, Religion, Virtues and Vices of the People: Comprising also a Complete Series of Historical Documents and Remarks, from the End of the War, in 1783, to the Election of the President, in March, 1801, 12 volumes (London: Printed for Cobbett & Morgan, 1801);

Letters to the Right Honourable Henry Addington,—on the Fatal Effects of the Peace with Buonaparte, Particularly with Respect to the Colonies, the Commerce, the Manufactures, and the Constitution of the United Kingdom (London: Cobbett & Morgan, 1802);

Important Considerations for the People of This Kingdom (London: Printed by C. Rickaby, 1803);

Four Letters to the Chancellor of the Exchequer; Exposing the Deception of His Financial Statements, and Shewing the Fatal Tendency of the Peace of Amiens with Respect to Public Credit. Submitted to the Stockholders of Great Britain (London: E. Harding [etc.], 1803);

The Political Proteus. A View of the Public Character and Conduct of R. B. Sheridan, Esq. as Exhibited in I. Ten Letters Addressed to Him; II. Selections from His Parliamentary Speeches from the Commencement of the French Revolution; III. Selections from His Speeches at the Whig Club, and Other Public Meetings (London: Cox, Son & Baylis, 1804);

Porcupine Revived; or, An Old Thing Made New, Being an Argument against . . . a War with England; an Exposition of the Absurdity of Sending Albert Gallatin to Treat with the British, with Additional Notes (New York: Printed for the publisher, 1813);

The Pride of Britannia Humbled; or, The Queen of the Ocean Unqueen'd, by "the American Cock Boats," and "the Fir Built Things, with Bits of Striped Bunting at Their Mast Heads" . . . Illustrated and Demonstrated by Four Letters Addressed to Lord Liverpool on the Late American War, edited by Thomas Branagan (New York: T. Boyle/Philadelphia: Wm. Reynolds/Baltimore: J. Campbell, 1815);

Paper against Gold and Glory against Prosperity; or, An Account of the Rise, Progress, Extent, and Present State of the Funds and of the Paper-Money of Great Britain; and also of the Situation of That Country as to Its Debt and Other Expenses; Its Navigation, Commerce, and Manufactures; Its Taxes, Population, and Paupers; Drawn from Authentic Doc-

uments, and Brought down to the End of the Year 1814, 2 volumes (London: Printed by J. M'Creery, 1815); republished as *Paper against Gold; or, The History and Mystery of the Bank of England, of the Debt, of the Stocks, of the Sinking Fund, and of All the Other Tricks and Contrivances Carried on by Means of Paper Money* (New York: John Doyle, 1834);

An Address to the Clergy of Massachusetts. Written in England, Nov. 13, 1814 (Boston: Printed at the Yankee office, 1815);

Letters on the Late War between the United States and Great Britain: Together with Other Miscellaneous Writings, on the Same Subject (New York: Published by J. Belden & Co., Van Winkle & Wiley, printers, 1815);

To the Journeymen and Labourers of England, Wales, Scotland, and Ireland, on the Cause of Their Present Miseries; on the Measures Which Have Produced That Cause; on the Remedies Which Some Foolish and Some Cruel and Insolent Men Have Proposed; and on the Line of Conduct Which Journeymen and Labourers Ought to Pursue in Order to Obtain Effectual Relief, and to Assist in Promoting the Tranquility, and Restoring the Happiness of Their Country (Coventry: Printed & sold by J. Aston, 1816);

Two Letters Addressed to Sir F. Burdett, by W. Cobbett, on the Subject of Reform (Coventry: Printed & sold by J. Aston, 1816);

A Letter Addressed to Mr. Jabet, of Birmingham, Shewing That He Richly Merits the Indignation of All the Labouring People in the Kingdom, and of His Townsmen, the People of Birmingham in Particular, and That the Late Disturbances in That Town Have Arisen from the Provoking Falsehoods Published and Posted up by Him (Coventry: Printed & sold by J. Aston, 1816);

Mr. Cobbett's Address to His Countrymen, on His Future Political Works; and on the State of Their Political Affairs (London: Printed by R. Carlile, 1817);

Cobbett's Address to the Americans (London: Printed by Hay & Turner & published by J. Duncombe, 1817);

A Grammar of the English Language, in a Series of Letters. Intended for the Use of Schools and of Young Persons in General; but, More Especially for the Use of Soldiers, Sailors, Apprentices, and Plough-Boys (New York: Printed for the author by Clayton & Kingsland, 1818; London: Printed for the author & sold by T. Dolby, 1819);

A Year's Residence in the United States of America (London: Sherwood, Neely & Jones, 1818; New

York: Printed for the author by Clayton & Kingsland, 1818);

Long Island Prophecies (London, 1819);

The Life of Thomas Paine, Author of the "Age of Reason," &c. as Published with the Observations of William Cobbett: To Which Are Subjoined, Some Additional Facts, Describing His Last Years and Miserable End (Durham: Printed by F. Humble, 1819);

The American Gardener; or, A Treatise on the Situation, Soil, Fencing and Laying-out of Gardens; on the Making and Managing of Hot-beds and Greenhouses; and on the Propagation and Cultivation of the Several Sorts of Vegetables, Herbs, Fruits and Flowers (Claremont, N.H.: Claremont Manufacturing Co., 1819; London: C. Clement, 1821); republished with revisions as *The English Gardener* (London: The author, 1829);

An Answer to the Speech of the Attorney-General, against Her Majesty the Queen (London, 1820);

Cobbett's Sermons on 1. Hypocrisy and Cruelty. 2. Drunkenness. 3. Bribery. 4. Oppression. 5. Unjust Judges. 6. The Sluggard. 7. Murder. 8. Gaming. 9. Public Robbery. 10. The Unnatural Mother. 11. Forbidding Marriage. 12. Parsons and Tithes (12 monthly parts, London: C. Clement, 1821-1822; 1 volume, London: J. M. Cobbett, 1823); expanded as *Thirteen Sermons* (New York: J. Doyle, 1834);

Cottage Economy: Containing Information Relative to the Brewing of Beer, Making of Bread, Keeping of Cows, Pigs, Bees, Ewes, Goats, Poultry, and Rabbits, and Relative to Other Matters Deemed Useful in the Conducting of the Affairs of a Labourer's Family (7 parts, London: C. Clement, 1821-1822; New York: S. Gould & son [etc.], 1824);

The Farmer's Wife's Friend; or, The Way for the Farmer's Wife to Assist in Saving Her Family from Ruin (London: Printed & published by C. Clement, 1822);

Cobbett's Collective Commentaries; or, Remarks on the Proceedings in the Collective Wisdom of the Nation, during the Session Which Began on the 5th of February, and Ended on the 6th of August in the 3rd Year of the Reign of King George the Fourth, and in the Year of Our Lord 1822 (London: Printed for J. M. Cobbett, 1822);

A French Grammar; or, Plain Instructions for the Learning of French. In a Series of Letters (London: C. Clement, 1824; New York: J. Doyle, 1824);

A History of the Protestant "Reformation," in England and Ireland; Showing How That Event Has Impoverished and Degraded the Main Body of the People in Those Countries. In a Series of Letters, Addressed to All Sensible and Just Englishmen (16 monthly parts, London: Printed & published by Charles Clement, 1824-1826; 1 volume, Philadelphia: Printed by Joseph R. A. Skerrett, 1825);

The Woodlands; or, A Treatise on the Preparing of Ground for Planting (London: Printed by William Cobbett, 1825);

Gold for Ever! Real Causes of the Fall of the Funds: also, Wholesome Advice to Holders of Funds, Scrip, Shares, and All Sorts of Paper-Money (London: C. Clement, 1825);

Big O and Sir Glory; or, "Leisure to Laugh." A Comedy. In Three Acts (London: J. Dean, 1825);

Cobbett's Poor Man's Friend; or, A Defence of the Rights of Those Who Do the Work and Fight the Battles (London: A. Cobbett, 1826; New York: J. Doyle, 1833);

Mr. Cobbett's Petition to the King, in Favour of the Distressed Manufacturers (London: W. Cobbett, 1826);

Cobbett at the King's Cottage. The Petition of William Cobbett to His Majesty King George the Fourth, with a Detail of His Endeavour to Deliver the Petition in Person to His Majesty, at the Cottage, Near Windsor, on Saturday, July 29, 1826 (London: J. Fairburn, 1826);

Usury; or Lending at Interest (London, 1826);

The Protestant Reformation. Part Second: Containing a List of the Abbeys, Priories, Nunneries, Hospitals and Other Religious Foundations in England and Wales, and in Ireland, Confiscated, Seized on, or Alienated, by the Protestant Reformation Sovereigns and Parliaments (London: W. Cobbett, 1827);

A Treatise on Cobbett's Corn, Containing Instructions for Propagating and Cultivating the Plant, and for Harvesting and Preserving the Crop; and also an Account of the Several Uses to Which the Produce Is Applied, with Minute Directions Relative to Each Mode of Application (London: W. Cobbett, 1828);

Noble Nonsense! or, Cobbett's Exhibition of the Stupid and Insolent Pamphlet of Lord Grenville (London: Printed & published by W. Cobbett, 1828);

A Letter to . . . the Pope, on the Character, the Conduct and the Views, of the Catholic Aristocracy and Lawyers of England and Ireland (London: W. Cobbett, 1828);

A Letter from William Cobbett on the American Tariff (London, 1828);

Advice to Young Men, and (Incidentally) to Young

Women, in the Middle and Higher Ranks of Life. In a Series of Letters, Addressed to a Youth, a Bachelor, a Lover, a Husband, a Father, a Citizen, or a Subject (14 parts, London: The author, 1829-1830; 1 volume, New York: J. Doyle, 1831);

The Emigrant's Guide; in Ten Letters, Addressed to the Tax-payers of England; Containing Information of Every Kind, Necessary to Persons Who Are about to Emigrate; Including Several Authentic and Most Interesting Letters from English Emigrants, Now in America, to Their Relations in England (London: The author, 1829);

Rural Rides in the Counties of Surrey, Kent, Sussex, Hampshire, Wiltshire, Gloucestershire, Herefordshire, Worcestershire, Somersetshire, Oxfordshire, Berkshire, Essex, Suffolk, Norfolk, and Hertfordshire: with Economical and Political Observations Relative to Matters Applicable to, and Illustrated by, the State of Those Counties Respectively (London: W. Cobbett, 1830);

Plan of Parliamentary Reform; Addressed to Young Men of England (London: W. Strange, 1830);

History of the Regency and Reign of King George the Fourth, 2 volumes (London: W. Cobbett, 1830-1834);

Eleven Lectures on the French and Belgian Revolutions, and English Boroughmongering: Delivered in the Theatre of the Rotunda, Blackfriars Bridge (London: W. Strange, 1830);

Good Friday; or, The Murder of Jesus Christ by the Jews (London: Published by the author, 1830);

A Spelling Book, with Appropriate Lessons in Reading and with a Stepping-stone to English Grammar (London: Cobbett, 1831);

Cobbett's Manchester Lectures, in Support of His Fourteen Reform Propositions (London: Cobbett, 1832);

Mr. Cobbett's Address to the Tax-payers of England and Scotland, on the Subject of the Seat in Parliament (London: W. Cobbett, 1832?);

A Geographical Dictionary of England and Wales (London, 1832);

Cobbett's Tour in Scotland; and in the Four Northern Counties of England: in the Autumn of the Year 1832 (London: Cobbett, 1833);

Popay the Police Spy; or, A Report on the Evidence Laid before the House of Commons by the Select Committee Appointed to Inquire into the Truth of th[e] Allegations of a Petition, Presented by Mr. Cobbett, from Members of the National Union of the Working Classes (Resident in Camberwell and Walworth), in Which They Complained That Policemen

Were Employed as Government Spies (London: Cleave, 1833);

A New French and English Dictionary (London, 1833);

The Flash in the Pan; or, Peel in a Passion (London: W. Cobbett, 1833?); .

Life of Andrew Jackson, President of the United States of America (New York: Harper, 1834; London: Printed by Mills, Jowett & Mills, 1834);

Cobbett's Legacy to Labourers; or, What Is the Right Which the Lords, Baronets, and Squires, Have to the Lands of England? In Six Letters, Addressed to the Working People of England (London: Printed by Mills & Sons, 1834; New York: J. Doyle, 1835);

Four Letters to the Hon. John Stuart Wortley; in Answer to His "Brief Inquiry into the True Award of an Equitable Adjustment between the Nation and Its Creditors" (London: Cobbett, 1834);

The Malt-Tax Kept upon the Backs of the People by the Whigs (London?: Printed by W. Cobbett, 1835?);

The Life of W. Cobbett, Esq., M. P. for Oldham. Written by Himself (London: Published for the proprietor by W. Strange, 1835);

Cobbett's Legacy to Parsons; or, Have the Clergy of the Established Church an Equitable Right to the Tithes, or to Any Other Thing Called Church Property, Greater than the Dissenters Have to the Same? And Ought There, or Ought There Not, to Be a Separation of the Church from the State? In Six Letters, Addressed to the Church-Parsons in General, Including the Cathedral and College Clergy and the Bishops (London: Cobbett, 1835; New York: John Doyle, 1835);

Surplus Population, and Poor-Law Bill. A Comedy, in Three Acts. As Performed by Desire of Mr. Cobbett, at Normandy Farm, a Few Weeks before His Death. By the Late Wm. Cobbett (London: Published at Cobbett's Register Office, 1835?);

Cobbett's Legacy to Peel; or, An Inquiry with Respect to What the Right Honourable Baronet Will Now Do with the House of Commons, with Ireland, with the English Church and the Dissenters, with the Swarms of Pensioners, &c., with the Crown Lands and the Army, with the Currency and the Debt. In Six Letters (London: Published at Cobbett's "Register" Office, 1836);

Cobbett's Legacy to Lords: Being Six Lectures on the History of Taxation and Debt in England. To Which Is Subjoined a Scheme of Substitution for Taxes, with additions by William Cobbett, Jr. (London: H. J. Tresidder, 1863);

Cobbett: Selections, with Hazlitt's Essay and Other Criti-

cal Estimates, edited by A. M. D. Hughes (Oxford: Clarendon Press, 1923);

The Opinions of William Cobbett, edited by G. D. H. and Margaret Cole (London: Cobbett Publishing Co., 1944);

The Autobiography of William Cobbett: The Progress of a Plough-boy to a Seat in Parliament, edited by William Reitzel (London: Faber & Faber, 1947).

OTHER: *Impeachment of Mr. LaFayette: Containing His Accusation, Stated in the Report of the Extraordinary Commission to the National Assembly on the 8th of August, 1792, Supported by Mr. Brissot; and His Defence by Mr. Vaublanc: with a Supplement Containing the Letters and Other Authentic Pieces Relative Thereto*, translated from the French by Cobbett (Hagerstown: Printed by Stewart Herbert, 1794);

Georg Friedrich von Martens, *Summary of the Law of Nations, Founded on the Treaties and Customs of the Modern Nations of Europe*, translated from the French by Cobbett (Philadelphia: Published by Thomas Bradford, 1795);

William Playfair, *The History of Jacobinism, Its Crimes, Cruelties and Perfidies: Comprising an Inquiry into the Manner of Disseminating, under the Appearance of Philosophy and Virtue, Principles Which Are Equally Subversive of Order, Virtue, Religion, Liberty and Happiness*, appendix by Cobbett as Peter Porcupine (Philadelphia: W. Cobbett, 1796);

Edmund Burke, *A Letter from the Right Honourable Edmund Burke to a Noble Lord, on the Attacks Made upon Him and His Pension, in the House of Lords, by the Duke of Bedford, and the Earl of Lauderdale, Early in the Present Session of Parliament*, preface by Cobbett as Porcupine (Philadelphia: Printed for B. Davies, H. & P. Rice & J. Ormrod, 1796);

Pierre Auguste Adet, *The Gros Mousqueton Diplomatique; or, Diplomatic Blunderbuss*, preface by Cobbett as Porcupine (Philadelphia: W. Cobbett, 1796);

Johann Friedrich Anthing, *History of the Campaigns of Prince Alexander Suworow Rymnikski, Field-Marshal-General in the Service of His Imperial Majesty, the Emperor of All the Russias, with a Preliminary Sketch of His Private Life and Character*, translated from the German by Cobbett (New York: Printed by C. & R. Waits for Wm. Cobbett, 1800);

Martens, *A Compendium of the Law of Nations, Founded on the Treaties and Customs of the Mod-*

ern Nations of Europe: To Which Is Added, a Complete List of All the Treaties, Conventions, Compacts, Declarations, &c. from the Year 1731 to 1788, Inclusive, Indicating the Several Works in Which They Are to Be Found, translated and the list of treaties, etc., brought down to June 1802 by Cobbett (London: Cobbett & Morgan, 1802);

William Forsyth, *A Treatise on the Culture and Management of Fruit Trees*, introduction and notes adapting the rules of the treatise to the climates and seasons of the U.S.A. by Cobbett (Philadelphia: J. Morgan, 1802);

Jean Gabriel Peltier, *The Empire of Germany Divided into Departments, under the Prefecture of the Elector of * * * * *To Which Is Prefixed, a Memoir on the Political and Military State of the Continent, Written by the Same Author*, translated from the French by Cobbett (London: Printed for E. Harding, 1803);

Forsyth, *An Epitome of Mr. Forsyth's Treatise on the Culture and Management of Fruit Trees. Also, Notes on American Gardening and Fruits: with Designs for Promoting the Ripening of Fruits, and Securing Them as Family Comforts: and Further, of Economical Principles in Building Farmers' Habitations. By an American Farmer*, edited by Cobbett (Philadelphia: Printed by T. L. Plowman for J. Morgan, 1803);

Jethro Tull, *The Horse-hoeing Husbandry; or, A Treatise on the Principles of Tillage and Vegetation, Wherein Is Taught a Method of Introducing a Sort of Vineyard Culture into the Corn-fields, in Order to Increase Their Product and Diminish the Common Expense*, introduction by Cobbett (London: W. Cobbett, 1829);

William M. Gouge, *The Curse of Paper-Money and Banking; or, A Short History of Banking in the United States of America, with an Account of Its Ruinous Effects*, introduction by Cobbett (London: Printed by Mills, Jowett & Mills, 1833).

William Cobbett was a British subject who fled to the United States in 1793 as a refugee from the violence of the French Revolution. While living in America, Cobbett became embroiled in the political discussions that polarized communities and generated much forceful political writing. On one side there were the Republicans, followers of Thomas Jefferson, believers in a decentralized government under which the states would retain great powers unto themselves. On the other side were the Federalists, led by Alexander Hamilton, who favored

The Jolly Farmer Tavern in Farnham, Surrey, England, where Cobbett was born

a strong central government and tight control over economic resources.

Into this conflict came William Cobbett, who valued the monarchy of England, treasured an orderly progression of public affairs, and abhorred the chaos created by revolution. He loathed what he had seen in France and it disturbed him to think that the Jeffersonians would lend any support to that "rabble." Most of all, he feared that if Jefferson and his advocates carried the day, an alignment of the United States with revolutionary France would work to the detriment of England.

While Cobbett was in America he was one of the most persuasive public voices. His writing was voluminous, and like much of the writing in the newspapers and pamphlets of that period, it was often vituperative. But it is important to view Cobbett's work as the work of an individual, an Englishman, not a Federalist (though he sided with the Federalists) or an anti-Jeffersonian (though he was that, too). He was a defender of England, and his only concern with American events was how they might affect England.

Cobbett was one of the best writers of his time, one of the best thinkers, a most careful grammar-

ian, a brilliant rhetorical strategist, and extremely prolific. A master of stinging satire, Cobbett was a pugnacious—some say a vicious—writer, given to invective. In the end, the ordinary diction, the unrelenting logic and clarity of his prose made Cobbett a formidable ally or enemy.

A comparison of Cobbett's writings in America and his later work in England seems to reveal a fundamental contradiction in his thought. Why, for example, was he not aligned with Jefferson, whose philosophies were certainly compatible with Cobbett's agrarian vision of an orderly society built on the value of the individual, the farmer, the laborer, and the artisan? More careful examination, however, reveals a basic consistency in Cobbett's outlook. Cobbett was a man of simple birth, who saw himself as a champion of and adviser to other simple folk; he longed for social, political, economic, and agricultural order. He fought to preserve an order that he had grown up with and that he attributed to the glorious traditions of England. All he ever really wanted was the preservation of a preindustrial England, which, by the time he lived and wrote, was no longer a reality. He attacked American libertarianism from the point of view of an idealized, agrarian England. When he returned to England in 1800 and found that it did not accord with his ideal, he then attacked the establishments of England and was forced to seek refuge in the United States again in 1817.

Cobbett was born in Farnham, in the county of Surrey, in the south of England. There is some dispute about the exact date of his birth. He himself reports it in three separate pieces of writing, as 9 March 1766. Various biographies and reference works give the date as March 1762 or 1763, with the 1762 date occurring more frequently. His father had been a farmer but at the time of Cobbett's birth was an innkeeper. Cobbett described his father as somewhat learned for a man of his rank. When his father had been a small boy he had driven a plough, earning two pence a day. The earnings went to pay the expenses of an evening school where he learned as much as he could, especially in mathematics and surveying. Cobbett wrote that this little learning accounted for the respect and status given his father within their humble circle.

Cobbett knew no ancestors beyond his grandfather, a day laborer who had worked for the same farmer for forty years. Cobbett recounted his childhood visits to the thatched cottage of his grandparents. Later, in America, Cobbett made a devastating comparison of his own humble background with what he described as Benjamin Franklin's cherished fantasies of a noble lineage. Cobbett, like his father and grandfather, grew up working the soil. "My first occupation was driving the small birds from the turnip-seed, and the rooks from the peas. When I first trudged a-field, with my wooden bottle and my satchel swung over my shoulders, I was hardly able to climb the gates and stiles; and, at the close of the day, to reach home, was a task of infinite difficulty." His was a country life and a simple life. Cobbett wrote that he had no political awareness as he was growing up: "We were like the rest of the country people of England; that is to say, we neither knew nor thought any thing about the matter."

Cobbett, like his father, had little formal education. He had a faint recollection of attending a school taught, unsuccessfully, by an old woman. It was Cobbett's father who, on winter evenings, taught him and his brothers to read and to write. Since his father had less than a perfect understanding of grammar, Cobbett, while forced to memorize the rules, did not advance much in this area. He did credit his father with a respectable effort in the area of mathematics.

Cobbett first left home at the age of twenty. He tried to enlist in His Majesty's Navy, having gotten his first glimpse of the sea while visiting in Portsmouth. Cobbett got as far as boarding the *Pegasus* and telling the captain that he was ready to sign up. The captain concluded that the young man was running from some difficulty and told him that life at sea was much rougher than anything he could then be facing. Cobbett left the ship but did not return to his plough until he had tried to sign up with the port-admiral, who also turned him down. When he did leave home, in May 1783, his departure seems to have been a lark. When he reached the London turnpike on his way to the Guildford fair, a stagecoach came upon him. With little money and no plan, he made his way to London. A fellow traveler took him in and found him a job as a clerk in the office of an attorney. The work became for Cobbett a hell on earth. He wrote of this experience that just about the time that the attorney had become satisfied with him, he had become dissatisfied with the attorney, praying: "Gracious heaven! if I am doomed to be wretched,

Caricature by James Gillray of Cobbett "pledging his soul to the devil" in order to convince a judge of the truth of his allegations of corruption in the British army

bury me beneath Iceland snows, and let me feed on blubber; stretch me under the burning line, and deny me thy propitious dews; nay, if it be thy will suffocate me with the infected and pestilential air of a democratic club-room; but save me from the desk of an attorney!"

About this time Cobbett saw an ad for His Majesty's Marine Service; not having gotten the notion of the sea out of his head, but having had his fill of the scrivener's life, he went to Chatham and enlisted. It turned out that he had enlisted in a marching regiment, not in a marine unit at all. Fortunately for his later career as an editor and writer, he was assigned to work for the commandant of the garrison as a copyist. The commandant, in some exasperation with Cobbett, commended some grammar to his study. During his time at Chatham, Cobbett joined a circulating library at Brompton: "The library was not very considerable, it is true, nor in my reading was I directed by any degree of taste or choice. Novels, plays, history, poetry, all were read, and nearly with equal avidity." He did, however, follow the commandant's urging and began a serious study of grammar. He got a copy of Lowth's grammar, read and reread it, copied it several times, and memorized its contents. While on sentry duty he would recite grammar. Not only did he master the grammar of his mother tongue, he believed that his endeavors improved his memory—a quality that others would later remark.

From 1784 to 1791, Cobbett served with the Fifty-fourth Infantry Regiment in Nova Scotia, where he witnessed and documented a number of abuses and examples of corruption within the military service. Cobbett intended to correct this situation. Upon his discharge with the rank of sergeant-major in 1791, he went to London to place complaints before the government. No immediate action was taken. He continued to raise questions and lodge complaints. During his time in London, and just prior to his wedding to Nancy Ann Reid on 2 February 1792, Cobbett is believed to have worked with others in writing *The Soldier's Friend*, an account of the private soldier's grievances and an exposé of army corruption. This work is considered by some to be the earliest extant sample of Cobbett's writing.

Finally, a hearing was scheduled. Cobbett wanted the corrupt officers court-martialed, plain and simple; it had not occurred to him how high the corruption might reach. When the trial began and the call came for the accuser to stand forward to make his charge, Cobbett saw the guards at ready

and realized that it was certain that he would lose the case; so, quickly, he slipped out and retreated to France.

The Cobbetts arrived in France in March 1792. Cobbett took up the learning of French and remained happily situated until September. He had planned to remain in France until the spring of 1793, spending the winter in Paris. En route to Paris, however, he learned at Abbeville that the king had been dethroned and his guards murdered. Cobbett said later: "I saw that a war with England was inevitable, and it was not difficult to foresee what would be the fate of Englishmen in that country." The Cobbetts turned immediately for Havre-de-Grace, with the hope of finding passage for America.

Cobbett happened upon America as she found herself in the midst of great decisions. The disputants of the period were the Federalists and the Republicans, each fearing dire consequences for the nation should the other party prevail. Both parties had strong, intelligent, capable, and sincere leadership; and both parties had vigorous publications to propagate the party line. There may never have been a time in American history when

Caricature by Gillray of Cobbett making his escape to France when he realized that the court-martial of several officers on his charges of corruption would go against him

the opportunities for a man of words have been greater. In looking at Cobbett's American experience one must not forget that he came to America out of the anarchy of France and the early days of bloody revolution. In addition, one must keep in mind that this was not Cobbett's first experience in the New World; he had served with the British forces for seven years in Nova Scotia, a Loyalist bastion. These experiences had left an indelible mark and inclined him toward the conservative Federalist side.

Cobbett and his wife settled first in Wilmington, Delaware. It had been their intention to set up a school in America, but Cobbett found so many French emigrés who wanted to be taught English that he was able to make a sufficient living by going to their boarding houses and giving lessons. In fact, Cobbett found America a very good place for getting money, at least for a person who was industrious and enterprising; and few persons were more industrious than Cobbett. His description of America makes it plain that he did not think highly of the place: "The land was bad—rocky—houses wretched—roads impassable after the least rain. Fruit in quantity, but good for nothing. One apple or peach in England or France was worth a bushel of them. The seasons were detestable. All burning or freezing. There was no Spring or Autumn. The weather was so very inconstant that you were never sure for a single hour at a time. The whole month of March was so hot that we could hardly bear our clothes, and three parts of the month of June there was a frost every night, and so cold in the daytime, that we were obliged to wear great-coats. The people were worthy of the country—a cheating, sly, roguish gang. Yet strangers made fortunes in spite of all this, particularly the English. The natives were by nature idle, and sought to live by cheating, while foreigners, being industrious, sought no other means than those dictated by integrity, and were sure to meet with encouragement even from the idle and roguish themselves; for, however roguish a man may be, he always loves to deal with an honest man."

By spring of the next year Mrs. Cobbett had grown to dislike the Frenchmen who insisted on living with them while Cobbett taught them English. She also disliked Wilmington, so the Cobbetts moved to Philadelphia. It was about this same time, in February 1793, that Cobbett began to write for publication. His first work was a translation of a French pamphlet about the impeachment of Lafayette, prefaced and annotated by Cobbett with, as he said, "most scrupulous impartiality." His next

work, however, exhibits a marked change. There is no impartiality in *Observations on the Emigration of Dr. Joseph Priestley* (1794). This work was provoked by the enthusiastic welcome given by some Americans to this radical exile from Birmingham. Cobbett now publicly began to show his anti-Republicanism and became in print what he had long been in person—a stout defender of the old order, of monarchy, of England. He had had direct experience of the revolution during his short stay in France and thought that anyone who set France up as an ideal was lacking in good sense and dangerous.

Cobbett wrote a series of pamphlets in which he severely criticized the French revolutionists and their sympathizers. By February 1795, *Observations on the Emigration of Dr. Joseph Priestley* was into the third edition and the reprints in England had great circulation and influence. During this year he wrote three more pamphlets: *A Bone to Gnaw, for the Democrats*, a two-part attack on British exiles and their American sympathizers; *A Kick for a Bite*, in answer to a female critic; and *A Little Plain English, Addressed to the People of the United States*, a bitter but effective assault on those who opposed the British treaty. Cobbett wrote about his efforts between 1794 and 1800: "My labours were without intermission. During that space there were published from my pen about twenty different pamphlets, the whole number of which amounted to more than half a million copies. During the three last years, a daily paper [*Porcupine's Gazette*], surpassing in extent of numbers any ever known in America, was the vehicle of my efforts; and, by the year 1800, I might safely have asserted, that there was not in the whole country, one single family, in which some part or the other of my writings had not been read; and in which, generally speaking, they had not produced some degree of effect favourable to the interests of my country."

Thomas Bradford, a Philadelphia bookseller and publisher, hired Cobbett in 1795 to report the proceedings of the U.S. Congress. The product of this work was *A Prospect from the Congress-Gallery*, a most successful pamphlet. The relations between publisher and author had become strained in the process and Cobbett was not satisfied with the terms he got from Bradford. After completing the assignment, he tried to negotiate with other publishers. His efforts were not successful, so he decided to start his own publishing venture. He started the *Political Censor*, a monthly publication, which ran until March 1797.

In August 1796, Cobbett, in an effort to defend himself from an angry Bradford, wrote an autobiographical account, *The Life and Adventures of Peter Porcupine, with a Full and Fair Account of All His Authoring Transactions; Being A Sure and Infallible Guide for All Enterprising Young Men Who Wish to Make a Fortune by Writing Pamphlets*. Below the title Cobbett looses one of his typical barbs, a quote from Shakespeare: "Now, you lying varlets, you shall see how a plain tale will put you down." The title and the quote provide an indication of the vigor of his attack.

This was also the year in which Cobbett came out with his attack on Thomas Paine. His treatment of Paine, at this time and later, serves as the measure of the changes in Cobbett's politics; at the same time, his treatment of Paine indicates the essential changelessness of Cobbett's basic principles. In 1796, Cobbett could not abide Paine's politics or philosophy; consequently, he published the extremely critical *Life of Thomas Paine* in the *Political Censor*. Later, when imprisoned in Newgate Prison in London from 1810 to 1812, he wrote his *Paper against Gold* (1815) and offered it to the memory of Paine. Seven years later, living on Long Island to escape increasing harassment from the official quarters of England, Cobbett's last activity before going home was to dig up Paine's bones and take them back to England for honor and burial.

Cobbett established *Porcupine's Gazette and Daily Advertiser* in March 1797 to replace the *Political Censor*. *Porcupine's Gazette* was a four-page daily. The 24 August 1797 issue stated that the *Gazette* started with 1,200 subscribers and by August had 2,400 subscribers. The farewell number of this paper was issued from New York in January 1800. It was also Cobbett's farewell to the United States. Cobbett said that he started the *Gazette* with John Adams's presidency and that it had been his intention that the paper would serve Adams to the fullest extent.

The newspapers of the 1790s are too often judged by criteria imposed after the fact. The primary role of the press at that time was to provide a place to articulate ideas and political positions. Every cause had its writers, its editors, its publishers. The publications were diverse—newspapers, pamphlets, books, circulars. The purpose of publishing was to persuade the unaligned, to reassure the converted, and to undermine the thinking and articulation of the opposition. Ridicule was a tool to assail the opponent; so were satire and forceful language. These devices met the needs of the publications' constituencies. These publications were provocative and they were meant to provoke. They

led the discussions, heated the arguments, and set the agendas. *Porcupine's Gazette* was one such publication. Other Federalist papers of that time were John Fenno's *Gazette of the United States* and Noah Webster's *Commercial Advertiser* and *Spectator*. Opposing the Federalists was Benjamin Franklin Bache and his *Aurora*. Bache and Fenno disagreed to such an extent that they brawled in the street. Bache, the grandson of Benjamin Franklin, had picked up the Republican crusade from the faltering *National Gazette*, edited by Philip Freneau.

None of these editors was mild-tempered in his writing. Bache wrote with what today would be considered imprudent jubilation when George Washington left office. In his editorial of 6 March 1797 he called Washington "the man who is the source of all the misfortunes of our country," and went on to say that Washington was "this day reduced to a level with his fellow citizens, and is no longer possessed of power to multiply evils upon the United States. . . ." On 14 November 1797, Cobbett wrote about Bache: "This atrocious wretch (worthy descendant of old Ben) knows that all men of any understanding set him down as an abandoned liar, a tool and a hireling; and he is content that they should do so. . . ."

Such vigorous language characterized all the papers of the period. Presidents were referred to as infidels. Opponents were likened to reptiles or devils. Their use of the word *evil* was frequent. By twentieth-century standards of journalism, the language, the content, and the treatment may seem excessive, reckless, and intemperate. *Porcupine's Gazette* was hardly atypical of the publications of that period; Cobbett may simply have been one of the better tacticians, knowing exactly how to aim his pen and sharpen his words to pierce his opponents.

During his career in America Cobbett was always near or thoroughly mixed up in trouble. His first trial for libel took place in early 1797. As soon as he was acquitted, he wrote *The Democratic Judge*, an account that made Chief Justice McKean look not only foolish but also criminal. His most serious conflict with the established powers came when Cobbett harshly criticized the medical practices and competence of Dr. Benjamin Rush. At the time, yellow fever was raging throughout Philadelphia. Rush's treatment of preference was to bleed his patients and to practice other purgative measures. Cobbett thought Rush's frequent bleedings an unsound practice and called him "Dr. Sangrado," after the doctor in *Gil Blas* who thought that blood was not really necessary for life. Circulation of the

Front page of Cobbett's pro-Federalist Philadelphia newspaper

Gazette soared as a result of this attack, but Rush sued for libel in 1797. The case did not come to trial until 1799, when it was decided against Cobbett and a $5,000 fine was levied against him. His assets in Philadelphia were seized, though he had already suspended publication of the *Gazette* and moved to New York to try a bookselling business. While in New York he published five issues of the *Rush-Light*, a monthly denunciation of his persecutors. The irony of this trial and the conviction is that Cobbett was right; his real crime was that he had attacked a bluestocking luminary, not another editor or publisher or politician. "The Americans, under pretenses the most false, by the violent mockery of judicial proceedings, by openly avowed and boasted of perjury, robbed me of earnings, left me to begin anew with a family dependent solely upon my exertions, and cruelly persecuted several of my friends. For the sake of these friends more than for my own sake I hate the unprincipled nation."

In disgust, Cobbett returned in 1800 to En-

Cobbett, after his return to England in 1800, writing his Weekly Political Register, *the most successful of his periodicals (The Bodley Head)*

gland, but it was an England quite different from that of his youth and his memories. He opened a book shop and continued publishing the works of Peter Porcupine, which eventually ran to twelve volumes. He founded the *Weekly Political Register,* one of the fourteen or more periodicals he started during his lifetime. The *Register* was Cobbett's biggest success and had reached eighty-eight volumes by the time Cobbett died in 1835.

Between 1806 and 1816 Cobbett's break with the British establishment became final. It was during this period that Cobbett was imprisoned at Newgate Gaol because of his outraged writing on the flogging of British militiamen by German mercenaries. He was fined £1,000 and sentenced to two years' imprisonment—every day of which he served, even though friends raised money for bail. He continued writing and operated his publishing interests from prison with the help of his wife, his sons and daughters, and friends. By 1816, Cobbett was writing increasingly of the need for reform and found himself increasingly in the disfavor of officialdom. To further his constituency, he took his appeal directly to the working class with a cheap edition of the *Register*. His opponents called it "Cobbett's Two-Penny Trash," and, typically, Cobbett began publishing it under that name, getting his words and ideas into every working-class club and meeting house. So unpopular was this publication with the officials that it was not unusual for sellers of the *Two-Penny Trash* to be hauled in and flogged by local magistrates. In January 1817 the Power of Imprisonment Bill was passed by Parliament; the law made it easier to successfully prosecute seditious writing and allowed the suspension of habeas corpus. Cobbett was the intended target of the law. In March, he returned to America. He leased a farm on Long Island and lived there for two years. During this time he continued publishing the *Register* and wrote his *Grammar of the English Language* (1818) and *A Year's Residence in the United States of America* (1818).

Cobbett returned to England in 1819 at the age of fifty-seven. In January 1820, he began *Cobbett's Evening Post.* In 1821 he began a popular series of monthly political sermons. The next year Cobbett started the *Parliamentary Register* and published the last of seven parts of *Cottage Economy.* The latter was one of his most popular books and was one that allowed him to vent fully his hatred of the Industrial Revolution. Balancing all the bile and scorn in this piece is Cobbett's love for the simple, independent English cottager. During this time he also bought a large share of the *Statesman*, a daily, and became a major contributor to the paper. In 1823, Cobbett left the *Statesman* and started the *Norfolk Yeoman's Gazette*, a paper that lasted only a few weeks. In 1824, he began *The Woodlands* (1825), a manual for planters, one of his many writings on agriculture, a matter of great importance to him throughout his life. Cobbett's *Poor Man's Friend* came out in 1826. The next year, he completed part two of his *History of the Protestant "Reformation," in England and Ireland*; the first part had been published in sixteen monthly installments from 1824-1826. This work was written in order to support Catholic Emancipation rather than for purely historical reasons. In 1828 Cobbett published his *Treatise on Cobbett's Corn,* an attempt to popularize the growing of Indian corn. He followed this with *The English Gardener,* a work similar to the earlier *American Gardener* (1819), and began the fourteen parts of *Advice to Young Men* (1829-1830). The last work of this prolific period was *Rural Rides* (1830), a day-to-day account of Cobbett's travels in England since 1821.

The years 1830 to 1835 were a time of intense political activity and fame for Cobbett. Between 1830 and 1832 he issued a monthly *Two-Penny*

Sketch by Daniel Maclise of Cobbett in Parliament

Trash. He was elected to Parliament for the borough of Oldham in 1832, when he was seventy years of age; he was a distinguished member but had little influence. Between 1830 and 1834 he published the two volumes of his *History of the Regency and Reign of King George the Fourth* and wrote *Cobbett's Tour in Scotland* (1833). On 25 May 1835, Cobbett suffered a heart attack while debating a tax issue in Parliament. He died at his home in Ash, Surrey, on 18 June 1835.

How is it that Cobbett became so embroiled in American politics and in the highly politicized press of the day? Cobbett commented on this in *The Life and Adventures of Peter Porcupine*: "Several persons . . . seem to think that it was impertinent in me to meddle with the politics here, because I was an Englishman. I would have these good people to recollect, that the laws of this country hold out to foreigners an offer of all that liberty of the press which Americans enjoy, and that, if this liberty be abridged, by whatever means it may be done, the laws and the constitution, and all together, is a mere cheat; a snare to catch the credulous and enthusiastic of every other nation; a downright imposition on the world. . . . When an act is passed for excluding Englishmen from exercising their talents, and from promulgating what they write, then will I desist; but, I hope, when that time arrives, no act will be passed to prevent people from emigrating back again."

Cobbett from the first felt that, in the America of the 1790s, England had few to speak up for her. He did not think that America should become embroiled in the French revolution or be at odds with England over France. But, most of all, he thought someone should stick up for England, and he appointed himself to be that person.

He consistently, no matter how the political environments and ideologies changed, believed in the rank and order of society, that change should come about through peaceful reform. He always worked to restore the system that he had known as a boy. In his later years he wrote: "I am no republican in principle, any more than I am in law or allegiance. I hold, that this, which we have [in England] is the best sort of government in the world. I hold that a government of king, lords, and commons, the last of which chosen by all men, who are of full age, of sound mind, and untainted by indelible crime, is the best of governments. I lived eight years under the republican government of Pennsylvania; and I declare, that I believe that to have been the most corrupt and tyrannical government that the world ever knew; added to which

The tomb of Cobbett and his wife at Farnham

were the lowness, the dirtiness of the villainy, the vulgarity, the disregard of all sense of morality and of honour, making the whole thing so disgusting, as to drive an Englishman half mad at the thought of ever seeing his country subjected to such rulers."

While Cobbett undoubtedly provided one of the strongest, most articulate voices for the Federalists, he was through and through a Tory, a man of and for England. It took only a few years after his return to England for him to learn that the England he had so staunchly defended on American soil no longer existed. Upon this discovery he turned his prose with equal ability, enthusiasm, and bite to the subject of reform.

Letters:

The Life and Letters of William Cobbett in England and America, edited by Lewis Saul Benjamin, 2 volumes (London & New York: Lane, 1913);

Letters from William Cobbett to Edward Thornton, Written in the Years 1797 to 1800, edited by G. D. H. Cole (London & New York: Oxford University Press, 1937);

Letters of William Cobbett, edited by Gerald Duff (Salzburg: Institut für Englische Sprache und Literatur, 1974).

References:

Marjorie Bowen, *Peter Porcupine; A Study of William Cobbett, 1762-1835* (London & New York: Longmans, Green, 1936);

Gerald Duff, *William Cobbett and the Politics of Earth* (Salzburg: Institut für Englische Sprache und Literatur, 1972);

Pierce Welch Gaines, *William Cobbett and the U.S., 1792-1835* (Worcester, Mass.: American Antiquarian Society, 1971);

Dorothy Catherine Johnson, *Pioneers of Reform* (London: Methuen, 1929), pp. 23-55;

John W. Osborne, *Cobbett, His Thought and His Times* (New Brunswick, N.J.: Rutgers University Press, 1966), p. 272;

Morris Leonard Pearl, *William Cobbett: A Bibliographical Account of His Life and Times* (Folcroft, Pa.: Folcroft Press, 1970);

James Sambrook, *William Cobbett* (London & Boston: Routledge & Kegan Paul, 1973).

Papers:

The 1947 edition of *The Autobiography of William Cobbett,* edited by William Reitzel, thanked "H. W. Cobbett, Esq." of Manchester for the use of the Cobbett papers then in his possession. It is not known what later disposition was made of them. The American Antiquarian Society has Cobbett's account book. The New York Public Library, the Yale University Library, and the Houghton, Kress, and Widener Libraries at Harvard University all have Cobbett collections.

Daniel H. Craig

(3 November 1811-5 January 1895)

Richard A. Schwarzlose
Northwestern University

MAJOR POSITION HELD: General agent, New York Associated Press (1851-1866).

BOOKS: *Craig's Business Directory and Baltimore Almanac for 1842* (Baltimore: Dan'l H. Craig, 1842);

A Review of "An Exposition of the Differences Existing between Different Presses and Different Lines of Telegraph, Respecting the Transmission of Foreign News, Being a Letter and Accompanying Documents, Addressed to the Government Commissioners of the Nova Scotia Telegraph" (Halifax, Nova Scotia, 16 March 1850);

Letter to F. M. Edson on the House Telegraph Line (N.p., 5 April 1853);

"The American Telegraph Company and the Press," A Reply to the Falsehoods of the Executive Committee (New York?, 7 July 1860);

Associated Press, Annual Report of the General Agent (N.p., 1 January 1863?);

The Convicted Libeller (N.p., 6 February 1863);

Craig's Manual of the Telegraph, Illustrating the Electro-Mechanical System of the American "Rapid" Telegraph Co. of New York, Designed for Use in Schools, Business Colleges, Counting Rooms and the Home Circle (New York: John Polhemus, 1879);

Answer of Daniel H. Craig, Organizer and Manager of the New York Associated Press, 1850 to 1867, and Originator and Promoter of Machine or Rapid Telegraphing, to the Interrogatories of the U.S. Senate Committee on Education and Labor at the City of New York, 1883 (New York, 1883);

Startling Facts! Practical Machine Telegraph, One Thousand Words per Minute (N.p., 1888?);

Machine Telegraph of To-day (N.p., August 1888, June 1890, September 1891).

OTHER: "Letter from D. H. Craig," in Robert Squires, *Report of the Executive Committee of the National Telegraph Co. to Subscribers of Its Stock on Little's Automatic System of Fast Telegraphy* (New York: Fisher & Field, 1869), pp. 7-20.

PERIODICAL PUBLICATION: "Automatic Telegraphy," *Scientific American*, 24 (1 January 1871): 4.

A resourceful self-made journalist and businessman, Daniel H. Craig built the Associated Press into a national news monopoly during the decade preceding the Civil War. Shrewdly practicing the arts of business correspondence, investment, and news gathering, Craig systematized and expanded the amorphous AP news agency which six leading New York City newspapers had gradually improvised during the few years before Craig took it over in 1851. So successful were Craig's efforts at eliminating competition, building a system of reporters and clients, and providing a news report which newspaper editors came to view as indispensable, that his wire service became the vehicle by which President Lincoln's administration released dispatches and announcements to the public during the Civil War, breaking the tradition of Washington papers serving as presidential mouthpieces. At the same time, Craig took a decisive role in the development of telegraphy, thereby both amassing a personal fortune and protecting the telegraph circuits he needed to transmit his daily news reports.

Daniel H. Craig

Daniel Hutchins Craig was born on 3 November 1811 in Rumney, New Hampshire, the youngest of eight children of Daniel and Pamela Hutchins Craig. His father fought in the War of 1812 and his grandfather, Alexander Craig, had been a soldier in the Revolutionary War. At the age of twelve Craig began a printing apprenticeship in the *Gazette* office in Plymouth, New Hampshire. When that newspaper failed a few years later, he completed his apprenticeship at the *Gazette* in Lancaster, Massachusetts. Moving to Boston in 1832 Craig became a journeyman printer, attempting unsuccessfully to establish a daily one-cent newspaper in advance of the appearance on 3 September 1833 of the *New York Sun*, considered the first successful penny paper in the United States. He married Helena Croome of England on 6 November 1834 at the South Congregational Society.

For four years beginning in 1840 Craig was a printer in Baltimore, where he edited *Craig's Business Directory and Baltimore Almanac for 1842*. A second volume of the directory was printed for 1843, but under the direction of Robert Semmes. More importantly, Craig's brief stay in Baltimore launched him on his news-gathering career. Working with Arunah S. Abell, editor of the *Baltimore*

Sun, a penny paper founded in 1837, Craig developed a system for delivering news dispatches from distant cities via carrier pigeons. In the summer of 1842, when the *New York Sun* moved into a six-story building, it built a pigeon house on its roof. Craig's news pigeons had penetrated New York City journalism and were also beginning to serve other newspapers and market speculators there and elsewhere in the East.

While some newspapers made occasional use of the pigeons and a few used them regularly, speculators were more consistent and lucrative customers of Craig's pigeon service, and the news which speculators craved above all else in advance of the general public was of British and Continental markets, which still played the tune to which American business danced. To meet this need Craig returned to Boston, where European news had been regularly delivered by the new transatlantic steamers of the Cunard line since mid-1840. (Cunard service was not extended to New York City until 1848.) Craig moved back to Boston in 1844; he is listed in the tax records as a printer from then until 1849, but he was also developing his news service, using African carrier pigeons which he kept at his home in Roxbury. Craig later described his operation: "I carried my birds by land to Halifax to meet the incoming Cunard steamers, and then took passage for Boston. After gathering news from London and Liverpool journals, I printed it on tissue paper, with small type, in my state-room, fastened it to the legs of the birds, and at the proper time flew them from the decks or port holes of the steamers."

A history of the *Boston Herald*, published in 1878, says that Craig carried three birds on each trip—each presumably bound for a different destination—which were released when the ship came within fifty miles of land, reaching Boston several hours in advance of the Cunarder. Craig's dispatches were received at the *Boston Daily Mail* office, where, after an "extra" edition of the *Mail* was printed, the nameplate was changed to read "New York Herald Extra" and another press run was done. The *Herald*s were shipped by fast coastal steamer to New York City for distribution. The *Herald* had won Craig's services over several other New York newspaper bidders by offering him $500 for each hour he could get the news to the paper ahead of its competition.

As Craig was perfecting his carrier pigeon system in 1844, however, Samuel F. B. Morse erected the nation's first telegraph line. Faster than pigeons and capable of longer news dispatches, telegraphy in time would supplant Craig's operation unless he could link his pigeon service to its pioneer circuits. Craig made such a proposal in 1845 to F. O. J. Smith, holder of the franchise to construct a Morse telegraph system northeast from New York City through Boston to the Canadian border. But because both men foresaw the growing significance of controlling the North American flow of foreign news being delivered by Cunarders, they not only could find no common ground in 1845 but became bitter enemies in a war over control of foreign news which lasted for five years.

During the 1840s Craig fathered three children. The first was a daughter, Ida G., born in Baltimore in 1843 or 1844. Frank H. was born in Boston and died from cholera infantum on 18 August 1846 at the age of one year and five months. William L. was born in 1848.

In 1846, spurred by the Oregon boundary question, repeal of the British Corn Laws, and war with Mexico, leading New York and Boston editors took renewed interest in foreign news and began organizing systems to expedite news delivery, using coastal ships, railroad expresses, and the telegraph where available. While New York papers' agents awaited the Cunarders in Boston, Craig's pigeons continually beat the steamers to port, giving speculators and Craig's newspaper clients the edge on foreign news. After some New York papers petitioned Cunard for help, Craig's pigeons were occasionally seized or shot at by Cunard captains, but his birds succeeded more frequently than not. This rivalry continued sporadically until March 1848, when news of the European revolutions compelled New York editors to move decisively into the field of news gathering. In April 1848, five leading New York newspapers, the nucleus of the eventual New York Associated Press, chartered the coastal steamer *Buena Vista* and dispatched her to Nova Scotia waters to gather European news from inbound Cunarders. Craig responded to this competition by booking his return passages from Halifax on the *Buena Vista*, flying his pigeons from her decks, and beating her patron newspapers with the news several times. Within three months the New York papers broke off their costly and self-defeating steamer venture, turning instead to encouraging the erection of telegraph lines between Boston and Halifax.

Between mid-1848 and early 1849 Craig had the foreign news field to himself, while a strand of telegraph line inched northeastward toward Halifax. Casting Craig's trafficking with speculators as sinister and unethical, the New York press had con-

vinced the provincial governments of New Brunswick and Nova Scotia to erect telegraph lines which would deliver foreign news to the general public and newspapers as rapidly as speculators could receive it. On 13 February 1849 the line was completed from New York City to Saint John, New Brunswick, across the Bay of Fundy from the Nova Scotia shoreline, and Craig prepared to race John T. Smith, the New York papers' agent and an associate of F. O. J. Smith, for use of the line. Each agent engaged a string of express horses to cross Nova Scotia and steamers to plow through the Bay of Fundy to Saint John. A Cunard steamer arrived in Halifax on 21 February, setting off a spectacular express dash which the resourceful Craig easily won. The New York editors immediately offered Craig the job as their Halifax agent for foreign news, which he accepted and held almost continuously until he was called to New York City to become agent of the New York Associated Press in 1851. John T. Smith, attempting to regain the AP's business, challenged Craig on the next Cunard arrival, was soundly beaten, and temporarily retired from the field.

When the telegraph line was completed to Halifax on 9 November 1849 Smith reappeared and beat Craig in the short dash to the Halifax telegraph office by securing his bundle of European papers first. This defeat cost Craig his New York AP job, and he promptly devised a scheme to get it back. While publicly announcing his intention to intercept the next Cunarder in a small boat beyond Halifax and express his bundle of European papers from the Nova Scotia coast to the telegraph office by fast horse, Craig secretly enlisted an accomplice to create a subterfuge. While Craig's small boat was collecting his bundle of European papers from the next Cunarder off the Nova Scotia coast, the accomplice took a bundle of old European papers prominently displaying the papers' names but hiding their dates, gave the bogus bundle a good soaking in a secluded area of the coastline, raced to the telegraph office, threw the dripping bundle onto the counter, and announced that it was Craig's European papers. A few minutes later John T. Smith arrived with his papers, was informed that he had been beaten by Craig, returned to the Cunarder without filing any news, and booked passage for Boston, a beaten man. Carrying the current papers from the small boat, Craig later arrived at a leisurely pace, filed his two-column synopsis of foreign news, and reclaimed his AP job.

Although holding the Morse telegraph franchise between New York City and Canada, F. O. J. Smith faced growing competition in his territory during the late 1840s from new telegraph companies utilizing other inventions. To retain AP's business in foreign news transmission, Smith had to convince the Nova Scotia telegraph authorities to recognize his agent at Halifax rather than Craig. In a forty-six-page pamphlet, *An Exposition of the Differences Existing between Different Presses and Different Lines of Telegraph, Respecting the Transmission of Foreign News*, published in February 1850, Smith attempted to discredit Craig, claiming that Craig had cut telegraph lines to prohibit competitors' dispatches from beating his, that his past trafficking with speculators disqualified him as a news gatherer for the press and public, and that he had privately threatened to resume carrier pigeon service of market news to speculators while continuing as AP agent. Replying the following month in his own pamphlet, Craig said, "I cannot doubt but that you will spurn the senseless remarks of Mr. Smith. . . . [N]o person, save a knave or a fool, would presume to urge objections against the arrangements between the Telegraph and the Press. . . . [N]either F. O. J. Smith, any portion of the public press, yourself or friends, nor the devil himself shall ever drive me from any position that I may see fit to assume." When the Nova Scotia company reiterated its recognition of Craig as AP's agent, Smith forbade the transmission of Craig's news dispatches on his lines. AP then encouraged construction of competing lines paralleling Smith's, and in June 1850 Smith's threat to Craig and the newspapers was neutralized by completion of an alternative line to the Canadian border.

Within a year of F. O. J. Smith's defeat, AP's executive committee asked Craig to move to New York City to replace Dr. Alexander Jones as general agent of the New York Associated Press. Jones, a pioneer in telegraphic news reporting and New York AP agent for about two years, stepped down on 19 May 1851 "after having devoted," he later said, several years "of unremitting health-wearing toil to the business." The thirty-nine-year-old Craig and his family moved into a house in Brooklyn, Craig making the daily trip to his office at 3 Hanover in lower Manhattan by one of the five steamer ferries plying the East River. The New York Associated Press he took charge of was still materializing as a partnership of the city's six leading morning papers—the *Journal of Commerce, Courier and Enquirer, Sun, Herald, Express,* and *Tribune*—to secure foreign, domestic, and harbor news principally for the use of the partners. The *New York*

Times became the seventh partner when it was founded on 18 September 1851. Although it was only one of six regional or local APs in 1851 (others existing in Boston, Philadelphia, Baltimore, the Southern states, and upstate New York), the New York Associated Press controlled the flow of foreign, Washington, and most domestic news to all the APs by virtue of its central location in the developing telegraph network. Craig inherited Jones's string of about fifteen correspondents scattered among major Eastern cities. He also inherited a competitor, the Abbot and Winans news agency, closely allied with the Morse telegraph system and serving about half of the nation's daily newspapers by late 1852. Twelve years later, Craig noted in an annual report to his New York editors that when "I commenced with you in 1851 all the papers in the city, except the six regular morning journals were violently hostile to the interests of the Association, whilst outside of the city, fully four fifths of all the papers sustained an opposition News Association."

Craig's prinicipal responsibility was to gather a daily telegraphic news report for his handful of patron editors. With many editors and Morse telegraphers aligned against him, thus limiting his sources of news and channels of transmission, Craig's mission in 1851 was twofold; to eliminate Abbot and Winans by offering a superior news report and to encourage development of telegraph companies friendly to the AP and opposing the Morse system. Neither was a modest undertaking, but together they required an organizer and manipulator of rare skill. Craig "did not increase the number of his personal friends," Frederic Hudson, a member of the AP executive committee which hired Craig as general agent, wrote twenty years later, "but amid all the trials he fought the battles mildly, pleasantly, and gentlemanly in conversation, but savagely, bitterly, and ruthlessly on paper. His correspondence was always a full-charged galvanic battery . . . but he was a faithful worker, a prompt news collector, an excellent executive officer, always on duty. . . ." Telegraph developer and historian James D. Reid portrayed Craig's business manner in even more graphic terms. Craig was "a cool, shrewd, indefatigable man, to whom processes were valuable only as they secured success. His manners were peculiar and unique. He preserved at all times the placidity of a summer's morning. His speech was as gentle and suave and courtly as if the world had made him its exceptional favorite, and he was its benignant son. Beneath this calm exterior there was a fertility of resource, a capacity of terse Saxon, especially with his pen, and an energy and force of will, which, for a time, made him a very prominent factor in the telegraphic enterprises of the period."

Improving the news report required the careful selection of trustworthy correspondents, the expansion of the the news report's length and diversity, an increase in the number of distant editors willing to supply local items to his agency, and a lean and factual approach to the news which kept telegraph tolls down and did not offend subscribing editors. Describing his efforts to enlist cooperative editors and telegraphers, Craig said in 1883, "I visited all the leading editors of the country and the managers of the numerous telegraphic companies and explained to them my purpose to establish a complete system for reporting the details of all important news by telegraph. I found a large majority of the editors violently opposed to my views, and [the Morse telegraph people] did all in their power to defeat my purpose of combining the whole daily press of the country in sustaining one substantial telegraph news organization." "After years of effort," Craig wrote in 1863, "we succeeded and compelled the Editors to abandon their arrangements and come into ours."

The factual and nonpartisan style which became the trademark of wire service reporting was outlined in an instruction sheet for prospective correspondents prepared by Craig in 1854: "We want only the *material facts* in regard to any matter or event, and those facts in the fewest words possible compatible with a clear understanding of the correspondent's meaning. All expressions of opinion upon any matter; all political, religious, or social biasses [sic] and especialy [sic] all *personal feeling* on any subject on the part of the Reporter, must be kept out of his despatches [sic]. Be brief and to the point. Omit all superfluous words."

Craig's daily dependence on telegraphic transmission of his news reports compelled him to take a role in the telegraph's development at several crucial moments. Unable to convince his New York editors to participate in telegraph construction—except for underwriting a line between Sandy Hook, at the mouth of New York Harbor, and Manhattan—Craig took the plunge twice for personal gain and for his patrons' protection. When a patent infringement decision reduced the telegraph companies between New York and Boston from three to two, one of them controlled by his old nemesis F. O. J. Smith, Craig and two associates purchased the second line in 1853 for $40,000. Three years later Craig leased the line to the rap-

idly growing American Telegraph Company, which after two more years purchased the line from Craig, with assurances that AP's news traffic would be protected on the circuit. This association with American brought Craig into contact with Cyrus W. Field, whose briefly successful transatlantic cable in 1858 gave preferential treatment to AP news bulletins from England. When this first cable failed, Craig leased a line across Newfoundland from Field to carry AP foreign news dispatches gathered by AP boats intercepting Cunard steamers off the Newfoundland coast.

Of his various infiltrations of telegraphy, however, none was more significant than Craig's unearthing and exploiting of a new telegraphic instrument invented by Kentucky music professor David E. Hughes. After bringing the Hughes device East for improvement by a competent mechanic, Craig offered it to the American Telegraph Company and Western Union, the latter still a regional company occupying portions of New York and Pennsylvania and the states of Ohio, Indiana, Michigan, and Wisconsin. The Hughes instrument, which was secure from patent infringement claims, gave these two companies the leverage they needed to subdue the Morse system and to emerge as the two giants of telegraphy at the start of the Civil War. The purchase of American by Western Union in June 1866 established the latter as the nation's first industrial monopoly.

Craig's fervent work in journalism and telegraphy led to the death of the Abbot and Winans agency in 1855. Except for an unsuccessful bid by some American Telegraph Company officials to set up a competing wire service in 1859-1860, Craig ruled over an Associated Press news monopoly during the rest of his tenure as general agent. Daily gathering all the nationally available telegraphic news dispatches, assembling them for his famous New York editors, and abbreviating them for redistribution to papers outside the city, Craig sat at the center of a vast two-way news network.

When Abraham Lincoln went to Washington, D.C., in 1861 for his first inaugural and found no Eastern publishers he could trust with his administration's announcements, the new president turned to the AP as his pipeline to the press and people of the North. His decision ended a seventy-two-year practice of releasing presidential statements through selected newspapers. In the Civil War setting of censorship, sectional patriotism, and highly visible newspaper correspondents, Craig appeared content to serve Lincoln in this way and to leave the bulk of battlefield coverage to reporters for the newspapers. For some Midwestern editors, however, who relied on Craig's reports because they could not send correspondents to the war zones, AP's terse and semiofficial wartime reports were a cause for severe criticism. These complaints eventually led to formation of the Western Associated Press, occupying territory between Pittsburgh and St. Louis, the Great Lakes and the Ohio River Valley and reaching for a role in the control of the AP system by the end of Craig's term with AP.

The end of the Civil War did not bring peace to news gathering. Many new newspapers clamored for AP news, but most were kept out by local competitors already belonging to AP. Discontent surfaced among the New York AP members because a "ring" of four weaker papers, the *Journal of Commerce, Times, Express,* and *Sun,* limited the enterprise of their stronger partners, the *Tribune, Herald,* and *World.* (The *World* had replaced the *Courier and Enquirer* in 1861.) The Western AP, emerging from the war fully organized and representing fifty Midwestern papers by late 1867, insisted on a status equal to the New York AP. Perhaps most significant, however, was the creation on 12 June 1866 of the Western Union monopoly, a gigantic new telegraphic force which made newspaper and wire service bickering seem petty and self-defeating. Fearing that these quarrels among newspaper editors would endanger revenue from regular news transmission and seeing an opportunity to wrest news gathering from newspaper control, Western Union managers, according to Craig, "expressed a desire to have me form a general news company, and give them one share more than one-half of it, pledging themselves to leave the absolute control of the organization in my hands." Word of the conspiracy reached the New York AP, which fired Craig on 5 November 1866 "for endeavoring," the *New York Tribune* later said, "while receiving pay from the New York Associated Press, to subvert it, and make a new organization which would make him the arbiter of news in America."

Although Western Union quietly backed away from the scheme after its details were revealed, Craig gained the support of the Western AP and formed the United States and European Telegraph News Association, which moved its first news report on 25 November 1866. Able in two months to attract patronage from a remarkably large number of papers, including most of the Western AP and a New York AP partner, the *World,* Craig's new wire service was, however, only a pawn in Western AP's campaign to elicit concessions from the New York AP. On 11 January 1867 the two APs and Western Union signed contracts ending hostilities and effectively killing Craig's new association. After fifteen years of forging and operating a news monopoly and of influencing the course of telegraphy, AP's "boss and dictator," as the *Chicago Tribune's* Joseph Medill once called him, was ignominiously consigned to the backwaters of business at the age of fifty-five, defeated by the schemes of the same Western Union he had assisted with the Hughes device a decade earlier.

Reportedly worth between $75,000 and $100,000 in mid-1866 but having built a large home in Brooklyn in 1860 and a twenty-five-room mansion on an eighty-acre estate near Peekskill, New York, during the war, Craig suddenly found himself overextended and declared bankruptcy in 1869. His more modest circumstances, however, did not prevent him from speculating in new telegraphic devices and systems. He promoted the illfated National Telegraph Company in 1869 and a system for "high-speed automatic" telegraphy during the 1870s. In 1879 he organized the American Rapid Telegraph Company to put his automatic system to work in the hope of attracting either some telegraphic business or a merger with Western Union. Neither occurred, and the company went under in 1884 when a bank scare stripped it of its loan capital. Craig occasionally promoted his automatic or "machine" telegraphic system in pamphlets and letters to wire service leaders during the next ten years, but the worlds of news gathering and telegraphy had passed him by. At the age of eighty-three Craig died while sitting quietly in his home in Asbury Park, New Jersey, on 5 January 1895. He was buried in Green-Wood Cemetery in Brooklyn.

When it moved its patronage from Craig's AP to Abbot and Winans in 1851, the *Boston Evening Transcript* editorially chirped, "Business is business, Mr. Craig." He did not need to be reminded, for seldom has journalism harbored a craftier, more accomplished businessman than Craig. Operating in a climate of sharp and reckless business practice, having to devise new methods of news gathering as he made his way through a rapidly changing and often hostile telegraphic setting, and yet functioning merely as the "agent" of a few leading newspapers, Craig within five years eliminated an entrenched competitor, created a wire service of national proportions, and tipped the balance in favor of telegraph proprietors friendly to his AP. A man of vast personal resourcefulness, Craig's shrewd business dealings for fifteen years in New

York City's high-pressured atmosphere contrast sharply with his seven previous years of success in the coarse and physically demanding craft of dashing after foreign news with pigeons, horses, and boats in remote and even dangerous regions. His premature departure from journalism resulted from his failure to recognize that his combative and adventuresome prewar methods were ineffective in a postwar business community which shunned competition and whose methods were incorporation, stock issues, and delicate, often secret, negotiations. Craig's pamphlets and parade of "startling" new telegraphic devices were anachronistic in a postwar world ruled by mammoth money, market manipulation, and monopoly.

References:

American Telegraph Company, Executive Committee, *Reply of the Executive Committee to the Pamphlet of D. H. Craig* (N.p., 24 August 1860);

American Telegraph Magazine, 1 (1852-1853);

Jesse A. Barney, *Rumney Then and Now, History* (Rumney, N. H.: The town, 1967);

Fourth Estate, 2 (10 January 1895): 5;

Granite Monthly, 18 (February 1895): 124;

Alvin F. Harlow, *Old Wires and New Waves, The History of the Telegraph, Telephone, and Wireless* (New York: D. Appleton-Century, 1936), pp. 172-200, 245-248, 323-324, 415-416;

Amos Kendall, *Circular, To the Stockholders of the American Telegraph Company* (N.p., 27 August 1860);

Peter R. Knights, *The Press Association War of 1866-67*, Journalism Monograph no. 6 (Austin, Tex.: Association for Education in Journalism, December 1967);

Joseph Medill, banquet address, *Associated Press of Illinois Annual Report* (1896), pp. 154-158;

Andrew D. Merkel, "Co-operative Newsgathering in Nova Scotia," *Nova Scotia Historical Society Collections*, 28 (1949): 51-60;

New York Herald, 6 January 1895, p. 12;

John W. Regan, "The Inception of the Associated Press," *Nova Scotia Historical Society Collections*, 19 (1918): 93-114;

James D. Reid, *The Telegraph in America, Its Founders, Promoters and Noted Men* (New York: Derby Brothers, 1879), pp. 341-370, 407-425;

F. O. J. Smith, *An Exposition of the Differences Existing between Different Presses and Different Lines of Telegraph, Respecting the Transmission of Foreign News, Being a Letter and Accompanying Documents, Addressed to the Government Commissioners of the Nova Scotia Telegraph* (Boston: Dutton & Wentworth, 22 February 1850);

William Henry Smith, Appendix to *Proceedings of the Western Associated Press, at the Twelfth Annual Meeting, Held at Detroit, July 19, 1876* (Detroit, 1877), pp. 25-81;

The Telegrapher, 3 (November-December 1866);

Robert Luther Thompson, *Wiring a Continent, The History of the Telegraph Industry in the United States, 1832-1866* (Princeton: Princeton University Press, 1947), pp. 217-239, 303-310, 335-342;

U.S. Congress, Senate, Committee on Education and Labor, *Report of the Committee of the Senate upon the Relations between Labor and Capital, and Testimony Taken by the Committee*, 4 volumes, 48th Congress, 2d session, 1885, 2:1265-1283.

Papers:

Three letters concerning family business constitute the Daniel H. Craig Papers at the New York Public Library, New York City. A scattering of Craig's letters are in the Ezra Cornell Papers, John M. Olin Research Library, Cornell University, Ithaca, New York; the Horace Greeley Papers, New York Public Library; the Marshall Lefferts Papers, New York Historical Society, New York City; the F. O. J. Smith Papers, Maine Historical Society, Portland; and the William Henry Smith Papers, Indiana Historical Society, Indianapolis. Numerous entries on Craig are in the credit report ledgers of the Dun & Bradstreet Collection, New York City Series, Baker Library, Harvard University, Cambridge.

George William Curtis

(25 February 1824-31 August 1892)

James S. Featherston
Louisiana State University

See also the Curtis entry in *DLB 1, The American Renaissance in New England.*

MAJOR POSITIONS HELD: Travel writer and critic, *New York Tribune* (1851-1852); political editor, *Harper's Weekly* (1863-1892).

BOOKS: *Nile Notes of a Howadji* (New York: Harper, 1851); republished as *Nile Notes. By a Traveller* (London: Bentley, 1851);

The Howadji in Syria (New York: Harper, 1852); republished as *The Wanderer in Syria* (London: Bentley, 1852);

Lotus-Eating: A Summer Book (London: Bentley, 1852; New York: Harper, 1852);

The Potiphar Papers (New York: G. P. Putnam, 1853);

Prue and I (New York: Dix, Edwards, 1856; Edinburgh: D. Douglas, 1892);

Our Best Society (New York: G. P. Putnam, 1856);

The Duty of the American Scholar to Politics and the Times: An Oration, Delivered on Tuesday, August 5, 1856, before the Literary Societies of Wesleyan University, Middletown, Conn. (New York: Dix, Edwards, 1856);

An Address, Vindicating the Right of Woman to the Elective Franchise (New York: Munson, 1858);

Reviewer Reviewed; A Few Remarks upon "Four Papers from the Boston Courier" Concerning Theodore Parker, Ralph Waldo Emerson, George William Curtis and the Abolitionists (Boston: Kent, 1858);

Trumps. A Novel (New York: Harper, 1861);

An Oration on the Annals of Rhode Island and Providence Plantations, by the Rev. Francis Vinton, D.D., and A Rhyme of Rhode Island and the Times, by George William Curtis, Esq., Delivered before the Sons of Rhode Island in New York, May 29, 1863 (New York: Printed for the association by C. A. Alvord, 1863);

The President. Why He Should Be Re-elected (New York: Daniel W. Lee, stationer & printer, 1864);

Equal Rights for All (Rochester, N.Y.: New York State Constitutional Convention, 1867); republished as *Equal Rights for Women* (New York: Office of "The Revolution," 1868);

Fair Play for Women. An Address Delivered by George William Curtis, before the American Woman Suffrage Association, Steinway Hall, New York, May 12, 1870 (Boston: Woman's Journal office, 1870);

Opening Address at the New York Meeting, 1874, by G. W. Curtis. The Work of Social Science in the United States, by F. B. Sanborn (Cambridge, Mass.: American Social Science Association, 1874);

Burgoyne's Surrender: An Oration Delivered on the One Hundredth Anniversary of the Event, October 17,

George William Curtis in 1862

1877, at Schuylerville, N.Y. (New York: Baker & Goodwin, 1877);

The Public Duty of Educated Men. The Oration of the Honorary Chancellor of Union University, Hon. George William Curtis, LL.D., Delivered at the Commencement of Union College, June 27th, 1877 (Albany, N.Y.: J. Munsell, printer, 1878);

The Life, Character and Writings of William Cullen Bryant. A Commemorative Address Delivered before the New York Historical Society at the Academy of Music, December 30, 1878 (New York: Scribners, 1878);

Essays from the North American Review, edited by Allen Thorndike Rice (New York: D. Appleton, 1879);

Machine Politics and the Remedy: A Lecture Delivered in Chickering Hall, New York, May 20th, 1880 (New York: Independent Republican Association, 1880);

Robert Burns: An Address by George William Curtis at the Unveiling of the Statue of the Poet, in Central Park, New-York, October 2, 1880 (New York: For private circulation, 1880);

The Progress of Reform: An Address Delivered at the Annual Meeting of the National Civil-Service Reform League (New York: Published for the National Civil-Service Reform League, 1883);

An Address at the Unveiling of the Statue of George Washington, upon the Spot Where He Took the Oath as First President of the United States (New York: Harper, 1883);

Wendell Phillips, by George William Curtis, and The War for the Union, by Wendell Phillips (New York: J. B. Alden, 1884);

The Year's Work in Civil-Service Reform: An Address Delivered at the Annual Meeting of the National Civil-Service Reform League (New York: Published for the National Civil-Service Reform League, 1884);

Civil-Service Reform under the Present National Administration: An Address Delivered at the Annual Meeting of the National Civil-Service Reform League August 5, 1885 (New York: Published for the National Civil-Service Reform League, 1885);

The Situation: An Address Delivered at the Annual Meeting of the National Civil-Service Reform League, August 4, 1886 (New York: Published for the National Civil-Service Reform League, 1886);

The Reason and the Result of Civil-Service Reform: An Address Delivered before the National Civil-Service Reform League at Its Annual Meeting Held May 29, 1888 (New York: Published for the National Civil-Service Reform League, 1888);

Address Prepared for the Annual Meeting of the New York Civil-Service Reform Association (May 1, 1889), by the President (New York: Published for the Civil-Service Reform Association, 1889);

From the Easy Chair, 3 volumes (New York: Harper, 1891-1894);

Washington Irving: A Sketch (New York: The Grolier Club, 1891);

James Russell Lowell: An Address (New York: Harper, 1892);

"Party and Patronage": An Address Prepared for the Annual Meeting of the National Civil-Service Reform League (April 28, 1892). By the President (New York: Published for the National Civil-Service Reform League, 1892);

Other Essays from the Easy Chair (New York: Harper, 1893);

Orations and Addresses of George William Curtis, edited by Charles Eliot Norton (New York: Harper, 1894);

Literary and Social Essays (New York: Harper, 1894);

Emerson (New York & London: Putnam's, 1896);

Hawthorne (New York & London: Putnam's, 1896);

Longfellow (New York & London: Putnam's, 1896);

Ars Recte Vivendi: Being Essays Contributed to "The Easy Chair" (New York & London: Harper, 1898).

OTHER: Andrew Jackson Downing, *Rural Essays*, edited by Curtis (New York: G. P. Putnam, 1853);

Theodore Winthrop, *Cecil Dreeme*, biographical sketch of Winthrop by Curtis (New York: Holt, 1876);

Modern Ghosts: Selected and Translated from the Works of Guy de Maupassant, Pedro Antonio de Alarcón, Alexander L. Kielland, Leopold Kompert, Gustavo Adolfo Becquer, and Giovanni Magherini-Graziani, introduction by Curtis (New York & London: Harper, 1890);

The Writings of John Lothrop Motley, edited by Curtis (New York & London: Harper, 1900);

The Correspondence of John Lothrop Motley, edited by Curtis (New York & London: Harper, 1900);

A Pocket Book of the Early American Humorists, edited by Curtis (Boston: Small, Maynard, 1907).

George William Curtis, a man of great versatility, high ideals, and immense charm, was widely admired as a journalist, author, orator, educator, reformer, and political leader during the last half of the nineteenth century. As a journalist, he wrote for the *New York Tribune* before becoming an editor and writer for the short-lived *Putnam's Monthly*. He was a columnist for *Harper's Monthly* and political editor for *Harper's Weekly* for many years and contributed to other magazines and newspapers. As an author, Curtis produced fiction as well as books of essays, travel, satire, and biography; he also wrote poetry. Curtis was one of the nation's most popular orators, a speaker of great courage who was not afraid to face down a mob. Although he had little formal education, Curtis served as a regent and later as chancellor of the University of the State of New York. He was a leader in Republican party politics, both nationally and in New York State, and he was a tireless worker for civil service reform.

Curtis was born on 25 February 1824 in Providence, Rhode Island, near Brown University, an institution that would later deny him admission but would still later confer upon him two honorary degrees. His father, the elder George Curtis, a successful banker, was descended from the first settlers of Massachusetts; his mother, born Mary Elizabeth Burrill, was the daughter of a United States senator from Rhode Island. After only five years of marriage the mother died, leaving her grief stricken husband to care for George and his older brother, James Burrill Curtis, who was usually called by his middle name.

For the next several years, the father managed to rear the boys with the help of relatives. In 1830 he sent them to a boarding school in Jamaica Plains, near Boston, where George remained from the ages of five to eleven. In 1835 the father married Julia B. Bridgham, also a member of a prominent Rhode Island family. The father was thirty-eight at the time of his second marriage; his bride was twenty-four. She was charming, talented, and vivacious and was more of a companion than a stepmother to the boys. Even after she had four boys of her own, she continued to shower affection on her two stepsons.

Curtis and Burrill returned to Providence when their father remarried, and Curtis continued his schooling there. In 1836 Burrill was admitted to Brown University; he attended for four years but did not graduate. The university rejected George two years later, after he dismally failed the entrance examinations. George, however, continued to acquire an education through reading and seeking out such literary men and women as Ralph Waldo Emerson, Richard Henry Dana, John Neal, and Margaret Fuller when they happened to visit Providence.

In 1839 the Curtis family moved to New York City, and George, then only fifteen, decided to give up his studies and enter the business world. He worked for one year at an importing firm and then gladly returned to his studies. He later said that he read the "usual college courses" under the direction of tutors. In the spring of 1842 he and his brother went to Brook Farm in West Roxbury, Massachusetts, for a stay of eighteen months. Brook Farm was a cooperative community established by a group eager to put transcendental religious principles into action. Work was to be shared among all, selfishness eliminated, and a practical Christianity established. Brook Farm was also a school, a good one, with its teachers including some of the more learned Americans of the time. The Curtis brothers, described as looking like "two young Greek gods," profited greatly from their Brook Farm experience, developing physically through farm labor and furthering their intellectual and moral education.

After returning home for a year, the brothers went to Concord, Massachusetts, to do farm work and associate with such men as Emerson, Nathaniel Hawthorne, Henry Thoreau, Bronson Alcott, Ellery Channing, and George P. Bradford. The brothers helped Thoreau build his cabin at Walden Pond. George spent many hours with Hawthorne, whom he grew to admire more and more. He frequently visited Emerson, a man he likened to "Plato and Bacon, and the other great teachers." He was greatly influenced by Emerson, particularly by Emerson's individualism, and to a lesser degree by Hawthorne and Thoreau. During some of his leisure time at Concord, George wrote poetry, including "Autumn Song," which was published in the Brook Farm paper, the *Harbinger*, 4 October 1845.

George and Burrill Curtis next decided to take a "grand tour" of Europe. As a biographer Gordon Milne later wrote: "Though many people might criticize their leisurely and unorthodox preparation for life, George and Burrill regarded it as a truly liberal education. Fortunately, their kind and patient father was willing to foot the bill." George sailed from New York on 1 August 1846 on the packet ship *Nebraska*; Burrill followed in the fall. After twenty-eight days at sea, the *Nebraska* reached the strait of Gibraltar and sailed into the Mediterranean past Barcelona to Marseilles. George toured France, Italy—where Burrill joined him in Rome in December—Germany, Austria, Switzerland, Holland, and elsewhere before sailing to Malta and then visiting Egypt, Jerusalem, and Syria. In the summer of 1849 George and Burrill parted company, with George returning home and

Burrill remaining in Paris to enjoy the life of an artist. Burrill later became an Anglican clergyman.

During his travels, George Curtis began his journalistic career by writing letters to the *New York Tribune*. He also was gathering material for several books which would be published within two years after his return. The first book, *Nile Notes of a Howadji—Howadji* is Arabic for traveler—was begun during the summer of 1850 and completed early in the winter. It was published in March 1851 by Harper and Brothers in the United States and simultaneously by Richard Bentley in London. Despite its florid style and sentimentality, the book was warmly received and critically acclaimed. As William Dean Howells later commented: "How well that luscious expression, those gaudy alliterations, those vague allusions, those melting hues, that sadness and sweetness of the young poet's spirit satisfied the utmost desire of the time." With the publication of this first book, Curtis found himself

to be a "kind of lion," and he was wined and dined in New York, Providence, and Boston. He also was given an assignment by the *Tribune* to tour summer resorts in the eastern United States and send back articles. During this time, some of his friends began calling him "Howadji." A second book of his travels, *The Howadji in Syria*, was published in April 1852, again by Harper and Bentley. The reviewers again commented favorably, particularly those abroad: *The London News* called it an "unrhymed poem," and the *London Morning Herald* gushed that it was "another fragant record of Oriental life by the delightful pen which dropped spices and honey so luxuriantly in the unmatched *Nile Notes of a Howadji*." Meanwhile, Curtis was writing art and music criticism for the *Tribune* and revising the articles about his tour of the resorts for publication in book form. This book, *Lotus-Eating: A Summer Book*, appeared in London in June 1852 and was published in the United States two months later. Although

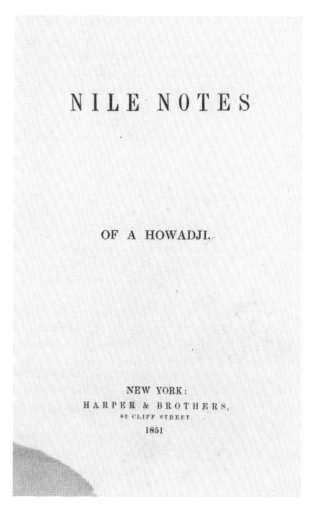

Illustrated title page and title page for Curtis's first book

filled with rhapsodic descriptions and literary allusions, the book is written in a more restrained and simpler style than his previous ones and anticipates the "clear, smooth prose" of his later works. During the summer of 1852 Curtis also wrote articles on Emerson, Hawthorne, Henry Wadsworth Longfellow, and George Bancroft for *Homes of American Authors,* a project conceived by the publisher George P. Putnam.

Putnam brought out a new magazine, *Putnam's Monthly,* in January 1853. The editorial board consisted of Charles F. Briggs, Parke Godwin, and Curtis. Curtis contacted his friends Emerson and Hawthorne, whose names, he knew, would lend tremendous prestige to the new magazine. Hawthorne never contributed but many others did, including Emerson, Thoreau, Longfellow, James Russell Lowell, Herman Melville, and John Greenleaf Whittier. Thoreau, incidentally, twice objected heatedly when Curtis deleted passages from his work. Thoreau demanded that his series "A Yankee in Canada" be discontinued after three parts of it had been published; he also asked that the manuscript be returned. Thoreau again objected and asked that the manuscript be returned when alterations were made in his series "Cape Cod."

Putnam's Monthly lasted only four years despite its high quality; its failure was attributed to a lack of mass appeal rather than faulty business management. Curtis himself believed the magazine was too highbrow to attract a large readership. Curtis wrote poems, art and music criticism, book reviews, travel articles, stories, and essays for the new magazine, as well as reading manuscripts and correcting proofs.

During this period, Curtis found time to start on another occupation: lecturing. It was probably money that lured him to the lecture platform. The "lyceum," or lecture series, had become a popular institution among Americans thirsty for culture and knowledge. Towns throughout the East and Middle West sponsored talks on any and all subjects by famous lecturers. A lecturer could earn as much as $2,000 in a relatively short season, a substantial sum in those days. Curtis took his first lecture tour early in 1853 through New York State, and he pleased audiences from the start. Milne explained Curtis's success as a lecturer: "His fame as an author had preceded him, and the many who read and enjoyed the Howadji books were prepared to be well disposed toward him. Even if not prepared, the audience, particularly the women, were quickly won over by his attractive appearance, his slim and faultlessly dressed figure, his ruddy complexion,

deep blue eyes, wavy hair and ready smile." Curtis was also blessed with a "resonant and mellifluous" voice.

In addition to his work with *Putnam's Monthly* and his lectures, Curtis took on still another task when he agreed to write the "Easy Chair" column for *Harper's Monthly,* beginning in October 1853. He shared the column with Donald G. Mitchell at first, but he wrote it alone beginning in April 1854. Curtis would write the monthly column for nearly forty years, except for a six-month period of illness in 1873 when Thomas Bailey Aldrich and Dr. Samuel Osgood filled in for him. The tone of Curtis's columns was almost conversational as he discussed an endless variety of subjects. He reminisced; analyzed current events; commented on music, drama, and literature; presented biographical sketches; and urged support of good causes. His style was smooth and urbane, but his moods varied from critical to humorous, grave to fanciful. During 1853 Curtis also published *The Potiphar Papers,* a series of satirical sketches lampooning New York social life.

His opposition to slavery drew Curtis into the political arena during the presidential race between James Buchanan and John C. Frémont in the summer of 1856. Buchanan favored compromise with the Southern slavery forces while Frémont, who was endorsed by the newly organized Republican party, was vehemently opposed to compromise. Curtis campaigned for Frémont, speaking first on Staten Island, then in Yonkers with William Cullen Bryant, and in upper New York State. Curtis continued campaigning, denouncing the moral and economic curse of slavery, into the fall while traveling through New England, Pennsylvania, New Jersey, and New York. Although his efforts for Frémont failed, Curtis comforted himself with the knowledge that the antislavery movement had gained an unstoppable momentum.

During the summer of 1854, while vacationing at Newport, Rhode Island, Curtis had fallen in love with Anna, the eldest daughter of Francis George Shaw. Curtis was a friend of the family and had known Anna previously, but she was no longer the "tomboyish" child he remembered: she was a tall and handsome young woman, and Curtis was enraptured. They became engaged the following year and were married on 26 November 1856 at a Unitarian church on Staten Island, where the Shaw family had been living elegantly, but not ostentatiously, for some years and where the newlyweds also made their home. Their union was to produce a son and two daughters. Earlier in 1856, Curtis

Curtis's wife, Anna Shaw Curtis

had published *Prue and I,* a collection of fictional sketches which had previously appeared in *Putnam's Monthly.*

During the winter and spring of 1856-1857 Curtis devoted most of his time to his duties at *Putnam's Monthly.* The old management had failed, and Curtis had taken over the magazine with new partners. Curtis was unable to save the magazine, and he lost all of the money he had invested along with between $60,000 and $70,000 of his father-in-law's money. Shaw was convinced that his son-in-law would repay him, and Curtis eventually did even though it meant more and more snow-stalled trains and grubby hotels as he increased his number of lectures.

By 1857 Curtis had been writing the "Easy Chair" columns in *Harper's Monthly* for four years. Now he decided to take on another task for Harper and Brothers and write a column for the big circulation *Harper's Weekly.* The new column, "The Lounger," was similar to but more superficial than the "Easy Chair" essays, and it continued for only six years. Curtis commented on a wide variety of subjects in "The Lounger," and he entertained and informed his readers, which was all he had set out

to do. He continued his lecture tours, contributed to the *Atlantic Monthly,* and worked on a novel, *Trumps,* which was published in 1861.

Although he sometimes spoke on literary matters, Curtis increasingly dealt with politics, and he joined such orators as Henry Ward Beecher and Wendell Phillips in speaking out against slavery. He sometimes faced hostile crowds. In Philadelphia on 15 December 1859, a mob estimated from "four to six to eight thousand" people milled outside the lecture hall. Proslavery forces inside the hall heckled the speaker. Bricks were thrown through the windows, and two attempts were made to set fire to the building. Although there were 500 policemen on duty and many arrests were made, tumult prevailed. Despite the turmoil, Curtis delivered his speech calmly and left unharmed. It was a courageous performance.

Curtis rose to national political prominence in the years from 1860 to 1865, and he was once described as "the most distinguished citizen in public life who has never held public office." He attended the Republican national convention in Chicago during May 1860 as a member of the New York delegation and electrified the convention with an antislavery speech insisting that the "all men are created equal" phrase from the Declaration of Independence be included in the Republican platform. He campaigned throughout the summer and fall of 1861 for Abraham Lincoln, and the following year he was elected as a delegate to the New York State Republican convention. Also in 1862 he won the Republican nomination for representative to Congress but was defeated in the election because his district was heavily Democratic. As the Civil War progressed, Curtis became deeply concerned about the care of liberated slaves. Curtis and his father-in-law helped to establish the Freedmen's Bureau to educate the ex-slaves in their duties as citizens. Because of his age and his responsibilities as the father of a family of five, Curtis never served in the military, but he vigorously supported the Union war effort in his writings and lectures.

In December 1863 Curtis suspended his "Lounger" column in *Harper's Weekly* and became its political editor, a post he was to hold until his death nearly thirty years later. Journalism historian Frank Luther Mott had this to say about Curtis's role at *Harper's Weekly:* "Curtis, recognized as the editorial head of the paper, was in reality purely a political editor. He was responsible for two or three editorials a week, and he did this work without the least trouble or responsibility for the details of the

Curtis's home on Staten Island

paper, and with no necessity of even being at the office. During his service with the *Weekly*, therefore, a succession of managing editors attended to such details. . . ." Curtis was perfectly content with his dual role as "Easy Chair" columnist for the *Monthly* and political editor of the *Weekly*. He enjoyed freedom from editorial chores along with the freedom to say what he wished. His salary, estimated at as much as $25,000 a year, was princely for the times. He turned down other attractive offers, including the editorship of the *New York Times*.

In 1864 Curtis assumed still another role, this time as an educator, when he was named a regent of the University of the State of New York. Despite the name, this was not a college of higher learning but an organization which supervised the state's system of education. Curtis worked hard over the years for educational improvements, fostering among other projects adult university extension courses.

The affluent Curtis family now alternated its residences between Staten Island and a summer home in the Berkshire hills in Ashfield, Massachusetts. Curtis was active in local affairs at both places. His supporters in 1856 urged that Curtis be given an important foreign post, preferably the ministry to France, but Curtis was instead offered the less desirable position of minister to Egypt, and he turned it down. He was considered for but failed to win a Republican nomination for United States senator from New York in 1866. In 1869 he was nominated by acclamation at the Republican convention for secretary of state of New York, but he rejected the nomination. During May and part of June he served as a professor at the newly organized Cornell University in Ithaca. The following year, he was proposed as the Republican candidate for governor of New York, and he let his name stand, but Curtis lost the nomination to another candidate. During these years, Curtis also battled for woman's suffrage and became interested in civil service reform.

President Grant appointed a commission to study civil service reform, with Curtis as chairman,

Curtis's summer home in Ashfield, Massachusetts

in 1871. The commission spent many months in Washington preparing rules and regulations, and Grant approved its work. Curtis was dissatisfied with Grant's efforts to follow the commission's recommendations, although he did not question the president's good intentions. He resigned as chairman of the commission, and on 18 March 1873 he wrote Grant: "As the circumstances under which several appointments have been recently made seem to me to show an abandonment of both the spirit and letter of the Civil Service regulations, I respectfully resign my position as a member of the advisory board of the Civil Service." However, Curtis continued his fight for civil service reform.

Curtis supported Rutherford B. Hayes as the Republican presidential candidate in 1876, and after his victory Hayes sought Curtis's advice on civil service reform. Through his secretary of state, William Evarts, Hayes offered Curtis his choice of diplomatic posts. Curtis turned down the attractive offer. Hayes also revived the defunct Civil Service Commission and tried to put into effect the rules

formulated by Curtis. Hayes found his efforts at reform thwarted at times by a hostile Congress, and progress proceeded much too slowly to suit Curtis. James Garfield became the Republican presidential candidate in 1880, and after his victory he surprised Curtis by endeavoring to carry out civil service reform. After Garfield was mortally wounded by a disappointed office-seeker in the summer of 1881, public sentiment was aroused against the spoils system. When Chester Arthur succeeded Garfield, he recommended an appropriation to renew the work of the Civil Service Commission. Arthur also endorsed the Pendleton Bill, which set up a civil service merit system earlier recommended by Curtis.

Curtis continued his lectures, his column in *Harper's Monthly*, and his work for *Harper's Weekly* during his political and civil service reform efforts. Although he was free to say what he wished in editorials in *Harper's Weekly*, he did not have control of overall policy, and at times this created problems. Curtis was particularly distressed when an article appeared in February 1875 severely criticizing his friend Carl Schurz. He protested to the publishers and was given broader supervisory powers. Difficulties still arose, however. Curtis was occasionally at odds with the management but frequently at odds with Thomas Nast, *Harper's Weekly*'s political cartoonist. According to Milne, "The two men were temperamentally very different. Nast was brusque, Curtis suave and kindly, and they used methods which were diametrically opposed. Nast tried 'to hit the enemy between the eyes and knock him down;' Curtis treated his opponents much more gently. . . . The shrewd Harper brothers, aware that both Curtis and Nast had large followings, kept the two together, allowing them, insofar as possible, to pursue independent courses, and stepping in when necessary to preserve peace." Nast sometimes used cartoons as brass knuckles, and Curtis did not believe that "the cartoon was a gentleman's weapon—at least not a weapon to be used on a gentleman."

Meanwhile, Curtis's "Easy Chair" columns were widely read and admired and were published in books. His patriotic addresses and eulogies were widely acclaimed. On the political front, a climactic event came in 1884 when Curtis, Schurz, E. L. Godwin, R. H. Dana III, and others bolted the Republican party and formed an independent group familiarly known as the "Mugwumps" in opposition to James Blaine, the Republican presidential nominee. The Mugwumps threw their support to the Democratic candidate, Grover Cleveland, and some of them, chiefly Curtis and Schurz, spoke on behalf of Cleveland throughout the summer and fall.

In 1886 Curtis was named vice-chancellor of the University of the State of New York, and four years later he became chancellor. In the summer of 1892 he was stricken by an illness which his doctors could not diagnose but which apparently was cancer of the stomach. He lingered through August, "cheerful and coherent until the end." He died at 2:40 A.M. on 31 August 1892 at the age of sixty-eight, with his family at his bedside; he was buried in New Dorp Cemetery, Staten Island. His reputation remained at its zenith for some years after his death. During the 1890s, his work was collected and reprinted, poems were written in his memory, and articles appeared in periodicals throughout the country. During the early years of the twentieth century the emphasis began to shift from Curtis as a literary and journalistic figure to Curtis as a political person.

Curtis's books are seldom read today, and his contributions to journalism have been largely forgotten. The late Frank Luther Mott described Curtis as a gentle, aristocratic essayist who was a "critic of his times" but who lacked "the stuff of which great popular editors are made."

Letters:

Early Letters of George Wm. Curtis to John S. Dwight: Brook Farm and Concord, edited by George Willis Cooke (New York & London: Harper, 1898).

References:

Edward Cary, *George William Curtis* (Boston & New York: Houghton Mifflin, 1894);

Parke Godwin, *George William Curtis: A Commemorative Address* (New York: Harper, 1893);

Gordon Milne, *George William Curtis: The Genteel Tradition* (Bloomington: Indiana University Press, 1956);

Frank Luther Mott, *A History of American Magazines 1850-1865* (Cambridge: Harvard University Press, 1938);

Mott, *A History of American Magazines 1865-1885* (Cambridge: Harvard University Press, 1938).

Papers:

George William Curtis's letters are held by the Abernethy Library, Middlebury College, Middlebury, Vermont; the Boston Athenaeum; the Boston Public Library; Brown University Library; Fruitlands Museum and Harvard College Library, Harvard University; the George William Curtis Collection, Ashfield, Massachusetts; the Huntington Library; Henry Wadsworth Longfellow House, Cambridge, Massachusetts; the Library of Congress; the Massachusetts Historical Society; the New York Public Library; the Paulist Fathers, New York; the Mrs. Pierre Jay Collection, New York; the Rutherford B. Hayes Memorial Library, Fremont, Ohio; and the Staten Island Institute of Arts and Sciences, New York.

John M. Daniel

(24 October 1825-30 March 1865)

Charles A. Fair
Sam Houston State University

MAJOR POSITION HELD: Editor in chief, *Richmond* (Va.) *Examiner* (1848-1853; 1860-1865).

BOOK: *The Richmond Examiner During the War; or, Writings of John M. Daniel, With a Memoir of His Life by His Brother,* edited by Frederick S. Daniel (New York: Printed for the author, 1868).

As the editor in chief of the Democratic newspaper in intensely Whig Richmond, Virginia, John M. Daniel became a major editorial leader nationally for his party and a much-hated man by his detractors. A political activist, Daniel was an ardent defender of slavery, a champion of Southern rights, and an advocate of sovereignty for the Confederate states. He was also among the loudest voices speaking out against the leadership of President Jefferson Davis.

Daniel's roots were in the law. Although he was the son of a country doctor, his ancestry included Thomas Stone, a lawyer and a signer of the Declaration of Independence; and his great-uncle, with whom he lived as a teenager, was Justice Peter V. Daniel of the United States Supreme Court.

John Moncure Daniel was born in Stafford County, Virginia, on 24 October 1825 to John Moncure and Elizabeth Mitchell Daniel. At age fifteen, he went to live with his father's uncle, the jurist, in Richmond. The youth had no formal education but had ready access to the private libraries of neighbors and often wrote comments in the margins of the borrowed books. A decision was made for him to pursue a career in law, and he was sent to Fredericksburg, Virginia, to read law under the tutelage of Judge John Tayloe Lomax. When his father died in 1845, Daniel returned to Richmond to find a job and help raise his brother; he abandoned his plans for a career as a lawyer.

Daniel secured a job as librarian in a small library operated by the Patrick Henry Society. Although the job paid only $100 per year, it did permit him to feed his passion for reading. He also began writing articles, and a friend encouraged him to submit some of them to a newspaper. As a result of his submissions, Daniel was offered the editorship of a monthly agricultural magazine, the *Southern Planter.* He worked there but a short while before he was asked to write for the new Democratic newspaper, the *Richmond Semi-Weekly Examiner,* which was published by Bennett M. DeWitt and J. J. Wright. An issue of the paper in December 1847 noted that "John M. Daniel, Esq. is connected with the editorial department of this paper." Within a few months, he became editor in chief and part proprietor.

In the 1840s the Democrats were in power in both Washington and Virginia, but the city of Richmond was a Whig stronghold. "Hence, the *Examiner,* during the first state of its existence, encountered many enemies, mostly political, not a few personal, owing to the style in which it was conducted," Daniel's biographer-brother Frederick S. Daniel wrote.

John M. Daniel was one of the last of the nineteenth-century American journalists who practiced a personal approach to the news. His paper reflected his personality, and little was published without his personal touch. Judge Robert W. Hughes, who edited the *Examiner* in Daniel's absence, said that "Mr. Daniel was even a better editor than writer. He corrected and strengthened everything which went into the columns; often not accepting advertisements."

Daniel took on the task of leading the Democratic party with eagerness. "With all of the enthusiasm of youth, and all of the consciousness of his journalistic powers, he enlisted under its banner, confident of being on the high road to promotion," Hughes said. Daniel was not one to mince words, and "the effect of such a violently offensive system was to enhance the prospects of the party and of the paper, but also, as well, to create for the editor a host of personal enemies, some of which, suffering from the incurable wounds produced by his ridicule and sarcasm, entertained towards him an intense and bitter animosity as long as he lived," his brother recalled.

One writer of that time, a Dr. Peticolas, said

that Daniel "was no sooner engaged in a newspaper controversy than he forgot, or at least threw behind him, the sense even of decency and heaped upon his adversary epithets which ought never to have defiled the columns of a respectable journal. . . . It is not unsafe to assert that he never had a friend with whom, at some time, he did not have a misunderstanding."

George W. Bagby, who wrote editorials for Daniel, recalled that as soon as Daniel arrived at the newspaper office, he would lay a Derringer, "which he carried in his hand for any emergency," on a large table in the middle of the room. After lighting a cigar, Daniel would read the proofs of news articles, legislative or Congressional proceedings, editorials, and even proofs of the ads. Bagby said that Daniel "was the only newspaper proprietor I ever heard of who would throw out, without hesitation, paying advertisements, sometimes of much importance to advertisers, in order to make room for editorials, or for contributions which particularly pleased him."

He did not throw out too many advertisements, however, because his newspaper prospered, and Daniel enjoyed his wealth. He had a large three-story brick home; his three slaves resided in a four-room building behind the house. He also had two rooms on the second floor of the *Examiner* building, where he would seat himself in a sort of barber's chair and receive visitors to the newspaper.

Many considered the *Examiner*, under Daniel's control, to be the most influential newspaper in the South. Among those admirers were Richmond poet-author Edgar Allan Poe and President Franklin Pierce. Poe, whom Daniel had assisted financially, revised his principal poems for publication in the *Examiner,* and, at the time of his death in 1849, was under contract to furnish literary articles for the newspaper. Pierce was pleased enough with the support the *Examiner* had provided the Democratic party that he appointed Daniel chargé d'affaires to the court of Victor Emmanuel II, king of Sardinia. Daniel sold the *Examiner* but retained a right to buy it back upon his return from Europe. While in Turin, Daniel was as outspoken about political affairs as he had been in Richmond. He demanded the same immunities for an Italian naturalized in the United States as for any other American visiting Italy and threatened a disruption of diplomatic relations if his demand was not met. Secretary of State William L. Marcy did not support this threat, however. Daniel again made headlines when he escorted an uninvited guest to a royal ball in Turin; this resulted in a scandal heard throughout Europe. He turned down a request by Giuseppe Garibaldi to have the United States annex Nice, claiming that such a move would be a violation of the Monroe Doctrine. His last skirmish in Turin came after a letter he had written to a Richmond friend was imprudently published in the United States and in Europe. The letter belittled some members of the royal court and prompted Daniel to offer to resign his diplomatic post. The offer was not accepted.

What did bring Daniel back to the United States in 1860 was word that South Carolina was planning to secede from the Union. Daniel again took up the editorial reins of the *Richmond Examiner.* He believed in the right to secede but thought that the action of the first few states to secede was a blunder, because it compelled all slave states to withdraw from the Union. Still, he was considered by some to be the earliest apostle of secession in Virginia. Indeed, he said that the breakup of the Union "has got to come to this at last, and the sooner, the better." He called for Jefferson Davis, the president of the Confederacy, to move his headquarters from Montgomery, Alabama, to Richmond—"the real capital"—and estimated that such a move would be worth 50,000 troops for the South.

Soon after Davis arrived in Richmond, however, Daniel began to see signs of governmental mismanagement; he concluded that Davis was not the man to lead the Confederacy. The *Examiner,* by then a daily newspaper, became the champion of Southern rights and was one of the few voices calling for sovereignty. His attacks on the Davis administration became more strident. Despite the protests of President Davis, Daniel advocated military conscription, then volunteered to go to the battlefields as an aide first to General John B. Floyd and then to General Ambrose P. Hill. Daniel received the rank of major, and his editorials were reportedly read to the troops in the field.

Daniel went to war to find glory and to gain some visible sign that he had served. "I hate pain; I cannot bear it, and yet I should like to be able to show an honorable scar in this cause," he wrote. He got his wish in June 1862, when he was wounded in action near Mechanicsville, northeast of Richmond. Daniel and his valet and cook—both slaves—returned to Richmond. Daniel supported the institution of slavery and felt that Negroes should not be considered men in the same sense as whites.

His wounded arm earned him a second wound in 1864. After a bitter editorial attack upon the Davis administration, and particularly its treasurer, Edward A. Elmore, Daniel was challenged to a duel, one of nine he fought in his life. Daniel was unable to raise his pistol, and Elmore shot him in the foot.

As the summer of 1864 came, Daniel was losing all hope that the South could win the war. He began calling for peace by negotiation. Although he was less than forty years old, his health began to fail, and by the summer's end, he rarely wrote for the *Examiner.* Early in 1865, he won a bout with pneumonia but contracted acute phthisis, a form of tuberculosis.

He died on 30 March 1865, three days before the collapse of the Confederacy that he had predicted. The last issue of the *Examiner,* printed on the day before the Confederate troops fled Richmond, published his obituary. In their desire to leave nothing of value behind, the fleeing troops set fire to much of the city and the *Examiner* office was destroyed in the blaze.

Although some of Daniel's views were unpopular, his sense of professionalism and his journalistic ethics were rare in his day. Daniel castigated Confederate generals for trying to get inaccurate reports of battles into print and fought for access and for objective reporting of the war. He also set some simple but demanding standards for newspaper writers. "Write plain English," he said. "It is good enough to convey all that you should have to say."

References:

Dr. George W. Bagby, *John M. Daniel's Latchkey, A Memoir of the Late Editor of the Richmond Examiner* (Lynchburg, Va.: J. P. Bell, 1868);

R. W. Hughes, *"Editors of the Past." Lecture of Judge Robert W. Hughes, Delivered Before the Virginia Press Association, at Their Annual Meeting at Charlottesville, Va., on the 22d of June, 1897* (Richmond, Va.: W. E. Jones, printer, 1897).

Benjamin Henry Day

(10 April 1810-21 December 1889)

Nickieann Fleener
University of Utah

MAJOR POSITIONS HELD: Founder, publisher, and editor, *New York Sun* (1833-1838).

Benjamin Henry Day revolutionized American journalism with the introduction of the *New York Sun.* Costing one cent and emphasizing local news and humorous human interest stories, the *Sun* was intended for an audience largely ignored by the other New York newspapers, which cost six cents and stressed national economic and political news. Penny papers had been tried before, but all had failed. With the *Sun,* Day proved that a penny paper could be successful and that a much wider audience for American newspapers existed than had previously been imagined. By choosing stories with high human interest value and strong local ties over stories about national political or economic issues, Day redefined newsworthiness. In addition, he brought the "London Plan" of newspaper distribution, under which newsboys hawked newspapers in the streets, to America. Day's unique news formula and his use of direct marketing techniques were highly successful, and within two years the *Sun* had the highest daily circulation of any newspaper in the world.

Day was born in Springfield, Massachusetts, in 1810 to Henry Day, a hatter, and Mary Ely Day. His ancestors Robert and Mary Day had come to Massachussets from England in 1634 and eventually helped found Hartford, Connecticut. Day's mother was a direct descendant of William Brewster, fourth signer of the *Mayflower* Compact.

In 1824, when he was fourteen, Day was apprenticed to Samuel Bowles of the *Springfield Republican.* Day was one of that newspaper's first apprentices and remained with the *Republican* for six years learning the printing trade. Because he joined the *Republican* so soon after the paper's

Benjamin Henry Day

founding, Day was able to view closely the growing pains a newspaper endured as it struggled to establish itself. The editorial formula that initially guided the *Republican* was typical of the times. As historian Richard Hooker observed, the paper contained "a miscellaneous assortment of family reading suited to the taste of the period . . . news about pretty much everything but the life of Springfield itself." Bowles was new to Springfield and as his familiarity with the community grew so did the number of *Republican* column inches devoted to local news. Gradually, Day found himself setting fewer items copied from other newspapers and more items about local events, such as the annual Fourth of July celebration and improvements to navigation on the nearby Connecticut River. Typical of the local items was a paragraph about the formation of a Springfield branch of the American Colonization Society, an organization devoted to solving racial problems by helping blacks to settle elsewhere. The story noted that "a respectable meeting of gentlemen met at the old court house and adopted resolutions to promote the 'colonizing' with their consent, free people of color resident in our country, in Africa or such other places as Con-

gress shall deem expedient." Day also saw Bowles include light, humorous items, such as: "We shall publish no marriage unless the writing is accompanied by a piece of the wedding cake, and a little wine if convenient—but we are not particular as to that." And Day observed the consequences of the *Republican*'s politicization when the newspaper lost a lucrative government printing contract after Andrew Jackson's election because the paper had supported John Quincy Adams during the campaign. Thus, when Day finished his apprenticeship in 1830 and went to New York to work as a compositor in the offices of the *Evening Post,* the *Journal of Commerce,* and the *Commercial Advertiser,* he carried with him not only knowledge of the printing trade but also knowledge of how a newspaper evolved and adapted to its environment.

At the *Journal of Commerce,* Day worked beside David Ramsey, a compositor who strongly believed that a penny paper could survive. Apparently Ramsey and Day passed much time in the composing room discussing Ramsey's belief that the public would respond enthusiastically to an inexpensive paper which emphasized human interest stories over politics. The idea was not uniquely Ramsey's: penny papers had been tried in Boston, Philadelphia, and New York, but all had failed. Nevertheless, Ramsey's unyeilding faith in the idea impressed Day. According to historian Frank O'Brien, Ramsey even intended to call his paper the *Sun.*

On 13 September 1831, Day married Eveline Shepard. The Days had three sons and one daughter. One son, Benjamin Day, Jr., invented the ben-day engraving process used for shading in printing illustrations. Another son, Clarence Shepard Day, was the model used by his son Clarence Shepard Day, Jr., in his book *Life With Father* (1935). Day opened his own print shop with money saved from his employment. He began the business with very little capital, and as economic conditions tightened, he found himself in a difficult position. Adding to a general depression and a financial panic was a virulent cholera epidemic which hit New York in 1832 and killed more than 35,000 people. Day's business floundered. In what one historian described as an act of desperation, Day decided to publish a newspaper along the lines of his earlier conversations with Ramsey. Day discussed his plans with fellow printers Arunah S. Abell and William M. Swain. Both men actively discouraged Day from trying the experiment. In fact, Swain told Day that the *Sun* would ruin him financially rather than save him. Nevertheless, Day went ahead. Although Day had the courage to try the experiment, he had little faith that it would succeed.

Day created the first issue of the *New York Sun* virtually single-handedly. He had no extra capital to invest in the paper, but he did have his press, type, paper, and newspaper experience. In a small room in his 222 William Street office, Day set the type, ran the presses, and folded the paper to make the 3 September 1833 issue of the *Sun* a reality.

The first edition of the four-page paper carried the *Sun*'s editorial philosophy: "The object of this paper is to lay before the public, at a price within the means of every one, all the news of the day, and at the same time afford an advantageous medium for advertising." Each of the first issue's four pages measured 11 1/4 inches by 8 inches. The initial press run was 1,000 copies. The cost was one cent per copy or three dollars a year paid in advance. The paper was set in a plain agate face. The first column of the front page of the three-column-format paper was packed with advertisements Day had borrowed from other newspapers for effect. The ads primarily focused upon commerce and stressed ship arrivals and departures. For example, Fish, Grinnell and Co. announced that it had a ship bound for Liverpool that was ready to receive cargo; K. E. Collins announced that it had "the very fast-sailing coppered ship Nashville" ready for an 8 September journey to New Orleans; and Captain Vanderbilt promised passengers that he would transport them from New York City to Hartford, Connecticut, aboard his "splendid low-pressure steamboat Water Witch" every Tuesday, Thursday, and Saturday for one dollar, leaving at six o'clock in the morning and arriving by seven o'clock the same evening. The lead news story on the front page was a humorous dialogue between an unidentified Irish military officer and "a young student of his acquaintance" about dueling. The second front-page story described carved miniatures that had fascinated famous individuals, recounting in detail the fascination a set of 1,600 dishes held for Pope Paul V. The dishes "were all perfect and complete in every part, yet so small and slender that the whole could be easily enclosed in a case fabricated in a peppercorn of the ordinary size! The Pope is said to have himself counted them, but with the help of a pair of spectacles, for they were so very small as to be almost invisible to the naked eye." A short item from Vermont about a boy who had whistled himself ill completed the first page. Pages two and three carried brief items reprinted from out-of-town newspapers, and police court reports apparently lifted from the *New York Courier and*

Enquirer. Page four featured a poem, a bank note table, and more advertisements, either made up or borrowed from other newspapers.

While quite similar in overall editorial emphasis to the first issue, the second issue contained an important item: an advertisement informing the unemployed that "a number of steady men can find employment by vending this paper. A liberal discount is allowed to those who buy to sell again." Day's "liberal discount" consisted of a sixty-seven cents charge per hundred papers if the carrier could pay in advance and seventy-five cents per hundred if the carrier had to buy on credit. Young men and boys quickly began appearing at the *Sun* office and Day sent them into the streets to hawk his paper. The *Sun*'s carriers boisterously yelled the virtues of the paper and highlighted the news. As one historian said, "they brought the paper to the people." While such flamboyant and direct marketing techniques were common in London, they had not previously been applied to the American newspaper industry. This introduction of the "London Plan" distribution scheme no doubt brought considerable attention to the fledgling paper and helped build sales.

Sometime during the *Sun*'s first week, an unemployed printer named George Wisner asked Day for work. In an 1883 interview in the *Sun*, Day recalled the meeting this way: "Wisner came to me and said that if I would give him $4 a week he would get up early every morning and do these police reports. The court was held at 4 o'clock.... He agreed to attend it regularly and write out what was interesting, besides working daytimes at setting type and doing whatever else he could." Written in the humorous, flippant, and sometimes moralistic tradition of London's Bow Street court reports, Wisner's popular column rapidly became a keystone of the *Sun*'s success and representative of the paper's commitment to writing news in a way that would appeal to a new audience. Typical of the police court stories is this brief item from July 1835: "William Luvoy got drunk because yesterday was so devilish warm. Drank 9 glasses of brandy and water and said he would be cursed if he wouldn't drink 9 more as quick as he could raise the money to buy it with. He would like to know what right the magistrate had to interfere with his private affairs. Fined $1—Forgot his pocketbook, and was sent over to Bridewell." Another item from the same column read, "Patrick Ludwick was sent up by his wife, who testified that she had supported him for several years in idleness and drunkenness. Abandoning all hopes of a reformation in her hus-

Front page of first issue of the first successful penny newspaper

band, she bought him a suit of clothes a fortnight since and told him to go about his business, for she would not live with him any longer. Last night he came home in a state of intoxication, broke into his wife's bedroom, pulled her out of bed, pulled her hair, and stamped on her. She called a watchman and sent him up. Pat exerted all his powers of eloquence in endeavoring to excite his wife's sympathy, but to no purpose. As every sensible woman ought to do who is cursed with a drunken husband, she refused to have anything to do with him hereafter—and he was sent to the penitentiary."

The light, human interest style of the police reports was representative of the characteristics which set the *Sun* apart from the other newspapers of the time. Day had not intended his paper to compete directly with the other New York papers. Emphasizing national, economic, and political news, the eleven other New York dailies published in 1833 all sold for six cents a copy and had a combined daily circulation of just over 25,000. Edited primarily for the mercantile class, these papers basically defined news as that which told of significant events in the marketplace. Day's news formula was radically different; he was reaching for an audience that did not normally buy or read the mercantile papers. He guessed that an audience existed for a newspaper that was inexpensive in price and that stressed local news and human interest stories. Day's guess was a good one: the *Sun*'s circulation and advertising revenue very quickly began to rise. Shortly after Wisner joined the newspaper, he and Day struck an agreement whereby Wisner would share in the profits if the paper were to become a success. Under the arrangement, Day retained Wisner's share until it amounted to enough to pay for half the paper. The profits were such that by the spring of 1834, Wisner became joint owner with Day.

Wisner's police reports, while perhaps the most popular early feature of the paper, were also representative of the shift which rapidly took place in the editorial focus of the *Sun*. From the initial issues packed with reprints, the *Sun* rapidly evolved into a paper full of original material. During its initial week of publication the *Sun* began to run editorials. One of these early editorials praised the British government for abolishing slavery in the West Indies, speculating that this action would "form a brilliant era in the annals of the world" and "circle with a halo of imperishable glory the brows of the transcendent spirits who wield the present destinies of the British Empire." The editorial concluded with a call for America to follow

Britain's example and free her own slaves. While the *Sun* would speak consistently against slavery, differing beliefs concerning the manner in which the institution should be eliminated increasingly alienated Day from Wisner. While Day opposed slavery, he also abhorred the abolitionists' tactics. In an editorial published on 10 September 1833, Day criticized slavery but also harshly attacked the abolitionists' methods. On the other hand, Wisner was a staunch abolitionist. Day explained later that Wisner "was a pretty smart fellow, but he and I never agreed. We split on politics. You see, I was rather Democratic in my notions; Wisner, whenever he got a chance, was always sticking in his damned little Abolition articles."

In addition to its editorials and human interest items, the *Sun* quickly began to include theater reviews and illustrations. It is interesting to note that the first illustration in the *Sun* was a two-column cut of the late Sir William Herschel's forty-foot telescope. Sir William's son, Sir John, and his telescope would figure prominently in the famous Moon Hoax series two years later. The uniqueness of Day's news judgment is shown by his treatment of John Quincy Adams's presidential nomination by the Anti-Masonic party in the 17 September 1833 issue. Day gave little space to the story and inserted it on an inside page. For the other New York dailies, this was a front-page story. In the same issue, Day gave more emphasis to a story about the reduction in the number of pounds of coal in a ton. Since many of his readers were low-income individuals who relied upon coal for heat, Day apparently perceived that they would be more interested in this story than in the Adams nomination. This choice of a story with either high human interest values or strong local ties over a story about national politics or economic issues became a central tenent of Day's news policy. For example, on 23 September 1833 the *New York Globe* ran six full columns about President Andrew Jackson's decision to deposit federal funds with state banks and thereby ruin the United States Bank; the *Sun* devoted one sentence to the event and the controversy it engendered. The *Sun* used only two lines to describe William Duane's removal as secretary of the treasury but devoted a quarter of a column to the American Museum's daily feeding of its anaconda. On 21 September 1833 Day changed the paper's title emblem. The original eagle logo was replaced by the sun rising over hills and the ocean.

Day designed the *Sun* to appeal to a large readership which had been uncultivated by the other editors. This formula proved successful: by the end of the *Sun*'s first month, the newspaper had a daily circulation of around 1,200, and both circulation and advertising revenues were increasing steadily. This success was editorially reflected in the 9 November 1833 issue when the *Sun* proclaimed that "its success is now beyond question and it has exceeded the most sanguine anticipations of its publishers in its circulation and advertising patronage.... Although of a character (we hope) deserving the encouragement of all classes of society, it is more especially valuable to those who cannot well afford to incur the expense of subscribing to a 'blanket-sheet' and paying ten dollars per annum. In conclusion, we may be permitted to remark that the penny press, by diffusing useful knowledge among the operative classes of society, is effecting the march of intelligence to a greater degree than any other mode of instruction. Day used part of the paper's initial profits to buy a new press and proudly announced in December 1833 that the paper had installed "a machine press on which one thousand impressions can be taken in an hour. The daily circulation is now nearly four thousand." Also in December 1833, Day again changed the paper's logo: the emblem of the sun rising over hills and sea was replaced with a printing press shedding symbolic light over the earth.

In spite of increasing prosperity and the new press, the *Sun* changed little in physical appearance throughout 1834. The paper retained its original page size and rarely ran to more than four pages. Editorially, too, Day continued the newspaper on the path which had proven successful. Page one was typically devoted to advertising and the serialization of a novel or some other multipart story. One of the most popular early serials was "The Life of Davy Crockett," purportedly written by Crockett himself. Pages two through four were devoted to short items written in a highly condensed form and sometimes printed under small italic phrases which functioned as headlines, such as *Ingratitude of a Cat* and *Wonderful Antics of Fleas.* Typical news items included: "It was rumored in Washington on the 6th that a duel would take place the next day between two members of the House," "James G. Bennett has become sole proprietor and editor of the Philadelphia *Courier,*" and "The Hon. Daniel Webster will leave town this morning for Washington." A longer story might read: "Sudden Death— Ann McDonough, of Washington Street, attempted to drink a pint of rum on a wager, on Wednesday afternoon last. Before it was half swallowed Ann was a corpse. Served her right. Bayington, the murderer, we learn by a contemporary,

was formerly employed in this city on the *Journal of Commerce.* No wonder he came to an untimely fate." By November 1834 the *Sun*'s circulation had reached 10,000. Such success was not unnoticed by the other New York dailies. James Watson Webb of the *Courier and Enquirer* editorially bemoaned the triumph of "penny trash"; Day replied in the *Sun* that the public had been "imposed upon by ten-dollar trash long enough." Politically, the *Sun* remained independent; socially, the paper crusaded against the filth of the city's debtors' prison and attacked conditions which it believed had contributed to that summer's cholera epidemic. Also during 1834, the *Sun* experienced its first serious penny competition in the *New York Transcript.* The *Transcript* imitated the *Sun* by emphasizing human interest items, humorous court reports, crime stories, and sports news.

At the end of 1834 Day again invested some of the paper's profits in technological improvements. He became the first newspaper editor to install new steam-driven Napier presses. On 1 January 1835 he changed typefaces and slightly increased the paper's page size. He also changed from a three-column to a four-column format. The 1 January 1835 issue also carried for the first time the motto "It Shines For All."

In the spring of 1835 Wisner and Day were indicted for criminal libel as a result of an editorial contention that one of the *New York Transcript*'s editors had passed a bogus three-dollar bill and that another editor of the rival paper "walked on both sides of the street like a two-penny postman." Day did not seem shaken by the indictment. In fact, in one editorial he discussed other prominent journalists who had been similarly charged and concluded that "the greatest men in the country have some time in the course of their lives been indicted." The indictment was eventually dismissed. Later in 1835 Day traveled to Westchester County to cover one of the more notorious trials of the day, in which Matthias the Prophet was charged with poisoning Elijah Pierson. Because of the notoriety of the individuals involved, most New York newspapers sent representatives to cover the case. Day became acquainted with Richard Adams Locke, who was covering the trial for Webb's *Courier and Enquirer.* Day was impressed with Locke's writing skills and after the trial hired Locke on a free-lance basis to write a series of articles about Matthias. The articles were subsequently published in pamphlet form.

Shortly after Day returned from Westchester County, Wisner's health failed and he told Day that

The first Sun *office: arrow points to 222 William Street, New York City*

he wanted to leave New York. Day bought Wisner's share in the *Sun* for $5,000. Wisner settled in Michigan and eventually recovered. While Wisner was in the process of leaving the *Sun,* Locke came to the newspaper's offices and told Day that Webb had fired him because of the articles he had written for the *Sun.* Day immediately hired Locke at a salary of twelve dollars a week. Late in August 1835 Locke's most famous series began appearing in the *Sun.* The series started innocently enough in the form of a short paragraph announcing that "astronomical discoveries of the most wonderful description" had just been made by Sir John Herschel in South Africa by means of an advanced telescope. Four days later, three columns of the *Sun*'s front page were devoted to detailed background stories describing the telescope and giving a history of both Sir William's and Sir John's works. The stories stressed that Sir John had a driving ambition to make discoveries even greater than his father's. The next day's installment began with a recounting of Sir John's discovery of life on the moon. The descriptions of the moon's flora and fauna were numerous and richly detailed. One creature was described as being "a bluish lead color, about the size of a goat with a head and beard like him and a single horn slightly inclined forward from the perpendicular ... in elegance of symmetry it rivaled the antelope and like him it seemed an agile, sprightly creature running with great speed and springing from the green turf with all the unaccountable antics of the young lamb or kitten." Another creature had a "spherical form" and "rolled with great velocity across the pebbly beach." The moon was also inhabited by several species of birds and a bison-like creature. The report ended with clouds obscuring Herschel's view. This story caused an immediate stir. Most of the other New York papers bowed to the *Sun*'s ability to scoop the competition. The *Daily Advertiser* called the article one of the most important to appear in print for years. The *Mercantile Advertiser* said that the report seemed authentic and reprinted it in full. Other papers followed the *Mercantile Advertiser*'s example.

However, two of the six-penny papers, the *Courier and Enquirer* and the *Journal of Commerce,* which regularly exchanged editorial barbs with the *Sun,* said nothing about the stories.

The next day's installment introduced the *Sun*'s readers to new regions of the moon, stressing topography and naming places like the Lake of Death and the Vagabond Mountains. One of the most interesting animals described that day was the biped beaver, which resembled earth's beavers "in every other respect than its destitution of a tail and its invariable habit of walking upon only two feet. It carries its young in its arms, like a human being, and walks with an easy, gliding motion. Its huts are constructed better and higher than those of many tribes of human savages, and from the appearance of smoke in nearly all of them there is no doubt of its being acquainted with the use of fire."

The 28 August *Sun* contained the most sensational story of all: it described the man-bat inhabitants of the moon, who "averaged four feet in height, were covered except on the face, with short and glossy copper-colored hair, and had wings composed of a thin membrane, without hair, lying snugly upon their backs, from the top of the shoulders to the calves of the legs." This issue of the *Sun* attained the record-breaking single-day circulation of 19,360 copies. Day had to run the double-cylinder Napier presses for ten hours straight to satisfy the public's demand. In addition, the *Sun* was swamped with requests for back issues containing the earlier articles. Busy with these requests and with making certain that the overworked presses kept turning, Day gave Locke a free hand to deal with the story and kept the reproduction and distribution problems for himself.

Responding to public requests for reproductions of the illustrations which had accompanied the stories, Locke commissioned lithographers Norris and Baker to produce a set of individual prints. Locke and Day also worked together to produce a pamphlet containing the original stories. When the presses were not devoted to meeting the demand for the *Sun,* Day turned them to printing the pamphlet. The monographs were advertised at thirteen cents each or two for a quarter, and the lithographs at twenty-five cents a set. The series reached Europe about this time and was reprinted in English, French, and Scottish newspapers.

The final story in the moon series was published on 31 August; it described the discovery of a new set of man-bats. Shortly after this story appeared, Locke told an acquaintance who wrote for the *Journal of Commerce* that he had fabricated the stories. The *Journal* immediately denounced the series as a hoax. The *Sun*'s other rivals rushed to press to criticize the paper for fooling the public in such a manner. The *Sun* did not apologize for the hoax, but rather editorially took credit for "diverting the public mind, for a while, from that bitter apple of discord, the abolition of slavery." The public seemed to approve of the diversion because it did not abandon the *Sun.* A fan of Locke's writing, Edgar Allan Poe, called the series "the greatest hit in the way of sensation—of merely popular sensation—ever made by any similar fiction either in America or Europe." Poe also noted that "from the epoch of the hoax, 'The Sun' shone with unmitigated splendor. The start thus given the paper insured it a triumph. . . . Its success firmly established 'the penny system' throughout the country, and consequently we are indebted to the genius of Mr. Locke for one of the most important steps ever taken in the pathway of human progress."

Day realized the importance Locke's name could have in selling newspapers. In November 1835 the *Sun* announced that Locke was writing a series of articles, soon to appear, titled "Life and Adventures of Manuel Fernandez, otherwise Richard C. Jackson, convicted of the murder of John Roberts, and to be executed at the Bellevue Prison, New York, on Thursday next, the 19th instant." Once again the competition stood in awe of the *Sun*'s enterprise. Several reporters, including one from the *Courier and Enquirer* and one from James Gordon Bennett's recently founded one-cent *New York Herald,* had been trying for months to get interviews with Fernandez. But it was Locke who finally convinced Fernandez to tell his story, and he spent several hours each day for three weeks interviewing Fernandez in his cell. The series ran from 14 November to 25 November 1835 and again *Sun* sales increased.

Sales shot up again the following month for the paper's coverage of the 16 December 1835 fire which consumed about twenty blocks of New York City between Broad Street and the East River. The fire started late in the evening and all the *Sun* had the next morning was a paragraph which indicated that "a tremendous conflagration is now raging in the lower part of the city. . . . Several hundred buildings are already down, and the firemen have given out. God only knows when the fire will be arrested." The following morning, the *Sun* devoted more space to the fire. The story said that almost 700 buildings had been destroyed at a loss of over twenty million dollars. The writer described the tragedy, in part, as follows: "Where but thirty hours since was the rich and prosperous theater of a great and productive commerce, where enterprise and wealth energized with bold and commanding efforts, now sits despondency in sackcloth and a wide and dreary waste of desolation reigns. It seemed as if God were running in his anger and sweeping away with the besom of his wrath the proudest monuments of man. Destruction traveled and triumphed on every breeze, and billows of fire rolled over and buried in their burning bosoms the hopes and fortunes of thousands." The *Sun*'s fire coverage reaffirmed the paper's popularity, and the paper had to print an extra 7,000 copies to satisfy public demand. To accomplish this total run of 30,000 copies in one day, Day had to keep his presses running for nearly twenty-four hours nonstop. On the Monday following the fire, the *Sun* carried a map of the burned area. Copies of this edition plus copies of the earlier editions with fire stories were circulated worldwide.

On New Year's Day 1836 Day announced additional technological changes at the *Sun:* the paper remained at four pages, but the pages were increased in size to 14 inches by 20 inches. Day observed: "We are now enabled to print considerably more than twenty-two thousand copies on both sides in less than eight hours. No establishment in this country has such facilities, and no daily newspaper in the world enjoys so extensive a circulation." Day also boasted that the *Sun*'s circulation was more than double that of all the six-penny papers combined. Only two of the many penny papers that had sprung up in imitation of the *Sun* had survived. The exceptions to the heavy penny paper mortality were the *Transcript,* which lasted until 1839, and Bennett's *New York Herald.* Of the *Herald,* Day said that "the little world we opened has proved large enough for us both." In spite of this belief that the world was large enough for two successful penny papers, Day regularly swapped editorial gibes with Bennett. In one such attack, Day wrote: "Bennett, whose only chance of dying an upright man will be that of hanging perpendicularly upon a rope, falsely charges the proprietor of this paper with being an infidel, the natural effect of which calumny will be that every reader will believe him to be a good Christian."

Second only to Bennett as a target for Day's editorial ire was James Watson Webb, editor of the *Courier and Enquirer.* In January 1836 Webb accused Day of luring his newspaper's courier into the *Sun*'s office and opening the courier's sealed pouch, which contained a dispatch intended for Webb's eyes only. The dispatch contained the text of a special message which President Jackson had just delivered to Congress. Once again, the *Sun* had scooped the competition and printed the message first. Webb could not imagine how, ethically, the *Sun* could have received the story before his paper and editorially charged Day with misconduct. Day responded that he had received the story legitimately and that Webb's charge was only a hollow attempt to discredit him and his newspaper: "The insinuation of Webb that we violated the sanctity of a seal we hurl back in proud defiance to his own brow." Several days later, on 21 January, Day continued the controversy by charging that Webb and six other editors had hatched "a diabolical plot" against the *Sun* by forming in December 1835 a horse express between Washington and New York from which the penny press had been excluded. In response, the *Sun* and the *Transcript* had formed their own express.

Day responded with editorial astonishment when Webb physically assaulted Bennett on 19 January 1836; in the process, he managed to insult both the perpetrator and the victim of the attack: "We were astonished to learn last evening that Colonel Webb had stooped so far beneath anything of which we had ever conceived it possible for him to be guilty . . . to descend to a public personal chastisement of that villainous libel on humanity of all kinds, the notorious vagabond Bennett . . . that he could . . . have so far descended from himself as to come in public contact with the veriest reptile that ever defiled the paths of decency, we could not have believed." The following May, Webb made another physical assault upon Bennett. Day speculated that because of the number of public attacks Bennett had received there was not "a square inch of his body which has not been lacerated somewhere about fifteen times." While Day refrained from joining in the physical violence against Bennett, he was quick to attack Bennett editorially. Day particularly disapproved of Bennett's involvement in the Robinson-Jewett murder trial. Bennett had conducted his own investigation into the sensational murder of prostitute Helen Jewett and concluded that Richard Robinson was not guilty of the crime. He filled the *Herald* with his investigation and conclusions. Day criticized Bennett for his zealous trial coverage, and after Robinson's acquittal he declared that if one viewed the evidence calmly and dispassionately, Robinson's guilt was evident.

In September 1836 Locke left the *Sun* to establish his own penny paper with Joseph Price. Day editorially wished Locke success. But within the month, the two men were exchanging editorial punches over meal costs at the Astor House. Locke accused Day of unjustly criticizing the Astor House and suggested that the criticism was "set afloat by some person who was kicked out for not paying his bill." Day replied that the criticism was entirely justified because the prices were high; the service was poor, with "one hour and seven minutes" elapsing between order and arrival of the meal; and that the room was "so uncleanly as to be rather offensive." These battles were short lived because of the rather rapid demise of Locke's paper and Locke's subsequent employment as *Brooklyn Eagle* editor.

The *Sun*'s page size increased slightly in January 1836, but the paper maintained its four-page length. Editorially, the paper continued as in previous years. When flour prices doubled in February 1837, the *Sun* argued that the increase was the result of unfair market manipulation rather than natural causes. Public outrage against the increase was swift and vocal. Widespread agitation followed, which culminated in the 13 February 1837 bread riots. The *Journal of Commerce* accused the *Sun* of inciting the riots and suggested that the grand jury investigate Day. Day retaliated by asserting that the grand jury foreman, Philip Hone, had incited an 11 July 1834 riot against the abolitionists for a much less worthy reason than underlay the bread riots. Day also refused to back down from his original position on flour prices.

In late spring 1837 Day was sued for libel by lawyer Andrew S. Garr. The suit resulted from a story in the 3 May issue of the *Sun* which briefly mentioned that Garr had once been charged with conspiracy to defraud but did not point out that he had been acquitted. Garr sued Day for $10,000. On 15 June Day removed his name from the *Sun*'s masthead. The paper contained no explanation of the absence of Day's name and rumors circulated. About a week later, Day wrote in an editorial that the absence of his name paralleled no significant editorial change at the paper and that he intended to stay at his post. In February 1838 the libel case was heard and Garr won a $3,000 judgment against Day. In an editorial the day after the verdict was handed down, Day said that he had sold the *Sun* but he did not say to whom. The name of the new owner appeared for the first time on 28 June, when a notice appeared instructing those who wished to communicate with the *Sun* to do so through Moses Yale Beach. Beach was Day's brother-in-law and had worked as a *Sun* bookkeeper almost since the paper's inception. The purchase price was $40,000. In an 1883 interview Day said that selling the paper was "the silliest thing I ever did in my life. . . ."

Why, then, did Day sell the *Sun*? Historian O'Brien contended that the decision was basically an economic one. The paper was still making money, but the profit margin was declining sharply. By 1838 the *Sun* was big business. Day's records indicate that the weekly outlay for material and wages was close to $2,000. Even though the newspaper's circulation was very high (an average 30,000 a day), operating expenses outweighed circulation revenues by about $300 a week. To make a profit, this deficit had to be overcome through advertising revenue. But, because of a business depression and increasing competition for the advertising dollar, advertising revenues were harder to generate and some weeks Day found himself just breaking even. O'Brien pointed out that with the money Day had saved during the paper's most profitable years and the $40,000 he received from Beach, Day had a comfortable fortune. Day was only twenty-eight years old, and with such a financial cushion he could turn his energies in a direction which might yield a higher profit margin.

Day understood that what he had done with the *Sun* was significant, but he viewed its significance in terms of the effects he believed the newspaper had on its audience rather than the revolutionary effect it had on American journalism. In one of his editorials, Day said: "Since the *Sun* began to shine upon the citizens of New York there has been a very great and decided change in the condition of the laboring classes and the mechanics. Now every individual, from the rich aristocrat who lolls in his carriage to the humble laborer who wields a broom in the streets, reads the *Sun*. . . . Already can we perceive a change in the mass of the people. They think, talk, and act in concert. They understand their own interest, and feel that they have numbers and strength to pursue it with success. The *Sun* newspaper has probably done more to benefit the community by enlightening the minds of the common people than all the other papers together."

After Day sold the *Sun*, the paper continued to be a daily circulation leader for nearly twenty years. The Beach family hired good writers, installed the best presses, increased political news coverage, and kept the price of the paper at a penny. Moses Yale Beach retired in 1848 and turned the paper over to his sons, Moses Sperry Beach and Alfred Ely Beach. When his brother retired in 1852, Moses S. Beach became the *Sun*'s sole owner. In 1860 Beach sold the "goodwill" of the paper for $100,000 and leased its physical plant to Archibald Morrison, who used the paper as an evangelistic forum. With the marked change in editorial focus came a marked decrease in revenue and in 1861 the paper returned to Beach. During the Civil War, the *Sun* struggled for financial survival and for the first time raised its price to two cents. In early 1868 a stock company headed by Charles Dana bought the paper for $175,000. Under Dana's editorial leadership, the *Sun* shone brightly once more. After Dana's death in 1897, the paper passed through several hands until it settled within the grasp of Frank Munsey in 1916. Munsey promptly merged the *Sun* with another of his papers, the *New York Press*, and thus ended the independent identity of the paper started by Day eighty-three years before.

In 1840 Day reentered the newspaper business by establishing a penny paper called the *True Sun*. However, he sold the paper in a few months. Shortly thereafter, he established another penny paper, the *Evening Tatler*, but it did not succeed. In 1842 Day and James Wilson founded *Brother Jonathan*, a monthly literary magazine. *Brother Jonathan* sold for one dollar a year and reproduced multivolume British novels complete in each issue. Eventually, the magazine became a weekly. Day supplemented these frequent editions with novels reprinted in inexpensive pamphlet form and with semiannual illustrated editions of *Brother Jonathan*. These special editions were among America's earliest successful illustrated periodicals, and O'Brien credits Day with giving birth to that media form as well as with ushering in the age of the penny press. Day continued *Brother Jonathan* for twenty years, until the Civil War caused a paper shortage in 1862;

Day then suspended publication and retired. He was financially comfortable and even after the war did not reenter professional life. Day's retirement lasted for twenty-seven years. He died of natural causes on 21 December 1889.

Day's life spanned almost eighty years. For nearly half those years, he was actively involved in journalistic endeavors; but his most significant contributions were compacted into a five-year period. Between 1833 and 1838, Day revolutionized American journalism. His success with the *Sun* redefined news and gave rise to many other newspapers. He brought newspapers to an audience that had largely been ignored. As O'Brien noted, Day "found New York journalism a pot of cold, stale water, and left it a boiling caldron, not so much by what he wrote as by the way in which he made his success. There were better newspapermen than Day before and during his time, plenty of them. They had knowledge and experience, they knew style, but they did not know people." As Day told Robert Hoe in 1851, he remade American journalism "more by accident than design."

References:

50 Great Pioneers of American Industry (Maplewood, N.J.: C. S. Hammond, 1964), pp. 19-21;

Richard Hooker, *The Story of an Independent Newspaper* (New York: Macmillan, 1924);

New York Sun One Hundredth Anniversary, 1833-1933 (New York: The *Sun*, 1933);

Frank O'Brien, *The Story of the Sun* (New York: Appleton, 1928).

Felix Gregory de Fontaine

(1834-11 December 1896)

Jean Folkerts
Mount Vernon College

MAJOR POSITIONS HELD: War correspondent, *New York Herald* (1861), *Charleston (S.C.) Courier* (1861-1863), *Savannah (Ga.) Republican* (1864-1865); publisher, *Daily South Carolinian* (Columbia) (1864-1865); managing editor, *New York Telegram* (1868-1871); financial editor, drama critic, *New York Herald* (1871-1895).

BOOKS: *Trial of the Hon. David E. Sickles for Shooting Philip Barton Key . . . February 27th, 1859* (New York: R. M. DeWitt, 1859);
History of American Abolitionism: Its Four Great Epochs, Embracing Narratives of the Ordinance of 1787, Compromise of 1820, Annexation of Texas, Mexican War, Wilmot Proviso, Negro Insurrections, Abolition Riots, Slave Rescues, Compromise of 1850, Kansas Bill of 1854, John Brown Insurrection, 1859, Valuable Statistics, &c., &c., &c., Together with a History of the Southern Confederacy (New York: D. Appleton, 1861);
Marginalia; or, Gleanings from an Army Note-book, as "Personne" (Columbia, S.C.: Steam Power-press of F. G. De Fontaine & Co., 1864);
The Hoffman House (New York, 1880);
De Fontaine's Condensed Long-hand and Rapid Writer's Companion, for the Use of Type Writers, Telegraphers, Corresponding Clerks (New York: American News Co., 1886);
Army Letters of Personne, 1861-1865 (Columbia, S.C.: War Record Publishing Co., 1897).

OTHER: *A Cyclopedia of the Best Thoughts of Charles Dickens*, edited by De Fontaine (New York: E. J. Hale, 1873); republished as *The Fireside Dickens* (New York: G. W. Carleton, 1883);
Birds of a Feather Flock Together; or, Talks with Sothern, edited by De Fontaine (New York: G. W. Carleton, 1878).

PERIODICAL PUBLICATIONS: "Shoulder to Shoulder: Reminiscences of Confederate Camps and Fields," as "Personne," *XIX Century*, 1-2 (June 1869-January 1870);

"The First Day of Real War," *Southern Bivouac* (July 1886): 73-79.

Born in Boston and trained as a journalist on the *Boston Herald* and the *New York Herald*, Felix Gregory de Fontaine became one of the South's leading war correspondents. Although he apparently had no ties to the South before the war began, after he arrived in Charleston, South Carolina, to cover the firing on Fort Sumter for his Southern-sympathizing employer, James Gordon Bennett, de Fontaine became and remained loyal to the Southern cause. He endured illness and danger while reporting the war, and he remained optimistic about the Confederacy even after the South's demise was ensured.

De Fontaine, along with Peter W. Alexander of the *Savannah (Ga.) Republican*, "stood head and shoulders" above other correspondents in the South, according to J. Cutler Andrews, author of *The South Reports the Civil War*. While the source of de Fontaine's Southern sympathy was not recorded, most European nations sympathized with the South, and de Fontaine's father's connection to France may have influenced him. Also, he had worked in Washington, D.C., for the *New York Herald*, and may have been introduced to the Southern point of view there.

During the war he covered most of the major campaigns. He was with Gen. Robert E. Lee in northern Virginia; he covered most of the Tennessee campaign; he left Atlanta as it fell in September 1864; and he was in South Carolina in 1865 when Gen. William T. Sherman's troops invaded Columbia.

De Fontaine's strength as a reporter in the field was displayed in his social commentary as well as in his battle coverage. Throughout his career he wrote vividly of camp life. He described firing along picket lines, army diet and recreation, terrain, illness, and the need for blankets and clothing. During the early period of the war, de Fontaine often described the enthusiasm Southerners displayed, and his loyalty in later years caused him to describe better conditions than actually existed. During the latter years of the conflict de Fontaine published his own newspaper, the *Columbia Daily South Carolinian*. He remained in South Carolina until about 1868, when he returned to New York to continue his career in journalism; but he chose the South for his retirement, and died there in 1896.

De Fontaine was born in 1834 to a French nobleman, Louis Antoine de Fontaine, who had immigrated to the United States four years earlier, and an American mother who was related to the Revolutionary War hero Ethan Allen.

He was educated privately, and early in his journalism career gained distinction as one of the first reporters to learn shorthand. As a congressional reporter in Washington, he compiled official reports of two famous murder trials—the trial of Harvard Professor John H. Webster, who was found guilty of murder after the victim's false teeth were found in his furnace; and the trial of Congressman Daniel E. Sickles for the killing of Philip Barton Key. De Fontaine's shorthand ability enabled the results of the Sickles trial to be published in pamphlet form within an hour after the trial concluded in 1859.

In early April 1861, de Fontaine arrived in Charleston. He made friends with the commanding Confederate general from New Orleans, P. G. T. Beauregard, who shared de Fontaine's French heritage. Beauregard gave him permission to file a telegraphic dispatch of the bombardment of Fort Sumter to the *New York Herald*. From that point on, de Fontaine, who wrote under the pseudonym "Personne," was accepted as a major Civil War correspondent. He wrote for the *Herald*, for the *Charleston Courier*, for the *Savannah Republican*, and for the *Daily South Carolinian*, which he founded in Columbia in 1864. In addition to covering the war, he also wrote a series of articles for the *New York Herald* on the history of abolitionism. These articles were published in 1861 in book form as *History of American Abolitionism*. He was not only the first to cover the war but one of the last Confederate voices to be stilled.

When the bombardment of Fort Sumter began on 12 April, de Fontaine described not only the battle, but the tenor in Charleston as well. "Lights flash on as if by magic from the windows of every house," he wrote, "and in the twinkling of an eye, as it were an agitated mass of people are rushing impetuously toward the water front of the city." De Fontaine said that citizens whose dignity usually was unimpeachable "are at the top of their speed dressing as they run, and sending up wild hurrahs as if they must have some such safety-valve for the enthusiasm or be suffocated. There are men *sans* coats, women *sans* crinoline, and children in their night-gowns."

After the attack on Fort Sumter, de Fontaine traveled north to Richmond. In May he wrote to the *Courier* from North Carolina that troops traveling to Virginia by railroad were cheered by "Crowds of women with ribbons and rosettes attached to their coats and secession flags in their hats, who extended ovations while floral offerings from their feminine hands were brought into the cars."

Active in writing reports from the capital city, he barely made it to the battleground of the first Battle of Bull Run. He arrived on the morning of 21 July 1861, in time to join a group of correspondents who viewed the battle from a nearby hill. He covered the Confederate victory for the Southern Associated Press, the principal news agency in the South at the start of the war. Dissatisfaction with that agency's service led to the formation of the Press Association of the Confederate States of America in March 1863.

In the fall of 1861 de Fontaine was at Fairfax, Virginia, when President Jefferson Davis came to discuss a forward movement to interfere with a planned Federal spring campaign against Richmond. Confederate Gen. Joseph E. Johnston's troops subsequently launched an offensive but retreated from the Potomac. De Fontaine cast the retreat favorably, claiming that the new position at Centreville would provoke Maj. Gen. George B. McClellan into attacking. The attack came in less than a week, with no correspondent accompanying the Confederate troops at Ball's Bluff. But de Fontaine later interviewed participants, then described for the *Richmond Dispatch* a "horde of pigs feasting on Yankee corpses that had been buried in shallow graves."

De Fontaine described the Confederate garrison at Harpers Ferry, West Virginia, commenting on the quality of the troops, which included "some of the wealthiest and most influential citizens of Alabama and Mississippi—lawyers, doctors, professors, editors, printers, merchants, and planters, along with a strong infusion of the sturdy yeoman element." He regarded Kentuckians as separate from these Southern gentlemen, describing them as robust, splendid marksmen, independent, careless but not ungraceful. De Fontaine said that the Kentuckians had arrived without arms, but when the garrison offered to provide them with muskets, they protested, saying that they did not know how to fire them. The Kentuckians, according to de Fontaine, said that if they could not have rifles, they would rather "throw rocks." De Fontaine remained with the army in northern Virginia until December, when he learned that the troops were moving into permanent winter quarters. He then returned to South Carolina.

In the spring of 1862, de Fontaine returned to the field with Gen. Albert Sidney Johnston and General Beauregard along the Tennessee-Mississippi line, where he covered Johnston's surprise attack on 6 April at Shiloh. After two days of fighting, the Confederates withdrew toward Corinth, Mississippi. Beauregard sent the first official descriptions of the battle, claiming a "complete victory," and de Fontaine said, "Our troops are in admirable spirits and ready for another fight." But the battle took a heavy toll on Confederate troops. De Fontaine wrote accounts of the bloodbath while sitting on a hotel floor in Corinth, with the dead and dying surrounding him. "Groans fill the air," he wrote, "surgeons are busy at work by candlelight. . . . The atmosphere is fetid with the stench of wounds, and the rain is pouring down upon thousands who yet lie out upon the bloody ground of Shiloh." De Fontaine stayed with the Corinth campaign in northeastern Mississippi after the Battle of Shiloh, describing how soldiers and correspondents suffered from "chills" caused by dysentery, pneumonia, and measles.

At the conclusion of the Corinth campaign, de Fontaine headed for Memphis, primarily because Beauregard had issued an order to the press to leave the army and not to remain within twenty-five miles of the area. De Fontaine speculated that Beauregard's order resulted from a *Memphis Appeal* account of his planned retreat from Corinth and the direction of troop movement. This critical issue had also caused General Johnston to expel the press from his command. The press protested and newspaper editors meeting in Atlanta in March 1862 appointed a committee, including de Fontaine, to draft resolutions criticizing Johnston's approach.

Early that summer de Fontaine, carried to the battle from a sickbed, watched crowds line the bluffs to view the naval battle for control of Memphis. The North prevailed. After being warned by a friend that Federal troops were looking for him, de Fontaine disguised himself as a farmer and left the city at night in a horse-drawn carriage and went south to Hernando, Mississippi. From there he returned to South Carolina to recover his health.

By July, however, de Fontaine had recovered sufficiently to cover the Battle of the Seven Days near Richmond. De Fontaine found Richmond in a state of confusion, with countless wounded. He visited the battlefield, interviewed officers, and compared conflicting accounts, trying to reconstruct military events that had taken place over thirty to forty miles. Reporting was severely restricted, because the brigade commander said he would arrest any soldier who gave information to a reporter before the official report was completed. While Lee repelled McClellan, he lost 20,000 men.

Lee remained worried throughout July about McClellan's presence near Richmond. De Fontaine speculated in the *Courier* that the South was ready to move from a defensive to an offensive strategy and inferred that Lee was about to march north. The first step in this offensive took place on 9 August, near Culpepper, Virginia, when Stonewall Jackson attacked Northern troops at Cedar Mountain. The Southern press claimed victory. Marching with Lee's army, de Fontaine said, "We live on what we can get—now and then an ear of corn, fried green apples, or a bit of ham fried on a stick, but quite as frequently do without either from morning until night." De Fontaine was with Confederate forces as they reached Thoroughfare Gap. He described the gap as "a rude opening through the Bull Run Mountains, varying in width from one hundred to two hundred yards. . . . It is a place where a thousand determined troops could hold at bay for weeks ten times their number." Southern troops managed to penetrate the gap and marched southeast to join Jackson for the second battle of Manassas. Richmond waited several days for Lee's report that they had attacked McClellan and Pope and routed "them with immense loss." "Personne's" account was written three days after the battle, and Andrews credits it as being probably the best account that appeared in the Confederate press.

In early September, when Lee crossed the Potomac near Leesburg to march north, de Fontaine witnessed the arrival of the army in the town and its cordial reception. He wrote, "The doorways and curb stones are like living bouquets of beauty. Everything that wears crinoline or a pretty face is out, and such shouts and wavings of handkerchiefs and hurrahs by the overjoyed gender never emanated from human lips."

Meanwhile, McClellan intercepted a dispatch from Lee, indicating that Southern troops were momentarily divided. The plan was for several Confederate forces to converge at Harpers Ferry, but delays prevented them from doing so. Jackson, meanwhile, captured Harpers Ferry, and Lee concentrated his army near Sharpsburg, overlooking a tributary of the Potomac called Antietam Creek. De Fontaine was there to provide an eyewitness account of the battle, in which Lee's army faced odds of more than two to one. On 18 September Lee's army retreated into Virginia, bringing the Maryland campaign to an end. De Fontaine's account of Antietam described the carnage that took place but gave a misleading impression of the significance of the battle.

It was late October before the Army of the Potomac regrouped and began to march southward east of the Blue Ridge. De Fontaine was dragged for about fifty yards by a frightened horse. Internal inflammation forced him to return to South Carolina and he was separated from Lee's army for the rest of 1862.

He rejoined Lee in January 1863 and was impressed with the army's improved health, discipline, and morale. His accounts were of theatrical productions in the camps; the occupation of Richmond by gamblers, courtesans, and transient visitors; and jokes soldiers played on one another. In June, when Lee's army moved into Pennsylvania, de Fontaine did not accompany it. He had returned to South Carolina to marry Georgia Vigneron Moore of Charleston. In so doing, he missed the Battle of Gettysburg.

That fall the correspondent joined Gen. Braxton Bragg on the Tennessee-Georgia border to cover President Jefferson Davis's visit to the dispirited troops. De Fontaine welcomed Davis's visit, hoping that it would "dispel the spirit of complaint which I am free to state prevails throughout the army."

De Fontaine then joined Gen. James Longstreet's command on its march into east Tennessee to support other Confederate troops in the desperate battles for control of Tennessee. "Personne's" account of Longstreet's unsuccessful attempt to storm the fortifications of Knoxville reached the *Courier* shortly before Christmas. Southern troops were in desperate circumstances that winter. De Fontaine wrote that 3,000 men were barefoot: "Some of them are officers high in rank. One whom I know is a Lieutenant Colonel. All of them are fighting men, who, but for this necessity, would be in the front rank in every hour of danger." He described their need vividly. "The surface of the ground is as hard as a rock, and at every step the frozen edges of earth cut into naked feet, until the path of the army may be almost said to have been tracked in blood." This report was the

last of the Tennessee campaign from "Personne," who left for Charleston to spend the winter at home and plan a newspaper venture with a partner, Henry Timrod.

Confederate soldiers fared no better the following summer than they had in the winter. De Fontaine, reporting for the *Savannah Republican*, arrived at the front lines of the Army of Tennessee. At the first battles of Atlanta he wrote he was too weary to describe the fighting in detail, and the possibility of his correspondence being intercepted between Atlanta and Macon by the enemy made it seem imprudent to do so. During the later stages of the battle his reporting was misleading, not revealing the extent of the Confederate loss. He left Atlanta at the end of July; the city fell in September.

By fall of 1864 newspapermen in Richmond were discouraged by what appeared to be further deterioration of Lee's army. In November de Fontaine, who since January had edited the *South Carolinian*, arrived at the capital to "have another try at reporting." He expressed an optimistic tone, assuring his readers that in Richmond not a single person expressed doubt or trepidation. Women were "attired with a richness and elegance," and restaurants served full menus. Andrews viewed de Fontaine's account as sheer propaganda, because the reporter neglected to mention the low civilian morale and the fact that only a few soldiers and speculators could afford the high prices charged in Richmond restaurants. By this time, even General Lee recognized that Richmond would fall soon to Union troops.

In early 1865 de Fontaine was again in South Carolina, warning Columbians of a possible invasion. Since Columbia was "the place where the convention met that took South Carolina out of the Union first," de Fontaine thought the city particularly vulnerable. Sherman invaded on 14 February 1865, and de Fontaine wrote about the occupation until his exit from the city. De Fontaine's press was burned in the fire that destroyed much of Columbia during Sherman's occupation. He moved to Charlotte, North Carolina, to resume publication of his newspaper, and as the local representative for the Press Association of the Confederate States, he wired that the enemy was moving toward Camden and Cheraw, South Carolina, and Fayetteville, North Carolina. He predicted that Federal troops would not attack Charlotte. His prediction proved true, and the troops bypassed the city.

In Charlotte, de Fontaine covered closing events of the war, according to Andrews, more "fully" and "circumstantially" than any other Southern reporter. In addition, "he had supplied the Confederate Associated Press with news dispatches which in one instance at least found their way to the intelligence service of General Lee."

De Fontaine acquired many Confederate records in April 1865 while publishing a newspaper at Chester, South Carolina. As union officials were about to take possession of the town, the quartermaster abandoned the records. According to one account, de Fontaine went to the depot with a cotton truck and carried away a load of stationery and records. Among the records were the provisional and permanent constitutions, Indian treaties, patent drawings, and official opinions of the attorney general. In 1883 one researcher wrote that de Fontaine recognized the monetary value of the records and sold most of them to other individuals who were interested in preserving them. W. W. Corcoran, millionaire philanthropist who established the Corcoran Gallery of Art in Washington, bought the original of the provisional constitution from de Fontaine and presented it to the Southern Historical Society.

De Fontaine remained in South Carolina at least until 1867, when he was secretary of a convention in Columbia to consider abuses of carpet-bag rule. Shortly afterward, he returned to New York, where he was editor of the *Telegram* for three years. He was financial editor of the *New York Herald* for seven years, then became dramatic and music editor. During this time he also edited a volume of selections from the works of Charles Dickens, wrote magazine articles about his experiences in the war, and wrote a book on shorthand. He remained at the *Herald* until he became ill, when he retired and returned to Columbia. He died of pneumonia on 11 December 1896.

References:

J. Cutler Andrews, *The South Reports the Civil War* (Princeton: Princeton University Press, 1970);

James A. Hoyt, "The Confederate Archives and Felix G. de Fontaine," *South Carolina Historical Magazine*, 57 (October 1956): 199-203;

James M. Merrill, "Personne Goes to Georgia: Five Civil War Letters," *Collections of the Georgia Historical Society*, 43 (June 1959): 202-211;

Edwin A. Perry, *The Boston Herald and Its History* (Boston, 1878), pp. 34-35;

Yates Snowden and H. G. Cutler, *History of South Carolina*, 5 volumes (Chicago & New York: Lewis, 1920), II: 884.

Joseph Dennie

(30 August 1768-7 January 1812)

Gary Coll
University of Wisconsin-Oshkosh

See also the Dennie entry in *DLB 37, American Writers of the Early Republic.*

MAJOR POSITIONS HELD: Editor, *Boston Tablet* (1795), *New Hampshire Journal: or the Farmer's Weekly Museum*, renamed *Farmer's Museum, or Lay Preacher's Gazette* in 1799 (Walpole, N.H.) (1796-1799), *Gazette of the United States* (Philadelphia) (1800).

BOOKS: *The Lay Preacher; or, Short Sermons, for Idle Readers* (Walpole, N.H.: Printed & sold by David Carlisle, Jun., 1796); collected and arranged by John E. Hall (Philadelphia: Harrison Hall, 1817);

A Collection of Essays, on a Variety of Subjects, in Prose and Verse (Newark, N.J.: Printed by John Woods, 1797);

The Spirit of the Farmers' Museum, and Lay Preacher's Gazette. Being a Judicious Selection of the Fugitive and Valuable Productions, Which Have Occasionally Appeared in That Paper, since the Commencement of Its Establishment (Walpole, N.H.: Printed for Thomas & Thomas by D. & T. Carlisle, 1801);

Sketches in Verse (Philadelphia: Printed for C. & A. Conrad by Smith & Maxwell, 1810);

The Poetry of the Port Folio, as Oliver Oldschool (Philadelphia: Harrison Hall, J. Maxwell, printer, 1818);

Brief Outline of the Life of Henry Clay, as Oldschool (Washington, D.C.: Whig Standard, n.d.).

OTHER: *The Plays of William Shakespeare . . . with the Corrections and Illustrations of Various Commentators,* edited by Dennie (Philadelphia: C. & A. Conrad/Baltimore: Conrad, Lucas, 1809).

Joseph Dennie was one of the first Americans to be considered a professional writer. Although his principal fame rests on his essays and literary criticism, he also earned journalistic renown as the editor of one of a class of rural newspapers which in the early years of the republic were often as well known and influential as their larger cousins in major port cities. Between 1796 and 1799 Dennie edited the *Farmer's Weekly Museum* in Walpole, New Hampshire, and made it a vehicle for some of his best writings—especially his Lay Preacher essays, which rank among the best essays ever produced in America. He also used the newspaper to disseminate his strong Federalist views on political life in the new nation. In 1800 he was hired as literary editor for the Federalist *Gazette of the United States* in Philadelphia, and the next year he founded and edited the weekly *Port Folio* magazine. Throughout his short career he was a controversial figure in American journalism because of his fiercely antidemocratic writings, outspoken adherence to Federalism, and strong attachment to and admiration for all things British. His editing skill and his ability to assemble around him a circle of persons with literary talents similar to his own made him also an influential figure.

Dennie's distaste for democracy can be traced to his childhood. He was born in 1768, the only child in a well-to-do Boston family created by the mingling of the Dennies, of Boston's merchant aristocracy, and the Greens, one of colonial America's foremost printing families. His childhood in Boston was filled with the turmoil of Patriot mobs and British troops. Before he was seven he witnessed the mob violence that resulted from the Boston Massacre, the Stamp Act crisis, and the Tea Party, as well as the day-to-day frictions that arose from the quartering of British troops in Boston. The revolution split his family; a cousin died from wounds received on Lexington Green as a member of the rebel side, and others in the family set sail for England, never to return. Although Dennie's father, Joseph, remained a Loyalist, he took his family from garrisoned Boston to rebel-controlled Lexington, where they lived uneasily in the charged atmosphere of patriotism. There his family's relative sophistication caused the young Dennie to develop a superior and aristocratic attitude toward his rustic Patriot neighbors. He carried this attitude throughout his life, and it found form as his often expressed hatred of American democracy, his distrust of the common people, and his continual championship of government by the elite.

Dennie's frailness, which dogged him throughout his life, caused him to be indulged by his mother, Mary, and this may have had a great deal to do with his later indolent, foppish, vain, and self-centered nature. His father suffered increasingly from a severe mental illness, and Dennie himself fought a recurring melancholia in his adult years. Both parents sought to supplement their son's crude New England schoolhouse education, and they maintained a home library of classical literary and philosophical works which Dennie read assiduously. His later writings were often filled with literary references, some of which were no doubt confusing to less well-educated readers.

His first job, as a clerk in a Boston merchant's counting room, convinced his parents that his future lay elsewhere, and he was sent to a clergyman to be prepared for entry into Harvard College. He was admitted as a nineteen-year-old sophomore in 1787, and his buoyant nature made him popular with his classmates. One of them thought Dennie "the most talented [in the class], taking light literature as a standard," but "negligent in his studies, and not faithful to the genius with which nature had endowed him." Actually, Dennie excelled in all of his subjects except science and math. An anecdote tells of his working on a problem for his landlady involving the cost of 7 3/4 pounds of mutton at 5 1/4 cents a pound. After spending more than a day figuring, he assured her that the butcher was "doubtless honest and she might safely pay her bill." His independent nature and some acts of insolence toward a faculty member caused him to be sent from the college in his senior year, demoted in class rank, and forced to apologize to gain readmission. These were humiliations he never forgave nor forgot. Although his college career was interrupted several times by illness, he was graduated in 1790, fitted for entry into law, medicine, or the ministry, but with a passion for literature and writing.

He chose to study law, which appeared to offer the best chance to make a living. He had misgivings: he did not think that he possessed profound legal talent, he thought that he was showy and superficial, and he admitted to a marked deficiency of judgment. But he thought that these deficiencies were compensated for by "boldness and glitter of fancy in the expression." His study was again interrupted several times by illness, and he began to refer in his letters to his nervous disorder, which he termed "quick vibrations." This illness apparently prevented him from concentrating on a subject for more than a short time, and it did not enhance his already meager legal talent. This disability, and his wish to write, quite naturally led him to an interest in the essay, a literary form popular at the time. The essay was short and did not require long periods of concentration. Dennie was imaginative, wrote in an easy style, and modeled his essays on those of the Britons Addison and Steele.

At the time there were many newspapers in the newly settled areas of Maine, New Hampshire, and Vermont, and their editors were continually on the lookout for material to fill their columns. In early 1792 Dennie began his newspaper career as a contributor of some short works to the *Morning Ray, or Impartial Oracle,* in Windsor, Vermont. The light and racy essays, entitled "The Farrago," poked gentle fun at the manners and morals of the time and the personal foibles of Dennie's friends and neighbors. The essays, which eventually numbered twenty-nine, relieved the tedium of life, amused their readers, and were well received. Some of them were first published in area newspapers other than the *Morning Ray,* and all were widely reprinted in New England newspapers. They drew attention to their young creator.

The next year was a good one for Dennie, and events during 1793 set him on his life's course. His legal practice in Charlestown, New Hampshire, was not a great success, and he was uncomfortable appearing before some of the politically connected but unlettered judges of the backcountry. He later looked back upon his early months of being a lawyer as the happiest of his life, but only because, as one biographer noted, he "slept soundly, unscared . . . by the spectre of poverty." His overall view of himself and the law was that he was trying to "batter down a mud wall with roses," and he knew that his future lay elsewhere.

In mid-1793 he was called upon to conduct the liturgy and read prayers and sermons for a small church in a nearby town whose minister had died. As a result of a successful effort the first week, the congregation contracted with Dennie to carry on for four months. Later he was urged to become

ordained and remain at the head of the congregation, and he gave the offer serious consideration. He viewed the clergyman's life as a more honest one than that of a lawyer, and the salary tempted him. As the months went by, however, he had second thoughts—as did the congregation, which did not wholeheartedly approve of his playing whist, smoking cigars, or joining other attorneys in local taverns for evenings of congenial amusement. His parents, to whom he felt indebted, were not happy to see his three years of study of the law go for naught, and the offer was allowed to die. Dennie took from the experience, however, something of the "suggestion and design" for his Lay Preacher essays, which would assure him literary fame.

In 1794 Dennie met and formed a literary partnership with Royall Tyler, another young lawyer. They headed their writings "From the Shop of Colon and Spondee," and the two authors soon became well known for satirical poetry and prose directed against such contemporary concerns as the revolution in France, the innumerable lotteries held by Harvard College to raise funds, Boston democrats, and, in general, foes of Federalism. The works, which first appeared in Josiah Dunham's *Eagle: or Dartmouth Centinel,* were widely reprinted in Federalist-sympathizing newspapers throughout the region. Dennie realized that people looked forward to reading his witty, optimistic, and fresh musings, and he started thinking about using his writing talent to augment his meager law income.

He first attempted to capitalize on his writing on a visit to Boston in 1795. He was warmly welcomed by some of his Harvard chums, who introduced him to other admirers of his essay style. While there, he sought out the major newspaper publishers in town, including Benjamin Russell and Isaiah Thomas, but they offered him no encouragement. He eventually arranged with a bookseller, William Spotswood, for publication of a weekly newspaper, the *Tablet,* to be the vehicle for his "Farrago" series, which he planned to continue. Spotswood was the publisher and Dennie the anonymous editor. The *Tablet* was patterned after the English *Spectator* and *Tatler,* and Dennie's essays imitated those of Addison and Steele. Dennie remained in the city long enough to get the project under way. He found his stay pleasant; he was witty and jovial, a lover of wine and good conversation, and he was much sought after for parties and dinners.

He returned to his law practice in Charlestown, but by the time he got around to writing some new "Farrago" essays, Spotswood notified him that the magazine had died after only thirteen weeks.

Its diverting rather than practical content might have offended some Bostonians, who were well known for their concern with industry and personal betterment. Perhaps, also, Dennie's sarcastic and humiliating references to Harvard College grated on Bostonians. Dennie was dejected, calling the dead periodical "my child" and writing to his mother that it would have succeeded anywhere in the world but in "your vile democracy."

In late 1795 Dennie moved his law practice to Walpole, New Hampshire, on the Connecticut River. The town was already served by three lawyers, so he was not drawn there solely by prospects of a potentially lucrative law practice. In fact, he was probably more interested in the town's newspaper, the *New Hampshire Journal: or the Farmer's Weekly Museum*, a literary sheet which had already reprinted some of his "Farrago" essays. When he arrived, he immediately offered to create some more entertaining essays for the newspaper, which was owned jointly by Isaiah Thomas and David Carlisle. In October 1795 the first of his Lay Preacher essays appeared in the pages of the *Farmer's Museum*. They soon became the newspaper's most popular feature. As did many authors of such productions at the time, Dennie introduced them with the claim that they were to "be useful, by exhibiting truth in a plain dress to the common people"; in fact, they established his nationwide literary reputation. He also developed for the newspaper a department of criticism called "Literary Intelligence" and wrote some political satires against New England Democrats. In a few months the newspaper had become well known as a Federalist sheet.

Thomas sold his interest in the newspaper to Carlisle in April 1796, and Dennie was immediately hired as editor at a salary of £110, which was more than he earned at law. He devoted his full time and energy to his new job and even locked his law office door to avoid being bothered by potential clients.

Under Dennie's direction, the *Museum* adopted the motto "Ho, every one, that thirsteth for novelty—come!" The newspaper was soon one of the most popular in New England, known for leadership in both politics and literature. Carlisle took charge of what Dennie called "tiresome" advertising and local news chores, while Dennie was responsible for all else. He and Tyler reopened their "Shop of Colon and Spondee" in the pages of the *Farmer's Weekly Museum* with some new antidemocratic political satires.

Dennie early on expressed his intention to conduct the newspaper as a "magazine in a minor form," and he filled its pages with poetry and prose.

Like other editors of the time, he hoped to be able to supply his readers with original material, but like the others he was soon driven to the paste pot to fill empty columns with reprints. He relied heavily on British periodicals and announced that he would reprint only exceptional American works. This brought criticism from readers who did not wish to see the pages of American periodicals monopolized by the productions of British pens. But Dennie was convinced that American literature had little to offer, and if American writers hoped to improve themselves, they would have to do so by imitating British literature and adopting British forms of education and government. He belittled American education and condemned the lack of patronage to support a native literature. "The silly vanity of a self-complacent American may be wounded at this blunt, but notorious truth," he admitted, but "let him deny it if he can." Dennie's growing Anglophilia was becoming more apparent, and his expression of it was becoming one of his favorite themes.

Dennie's own writings for the newspaper were sufficient, however, to give it distinction—especially his Lay Preacher essays, which he produced more or less regularly through 1796 and 1797. People seemed never to tire of reading these didactic musings. In 1796 Carlisle collected and printed a volume of about forty of them, thus assuring Dennie literary fame as "the American Addison." In fact, the slim *Lay Preacher* volume did more to make Dennie noteworthy than all of his other efforts. The essays were reprinted in nearly every newspaper on the continent—especially in the rural areas, where, according to journalism historian Joseph Tinker Buckingham, they were "welcomed by both editors and readers as a kind of 'God-send.'"

Rural readers liked the essays because most of them extolled the virtues of the farmer and his life and cast a dubious eye on anything more sophisticated than hard, honest work. They tended to hold up to view and find wanting those things that farmers did not or could not have. For example, in an essay entitled "Come my beloved, let us go forth into the field, let us lodge in the villages," Dennie wrote that cities were a "Morbid influence, turbid and full of taint," while villages offered "the pleasure of reading and reflecting." In another he wrote that "cutting tender grass is more easy than cutting unlucky cards; that the laborer with a corn basket on his shoulders is less burdened than the tipler with the load on his stomach. . . ." Other editorial topics that appeared in the Lay Preacher essays held up Franklin, Washington, Adams, and Hamilton for effusive approval, while ridiculing Tom Paine ("a loathsome, drunken atheist"), the Jesuits ("giant promise and pigmy pride!"), and women who scolded their husbands. Dennie also continually railed against "idols" such as women's looking glasses ("a great cheat of their time, and an artful flatterer of their beauty"), drinking glasses, pillows and wasting time asleep, and popularity, especially that of seekers for public office. His audience responded by buying his newspaper. By July 1797 Dennie had between 1,500 and 2,000 subscribers throughout the country, and he was offering readers even more than originally promised, including a separate page of his own literary criticisms, "The Dessert," which was extremely popular.

As time went on, his political articles began to draw the notice of important figures. Eventually, Dennie was supplied political intelligence from the very floor of Congress by Federalists General Lewis Morris and Jeremiah Smith of Vermont. Even the powerful Fisher Ames of Massachusetts occasionally sent contributions, all of which Dennie polished and inserted in his pages.

Dennie also improved the newspaper by searching out and encouraging contributors. "He is timorous," he wrote, "lest his readers should be nauseated with similar dishes, cooked by the same hand." He was, however, always the central figure around which others congregated. In 1797, in an attempt to create an environment in which good writing could flourish, he formed a literary club at Walpole composed, he said in a letter to Jeremiah Mason, of "lawyers, divines, quacks and merchants," many of whose members eventually wrote essays, poetry, and criticism for the *Museum*.

In 1798 the newspaper and Dennie's job were threatened. The major blow was a bankruptcy in which Dennie lost a year's salary and money he had invested in the firm. Thomas again took over the publication and reduced Dennie's salary from $500 to $400. Dennie's attitude toward the newspaper also began to change. He was growing tired of mainly local fame. He wanted national literary fame and money, and he hoped for political influence through patronage. He began to turn his attentions elsewhere, and the newspaper's fortunes declined. Things had not progressed beyond hope of redemption, however, before Dennie had temporary second thoughts, and though 1798 was not a good year for the newspaper, Dennie revived it in 1799 by more diligently mining the works of American essayists. In April 1799, in an attempt to capitalize on the popularity of the Lay Preacher

essays, its name was changed to the *Farmer's Museum, or Lay Preacher's Gazette*. In his renewed effort, Dennie began a series of biographies of noteworthy Americans and criticisms of American authors, replacing what had become an almost total concern with British figures. But he was irritated by the salary reduction, which prevented him from living in the manner he enjoyed, and he thought that he could capitalize on his national reputation as the "Erudite Walpole Fire-Brand." He made a run for Congress which netted him only six votes of several hundred cast and attributed the loss to a churlish democracy in which the talents of men were not as well recognized as they would be under a royal government. He received several offers to edit larger newspapers, including one from James White of Boston to edit the *Independent Chronicle* for $1,200 a year, three times his Walpole salary. Dennie wrote White that he would not accept $12 million a year to edit a politically independent newspaper.

He left Walpole in September 1799 for Philadelphia, having been hired to help edit John Ward Fenno's *Gazette of the United States*. Friends had also secured for him an appointment as secretary to Timothy Pickering, the secretary of state, which made Fenno's offer more appealing. Dennie's vanity insisted on the title of confidential assistant or confidential secretary. A lesser title, he made clear, was hurtful to his pride and might disgust his family. He eventually wrote his mother that he was "private and confidential secretary to the Secretary of State," at a salary of $1,000 a year. Further, William Cobbett, the English-sympathizing Federalist editor of *Porcupine's Gazette*, had offered to reprint the Lay Preacher essays in a better edition and to pay Dennie well for the copyright. So by the time he packed his belongings to leave for Philadelphia, Dennie envisioned literary fame and wealth, perhaps a future appointment as head of a foreign legation or even a government secretaryship. He was eager to begin. He wrote a college friend that he hoped only that he had "enough mortal time left . . . both for some fame and fortune."

In October 1799 he arrived in Philadelphia, which was to be his home for the remainder of his life. The city was then the most important in American politics, trade, literature, and medicine. It boasted among its residents two important American writers, Philip Freneau and Charles Brockden Brown. It was in the back of Dennie's mind to join their ranks as the country's best essayist, an endeavor for which he was already prepared because of the popularity of his Lay Preacher essays.

His job as Pickering's secretary paid him enough to live as a gentleman, and it provided access to official circles of both city and national government, including the president. Dennie had some income from the *Farmer's Museum,* for which he continued to write occasionally, and he could count on $800 a year as literary editor of Fenno's *Gazette.* He began to enjoy Philadelphia society.

The *Gazette* was an outlet for both his arch-Federalism and his literary criticism, which he often combined in a single essay. His editorship seemed to draw from him a rabid Anglophilia. He increasingly rejected American life, and his antipathy to democracy grew almost obsessive. Although his sentiments were doubtless partly the product of the often virulent party feeling of the period, the depth of his emotions was apparent in a Lay Preacher essay written at the end of 1799. In it he blamed yellow fever and all of the world's other ills on the "frantic madness of liberty, equality, fraternity" that had engulfed France and threatened to overcome America. He wrote his parents early in 1800 that if the American Revolution had not occurred, or if he had been born in London, his fame would have been greatly enhanced, and he would by that time have been worth three or four thousand pounds. "But in this Republic, this region covered with the Jewish and canting and cheating descendants of [the first American settlers] . . . what can men of liberality and letters expect but such icy polar treatment, as I have experienced?" After his move to the capital, he began to refer to "my countrymen, the natives of North Britain," and wrote: "I have a strong motive to love the nation. The English character is the most honest, the most generous, the most frank and liberal, and foul is that day in our calendar and bitterly are those patriotic, selfish and Indian traitors to be cursed who instigated the wretched populace to declare the 4th Day of July, 1776, a Day of Independence." In a letter to a friend, he referred to Americans as a "brute mass . . . despicably mean, weak and miserable." His feelings toward his countrymen hardened in the nation's capital, and he began to exhibit signs that he viewed himself as a tragic figure, ill-treated by events. This was not a healthy development, given his "quick vibrations" and his physical frailty. He was probably not prepared to handle such strong emotions in a sustained manner. Gradually the exuberance and wit of his youth were giving way to more serious concerns, which threatened to end in bitterness and disillusionment toward both himself and his country.

Of course, his days were not filled merely with pique over the hand life had dealt him, and he contributed whenever he could to letters and literary pursuits. His literary criticism, although by now not always gentle, was nonetheless to the point. He struck out at the florid writing characteristic of the times, and he continually urged others to "emulate a diction pure, simple, expressive and English." His generally good motives seem to have been weakened, however, by the fact that he continually overshot his mark. His criticism, when supplemented by his fierce antirepublicanism, became as ridiculous in others' eyes as those persons and works which were the object of his satires. One critic wrote that Dennie's "sarcasm will never convert dullness into ingenuity, nor will genius be bullied into exercise."

Although Dennie was a convivial man, by 1800 his conviviality extended little beyond the narrow circle of his elite Federalist friends. He joined wholeheartedly on their side in the newspaper editorial battles of the time and helped to earn the title "the Dark Ages of Partisan Journalism" for that period in journalism history. He was not convivial when he wrote, "the editor of the *Sun* is a blockhead, and an ass, and a True American," nor when he referred to William Duane, conductor of the Democrat sheet *Aurora,* as a "gin-drinking pauper" and to his newspaper as a "dull Democratic gazette, intolerably tedious, egregiously stupid, audaciously false, and unspeakably absurd."

He reserved for his most venomous outpourings, though, Thomas Jefferson, whom Dennie thought America's most dangerous man. He waged a never-ending war against the third president. In one of two pamphlets directed against Jefferson's presidential candidacy, Dennie wrote: "And I looked, and beheld a pale Horse; and his name that sat on him was death, and Hell followed with him." After Jefferson's election, Dennie predicted "some civil convulsion in the heart of our Republic." Eventually Dennie would be called to task for his increasingly shrill and strident words.

In the course of editing the *Gazette of the United States,* he tried also to arrange for further publication of his literary output. His understanding with Cobbett about the publication of a new edition of his Lay Preacher essays evaporated when Cobbett fled America one step ahead of an unfavorable libel judgment. Dennie considered leaving with Cobbett for London, where he thought he would be better appreciated than in his native land. But in the end, he decided to stay in Philadelphia.

His short stint as editor of the *Gazette* ended

when Fenno sold the newspaper, although Dennie stayed on until December 1800 as editor of the literary and miscellaneous departments. His job as secretary to Pickering ended with Pickering's ouster by Adams. The loss of his two sinecures did not seem to bother him greatly, although he was left with little income. He began once again to cast about for new opportunities.

Near the end of 1800, with financial backing from a Philadelphia bookseller, he advertised "A New Weekly Paper, to be conducted on an extensive and liberal plan, combining, in the manner of the TATLER, politics with essays and disquisitions on topics scientific, moral, humorous and literary." The proposed publication, to be called the *Port Folio*, was to look like a newspaper, if more literary in content than most. Dennie adopted the pen name "Oliver Oldschool, Esq." to signify that the editor would look to the happier days of the past. His pseudonym was a recognition of Dennie's reactionary outlook; he longed for a return to the days before American independence. "He would never asperse," he wrote, "the government, church or literature of England," but he made no such promise about his own country or its citizens. On the brighter side, he said that he hoped to relieve for his readers "the dryness of news, and the severity of political argument, with wholesome morals and gay miscellany."

The *Port Folio* surpassed even Dennie's expectations. It became the best such publication in America, owing largely to his cultivation of the ablest American essayists, storytellers, and poets and to his reprinting of the best English and even French writers. He even printed, for the first time anywhere, some important letters to the British novelist Tobias Smollett from James Boswell, David Hume, and William Pitt the Younger.

All of the Adams family subscribed to the *Port Folio*, and several were more actively involved. A particularly important series, which ran for almost a year, was John Quincy Adams's "Journal of a Tour through Silesia," which had the dual effect of attracting readers and of filling nearly an entire page each week. John Adams's youngest son, Thomas Boylston Adams, a friend and one of Dennie's Harvard classmates, was its secret business manager for several years. At the time, it was not unusual for the Adams connection not to be prominently featured, as most gentlemen, President John Adams especially, looked upon nonpolitical writing as "scribbling" and thought dabbling in literature a "positive disqualification for business."

Dennie contributed to the magazine for several years, until his editing chores grew too great for him to handle comfortably. He then gave up creating essays and conducting spirited literary criticisms for full-time editing. Politically, the stock-in-trade of the *Port Folio* was antidemocratic essays, of a type even more bitter and shrill than Dennie had yet exhibited. They included his fierce attack on the Declaration of Independence, "that false and flatulent and foolish paper," and they were supplemented by nasty anti-Jefferson essays, including republication of some particularly vile stories about Jefferson's supposed liaison with a slave. These stories, and statements such as "a democracy is scarcely tolerable at any period of national history . . . it is on trial here . . . and no honest man but proclaims its fraud, and no brave man but draws his sword against its force," all but forced the Republican administration to notice Dennie. Perhaps at Jefferson's direction, Dennie was indicted in July 1803 by a Pennsylvania grand jury and charged with "inflammatory and seditious libel." Although the trial was delayed until November 1805 and ended with Dennie's acquittal, it put Dennie and others on notice that there were boundaries to good taste in criticism, and Dennie emerged from the affair quieter and less strident. He did proclaim after the favorable verdict that he had triumphed in warfare with democracy, "a fiend more terrible than any that the imagination of the classical poets ever conjured up from the 'vasty deep' of their Pagan Hell." But then he seemed content—or tired—and let the matter rest.

The *Port Folio*'s major force, however, was as a literary endeavor. Dennie was able to assemble about him qualified writers and to ferret out interesting, significant, and lively material for his pages. By 1803 and 1804, Dennie's superlative editing and literary criticism had made it the best magazine yet published in America. When he ran short of sources, he encouraged the founding of a literary club in Philadelphia, the Tuesday Club, much as he had done earlier in Walpole. Like the members of the earlier Walpole group, most of the Tuesday Club's members were college-educated lawyers and Federalists, and most of them had literary ambitions. They provided some of the spark that kept the magazine going.

But time was running out. In 1802 Dennie had written his mother to lament that he had a "weak habit of body" and was "obliged to drudge for literature for a mere subsistence in this execrable country." His health continued to be precarious, and further deterioration by 1807 cut down on his contributions and his editing energy and forced

THE PORT FOLIO.

BY OLIVER OLDSCHOOL, ESQ.

"VARIOUS, THAT THE MIND
OF DESULTORY MAN, STUDIOUS OF CHANGE,
AND PLEAS'D WITH NOVELTY, MAY BE INDULGED."
COWPER.

VOL. I.]

PHILADELPHIA, SATURDAY. JANUARY 3d, 1801.

[No. 1.

TRAVELS.

FOR THE PORT FOLIO.

[The subsequent letter is the commencement of a series, which will be regularly published in this paper. It is unnecessary to dwell upon the general excellence of the following tour. It will be obvious to every intelligent reader that it has been made by no vulgar traveller, but by a man of genius and observation, who, in happy union, combines the power of selecting the most interesting and picturesque objects, and of describing them gracefully.]

JOURNAL OF A TOUR THROUGH SILESIA.

LETTER I.

Frankfort, on the Oder, 20th July, 1800.

As I have bespoken your company, upon our journey into Silesia, I begin this letter at our first resting station from Berlin. Hitherto, we have indeed seen little more than the usual Brandenburg sands, and perhaps you will find our tour as tiresome, as we have found it ourselves. I cannot promise you an amusing journey, though I hope it will prove so to us. My letters to you, on this tour, will be in the form, and serve as the substitute of a journal. They will, of course, be fragments, written at different times and places; nay, perhaps in different humours. Therefore, make up your account, to receive patiently all my tediousness.

On Thursday, the 17th inst. we left Berlin, just after three in the morning, and arrived here at about nine the same evening. The distance is ten German miles and a quarter; which you know is a very long day's journey in this country. In the course of a few years, it will be an easy journey of eight hours; for the present king, who has this very laudable ambition of improving the roads through his dominions, is now making a turnpike road, like that to Potsdam, the whole way hither; as yet, not more than one German mile of it is finished, and the rest of the way is like that, which on every side surrounds the Tolmer of modern times. As we approach within a few miles of Frankfort the country becomes somewhat hilly, and of course more variegated and pleasant than round Berlin; but we could perceive little difference in the downy softness of the ground beneath us, or in the idea of the pines within our view. Part of the country is cultivated, as much as it is susceptible of cultivation, and here and there we could see scattered spires of wheat, rye, barley, and oats shooting from the sands, like the hairs upon a head almost bald. We came through a few villages, and those few had a miserable appearance. A meagre composition of mud and thatch composed the cottages, in which a ragged and pallid race of beggars reside; yet we must not be unjust, and confess, that we passed by one nobleman's seat, which had the appearance of a handsome and comfortable house.

We arrived here just in time to see the last dregs of an annual *fair,* such as you have often seen in the towns of Holland, and as you know are customary in those of Germany. But we hear great complaints against the minister Struensee, for having ruined the value of the *fair,* by prohibiting the sale of foreign woollen manufactures, which have heretofore been the most essential articles of sale at this fair. This prohibition is for the sake of encouraging the manufactures of this country, a principle, which the government pursue on all possible occasions. They are no converts to the opinions of Adam Smith and the French economists, concerning the balance of trade, and always catch with delight at any thing which can prevent money from *going out of the country.* Of this disposition we have seen a notable instance in the attempts lately made here or producing sugar from beets, of which I believe you heard something while you were here, and about which much has been said and done since then. At one time we were assured beyond all question, that one mile square of beets would furnish sugar for the whole Prussian dominions. The question was submitted to a committee of the Academy of Sciences, who, after long examination and deliberation, reported, that in truth, sugar, and even brandy, could be produced from beets, and in process of time might be raised in great quantities; but that, for the present, it would be expedient to continue the use of sugars and brandies, such as had been in use hitherto. Since this report, we have heard little or nothing of beet sugar.

This is an old town, pleasantly situated, and containing about twelve thousand inhabitants, of which a quarter part are Jews. It is therefore distinguished by those peculiarities, which mark all European towns where a large proportion of Israelites reside, and to express which, I suppose, resort must be had to the Hebrew language. The English at least is inadequate to it; for the word *filth* conveys an idea of spotless purity, in comparison to the Jewish nastiness. The garrison of the town consists of one regiment. There is here likewise an university; and by the introduction of a letter from Berlin, we have become acquainted with two of the professors. The number of students is less than two hundred; and of them, one hundred and fifty are students of law; ten or fifteen of divinity; and not more than two or three of medicine. The library, the museum, and the botanical garden, the professors tell me, are all so miserable, that they are ashamed to show them.

The banks of the Oder, on one side, are bordered with small hills, upon which at small distances, are little summer-houses with vineyards, at which, during summer, many inhabitants of the town reside. On the other side, the land is flat, and the river is restrained from overflowing only by a large dyke, which has been built since the year 1785. At that time the river broke down the smaller dyke, which had, until then, existed and overflowed the country to a considerable extent. Prince Leopold of Brunswick, a brother of the present reigning duke, was then colonel of the regiment in garrison here, and lost his life in attempting to save some of the people, whom the inundation was carrying away. You have probably seen prints of this melancholy accident, and there is an account of it in the last edition of Moore's *Travels.* (I mean his first work.) There is a small monument erected in honour of the prince, upon the spot where his body was found. It was done by the free-masons of this place, of which society he was a member. But there is nothing remarkable in it. There is likewise in the burying ground a little monument, or rather tomb-stone, to *Kleist,* one of the most celebrated German poets, whom his countrymen call their Thomson. He was an officer in the service of Frederick the second, and was killed at the battle of Cunersdorf, a village distant only a couple miles from this place.

Just at the gate of the town, there is a spring of mineral water, at which a bathing house has been built, with accommodations for lodgers. This bath has been considerably frequented for some years past, and the physicians of the town say, that the waters are as good as those of Freyenwalde. I am willing to believe them as good as those of Toeplitz; for my faith in mineral waters in general, was not much edified by the success of our tour there last summer.

22d July. Still at Frankfort. We had left Berlin without being fully aware of the precise nature of the journey we had undertaken; and had not thought of taking with us furs, and winter-clothing for a tour in the dog-days. But one of the professors, whose acquaintance we have made here, had formerly gone the same journey; and from his representations, we have been induced to send back to Berlin for thick clothing, and this circumstance has prolonged our stay here a couple of days more than we at first intended. Yesterday we took a ride of three or four miles, to the country seat of a Mr. Schoening, the landrath of the *circle.* The functions of his office are to collect the territorial taxes within a certain district called a *circle,* which is a subdivision of the province. You know the importance and extent of this title of *rath* or *cavalier,* in the constitutions of the German states. It is a general name, designating every officer in all the subordinate parts of the administration; and sometimes a mere honorary title, which Frederic the second, by way of joke, once granted to a person, *upon condition* that he should never presume to give any *council.* For the principle upon which the name is founded is, that the person holding the office gives the king occasionally counsel, and the first part of it usually designates the particular department in which he gives it.

Mr. Schoening and his lady, received us with great kindness and hospitality. From the neighbourhood of their house, and on our return, we had the pleasure of agreeable prospects of the

First page of the first issue of Dennie's weekly magazine of essays, which he edited under the pseudonym "Oliver Oldschool, Esq."

him to turn increasingly to English journals for reprints. His rabid antidemocratic stand had cut him off from some important domestic writers, and he was by then ridiculing even fellow Federalists: he lampooned Noah Webster for working on a dictionary which attempted to establish an American standard of language to replace the British. His bitter political stands undoubtedly cost him some support.

He lost the *Port Folio* in 1808, although he stayed on as a salaried editor, paid for his prestige and management skills. After January 1809 the magazine was published by the firm of Inskeep and Bradford. Dennie was given to more and more frequent gloom and depression. In 1809 the magazine was changed to a monthly, and the new owners adopted a nonpartisan policy. It was evidence of Dennie's failing health that he did not noisily protest but merely replaced his pen name, Oliver Oldschool, Esq., with plain Joseph Dennie. After Dennie's death, his successor, Nicholas Biddle, resurrected the Oliver Oldschool name.

The *Port Folio*, like its founder, was sliding downhill. Dennie's health failed in the summer of 1811, and he was bedridden through the fall. He revived for a time near the end of the year but declined rapidly after the beginning of the New Year, and he died on 7 January 1812 "like a gentleman and a Christian," surrounded by a few close friends. He was forty-four.

Dennie's best newspaper effort was his editorship of the *Farmer's Weekly Museum;* he made that small country sheet a national force, one of the most reprinted newspapers of the day. Furthermore, it was Dennie's own writings, especially his Lay Preacher essays, that other editors reprinted. But even those essays, when collected, amounted to little more than a thin volume, and most of his newspaper work, including the "Farrago" series, was never collected. Dennie did not leave a great deal of material, and that which he did leave was written largely in the essay form, which even in the early 1800s was beginning to lose its popularity. Still, he was perhaps the best essayist in America when that form was still popular; he excelled with his contemporaries if not with posterity.

Probably Dennie's best claim to journalistic greatness is as an editor. He was able to gather about him talented writers and to encourage and develop their creativity. His cultivation of the best writers of the time for both the *Museum* and the *Port Folio* is a singular accomplishment; and he should be given credit for his sincere desire to criticize, elevate, and improve the tastes of others, even when doing so made him unpopular. Unfortunately, he will be remembered as the shrill and sometimes nasty little man who was a reactionary force in an increasingly democratic era, and who had the bad judgment to repeat some vile stories about the third president, which led to his indictment for libel.

Letters:

The Letters of Joseph Dennie, 1768-1812, edited by Laura Green Pedder (Orono, Me.: Printed at the University Press, 1936).

Biography:

Harold Milton Ellis, *Joseph Dennie and His Circle* (Austin: University of Texas, 1915).

References:

Joseph Tinker Buckingham, *Specimens of Newspaper Literature,* 2 volumes (Boston: Little, Brown, 1850), II: 74-202;

Annie Russell Marble, *Heralds of American Literature* (Chicago: University of Chicago Press, 1907), pp. 193-231;

Frank Luther Mott, *A History of American Magazines, 1741-1850* (New York: D. Appleton, 1930), pp. 223-246;

Fred Lewis Pattee, *The First Century of American Literature, 1770-1870* (New York: D. Appleton-Century, 1935), pp. 184-190, 210-212;

Randolph Randall, "Joseph Dennie's Literary Attitudes in the *Port Folio,* 1801-1812," in *Essays Mostly on Periodical Publishing in America,* edited by James Woodress (Durham, N.C.: Duke University Press, 1973).

Papers:

Joseph Dennie's papers are held by Harvard University.

Frederick Douglass
(February 1817-20 February 1895)

Sharon M. Murphy
Marquette University

See also the Douglass entry in *DLB 1, The American Renaissance in New England.*

MAJOR POSITIONS HELD: Editor, *North Star* (Rochester, N.Y.), renamed *Frederick Douglass's Paper* in 1851 (1847-1860), *Douglass' Monthly* (1858-1863), *New National Era* (Washington, D.C.) (1870-1874).

SELECTED BOOKS: *Narrative of the Life of Frederick Douglass, an American Slave. Written by*

Gale International Portrait Gallery

Himself (Boston: Published at the Anti-Slavery Office, 1845; Dublin: Webb & Chapman, 1845); enlarged as *My Bondage and My Freedom*, introduction by Dr. James M'Cune Smith (New York: Miller, Orton & Mulligan, 1855); enlarged again as *The Life and Times of Frederick Douglass, Written by Himself*, introduction by George L. Ruffin (Hartford, Conn.: Park, 1881); republished as *The Life and Times of Frederick Douglass, from 1817-1882, Written by Himself*, introduction by the Right Hon. John Bright, M.P., edited by John Lobb (London: Christian Age Office, 1882); revised as *Life and Times of Frederick Douglass, Written by Himself*, introduction by Ruffin (Boston: De Wolfe, Fisk, 1892);

Farewell Speech of Mr. Frederick Douglass, Previously to Embarking on Board the Cambria, *upon His Return to America, Delivered at the Valedictory Soiree Given to Him at the London Tavern, on March 30, 1847. Published, by Order of the Council of the Anti-Slavery League, from the Short-hand Notes of Mr. W. Farmer* (London: Ward, 1847);

Lectures on American Slavery (Buffalo, N.Y.: Reese & Co.'s Power Press, 1851);

Oration, Delivered in Corinthian Hall, Rochester, by Frederick Douglass, July 5th, 1852 (Rochester, N.Y.: Printed by Lee, Mann, 1852);

The Claims of the Negro Ethnologically Considered. An Address before the Literary Societies of Western Reserve College, at Commencement, July 12, 1854 (Rochester, N.Y.: Printed by Lee, Mann, 1854);

The Anti-Slavery Movement. A Lecture by Frederick Douglass, before the Rochester Ladies' Anti-Slavery Society (Rochester, N.Y.: Press of Lee, Mann, 1855);

Address by Frederick Douglass, and Poem by A. C. Hills Delivered at the Erection of the Wing Monument, at Mexico, Oswego Co., N.Y., September 11th, 1855 (Syracuse, N.Y.: J. G. K. Truair, 1855);

Two Speeches by Frederick Douglass: One on West India Emancipation, Delivered at Canadaigua, Aug. 4th, and the Other on the Dred Scott Decision, De-

*livered in New York, on the Occasion of the An-
niversary of the American Abolition Society, May
1857* (Rochester, N.Y.: C. P. Dewey, printer,
1857);

*Eulogy of the Late Hon. Wm. Jay, by Frederick Douglass,
Delivered on the Invitation of the Colored Citizens
of New York City in Shiloh Presbyterian Church,
New York, May 12, 1859* (Rochester, N.Y.:
Press of A. Strong & Co., 1859);

*U.S. Grant and the Colored People. His Wise, Just, Prac-
tical, and Effective Friendship Thoroughly Vindicated by Incontestable Facts in His Record from
1862 to 1872. Words of Truth and Soberness! He
Who Runs May Read and Understand!! Be Not
Deceived, Only Truth Can Endure!!!* (Washington, D.C., 1872);

*Address Delivered by Hon. Frederick Douglass, at the
Third Annual Fair of the Tennessee Colored Agricultural Association on Thursday, September 18,
1873, at Nashville, Tennessee* (Washington,
D.C.: New National Era and Citizen Print.,
1873);

*Oration by Frederick Douglass, Delivered on Occasion of
the Unveiling of the Freedmen's Monument in
Memory of Abraham Lincoln, in Lincoln Park,
Washington, D.C., April 14th, 1876. With an Appendix* (Washington, D.C.: Gibson Brothers,
printers, 1876);

*John Brown. An Address by Frederick Douglass, at the
Fourteenth Anniversary of Storer College, Harper's
Ferry, West Virginia, May 30, 1881* (Dover,
N.H.: Morning Star Job Printing House,
1881);

*The 21st Anniversary of the Emancipation of Slavery in
the District of Columbia: An Address* (Washington, D.C.: National Republican, 1883);

*Three Addresses on the Relations Subsisting between the
White and Colored People of the United States*
(Washington, D.C.: Gibson Brothers, print-
ers, 1886);

*Lecture on Haiti. The Haitian Pavilion Dedication Cer-
emonies Delivered at the World's Fair, in Jackson
Park, Chicago, Jan. 2d, 1893* (Chicago, 1893);

*Address by Hon. Frederick Douglass, Delivered in the
Metropolitan A.M.E. Church, Washington, D.C.,
Tuesday, January 9th, 1894, on the Lessons of the
Hour. In Which He Discusses the Various Aspects
of the So-Called, but Mis-Called, Negro Problem*
(Baltimore: Press of Thomas & Evans, 1894);

*Negroes and the National War Effort, an Address by
Frederick Douglass*, foreword by James W. Ford
(New York: Workers Library Publishers,
1942);

Frederick Douglass: Selections from His Writings, edited

by Philip S. Foner (New York: International
Publishers, 1945);

*The Frederick Douglass Papers: Series One: Speeches,
Debates, and Interviews. Volume I: Eighteen-Forty-
One to Eighteen-Forty-Six*, edited by John W.
Blassingame (New Haven: Yale University
Press, 1979).

Frederick Douglass's life encompassed slavery
and freedom, absolute poverty and international
fame and gentility. Though he made his escape
from slavery at the age of twenty-one, he spent his
remaining fifty-seven years fighting that institution
through oratory and the press. His *North Star* was
among the first successful black newspapers in the
United States, and his three autobiographical books
were early, stinging indictments written as first-per-
son accounts of life amid slavery.

His work as editor and writer served to counteract much of the antiblack, proslavery sentiment
of the rest of the American press system. One example of the latter, apocryphal though it may be,
is the retort by the editor of the famous *New York
Sun* when blacks wanted a retraction printed after
slanderous comments were published concerning
black businessmen. They were told that the *Sun*
shone for white men, not black; and if the gentlemen wanted anything printed they might as well
start their own newspaper.

Throughout his life, Douglass was a voice for
the unheard and a champion for the unprotected.
His life and his work demonstrate the best and the
most courageous in American activist, crusading
journalism. They show what the power of the press,
harnessed in the cause of the oppressed, could do.
In addition, they demonstrate what a noble creature the human individual is: determination, not
formal education, helped develop in him an ora-
torical power and a gift for persuasive writing
rarely matched in the journalism of his time.

He was born Frederick Augustus Washington
Baily, in Tuckahoe, Talbot County, Maryland, the
son of Harriet Bailey, a slave, and a white man
whose name he never learned. "From certain
events . . . the dates of which I have learned since,
I suppose myself to have born about the year 1817,"
he later wrote. Biographers have confirmed that
his mother was one of very few literate slaves.
Though the practices of slavery resulted in his removal from his mother at a very early age, Douglass
was deeply influenced throughout his life by his
memory of her.

He served in varying capacities under slavery,
as a house servant, a farm laborer, and a shipyard

worker. Because of his strong spirit and evident desire for freedom, he was sent to a slave-breaker to be trained, worked to death, or beaten into submission. One reason for this treatment was that he had learned a little bit of reading from the compassionate and well-intentioned wife of one of his masters, and had tried to pass on this learning by establishing a school under the trees for fellow slaves. Another reason was that he had been betrayed by another slave in a plan to escape. He did escape on 3 September 1838, using a borrowed sailor's suit and a sympathetic black freedman's "protection papers," which indicated that an individual described on the paper, slightly resembling Douglass, could move freely about the country.

Douglass, whose last master had been the foreman of a shipyard in Baltimore, made his escape from that city to Philadelphia, where, he wrote in his autobiography, he "lived more in one day than in a year of . . . slave life." The next day he moved on to New York City, where he married a freedwoman, Anna Murray, who had encouraged and financially supported his escape. Together they moved to New Bedford, Massachusetts, under the new surname of Douglass. His difficulties in finding work and the demeaning treatment he received at the hands of prospective employers and coworkers stayed in his memory and gave inspiration and impetus to his eventual work as an antislavery journalist and orator.

Douglass's experiences as a free man included tending furnaces, where he "often nailed a newspaper to the post near my bellows and read" while working. One newspaper of which he was a regular and avid reader was William Lloyd Garrison's *Liberator,* and he attended all the meetings of that editor's Abolitionist Society held in New Bedford. He did not long remain a quiet observer and, despite the danger which public notice might bring him, spoke before a society gathering in New Bedford's Christian Church on 12 March 1839, just over six months after his escape from slavery. Two years later he met Garrison in person and began the life of public speaking which was to propel him into public notice and to help propel the country into emancipation and universal suffrage. In addition to public addresses on slavery, he traveled with Stephen S. Foster promoting the *Liberator* and the *Anti-Slavery Standard.* Little did Garrison realize that such an arrangement would not only further the abolitionist cause but would also launch the career of one of black journalism's most prominent pioneers.

Beginning in August 1841, Douglass was part

Douglass's first wife, Anna Murray Douglass, who helped him to escape from slavery in 1838 (Moorland-Spingarn Research Center, Howard University)

of a national and international team of lecturers who took the cause of abolitionism into churches, town halls, and wherever groups of people, friendly or hostile, would listen. Between 1842 and 1847, the *Liberator* printed his letters and the texts of many of his lectures. His autobiography, *Narrative of the Life of Frederick Douglass, an American Slave,* written in 1845 to convince audiences of the truth of his assertions, put his freedom in jeopardy from bounty hunters who would have profited from returning him to his former master. Taking the advice of friends, he left his wife and four children in August 1845 and sailed for the British Isles. He spent two years in England, Ireland, and Scotland lecturing and corresponding with the *Liberator* and the *National Anti-Slavery Standard.* While he was in Europe, an edition of his autobiography, printed in Dublin, helped fund his travels and his antislavery lecturing. He also established a circle of friends and supporters who would remain loyal through-

Douglass in about 1844, portrait attributed to Elisha Hammond (National Portrait Gallery, Smithsonian Institution)

out his career. Their concern for his safety led several English friends to raise £150 to purchase his freedom papers. In addition to official freedom status, the two years in Europe gave Douglass a vision of liberty which was to haunt him upon his return to America on 20 April 1847.

He returned with the intention and the funds to establish a newspaper, but opposition by Garrison led him to put the thought aside and to rededicate himself to lecturing against slavery. But the editorial urge was strong, and in the 1 November 1847 issue of the *Ram's Horn*, a black newspaper, he announced plans for the *North Star*, which would "attack slavery in all its forms and aspects"; advocate "Universal Emancipation; exact the standard of public morality; promote the moral and intellectual improvement of the colored people; and . . . hasten the day of freedom to our three million enslaved fellow-countrymen." It would also create lasting ill will between him and Garrison, who considered Douglass ungrateful for abandoning the *Liberator* and the speaking engagements Garrison felt he was better suited for. The paper was to be published in Rochester, New York, with

subscriptions at two dollars per year.

That Douglass expected and counted upon the support of the free black community is attested to by a comment in the inaugural issue of the *North Star*. He wrote that he had long wanted to see "in this slave-holding, slave-trading and Negro-hating land" a newspaper "under the complete control and direction of the immediate victims of slavery and oppression." It was his belief that "the man who has *suffered the wrong* is the man to *demand redress* . . . the man who is STRUCK is the man to CRY OUT . . . he who has *endured the cruel pangs of slavery* is the man to *advocate Liberty.*"

Initial funding for the paper, $2,174, collected by supporters in England, did not go far enough; after six months of operation, Douglass acknowledged that he and partner Martin R. Delany had trouble getting subscriptions and support at home. He was especially disappointed by the lack of financial and moral backing from the black community; only one in five subscribers was black. At the same time, the *North Star* was "too free from party dictation to receive much support from any existing anti-slavery paper." This very apparent jab at the Garrisonians hints at the pain the rupture from Garrison must have caused him. In April 1848 Douglass mortgaged his home to keep the paper afloat.

Douglass's paper was very clearly marked with the imprint of its editor. The collaboration with Delany lasted only six months; thereafter, the paper was Douglass's work. Douglass sought freedom and self-determination for blacks and parted company with some leaders of the time who promoted sending blacks to Africa in the quest for freedom. When Henry Clay tried to revive the Colonization Society and to encourage blacks to end the "Negro problem" through voluntary expatriation, the *North Star* retorted, "We are at home here; and our staying here is evidence that we wish to stay here." Colonization was, Douglass wrote, "the twin sister of slavery."

The *North Star*, like Douglass himself, was not to be limited to the issues of emancipation and suffrage for black people. The paper's slogan was "Right is of no Sex—Truth is of no Color—God is the Father of us all, and we are all Brethren." In the second year of the paper Douglass was actively supporting woman suffrage and education, as well as married woman's rights. He spoke at the Seneca Falls convention in the summer of 1848.

Although by 1850 the paper had subscribers throughout the United States as well as in London, Liverpool, Derby, Dublin, Belfast, Edinburgh, and

The print shop in Rochester, New York, where Douglass's North Star *was published. The paper was renamed* Frederick Douglass's Paper *in 1851.*

Glasgow, its financial difficulties continued. Douglass finally was forced to seek a merger with Gerrit Smith's *Liberty Party Paper*. The new organ, named *Frederick Douglass's Paper*, appeared in June 1851. It survived until mid-1860.He selected the name as much to distinguish the paper from the many other "Stars" in the publishing firmament as to use what he knew was the prestige and drawing power of his name to attract subscribers and financial backers. The paper was similar to most contemporary abolitionist publications: a four-page, six-column weekly, heavy on exhortation and vigorous in style. Its contents included coverage of local and state antislavery meetings, submitted by unpaid correspondents; reports reprinted from other reformist publications; antislavery verse—most of it doggerel, but some by luminaries like Lowell and Whittier; book reviews and serialized novels; and advertisements, including the ever-popular patent medicine endorsements. One biographer has pointed to the high standard set by Douglass: "He would tolerate no grammatical debaucheries," and

typographical errors rarely occurred.

With the merger of the *North Star* and the *Liberty Party Paper*, the financial problems facing Douglass were temporarily lessened. Gerrit Smith, leader of the Liberty party, took over the debts of the *North Star* and pledged a monthly contribution to the support of *Frederick Douglass's Paper*, which was to serve as the official organ of the party. Douglass's work as an editor was accompanied by a continuing career as an antislavery lecturer and by the challenging and dangerous role he played as "conductor" of the Rochester branch of the Underground Railroad. He harbored fugitives overnight in his home, arranged for their safe passage to Canada, and often supplied funds for their journey.

Rather than support "solutions" to the problems of blacks such as colonization, Douglass promoted job training; an 1853 editorial was entitled "Learn Trades or Starve." But he was selective: young men should be apprenticed as farmers and mechanics, not as waiters, porters, and barbers, even then traditional positions for black free men.

In June 1858, on the advice of Julia Griffiths, an Englishwoman who had come to Rochester to help with the newspaper, Douglass introduced an additional publication, *Douglass' Monthly,* a magazine directed toward circulation in the British Isles. It was as much a recognition of the continuing devotion to the abolitionist cause there as a promotional effort. Funds were again running low, the Liberty party had fallen on lean economic times and could not be counted on for monthly contributions needed to pay expenses, and various fundraising efforts had netted little toward solvency. The monthly, with a yearly rate of two dollars, had as little success as other fund raisers had.

The death of *Frederick Douglass's Paper* came shortly after the forty-three-year-old Douglass returned from a second forced exile in England and Scotland, this time of six-month duration and occasioned by the John Brown raid at Harpers Ferry, Virginia, in 1859. Because Douglass had been sought out by Brown and had been a guest in Brown's home as the fiery reformer planned his insurrection, the editor was suspect and in danger of arrest and execution. Danger was nothing new to Douglass, an early civil rights activist who had been pitched off a train in Lynn, Massachusetts, in 1841 for refusing to ride in the Jim Crow car after he paid for a first-class coach seat. Citing delinquent subscribers, continuing expenses, and receipts "nearly zero" for the weekly, Douglass folded his weekly newspaper in mid-1860. But as he had pointed out five years before, the years and the dollars devoted to the paper had been worthwhile "in the development of my own mental and moral energies, and in the corresponding development of my deeply injured and oppressed people." As his second autobiography, *My Bondage and My Freedom* (1855) attests, Douglass's editorial work had forced him to look closely and continuously at the limitations placed on black existence in pre-1860 America. His lecturing with the Garrisonians had been directed against slavery and against union with slaveholding states. Gradually, however, he came to argue for the use of voting power to take advantage of what he felt was the antislavery nature of the Constitution. He promoted woman suffrage because of its inherent logic as well as because of the need to broaden the base of antislavery sentiment. In 1853 he had told the Rochester Women's Rights convention, "Someone whispers in my ear, that as teachers, women get one-fourth the pay men do, while a girl's tuition is the same as a boy's."

From Gerrit Smith's abolitionist Liberty party,

Douglass moved to action within the Republican party. He was initially dissatisfied with Abraham Lincoln's cautious handling of the slavery controversy, considering him cowardly and ignoble. When Lincoln issued a call to arms following the attack on Fort Sumter in 1861, Douglass urged black men to form companies of militia to aid in the Union effort. When the president resisted enlistments by black men into the army (despite the fact that it was customary to accept blacks into the navy), Douglass saw more of the bowing to expediency which angered him.

The final straw was Lincoln's recommendation to Congress in 1861 of colonization for slaves and free blacks. Douglass wrote that he was "bewildered by the spectacle of moral blindness, infatuation and helpless imbecility which the government of Lincoln represents." He did little to soften his criticisms until the Emancipation Proclamation was finally published on 1 January 1863. Then, he took up the cause of black troops. Not only did he urge enlistment in the pages of the *Monthly* but he actively worked as a recruiter. The first man he signed up for the Massachusetts Fifty-fourth and Fifty-fifth Negro Regiments was his youngest son, Charles, followed closely afterward by his eldest son, Lewis. His argument was that "liberty won only by white men will lose half its lustre."

But when he began hearing reports of black soldiers receiving lower pay than whites, and of captured black soldiers being sold into slavery, he took his grievances to the White House. Lincoln agreed to consider military commissions for blacks and asked for the editor's assistance. A short time later, Douglass was led by Secretary of War Stanton to believe that he would receive a commission in the army to do recruitment for black divisions. With this understanding, he returned to Rochester and prepared his valedictory issue of the *Monthly.* He was leaving journalism, he told his readers, but not because there was no longer need for or value in the work. "I have lived to see the leading presses of the country, willing and ready to publish any argument or appeal in behalf of my race, I am able to make," he wrote, and pointed to the accomplishments of his journalism: "It has done something towards battering down that dark and frowning wall of partition between the working minds of two races, hitherto thought impregnable." However, "I discontinue my paper, because I can better serve my poor bleeding country-men whose great opportunity has now come, by going South and summoning them to assert their just liberty. . . ."

Frontispiece and title page for Douglass's second autobiography

The commission never came, but Douglass continued to work for black enlistment. At the same time, his advice was sought by Lincoln in his reelection campaign. His political life had begun with involvement in the abolitionist movement, and the announcement of the Emancipation Proclamation had seemed to end one phase of his life's purpose. It had also given him reason to trust in Lincoln's basic honesty, and he became an informal consultant to the president in the months before his reelection. In this capacity he began pressing for black suffrage; he eventually saw that hope become a reality, though not in Lincoln's lifetime.

Such was the esteem in which Lincoln held Douglass that when guards sought to bar the black leader from the inaugural ball, Lincoln personally saw to it that he was admitted and, in welcoming him to the festivities, made quite clear Douglass's

standing in his estimation. Douglass half hoped for a cabinet or other government position under Lincoln but was disappointed.

Douglass's major contributions and, apparently, his greatest loves remained oratory and writing. In addition to his own papers, his works appeared in the *Washington Evening Star,* the *Journal of Social Science,* the *North American Review, Harper's Weekly, Cosmopolitan, Our Day, Century Magazine, Woman's Journal,* the *London Times,* and *Zion's Herald.* His lectures and speeches were heard in temples and town halls across the United States.

Douglass's journalistic career was resumed briefly in the *New National Era,* which he joined in 1870 as corresponding editor. The weekly venture, devoted to the "defence and enlightenment of the newly emancipated and enfranchised" black citizens of Washington, was supposed to be a cooperative effort, but save for his sons Lewis and Frederick, who had found jobs as printers at the *Era* when no one else would hire black trainees, Douglass soon found himself with little help he could count on. The business end of the paper went badly and, to prevent a noticeable failure of a black enterprise so soon after emancipation, Douglass bought the paper during the second year of its existence in what he later called a $10,000 misadventure, hoping that the drawing power of his name would bring needed support and circulation. He wanted to use the paper to lift "a standard . . . for my people which would cheer and strengthen them in the work of their own improvement and elevation." He also used its columns to scold and chide black scholars and professionals who he felt were not making contributions to the betterment of their fellows. It was not enough for them to be scholars and book-learned; they had to be givers as well as receivers, he insisted: "There is no question about it, the colored race are [*sic*] still on trial, and the inquiry is still made as to whether the colored man has within him the elements of a self-sustaining progress." In 1874 economics caused him to suspend publication of the *Era.*

Douglass served in various minor posts in government, including that of U.S. marshal of the District of Columbia under the Hayes administration, and recorder of deeds in the Garfield and Arthur administrations. In 1881 he published a third autobiography, *Life and Times of Frederick Douglass, Written by Himself,* which he updated in 1892. In the 1881 book, he philosophized about what he had learned from the failures of his journalistic ventures, "which to some extent has been heeded, for I have kept well out of newspaper undertaking since."

Douglass's wife died on 4 August 1882. On 24 January 1884 he married Helen Pitts. He was United States Minister Resident and Consul-general to the Republic of Haiti and chargé d'affaires to Santo Domingo between 1889 and 1891.

The very full life Frederick Douglass lived is reflected in his voluminous writing, and in the many speeches he delivered, reprinted in newspapers and often published in pamphlet form. Though a fire of mysterious origins destroyed his Rochester, N.Y., home in June 1872, and with it his complete collection of the newspapers he had poured his life into, collections of his letters and speeches, as well as excerpts from his papers, have survived. Other reflections of his contributions come in the tributes which poured in from across the country following his death of a heart attack

Douglass's second wife, Helen Pitts Douglass

on 20 February 1895. The *Sacramento Bee* called the seventy-eight-year-old activist/statesman "honest and sincere, therefore he commanded respect, attention, admiration, even though he frequently evoked bitter opposition." The *Boston Transcript* called him "a noted and notable man"; the *New York Mail and Express* characterized him as "the last conspicuous figure in that brilliant and picturesque group of anti-slavery agitators and orators . . . who will be gratefully and reverently remembered by all future generations." The *Indianapolis News* called him "the most distinguished of American negroes"; the *Washington Post* eulogized him as "one of the great men of the century measuring magnitude by the influence which he was enabled to exert"; and the *Chicago Advance* said Douglass was "for years the most picturesque and historically significant personality in America."

References:

Black Heritage Library Collection, *In Memoriam: Frederick Douglass* (Freeport, N.Y.: Books for Libraries Press, 1971);

Arna Bontemps, *Free at Last: The Life of Frederick Douglass* (New York: Dodd, Mead, 1971);

Charles W. Chesnutt, *Frederick Douglass* (Boston: Small, Maynard, 1899);

Philip S. Foner, *The Life and Writings of Frederick Douglass*, 4 volumes (New York: International Publishers, 1950-1955);

Frederic May Holland, *Frederick Douglass: The Colored Orator* (New York: Funk & Wagnalls, 1895);

Nathan Irvin Huggins, *Slave and Citizen: The Life of Frederick Douglass* (Boston: Little, Brown, 1980);

Diopkon J. Preston, *Young Frederick Douglass: The Maryland Years* (Baltimore: Johns Hopkins University Press, 1980);

Benjamin Quarles, *Frederick Douglass* (Washington, D.C.: Associated Publisers, 1948);

Quarles, ed., *Frederick Douglass* (Englewood Cliffs, N.J.: Prentice-Hall, 1968);

Victor Ullman, *Martin R. Delany: The Beginnings of Black Nationalism* (Boston: Beacon Press, 1971);

Booker T. Washington, *Frederick Douglass* (New York: Haskell House, 1968).

William Duane
(17 May 1760-24 November 1835)

Wm. David Sloan
University of Alabama

MAJOR POSITIONS HELD: Assistant editor (1796-1798), editor, *General Advertiser and Aurora* (Philadelphia) (1798-1822).

BOOKS: *A Letter to George Washington, President of the United States: Containing Strictures on His Address of the Seventeenth of September, 1796, Notifying His Retinquishment of the Presidential Office,* as Jasper Dwight, of Vermont (Philadelphia: Printed for the author, 1796);

A History of the French Revolution, from Its Commencement to the Complete Establishment of the Republic. Collected from the Best English and French Authorities, Interspersed with Original Articles Never Before Published; and Containing a Free Examination of the Dispute, between the French and American Republics (Philadelphia: Stewart & Rowson, 1798);

The History of France, from the Earliest Times, till the Death of Louis Sixteenth. From the French of Velly, Villaret, Garnier, Mezeray, Daniel, and Other Eminent Historians; with Notes, Critical and Explanatory; by John Gifford, Esq. And, Continued from the Above Period, until the Conclusion of the Present War, by a Citizen of the United States (Philadelphia: Printed for A. & J. G. Henderson by Bioren & Madan, 1798);

A Caution; or, Reflections on the Present Contest between France and Great-Britain, anonymous (Philadelphia: Bache, 1798);

A Report of the Extraordinary Transactions Which Took Place at Philadelphia, in February 1799, in Consequence of a Memorial from Certain Natives of Ireland to Congress, Praying a Repeal of the Alien Bill; Containing an Account of the Proceedings Which Produced the Memorial—the Assault on the Committee at St. Mary's Church.—and the Proceedings at the Mayor's Office, upon the Arrest of the Memorialists. A Copy of the Memorial. And, the Trial, with the Names of the Jury, the Evidence at Large, the Speeches of Counsel on Both Sides, and the Charge to the Jury (Philadelphia: Printed at the office of the *Aurora*, 1799);

An Examination of the Question, Who Is the Writer of the Two Forged Letters, Addressed to the President of the United States? Attributed to John Rutledge (Washington, D.C: Printed by William Duane & Son, 1803);

The Mississippi Question Fairly Stated, and the Views and Arguments of Those Who Clamor for War, Examined, in Seven Letters. Originally Written for Publication in the Aurora, at Philadelphia, as Camillus (Philadelphia: Printed by William Duane, 1803);

Mississippi Question. Report of a Debate in the Senate of the United States, on the 23d, 24th, & 25th February, 1803, on Certain Resolutions Concern-

ing the Violation of the Right of Deposit in the Island of New Orleans (Philadelphia: Printed by W. Duane, 1803);

Observations on the Principles and Operation of Banking; with Strictures on the Opposition to the Bank of Philadelphia, as Anti-Monopoly (Philadelphia: Helmbold, 1804);

Report of a Debate, in the Senate of the United States, on a Resolution for Recommending to the Legislatures [sic] *of the Several States, an Amendment of the Third Paragraph of the First Section of the Second Article of the Constitution of the United States, Relative to the Mode of Electing a President and Vice President of the Said States* (Philadelphia: Printed by William Duane, 1804);

An Epitome of the Arts and Sciences. Being a Comprehensive System of the Elementary Parts of an Useful and Polite Education: Upon the Plan of a Similar Work of R. Turner . . . Augmented and Improved, and Adapted to the Use of Schools in the United States, anonymous (Philadelphia: Printed by W. Duane, 1805);

Politics for American Farmers: Being a Series of Tracts, Exhibiting the Blessings of Free Government, as It Is Administered in the United States, Compared with the Boasted Stupendous Fabric of British Monarchy. Originally Written for, and Published in, the Aurora of Philadelphia, in the Beginning of 1807, anonymous (Washington, D.C.: Printed by R. C. Weightman for W. Duane, 1807);

Experience the Test of Government: in Eighteen Essays. Written during the Years 1805 and 1806. To Aid the Investigation of Principles, and Operation of the Existing Constitution and Laws of Pennsylvania, anonymous, attributed to Duane (Philadelphia: Printed by William Duane, 1807);

The American Military Library; or, Compendium of the Modern Tactics. Embracing the Discipline, Manoeuvres, and Duties of Every Species of Corps, Cavalry, Artillery of Position, and Horse Artillery; a Treatise on Defensive Works in the Field, the Exercise in Sea Coast Batteries, and Regular Fortifications. Adapted to the Use of the Militia of the United States, 2 volumes (Philadelphia: Printed by and for the author, 1807-1809);

A Military Dictionary, or, Explanation of the Several Systems of Discipline of Different Kinds of Troops, Infantry, Artillery, and Cavalry; the Principles of Fortification, and All the Modern Improvements in the Science of Tactics: Comprising the Pocket Gunner, or Little Bombardier; the Military Regulations of the United States; the Weights, Measures, and Monies of All Nations; the Technical Terms and Phrases of the Art of War in the French Language.

Particularly Adapted to the Use of the Military Institutions of the United States (Philadelphia: Printed & published by William Duane, 1810);

A Hand Book for Infantry: Containing the First Principles of Military Discipline, Founded on Rational Method (Philadelphia: Printed for the author, 1812);

A Hand Book for Riflemen; Containing the First Principles of Military Discipline, Founded on Rational Method; Intended to Explain in a Familiar and Practical Manner, the Discipline and Duties of Rifle Corps: Conformable to the System Established for the United States Military Force, and the Latest Improvements in the Modern Art of War (Philadelphia: Printed for the author, 1812);

Explanation of the Plates of the System of Infantry Discipline, for the United States Army; according to the Regulation of 19th March, 1813, anonymous (N.p., 1814);

The System of Infantry Discipline: According to the Regulation Established for the Army of the United States, anonymous (Philadelphia?, 1814);

The Two Americas, Great Britain, and the Holy Alliance, anonymous (Washington, D.C.: E. De Kraft, 1814);

A Hand Book for Cavalry (Philadelphia: Printed for the author, 1814);

A Visit to Colombia, in the Years 1822 and 1823, by Laguayra and Caracas, over the Cordillera to Bogota, and Thence by the Magdalena to Cartagena (Philadelphia: Printed by T. H. Palmer for the author, 1826).

OTHER: Jesse Higgins, Thomas Paine, and Joel Barlow, *Select Pamphlets,* compiled with contributions by Duane (Philadelphia, 1814);

Letters to Benjamin Franklin from His Family and Friends, 1751-1790, edited by Duane (New York: C. B. Robinson, 1859).

William Duane, who succeeded Benjamin Franklin Bache as editor of the *Aurora* in Philadelphia, was one of the central figures in the Republican party's attempts to wrest political power from the Federalists. Party adherents in the early Republic believed that the United States' political system required that parties appeal to public opinion, with newspapers being the most important medium for reaching the public. Among Republican newspapers, the most prestigious and consequential was the *Aurora*. It was considered the leading spokesman of the Republican national leadership and was looked to for guidance on Republican stands on major issues. When Duane died in 1835, the *New York Star* declared that "no man had in his time more influence."

Duane was born on 17 May 1760 near Lake Champlain, New York, where his parents, John and Anastasia Sarsfield Duane, natives of Ireland, had settled in 1755. His father died when William was five years of age, and in 1774 his mother returned with him to her hometown of Clonmel in Tipperary County, Ireland. When in 1779 he married a Protestant, Catharine Corcoran, his Catholic mother disinherited him. Forced to learn a trade, he took up printing. In 1787 he moved to India, where he founded the *Indian World*, a liberal Calcutta journal. His editorial criticisms of the practices of the East India Company and support of the grievances of army officers led to his being arrested without charge, dispossessed of his property, and deported to England without trial. Biographers disagree on the chronology of events during this part of his life. Some say he was deported in 1788 and then worked briefly as a Parliamentary reporter for the *General Advertiser* until it was acquired by the British government through a seditious libel trial in 1790. From then until 1796 he vainly attempted to recover his property, supporting himself as best he could (but living "a most precarious life") by free-lancing. Better documented evidence suggests that Duane was deported from India in 1794 and for the next two years devoted most of his time attempting to recover his confiscated property through Parliament and the courts. Failing, he moved to Philadelphia in 1796 and assumed the editorship of the newly established *True American*. Soon thereafter he accepted a job as assistant editor of the more prestigious and prosperous *Aurora*. Its editor, Benjamin Franklin Bache, had founded the *General Advertiser and Political, Commercial, Agricultural and Literary Journal* in 1790, when he was twenty-two years old. Four years later it had added the name *Aurora* and had soon become known by the shorter title.

Under Bache, grandson of Benjamin Franklin and a Republican of radical tendencies, the *Aurora* was the leading Republican newspaper for most of the 1790s. In September 1798 Bache died; his widow, Margaret, made provisions for continuation of the paper, and Duane was made editor. Duane's first wife also having died in 1798, he married Margaret Bache in 1800 and thereupon became proprietor of the *Aurora*. Under Duane the paper continued as the Republicans' leading journal and took on added stature. The *Aurora*'s position had been enhanced by Bache's prestige in leading Republican circles, and it was improved by Duane's writing ability. During a period characterized by partisan passion in both public and private affairs, Duane was noted for his hard-hitting style. Because of this style and because he exposed several dubious Federalist schemes and tactics, the *Aurora* became the bible of Republicans in Pennsylvania and much of the remainder of the nation. While Bache had spent approximately $20,000 of his own money to keep the paper solvent, Duane doubled the *Aurora*'s circulation within a year after assuming control and for a while made the paper financially successful.

In a number of major issues in the late 1790s, Duane assumed a leading role. He was one of the foremost opponents of the Alien and Sedition Acts of 1798, he uncovered and revealed a number of Federalist machinations to capture governmental power for themselves, and he was considered to have had a decisive influence on Thomas McKean's victorious campaign for Pennsylvania governor in 1799.

Because of his efforts and political importance, Duane became the object of considerable Federalist hatred and attempts to silence him. The *Aurora*'s leadership, Federalists feared, had horrendous consequences. A correspondent in the Federalist *Connecticut Courant*, describing the process by which Duane affected popular opinion, declared, "Whatever appeared in that [newspaper] was faithfully copied into the others. . . . Whoever has been careful enough to watch the progress of jacobinism [Republicanism] in the country, must have observed, that on every important subject, the sentiment to be inculcated among the democrats, has been first put into the Aurora. This was the heart, the seat of life. From thence the blood has flowed to the extremities by a sure and rapid circulation, and the life and strength of the paper have thus been supported and nourished. It is even astonishing to remark, with how much punctuality and rapidity, the same opinion has been circulated and repeated by these people, from the highest to the lowest." The editor of the *United States Oracle* in Portsmouth, New Hampshire, agreed that Republican papers throughout the country served "as sounding boards to the notes that issue[d] through the great 'speaking trumpet of the devil,' the Philadelphia Aurora." The *Gazette of the United States* declared that the *Aurora* was one of the "two mediums through which [the Republicans] convey their poison" to the public.

In 1799, Duane and three other Republicans attempting to get Philadelphia residents to sign a petition opposing the Alien Act were attacked by Federalists. One of the Republicans, Dr. James Reynolds, drew a gun—apparently for protection—at which time law officers arrived and arrested Duane and his companions for creating a seditious riot. When Duane complained about conditions in the Philadelphia jail, the *Gazette of the United States* commented, "What a pity there is no Gallows in Pennsylvania that he might have an opportunity of abusing his last enemy in this world." Later that year Duane was brutally attacked by a group of perhaps thirty men, including a number of Federalist-sympathizing off-duty militiamen. The band entered the *Aurora* office, and while some of the men held the pressmen and other staff members at bay with swords and guns, others grabbed Duane and beat him over the head with a pistol butt. He then was kicked downstairs and dragged into the courtyard, where the assault was repeated. Duane, kicked while lying senseless on the ground, might have been killed had not his sixteen-year-old son thrown himself across his father's body. A number of Republicans then arrived and dispersed the assailants. That night an armed guard of Republicans stationed themselves at the *Aurora* office to provide protection. In 1800 Duane wrote that he determined "it more prudent to remain at home than go abroad much, because every idea of Justice is out of the question for me . . . , and tho' I might be killed and my family ruined without justice . . . if I were to wound or kill one of them even in defending myself, a prison and a gibbet would be soon provided for me."

Duane—like several other editors—faced actions by opponents in Congress aimed at stifling his writing. The most notorious of such partisan assaults on editors was the attempt by the Federalist-controlled Senate to punish Duane for publishing the contents of a Federalist bill that would have created a thirteen-member committee to determine which electoral votes were to be allowed in the 1800 presidential election. Federalist senators were embarrassed by the bill's exposure in the *Aurora*, and they pushed through a resolution to investigate Duane for his "daring and high-handed breach of the privileges" of the Senate. The editor was commanded to appear before the Senate to answer for his conduct. His lawyers, however, refused because they believed that the ground rules laid down made an effective defense impossible. "I will not degrade myself," said Thomas Cooper, "by submitting to appear before the Senate with their gag in my mouth." Duane, who already had met once with the Senate for preliminary proceedings,

then wrote the body that he felt "bound by the most sacred duties to decline any further voluntary attendance." The Senate thereupon declared Duane in contempt and issued a warrant for his arrest. Even though Duane later claimed that he had remained in Philadelphia, often at his home, after the warrant was issued, the annoyed Federalists paid $300 to twenty-three constables in an unsuccessful attempt to capture the "obstinate democrat." Duane maintained that the entire episode was part of a Federalist plot to destroy the *Aurora* before the 1800 election.

Federalists so feared Duane that he was nearly indicted under the Alien Act. President John Adams lamented that "a group of foreign liars [that is, Republican editors, including Duane], encouraged by a few ambitious, native gentlemen, have discomfited the education, the talents, the virtues and the prosperity of the country." Secretary of State Timothy Pickering wrote Adams that although Duane pretended to have been born in America, he was "really a British subject, and, as an alien, liable to be banished from the United States." Adams agreed; yet though he fumed that "the matchless effrontery of Duane merits the execution of the Alien Law," Federalists never successfully exercised the law against Duane.

After the Federalists failed through the Alien Act, they tried to silence Duane by enforcing the Sedition Act against him. While his trial was pending, he declared, according to another Republican editor, that "neither persecution nor any other peril to which bad men may expose him can make him swerve from the cause of republicanism, or prove himself unworthy to be the successor of the descendant of Franklin." Although charged with libeling President Adams, Duane appeared unafraid of the Federalists, virtually daring them to try him. One reason for his boldness was that he claimed to possess a letter written by Adams which showed that Great Britain exercised an undue influence on the United States government. Duane's trial was postponed; on the very day of the postponement he was busy accusing Federalists of "secretly combining and covertly usurping the public power . . . [and] sapping the foundations of our freedom, prosperity, and national character." Upon becoming president, Jefferson had all suits under the Sedition Act dismissed before Duane could be brought to trial. In 1801 the editor finally was snared and served thirty days in jail on a charge of libeling a Federalist judge. This experience, however, did not muzzle him; instead, it made him even more determined to "reform" the court system and purge it of the influence of the "rich and well-born."

Even though such government actions were noteworthy because they pitted the power of a government controlled by partisans against editors of an opposing party, many more prosecutions were brought for civil libel of private individuals than for criminal libel of the government. By 1806 Duane had been sued between sixty and seventy times—perhaps more than anyone else in Philadelphia—and in each case by a Federalist.

Despite such heroics, Duane appears to have been personally ambitious and eager for government patronage. After Jefferson's election, the national capital was moved from Philadelphia to Washington, and Jefferson selected Samuel Harrison Smith's infant *National Intelligencer* as the national administration's organ. Although financial support and patronage were largely diverted from Duane to others, such as Smith, they were not cut off completely; but Duane incurred heavy expenses in operating the *Aurora* and in defending himself in the suits brought by Federalists. He reasoned that since his cause was the cause of Republicanism, it was only right that his party should share the expenses. Giving him printing and stationery patronage was one way it could help. Duane opened a stationery and printing shop in Washington with a view to receiving orders from the government, and solicited Jefferson and department heads. The president replied that "as to your proposition on the subject of stationery, I believe you may be assured of the favor of every department here." In July 1801 Secretary of the Treasury Albert Gallatin gave Duane a contract to deliver 400,000 sheets of paper to the Treasury Department. By September Duane also had acquired stationery contracts with Congress.

He was disappointed, however, in his attempt to receive congressional printing, and complained to Gallatin that House clerk John Beckley had awarded all House printing to Smith. Gallatin expressed his sympathy and told Jefferson that although aid certainly should have been given to Smith, the *National Intelligencer* editor should not have had a monopoly. He urged Jefferson to request department heads to buy more stationery from Duane. By February 1802, however, Duane still had not delivered all of the 400,000 sheets originally ordered for the Treasury Department, and Gallatin informed Jefferson that the department already had a surplus and would order no more from Duane. The editor heard through the grapevine that Gallatin had also accused him of over-

charging the government for stationery and had purchased stationery from another firm.

In 1803 Duane solicited support from senators in getting the Senate's printing order. The Federalist clerk of the Senate was then told that he should award the Senate's printing to Duane if he wished to keep his job. Duane took over the printing and continued the contract until 1806.

During this period Duane was also aided personally by Jefferson. "Duane is honest, and well intentioned, but over zealous," the president wrote in 1803. "These qualities harmonise with him a great portion of the republican body. He deserves therefore all the just and favorable attentions which can properly be shewn him." Jefferson bought books, stationery, and writing supplies for his own use from Duane, subscribed to the *Aurora*, and ordered printing.

From the base he had established as the Republicans' leading national journalist, Duane moved into a factional battle for control of Pennsylvania politics. The state's more powerful politicians were Governor McKean, Treasury Secretary Gallatin, Alexander James Dallas, George Logan, Michael Leib, Tench Coxe, and Peter Muhlenberg. These men contended for political supremacy in the state and formed shifting alliances to help them in their rivalries. When McKean, whom Duane had supported in his bid for the governorship, would not reward patronage seekers Duane recommended, Duane turned on him and formed an association with Leib. Their alliance was based more on circumstance than political affection, and one of their main motives was to avenge their insufficiency of patronage. The lack of state patronage made them even more determined to obtain some of the national spoils made available by Jefferson's election. They tried unsuccessfully to have a Philadelphia friend appointed secretary of the navy, and Duane recommended to Gallatin a list of potential appointees to clerkships in the State and Treasury Departments. Duane was particularly eager that the Federalist collector of the Philadelphia port be replaced with one of his supporters. Gallatin, finding himself more and more in disagreement with the Duane wing of the Republican party, was reluctant to do anything which would increase the editor's influence, and no important federal office was given to Duane or his friends. The collectorship went to a man so conservative that the Federalists earlier had considered him as a possible gubernatorial candidate.

Duane turned on Coxe, to whom he had given free use of the *Aurora*'s columns in 1800, in 1804 when Coxe attempted to contest Duane's and Leib's control of Philadelphia Republicanism. Duane suspected that Coxe had helped establish and support the rival *Philadelphia Evening Post* under the editorship of William McCorkel. The journal had been founded to defend McKean's administration and the Coxe faction, termed the "Tertium Quids" by Duane, against attacks in the *Aurora*. Siding with McKean and Coxe were Dallas, Muhlenberg, and Logan. In 1804 Gallatin joined Duane's Pennsylvania opponents in attempting to break the Duane-Leib alliance. Duane protested that "Washington City" was interfering too much in state politics and should limit its influence to finance and not meddle with local elections.

Dallas complained to Jefferson that the combative Duane's editorials had caused "a fatal division" in Pennsylvania's Republican ranks. The breach widened after the 1804 election, and Duane and Leib attempted to have the state constitution amended to curtail some of McKean's power and obtain some patronage for their faction. The "Quids," however, managed to defeat the move and get McKean reelected in 1805. Gallatin was displeased that McKean's narrow victory was accomplished only through the support of Federalists and blamed McKean's spoils system. In 1807 Duane was defeated in his race for the state Senate and decided not to run for office again. The following year, Duane, interesting himself more and more in military affairs, applied for a commission, to which Jefferson responded by appointing him a lieutenant colonel of rifles. Duane fancied himself a military authority and authored a number of undistinguished books, among them *A Military Dictionary* (1810), *A Hand Book for Riflemen* (1812), *A Hand Book for Infantry* (1812), and *The American Military Library* (1807-1809).

Duane's *Aurora* remained the leading national Republican paper throughout Jefferson's two terms. While the *National Intelligencer* was a source of news from the capital, the *Aurora*'s editorial comments were reprinted nationwide. "Duane's press," wrote a Madison supporter in 1808, "with all its indecency, is worth for our purposes all others. The circulation of his paper is so universal throughout the United States." That year, however, showing his independence from Republican leadership, Duane threatened Madison with throwing his support to Clinton if Madison did not dump Gallatin. Although Duane dropped the threat, Leib was more intransigent and did support Clinton, a move which did not help the Duane-Leib alliance. Duane, however, also eventually turned on Madison. His

differences with the national Republican leadership, including even Jefferson, and his political battles in Pennsylvania gradually wore away Duane's journalistic stature. In the state elections of 1811, the "Quids" easily got McKean reelected as governor. The aid that John Binns of the *Democratic Press* in Philadelphia had given to McKean helped him replace Duane as the state's leading Republican editor.

Duane remained dissatisfied with his financial treatment by Republicans and in 1811 threatened to try to improve his fortunes by changing parties. Jefferson wrote various Republicans in an effort to find bank loans or other financial support for the *Aurora*. Duane was mollified, but he perpetually faced ups and downs in running the *Aurora*. Diminished in importance, the newspaper also found its patronage and advertising revenues gradually decreasing. Duane continued as editor until 1822. At the time of his retirement, delinquent subscribers owed $80,000, and Duane allowed the *Aurora* to cease. He toured South America in 1822 and 1823. On his return to the United States, he tried unsuccessfully to revive the *Aurora* to fight the Second Bank of the United States. In 1823 he was appointed principal clerk for the eastern district of the Pennsylvania Supreme Court, serving in that position until his death.

Why Duane, like many other partisan editors of the period, made the sacrifices he did is not difficult to explain. It was not because of remuneration from politicians or the financial rewards of running a paper. He did so because he believed fervently in the cause he supported. While most historians have been critical of the party press of the Federalist-Republican period, Duane and other editors believed that they had at least tried to do their duty as journalists. Years after the period had passed, Jefferson—reflecting on the struggle of the late 1790s that did so much to shape the American political system—wrote Duane, "I have not forgotten the past, nor those who were fellow-laborers in the gloomy hours of federal ascendancy, when the spirit of republicanism was beaten down, its votaries arraigned as criminals, and such threats denounced as posterity will never believe."

References:

Ray Boston, "The Impact of 'Foreign Liars' on the American Press (1790-1800)," *Journalism Quarterly*, 50 (Winter 1973): 722-730;

Allen Cullen Clark, "William Duane," *Records of the Columbia Historical Society*, 9 (1906): 14-62;

Jonathan Daniels, *They Will Be Heard* (New York:

McGraw-Hill, 1965), pp. 41-57;

Worthington C. Ford, "The Letters of William Duane," *Proceedings of the Massachusetts Historical Society*, second series, 20 (1906): 257-394;

Benjamin Ellis Martin, "Transition Period of the American Press—Leading Editors Early in

This Century," *Magazine of American History*, 17 (April 1887): 273-294;

Wm. David Sloan, "The Party Press: The Newspaper Role in National Politics," Ph.D. dissertation, University of Texas at Austin, 1981.

John Dunlap

(1747-27 November 1812)

Dwight L. Teeter, Jr.
University of Texas at Austin

MAJOR POSITION HELD: Publisher, *Pennsylvania Packet, or the General Advertiser* (Philadelphia), renamed *Pennsylvania Packet and Daily Advertiser* in 1784 (1771-1794).

John Dunlap's place in the journalism history of North America is secure: he was the first American to publish a successful daily newspaper. He was memorable, however, for other reasons as well. Inspection of Dunlap's career reveals a canny businessman, soldier, politician, and speculator who worked adroitly in late-eighteenth-century Philadelphia to establish a substantial fortune. Dunlap achieved financial success by mixing public pursuits with his printing business.

Dunlap was born in Tyrone, County Strabane, Ireland, in 1747, and was sent to Philadelphia in 1757 to be apprenticed to his uncle, printer-bookseller William Dunlap, who had just moved to Philadelphia as postmaster after serving in a similar position in Lancaster, Pennsylvania. In 1766 William Dunlap sold his stock of books and put his printing house in the care of his nineteen-year-old nephew. After two years of religious studies in England, William Dunlap became an Anglican priest and took charge of the parish of Stratton in King and Queen County, Virginia, selling his shop and equipment to his nephew.

John Dunlap doubtless had to pay for the printing shop in installments, and his first years as proprietor were financially arduous. His friend, Dr. Benjamin Rush, in 1812 recalled Dunlap's early struggles: "So humble was his beginning that he slept on a blanket under his counter, and ate pepper pot only bought in the market from his inability

to purchase a bed or other food." Dunlap made ends meet during his early years by printing sermons; he may also have printed pamphlets, handbills, "single advertisements," and books.

In November 1771 Dunlap began publishing the weekly *Pennsylvania Packet, or the General Advertiser*. In the 1770s beginning a newspaper was a venture for only the optimistic and industrious. Newspapers brought small financial returns in terms of the amount of materials and labor needed to produce them. On the other hand, newspapers were useful in advertising a printing house's other services and wares: job printing, bookselling, stationery, account books, ink, quill pens, medicines, and so on. On 4 February 1773 Dunlap married Mrs. Elizabeth Hayes Ellison of Liverpool.

In the *Packet*'s first several years, Dunlap printed few controversial items, and the paper survived without garnering any major printing business from the Pennsylvania Assembly. By 1775 the *Packet* was full of advertisements and appeared to be competing solidly with the *Pennsylvania Journal*, published since 1742 by William Bradford III and after 1776 in partnership with his son, Thomas.

Also providing experienced competition was the *Pennsylvania Gazette*, Benjamin Franklin's former property. In 1775 the *Gazette* was published by the partnership of William Hall, David Hall, Jr., and William Sellers. The *Gazette* received almost half of the Assembly's printing business that year. But Henry Miller, publisher of the German-language *Philadelphische Staatsbote*, which was more outspoken against imperial policies of the English than the *Gazette*, earned more by printing for the

Assembly from 1771 to 1775 than did the firm of Hall and Sellers.

During the first four months of 1775, Philadelphia became the center of the greatest newspaper activity in the American colonies. Three new newspapers were founded: Benjamin Towne's triweekly *Pennsylvania Evening Post* first appeared on 25 January 1775; three days later, James Humphreys, Jr., started his weekly *Pennsylvania Ledger*, initially cautious in tone; the third new entry, the *Pennsylvania Mercury*, published weekly by Enoch Story and Daniel Humphreys, first appeared on 7 April 1775. The *Mercury* was an openly Tory sheet which received financial backing (as had William Goddard's *Pennsylvania Chronicle*, which had halted publication in 1774) from merchant-politicians Thomas Wharton, Sr., and Joseph Galloway. The *Mercury* was destroyed by fire on the last day of 1775; Story later asserted that the fire was set by "the infatuated populace." Daniel Humphreys fled the city late in 1776 after Towne accused him of having run a Tory newspaper.

Publications with Tory leanings operated on borrowed time in Philadelphia in 1775. With the armed conflict at Lexington and Concord on 19 April 1775, anti-British sentiment flared. Revolutionary stirrings were altering the old political order in Pennsylvania, and Dunlap made these dislocations work to his advantage. The young printer was admitted to membership as a cornet— the lowest commissioned rank—in the First Troop of the Philadelphia Light-Horse. This unit was sometimes termed the "Silk Stocking Cavalry"; its members included some of Philadelphia's most prominent names. Although such contacts doubtless were good for business, Dunlap was characterized as a good soldier for his part in the fighting in the campaign of 1776-1777 at the Battles of Princeton and Trenton.

In 1776 Dunlap's career as an official printer to government began. This timely appointment secured Dunlap's position in history as the first to print the Declaration of Independence. This printing of the declaration, in broadside form, was signed by John Hancock and Charles Thomson, president and secretary of Congress, respectively, and sent to colonial legislatures and European governments. Ironically, Towne's triweekly *Post* published an insert with the text of the declaration on 6 July, thus beating Dunlap's own *Packet*, which next appeared on 8 July.

From mid-1776 until March 1777, Dunlap worked for the Council of Safety, the interim body which served as Pennsylvania's executive during the hiatus between colonial authority and the adoption of the Pennsylvania Constitution of 1776. He printed loyalty oaths for the council which were administered by the militia, including the Philadelphia Light-Horse. Under Pennsylvania law, if Tories or Quakers would not sign oaths to be loyal to the new government, their properties were confiscated and sold at auction.

Ownership of land and buildings was a major concern of Dunlap's. In 1774 he had purchased 600 acres in Northumberland County for thirty-six pounds, a substantial amount of money at the time. Dunlap did not pay cash, however; the seller, Jesse Lukens, received the thirty-six pounds in printing, stationery, and books. After 1776 Dunlap joined with Philadelphia merchants Thomas Lawrence and James Budden to buy up confiscated Tory and Quaker property. Dunlap's central position as a printer-entrepreneur is worth noting: Dunlap printed some of the Pennsylvania currency; that currency was depreciating rapidly during the War of Independence; thus the land speculators—Dunlap among them—could use the depreciating state or Continental currency in payment for desirable dwellings and parcels of land.

In 1779 Dunlap bought lots at the corner of Arch and Fifth Streets in Philadelphia and did well financially by renting out the houses on those lots. A shabbier purchase involved houses on a tiny thirty-by-seventy-foot lot on Fifth Street between Market and Arch Streets. Dunlap described these dwellings as "several old Tenements of little value, rented to poor people, from December 23, 1779, to March 18th, 1784. From them was received One hundred pounds and Taxes."

Dunlap's land purchases, however, made him much more than an eighteenth-century landlord. In 1779 he was one of the foremost buyers of the holdings left behind by Pennsylvania Tory politician Joseph Galloway. His biggest effort at land speculation involved the purchase in 1788 of 131,000 acres in Kentucky. Papers for this sale were signed by Governor Edmund Randolph of Virginia, a tenant in a Dunlap rental property in earlier years.

Although land speculation caught his attention, Dunlap was primarily a printer. His newspaper and printing house survived the vicissitudes of the War for Independence remarkably well. As the British army bore down upon Philadelphia on 16 September 1777, Massachusetts member of Congress John Adams complained in his diary: "No newspaper this morning. Mr. Dunlap has moved or packed up his types. . . ." Dunlap was sending

Front page of Dunlap's Pennsylvania Packet *for 8 April 1776. In 1784 the* Packet *became the first successful daily newspaper in America.*

his printing equipment west in a wagon toward Lancaster, where the Pennsylvania Assembly was soon to meet. Congress left Philadelphia a few days later, next meeting in York on 30 September.

Dunlap remained in Lancaster to print for the Assembly; Hall and Sellers of the *Gazette* moved to York to become the printers to Congress. The businesslike Dunlap, however, soon got a share of the congressional printing, succeeding Robert Aitken as the printer of the journals of Congress. Dunlap, evidently possessing more printing equipment than his competitors, set up a press in York, but news soon came that the British would be leaving Philadelphia in June 1778.

After the interim printing at Lancaster, the *Packet* on 4 July 1778 became the first of the newspapers which had fled the British occupation to resume publication in Philadelphia. Although the *Packet*, now a tri-weekly, prospered upon returning to Philadelphia, Congress was displeased with Dunlap's progress in printing the journals. By early 1779 complaints were heard in Congress that the printer's charges were "very enormous"; it is possible, however, that the real problem was that the *Packet* had published indiscreet writings by Thomas Paine in 1779 which revealed that France had been providing aid to the revolutionists before its alliance with the United States became official.

Dunlap was replaced as printer of the journals of Congress, but the separation may not have been complete. Taking over was his friend, sometime apprentice and employee, and future partner, David Chambers Claypoole.

During 1778 and 1779 Dunlap seems to have done more printing for the Pennsylvania Assembly than any other printing house, but he had his eye on bigger and better printing deals. In 1777 he had set up a newspaper in Baltimore, run by James Hayes, Jr., a young former apprentice. Dunlap's *Baltimore Gazette* faced stiff competition from the Goddards' *Maryland Journal*, and by 1779, shortages of paper and other printing supplies forced suspension of Dunlap's Baltimore venture.

Dunlap turned ambitions further South to Virginia. The disruptions of the war had left Virginia without a public printer in 1779 and 1780, and Governor Thomas Jefferson asked his state's delegates to Congress to find a printer from among those then active in Philadelphia. Jefferson recommended that Dunlap's agent in Virginia obtain the postmastership in Richmond, observing that the postmaster's job would bring business to the printing house plus an exemption from militia duties.

Again relying on his young associate Hayes, Dunlap loaded a press and printing materials onto the *Bachelor*, a ship southbound on Chesapeake Bay. Ill fortune dogged this venture, as a storm drove the ship aground and the equipment was captured by the British. Dunlap and Hayes then shipped printing materials to Virginia overland, using three wagons. Finally, after waiting out a paper shortage, Hayes began publishing the *Virginia Gazette, or the American Advertiser* in Richmond on 22 December 1781.

By the 1780s Dunlap had the financial leverage and the social acceptance to be a major business force in Philadelphia, the new nation's largest city. While Dunlap busily converted depreciating paper currency into real property in 1780, Claypoole continued as printer to Congress. Late in 1780, if not before, Claypoole and Dunlap were partners in publishing the *Packet:* from 17 October 1780 until 12 June 1781, the *Packet*—which became a semiweekly in 1780 and returned to triweekly publication in 1781—bore the imprint of "John Dunlap and David C. Claypoole." During the remainder of 1781 and through the first half of 1784, Claypoole's name appeared alone as the *Packet*'s publisher. On 21 September 1784, when the *Packet* became a daily newspaper, Dunlap's name again joined Claypoole's as copublisher. Although Dunlap was not the first to publish a daily newspaper in the United States—Benjamin Towne had converted his pathetic *Pennsylvania Evening Post* into a daily in 1783—the *Packet* was the first daily to be successful. Towne's paper, a puny, half-sized, virtual caricature of a newspaper, folded about a month after the *Packet* started daily publication on 21 September 1784. The paper's name changed with its publication frequency, becoming the *Pennsylvania Packet and Daily Advertiser*. The daily *Packet* was full-sized (for its time) and was packed with advertisements and government announcements, as well as essays clipped from English papers, news reports, and letters. On 19 September 1787 the *Packet* was devoted to the first printing of the new U.S. Constitution.

Dunlap had a continuing interest in military and political as well as financial matters. In 1780 he subscribed £4,000 to the Bank of the United States, which was chartered, at least in part, to provide supplies for the army. He was elected to the rank of first lieutenant in Philadelphia's historic City Cavalry or Light Horse in 1781 and was a member of that city's Common Council from 1789 to 1792. In 1794 he was promoted to captain and then to major and commanded all cavalry during the Whiskey Insurrection campaign that year.

Dunlap's financial acumen and perseverance led to fame as the founder of the nation's first successful daily. He was an eighteenth-century printer-entrepreneur who deftly used his governmental connections to build a substantial fortune. His death on 27 November 1812 was attributed to apoplexy. His friend Dr. Rush wrote that Dunlap "by his business but chiefly by [land] speculation had accumulated an estate valued at between $300,000 and $400,00." Dunlap was known as a man who gave generously to charity, but he was no saint. Rush wrote of him: "In his family he was less amiable and respectable than in society. Towards the close of his life he became intemperate so as to fall in the street."

References:

Julian P. Boyd, ed., *The Papers of Thomas Jefferson*, 18 volumes (Princeton: Princeton University Press, 1950), III: 579-580n.;

Benjamin Rush, *The Autobiography of Benjamin Rush: Travels Through Life* (Princeton: Princeton University Press, 1948);

Joseph Scharf and Thompson Westcott, *History of Philadelphia, 1690-1884,* 3 volumes (Philadelphia, 1884), I: 338;

Arthur M. Schlesinger, *Prelude to Independence: The Newspaper War on Britain, 1764-1776* (New York: Knopf, 1958), pp. 164-165, 282, 290, 296);

Earl G. Swem, "A Bibliography of Virginia, Part II," *Bulletin of the Virginia State Library,* 10 (1917): 1069;

Dwight L. Teeter, Jr., "John Dunlap: The Political Economy of a Printer's Success," *Journalism Quarterly,* 52 (Spring 1975): 3-8, 55;

Teeter, "Press Freedom and the Public Printing: Pennsylvania 1775-83," *Journalism Quarterly,* 45 (Autumn 1968): 445-451.

Benjamin Edes
(14 October 1732-11 December 1803)

Sallie A. Whelan
Louisiana State University

MAJOR POSITION HELD: Editor, *Boston Gazette and Country Journal* (1755-1798).

Benjamin Edes, one of the most influential political writers and newspaper publishers of the period of the American Revolution, published the *Boston Gazette and Country Journal* for forty-three years with his partner, John Gill. The *Gazette* served as the organ of the Patriots. Edes fought British policy through written attacks on the Stamp Act, the tea tax, the Townshend Acts, and other oppressive measures. Called the "trumpeters of sedition," Edes and Gill were constantly under attack by British officials and Loyalists but were never silenced.

Edes was born on 14 October 1732 in Charlestown, Massachusetts, to Peter and Esther Hall Edes. After a small amount of schooling in Charlestown, Edes married Martha Starr in 1754. He and Gill took over the *Boston Gazette and Country Journal* on 7 April 1755.

The *Gazette* had been established on 21 December 1719 by William Brooker, who was then postmaster of Boston. Five successive postmasters edited the weekly before it was passed on to Edes and Gill. The two young printers set up their shop on the corner of Court Street and Franklin Avenue.

Edes and Gill's political involvement began on a rather timid note but did not remain so for long. In 1757 the Massachusetts-imposed stamp tax was repealed. That same year, Boston selectmen commissioned Edes and Gill to print the votes of the town in the *Gazette*. Along with the commission came a warning from the city officials saying that if the *Gazette* continued to publish attacks on people's "religious principles," the partners "must Expect no more favours from Us." This was one of the last times the printers heeded warnings and threats from government officials.

With the end of the French and Indian War in 1763 came a slump in trade, partially due to British efforts to stop all smuggling. Especially hard hit was the port city of Boston. Resentment in the colonies began to rise and came to a head with the introduction of the Stamp Act in 1765. The act imposed a tax of two shillings on every advertisement and a tax of from a half-penny to a penny on newspapers, according to size; the publisher's name was required to appear on every newspaper. Colonial papers used a number of methods to avoid paying the tax: some ceased publication while others published issues without the publisher's name. Edes retaliated by publishing the *Gazette* with a skull and crossbones on the front page.

Edes was a member of the "Loyal Nine," who secretly controlled the Sons of Liberty. The Sons of Liberty launched some of the bitterest attacks on the Stamp Act through the *Gazette*, and the *Gazette* office soon became a meeting place for those opposed to British policy. Patriots such as Samuel Adams, his cousin John Adams, Joseph Warren, Josiah Quincy, Thomas Cushing, Samuel Cooper, James Otis, and John Hancock regularly contributed material to Edes. John Adams said that it was a "curious employment": they were "cooking up paragraphs, articles, & occurrences &c., working the political machine!"

In his diary, John Adams described a relatively calm meeting of the Sons of Liberty on 15 January 1766:

> Spent the evening with the Sons of Liberty at their own apartment in Hanover Square near the tree of liberty. It was a counting-room in Chase and Speakman's distillery, a very small room it is.
>
> John Avery, distiller or merchant, of a liberal education, John Smith, the brazier, Thomas Crafts, the painter, Edes, the printer, Stephen Cleverly, the brazier, Chase, the distiller, Joseph Field, master of a vessel, Henry Bass, George Trott jeweller, were present. I was invited by Crafts and Trott to go and spend an evening with them and some others. Avery was mentioned to me as one. I went, and was very civilly and respectfully treated by all present. We had punch, wine, pipes and tobacco, biscuit and cheese, &c. I heard nothing but such conversation as passes at all clubs, among gentlemen, about the times.
>
> No plots, no machinations. They chose a committee to make preparations for grand rejoicings upon the arrival of the news of a repeal of the Stamp Act, and I heard afterwards they are to have such illuminations, bonfires, pyramids, obelisks, such grand exhibitions and such fireworks as were never

before seen in America. I wish they may not be disappointed.

The Liberty Tree was a large oak that had been planted in 1646; six of the men present at the Sons of Liberty meeting on 15 January were said to have hanged the effigy of a stamp officer and a jackboot on the Liberty Tree on 14 August 1765. The Tories of Boston thought it was significant that the "Liberty Boys" met near a supply of liquor, such as Chase and Speakman's distillery, because they believed that the group's courage arose mainly "from the steams of their poisonous rum." Loyalists continually tried to suppress the powerful Patriot press. On 29 February 1768 the *Gazette* published an article criticizing the unnamed but clearly implied Governor Bernard for his "obstinate Perseverance in the Path of Malice." The article ended with these words and an excerpt from a 1676 poem by John Wilmot, earl of Rochester: "Men totally abandoned to Wickedness, can never merit our Regard, be their Stations ever so high. 'If such Men are by God appointed, The Devil may be the Lord's anointed.' " Bernard sought action from the legislature against Edes and Gill for a "breach of privilege tending to overthrow all government." He gained support from the Council; the popular branch, however, would not go along, saying that Bernard had not been specifically named in the article. Edes and Gill had won a battle for the press when the House of Representatives declared that "the Liberty of the Press is a great Bulwark of the Liberty of the People: It is therefore the incumbent Duty of those who are constituted the Guardians of the People's Rights to defend and maintain it."

Edes and Gill's attacks on Bernard did not stop there. They dealt the final blow in April 1769 when they, along with the *Evening-Post*, printed in pamphlet form Bernard's confidential letters to the British ministry describing conditions in Massachusetts. Resentment toward Bernard grew in Boston after the publication of the letters, and finally the British ministry recalled him. He set sail on 1 August, never to return. The *Gazette* declared that for the past nine years, Bernard "has been a Scourge to this Province, a Curse to North America, and a Plague to the whole Empire."

Because of their bold attacks on the government, Edes and Gill were frequent targets themselves. Many newspapers outside Massachusetts did not support the brand of journalism practiced there. On 2 November 1772 the *Gazette* reported that Peter Livius, a bitter foe of New Hampshire's Tory governor, had been named chief justice of

First and second pages of Benjamin Edes and John Gill's Boston Gazette *for 12 March 1770, with an inflammatory account of the Boston Massacre. The coffins, inscribed with the initials of the four victims of the massacre who had died to that point, were engraved by Paul Revere.*

The 29th Regiment have drawn off to us, and the 14th Regiment are following them, so that we expect the Town will soon be clear of all the Troops. The Wisdom and true Policy of his Majesty's Council and Col. Dalrymple the Commander appear in this Measure. Two Regiments in the midst of this populous City; and the Inhabitants justly incensed: Those of the neighbouring Towns actually under Arms upon the first Report of the Massacre, and the Signal only wanting to bring in a few Hours to the Gates of this City many Thousands of our brave Brethren in the Country, deeply affected with our Distresses, and to whom we are greatly obliged on this Occasion—No one knows where this would have ended, and what important Consequences even to the whole British Empire might have followed, which our Moderation and Loyalty upon so trying an Occasion, and our Faith in the Commander's Assurances have happily prevented.

Last Thursday, agreeable to a general Request of the Inhabitants, and by the Consent of Parents and Friends, were carried to their Grave in Succession, the Bodies of Samuel Gray, Samuel Maverick, James Caldwell, and Crispus Attucks, the unhappy Victims who fell in the bloody Massacre of the Monday Evening preceding!

On this Occasion most of the Shops in Town, were shut, all the Bells were ordered to toll a solemn Peal, as were also those in the neighboring Towns of Charlestown Roxbury, &c. The Procession began to move between the Hours of 4 and 5 in the Afternoon; two of the unfortunate Sufferers, viz. Mess. James Caldwell and Crispus Attucks, who were Strangers, borne from Faneuil-Hall, attended by a numerous Train of Persons of all Ranks; and the other two, viz. Mr. Samuel Gray, from the House of Mr. Benjamin Gray, (his Brother) on the North-side the Exchange, and Mr. Maverick, from the House of his distressed Mother Mrs. Mary Maverick, in Union-Street, each followed by their respective Relations and Friends: The several Hearses forming a Junction in King-Street, the Theatre of that inhuman Tragedy! proceeded from thence thro' the Main-Street, lengthened by a immense Concourse of People, so numerous as to be obliged to follow in Ranks of six, and brought up by a long Train of Carriages belonging to the principal Gentry of the Town. The Bodies were deposited in one Vault in the middle Burying-ground: The aggravated Circumstances of their Death, the Distress and Sorrow visible in every Countenance, together with the peculiar Solemnity with which the whole Funeral was conducted, surpass Description.

A military watch has been kept every night at the town house and prison, in which many of the most respectable gentlemen of the town have appeared as the common soldier, and night after night have given their attendance.

A Servant Boy of one Manwaring the Tide-waiter from Quebec is now in Goal, having deposed on himself, that the Order and Encouragement of his Superiors had discharged a Musket several Times from one of the Windows of the House in King-Street, hired by the Commissioners and Custom House Officers to do their Business in; more than one other Person swore upon Oath, that they apprehended several Discharges came from that Quarter.—It is not improbable that we may soon be able to account for the Assassination of Mr. Otis some Time past; the Message by Wilmot, who came from the same House to the infamous Richardson before his firing the Gun which kill'd young Snider, and to open up such a Scene of Villainy acted by a dirty Banditti, as must astonish the Public.

It is supposed that there must have been a greater Number of People from Town and Country at the Funeral of those who were massacred by the Soldiers, than were ever together on this Continent on any Occasion.

A more dreadful Tragedy has been acted by the Soldiery in King-Street, Boston, New-England, than was sometime since exhibited in St. George's Field, London, in Old England, which may serve instead of Beacons for both Counties.

Had those worthy Patriots, not only represented by Bernard and the Commissioners as a Faction, but as aiming at making a Separation between Britain and the Colonies, had any Thing else in Contemplation than the Preservation of our Rights, and bringing Things back to their old Foundation—What an Opening has been given them?

Among other Matters in the Warrant for the annual Town-Meeting this Day, is the following Clause, viz. "Whether the Town will take any Measures that a public Monument may be erected on the Spot where the late Tragical Scene was acted, as a Memento to Posterity, of that horrid Massacre, and the destructive Consequences of Military Troops being quartered in a well regulated City."

The Transactions of the Town Meetings in Waltham, Dedham, Bridgwater, &c. compos'd for this Days Paper, we are oblig'd to postpone for want of Room.

BOSTON-GOAL, Monday, 12th March 1770.

Messieurs Edes & Gill,

PERMIT me thro' the Channel of your Paper, to return my Thanks in the most Publick Manner to the Inhabitants in general of this Town—who throwing aside all Party and Prejudice, have with the utmost Humanity and Freedom stept forth Advocates for Truth, in Defence of my injured Innocence, in the late unhappy Affair that happened on Monday Night last: And to assure them, that I shall ever have the highest Sense of the Justice they have done me, which will be ever gratefully remembered, by

Their much obliged and most obedient humble Servant,
THOMAS PRESTON.

Last Thursday last a Committee from the Town of Roxbury waited upon his Honor the Lieut. Governor with the following Petition, viz.

To his Honor THOMAS HUTCHINSON, Esq; Lieutenant Governor and Commander in Chief in and over the Province of Massachusetts Bay.

THE Inhabitants of Roxbury in Town-Meeting lawfully assembled, beg leave humbly to represent to your Honor, that they have often heard, and many of them seen, with pity and concern, the very great inconveniencies and sufferings of our fellow-subjects and countrymen, the inhabitants of the Town of Boston, occasioned by several regiments of the King's troops being quartered in the body of that town for many months past: in a peculiar manner we desire to express our astonishment, grief and indignation, at the horrid and barbarous action committed there last Monday Evening, by a party of those troops, by firing with small arms, in the most wanton, cruel and cowardly manner, upon a number of unarmed inhabitants of said town, whereby four of his Majesty's liege subjects have lost their lives, two others are supposed to be mortally wounded, and several besides badly wounded and suffering great pain and distress; and the town still alarmed and threatned with further and greater mischief: We therefore truly sympathizing with our distressed brethren the inhabitants of said town of Boston, heartily unite with them, in praying your Honor would exert your authority to remove all the troops out of that town immediately; for we cannot, after what has happened, think it can possibly consist with the peace, order and safety of the inhabitants of that or any other town within this province, or his Majesty's real service, to have those troops, or any other, quartered among them. And your Petitioners is in duty bound, &c.

Roxbury March 8, 1770. Unanimously Voted, That Joseph Williams, Esq; Mr. Eleazer Weld, Mr. John Williams, jun. Mr. John Child, Mr. Nathaniel Ruggles, Capt. William Heath, and Major William Thompson, be a Committee to wait upon his Honor forthwith, in behalf of this Town, with the above Petition.

Attest. SAMUEL GRIDLEY, Town-Clerk.

To the above PETITION his Honor returned the following Answer.

Gentlemen,

I Have no Authority to order the King's Troops from any Place where they are posted in his Majesty's Order, or the Order of the Commander in Chief of his Forces here: Every thing that is in my Power to do, with respect to any alteration of the Place of Quartering those Troops, has already been done by me in Pursuance of the unanimous Advice of His Majesty's Council. T. HUTCHINSON.

To the Inhabitants of the Town of Roxbury.
Boston, the 9th of March, 1770.

Last Monday Evening died at his Seat in Chelsea, and on the Friday following was very decently inter'd in this Town, the Honorable SAMUEL WATTS, Esq; formerly one of his Majesty's Council for this Province, and for many Years past one of the Judges of the Court of Common Pleas for this County: The Duties of both of which Offices he discharg'd to general Acceptance, with Firmness and Integrity. And as he lived, so he died, a lover of all Mankind, a friend to his Country, and a truly honest Man.

The 1st Instant died at Newbury, aged 61, MICHAEL DALTON, Esq; a principal Merchant in that Town.

A Gentleman in Carolina, in a Letter to his Friend in Boston, in Answer to one inclosing the last Budget of Letters from Governor Bernard, &c. has the following Passage.

"We have no Precautions, no Noise, but I hope every Thing is operating here, as well as in every other Part of the Continent, to bring about the Events so generally wished for; I pray God to hasten them. Bernard and his Associates will want an H——ll as much hotter for them, than for common Sinners, as Nebuchadnezar's fiery Furnace was, and rare Ecclesiasticks Continuance there."

Thursday the 5th of April next, is appointed by Authority, to be observ'd as a Day of public Fasting and Prayer, thro'out this Province.

We hear from Rutland; That at their annual Meeting on Monday last, John Murray, Esq; was excluded every Office in that Town, Surveyor of the High Ways excepted.

The WATCHMAN, No. II. is come to Hand and will have a Place in our next.

NEW-YORK, March 1.

The 16th Regiment now here are ordered to be got ready to embark for Pensacola; and we hear they are to be replaced by the 14th Regiment now in Boston.

Some People observe, that a late American State prisoner was sent to Goal chiefly by a French Interest, and thence conclude that there is no prospect of a speedy Rupture with France.

THE Effects of Peter Boarn, late of Boston, Mariner, deceas'd, being represented Insolvent, and six Months allowed the Creditors to bring in their Claims and prove their Debts—The Commissioners appointed by the honorable Foster Hutchinson, Esq; Judge of Probate for the County of Suffolk, to receive and examine said Claims—GIVE NOTICE, That they shall attend that Service at the Sign of the Ferry-Boat, near Charlestown-Ferry, Boston, from the Hours of 5 to 8 o'Clock, on the last Thursday of this and the five following Months.

Boston, March 1, 1770

TO BE SOLD BY

John Baker,

At his Store in Back-Street,

A few Bags of the best Cocoa, also choice Chocolate by the Hundred or smaller Quantity

Drifted from Point Shirley, about a Fortnight ago, a MOSES built BOAT. Whoever will bring her to said Baker, shall be satisfied for their Trouble.

Brimstone in Boxes, Cod Lines and Twine by the Cask or Dozen, to be Sold very cheap at the Store No. 9, on the Long Wharff.

---

that province. The *New Hampshire Gazette*, published by Daniel Fowle, doubted the truth of the report and told its readers that the article had most likely been "fabricated" by "geniuses who can upon any occasion set [in] their own Chimney Corners and Write a Letter from London." In a later issue, the New Hampshire paper said that "Edes and Gill, or some of their Hireling Writers," had "become so accustomed to Libel and Defamation, that they never take up a Pen without charging it with Poison of Scandal and Detraction." The *Boston Gazette* had been correct in its report, however, because the British ministry had issued a warrant for the appointment and had withdrawn it later. Publisher James Rivington labeled the Boston paper "Monday's Dung Barge" from "Schism Lane" after Edes and Gill called his *New York Gazette* "dirty" and "malicious."

These attacks from government officials and newspapers seemed to add fuel to Edes and Gill's work. Their firm was the leading printer in America between 1764 and 1783. During the period from 1764 to 1776, they led colonial firms in the production of political pamphlets, producing sixteen percent of the total; they also led in the number of political pamphlets reprinted. The *Gazette* reported a record-breaking weekly circulation of 2,000 between mid-1774 and April 1775. Not all viewed these figures as signs of quality, however; in 1770 Bernard's successor, Governor Hutchinson, wrote, "The misfortune is that seven eights of the people read none but this infamous paper."

The Royalists had a favorite joke about Edes: a Negro happened to be in the *Gazette* office when Edes was complaining about the scarcity of news. "Well, if you've nothing new, Massa Edes," the slave was supposed to have said, "I s'pose you print the same dam' old lie over again."

The Boston Massacre of March 1770 provided an excellent opportunity for Edes to further arouse the already enraged Bostonians. On 5 March 1770 a group of soldiers passing not far from the *Gazette* office were met by a club-armed crowd who deeply resented their presence and refused to let them pass. In the confusion a child was hit with a soldier's musket butt and more citizens joined the crowd. More soldiers came forth and shots were fired. When the smoke cleared, four civilians lay fatally wounded. Seven days later, when the victims of the massacre were buried, Edes and Gill bordered their report of the event with heavy black rules. They also printed a picture of four large coffins; upon each coffin were the initials of one of the men shot to death, along with a skull

and crossbones. The coffins were engraved by Paul Revere, a fellow member of the Sons of Liberty. Edes wrote the account of the massacre, beginning, "The Town of Boston affords a recent and melancholy Demonstration of the destructive Consequences of quartering Troops among citizens in a Time of Peace." The story and the accompanying illustrations did much to arouse the Sons of Liberty to action. When a fifth rioter died several days later, a special cut was devoted to him in the next issue.

It was in Edes's house that the Boston Tea Party was planned. On the day the first of the tea ships arrived from England, 19 November 1773, a large protest meeting was held in Boston. It was resolved that the tea be returned to the place from which it came. Edes printed this protest in the *Gazette* but also played a more important role than that of printer. He and Gill recruited armed patrols who watched the ships day and night to prevent them from unloading their cargo. Edes served as a member of the guard and, as a member of the Loyal Nine, he maintained communications from the top Patriot leaders to the rank and file. On 16 December, as Governor Hutchinson continued to demand that the ships be allowed to unload, a group of men gathered at Edes's house on Brattle Street. Edes's son Peter mixed punch while the conspirators waited for nightfall. Adjourning after dark to the *Gazette* office, the men painted their faces and donned feathered headdresses. They waited for a one-sentence signal that Samuel Adams was to give at a meeting house some blocks away where 7,000 angry Bostonians stood. When Adams received word that Governor Hutchinson had refused to send the ships away, he spoke the words everyone was waiting to hear: "This meeting can do nothing more to save the country." Word spread quickly to the printing office. Joined by others along the way, the group worked for three hours dumping tea from the 342 chests on board.

No published report of Edes's participation appeared in either Patriot or Loyalist papers. The *Gazette* published a warning with its report of the incident, however, saying that any officials attempting to seize the printers for questioning and trial could expect to fall "into the pit they are digging for others." No one touched Edes or Gill, but the threat of arrest remained.

General Gage circulated the following letter, written by a group of Tories in September 1774, among British troops in Boston, urging them to seek out certain troublemakers:

TO THE OFFICERS AND SOL

DIERS OF HIS MAJESTY'S TROOPS IN
BOSTON.

It being more than probable that the
King's standard will soon be erected from
rebellion breaking out in this Province, it's
proper that you soldiers should be ac-
quainted with the authors thereof, and of all
the misfortunes brought upon the Province.
The following is a list of them, viz.: Messrs.
Samuel Adams, James Bowdoin, Dr. Thomas
Young, Dr. Benjamin Church, Capt. John
Bradford, Josiah Quincy, Major Nathaniel
Barber, William Molineux, John Hancock,
William Cooper, Dr. Chauncy, Dr. Cooper,
Thomas Cushing, Joseph Greenleaf, and
William Denning. The friends of your King
and country and of America hope and expect
it from you soldiers, the instant rebellion
happens, that you will put the above persons
to the sword, destroy their houses, and plun-
der their effects! It is just that they should
be the first victims to the evils they have
brought upon us. (signed) A FRIEND TO
GREAT BRITAIN AND AMERICA.

N.B.—Don't forget those trumpeters of
sedition, the printers Edes and Gill, and
Thomas.

Edes, like other Patriot printers, was forced
to leave Boston. Edes made his escape with an an-
tiquated press and types and resumed publication
of the *Gazette* on 5 June 1775 at Watertown. Edes's
son Peter and Gill, who had remained in Boston,
were arrested by the British and held for several
weeks until they posted bail not to leave town. Edes
reported the triumphant news of the English surrender on 19 October 1781 in a broadside with one
of the few headlines printed during colonial
times—"CORNWALLIS TAKEN!"

Edes and his sons Peter and Benjamin ran the
paper until 1794, when Edes resumed sole control.
Edes brought the *Gazette* back to Boston in October
1776, but he could not gather the support and the
contributors that he had once relied on. The paper's mission had apparently been accomplished.
Gill started a second Boston paper on 30 May 1776.
The *Constitutional Journal* ran until 1787.

Edes discontinued the *Gazette* on 17 September 1798, after forty-three years; he closed his
printing business a short time afterwards. His last
years were spent in ill health and poverty, and he
died in obscurity on 11 December 1803.

Edes had been one of the most active and

influential journalists of the revolutionary period.
Using the *Boston Gazette* as their voice, Edes and
other Patriots aroused the support of the people
against British oppression. Edes's writings were reprinted in other colonial newspapers and widely
read all along the seaboard. He was involved in
reporting events during an extremely stormy period of American history and remained true to the
cause of independence and freedom throughout.

John Adams in 1765 paid tribute to Edes and
Gill: "None of the means of information are more
sacred, or have been cherished with more tenderness and care by the settlers of America, than the
press. Care has been taken that the art of printing
should be encouraged and that it should be easy
and cheap and safe for any person to communicate
his thoughts to the public. And you, Messieurs
printers, whatever the tyrants of the earth may say
of your paper, have done important service to your
country by your readiness and freedom in publishing the speculations of the curious. The stale, im-
pudent insinuations of slander and sedition, with
which the gormandizers of power have endeavored
to discredit your paper, are so much the more to
your honor.... And if the public interest, liberty,
and happiness have been in danger from the ambition or avarice of any great man, whatever may
be his politeness, address, learning, ingenuity, and,
in other respects, integrity and humanity, you have
done yourselves honor and your country service by
publishing and pointing out that avarice and ambition. Be not intimidated, therefore, by any terrors, from publishing with the utmost freedom."

References:

John Adams, *Works of John Adams*, edited by Charles
    Francis Adams, 10 volumes (Boston: Little &
    Brown, 1850-1856), II: 178; III: 457;

Bernard Bailyn and John B. Hence, *The Press and
    the American Revolution* (Worcester: American
    Antiquarian Society, 1980), pp. 367-368;

Jonathan Daniels, *They Will Be Heard* (New York:
    McGraw-Hill, 1965), pp. 26, 30, 34;

John C. Miller, *Sam Adams: Pioneer in Propaganda*
    (Stanford, Cal.: Stanford University Press,
    1936), pp. 52, 138;

Arthur Schlesinger, *Prelude to Independence: The
    Newspaper War on Britain 1764-1776* (New
    York: Knopf, 1958), pp. 96, 157, 225, 227;

William V. Wells, *The Life of Samuel Adams* (Boston:
    Little & Brown, 1865), p. 250.

George Henry Evans

(25 March 1805-2 February 1856)

James Stanford Bradshaw
Central Michigan University

MAJOR POSITIONS HELD: Printer, *Free Enquirer* (New York) (1828-1832); editor and publisher, *Working Man's Advocate* renamed *Young America* in 1845 (New York) (1829-1837, 1844-1849), *The Man* (New York) (1834-1835), *The Radical* (Granville, N.J.) (1841-1843).

George Henry Evans is noted chiefly as the editor and publisher of the *Working Man's Advocate*, the second labor paper established in the United States. For a period in the 1830s, it was the most widely copied and quoted workingman's paper in the country. But Evans's most remarkable single achievement—one which he did not live to see realized—was the passage in 1862 of the Homestead Act, permitting free grants of public land to those who actually settled on the land. The founder, leading spirit, chief ideologue, and propagandist of the National Reform Association, he argued from a deeply held belief that a portion of land was the birthright of every man. His ideas are said to have influenced Henry George, the later social and political philosopher, and are still embedded in American thinking on land reform.

Evans was born on 25 March 1805 near Bromyard, Herefordshire, England, to George and Sarah White Evans. His father, an officer in the Napoleonic wars, was proprietor of a brick-making establishment; his mother was the daughter of a well-to-do family of yeomen. A brother, Frederick Evans, born in 1808, later became the chief elder of the Shaker movement in the United States. In 1820, the father—his wife had died—left England, joining two brothers who had established themselves at Chenango Point, now Binghampton, New York. After a year there, during which the father remarried, the family moved to a farm on the Oswego turnpike near Ithaca, then a village of 800.

With a good English elementary education behind him, young George Henry, having turned sixteen, was apprenticed to A. P. Searing, a printer who published books and the weekly *Ithaca Journal*. Ithaca had a reputation as a center of free thought and while there, Evans probably had access to the writings of Thomas Paine, who became one of his idols. Later, he collected and printed some of Paine's miscellaneous writings and was a leading member of the Thomas Paine Society in New York. Near the end of his apprenticeship, in 1824, Evans joined another youth, L. B. Butler, in publishing the biweekly *Museum and Independent Corrector*, a chatty free thought paper. The paper may have lasted until 1827, when Evans left for New York to become a printer and writer for George Houston's *Correspondent*, also a free thought periodical. By March 1828, that paper was carrying the notice that it was printed by the "George H. Evans Printing Co." at successive addresses, including that of the Institute of Practical Education, directed by Robert Jennings.

That association led Evans to a further stage in his career. Jennings was a friend and associate of Frances Wright, a bright and beauteous Scotswoman who had a long love affair with America. By mid-1828, she had virtually abandoned one of her most quixotic and ambitious undertakings—a communal settlement at Nashoba, Tennessee, near Memphis, where she sought to have Negro slaves work out their own freedom and independence; the anticipated—but unrealized—proceeds from the farm were to go to pay their purchase price. She came to New Harmony, Indiana, a commune backed by the wealthy English industrialist Robert Owen. The community had a functioning but money-losing newspaper, the *New Harmony Gazette*. She and Owen's son, Robert Dale Owen, took over the editorship of the paper, ultimately renaming it the *Free Enquirer*. As its fame spread, due to Wright's growing notoriety as a lecturer (women simply did not give public lectures in the 1820s), she determined to move it to New York. Through Jennings, Evans became its printer, a post in which he continued (with the exception of a few issues) until the paper changed ownership in 1832.

In the *Free Enquirer*, Owen and Wright made favorable references to the *Mechanics' Free Press*, the first true labor paper in the United States, started in Philadelphia in 1828. In 1829 a labor movement, whose component groups had succeeded in reducing the workday from twelve hours or more to ten, arose in New York. One of its cardinal aims was to maintain the ten-hour day in opposition to employers who wanted to return to the earlier system. The movement's other interests included the passage of a mechanics' lien law, giving workmen legal claims to pay for work they had done under contractors, who sometimes refused such pay; an end to imprisonment for debt; abolition of the militia system, which required military service without pay under penalty of fine or jail, and which bore most harshly upon low-paid workers who could not afford to buy their way out; and improved educational opportunities for children of the poor and middle classes. The movement entered the political arena as the Working Men's party in October 1829.

While the *Free Enquirer* was useful in the ensuing political campaign of the new party, which entered candidates for New York City and some state political offices, another newspaper was needed. The commercial papers of the city could not be counted upon to support so "radical" a movement. Accordingly, and probably with some financial support from Owen and Wright, Evans brought out on Saturday, 23 October 1829, the first issue of the *Working Man's Advocate*, a five-column, four-page weekly. Its "flag" carried the note "edited by a Mechanic" (Evans). The name *Working Man's Advocate*, he recalled later, was adopted "on the spur of the moment," despite objections by some that it was too exclusive. The paper's goal, a prospectus said, was to prevent "any further encroachments on our equal rights," and seek "the means by which all may be placed . . . on an equal footing."

Evans then was twenty-four years old. On 4 November 1829 he became an American citizen. He was described as a person of "full middle size, regular features, broad forehead." He was said to be "mild and courteous in his intercourse," speaking in "a plain and clear manner," never allowing himself "to arise to a passion," and remarkable for his "great evenness of temper." These personal characteristics carried over into his columns in the *Advocate*. He had an intellectual seriousness which he felt was shared by his workingmen subscribers. A continuing appeal of the *Advocate*, certainly, was what he thought on specific issues of interest to his readers.

The workingmen's movement, after achieving a startling showing in the 1829 elections in New York City, was subject to divisive pressures. It ultimately split into three factions, the largest of which was associated with Owen and Evans; an-

other with the Tammany Democrats; and a third with the supporters of Thomas Skidmore, a radical mechanic. To counter these pressures and prepare for the 1830 elections, the leaders in the Owen-Evans wing decided a daily newspaper was needed. A $3,000 credit was arranged through Camilla Wright, Frances's sister, and in February, the *New York Daily Sentinel* appeared, published by a group of six printers which ultimately included Evans. Essentially, Owen edited it, although he sought to hide this fact. Evans's primary responsibility continued to be the weekly *Advocate*. By June, however, the *Advocate*—which printed material from the *Sentinel*—was describing itself as the "country edition" of that paper. One student of the workingmen's movement, Helene Zahler, has identified over fifty other newspapers in the East, the South, and the Midwest which endorsed, sympathized with, and imitated the *Advocate*. Yet its circulation probably never passed the 2,000 mark; and in keeping with Evans's expressed philosophy that a newspaper should be a carrier of ideas and should not depend for its success (as many did) on official advertisements, it never attracted any great quantity of advertising.

In 1830 the *Sentinel* called for an association of editors which would work for "fairness, temperate argument and courteous language, and against party abuse, personalities, and misrepresentation of opinion." This was perhaps the first time that such an association had been suggested. A few other papers endorsed the idea, but it was not acted upon. The *Sentinel* passed in 1831 to the joint proprietorship of Evans and William J. Stanley, and in 1832 to Evans alone. He discontinued it in July 1833 because of "insufficient patronage."

The 1833 success of Benjamin Day—who had worked with Evans on the *Sentinel* and remained a friend—and his *Morning Sun* led Evans on 18 February 1834 to bring out his own "penny paper"— *The Man*. It soon attained a circulation of over 2,000 and was active in support of President Andrew Jackson's battle against the Bank of the United States. The *Working Man's Advocate*, which remained a weekly, drew heavily on the daily material in *The Man*, and, as with the *Sentinel*, was termed its "country" edition. The advent of James Gordon Bennett's *New York Herald* in 1835, however, increased the bitter competition among the penny papers, and with economic conditions weakening, Evans was forced to discontinue the daily. Later that year, he moved to Rahway, New Jersey, and published the *Advocate* there for several months. Already ill from overwork, he found the damp climate of Rahway unhealthy for himself and his family, and in 1836 he moved to Granville Township in Monmouth County, New Jersey, where he had purchased a forty-acre farm in 1832. Early in 1837, he suspended the *Advocate* and devoted himself to farming.

But in 1841, as he regained his health, he came out with a new publication, *The Radical*, a three-column monthly, which he printed at Granville. It was, he said, a continuation of the *Working Man's Advocate*, "devoted to the abolition of the land monopoly and other democratic reforms." In its sporadic numbers, he stated his own "doctrine" on the question of the public lands, which had been perturbing the U.S. Congress. He stressed that land "should not be a matter of traffic, gift or will," and that the public lands of the United States should be given free to actual settlers. In Evans's conception, settlers who received public land in the newer states would be entitled to bequeath only 160 or 320 acres to their heirs. These holdings would be absolutely inalienable, with sale or mortgage prohibited. If other holdings from public lands were sold, the price should only be for the improvements made on them. Evans never fully elaborated on this point, as he believed that the public lands were so vast that they could meet the demands of settlers for the next 200 years. In Evans's ideas were the seeds of the 1862 Homestead Act. Other reforms on the seventeen-item list included the right of all citizens to vote; election of all government officers by the people; a district system of elections; direct election of the president and vice-president by the people, throughout the nation, on the same day; direct taxation; and submission of all laws to the vote of the people.

In 1844, despite his announced distaste for city living, he returned from Granville to New York City. There, with a group of friends, he launched the National Reform Association. It agitated for freedom of the public lands; exemption of homesteads from legal seizure for debt, nonpayment of taxes, or even failure to complete the appropriate land claims; and limitations on the purchase and ownership of private lands. The proposals were presented to the political candidates of all parties. If the candidate pledged to support the principles, the National Reformers would vote for him; if there was no pledge, they would withhold their votes. Clearly, the National Reformers were an early special interest group. Two papers carried the message of the National Reformers to the public: *People's Rights*, a triweekly published in John Windt's shop, and the *Working Man's Advocate* (New Series), which Evans printed and edited. The *Advocate* was termed the "country edition" of *People's Rights*.

Although the National Reformers were few in number, between 400 and 500 by mid-1844, they were extremely vocal, holding public meetings in the city's parks and circulating petitions and "agrarian pledges." The idea that every citizen had a "right" to land was popular, even among workers who had no intention of moving West. It also provided a justification for frontiersmen who chafed at government insistence on land sales and resented the huge profits of land speculators. Ultimately, over 600 of the 2,000 newspapers in the United States were to endorse the idea of "free" homesteads. In large part, this was due to Evans's adroit propagandizing. His converts included Horace Greeley, whose own *New York Tribune* had far more influence than Evans's low-circulation *Advocate*.

The land issue, however, became inseparably linked with the slavery controversy. The North and the West, to prevent the spread of slavery, wished to keep it out of the new states which were joining the Union. Low- or no-cost 160-acre homesteads, whose settlers would till their own land, were a way of assuring that slavery would not spread. So the Free Soil party—the name has a double significance, free of slavery and free land—emerged in the mid-1840s. It combined the interests of the older Liberty party, the National Reformers, the Barnburning (liberal) Democrats, and the antislavery Whigs. After Free Soil candidate Martin Van Buren provided a crucial margin against Democrat Lewis Cass in the 1848 presidential election, resulting in the election of Whig candidate Zachary Taylor, the Free Soilers were succeeded in 1854 by the new Republican party.

During this tortured period, Evans maintained a friendship and exchanged letters with Gerrit Smith, a New York landowner and philanthropist who was active in the antislavery movement. Smith even advanced some small sums for the support of the *Advocate*'s work. Evans consistently supported liberal causes, including the case of Governor Thomas Dorr of Rhode Island, who was arrested and imprisoned by his opposition after supporting suffrage reforms. He also took the side of the "renters" in upper New York State in the long, drawn out struggle with the landholding patroons, who sought to collect back rents on farms tilled for generations by single families. The Oregon territory, he said, might be a good place to start his "experiment" with homestead farms. In the debate over the annexation of Texas, he stressed that a condition should be that it "abolish the land monopoly to prevent white slavery, and provide for the speedy extinction of black slavery."

Still, the *Advocate* was not a paying proposition, and for some weeks in late 1844, in an effort to solve its financial problems, Evans merged it with the *Subterranean*, published by the flamboyant and irrepressible Mike Walsh, who headed a group of young Democrats known as "the Spartan Band." The arrangement ended when Walsh was jailed for libel and complained that Evans—left in charge of the printing—had censored his comments on the case.

As a part of the process of informing and educating his readers, Evans—as in his earlier papers—reprinted substantial excerpts from British working-class newspapers. In this he was relatively unique, since most American editors preferred to use the older, elite British press. The "Young England" movement, in which Benjamin Disraeli and others sought to protect both landholders and workingmen, attracted him. In 1845 he closed out the final volume of the *Advocate* and retitled the paper *Young America* as "more expressive" of the land reform movement. During that spring and summer, he took a leading role in agitation which resulted in the calling of a "National Industrial Congress" of labor and reform groups in Boston in 1846. The periodic congresses, held in various cities, have been viewed as a significant predecessor of labor unions and a continuing force for liberal principles.

Young America, meanwhile, pressed forward on the issue of free public land. In the fall of 1845 the National Reform candidates showed substantial gains in the New York elections and saw their proposal formally endorsed by Horace Greeley, who, during a brief congressional term in 1848, introduced his own version of a "homestead" bill. With the *Tribune* and other papers taking up the free public land issue, the role of Evans and *Young America* began to diminish. Gaps in publication of the paper began to occur, and it ceased publication in 1849. By that year, Evans evidently had retired to his New Jersey farm. His wife, Laura, who had borne him a son and two daughters, died the same year, and over her grave he put a marker with this touching inscription: "She bore, without murmuring, all the privation necessary for the cause her husband espoused, and now while we mourn the vacant chair, she sleeps calmly, with the branches above waving a requiem over her grave. . . ."

Left with one daughter, Edwina, who was only six, and another, Frances, only eight, Evans re-married. His second wife, Mary Ann, survived until 1876. His son, George Henry, Jr., twice enlisted in New Jersey regiments during the Civil War but never attained the distinction of his father.

Evans caught a severe cold while working on his farm in January 1856 and died in his home on 2 February, just two months short of his fifty-first birthday. His passing went almost unremarked, although the *New York Tribune* carried a two-line notice on 9 February. On his death, Evans owed nearly $3,000, with assets valued at only $1,038. These included two printing presses, one power and one hand; two type cases; and some stereotype plates, together valued at $100. A "lot" of bound newspapers, probably his complete files of the *Advocate* and other papers, was valued at one dollar. All his effects were sold or dispersed. His creditors ultimately received sixty-one cents on the dollar for their claims.

In 1874 the officers of the National Reform Association—by then renamed the Land Reform Association—visited his grave in Wood Cemetery in Keansburg. They discussed the possibility of erecting a monumental bust to him in Prospect Park or Central Park in New York City. Other plans were to celebrate his birthday every year and to republish some of his writings. All of these plans came to nothing.

In 1984 a Keansburg Eagle Scout, Trevor Kirkpatrick, dug Evans's tombstone out from a mound of detritus in the abandoned and vandalized cemetery. The inscription, placed there by his widow, reads: "G. H. E. The Radical. The great object of his life was to secure homes for all by abolishing the traffic in land and limiting the individual possession of it. As editor of The Man, The Radical, The People's Rights, and Young America, he triumphantly vindicated the right of every human being to a share of the soil, as essential to the welfare and permanence of the Republic."

George Henry Evans remains a significant figure in American journalism and American political development. His newspapers provide major touchstones for an understanding of the Jacksonian era, when the "new nation" came to fruition. Certainly he spurred the development of a powerful labor press. Without him, the Homestead Act might never have been passed, and he had a decided role in the movement toward the formation of the Republican party. The loss of his personal papers has deterred any detailed study of his political thinking, which was derived from his idols Thomas Paine, Thomas Jefferson, and John Locke. His role as a political activist and propagandist is worthy of close examination, as are his links with the British reform movement and his unrecognized work in printing American editions of liberal books and tracts.

He was, too, a new kind of editor-publisher, a transitional figure between the hack political printer-editors of the early Federal period and the personal-independent editors who emerged with the spread of the popular press. Devoted to ideas and causes and consecrated to the promotion of the common welfare, he was, with the possible exceptions of William Leggett and Horace Greeley, the most progressive journalistic influence of his era.

References:

John R. Commons, ed., *A Documentary History of American Industrial Society*, 10 volumes (Cleveland: A. H. Clark, 1910-1911), V: 46; VII: 30-33, 46, 288-291, 293-305, 308, 325-327, 331-340, 344-345, 352-356, 358-362, 362-364; VIII: 23-27, 91-94, 288-303;

Commons, David J. Saposs, Helen L. Sumner, E. B. Mittelmas, H. E. Hoagland, John B. Andrews, Selig Perlman, *History of Labor in the United States*, 4 volumes (New York: Macmillan, 1926-1935), I: 10, 234, 237-284;

Water Hugins, *Jacksonian Democracy and the Working Class* (Palo Alto, Cal.: Stanford University Press, 1960), pp. 6, 12, 16-18, 24-26, 29, 31, 32-35, 37, 38, 40, 66, 73-75, 85-88, 91-94, 100-112, 119, 136-160, 164, 177, 179, 185, 190, 195, 222, 226, 241;

Newman Jeffrey, "Social Origins of George Henry Evans, Workingman's Advocate," M.A. thesis, Wayne State University, 1960;

Richard W. Leopold, *Robert Dale Owen* (New York: Octagon Books, 1969), pp. 7, 72, 89-94, 119, 214-216, 302;

Lewis Masquerier, *Sociology, or The Reconstruction of Society, Government and Property* (New York: By the author, 1877), pp. 93-99, 204-207;

Edward Pessen, *Most Uncommon Jacksonians: The Radical Leaders of the Early Labor Movement* (Albany, N.Y.: State University Press, 1967), pp. 9, 16-19, 22, 24, 25, 28, 58, 63, 70-71, 107-113, 116-117, 119, 120, 122, 124, 125, 127, 146, 148, 161, 167, 169-170, 175, 179, 180, 185-186, 189-193;

Arthur M. Schlesinger, Jr., *The Age of Jackson* (New York: Little, Brown, 1945), pp. 33, 138, 140, 182, 185, 198, 212, 286, 308, 318, 347-348, 356, 407, 409-410, 429, 499;

Helene S. Zahler, *Eastern Workingmen and National Land Policy, 1829-1862*, Ph.D. dissertation, Columbia University, 1941.

John Fenno

(23 August 1751-14 September 1798)

Wallace B. Eberhard
University of Georgia

MAJOR POSITIONS HELD: Editor and publisher, *Gazette of the United States* (New York; moved to Philadelphia in 1790), renamed *Gazette of the United States and Evening Advertiser* in 1793 (1789-1798).

The press of the early American nation was one of fierce partisanship and rivalry, and the editorship of John Fenno represents that era of American journalism. The son of Ephraim and Mary Chapman Fenno, Fenno was born in Boston on 23 August 1751. His father engaged in the business of dressing leather, while selling cakes and ale on the side. The Old South Writing School on Boston Common was the scene of Fenno's early education; after graduating some time around 1768, young Fenno became an "usher"—assistant teacher—at the school, under the supervision of Samuel Holbrook. A lifelong friendship with one of the school's masters, Joseph Ward, fourteen years senior to Fenno, was struck up during this period. The Ward-Fenno letters provide insight into the friendship, the times, the character, and the editorship of Fenno. He apparently left the school's employ about 1774, and the following fifteen years are not well documented. It may be that he served a period of service during the Revolutionary War as secretary to Gen. Artemas Ward, but this is in dispute. He took Mary Curtis (or Curtiss—sources differ on the spelling) of Needham, Massachusetts, as his wife on 8 May 1777; he called her "Polly." She was the daughter of Nova Scotia Loyalists who had fled to Boston. His next job apparently was in the inn and livery business in Boston, then as an editorial assistant of some kind for Benjamin Russell, editor of the *Massachusetts Centinel*. A venture into the dry goods business, underwritten by his wife's wealthy uncle, Obadiah Curtis, failed. Fenno apparently imported too much and made too little profit.

Fenno obtained the backing of some Boston Federalists for a printing venture and moved to New York, then the seat of the national government. He carried a letter from one of his patrons, Christopher Gore, a relative of his wife, to Rufus King, leader of the New York Federalists. Gore was a member of the Massachusetts House of Representatives; other prominent backers included James Bowdoin, later governor of Massachusetts, and Jonathan Mason, also a member of the Massachusetts House. Fenno's prospectus to supporters made plain his political stance. He would publish "a continued series of Essays in vindication and support of the Federal Constitution [and] its several parts, connections and dependencies." It was "obvious," he continued, that during the early years of the new government "many difficulties will arise; these can be abated by no method so effectively as a well conducted press, the production of which shall be under the direction of characters who are fully in the Federal interest. . . ." The initial sum pledged by Gore and others as a loan for two years was about £230. Fenno launched the semiweekly *Gazette of the United States* on 11 April 1789. In the issues dated 15 and 27 April, he declared to readers that his newspaper would publish "essays upon great subjects of government in general" and would try to "hold up the people's own government in a favorable light" and "by every exertion, to endear the GENERAL GOVERNMENT to the people." His opening partisan ruffles and flourishes were typical of the press of the day: with few exceptions the editorial objective was to support one or another political party; news and editorial impartiality emerged much later in the history of American journalism.

Fenno's newspaper was published from three successive locations in New York until the govern-

ment moved to Philadelphia in 1790. The final issue published in New York was dated 13 October of that year. The *Gazette* resumed publication in Philadelphia on 3 November 1790, with offices at 69 Market Street, the first of three addresses for the newspaper in that city. The business grew slowly; Fenno had only 600 subscribers by July 1789, with revenues that barely covered the basic printing expenses. Still, new subscriptions trickled in, though not all subscribers paid their accounts regularly. The management of the paper, Fenno wrote to Ward, "is a task of such magnitude that few persons ever before undertook its equal—it employs all my time—it absorbs my whole attention in such a manner that I have not known a pleasing moment of relaxation since you were here. . . ."

Fenno was indeed immersed in the *Gazette* and the politics that led to its birth. His paper was patently pro-Federalist, written for upper-class merchants, manufacturers, wealthy farmers, and shipping interests. The contributors included John Adams, Rufus King, and the guiding light of the *Gazette*, Alexander Hamilton. Hamilton frequently invited Fenno to his library, where he dictated material which was published either anonymously or pseudonymously. Historians have declared Hamilton to have been a "natural journalist and pamphleteer." While the *Gazette* was partisan, it was less vitriolic than some of its competitors. The *Gazette*'s constant drumming on Federalist themes eventually got to Thomas Jefferson, who launched the *National Gazette* with the fiery poet-patriot Philip Freneau as editor. Jefferson had confided to a friend in Paris that the "Tory paper, Fenno's, rarely admits any thing which defends the present form of government in oposition to his desire of subverting it, to make way for a King, Lord and Commons." He also wrote that the *Gazette of the United States* was "disseminating the doctrine of monarchy, aristocracy, and the exclusion of the people." The two *Gazettes* traded charges about which editor was most subservient to which faction of government. The clash of Hamilton and Jefferson through the two newspapers eventually caused an exasperated President Washington to ask Jefferson to fire Freneau. Jefferson refused in an eloquent letter that contained a robust defense of a free press: "No government ought to be without censors; and where the press is free, no one ever will."

Fenno outlasted Freneau, who folded his paper in 1793. Still, Fenno's financial position was precarious at best, and he suspended publication for three months that year, partially because of lack

Gazette of the United States.

NUMBER I.　　　　　WEDNESDAY, April 15, 1789.　　　　　PRICE IX PENCE.

PLAN
OF THE
GAZETTE of the UNITED STATES.
A NATIONAL PAPER.

To be published at the SEAT of the FEDERAL GOVERNMENT, and to consist in part to publish the following Objects, viz.

I. EARLY and authentick Accounts of the PROCEEDINGS of CONGRESS—LAWS, ACTS, and RESOLUTIONS communicated so as to form an HISTORY of the TRANSACTIONS of the FEDERAL LEGISLATURE, under the NEW CONSTITUTION.

II. IMPARTIAL SKETCHES of the Debates of CONGRESS.

III. ESSAYS upon the great subjects of Government in general, and the federal Legislature in particular; also upon the national and local affairs of the AMERICAN CITIZENS, as founded upon the Federal or State Constitutions, also upon every other Subject, which may appear suitable for a newspaper discussion.

IV. A SERIES of PARAGRAPHS, calculated to catch the "living manners as they rise," and to point the publick attention to Objects that have an important reference to domestick, social, and publick happiness.

V. The Interests of the United States, as connected with their literary Institutions—religious and moral Objects—Improvements in Science, Arts, EDUCATION and HUMANITY—their foreign Treaties, Alliances, Connections, &c.

VI. Every species of INTELLIGENCE, which may affect the commercial, agricultural, manufacturing, or political INTERESTS of the AMERICAN REPUBLICK.

VII. A CHAIN of DOMESTICK OCCURRENCES, collected through the Medium of an extensive Correspondence with the respective States.

VIII. A SERIES of FOREIGN ARTICLES of INTELLIGENCE, so connected, as to form a general Idea of publick Affairs in the eastern Hemisphere.

IX. The STATE of the NATIONAL FUNDS, also of the INDIVIDUAL GOVERNMENTS—Courses of Exchange—Prices Current, &c.

CONDITIONS.
I.

THE GAZETTE of the UNITED STATES shall be printed with the same Letter, and on the same Paper as this publication.

II.

It shall be published every WEDNESDAY and SATURDAY, and delivered, as may be directed, to every Subscriber in the city, on those days.

III.

The price to Subscribers (exclusive of postage) will be THREE DOLLARS per annum.

IV.

The first semi-annual payment to be made in three months from the appearance of the first number.

SUBSCRIPTIONS

Will be received in all the capital towns upon the Continent: also at the City-Coffee-House, and at No. 86, William-Street, until the 1st of May, from which time at No. 9, Maiden-Lane, near the Oswego-Market, New-York.

N. B. By a new Arrangement made in the Stages, Subscribers at a distance will be duly furnished with papers.

POSTSCRIPT.—A large impression of every number will be struck off, so that Subscribers may always be accommodated with complete Sets.

To the PUBLICK.

AT this important Crisis, the ideas that fill the mind, are pregnant with Events of the greatest magnitude—to strengthen and complete the UNION of the States—to extend and protect their COMMERCE, under equal Treaties yet to be formed—to explore and arrange the NATIONAL FUNDS—to restore and establish the PUBLICK CREDIT—and ALL under the auspices of an untried System of Government, will require the ENERGIES of the Patriots and Sages of our Country.—Hence the propriety of increasing the Mediums of Knowledge and Information.

AMERICA, from this period, begins a new Era in her national existence—"THE WORLD IS ALL BEFORE HER"—The wisdom and folly—the misery and prosperity of the EMPIRES, STATES, and KINGDOMS, which have had their day upon the great Theatre of Time, and are now no more, suggest the most important Mementos—These, with the rapid series of Events, in which our own Country has been so deeply interested, have taught the

EPITOME OF THE PRESENT STATE OF THE UNION.

NEW-HAMPSHIRE,

WHICH is 180 miles in length, and 60 in breadth, contained, according to an enumeration in 1787, 102,000 inhabitants—is attached to the federal Government—engaged in organizing her militia, already the best disciplined of any in the Union—encouraging the domestick arts—and looking forward to the benefits which will result from the operations of the New Constitution. New-Hampshire, from her local advantages, and the hardihood of her sons, may anticipate essential benefits from the operation of equal commercial regulations.

MASSACHUSETTS,

450 miles in length, and 160 in breadth, contained, according to an enumeration in 1787, 360,000 inhabitants—Since the tranquility of the State was restored by the suppression of the late insurrection, the whole body of the people appears solicitous for the blessings of peace and good government. If any conclusion can be drawn from elections for the Federal Legislature, this State has a decided majority in favour of the New Constitution. The great objects of Commerce, Agriculture, Manufactures, and the Fisheries, appear greatly to engage the attention of Massachusetts. Fabrication of Cotton, coarse Woolens, Linens, DUCK, IRON, Wood, &c. are prosecuting with success—and by diminishing her imports, and increasing her exports, she is advancing to that rank and importance in the Union which her extent of territory—her resources—and the genius and enterprise of her citizens entitle her to—and although the collision of parties, at the moment of Election, strikes out a few sparks of animosity, yet the decision once made, the "Calumet of Peace" is smoked in love and friendship—"and like true Republicans they acquiesce in the choice of the Majority."

CONNECTICUT,

81 miles in length, and 57 in breadth, contained, agreeably to a Census in 1782, 209,150 inhabitants, enjoying a fertile soil, this truly republican State is pursuing her interest in the promotion of Manufactures, Commerce, Agriculture, and the Sciences—She appears to bid fair, from the peaceable, loyal, and federal Character of the great body of her citizens—from the Enterprise of her men of wealth, and other favourable circumstances, to attain to a great degree of opulence, power, and respectability in the Union.

NEW-YORK,

350 miles in length, and 300 in breadth, contained, agreeably to a Census in 1786, 238,897 inhabitants, This State appears to be convulsed by parties—but the CRISIS is at hand, when it is hoped, that the "Hatchet" will be buried. Exertions on one side are making for the re-election of Gov. CLINTON, and on the other for the introduction of the Hon. Judge YATES to the chair—both parties appear sanguine as to their success. It is ardently to be wished, that temper and moderation may preside at the Elections; and there can be no doubt of it, as that Freedom, for which we fought and triumphed, depends so essentially upon a FREE CHOICE.—It is greatly regretted, that this respectable and important member of the federal Republick, should not be represented in the Most Honourable Senate of the United States. New-York, however, is rising in her federal character, and in manufacturing, agricultural, and commercial consequence; Evidenced in her federal elections—her plans for promoting Manufactures, and the increase of her Exports.

NEW-JERSEY,

160 miles in length, and 52 in breadth, contained, by a Census in 1784, 149,435 inhabitants. This

tions are now permitted by law—and the city has been incorporated: Experience will determine the eligibility of the two latter transactions.

DELAWARE,

92 miles in length, and 16 in breadth, by a Census in 1787, contained 37,000 inhabitants. This State, though circumscribed in its limits, derives great importance from its rank in the Union—attached to the New Constitution, and having the honour to take the lead in its adoption, there is no doubt of its giving efficacy to its righteous administration.

MARYLAND,

134 miles in length, and 110 in breadth, by a Census taken in 1782, contained 253,630 inhabitants. From its favourable situation in the Union, this State bids fair for prosperity, wealth, and eminence. Warmly attached to the New Constitution, and enjoying a central situation, the publications there have teemed with tempting inducements to Congress, to make Baltimore the Seat of the Federal Legislature.

VIRGINIA,

758 miles in length, and 224 in breadth—by a census taken in 1782, contains 567,614 inhabitants. From the natural ardour of her sons in the cause of freedom, is frequently convulsed in her elections, and has been torn by factions.—Possessing an extensive territory and a vast income, her funds are placed on a respectable footing; but as her representation in the federal legislature is decidedly attached to the union and the new constitution—there is now no doubt but that she will see her interest and glory finally connected with a few temporary sacrifices upon the principles of mutual concession.

SOUTH-CAROLINA,

200 miles in length, and 125 in breadth—and contains, by a census in 1787, 180,000 inhabitants, an important member of the union, has appeared barely to vibrate between opposing sentiments—Her attachment to national measures we doubt not will evidentally discover itself when all tender laws and pine barrens shall be done away. The prohibition of the importation of slaves, and the provision lately made for the reduction of her foreign debt are federal traits—add to these that their electors have given an unanimous vote for his Excellency GENERAL WASHINGTON, as President of the United States—by which the memorable circumstance is authenticated, that the voice of the WHOLE CONTINENT has once more called our FABIUS MAXIMUS to rescue our country from impending ruin.

GEORGIA,

600 miles in length, and 250 in breadth,—by a Census in 1787, contained 98,000 inhabitants. This State is completing her federal character by conforming her state constitution to that of the union—and being the youngest branch of the family... and a frontier—she will doubtless experience the supporting and protecting arm of the federal government.

FOREIGN STATES.

RHODE-ISLAND,

Is 68 miles in length, and 40 in breadth, and by a Census taken in 1783, contained 51,896 inhabitants. This state has again refused to accede to a union with her sister states, and is now wholly estranged from them; and from appearances, will long continue so, unless the measure of the iniquity of her "KNOW YE" gentry should be speedily filled up—or the delusion which has so long infatuated a majority of her citizens, should be removed.—Anxious of enjoying the protection of the union, the inhabitants of Newport, Providence and other places, are determined to sue for its protection, and to be annexed to Massachusetts

Front page of the first issue of Fenno's rabidly pro-Federalist Gazette of the United States

of finances and partially because of the yellow fever epidemic in Philadelphia.

It was a grim period in the capital's history. Fenno wrote Ward that the death toll was estimated at 3,000 between 1 August and 14 October 1793, with deaths sometimes occurring at the rate of 100 a day. Though he was in the midst of it, Fenno refused to join the throng of citizens who evacuated the city to wait for the epidemic to abate. The panic was so powerful, Fenno wrote, "that Husbands deserted their wives; wives their husbands; children their parents. . . ." Miraculously, Fenno, his wife, and their fourteen children survived, though some of the children became seriously ill.

Support from Hamilton in 1793 rescued Fenno from possible bankruptcy, and government printing contracts kept the newspaper afloat; but it never exceeded a circulation of 1,400, and about 400 of those were free copies or exchanges. His editorial wars kept him in the political forefront, and he converted the paper from semiweekly publication to an evening daily in December 1793, under the revised title *Gazette of the United States and Evening Advertiser.* Occasionally he was required to defend himself in street brawls with local office seekers, such as Israel Isreal of Philadelphia, or other editors, such as Benjamin Franklin Bache, grandson of Benjamin Franklin and publisher of the *Aurora* in Philadelphia. The bout with Isreal was judged to be something of a draw; in the other fight, Bache apparently got the best of it with the aid of a cane.

Fenno's letters to Ward with few exceptions were full of optimism, enthusiasm, and good spirits, even when the financial fortunes of the *Gazette* seemed at low ebb. On 28 July 1798 he wrote Ward about the extreme heat in Philadelphia, "upwards of 90 for three or four days past. It is notwithstanding very healthy. Indeed it is always healthy here in July." But another epidemic of fever soon raged in Philadelphia. Fenno wrote in late August that it seemed to be abating and, according to a physician friend, assuming "a milder form." The mortality rate was near that of the 1793 epidemic. Although many had fled the pestilence, Fenno again stayed. "As it is my duty to continue here so long as other printers remain at their posts, I shall remain here also, trusting in that almighty power which has so graciously protected me and mine heretofore." But this time, the fever hit him, too: he died on 14 September 1798, with "all his blooming virtues thick upon him," as *Russell's Gazette* of Boston commented later. His eldest son, John Ward Fenno, then nineteen, took over the *Gazette,* continuing it for two years with the same strong pro-Federalist edge that had prevailed during his father's editorial reign. After that, the paper had various editors until it was merged out of existence in 1818.

References:

John B. Hench, ed., "Letters of John Fenno and John Ward Fenno, 1779-1800," *Proceedings, American Antiquarian Society,* 89 (1979): 299-368; 90 (1980): 163-234;

Jerry W. Knudson, "Political Journalism in the Age of Jefferson," *Journalism History,* 1 (Spring 1974): 20-23;

Wm. David Sloan, "The Early Party Press: The Newspaper Role in American Politics, 1788-1812," *Journalism History,* 9 (Spring 1982): 18-23.

Benjamin Franklin

Michael Kirkhorn
University of Kentucky

See also the Franklin entry in *DLB 24, American Colonial Writers, 1606-1734.*

BIRTH: Boston, Massachusetts, 17 January 1706, to Josiah and Abiah Folger Franklin.

MARRIAGE: 1 September 1730 to Deborah Read; children: William (born out of wedlock), Francis Folger, Sarah.

MAJOR POSITIONS HELD: Typesetter, contributor, nominal editor, *New-England Courant* (Boston) (1721-1723); editor and publisher, *Pennsylvania Gazette* (Philadelphia) (1729-1748); publisher, *Philadelphische Zeitung* (1732); copublisher, *Pennsylvania Gazette* (1748-1766).

DEATH: Philadelphia, Pennsylvania, 17 April 1790.

SELECTED BOOKS: *A Dissertation on Liberty and Necessity, Pleasure and Pain . . .* (London, 1725);
A Modest Enquiry into the Nature and Necessity of Paper-Currency . . . (Philadelphia: Printed & sold at the New Printing-Office, 1729);
Poor Richard, 1733. An Almanack . . . , as Richard Saunders, Philom. (Philadelphia: Printed & sold by B. Franklin, 1732);
Poor Richard, 1734. An Almanack . . . , as Saunders (Philadelphia: Printed & sold by B. Franklin, 1733);
Poor Richard, 1735. An Almanack . . . , as Saunders (Philadelphia: Printed & sold by B. Franklin, 1734);
Some Observations on the Proceedings against The Rev. Mr. Hemphill; with a Vindication of His Sermons (Philadelphia: Printed & sold by B. Franklin, 1735);
A Letter to a Friend in the Country, Containing the Substance of a Sermon Preach'd at Philadelphia, in the Congregation of The Rev. Mr. Hemphill, Concerning the Terms of Christian and Ministerial Communion (Philadelphia: Printed & sold by B. Franklin, 1735);

A Defense Of the Rev. Mr. Hemphill's Observations: or, An Answer to the Vindication of the Reverend Commission . . . (Philadelphia: Printed & sold by B. Franklin, 1735);
Poor Richard, 1736. An Almanack . . . , as Saunders (Philadelphia: Printed & sold by B. Franklin, 1735);

Courtesy of Mr. Arthur J. Sussel

Poor Richard, 1737. An Almanack . . ., as Saunders (Philadelphia: Printed & sold by B. Franklin, 1736);

Poor Richard, 1738. An Almanack . . ., as Saunders (Philadelphia: Printed & sold by B. Franklin, 1737);

Poor Richard, 1739. An Almanack . . ., as Saunders (Philadelphia: Printed & sold by B. Franklin, 1738);

Poor Richard, 1740. An Almanack . . ., as Saunders (Philadelphia: Printed & sold by B. Franklin, 1739);

Poor Richard, 1741. An Almanack . . ., as Saunders (Philadelphia: Printed & sold by B. Franklin, 1740);

Poor Richard, 1742. An Almanack . . ., as Saunders (Philadelphia: Printed & sold by B. Franklin, 1741);

Poor Richard, 1743. An Almanack . . ., as Saunders (Philadelphia: Printed & sold by B. Franklin, 1742);

Poor Richard, 1744. An Almanack . . ., as Saunders (Philadelphia: Printed & sold by B. Franklin & Jonas Greene, 1743);

An Account Of the New Invented Pennsylvanian Fire-Places . . . (Philadelphia: Printed & sold by B. Franklin, 1744);

Poor Richard, 1745. An Almanack . . ., as Saunders (Philadelphia: Printed & sold by B. Franklin, 1744);

Poor Richard, 1746. An Almanack . . ., as Saunders (Philadelphia: Printed & sold by B. Franklin, 1745);

Poor Richard, 1747. An Almanack . . ., as Saunders (Philadelphia: Printed & sold by B. Franklin, 1746);

Plain Truth: or, Serious Considerations On the Present State of the City of Philadelphia, and Province of Pennsylvania, as a Tradesman of Philadelphia (Philadelphia: Printed by B. Franklin, 1747);

Poor Richard improved: Being an Almanack and Ephemeris . . . for the Bissextile Year, 1748 . . ., as Saunders (Philadelphia: Printed & sold by B. Franklin, 1747);

Poor Richard improved: Being an Almanack and Ephemeris . . . For the Year of Our Lord 1749 . . ., as Saunders (Philadelphia: Printed & sold by B. Franklin & D. Hall, 1748);

Proposals Relating to the Education of Youth in Pensilvania (Philadelphia, 1749);

Poor Richard improved: Being an Almanack and Ephemeris . . . For the Year of Our Lord 1750 . . ., as Saunders (Philadelphia: Printed & sold by B. Franklin & D. Hall, 1749);

Poor Richard improved: Being an Almanack and Ephemeris . . . For the Year of Our Lord 1751 . . ., as Saunders (Philadelphia: Printed & sold by B. Franklin & D. Hall, 1750);

Experiments and Observations on Electricity, made at Philadelphia in America . . ., part 1 (London: Printed & sold by E. Cave, 1751);

Poor Richard improved: Being an Almanack & Ephemeris . . . For the Year of Our Lord 1752, as Saunders (Philadelphia: Printed & sold by B. Franklin & D. Hall, 1751);

Poor Richard improved: Being an Almanack and Ephemeris . . . For the Year of Our Lord 1753 . . ., as Saunders (Philadelphia: Printed & sold by B. Franklin & D. Hall, 1752);

Supplemental Experiments and Observations on Electricity, Part II. Made at Philadelphia in America . . . (London: Printed & sold by E. Cave, 1753);

Poor Richard improved: Being an Almanack and Ephemeris . . . For the Year of Our Lord 1754, as Saunders (Philadelphia: Printed & sold by B. Franklin & D. Hall, 1753);

Some Account of the Pennsylvania Hospital . . . (Philadelphia: Printed by B. Franklin & D. Hall, 1754);

New Experiments and Observations on Electricity. Made at Philadelphia in America . . ., part 3 (London: Printed & sold by D. Henry & R. Cave, 1754);

Poor Richard improved: Being an Almanack and Ephemeris . . . For the Year of Our Lord 1755 . . ., as Saunders (Philadelphia: Printed & sold by B. Franklin & D. Hall, 1754);

Poor Richard improved: Being an Almanack and Ephemeris . . . For the Year of Our Lord 1756 . . ., as Saunders (Philadelphia: Printed & sold by B. Franklin & D. Hall, 1755);

Poor Richard improved: Being an Almanack and Ephemeris . . . For the Year of Our Lord 1757 . . ., as Saunders (Philadelphia: Printed & sold by B. Franklin & D. Hall, 1756);

Poor Richard Improved: Being an Almanack and Ephemeris . . . For the Year of Our Lord 1758 . . ., as Saunders (Philadelphia: Printed & sold by B. Franklin & D. Hall, 1757);

Father Abraham's Speech To a great Number of People, at a Vendue of Merchant-Goods; Introduced to The Publick By Poor Richard (A famous Pennsylvanian Conjuror and Almanack-Maker) . . . (Boston: Printed & sold by Benjamin Mecom, 1758); republished as *The Way to Wealth, as clearly shewn in the Preface of An Old Pennsylvania Almanack, Intituled, Poor Richard Improved* (London: Printed & sold by H. Lewis, 1774;

London: Printed & sold by R. Snagg, 1774);

The Interest of Great Britain Considered, With Regard to her Colonies, And the Acquisitions of Canada and Guadaloupe. To which are added, Observations concerning the Increase of Mankind, Peopling of Countries, &c. (London: Printed for T. Becket, 1760; Boston: Printed by B. Mecom, 1760);

A Narrative of the Late Massacres, in Lancaster County, of a Number of Indians, Friends of this Province, By Persons Unknown . . . (Philadelphia: Printed by Anthony Armbruster, 1764);

Cool Thoughts on the Present Situation of Our Public Affairs . . . (Philadelphia: Printed by W. Dunlap, 1764);

Remarks on a late Protest Against the Appointment of Mr. Franklin an Agent for this Province (Philadelphia: Printed by B. Franklin & D. Hall, 1764);

Oeuvres de M. Franklin, 2 volumes, edited by Jacques Barbeu-Duborg (Paris: Quillau, 1773);

Political, Miscellaneous, and Philosophical Pieces . . . , edited by Benjamin Vaughan (London: Printed for J. Johnson, 1779);

Observations on the Causes and Cure of Smokey Chimneys (London: Printed for J. Debrett, 1787);

Philosophical and Miscellaneous Papers. Lately written by B. Franklin, LL.D., edited by Edward Bancroft (London: Printed for C. Dilly, 1787);

Rules for Reducing a Great Empire to a Small One (London: Printed for James Ridgway, 1793);

Autobiography of Benjamin Franklin, first complete edition, edited by John Bigelow (Philadelphia: Lippincott/London: Trübner, 1868);

Benjamin Franklin Experiments. A New Edition of Franklin's Experiments and Observations on Electricity, edited by I. Bernard Cohen (Cambridge: Harvard University Press, 1941);

Benjamin Franklin's Autobiographical Writings, edited by Carl Van Doren (New York: Viking, 1945);

Benjamin Franklin's Memoirs. Parallel Text Edition, edited by Max Farrand (Berkeley: University of California Press, 1949);

Benjamin Franklin: His Contribution to the American Tradition, edited by Cohen (New York: Bobbs-Merrill, 1953);

Franklin's Wit and Folly: The Bagatelles, edited by Richard E. Amacher (New Brunswick: Rutgers University Press, 1953);

The Autobiography of Benjamin Franklin, edited by Leonard W. Labaree, Ralph L. Ketcham, and others (New Haven: Yale University Press, 1964);

The Political Thought of Benjamin Franklin, edited by

Ketcham (Indianapolis: Bobbs-Merrill, 1965);

The Bagatelles from Passy by Benjamin Franklin, Text and Facsimile (New York: Eakins Press, 1967);

The Autobiography of Benjamin Franklin, A Genetic Text, edited by J. A. Leo Lemay and P. M. Zall (Knoxville: University of Tennessee Press, 1981).

Collections: *The Works of Dr. Benjamin Franklin,* 6 volumes, edited by William Duane (Philadelphia: Duane, 1808-1818);

Memoirs of the Life and Writings of Benjamin Franklin, 3 volumes, edited by William Temple Franklin (London: Henry Colburn, 1817-1818);

The Works of Benjamin Franklin, 10 volumes, edited by Jared Sparks (Boston: Hilliard, Gray, 1836-1840);

The Writings of Benjamin Franklin, 10 volumes, edited by Albert Henry Smyth (New York: Macmillan, 1905-1907);

The Papers of Benjamin Franklin, edited by Leonard W. Labaree, Whitfield J. Bell, Jr., and others, 23 volumes to date (New Haven: Yale University Press, 1959-   );

The Complete Poor Richard Almanacs published by Benjamin Franklin, edited by Bell (Barre, Mass.: Imprint Society, 1970).

Irrepressibly inventive, gifted with a "marvellous range," Benjamin Franklin, an admiring biographer observed, was "a harmonious human multitude." To his contemporaries he seemed prodigious. To us, living in an age of occupational specialties, the abundance and variety of his activities appear phenomenal. He was never idle. On a sea voyage, noticing how the captain trimmed the ship, Franklin devised experiments, Carl Van Doren reported, "to determine the best form of hull, the proper position of the masts, the form and size of the sails, and the right disposition of the freight." When the ship nearly ran aground, Franklin decided that lighthouses were needed along the American coast. He "could contemplate nothing without wishing to improve it."

This image of Franklin studying the rigging of an ordinary merchantman embarked on an ordinary voyage, drawing from these observations the substance of more inventions, is merely a snapshot from the album of his accomplishments. He was editor of two of the American colonies' finest newspapers, the *New-England Courant* and the *Pennsylvania Gazette.* He was a versatile and popular writer; the inventor of the Franklin stove and the lightning rod; and the organizer of the American Philosophical Society, the first public library, and the first fire department. As a youth he was an expert swimming instructor who devised hand paddles to strengthen his stroke. Late in life he became one of the new republic's great diplomats. He was scientist, soldier, patriot, and navigator. He respected no boundaries, and in all of his activities he displayed a cheerful, willing nature which sometimes overflowed in the sort of playfulness which is illustrated in some of his occasional writings, such as his "Drinker's Dictionary," where he listed 226 terms describing intoxication: ". . . nimptopsical . . . as stiff as a ringbolt . . . coguy . . . jambl'd . . . scalt his head pan . . . pidgeon eyed . . . priddy. . . ."

This American who would become a reviled enemy of the British monarchy sprang from a family which lived peaceably for 300 years at Ecton, in Northhamptonshire, on a thirty-acre freehold. Franklin's father, Josiah, crossed the Atlantic Ocean with his first wife and three children and settled in New England about 1682. Josiah's second wife, Abiah Folger, who bore ten of his seventeen children, was Benjamin's mother. He was born in Boston in 1706.

He was brought up in a community ruled by the stringencies of Puritanism, and while he con-

formed, observing the stringent admonitions of Cotton Mather ("Stoop!," Mather told him, to avoid "the hard thumps of life"), he spent much of his early life shedding the inherited severities, discarding the harshness which restricted his grace.

His father removed him from grammar school after only one year because, Franklin later recalled, "having so large a family he could not well afford" to pay for schooling. Placed in a presumably less expensive school, Franklin failed arithmetic. So, at the age of ten, he joined his father in his trade of tallow chandler and soap boiler. Bored, Franklin found outlets for his energy. In his famous *Autobiography* (1868) he recounted an exploit in which he led some playfellows in the construction of a stone wharf at the edge of a salt marsh. Unfortunately, the stones were intended for construction of a house. Discovered, Franklin "pleaded the usefulness of the work," but his father convinced him that "nothing was useful which was not honest."

Noticing his son's bookishness (he was reading Bunyan, Plutarch, and Defoe), and hoping to restrain his desire to go to sea, Benjamin's father persuaded the reluctant twelve-year-old—"I stood out [refused] some time"—to sign indentures binding him as apprentice in his elder brother James's printing business until he was twenty-one years of age. "In a little time I made great proficiency in the business, and became a useful hand to my brother," he recalled.

Soon, the reader became a writer. He wrote a poem called "The Lighthouse Tragedy" and a sailor song about Blackbeard the pirate. James Franklin encouraged his younger brother and sent the boy out to sell the poems in the town. The first sold wonderfully, Franklin recalled, but his father ridiculed the writing and told Benjamin that poets were usually beggars. This harsh criticism killed the poet in Franklin, but before long he was working diligently at prose. He would read an article in the *Spectator,* lay it aside, and try several days later to write the same article as well as the *Spectator*'s writer had written it. When he finished he would compare his work with the published version and make the necessary corrections. These exercises he practiced before or after work, or on Sundays, when he did his best to avoid worship.

Meanwhile, James Franklin was planning his own career. A successful young businessman gifted with the Franklin family's audacity, on 7 August 1721 James began publication of the *New-England Courant,* a paper intended to set staid Boston on its ear. James Parton, one of Benjamin Franklin's

THE BIRTH PLACE OF FRANKLIN.
WHICH STOOD IN MILK STREET, OPPOSITE THE OLD SOUTH CHURCH, BOSTON

The house in Boston where Franklin was born in 1706

biographers, wrote that Bostonians, "accustomed to the monotonous dullness of the *News Letter* and the monotonous respectability of the *Gazette*," were delighted, more often horrified, and universally amazed by "this weekly budget of impudence and fun"—the "most spirited, witty, and daring" of all colonial newspapers.

An observer of James's incitements of the local civic leadership, including an outraged clergy, the unappreciated apprentice continued to set type, work at the press, and distribute the *Courant*. James felt no strong affection for his younger brother, and when Benjamin, who had been perfecting his prose style, wished to publish an essay in the newspaper, he had to resort to a ruse, slipping the manuscript—written under the pseudonym "Silence Dogood"—under the door of the printing shop at night. The next morning, overhearing the approval expressed by James and some *Courant* contributors as they read the essay, Franklin experienced "exquisite pleasure." Encouraged, he wrote several more essays.

The fourteen *Courant* articles signed "Silence Dogood" provide a remarkable example of Franklin's precocious shrewdness about human nature. In Mrs. Silence Dogood, widow of a country parson, Franklin invented a woman who was clever, sensible, and penetrating in her understanding of her neighbors—and even of her departed husband. Of the "Reverend Master," she observed, in the *Courant* for the week of 9 April to 16 April 1722: "There is certainly scarce any Part of a Man's Life in which he appears more silly and ridiculous, than when he makes his first Onset in Courtship." Through "Love, or Gratitude, or Pride, or All Three," she nevertheless consented to marry this awkward character, with whom she lived "in the Heighth of conjugal Love and mutual Endearments" for nearly seven years. And she would have married again after his death, but she seemed to find quiet satisfaction passing away her time "in Conversation, either with my honest Neighbor *Rusticus* and his Family, or with the ingenious Minister of our Town, who now lodges at my House, and by whose Assistance I intend now and then to beautify my Writings with a Sentence or two in the learned Languages, which will not only be fashionable, and pleasing to those who do not understand [it], but will likewise be very ornamental."

This "Enemy to Vice, and Friend to Vertue, . . . Forgiver of *private* Injuries," and "hearty Lover of the Clergy and all good Men," this "mortal Enemy to arbitrary Government & Unlimited Power," was also gifted at satire. For the *Courant* of 7 May

One of Franklin's fourteen "Silence Dogood" letters, published in his brother James's New-England Courant *while Benjamin worked on the paper as an apprentice*

to 14 May 1722, she provided a report of a dream she had while asleep beneath an apple tree in her orchard. The article satirizes Harvard College and the young "Dunces and Blockheads" congregated there through an elaborate account of the "Tribe" of scholars who with little success climb the throne of learning and again descend to make their way along the obscure paths of life: "SOME I perceiv'd took to Merchandising, others to Travelling, some to one Thing, some to another, and some to Nothing; and many of them from henceforth, for want of Patrimony, liv'd as poor as church Mice, being unable to Dig, and asham'd to beg, and to live by their Wits it was impossible." The greater number, beckoned by *Pecunia*, took "a large beaten path" to the Temple of Theology.

Soon, the political outspokenness of the *Courant* landed James in hot water. He was censured and imprisoned in the summer of 1722 and released after a month with the provision that he "should no longer print the paper called the *New England Courant.*" To evade the edict, James gave his younger brother nominal control of the *Courant*, discharging him from his previous indentures with the provision that he would secretly sign new ones. James announced to the readers of the paper that he had "entirely dropt the undertaking," and a new prospectus for the paper was presented, marked, as Parton has observed, with the style of the "laughing philosopher" Benjamin Franklin. The new *Courant*, the prospectus said, would "entertain the town with the most comical and diverting incidents of human life"; it would also contain "a grateful interspersion of more serious morals," but only those "which may be drawn from the most ludicrous and odd parts of life."

Franklin's period of notoriety among the goads whom Parton called the "gay Couranters" was cut short by his older brother's bad-tempered and perhaps envious abusiveness. They quarreled violently, and Benjamin left. It is a tribute to his fair-mindedness that he questioned his decision to escape indenture, to claim his freedom. "It was not fair in me to take this advantage," he wrote, "and this I reckon one of the first errata of my life; but the unfairness of it weighed little with me, when under the impressions of resentment for the blows his passion too often urged him to bestow upon me, though he was otherwise not an ill-natured man; perhaps I was too saucy and provoking."

James could not enforce the secret indentures that bound his brother to the *Courant* without admitting that he had been editing the paper himself all along, but he took revenge by preventing Benjamin from finding other employment in Boston. When other masters refused to give him work, Franklin decided to abandon Boston. He sold some books, caught a sloop for New York, and landed in the city three days later—"a boy of but seventeen, without the least recommendation to or knowledge of, any person in the place, and with very little money in my pocket."

From New York the boy was directed to Philadelphia, where, he was told by the printer William Bradford, he might find a place in Bradford's son Andrew's printing shop as a replacement for Aquila Rose, who had recently died. After a strenuous voyage he arrived, frazzled, in Philadelphia: "I was dirty from my journey; my pockets were stuffed out with shirts and stockings, and I knew no soul nor where to look for lodging. I was fatigued with traveling, rowing, and want of rest; I was very hungry; and my whole stock of cash consisted of a Dutch dollar, and about a shilling in copper."

Andrew Bradford needed no help, but Franklin found employment in the shop of another printer Samuel Keimer. As a young printer of skill and resource, he soon caught the attention of Sir William Keith, the governor of Pennsylvania. Keith persuaded Franklin to return to Boston and ask his father to assist him in establishing his own printing shop in Philadelphia. The elder Franklin declined to offer immediate assistance but promised to help Benjamin if, by the age of twenty-one, he had saved nearly enough to establish a business. He warned his son to repress his satirizing impulses and earn the respect of the citizens of Philadelphia.

Franklin heeded that advice. Philadelphia became his home, the city to which he would return again and again, a city which benefited greatly from his reforms and from his ingenuity, the city where he died on 17 April 1790 and was carried to his grave in a procession which included Philadelphia's politicians, printers, philosophers, physicians, judges, lawyers, bankers, and clergy. But he began his service to the city with a trip abroad.

Assuming, as he had been assured by Keith, that he enjoyed the governor's wholehearted support, Franklin arranged to travel to London to buy equipment to set up his own printing business in Philadelphia. On 5 November 1724, carrying letters of credit to buy types, paper, and a press from Keith's London friends, Franklin sailed for England. By the time he discovered that Keith's letters were worthless, Franklin was in London with no more than ten pounds sterling in his pocket. Advised to seek work in a London print shop, he immediately found a position at Palmer's, a well-known printing house in Bartholomew Close, where he was known as the "Water-American" for his habit of drinking water rather than the pints of

Sir William Keith, governor of Pennsylvania—romantically depicted in armor—who encouraged Franklin to set up a printing business in Philadelphia. Franklin went to London to buy equipment carrying letters of credit from Keith; the letters turned out to be worthless (Historical Society of Pennsylvania).

beer which his fellow printers consumed at intervals through the workday. In his autobiography, Franklin was charitable—some say too charitable—about Keith's betrayal. "It was a habit he had acquired," Franklin observed. "He wished to please everybody; and, having little to give, he gave expectations."

In London, Franklin improved his skill as a printer and met some interesting people, whom he impressed with his ability at repartee and with some unexpected abilities (he was, for example, an expert swimmer and a teacher of swimming). He also wrote and printed a short metaphysical treatise, *A Dissertation on Liberty and Necessity, Pleasure and Pain* (1725), in reply to a work he had been assigned to set in type. He returned to Philadelphia in October 1726 a worldlier and more confident young man

than he had been eighteen months before.

After working as a clerk for a merchant named Denham, Franklin returned to Keimer's shop. He gathered together some of his fellow printers and a few others (a mathematician, a surveyor, a shoemaker, and a carpenter among them) in a society known as the Junto. This polite and sensible debating society, which met each Friday evening, provided Franklin with delight and intellectual satisfaction for many years. Its membership was limited to twelve, and its offshoots, clubs called the Vine, the Union, and the Band, enriched the cultural life of the city.

Franklin derived considerably less pleasure from his relationship with his employer, Keimer. The older printer apparently had wanted an efficient and skilled man to train the five inexperienced employees in his shop. That having been accomplished, Keimer began to find fault with Franklin. In 1728, noticing Franklin at a window watching a commotion in the street, Keimer used the pretext to abuse the young printer, provoking a fight which ended with Franklin leaving the shop. A friend, Hugh Meredith, persuaded Franklin not to return to Boston, and Franklin and Meredith began a printing business of their own with some support from Meredith's father. George House, a member of the Junto, brought in the first customer, a farmer who paid five shillings for an advertisement. Another Junto member, Joseph Breintnall, obtained business for Franklin and Meredith from the Quakers, who wanted printing done for their society.

Franklin and Meredith made plans to start a newspaper to compete with Andrew Bradford's *American Weekly Mercury*, the only newspaper in the city. George Webb, to whom Franklin had confided his plans for a newspaper, revealed the secret to Keimer, who responded by starting the *Universal Instructor in All Arts and Sciences: and Pennsylvania Gazette* on 24 December 1728. The first part of the paper's name derived from Keimer's intention to serialize in it all of Ephraim Chambers's *Cyclopaedia; or, An Universal Dictionary of the Arts and Sciences* (1728), beginning with the letter *A*. In order to keep himself from being shut out of the newspaper business in Philadelphia, Franklin devised a crafty scheme to ruin Keimer. He and Breintnall wrote a series of satirical essays in Addisonian style, the Busy-Body papers, for Bradford's *Mercury*. The essays both ridiculed Keimer and drew readers to the rival paper. Finally, on 25 September 1729, Keimer sold his paper to Franklin and Meredith.

When the paper appeared under its new own-

THE

Pennſylvania GAZETTE.

Numb. XL.

Containing the freſheſt Advices Foreign and Domeſtick.

From Thurſday, September 25. to Thurſday, October 2. 1729.

THE Pennſylvania Gazette being now to be carry'd on by other Hands, the Reader may expect ſome Account of the Method we deſign to proceed in.

Upon a View of Chambers's great Dictionaries, from whence were taken the Materials of the Univerſal Inſtructor in all Arts and Sciences, which uſually made the Firſt Part of this Paper, we find that beſides their containing many Things abſtruſe or inſignificant to us, it will probably be fifty Years before the Whole can be gone thro' in this Manner of Publication. There are likewiſe in thoſe Books continual References from Things under one Letter of the Alphabet to thoſe under another, which relate to the ſame Subject, and are neceſſary to explain and compleat it; theſe taken in their Turn may perhaps be Ten Years diſtant; and ſince it is likely that they who deſire to acquaint themſelves with any particular Art or Science, would gladly have the whole before them in a much leſs Time, we believe our Readers will not think ſuch a Method of communicating Knowledge to be a proper One.

However, tho' we do not intend to continue the Publication of thoſe Dictionaries in a regular Alphabetical Method, as has hitherto been done; yet as ſeveral Things exhibited from them in the Courſe of theſe Papers, have been entertaining to ſuch of the Curious, who never had and cannot have the Advantage of good Libraries; and as there are many Things ſtill behind, which being in this Manner made generally known, may perhaps become of conſiderable Uſe, by giving ſuch Hints to the excellent natural Genius's of our Country, as may contribute either to the Improvement of our preſent Manufactures, or towards the Invention of new Ones; we propoſe from Time to Time to communicate ſuch particular Parts as appear to be of the moſt general Conſequence.

As to the Religious Courtſhip, Part of which has been retal'd to the Publick in theſe Papers, the Reader may be inform'd, that the whole Book will probably in a little Time be printed and bound up by it ſelf; and thoſe who approve of it, will doubtleſs be better pleas'd to have it entire, than in this broken interrupted Manner.

There are many who have long deſired to ſee a good News-Paper in Pennſylvania, and we hope thoſe Gentlemen who are able, will contribute towards the making This ſuch. We ask Aſſiſtance, becauſe we are fully ſenſible, that to publiſh a good News-Paper is not ſo eaſy an Undertaking as many People imagine it to be. The Author of a Gazette (in the Opinion of the Learned) ought to be qualified with an extenſive Acquaintance with Languages, a great Eaſineſs and Command of Writing and Relating Things cleanly and intelligibly, and in few Words; he ſhould be able to ſpeak of War both by Land and Sea; be well acquainted with Geography, with the Hiſtory of the Time, with the ſeveral Intereſts of Princes and States, the Secrets of Courts, and the Manners and Cuſtoms of all Nations. Men thus accompliſh'd are very rare in this remote Part of the World; and it would be well if the Writer of theſe Papers could make up among his Friends what is wanting in himſelf.

Upon the Whole, we may aſſure the Publick, that as far as the Encouragement we meet with will enable us, no Care and Pains ſhall be omitted, that may make the Pennſylvania Gazette as agreable and uſeful an Entertainment as the Nature of the Thing will allow.

The Following is the laſt Meſſage ſent by his Excellency Governour Burnet, to the Houſe of Repreſentatives in Boſton.

Gentlemen of the Houſe of Repreſentatives,

IT is not with ſo vain a Hope as to convince you, that I take the Trouble to anſwer your Meſſages, but, if poſſible, to open the Eyes of the deluded People whom you repreſent, and whom you are at ſo much Pains to keep in Ignorance of the true State of their Affairs. I need not go further for an undeniable Proof of this Endeavour to blind them, than your ordering the Letter of Meſſieurs Wilks and Belcher of the 7th of June laſt to your Speaker to be publiſhed. This Letter is ſaid (in Page 1 of your Votes) to incloſe a Copy of the Report of the Lords of the Committee of His Majeſty's Privy Council, with his Majeſty's Approbation and Order thereon in Council. Yet theſe Gentlemen had at the ſame time the unparallell'd Preſumption to write to the Speaker in this Manner: You'll obſerve by the Concluſion, what is propoſed to be the Conſequence of your not complying with His Majeſty's Inſtruction. The whole Matter to be . . .

First page of the first issue of Franklin's Pennsylvania Gazette, *which he purchased from his rival, Samuel Keimer, after driving Keimer out of business*

ership on 2 October, the title had been shortened to *Pennsylvania Gazette*, the serialized encyclopedia was gone, and the paper was livelier and better printed.

To the editing of the *Gazette* Franklin applied his lively temperament and his shrewd business sense. All news was stale, by modern standards, and Franklin followed the practices of other editors, publishing articles from English newspapers or other colonial papers, along with items drawn from conversations with ship captains or correspondence from commercial agents in other lands or friends traveling abroad. His newspaper resembled others also in its makeup, the first page being devoted to European news; the second to local news and letters; the third and fourth pages, added in the summer, carrying advertisements, political or commercial news, or information about shipping. He printed letters from readers, some so cleverly written that one must ask how much help the writers had from the editor; it was common practice at the time in English and American newspapers for editors to write anonymously or pseudonymously to their own papers. Franklin leavened the serious letters on religious or social matters with witty and light hearted letters.

He espoused freedom of the press and impartiality. When, in 1731, an advertisement annoyed some members of the clergy, Franklin published his "Apology for Printers," in which he professed that printers had a special responsibility to sustain the competition of ideas. "Printers are educated in the belief," Franklin wrote, "that when men differ in opinion, both sides ought equally to have the advantage of being heard by the public; and that when truth and error have fair play, the former is always an overmatch for the latter."

As Franklin obtained a contract to print paper currency, opened a bookstore and a stationer's shop, and in other small ways began to build his reputation as a businessman, he paid close attention to his manner and appearance. "I drest plainly," he recalled; "I was seen at no places of idle diversion. I never went out a fishing or shooting; a book, indeed, sometimes debauch'd me from my work, but that was seldom, snug, and gave no scandal; and, to show that I was not above my business, I sometimes brought home the paper I purchas'd at the stores thro' the streets on a wheel-barrow. Thus being esteemed an industrious, thriving young man, and paying duly for what I bought, the merchants who imported stationery solicited my custom; others proposed supplying me with books, and I went on swimmingly."

Keimer's business failed, and he moved to Barbados in 1729; shortly thereafter his profligate successor also failed and also moved to Barbados. Franklin then had only one competitor, the "rich and easy" Bradford. But he had other matters on his mind. He attempted a courtship but found that a young printer, still in debt, was not valued as a prospective son-in-law. He sought other marital opportunities but was not immediately successful. "In the meantime," he wrote, "that hard-to-be-governed passion of youth hurried me frequently into intrigues with low women that fell in my way, which were attended with some expense and great inconvenience, besides a continual risk to my health by a distemper which of all things I dreaded, though by great good luck I escaped it." He returned to Deborah Read, whom he had courted before his journey to London, and on 1 September 1730 the two entered into a common-law marriage. Deborah was already married to John Rogers, who had deserted her and disappeared; had she and Franklin been formally married, and had Rogers returned, Deborah could have been charged with bigamy—at that time a capital offense.

An illegitimate son, William Franklin, was born in 1731. William grew up to become royal governor of New Jersey and was estranged from his father; they may have been reconciled late in Benjamin's life. The identity of his mother remains a matter for speculation. William's son, William Temple Franklin, became Franklin's secretary, traveled with him to France, and accompanied him on his return to the United States in 1785.

Franklin's civic duties multiplied after his marriage. In 1731 he founded the first subscription library in the colonies, the mother of all free libraries in the United States. Franklin was a busy and versatile businessman. He printed books, tickets, leases, bills of sale and lading, contracts, and other legal papers; he sold books he received from England; in his stationer's shop he sold ink, paper, pens, fountain pens, compasses, scales, and slates; he bought rags to make paper and sold soap, as well as chocolate, palm oil, cheese, fish, and "Senaka Rattlesnake Root, with directions how to use it in the Plurishy. . . ."

Meredith finally decided that he had been cut out to be a farmer rather than a printer. He moved to North Carolina, leaving the business in Franklin's hands, and on 11 May 1732, the *Gazette* appeared for the first time under Franklin's name alone. The paper was profitable, business was good; the twenty-six-year-old Franklin was emerging from debt, which he always dreaded as a form of

Franklin's illegitimate son, William, who became royal governor of New Jersey and took the British side in the American Revolution (Collection of Mrs. J. Manderson Castle)

slavery. In Philadelphia there were the Junto and the library, monuments to his youthful industry. On 20 October of the same year his son Francis Folger was born. Franklin would be devastated four years later by Francis's death from smallpox; but for the present, life continued swimmingly. New projects emerged—in December 1732 one for which Franklin is known to all who know anything at all about him: *Poor Richard's Almanack.*

The almanac was an indispensable item in colonial America. It contained astrological forecasts, calendars, recipes, jokes, poems, maxims, moon and tide changes, and all sorts of practical information. A printer who produced a successful almanac could expect to make some money. Franklin's almanac, featuring the imaginary astrologer Richard Saunders (Poor Richard), quickly surpassed all the others on the market. The almanac opened with these words by Poor Richard: "I Might in this place attempt to gain thy Favour by declaring that I wrote Almanacks with no other View than that of the publick Good; but in this I

should not be sincere, and men are now-a-days too wise to be deceiv'd by Pretences how specious soever. The plain Truth of the Matter is, I am excessive poor, and my Wife, good Woman, is, I tell her, excessive proud; she cannot bear, she says, to sit spinning in her Shift of Tow, while I do nothing but gaze at the Stars; and has threat'ned more than once to burn all my Books and Rattling-Traps (as she calls my Instruments) if I do not make some profitable Use of them for the good of my Family. The Printer has offer'd me some considerable share of the Profits, and I have thus begun to comply with my Dame's desire."

The Franklin almanac became an institution, a profitable one. It sold 10,000 copies a year. After 1746 it was called *Poor Richard improved,* and it was larger than ever. The almanacs contained some of Franklin's better-known adages, but as Carl Van Doren has observed, not all of these adages were "on the side of calculating prudence." Among those which revealed the "saucy" and somewhat imprudent Franklin, Van Doren listed these: "Never spare the parson's wine nor the baker's pudding." "Avarice and happiness never saw each other. How then should they become acquainted?" "There's more old drunkards than old doctors." More char-

Franklin's son Francis Folger, who died in 1736 of smallpox (Collection of Mrs. J. Manderson Castle)

Poor Richard, 1733.

A N

Almanack

For the Year of Chrift

1733,

Being the Firft after LEAP YEAR:

And makes fince the Creation	**Years**
By the Account of the E ftern Greeks	7241
By the Latin Church, when ☉ ent ♈	6932
By the Computation of *W W*	5742
By the *Roman* Chronology	5682
By the *Jewifh* Rabbies	5494

Wherein is contained

The Lunations, Eclipfes, Judgment of the Weather, Spring Tides, Planets Motions & mutual Afpects, Sun and Moon's Rifing and Setting, Length of Days, Time of High Water, Fairs, Courts, and obfervable Days.

Fitted to the Latitude of Forty Degrees, and a Meridian of Five Hours Weft from *London,* but may without fenfible Error ferve all the adjacent Places, even from *Newfoundland* to *South-Carolina.*

By *RICHARD SAUNDERS*, Philom.

PHILADELPHIA:
Printed and fold by *B FRANKLIN,* at the New Printing Office near the Market

Title page for the first issue of Franklin's famous almanac

acteristic are: "Deny self for self's sake." "An old young man will be a young old man." "Now I have a sheep and a cow, everybody bids me good morrow." "Fish and visitors smell in three days." "Poverty, poetry, and new titles of honour make men ridiculous." "Fly pleasures and they'll follow you." "Eat to please thyself, but dress to please others." "A house without a woman and a firelight is like a body without soul or sprite." "A ship under sail and a big-bellied woman are the handsomest two things that can be seen in common." "Early to bed and early to rise makes a man healthy, wealthy, and wise." "Keep thy shop and thy shop will keep thee." "Creditors have better memories than debtors."

"For want of a nail the shoe is lost; for want of a shoe the horse is lost; for want of a horse the rider is lost." "In the affairs of this world, men are saved not by faith but by the want of it."

Not all of Franklin's enterprises were successful. In May 1732 he decided to provide a German-language newspaper for Philadelphians of German ancestry, of whom there were many. The editor was Louis Timothée, a French protestant newcomer, encouraged in his career by the Junto. But when only fifty subscribers responded, *Philadelphische Zeitung* was scrapped six weeks after its first issue.

Timothée, who Anglicized his name to Lewis Timothy, moved late in 1733 to South Carolina, where, through agreement with Franklin, who was to pay one-third of the expenses and take one-third of the profits for six years, the journeyman printer revived the *South Carolina Gazette*. When Timothy died, his widow carried on the partnership.

After 1732 Van Doren remarked, "the separate currents of Franklin's life drew gradually together in the single, broad stream which was his character moving through history." His increasing intellectual interests and the spreading breadth of his spirit and influence did not, however, detract from his business activity. By 1734 he was public printer for Delaware and New Jersey, and later he served the same function for Maryland. In 1736 he was appointed clerk of the Pennsylvania Assembly, and by holding that post until 1751 he was able to assure a flow of government printing to his shop. In 1737 he became postmaster at Philadelphia. He learned French, Italian, Spanish, and German. Languages were valuable for the printer, but his assiduousness indicates something more about that happy, endless curiosity which marked his life. No matter how busy or preoccupied he may have been, Franklin always spent some time each day in the library he had founded. His daughter Sarah was born in 1743.

Toward the mid-1740s the colonies felt increasing anxiety over the warring of the European powers, which was bound to have consequences in the dependencies of the New World. Pennsylvania lagged in military preparation. In 1746 Franklin visited Boston and, impressed by the military preparedness of the people of Massachusetts, upon his return wrote an essay warning Pennsylvanians of their vulnerability to the great Indian tribes and to the French. He then called a meeting, urging citizens to form an Association for Defense. Twelve hundred volunteered immediately, ten thousand within a few days; a regiment was formed in Phil-

✠(No. I.)✠

Philadelphifche Zeitung.

SAMBSTAG, den 6 Mey. 1732.

An alle teutfche Einwohner der Provintz Peunfylvanien.

NACHDEM ich von verfchiedenen teutfchen Einwohnern diefes Landes bin erfuchet worden, eine teutfche Zeitung ausgehen zu laffen, und ihnen darinnen das vornehmfte und merckwürdigfte neues, fo hier und in Europa vorfallen möchte, zu communiciren; doch aber hierzu viele mühe, groffe correfpondentz und auch Unkoften erfordert werden: Als habe mich entfchloffen, denen teutfchen zu lieb gegenwärtiges Specimen davon heraus zu geben, und ihnen dabey die Conditiones welche nothwendig zu der continuation derfelben erfordert werden, bekent zu machen.

Erftlich, müften zum wenigften, um die unkoften die darauf lauffen, gut zu machen, 300 ftücks können gedruckt und debitiret werden, und müfte in jeder Townfhip dazu ein mann ausgemachet werden, welcher mir wiffen lieffe, wie viel Zeitungen jedes mahl an ihn müften gefandt werden, und der fie dan weiters einen jeglichen zuftellen und die bezahlung davor einfordern müfte.

Vor jede Zeitung mufs jährlich 10 Shillinge erleget, und davon alle quartal 2 fh. 6 d. bezahlet werden.

Dagegen verfpreche ich auf meiner feite, durch gute Correfpondentz die ich in Holland und England habe allezeit das merkwürdigfte und neuefte fo in Europa und auch hier paffiret, alle

woce einmahl, nemlich Sonnabends in gegenwärtiger form einer Zeitung, nebft denen fchiffen fo hier abgehen und ankommen, und auch das fteigen oder fallen des Preiffes der Güter, und was fonft zu wiffen dienlieb bekandt zu machen.

Advertiffemente oder Bekant machungen, welche man an mich fchicken möchte, follen das erfte mahl vor 3 fhill. 3 mahl aber vor 5 fhil: hinein gefetzet werden.

Und weil ich nützlich erachte die gantze befchreibung der aufrichtung diefer provintz, mit allen derfelben privilegien, rechten und gefetzen, bey ermangelung genugfamer Neuigkeiten, darinen bekandt zu machen; folte nicht undienlich feyn, dafs ein jeder, zumahl wer kinder hat, diefe Zeitungen wohl bewahre, und am ende des jahres an einander heffte; zumahl da folche dann gleichfam als eine Chronica dienen können, die vorigen Gefchichte daraus zu erfehen, und die folgende defto beffer zu verftehen.

Auch wird anbey zu bedencken gegeben, ob es nicht rahtfam wäre, in jeder groffen Townfhip einen reitenden Boten zu beftellen, welcher alle woche einmahl nach der ftadt reiten und was ein jeder da zu beftellen hat, mit nehmen könne.

So bald nun die obgemeldte anzahl der Unterfchreiber vorhanden, welche fo bald als möglich erfuche in Philadelphia

Front page of Franklin's German-language newspaper, which was edited by Louis Timothée. The paper lasted only six weeks.

adelphia and Franklin was elected colonel, a post he declined for lack of soldierly experience. However, he began a lottery to buy cannon and he designed some military insignia.

In 1745, at the University of Leyden, Holland, a discovery was made which had the consequence of persuading Benjamin Franklin to give up his businesses and devote a period of his life to scientific study. The Dutch experimenters had managed to produce electricity by friction, but until this year they had found no way to collect and retain it. Then, through an accident which flattened Cuneus, one of the researchers, the Leyden jar was discovered, and immediately it became a sensation. This bottle half full of water, connected to a friction machine and producing manmade electrical shocks, apart from its immense scientific value, was touted through Europe as a cure for all ailments, including double chins and hairlessness. Franklin saw his first electrical experiments in Boston in 1746 and, as one biographer noted, for a

time he was lost to all other worlds.

"I never was before engaged," Franklin wrote, "on any study that so totally engrossed my attention and my time as this has lately done; for, what with making experiments when I can be alone, and repeating them to my friends and acquaintances, who, from the novelty of the thing, come continually in crowds to see them, I have, during some months past, had little leisure for anything else."

In 1748 Franklin sold his printing office, almanac, and newspaper to his associate, David Hall, who was to make annual payments of £1,000 sterling on the price of £18,000. Franklin, with an annual income from his estate of about $3,500, and $750 more from his political offices, could retire comfortably. He moved from the busy center of Philadelphia to Second and Race Streets, near the outskirts of town.

In his pursuit of the mysteries of electricity, Franklin was no dilettante. The Leyden jar was nothing more than a bottle with a wire piercing its cork. Franklin and his fellow experimenters analyzed the workings of electricity through the jar, made a primitive battery consisting of eleven panes of sash-glass with thin leaden plates pasted on each side, and then developed, as a more efficient replacement for the battery, a series of connected Leyden jars. Franklin summarized the winter's work in a letter proposing a celebratory party on the banks of the Schuylkill at which a turkey "is to be killed for our dinner by the *electrical shock,* and roasted by the *electrical jack,* before a fire kindled by the *electrical bottle;* when the healths of all the famous electricians in England, Holland, France, and Germany are to be drunk in *electrified bumpers,* under the discharge of guns from the *electrical battery.*"

Title page for Franklin's second book on his electrical experiments, with the key word misspelled (Yale University Library)

Looking to the sky for the source of this wonderful energy, he described an experiment in which a miniature lightning-rod had drawn off electricity from an artificial thunderstorm and speculated that rods fixed to the highest parts of houses, churches, and ships might draw electricity harmlessly from clouds before damage was done. It was 1752, following a period of patient experimentation and careful deduction, before Franklin flew the famous kite which carried a piece of sharpened iron wire into a June storm. At the end of the hempen string which held the kite, he fastened a key, and waited in a shed for indications that electricity was being transmitted from a thundercloud to a Leyden jar prepared for the collection of the energy. After a time, the Leyden jar was charged with electricity; and as he noticed the fibers of the

One of Franklin's many inventions: the armonica, a musical instrument consisting of glass hemispheres rotated through a trough of water and rubbed with the finger to produce tones

hempen string rise and then touched his knuckles to the key, detecting the flow of current, Franklin was, one writer observed, the happiest philosopher in Christendom.

In 1753 Franklin was appointed joint deputy postmaster general for the American colonies with William Hunter of Virginia, and he swiftly applied his energy and imagination to the complicated task of providing a better postal service. He saw that the mails could be one way to unite the colonies. He made a survey trip through the colonies, and as he broadened his contacts, receiving honorary degrees from Harvard and Yale, chatting with merchants about the postal service and with professors about science, he began to consider more seriously the idea that the colonies should be united in a federation. He wrote in the *Gazette* of the prospect for federation and, in one of the earliest American political cartoons, portrayed division as a serpent cut into segments—each segment representing a colony—with the motto "Join or Die."

The need for union was further reinforced by his experience as a commissioner of the government of Pennsylvania in negotiations with the Six Indian Nations, intended to study means of defense in case of attack by the French. Franklin believed that effective defense would require a union of the colonies under the protection and guidance of England. He proposed that a military governor general appointed by the king should guide the defense of the American colonies, while domestic affairs would be decided by an interco-

One of the first American political cartoons, drawn by Franklin for the Pennsylvania Gazette *of 9 May 1754, urging the uniting of the colonies into a federation*

lonial parliament. A few foresightful citizens responded approvingly, but most clung to traditional ways and rights.

In 1755 the blustering General Edward Braddock arrived from England with an army which was to defend the colonies from the French. The Quakers agitated against involvement in a war, while Braddock threatened to quarter soldiers in the homes of citizens. In the midst of this threat of hostilities between British soldiers and Pennsylvania colonists, Franklin tactfully intervened, offering to provide wagons and carriages to carry the troublesome army's supplies off to the frontier, where Braddock intended to take Niagara, Frontenac, and Fort Duquesne from the French—with whom he was sure some Pennsylvanians were collaborating.

Displaying an astuteness surprising in a man without military experience, Franklin questioned Braddock's optimism. He knew that Braddock's army would stretch for four miles along the narrow road through the wilderness, and he warned the general against Indian ambushes, which might cut the army "like a thread into several pieces." Braddock smiled tolerantly and replied that the king's regular army feared no savages.

The massacre of Braddock's army along the line of march which had been shortened—but not sufficiently—due to Colonel George Washington's urgings is a familiar story. Franklin's help to the doomed army earned him a unanimous vote of thanks from the Assembly of Pennsylvania. Franklin was never paid the full amount for his services, but in the ensuing period of massacre and terror

along the northwestern frontier he received a general's commission and led a military expedition.

The remnants of Braddock's army had fled back to Philadelphia; the frontier was unprotected. Franklin was given a small force which marched cautiously to the pillaged town of Gnadenhutten. There Franklin directed his men to cut palisades for a fort. The fort completed, Franklin's men scoured the countryside; they found concealed encampments but no Indians. Unsuccessful in his attempt to meet the enemy, Franklin established a garrison at "Fort Allen" and returned to Philadelphia on 10 February 1756, after two months' service in the field. The firing of guns during the celebration of the return of the militia broke several glasses of Franklin's electrical apparatus. Nine months after Franklin left Gnadenhutten, a party of Indians attacked Fort Allen, killed or scattered the garrison, and burned the village again.

A new dispute awaited Franklin and offered him the opportunity to gain even greater honor, this time as a diplomat. The Pennsylvania Assembly in 1756 was smoldering with resentment against Thomas and Richard Penn, who, granted twenty-six million acres of land worth fifty million dollars, refused to submit to taxation for defense of the colony against Indians. By passing an uncooperative and unsympathetic Governor Denny, the Assembly voted in 1756 to send two commissioners to England to present its grievances before the king. The commissioners were to be Assembly Speaker A. Isaac Norris and Franklin. Norris declined; Franklin, leaving his wife behind because of her fear of the sea, prepared at once to sail with his son William. After a long voyage, he arrived in London on 27 July 1757.

In Great Britain Franklin was cordially and generously welcomed by all he encountered—except for the royal representatives with whom he had been sent to negotiate. From their haughty insistence on the inferior status of the distant colonies Franklin learned those lessons which he later applied in his revolutionary writings, notably his "Rules by Which a Great Empire May be Reduced to a Small One" (1773), satirical advice to royal ministers which contained this passage: "Take special care the provinces are never incorporated with the mother country; that they do not enjoy the same common rights, the same privileges in commerce; and that they are governed by *severer* laws, all of *your enacting,* without allowing them any share in the choice of the legislators."

Lord Granville, president of the King's Council, told Franklin that colonists should consider the king's instructions to colonial governors as having the force of law, even if the colonial assemblies had had nothing to say about their formulation. Colonists were not at liberty to disregard these instructions but had to obey them, Granville said. Franklin replied that he had thought that the colonial assemblies made laws for the colonies. "This was new doctrine to me," he said.

Obviously, this would be a lengthy diplomatic mission, and Franklin settled in comfortably. He remained for five years and adopted a routine which permitted travel each summer, the most agreeable trip coming in 1758 when he visited the University of Cambridge, dining and conversing with the chancellor, the heads of the colleges, and the professors, and experimenting in the reduction of temperature through evaporation with Professor Hadley.

Franklin's diplomatic mission ended inconclusively, but his reputation as a philosopher and scientist was growing. In 1762, as he waited for a berth in a safe convoy—England and France were at war—to carry him back to Philadelphia, he was awarded a doctor of civil laws degree by Oxford University. At the same ceremony, his son William, soon to be appointed royal governor for New Jersey, was awarded the degree of master of arts. Shortly thereafter, a convoy of ten ships with a man-of-war as escort set sail for Philadelphia, called at Madeira, and arrived in Philadelphia the first of November. The sadness of London friends at his departure was offset by the rejoicing of his Philadelphia friends, who filled his house from morning to night after his return.

He was not to remain home for long. In 1764 he accepted another envoy assignment to England, once again to place the feuding between the Pennsylvania Assembly and the Penns before the agents of the crown and to relay to the king the Assembly's opposition to the proposed Stamp Act. Deborah refused once again to cross the ocean. Franklin expected to be away for ten months, but as his career became enmeshed in the prelude to the Revolutionary War, his return was delayed; he stayed away for ten years, returning on the eve of the revolution.

When he arrived in London on 10 December 1764 he quickly joined the other colonial agents in opposition to the Stamp Act, which Franklin called the "mother of mischiefs." The Americans failed; the Stamp Act was passed overwhelmingly by Parliament. The angry resistance to the Stamp Act persuaded Parliament to repeal it early in 1766, and Franklin celebrated by sending his wife a gown, remarking that if trade between Britain and the colonies had ceased as a consequence of the Stamp Act, he would have been proud to have been clothed once again "in woolen and linen of my wife's manufacture." He requested permission to return home; the Assembly responded by appointing him agent for another year.

Neither the labors of diplomacy nor his longing for home and family deterred Franklin's studies. "A complete statement of Dr. Franklin's philosophical investigations at this period of his life would fill a volume," Parton said. ". . . Never was his mind more on the alert or more successfully employed. We see him expatiating in his letters upon such diverse topics as chimneys and swimming; metallic roofs and spots on the sun; the average fall of rain and fireproof stairs; the torpedo, the Armonica (harmonica), and the northwest passage; the magnet and improved carriage wheels; glass-blowing, Prince Rupert's drops, and the Aurora Borealis; the inflammatory gases and the effect of vegetation upon air and water. Nothing escaped him that transpired in philosophical circles, and his remarks on subjects agitated therein were always valuable, and frequently original." His persistence, brilliance, and versatility were ever more widely acknowledged. When Franklin visited France in 1767, he met scholars, philosophers, politicians, and the king, who greeted him warmly. Much of Franklin's subsequent correspondence in the period before he returned to America was devoted to French philosophy, especially to the group called the Physiocrats.

In the increasingly venomous atmosphere of London before the revolt of the American colonies, Franklin learned to despise the intransigence of the England which once he had esteemed. When all his petitions had failed and after he had been reviled by officials of the crown (a reviling which earned him great favor in the colonies), he took his grandson, William Temple Franklin, aboard the *Pennsylvania Packet* and on 25 March 1775 they embarked upon a pitching sea—a "tired and vanquished old widower"—Deborah had died the year before—leaning, in Van Doren's words, "on the arm of his slender, supple grandson. . . ."

The Franklin who returned, finally, to Philadelphia, was "old only in years," Parton observed, and not aged mentally or in spirit. "Writers of the period describe him as having grown portly, and he himself frequently alludes jocularly to his great bulk. He had discarded the cumbersome wig of his earlier portraits, and wore his own hair, thin and gray, without powder or pigtail. His head being

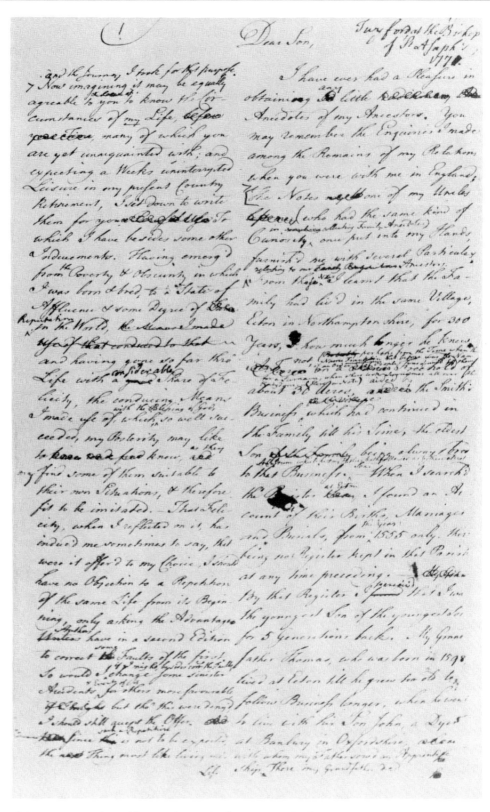

The first page of the manuscript of Franklin's autobiography, begun in England in August 1771 in the form of a long letter to his son William. Franklin folded the pages lengthwise into two columns and wrote the text in the right-hand column, leaving the left-hand column blank for afterthoughts and revisions. Almost all of the 230 pages of the manuscript—including this one—contain such revisions. Franklin continued to work on the autobiography until his death (Henry E. Huntington Library and Art Gallery).

remarkably large and massive, the increased size of his body was said to have given proportion as well as dignity to his frame. His face was ruddy, and indicated vigorous health. His countenance expressed serenity, firmness, benevolence; and easily assumed a certain look of comic shrewdness, as if waiting to see whether his companion had 'taken' a joke. . . . In conversation, he excelled greatly in the rare art of listening, and seemed devoid of the least taint of a desire to shine. His was a weighty and expressive silence, which elicited talk, not quelled it; and his taciturnity gave to his utterances, when he did speak, the character of events to be remembered and reported."

Among Franklin's contributions to the revolutionary cause, none outshone the letter of recommendation which eased the emigration from England of the bedeviled Thomas Paine, whose famous pamphlet, *Common Sense*, appeared on 10 January 1776. By that time Franklin had been busily employed for several months as postmaster general as the colonies organized for war.

Franklin did not spare himself. Seventy years old, he nevertheless joined a commission appointed by the Continental Congress which went by sloop, jolting country wagon, and boat to Montreal to persuade Canada to join the Union. The mission was hopeless, and Franklin suffered so severely from the wintry journey that he thought he might die. Asked upon his return to join the committee of five elected to draft the Declaration of Independence, he willingly complied and signed the finished document with a flourish. The same month, he was elected to Congress, and then was voted president of the Pennsylvania Constitutional Convention. It was a blow for the old patriot to learn that his son William, a firm Royalist, had been removed as royal governor of New Jersey and imprisoned. Later William retired in England with a life pension in appreciation for his service to the crown.

Encouraged by the promise of support from France, the beleaguered Continental Congress decided in 1776 to send a commission to Paris, consisting of Silas Deane, Arthur Lee, and Franklin. Now past seventy, Franklin, accompanied by his young grandsons, William Temple Franklin and Benjamin Franklin Bache, the son of his daughter Sarah, left for Europe on 26 October 1776 aboard the sloop *Reprisal*.

In France, the aging Franklin performed his final diplomatic service and enjoyed the experience immensely. He perceived, one biographer said, "that he was going to have the time of his life. This was the kind of *milieu* which all his life he had

Franklin on his diplomatic mission to France. On the wintry voyage across the Atlantic, he had worn a fur hat to keep his head warm; finding that this headgear gave him the appearance in French eyes of a simple backwoodsman, he often wore it when he wished to cultivate that impression (Yale University Art Gallery).

craved and one for which he had unconsciously been preparing all his toilsome years in business, politics, science and diplomacy. Here was Paris at the zenith of its exhilaration at getting rid of Louis XV and acquiring as its new monarchs the amiable Louis XVI and the charming if irresponsible Marie Antoinette. It was a Paris ready to hope and adore. It was especially in the mood to adore Franklin, and Franklin sagaciously decided to put nothing in its way. He swept his memory clean of all the shrivelling maxims of Poor Richard and gathering up the thirteen Virtues of his quondam creed—including Temperance, Silence, Order, Frugality and Moderation—he dropped them through a hole in his mind and closed the lid upon them with a barely muffled thud."

Franklin, aided by William Temple Franklin, the older of his two grandsons, set to work immediately writing pamphlets to further bend

French opinion toward aid, including money, for the American Revolution. The desperation of the envoys was lifted somewhat when Jonathan Loring Austin arrived at Franklin's home in Passy on 4 December 1777 to announce that General Burgoyne and his entire army had surrendered. Two months later the American commissioners signed, with members of the government of France, a Treaty of Amity and Commerce and a Treaty of Alliance between France and the United States—a great triumph for Franklin.

Eventually, Franklin became the sole plenipotentiary, and he lived comfortably and happily. In 1778 his wine list included 1,040 bottles, mostly French but including 148 bottles of Xeres, for he loved Spanish wines. He ate plentifully and kept his medicine chest stocked with quinine, Peruvian bark, Spanish licorice, anise seed, alkali, gargles, and manna. His neighbors were devoted to him and—always a lover of female companionship—he enjoyed the attention of a number of delightful women, including Madame d'Hardancourt Brillon, who invited him to her home twice and three times weekly; Madame Helvétius, with whom he dined at least once a week; and the Countess d'Houdetot, once beloved of Jean Jacques Rousseau and the patron of Michel Guillaume Jean de Crèvecoeur, who immigrated to the United States and wrote the invaluable *Letters from an American Farmer* (1782). The witty Madame Brillon inspired Franklin to write some of his most graceful short pieces, including the "Bagatelles" which he printed on his private press in the basement of his house at Passy. Among these were *The Story of the Whistle, The Ephemera, The Petition of the Left Hand, The Handsome and Deformed Leg, Dialogue Between Franklin and the Gout,* and *The Morals of Chess.*

He was so addicted to chess that he once started a game in Madame Brillon's bathroom and, apparently, went on playing long after she had finished her bath. Later he apologized that "in forgetting everything else by our too great attention to chess, we have inconvenienced you very much by keeping you so long in the bath."

Several times, Franklin had asked permission to return home. On 7 March 1785 Congress granted his petition, and appointed Thomas Jefferson to replace him as plenipotentiary. Asked by Count de Vergennes if he was the man who would "replace Dr. Franklin," Jefferson replied: "I am only his successor, sir; no one can replace him."

Too feeble to go to Versailles for a leave-taking ceremony, Franklin received from the king a parting gift of the king's portrait circled twice with

The portrait of Louis XVI that was given to Franklin by the doomed king on Franklin's departure from France in 1785. The portrait was originally contained in a frame studded with 408 diamonds; the gems were later sold by Franklin's family (American Philosophical Society).

408 diamonds. The queen's litter carried him to Havre. He was met at Southhampton by William Franklin, with whom he had been reconciled. On 28 July 1785 he set sail for home, after nine years in France. At the end of his voyage, cannonades, cheers, and hurrahs greeted him at the Market Street wharf. Finding his family safe and well, he expressed his gratitude in his diary: "God be praised and thanked for all his mercies."

He joined actively in the proceedings of the Constitutional Convention, which assembled at Philadelphia in 1787, and in the same year he was elected president of the Pennsylvania Executive Council. In his eighty-second year his health began to fail, but his spirit did not: he wrote several articles arguing for the abolition of slavery and for the improvement of life for black Americans.

On 17 April 1790 Franklin died. The funeral procession to the old Christ Church burial ground was the greatest ever seen in Philadelphia. His cheerful nature is preserved in an epitaph written in 1728, when he was twenty-two years old, and never used on his grave:

The Body of
B Franklin Printer,
(Like the Cover of an Old Book
Its Contents torn out
And Stript of its Lettering & Gilding)
Lies here, Food for Worms.
But the Work shall not be lost;
For it will, (as he believ'd) appear once more,
In a new and more elegant Edition
Revised and corrected,
By the Author.

Letters:

Les Amitiés américaines de Madame d'Houdetot, d'après sa correspondance inédite avec Benjamin Franklin et Thomas Jefferson, edited by Gilbert Chinard (Paris: E. Champion, 1924);

"My Dear Girl": The Correspondence of Benjamin Franklin, Polly Stevenson, Georgiana and Catherine Shipley, edited by James M. Stifler (New York: Doran, 1927);

The Letters and Papers of Benjamin Franklin and Richard Jackson, 1753-1785, edited by Carl Van Doren (Philadelphia: American Philosophical Society, 1947);

Benjamin Franklin and Catherine Ray Greene: Their Correspondence, edited by William G. Roelker (Philadelphia: American Philosophical Society, 1949);

Benjamin Franklin's Letters to the Press, 1758-1775, edited by Verner W. Crane (Chapel Hill: University of North Carolina Press, 1950);

"Franklin's Letters on Indians and Germans" and "Franklin and Jackson on the French War," edited by A. O. Aldridge, in American Philosophical Society *Proceedings,* 94 (August 1950): 391-395, 396-397;

The Letters of Benjamin Franklin and Jane Mecom, edited by Carl Van Doren (Princeton: Princeton University Press, 1950);

" 'All Clear Sunshine!' New Letters of Franklin and Mary Stevenson Hewson," edited by Whitfield J. Bell, Jr., in American Philosophical Society *Proceedings,* 100 (December 1956): 521-536;

Mr. Franklin: A Selection from His Personal Letters, edited by Leonard W. Labaree and Bell (New Haven: Yale University Press, 1956).

Bibliographies:

Paul Leicester Ford, *Franklin Bibliography: A List of*
Books Written by, or Relating to, Benjamin Franklin (Brooklyn: Historical Printing Club, 1889);

I. Minis Hays, *Calendar of the Papers of Benjamin Franklin in the Library of the American Philosophical Society,* 6 volumes (Philadelphia: University of Pennsylvania Press, 1908);

C. William Miller, *Benjamin Franklin's Philadelphia Printing, 1728-1766. A Descriptive Bibliography* (Philadelphia: American Philosophical Society, 1974).

Biographies:

James Parton, *Life and Times of Benjamin Franklin,* 2 volumes (Boston: Mason Brothers, 1864);

Carl Van Doren, *Benjamin Franklin* (New York: Viking, 1938);

Carl L. Becker, *Benjamin Franklin, A Biographical Sketch* (Ithaca: Cornell University Press, 1946);

A. Owen Aldridge, *Benjamin Franklin: Philosopher and Man* (Philadelphia: Lippincott, 1965);

Claude-Anne Lopez, *Mon Cher Papa: Franklin and the Ladies of Paris* (New Haven: Yale University Press, 1966);

Catherine Drinker Bowen, *The Most Dangerous Man in America: Scenes from the Life of Benjamin Franklin* (Boston: Little, Brown, 1974);

Lopez and Eugenia W. Herbert, *The Private Franklin: The Man and His Family* (New York: Norton, 1975);

David Freeman Hawke, *Franklin* (New York: Harper & Row, 1976);

Ronald W. Clark, *Benjamin Franklin: A Biography* (New York: Random House, 1983).

References:

Richard E. Amacher, *Benjamin Franklin* (New York: Twayne, 1962);

Amacher, "Humor in Franklin's Hoaxes and Satires," *Studies in Humor,* 2 (April 1975): 4-20;

Brian M. Barbour, ed., *Benjamin Franklin: A Collection of Critical Essays* (Englewood Cliffs, N.J.: Prentice-Hall, 1979);

Bruce I. Granger, *Benjamin Franklin, An American Man of Letters* (Ithaca: Cornell University Press, 1964);

Ralph W. Ketcham, *Benjamin Franklin* (New York: Twayne, 1965);

J. A. Leo Lemay, "Franklin's Suppressed 'Busy-Body,' " *American Literature,* 37 (November 1965): 307-311;

Lemay, ed., *The Oldest Revolutionary: Essays on Benjamin Franklin* (Philadelphia: University of Pennsylvania Press, 1976);

William E. Lingelbach, "B. Franklin, Printer—New Source Material," American Philosophical Society *Proceedings*, 92 (May 1948): 79-100;

Frank L. Mott and Chester E. Jorgenson, Introduction to *Benjamin Franklin: Representative Selections* (New York: American Book Company, 1936), pp. xiii-cxli;

Clinton Rossiter, "Benjamin Franklin," in his *Seedtime of the Republic* (New York: Harcourt, Brace, 1953), pp. 281-312;

Charles L. Sanford, ed., *Benjamin Franklin and the American Character* (Boston: Heath, 1955);

Arthur B. Tourtellot, *Benjamin Franklin: The Shaping of Genius, The Boston Years* (Garden City: Doubleday, 1977).

Papers:

By far the greatest collection of Benjamin Franklin's manuscripts is held by the American Philosophical Society Library, Philadelphia. Other sizable holdings are in the Stevens Collection, Library of Congress; the University of Pennsylvania Library; the Library of the Historical Society of Pennsylvania; and Yale University.

James Franklin

(4 February 1697-4 February 1735)

Jeffery A. Smith
University of Iowa

MAJOR POSITIONS HELD: Editor, *New-England Courant* (1721-1726), *Rhode-Island Gazette* (1732-1733).

BOOKS: *The Life and Death of Old Father Janus, the Vile Author of the Late Wicked Courant. A Satyr* (Boston: Printed & sold by J. Franklin, 1726);

The Rhode-Island Almanack for the Year 1728 Carefully Fitted, and Exactly Calculated to the Meridian of Newport, on Rhode-Island. Being the First Ever Published for That Meridian. By Poor Robin (Newport, R.I.: Printed by J. Franklin, 1727);

The Rhode-Island Almanack, for the Year 1729. . . . By Poor Robin (Newport, R.I.: Printed by J. Franklin, 1728);

Mr. Samuel Gorton's Ghost. . . . (Newport, R.I.: Printed by James Franklin, 1728);

The Rhode-Island Almanack for the Year 1730. . . . By Poor Robin (Newport, R.I.: Printed by J. Franklin, 1729);

The Rhode-Island Almanack for the Year 1732. By Poor Robin (Newport, R.I.: Printed by James Franklin, 1731);

The Rhode-Island Almanack for the Year, 1733. . . . By Poor Robin (Newport, R.I.: Printed by J. Franklin, 1732);

The Rhode-Island Almanack for the Year 1734. By Poor Robin (Newport, R.I.: Printed by J. Franklin, 1733);

MDCCXXXV. The Rhode-Island Almanack for the Year, 1735. . . . Fitted to the Meridian of Newport, . . . By Poor Robin (Newport, R.I.: Printed & sold by J. Franklin, 1735).

Although he did not attain the fame of his younger brother, Benjamin, James Franklin was America's first crusading editor and first major defender of press freedom. In the *New-England Courant*, the third continuous newspaper to appear in Boston and the fourth in the colonies, Franklin introduced an iconoclastic, saw-toothed style of journalism which outraged religious and political leaders in Massachusetts. The *Courant*'s correspondents, branded the "Hell-Fire Club" by their opponents, imitated leading English periodical writers to a large extent. They did, however, add an immediacy and a local angle to the kind of radical Whiggism displayed in *Cato's Letters* and a sarcastic bite to the type of urbane reasonableness made popular by the *Spectator*.

Born in Boston to Josiah and Abiah Folger Franklin, James Franklin traveled to England for an apprenticeship in the printing trade. He returned to Massachusetts in 1717 with a used press and began competing with five printers already es-

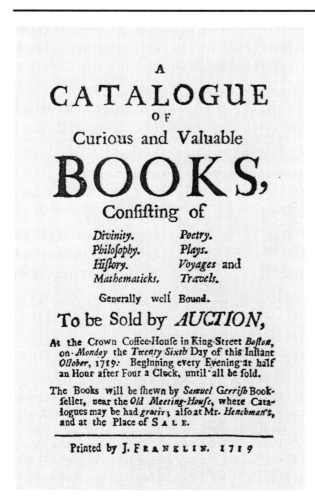

A
CATALOGUE
OF
Curious and Valuable
BOOKS,
Confifting of

Divinity.	Poetry.
Philofophy.	Plays.
Hiftory.	Voyages and
Mathematicks.	Travels.

Generally well Bound.

To be Sold by AUCTION,

At the Crown Coffee-Houfe in King-Street Bofton, on-Monday the Twenty Sixth Day of this Inftant October, 1719: Beginning every Evening at half an Hour after Four a Clock, until all be fold.

The Books will be fhewn by Samuel Gerrifh Book-feller, near the Old Meeting-Houfe, where Cata-logues may be had gratis; alfo at Mr. Henchman's, and at the Place of SALE.

Printed by J. FRANKLIN. 1719

Title page for a book catalogue printed by Franklin in his early days as a printer

tablished in Boston. He found some work turning out religious tracts and was soon encouraging his brother and newly acquired apprentice, Benjamin, to write and hawk Grub Street news ballads—a venture which ended after their Puritan father, Josiah, ridiculed the poetry and warned Benjamin that verse-makers were generally poor. By the end of 1719, James was printing the first issues of post-master William Brooker's *Boston Gazette,* the second regularly published newspaper in America. (The first was the *Boston News-Letter,* founded by John Campbell in 1704.) When Brooker lost his office in 1720, the newspaper also changed hands and the new postmaster, Philip Musgrave, gave the printing of the *Gazette* to Samuel Kneeland.

Out of a job, but not out of ideas, Franklin managed to keep his press busy in a city that was being racked by economic recession and the feuding of church and government factions. He printed pamphlets on both sides of a bitter fiscal policy debate, as well as the first music printed in bars in the colonies for Thomas Walter's *The Grounds and Rules of Musick* (1721). Signs of Franklin's personal political preferences began to appear in 1721 when he republished Daniel Defoe's *News from the Moon* and Henry Care's *English Liberties, Or the Free-Born Subject's Inheritance.* The reprinting of Defoe's piece, a clever satire of official suppression of criticism, coincided with an unsuccessful prosecution of bookseller Benjamin Gray for publishing an angry pamphlet on the colony's financial crisis and for disregarding an order of the Massachusetts Council that he not sell it. Care's *English Liberties,* a 228-page law book written from a libertarian perspective, purported to survey the past struggles of the English people against political oppression and religious bigotry.

If Franklin still lacked recognition as a printer of books and pamphlets, he quickly received public attention once he began publishing the *New-England Courant* in August 1721. "I remember his being dissuaded by some of his Friends from the Undertaking, as not likely to succeed," Benjamin later wrote in his autobiography, "one Newspaper being in their Judgment enough for America." The paper made its debut at a critical time, however, since the colony was experiencing an outbreak of smallpox and a controversy was developing over how to respond. A group of six ministers led by Cotton Mather advocated the novel practice of inoculation, while all of Boston's selectmen and all but one of the city's physicians believed that the method's use of artificial infection would only spread the deadly disease.

The first issue set the tone for the publication. The introductory essay, an imitation of the first *Spectator,* was written by John Checkley, an Anglican who more than once encountered censorship problems while trying to disseminate religious pamphlets which needled Boston's Puritan hierarchy. Checkley promised to report on his theological opponents,

> Who like faithful Shepherds take care of their *Flocks,*
> By teaching and practicing what's Orthodox,
> Pray hard against *Sickness,* yet preach up the POX!

Along with Checkley's piece the *Courant* offered an article by Dr. William Douglass, the only physician in Boston with a medical degree. Douglass blasted inoculation and complained that "Six Gentlemen of Piety and Learning" had decided to "very lavishly bestow all the fulsome common Place of

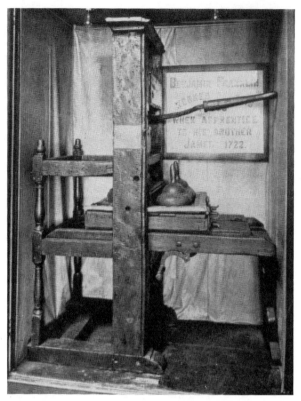

Franklin's printing press, now in possession of the Massachusetts Charitable Mechanic Association, Boston

London Journal essay on press freedom written by "Cato," the pseudonym of radical Whig authors Thomas Gordon and John Trenchard, which argued that the exposing of "publick Wickedness, as it is a Duty which every Man owes to Truth and his Country, can never be a Libel in the Nature of things."

For the next two months, as smallpox deaths among Boston's 12,000 inhabitants mounted toward an eventual total of 844, Franklin was content to fill the pages of the *Courant* with local wit and with extracts from Cato's writings which warned against being too confident in persons entrusted with power and which complained of court flatterers who think "Every Word they do not like, is a Libel; every Action that displeases them is Treason or Sedition." The medical debate died down considerably but flared again early in November when a *Courant* correspondent accused Cotton Mather of lying about the success of inoculation efforts in the city. Mather, New England's arch-Puritan, confronted the twenty-four-year-old printer on the street and delivered a brief, blazing sermon on the consequences of abusing ministers and serving the devil. Mather was clearly unnerved by public reaction to his ideas, and not without reason. In the early morning hours of the next day, someone threw a bomb through a window of his house. Tied to the lit fuse, which failed to work, was the message "I'll Inoculate you with this, with a Pox to you." The *Courant* printed Mather's account of the incident; the same issue mimicked his speaking style in a satirical endorsement of inoculation.

Attacks on the procedure were renewed in the *Courant*, and the paper also took aim at a number of new targets—including Philip Musgrave, who was giving space in his *Boston Gazette* to Mather and his supporters. Musgrave was accused of theft and incompetence in his handling of the postmastership and was repeatedly taunted for having a newspaper "Published by Authority." Unlike the *Gazette* and the *Boston News-Letter*, which the *Courant* also ridiculed, Franklin's newspaper made no pretense of being an official publication. Effective prior censorship had all but disappeared in Massachusetts and Franklin did not have to answer to a licenser. Since both the town government and the lower house of the legislature opposed inoculation and since the influence of the Bible Commonwealth's ministers had been declining for decades, Franklin's stand in the smallpox controversy was not particularly daring. The charges made against Musgrave, however, clearly moved the *Courant* in the direction of criticizing governmental activity.

Quack Advertisements" in their support for the procedure.

The ministers' immediate response, published a week later by Franklin, was a single issue of the *Anti-Courant* written by Cotton Mather's nephew, the Reverend Thomas Walter. Walter ridiculed Checkley's literary pretensions and characterized him as an "awkward Flogger" whose "Guts" were in his "Brains." Not to be outdone, and apparently stung by the *Anti-Courant*'s insults, Checkley wrote an essay for the third *Courant* describing Walter as having spent time in the bed of "two Sisters, of not the best Reputation" and as being inspired in his writing by rum and hard cider. Franklin printed Checkley's remarks, but two weeks later announced that he would not accept any more of his contributions. Seemingly shaken by the reaction of Boston's theocrats or perhaps by the threat of a libel suit, Franklin said that he was willing to print articles for and against inoculation provided that they were free of "malicious Reflections," and that in the future he intended to publish nothing "reflecting on the Clergy or Government, and nothing but what is innocently Diverting." In the next issue, however, he offered his readers a

*Cotton Mather, the Puritan minister who engaged in a contro-
versy with Franklin and the* New-England Courant *on the
merits of inoculation against smallpox. Mather, who favored
inoculation, was in the right (American Antiquarian Society).*

Franklin defended his journalistic conduct
several times in the winter of 1721-1722. Although
few if any of the news items and essays he printed
were favorable toward inoculation, he continued to
maintain that he would act impartially and accept
pieces from writers on both sides of the issue. Trading verbal punches with Cotton Mather and his
father, Increase, Franklin informed the religious
patriarchs that their condemnations of his newspaper were only increasing its circulation, and he
suggested that they mind their own business. He
portrayed himself as practicing a lawful trade and
said that their accusations and threats required that
responses be made in self-defense. The editor explained to his readers that the younger Mather and
his "hot-headed Trumpeters" were attempting to
destroy the *Courant* so that "he may reign Detractor
General over the whole Province, and do all the
Mischief his ill Nature prompts him to, without
hearing of it." Little was left for the Mathers to do
except for Increase to publicly cancel his subscription.

Franklin thus emerged practically unscathed
from the inoculation controversy; but there were,

nevertheless, ominous signs. The Mather faction
wanted the newspaper officially suppressed and a
correspondent from Portsmouth reported a rumor
that New Hampshire would outlaw the reading of
the *Courant* because it "sometimes sets forth the
Rights and Liberties of Mankind." A copy of the
issue with the paper's response to the Portsmouth
writer, which asked why the province did not elect
better representatives, was, as the *Courant* reported,
seized and burned at a New Hampshire public
house by the high sheriff, who was "fearing it might
infect the Inhabitants with a Desire of Liberty."

Franklin did have supporters, however. His
father had provided financial backing for the printing house and, once the inoculation controversy
was over, his brother Benjamin began his long journalistic career by submitting satirical and sometimes searing essays on Boston life which he signed
with the pen name "Silence Dogood." The *Courant*'s
early correspondents, most of whom had ties to the
Church of England, also furnished some of the
driving force that kept the paper lively and readable. One, a frequent contributor known only as
Mr. Gardner, advised the editor to continue to
"promote Enquiries after Truth, quicken and
rouze the Slothful, animate and inspire the Dull,"
and to remember "that Crimes are not lessen'd and
sanctifi'd because committed by Men in High Station, or of Reverend Name." Another form of endorsement came from the *Courant*'s growing list of
subscribers. In its eightieth issue on 11 February
1723, the weekly paper claimed to be printing a
"far greater" number of copies than its Boston competitors—which, if true, may have meant that it was
the most widely read periodical in the colonies,
since the only newspaper published outside the city
was Andrew Bradford's *American Weekly Mercury* in
Philadelphia.

The *Courant*'s editorial formula was unique
among the first American newspapers. In addition
to its irreverent essays, the paper entertained its
readers with brief accounts of fires, murders, illicit
sex, and mysterious occurrences. At the time of the
spring 1722 elections, the *Courant* ventured into
politics as correspondents reported on improper
efforts to influence voters. The paper urged the
voters to consider some of the past actions of their
representatives and to consider whether or not
their interests were being served. An anonymous
pamphlet published by Franklin, *English Advice to
the Freeholders*, pointed to several specific concerns,
including a recent attempt to pass a law to be used
against the press.

Shortly after the election, the legislature took

THE [N° 80

New-England Courant.

From MONDAY February 4. to MONDAY February 11. 1723.

The late Publisher of this Paper, finding so many Inconveniencies would arise by his carrying the Manuscripts and publick News to be supervis'd by the Secretary, as to render his carrying it on unprofitable, has intirely dropt the Undertaking. The present Publisher having receiv'd the following Piece, desires the Readers to accept of it as a Preface to what they may hereafter meet with in this Paper.

Non ego mordaci distrinxi Carmine quenquam, Nulla venenato Littera mista Joco est.

LONG has the Press groaned in bringing forth an hateful, but numerous Brood of Party Pamphlets, malicious Scribbles, and Billiogsgate Ribaldry. The Rancour and bitterness it has unhappily infused into Mens minds, and to what a Degree it has sowred and leaven'd the Tempers of Persons formerly esteemed some of the most sweet and affable, is too well known here, to need any further Proof or Representation of the Matter.

No generous and impartial Person then can blame the present Undertaking, which is designed purely for the Diversion and Merriment of the Reader. Pieces of Pleasancy and Mirth have a secret Charm in them to allay the Heats and Tumors of our Spirits, and to make a Man forget his restless Resentments. They have a strange Power to tune the harsh Disorders of the Soul, and reduce us to a serene and placid State of Mind.

The main Design of this Weekly Paper will be to entertain the Town with the most comical and diverting Incidents of Humane Life, which in so large a Place as Boston, will not fail of a universal Exemplification: Nor shall we be wanting to fill up these Papers with a grateful Interspersion of more serious Morals, which may be drawn from the most ludicrous and odd Parts of Life.

As for the Author, that is the next Question. But tho' we profess our selves ready to oblige the ingenious and courteous Reader with most Sorts of Intelligence, yet here we beg a Reserve. Nor will it be of any Manner of Advantage either to them or to the Writers, that their Names should be published; and therefore in this Matter we desire the Favour of you to suffer us to hold our Tongues: Which tho' at this Time of Day it may sound like a very uncommon Request, yet it proceeds from the very Hearts of your Humble Servants.

By this Time the Reader perceives that more than one are engaged in the present Undertaking. Yet is there one Person, an Inhabitant of this Town of Boston, whom we honour as a Doctor in the Chair, or a perpetual Dictator.

The Society had design'd to present the Publick with his Effigies, but that the Limner, to whom he was presented for a Draught of his Countenance, descryed (and this he is ready to offer upon Oath) Nineteen Features in his Face, more than ever beheld in any Humane Visage before; which so raised the Price of his Picture, that our Master himself forbid the Extravagance of coming up to it. And then besides, the Limner objected a Schism in his Face, which splits it from his Forehead in a

strait Line down to his Chin, in such sort, that Mr. Painter protests it is a double Face, and he'll have Four Pounds for the Pourtraiture. However, tho' this double Face has spoilt us of a pretty Picture, yet we all rejoiced to see old Janus in our Company.

There is no Man in Boston better qualified than old Janus for a Couranteer, or if you please, an Observator, being a Man of such remarkable Opticks, as to look two ways at once.

As for his Morals, he is a chearly Christian, as the Country Phrase expresses it. A Man of good Temper, courteous Deportment, sound Judgment; a mortal Hater of Nonsense, Foppery, Formality, and endless Ceremony.

As for his Club, they aim at no greater Happiness or Honour, than the Publick be made to know, that it is the utmost of their Ambition to attend upon and do all imaginable good Offices to good Old Janus the Couranteer, who is and always will be the Readers humble Servant.

P. S. Gentle Readers, we design never to let a Paper pass without a Latin Motto if we can possibly pick one up, which carries a Charm in it to the Vulgar, and the learned admire the pleasure of Construing. We should have obliged the World with a Greek strap or two, but the Printer has no Types, and therefore we intreat the candid Reader not to impute the defect to our Ignorance, for our Doctor can say all the Greek Letters by heart.

His Majesty's Speech to The Parliament, October 11. tho' already publish'd, may perhaps be new to many of our Country Readers; we shall therefore insert it in this Day's Paper.

His MAJESTY's most Gracious SPEECH to both Houses of Parliament, on Thursday October 11. 1722.

My Lords and Gentlemen,

I Am sorry to find my self obliged, at the Opening of this Parliament, to acquaint you, That a dangerous Conspiracy has been for some time formed, and is still carrying on against my Person and Government, in Favour of a Popish Pretender.

The Discoveries I have made here, the Informations I have received from my Ministers abroad, and the Intelligences I have had from the Powers in Alliance with me, and indeed from most parts of Europe, have given me most ample and current Proofs of this wicked Design.

The Conspirators have, by their Emissaries, made the strongest Instances for Assistance from Foreign Powers, but were disappointed in their Expectations: However, confiding in their Numbers, and not discouraged by their former ill Success, they resolved once more, upon their own strength, to attempt the subversion of my Government.

To this End they provided considerable Sums of Money, engaged great Numbers of Officers from abroad, secured large Quantities of Arms and Ammunition, and thought themselves in such Readiness, that had not the Conspiracy been timely discovered, we should, without doubt, before now have seen the whole Nation, and particularly the City of London, involved in Blood and Confusion.

The Care I have taken has, by the Blessing of God, hitherto prevented the Execution of their traiterous Projects. The Troops have been encamp'd all this Summer; six Regiments (though very necessary for the Security of that Kingdom) have been brought over from Ireland; the States General have given me assurances that they would keep a considerable Body of Forces ready ... ...

The 11 February 1723 issue of the New-England Courant, *announcing that James Franklin was no longer the publisher of the paper. Franklin's brother Benjamin was made nominal publisher of the* Courant, *and a fictitious character named "Old Janus" was designated as editor; in fact, James Franklin continued to exercise control over the paper. Franklin adopted this ruse to evade the order that he not publish a newspaper without official supervision.*

action against the *Courant*. Franklin was called before the Council to explain a sarcastic news item which implied that the government had been lax in its response to coastal pirates. Franklin as well as his apprentice proved uncooperative and both houses of the General Court agreed to imprison James Franklin for his "High affront" until the end of the session. While his brother remained in jail for a month, Benjamin Franklin temporarily took charge of the *Courant* and, as he related in his autobiography, "made bold to give our Rulers some Rubs." The younger Franklin published one of Cato's essays on freedom of expression which argued that officials were no more than the trustees of the people and that only the guilty ones feared liberty of speech.

James Franklin presented a physician's certification of his ill health and an apology in an unsuccessful effort to win early release, but once he got out of jail he showed no indications of debility or remorse. For two months he and his contributors represented the General Court's action as a violation of due process of law and decried the evils of tyrannical authority. In a poem probably written by Franklin, his appearance before the Council was parodied along the lines of Defoe's *News from the Moon*. Franklin, depicted as an artist who used only black and white to paint "ev'ry rougish Face," tells offended legislators:

> You own your selves the Draught is true,
> And yet can blame the Painter too.
> So homely Dames with ragged Faces,
> Lay all the Fault upon their Glasses.

The General Court took action again after the *Courant* of 14 January 1723 gave its readers a caustic essay on religious hypocrisy directed at the Mathers and letters deriding both sides in a breakdown of relations between the governor and legislature. Franklin was ordered not to publish any newspaper or pamphlet like the *Courant* without the prior approval of the secretary of the province. Franklin printed the next issue without submitting to censorship and mocked the action against him with a psalm on injustice and oppression. The Council ordered his arrest, but the sheriff reported back that he was unable to find him. The *Courant* then offered its absent editor droll suggestions on how to be inoffensive and characterized the steps taken against him as arbitrary and lawless. Franklin reappeared and the case was turned over to a grand jury. When he came out of hiding, Franklin established the fictitious "good Old Janus the Couranteer" as the editor of the paper and his apprentice brother as the publisher in order to avoid further infractions of the General Court's order that James Franklin be under supervision. This "flimsy Scheme," as Benjamin described it in his memoirs, continued even after the grand jury decided in May 1723 not to indict, and after the apprentice ran away to Philadelphia later in the year.

After its victory for freedom of the press, the *Courant* gradually lost its initial spirit. It was discontinued in 1726 when Franklin decided to move his press to Newport, Rhode Island, a city without a printer. Before leaving Boston, he published *The Life and Death of Old Father Janus, the Vile Author of the Late Wicked Courant*, a rollicking, self-congratulatory poem which began:

> FAREWELL, old JANUS, since at last thy Doom,
> Which some have fear'd, but more desir'd, is come;
> Who in thy Life wast deem'd a Publick Pest,
> And whom bright Fame shall restlessly molest.

In Rhode Island, Franklin found a freer if somewhat less stimulating environment. He attacked religious persecution in Massachusetts with a poem titled *Mr. Samuel Gorton's Ghost* and wrote humorous and sometimes ribald "Poor Robin" almanacs which had an apparent influence on his brother's "Poor Richard." In 1732 James Franklin started the *Rhode-Island Gazette*, a paper which resembled the *New-England Courant*, but it did not prove profitable and lasted less than a year. After a long illness, Franklin died in 1735. His wife, Ann Smith Franklin, whom he had married on 4 February 1724, took over the printing house and ran it successfully with two daughters and a son. James Franklin, Jr., served an apprenticeship with his uncle Benjamin in Philadelphia and, in 1758, founded the *Newport Mercury*, a newspaper which lasted into the twentieth century.

James Franklin's *New-England Courant* was published for less than five years, but it represented the birth of literary and adversarial journalism in America. Franklin and his "Hell-Fire Club" stood in the way of medical progress as they crusaded against smallpox inoculation, and they sometimes substituted personal defamation for reason. The paper's contributors, however, strongly defended freedom of the press and practiced what they believed was their right to criticize religious and political authority.

References:
John B. Blake, "The Inoculation Controversy in

Boston: 1721-1722," *New England Quarterly*, 25 (December 1952): 489-506;

Leo P. Bradley, Jr., "The Press and the Declension of Boston Orthodoxy, 1674-1724," M.A. thesis, University of Washington, 1977;

T. H. Breen, *The Character of the Good Ruler, A Study of Puritan Political Ideas in New England, 1630-1730* (New Haven: Yale University Press, 1970), pp. 261-269;

Clarence S. Brigham, "James Franklin and the Beginnings of Printing in Rhode Island," *Massachusetts Historical Society Proceedings*, 65 (March 1936): 536-544;

Clyde A. Duniway, *The Development of Freedom of the Press in Massachusetts* (New York: Longmans, Green, 1906), pp. 83-103;

Worthington C. Ford, "Franklin's New-England Courant," *Massachusetts Historical Society Proceedings*, 57 (April 1924): 336-353;

Perry Miller, introduction to *The New-England Courant. A Selection of Certain Issues Containing Writings of Benjamin Franklin* (Boston: American Academy of Arts and Sciences, 1956), pp. 5-9;

Arthur B. Tourtellot, *Benjamin Franklin: The Shaping of Genius. The Boston Years* (Garden City: Doubleday, 1977);

C. Edward Wilson, "The Boston Inoculation Controversy: A Revisionist Interpretation," *Journalism History*, 7 (Spring 1980): 16-19, 40.

Philip Freneau

(2 January 1752-18 December 1832)

James Glen Stovall
University of Alabama

See also the Freneau entry in *DLB 37, American Writers of the Early Republic.*

MAJOR POSITIONS HELD: Editor, *New York Daily Advertiser* (1790-1791), *National Gazette* (Philadelphia) (1791-1793), *Jersey Chronicle* (1795-1796), *New York Time-Piece; and Literary Companion* (1796-1798).

BOOKS: *A Poem, on the Rising Glory of America; Being an Exercise Delivered at the Public Commencement at Nassau-Hall, September 25, 1771 . . .*, by Freneau and Hugh Henry Brackenridge (Philadelphia: Printed by Joseph Crukshank for R. Aitken, 1772);

The American Village, A Poem. To Which Are Added, Several Other Original Pieces in Verse . . . (New York: Printed by S. Inslee & A. Car, 1772);

American Liberty, A Poem . . . (New York: Printed by J. Anderson, 1775);

A Voyage to Boston. A Poem . . . (New York: Printed by John Anderson, 1775);

General Gage's Soliloquy (New York: Printed by Hugh Gaine, 1775);

General Gage's Confession, Being the Substance of His Excellency's Last Conference, with His Ghostly Father, Friar Francis . . . (New York: Printed by Hugh Gaine, 1775);

The British Prison-Ship: A Poem, in Four Cantoes . . . (Philadelphia: Printed by F. Bailey, 1781);

The Poems of Philip Freneau. Written Chiefly during the Late War (Philadelphia: Printed by Francis Bailey, 1786);

A Journey from Philadelphia to New-York, By Way of Burlington and South-Amboy. By Robert Slender, Stocking Weaver . . . (Philadelphia: Printed by Francis Bailey, 1787); republished as *A Laughable Poem; or Robert Slender's Journey from Philadelphia to New York, by Way of Burlington and South Amboy . . .* (Philadelphia: Printed for Thomas Neversink, 1809);

The Miscellaneous Works of Mr. Philip Freneau . . . (Philadelphia: Printed by Francis Bailey, 1788);

The Monmouth Almanac, for the Year M, DCC, XCV: Being the Third After, Leap Year; and the XIXth of American Independence ('Till the Fourth of July.) Calculated for the Meridian of New Jersey. (Longitude 35 Minutes, East from Philadelphia) and Latitude of 40 Degrees, 20 Minutes North.

Number I (Middletown Point, N.J.: Printed & sold by P. Freneau, 1794);

The Village Merchant: A Poem. To Which Is Added The Country Printer . . . (Philadelphia: Printed by Hoff & Derrick, 1794);

Poems Written between the Years 1768 & 1794 . . . (Monmouth, N.J.: Printed by the author, 1795);

Letters on Various Interesting and Important Subjects; Many of Which Have Appeared in the Aurora . . . , as Robert Slender (Philadelphia: Printed by D. Hogan for the author, 1799);

Poems Written and Published during the American Revolutionary War, and Now Republished from the Original Manuscripts; Interspersed with Translations from the Ancients and Other Pieces Not Heretofore in Print . . . , 2 volumes (Philadelphia: From the press of Lydia R. Bailey, 1809);

A Collections of Poems, on American Affairs, and a Variety of Other Subjects, Chiefly Moral and Political; Written between the Year 1797 and the Present . . . , 2 volumes (New York: Published by David Longworth, 1815);

Some Account of the Capture of the Ship "Aurora" . . . , edited by Jay Milles (New York: M. F. Mansfield & A. Wessels, 1899);

Unpublished Freneauana, edited by Charles F. Heartman (New York, 1918);

The Last Poems of Philip Freneau, edited by Lewis Leary (New Brunswick, N.J.: Rutgers University Press, 1945);

The Prose of Philip Freneau, edited by Philip M. Marsh (Metuchen, N.J.: Scarecrow, 1955).

Collection: *The Poems of Philip Freneau*, 3 volumes, edited by Fred Lewis Pattee (Princeton: Princeton University Library, 1902, 1903, 1907).

George Washington once used a cabinet meeting to rage at length about "that rascal Freneau." "He makes no regret that I had passed up an opportunity to resign the presidency," Washington said. "By God, he makes me wish that I was in my grave rather than in my present situation. How can he charge me with wanting to be a king? I'd rather be on my farm than emperor of the world. And besides all that," Washington added, "Freneau sends me not one but three of his newspapers every day—as if I would distribute them for him. He does it only to insult me."

The man who had sparked Washington's anger was Philip Freneau, editor of the *National Gazette* and one of the best journalists of his day. In the rough-and-tumble world of journalism during the first decade of the Constitution, Freneau was a leading voice against monarchy and for the basic rights of man. His pen made for him powerful enemies such as Washington and Alexander Hamilton but also established enduring friendships with men like Thomas Jefferson and James Madison. Indeed, Jefferson had occasion to defend Freneau to Washington by saying that Freneau's paper had "saved our Constitution, which was galloping fast into Monarchy."

Freneau was clearly one of the most important and influential editors of the 1790s. His *National Gazette* set the tone for newspapers of the day. He wrote with a wit and authority that exceeded those of most of his contemporaries, and the *National Gazette* was thought to be the most widely read and circulated and the most politically important journal published. Freneau was a staunch defender of freedom of the press even before that concept had been fully developed. For example, he was one of the first to insist that Congress open its debates to the press and the public, even when sensitive foreign policy matters were being discussed.

Freneau's influence extended beyond his work as an editor, however. Indeed, he thought of himself primarily not as a journalist but as a poet.

His literary work, particularly that from the 1780s and 1790s, has earned him the title of "Poet of the Revolution," and all of his life he sought to establish a uniquely American genre of literature. He believed that other poets of his day were placing too much emphasis on British forms and styles and was convinced that America had something of her own to offer the world.

In addition, Freneau had yet another love and area of expertise—the sea. Freneau found himself repeatedly drawn to the sea for its adventure and the inspiration it gave to his poetry. As a seaman and ship's captain he faced Britain's most formidable weapon, its navy, during the Revolutionary War, and in later years he turned again to the sea for livelihood when journalism, literature, and farming failed to sustain him.

Philip Morin Freneau was born on 2 January 1752 in New York City. His grandfather, André Fresneau, was a French Huguenot who settled in New York in 1707 and established a wine importing business. Fresneau's son Pierre married Agnes Watson of Freehold, New Jersey; they had two sons, Philip and Peter, and two daughters, Mary and Margaret. The family lived in a house on Frankfort Street and was surrounded by books, works of art, and many interesting, cultured visitors. Pierre Fresneau continued his father's importing business and managed to provide a comfortable environment for his family. He soon was able to acquire near Middletown Point, New Jersey, a plantation called "Mount Pleasant," which the family used during the summers and which later became Philip's permanent home. Pierre Fresneau (the *s* was dropped from the family name when he died) also provided private tutors for his children, and Philip did well at his studies. At fifteen, he was able to enter the sophomore class at the College of New Jersey in Princeton.

Freneau met people at Princeton who were to influence his actions and writings for the rest of his life. Among them were John Witherspoon, president of the college, and James Madison, later to be chief architect of the Constitution and fourth president of the United States. Witherspoon introduced Freneau to classical literature and fostered a taste for fine writing in his young student. Freneau was also influenced by the "independence" debates in which he participated at Princeton and quickly came to believe that America could produce its own literature. He and friends Madison, Hugh Henry Brackenridge, and William Bradford formed the American Whig Society as a rival to the British-oriented Tory Clio-Sophic Society. The ar-

guments between these groups drove Freneau to produce his first piece of political satire, "Father Bombo's Pilgrimage to Mecca," in which he poked fun at the intellectual pretensions of his rivals. Madison, whom some believe to have been Freneau's roommate at Princeton, was impressed with his friend's early skills as a poet and used some of Freneau's poems to instruct his own brothers and sisters in the rudiments of literature. Freneau was increasingly fascinated by the development of the American nation, and his poetry more and more was aimed at encouraging that development. In 1770 he wrote "Columbus to Ferdinand," a poem which explores the mood of Christopher Columbus as he prepares to sail westward. Possibly the best literature of his college years, however, was a collaborative effort with Brackenridge, "The Rising Glory of America," read by Brackenridge at the graduation exercises of 1771. It extolled the virtues of the new nation as a leader in a world progressing toward a millennium; America would be a land blessed with "sweet liberty!/Without whose aid the noblest genius fails,/And science irretrievably must die." The poem was apparently very well received by the audience on graduation day and was published in Philadelphia the following year.

Freneau's father had died the year before he entered Princeton, and upon graduation Freneau found that he would have to seek a practical source of income. He took a job as a schoolteacher on Long Island but was immediately so miserable that he left after only two weeks. Freneau could only think of himself as a poet. He tried to establish himself as such in 1772 with the publication of *The American Village*, a short collection of poems which was not particularly successful. Freneau's activities during the next three years are not well documented. He took another teaching job in Back Creek, Maryland, but by all evidence he still hated the teaching profession and thought himself ill used. He wrote Madison that teaching "worries me to death and by no means suits my giddy, wandering brain." By his own account, Freneau made enemies more easily than friends and developed an ill nature that sometimes fed upon stubbornness and large amounts of self-pity. Still, during these years Freneau constantly wrote poetry. He was profoundly affected by the increasing tension between the British and American colonies and developed a hatred for monarchy, organized religion, and special privilege, all of which he believed were tools of British tyranny.

As relations with the British deteriorated, Freneau found more uses for his poetic and satirical skill. In July 1775, with the British laying siege to Boston, Freneau published one of his most noted patriotic poems, *American Liberty*. It read in part:

> What breast but kindles at the martial sound?
> What heart but bleeds to feel its country's wound?
> For thee, blest freedom, to protect thy sway,
> We rush undaunted to the bloody fray....

This poem was followed by a number of satires aimed at the British, the most famous of which were *General Gage's Soliloquy* and *General Gage's Confession*, both published in 1775. These and other writings needled the British with their irony and wit and stirred loyal Americans in defense of the country. They cemented Freneau's reputation as the "Poet of the Revolution," but they produced little in the way of monetary gain. They also brought stinging attacks and rebukes from his contemporaries—attacks which deeply wounded the sensitive Freneau.

Believing that his first calling was to poetry and not to war, Freneau chose not to "rush undaunted to the bloody fray" but rather to seek refuge from the violence in the West Indies. He accepted a secretaryship to a prominent planter on Santa Cruz early in 1776. He used his two years abroad to create some of his best poetry and to become a pioneer in the new romantic movement. The beauty and solitude of his surroundings were a comfort and inspiration to him, but Freneau soon saw the darker side of his environment. He was familiar with slavery in his native land, but in the West Indies, with slaves outnumbering freemen twelve to one, laws suppressing blacks were harsh and cruelly administered. In his poem "The Jamaica Funeral," Freneau wrote about the "thirst for gold" and the "bloody malice" he found in these islands of paradise. The poet sought refuge in the romanticism of poems like "Santa Cruz," but he could not escape the world for long. He disliked what he saw around him, and back home, things were not going well for the American rebels. In July 1778 he returned to New Jersey.

Freneau found that the land around his home had recently been the site of a major battle, and the scars of war were readily apparent. He quickly enlisted in the state militia but soon saw that America had a desperate need for trained seamen. He had received such training on his voyages to and through the West Indies and had acquired an abiding love of the sea. In October he was commissioned as a sea privateer on the *Indian River*. Eluding the dangerous British naval machine, Freneau shuttled between the colonies and friendly ports in the Caribbean for four months. He was briefly recalled to duty as a soldier but soon returned to the sea as a master of the *John Couster*. Late in 1779, as part of the crew of the *Rebecca*, Freneau helped capture the *Britannia*, a brig filled with valuable merchandise.

In May 1780 Freneau sailed from Philadelphia as third mate aboard the *Aurora*. His ship was soon captured and he was placed on the prison ship *Scorpion*, moored in New York harbor. He and his fellow prisoners were brutally treated, and he was soon taken ill with fever. He was transferred to a hospital ship, the *Hunter*, where the conditions were just as bad. Some of his friends had heard of his fate and applied to the British for his release. That release came in July, after six weeks of imprisonment. He returned to his home in New Jersey and spent the rest of the war restoring his health. His experience as a British prisoner became one of the driving forces of the rest of his life. Not only did he produce the searing poem *The British Prison-Ship* (1781), which took the British to task for their mistreatment of America, but he also established himself as a chief opponent of the British and their sympathizers in the coming struggles to establish a new government in America.

As Freneau's strength returned, he turned his thoughts to writing again—and to making a living. During the war, and even during his time in the West Indies, he had contributed some pieces to the short-lived *United States Magazine*, published in Philadelphia by his Princeton collaborator Brackenridge and Francis Bailey. These publishers sought to provide a vehicle for the development of American literature, but their magazine fell victim to the fortunes of war. Bailey, a printer, began a new paper, the *Freeman's Journal*, and by April 1781 Freneau had joined its staff as an editor and contributor. The paper gave Freneau an outlet for his steady stream of poetry, most of which concerned the war, the praise of patriotic Americans, and the misanthropy of the British. Located in Philadelphia, the *Freeman's Journal* gave Freneau a wide audience which was sympathetic to what he was writing. Despite some victories, the war was not going particularly well for the Americans, and Freneau's poetry and prose put into words the feelings of many. Freneau did not allow Americans to forget what they were fighting for nor did he allow them to ignore the repulsiveness of the enemy. Freneau welcomed French soldiers and money; he would never forget that it was the French who gave Americans aid when their revolution was on the verge of collapse and that shortly after the French arrived, so did victory for the American cause. Freneau used his forum to mourn the deaths of brave Americans, to scourge the British, to celebrate hard-won victories, to censure American Tories, to praise the French, and to help his readers look to the future beyond the war. The volume, tone, and quality of these writings further establish his claim to the title of "Poet of the Revolution."

Besides his work for the *Freeman's Journal*, Freneau had taken a job as a postal clerk when he came to Philadelphia. The pay was extremely low, but the work was light and left him time for writing. By 1784, when the Treaty of Paris had been signed and fighting with the British had officially ceased, Freneau found that there was little left for him in Philadelphia. His writing and post office work could not sustain him, so in June he set sail for Jamaica.

Freneau spent much of the next five years at sea. In some ways, these years were more adventurous than his stint as a wartime sailor, although few details are known about his comings and goings. In his first year, he barely escaped death during a hurricane and shipwreck. By 1786 he was the captain of a merchant ship which made regular runs from the East Coast ports to the Caribbean. All the while, he wrote poetry, and in 1788 a volume of his poems and prose, *The Miscellaneous Works of Mr. Philip Freneau*, was published. This book contained few political works and much of what the author considered his best writing.

Freneau's life at sea was largely successful, and he might have continued with it had he not fallen in love with Eleanor Forman, the daughter of Samuel Forman, a wealthy New Jersey farmer and neighbor of the Freneaus. Freneau began writing pieces for the *Daily Advertiser* in New York City while he was courting Eleanor, and a month before their marriage on 15 April 1790 he accepted an editor's position with the paper. He stayed with that paper for eleven months before deciding that he would be happier, and possibly more prosperous, editing a paper of his own. While still contributing to the *Daily Advertiser*, Freneau drew up a prospectus for a weekly paper to be published from Monmouth County, New Jersey, where his home was located.

Plans for the paper were interrupted by a letter from Thomas Jefferson, sent at the behest of Freneau's old friend Madison, now a congressman from Virginia. Jefferson was then secretary of state, and his letter offered Freneau a job as a translator in the State Department. No mention was made of Freneau's starting a newspaper in Philadelphia, then the nation's capital city, but that thought was in the backs of Jefferson's and Madison's minds. The letter to Freneau said the salary for the translator's job was $250 a year, far too little for Freneau to consider, and there is no evidence that he even replied to Jefferson's offer.

Madison and Jefferson realized that they needed a newspaper and an editor of clearly Republican principles in Philadelphia. Alexander Hamilton and the Federalists already had John Fenno and the *Gazette of the United States* at their disposal, and the Republicans had nothing to match them. Madison knew that Freneau would provide a strong libertarian voice, and he decided not to let Freneau off the hook so easily. He visited Freneau in New York. Freneau raised many objections to his coming to Philadelphia, but Madison answered them all. He told Freneau that the job at the State Department would not be taxing or time-consuming; Freneau could start his own paper, and Madison and other friends would help solicit subscriptions; financing could be arranged to support Freneau in the capital. Men whose principles were opposed to those of Freneau were gaining strength; Freneau, Madison said, must join the fight.

Freneau hesitated. He had no ethical qualms about holding a government position and an editorship at the same time—such arrangements were common—but he was still not sure that he wanted to go to Philadelphia. Finally, however, after more urging from Madison, Jefferson, and Gen. Henry Lee, Freneau accepted. He began his official duties on 16 August 1791.

Freneau thus entered the most public, influential, and important part of his life. The government in Philadelphia was still finding its way. It was held together by the presence of George Washington, but its form was still uncertain. Freneau and his colleagues were determined to shape it in a republican mold and fight those who would follow the English model of government. The first thing he had to do was put his newspaper, the *National Gazette*, on a firm footing. As the name implies, Freneau sought to make his paper national in scope and circulation. This he did through the help of Madison, Jefferson, and others who solicited subscriptions. He soon had subscribers in every part of the country. The first edition of the paper appeared on 31 October 1791. The *National Gazette* came out on Mondays and Thursdays and printed foreign as well as domestic news (Freneau had access to much State Department intelligence

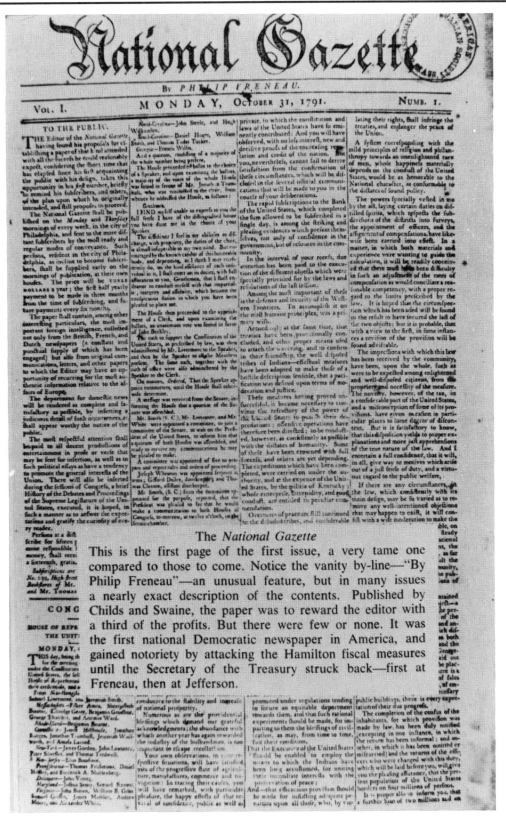

The National Gazette

This is the first page of the first issue, a very tame one compared to those to come. Notice the vanity by-line—"By Philip Freneau"—an unusual feature, but in many issues a nearly exact description of the contents. Published by Childs and Swaine, the paper was to reward the editor with a third of the profits. But there were few or none. It was the first national Democratic newspaper in America, and gained notoriety by attacking the Hamilton fiscal measures until the Secretary of the Treasury struck back—first at Freneau, then at Jefferson.

Front page of the first issue of Freneau's Republican newspaper, established at the urging of Thomas Jefferson and James Madison (Philip M. Marsh, Philip Freneau, *1967)* through Jefferson), political debates, government reports, book reviews, and advertisements.

It did not take long for Freneau to begin doing battle with Hamilton and the Federalists. The Republican bent of the paper was soon apparent and Hamilton's partisans wasted no time in attacking Freneau. The *American Mercury* in Hartford, Connecticut, called him "The blackguard's pattern, and the great man's fool,/The fawning parasite, and the union's tool." Freneau answered these personal attacks in kind, but the first issue to receive extended debate in the columns of the paper was the monarchical tendencies of the Federalists. Madison raised serious questions about these tendencies in the 2 April 1792 article entitled "The Union. Who are Its True Friends?" Freneau continuously satirized the way Federalist papers referred to the men of government as "Most Honorable" and to their wives as "Ladies." The issue of monarchy could not be taken lightly: there were a significant number of people in political circles who saw the establishment of a monarchy as a road to political order, and their best hope for such a monarch was George Washington. The president had no intention of accepting a crown, but that did not deter those who favored the idea; nor did it allay the fears of men like Freneau who opposed it.

The monarchy issue reflected a deeper issue that was the basis for most of the political debates of the decade—the amount of power that would rest with the federal government. With the Constitution in place, few argued that a national government was unnecessary. A "loose construction" of the Constitution, however, could place more power in the hands of fewer people. Hamilton, Fenno, John Adams, and Fisher Ames, a congressman from Massachusetts, favored this interpretation; Jefferson, Madison, and Freneau opposed it. Washington was caught in the middle of the fray and felt the heat from both sides.

Freneau showed no particular desire to attack Washington personally, but he did not shrink from the task when he felt it necessary. Freneau shared, with most others in America, a great respect for the man who had led the country to independence. He praised his virtue and courage. But Freneau believed that Washington was being duped by bad advisers, and he felt it necessary to lecture the president occasionally on relations with France and England and on the dangers of monarchy. He reminded Washington on one occasion that "principles, not men, ought ever to be the objects of republican attachments." Freneau believed these

attacks to be directed at the administration rather than at Washington himself.

For his part, Washington chose to believe that when his administration was criticized, the criticism was also meant for him personally. He was especially embittered by Freneau's implications that he was being duped by his advisers. He once wrote Jefferson, speaking of himself in the third person, "that in condemning the administration of the government they condemned him, for if they thought there were measures pursued contrary to his sentiment, they must conceive him too careless to attend to them or too stupid to understand them." With this basic misunderstanding of each other's position, the war of words between the president and the editor escalated.

Freneau's support of the French Revolution naturally followed from his past experience and his anti-English and antimonarchist sentiments. Louis XVI's execution elicited no sympathy for the king from Freneau: "It affects me no more than the execution of another malefactor," he wrote. Freneau felt that the U.S. should give unstinting support to the revolution, and he welcomed the new French ambassador, Edmond Genêt, known as Citizen Genêt, in 1793 with enthusiasm. Despite the popular acclaim Genêt received, Washington's government, with Jefferson's assent, declared its neutrality in the conflict between Britain and France. Genêt affronted the government by threatening to take his case directly to the people and by bypassing the secretary of state in his communication with the government. Thoroughly disgusted, Jefferson gave Genêt a sharp rebuke. In a measure of Freneau's independence from Jefferson, however, the *National Gazette* never abandoned Genêt. Freneau saw nothing wrong with Genêt's threat to appeal to the people: "Why all this outcry against Mr. Genêt, for saying he would appeal to the people? Is the president a consecrated character that an appeal from him must be considered criminal?" Washington, of course, did not appreciate these sentiments and told Jefferson he would not mind if the secretary of state fired Freneau. Jefferson refused to do so.

Jefferson's relationship with Freneau was one of the major controversies of Freneau's editorship. Freneau's writings were frustrating to the Federalists because of their inability to answer him adequately. Personal attacks on Freneau did not silence him. The Federalists decided that Freneau's position and credibility would have to be challenged. That challenge came from Hamilton in a letter signed "T.L.," printed in Fenno's *Gazette of the United States* in July 1792, in which Hamilton asked if it was right for an editor to accept a salary from the government and then criticize the policies of that government. This kind of attack continued and expanded to include Jefferson—who was the real target anyway—and his motives in encouraging Freneau to come to Philadelphia. Jefferson never answered these attacks publicly, but Freneau swore out an affidavit with the mayor of Philadelphia that he never received any direction from Jefferson in running the *National Gazette.*

Freneau found these attacks fairly easy to fend off because Hamilton never produced any evidence of an unseemly relationship between Freneau and Jefferson. In truth, there was none to be found. Freneau was a fiercely independent man who would not have taken kindly to advice on running his paper from Jefferson or anyone else. Jefferson was not inclined to give such advice and preferred to let the press go its own way. He said so in a famous letter to Washington which included the sentence: "No government ought to be without censors; and where the press is free, no one ever will."

The *National Gazette* remained unhurt by Hamilton's attacks, but Freneau could not defend it from other circumstances. In the fall of 1793 Philadelphia was struck by a yellow fever plague, and half the population fled to the countryside. Government and business offices were closed, and a general depression set in. Freneau was having trouble getting his subscribers to pay anyway, and these conditions made matters worse. Too, Jefferson had recently resigned as secretary of state, and Freneau thus lost his office and the small income he derived from it. Without the financial backing he needed, Freneau shut down the *National Gazette* in October, two years after he had begun.

The paper's failure was not connected with its editorial content. By all accounts it was one of the most interesting newspapers of its day, and it was one of the best weapons the Republicans had. The Federalists' obsession with criticizing Freneau and attacking his credibility were ample testimony to his effectiveness, and the praise Freneau received from his friends showed their satisfaction with him and the *National Gazette.*

Freneau returned to his family home in New Jersey and plotted his future course. His scheme of publishing a paper from Monmouth County was revived. During 1794, while putting together plans for this paper, he published an almanac which sold very well. He also produced a book of poetry which had only modest success. By late spring of 1795,

he was finally ready to return to journalism, and on 2 May the first issue of the *Jersey Chronicle* appeared. Much of the paper consisted of material reprinted from other papers, and the careful editing that had characterized the *National Gazette* was missing. Freneau was ever the radical republican, unreformed in his anti-English and antimonarchical views. He continued his criticisms of the Federalists, but the major issue of this short-lived paper was Jay's Treaty, in which Freneau believed that America had conceded too much to England. Freneau printed the whole treaty in his paper and criticized it sharply. After a year, the *Jersey Chronicle* perished from the same cause as the *National Gazette,* a lack of money to sustain it. Once again, Freneau had to look for employment.

Freneau joined business and political associates in New York in 1796 to issue the *Time-Piece.* This publication was more a literary journal than a newspaper, but Freneau made sure that politics was a major part of its content. He fenced with his old rival Fenno and with the acerbic pro-British editor William Cobbett. He criticized John Adams, who had been elected president, and he editorialized on social issues such as imprisonment for debt. The *Time-Piece,* like Freneau's other journalistic ventures, did not prosper, and by March 1798, he had disassociated himself from it. This action marked Freneau's final exit from full-time journalism. The next year he contributed a series of satiric letters to William Duane's *Aurora* in Philadelphia, but Freneau never returned to editing.

By the time he retired from journalism, Freneau was beginning to see some political victories. The Federalists had been routed in the 1800 election, and Republicanism was ascendant. The hated Alien and Sedition Acts, which the Federalists had used to try to silence the opposition, had expired, and editors were free to speak their minds.

Freneau went back to the one thing in life which had offered him some degree of financial success—the sea. For the next ten years he spent much of his time commanding a merchant ship. He made voyages to the Canary Islands and visited various ports in the Caribbean. Always he wrote poetry. In 1809 he prepared an edition of his poems to be sold by subscription. Among the subscribers were old friends Madison and Jefferson. In his letter requesting the subscription, Jefferson told Freneau, "Under the shade of a tree one of your volumes will be a pleasant pocket companion." Freneau's last appearance as a poet occurred during the War of 1812. He had written a number of patriotic verses to spur America on in its fight with

Britain, and he collected these and other poems into two volumes which were published in 1815.

Freneau planned to live the rest of his life as a farmer at the family home near Mount Pleasant, New Jersey. Not long after the war, the house burned, and many of Freneau's letters and papers were destroyed. The Freneau family moved to another farmhouse near Freehold, New Jersey. There they lived close to poverty for the next fifteen years. On 18 December 1832 Freneau was caught in a snowstorm while walking home and froze to death. He was eighty years old.

The life of Philip Freneau was largely a series of failures and frustrations, and this "Poet of the Revolution" has not received particularly kind attention from critics and biographers since his death. His reputation and his relationship with Thomas Jefferson have been called into question; his courage and patriotism have been criticized; and his poetry has been largely dismissed as crude and lacking in style. Even his sympathetic biographer Lewis Leary subtitled his 1941 work *A Study in Literary Failure.* The one time when Freneau was definitely not a failure was when he was editor of the *National Gazette.* During this two-year period, Freneau produced the liveliest, most readable newspaper of the day. Even his political opponents

directly or indirectly conceded the merits of the *National Gazette.* Jefferson may have overstated the case when he said that Freneau's paper had saved the Constitution from monarchy, but Freneau was the best editor of his time, and his influence on the early interpretation of the Constitution was profound.

Biographies:
Mary Austin, *Philip Freneau, The Poet of the Revolution* (New York: A. Wessels, 1901);
Lewis Leary, *That Rascal Freneau: A Study in Literary Failure* (New Brunswick: Rutgers University Press, 1941);
Jacob Axelrad, *Philip Freneau* (Austin: University of Texas Press, 1967).

References:
S. G. W. Benjamin, "Notable Editors between 1776 and 1800," *Magazine of American History,* 17 (January-June 1887): 1-28, 97-127;
P. L. Ford, "Freneau's *National Gazette,*" *Nation,* 60 (21 February 1895): 143-144;
Samuel Forman, *The Political Activities of Philip Freneau* (New York: Arno & the *New York Times,* 1970).

Hugh Gaine

(1726-25 April 1807)

Alfred Lawrence Lorenz
Loyola University in New Orleans

MAJOR POSITIONS HELD: Printer-editor, *New-York Mercury,* renamed *New-York Gazette; and the Weekly Mercury* in 1768 (1752-1783).

SELECTED BOOKS: *Gaine's Universal Register, or, American and British Kalendar for the Year 1777* (New York: H. Gaine, 1777);
The Journals of Hugh Gaine, Printer, edited by Paul Leicester Ford, 2 volumes (New York: Dodd, Mead, 1902).

On 17 December 1740, fourteen-year-old Hugh Gaine was taken by his father to the print shop at the sign of the Crown and Bible in Belfast's

Beaver Street, where he was apprenticed to the printers Samuel Wilson and James Magee. For young Gaine, born in 1726 near Belfast in Portlonone in the parish of Ahogkill, the articles of apprenticeship that were signed that day would serve as a passport to a long career as a printer and editor in America, to a measure of wealth, and to a place in history as a turncoat printer of the American Revolution.

Under the terms of his indenture, Gaine was apprenticed for six years; but Wilson and Magee dissolved their partnership in 1744, and Gaine soon after sailed for America. He settled in New York and was hired as a journeyman in the shop of James

Courtesy of Edward Wood, Jr.

Parker, printer-editor of the *New York Weekly Post-Boy*, with whom he worked for seven years.

Gaine left Parker in the spring of 1752 and opened his own shop under the sign of the Bible and Crown, and in August of that year began publication of the *New-York Mercury*. The *Mercury* was indistinguishable in appearance from other newspapers of the day, but editorially it was equal, if not superior, to most. The Patriot printer Isaiah Thomas, publisher of the *Massachusetts Spy*, rather backhandedly complimented it in writing later that "the collection of intelligence in this paper was not inferior to that of any paper published in the city." The New York historian James Grant Wilson observed that the *Mercury* "became by far the best newspaper in the colonies." In the beginning, Gaine's news consisted of brief items from other colonial and English newspapers reporting fires, natural disasters, robberies, and murders. He carried the verbatim proclamations of governors and mayors. But Gaine also relied heavily on authors of familiar essays to fill his columns, and their topics ranged widely; among them were religion, philosophy, the sciences, and love and marriage. But most of the writings were political, and almost from the beginning Gaine was embroiled in political conflicts. In 1753 the colony's Presbyterian faction attacked him for supporting the Episcopalian faction in a dispute over the financing and administration of King's College (later Columbia University). Not long after, he was chastised by the conservative Episcopalian-dominated New York Assembly for printing without authorization an extract from the assembly's proceedings. Subsequently, he sold the Presbyterians space in the *Mercury* to present their side of the question. Fifteen years later, when the Episcopalians sought a bishopric in the colonies, Gaine—himself an Episcopalian—allowed the Presbyterians no voice in the newspaper.

In spite of the conflicts, Gaine was successful. His newspaper, his adjunct printing activities, and his sale of books, paper, and sundries from his print shop brought him an increasing income. As Philip Freneau had him say in a lengthy satirical poem, "Hugh Gaine's Life," written at the end of the revolution,

> . . . I put up a press,
> And printed away with Amazing success;
> Neglected my person, and looked like a fright,
> Was bothered all day, and was busy all night,
> Saw money come in, as the papers went out. . . .

Gaine married Sarah Robbins in 1759. They had three children: Elizabeth, born in 1761; John R., born in 1762; and Anne, born in 1764. Sarah Gaine died soon after Anne's birth, leaving Gaine to raise the infants. In 1769 he married Cornelia Wallace; they had two daughters, Cornelia (date of birth unknown) and Sarah, born in 1772.

In the long struggle of the 1760s and 1770s against the British mercantile system, Gaine and his *Mercury* followed an erratic course. Like other printers, he would be severely burdened by the Stamp Act, and so he joined with the Whigs in fighting the act by publishing a variety of essays by American writers which condemned the measure as taxation without representation. After the act became effective on 1 November 1765, he defied it by printing his newspaper on unstamped paper with the heading "No Stamped Paper to be Had." This heading was substituted for the paper's title in the issues for 4, 11, and 18 November. On Par-

Front page of Gaine's New-York Mercury, *which switched back and forth from a Tory to a revolutionary position over the years*

liament's repeal of the stamp duties in 1766, he exulted.

The following year saw the enactment of the Townshend Acts, which levied duties on a variety of goods, including paper. Again Gaine stood in opposition to Parliament. He printed in the *Mercury* the eloquent series "Letters from a Farmer in Pennsylvania" by John Dickinson, the strongest arguments the colonials were to muster against the duties, and he supported the nonimportation movement to boycott British goods. But when the duties on all goods but tea were repealed, he opposed the Whigs and advocated that the boycott be lifted lest England employ even harsher methods against the colonists. He appeared to want to limit opposition within clearly defined bounds, and when the British retreated, he believed the Americans should fall back also.

Gaine's conservatism grew even more pronounced in the late 1760s. A contributing factor may well have been his appointment in 1768 as public printer of the province of New York, which carried with it a contract for official printing and also provided a measure of social status; he marked the event by changing the name of the newspaper to the *New-York Gazette; and the Weekly Mercury*, *Gazette* being the name assumed by other official colonial newspapers. Gaine was a property owner by that time, too; he held the deeds not only to his own shop and house in Hanover Square but also to a portion of a farm in Albany County. He also joined a partnership to build a paper mill on Long Island, a major enterprise in colonial New York.

At the same time, Whig opposition to the British became more violent, and Gaine abhorred violence. Riots in New York and Boston went unreported in the *Mercury*, or else the newspaper printed the Tory versions of the incidents. Gaine sided with the conservative assembly against the radical Whigs in 1770, when the latter sought a law which would have instituted the secret ballot in elections for assemblymen. In the same year, the *Mercury* was the voice of conservatism in the furor which resulted from the imprisonment of Alexander McDougall, a leader of the Whig group the Sons of Liberty, on charges of seditious libel. Gaine both defended the British common law of libel and heaped abuse on the Whig prisoner.

In the two-year calm that followed the repeal of the Townshend Acts the *Mercury* contained little political news. But it was drawn back into the political wars in 1773, when Parliament enacted the British East India Company Act. Since Gaine was not directly affected by the measure, he gave only perfunctory support to the resistance movement led by the tea merchants and importers. As opposition to the act grew throughout the colonies in November and December 1773, he strengthened his support; but with the violence of "tea parties" in Boston and New York that winter, he gave over his columns to essays abjuring violence and advocating an accommodation with the mother country.

An understanding with Great Britain was also the *Mercury*'s theme as the First Continental Congress convened in Philadelphia in September 1774. But while he articulated conservative opposition to another boycott of imports when the Congress adopted a stringent nonimportation agreement, he both publicized the agreement and allowed space to supporters of nonimportation. Nevertheless, because he did not fully support the work of the Congress, Gaine became the target of the more militant Whigs, some of whom branded him and his newspaper as enemies of the united colonies. He was not the convinced Tory that they imagined him to be, however, and, after the battles of Lexington and Concord in April 1775, he sided wholeheartedly with the Whigs.

Gaine took no position when the question of independence arose the following year; rather, he printed in the *Mercury* the most representative and articulate essays of the many who addressed the issue. When independence was declared, he accepted it readily and enthusiastically. His support of the Americans was such that when New York was threatened with a British invasion in September 1776, Gaine packed a press and some paper and type and fled with his family to Newark, where he enlisted the *Mercury* in the revolutionary cause.

The British occupied New York soon after. With its printers gone, the city was without a newspaper and Ambrose Serle, a young Englishman who had arrived with the fleet as Lord Richard Howe's secretary, accepted Governor William Tryon's request that he publish a new one. Gaine had left the Bible and Crown in the care of a clerk when he left, and Serle was able to use the shop, materials, and even the nameplate of the *Mercury* to provide the authorities with an official organ, a British version of the *Mercury*.

If Gaine, in Newark, thought that the Americans would shelter and support him he was disappointed. While he put a glowing face on the American activities in his *Mercury*, in reality he was suffering badly. His few remaining subscribers were scattered and did not pay their bills. Advertisers were practically nonexistent. The retreating American army appeared helpless in the face of

Gaine's New-York Mercury *for 4 November 1765, published in defiance of the Stamp Act. Two more issues appeared with this heading in place of the title before the act was repealed in 1766.*

British might. There was even discord among the leaders of the revolt. Disillusioned, Gaine returned to New York on the first of November. In Freneau's poem, he says that he,

> (after repenting of what I had done,
> And cursing my folly and idle pursuits)
> Returned to the city, and hung up my boots.

Gaine was allowed to resume printing the *Mercury*, but Serle retained editorial control. So scurrilous was the newspaper under Serle's direction and so successfully did he stay in the background that it was not he but Gaine who became the object of Whig hatred and who bore the brunt of American attacks on the Tory press. He was characterized in Patriot publications as "Hugh Lucre," as "a gentleman who can lie with ingenuity," and as "the greatest liar upon earth."

Gaine regained full control of the newspaper only after Serle sailed with Lord Howe's fleet in the summer of 1777. But he did not regain the trust of the British. When the arch-Tory printer James Rivington returned from exile in England, where he had been driven by angry mobs of the Sons of Liberty in 1775, the post of Royal Printer was given to him rather than returned to Gaine, and he superseded Gaine as the most hated of Tory printers. Gaine, nevertheless, was odious to the Patriots, and Freneau expressed their distaste for him in his poem "Hugh Gaine's Life," published in 1783.

Although the British slighted him in conferring honors on Rivington, Gaine placed the *Mercury* in the British ranks for the remaining seven years of their occupation of New York. He served them, also, by giving a room in his house to a naval officer and by performing duties in the city militia. Soon after the British sailed for home after their defeat, Gaine dropped the word *Crown* from the name of his shop and closed the *Mercury*. His final issue was dated 10 November 1783.

Gaine maintained his printing business until his death, publishing a variety of books ranging from stories for children to political tomes; he stocked an even greater variety of imported books on his shelves. He also entered into the new American society with no timidity. He was among those merchants who lent their prestige to urge that New York adopt the new federal Constitution and he took part in a grand parade celebrating its adoption. He was active in civic affairs and in professional activities; he was a founder of the American

Booksellers Association and served as its first president.

Gaine's last years were comfortable, for he had income from substantial real estate holdings in New York and owned a manor home in the country just north of New York City. With affluence came social recognition, and his daughters made marriages which reflected an upper-class social position.

Gaine died at age eighty-one in 1807 and was interred in the family plot in the Trinity Church burial ground in New York. In the history of American journalism he would come to be known as a minor figure, almost a curiosity because of his political wanderings and his apparent willingness to surrender principle for financial reward. James Grant Wilson perhaps best expressed the enduring view of him: "When with the Whigs, Hugh Gaine was a Whig; when with the Royalists, he was loyal; when the contest was doubtful, equally doubtful were the politics of Hugh Gaine." Nevertheless, Gaine had made a contribution of importance. For one thing, his *Mercury* was superior to most of its competitors—a fact attested to by its thirty-year life, if by nothing else—and as such it served as a model for other newspapers. Thus, Gaine helped to lay the basis for the journalism that would come later and he helped to instill in Americans the habit of newspaper reading. Perhaps more important, the *Mercury*, like most of its competitors, devoted itself to American issues in the period prior to the Revolution, and in so doing helped to forge a national identity which both foreshadowed and contributed to the making of a separate American nation. Indeed, it was Gaine's support in the *Mercury* of anti-British activities which helped to bring about the revolution on which he ultimately turned his back.

Biography:

Alfred Lawrence Lorenz, *Hugh Gaine: A Colonial Printer-Editor's Odyssey to Loyalism* (Carbondale: Southern Illinois University Press, 1972).

References:

S. G. W. Benjamin, "A Group of Pre-Revolutionary Editors," *Magazine of American History*, 17 (January 1887): 1-28;

Benjamin, "Notable Editors Between 1776 and 1800—Influence of the Early American Press," *Magazine of American History*, 17 (February 1887): 97-127;

Paul Leicester Ford, ed., *The Journals of Hugh Gaine,*

Printer, 2 volumes (New York: Dodd, Mead, 1902);

Charles R. Hildeburn, *Sketches of Printers and Printing in Colonial New York* (New York: Dodd, Mead, 1895), pp. 25, 153-154;

"Hugh Gaine, Irishman, Publisher," *Recorder*, 1 (April 1902): 1;

Fred Lewis Pattee, ed., *The Poems of Philip Freneau, Poet of the American Revolution*, 3 volumes (Princeton, N.J.: The University Library, 1902-1907), II: 201-214;

Lorenzo Sabine, *Biographical Sketches of Loyalists of the American Revolution with an Historical Essay*, 2 volumes (Boston: Little, Brown, 1864), I: 451-452;

Arthur M. Schlesinger, *Prelude to Independence: The Newspaper War on Britain, 1764-1776* (New York: Knopf, 1958), pp. 63-307;

Edward H. Tatum, Jr., ed., *The American Journal of Ambrose Serle* (San Marino, Cal.: The Huntington Library, 1940), pp. 113, 135, 176, 185, 187, 219, 283;

Isaiah Thomas, *The History of Printing in America*, 2nd edition, 2 volumes (Albany, N.Y.: American Antiquarian Society, 1874), I: 300-301, II: 109-110, 234-235;

James Grant Wilson, *The Memorial History of the City of New York*, 4 volumes (New York: New York History Co., 1893), IV: 137.

William Lloyd Garrison

David Paul Nord
Indiana University

See also the Garrison entry in *DLB 1, The American Renaissance in New England*.

BIRTH: Newburyport, Massachusetts, 10 or 12 December 1805, to Abijah and Fanny Lloyd Garrison.

MARRIAGE: 4 September 1834 to Helen Benson; children: George Thompson, William Lloyd, Jr., Wendell Phillips, Charles Follen, Helen Frances (Fanny), Elizabeth Pease, Francis Jackson.

MAJOR POSITIONS HELD: Editor, *Newburyport* (Mass.) *Free Press* (1826), *National Philanthropist* (Boston) (1828), *Bennington* (Vt.) *Journal of the Times* (1828-1829), *Baltimore Genius of Universal Emancipation* (1829-1830), *Boston Liberator* (1831-1865).

DEATH: New York, 24 May 1879.

BOOKS: *An Address. Delivered before the Free People of Color, in Philadelphia, New York, and Other Cities, during the Month of June, 1831* (Boston: Printed by S. Foster, 1831);

An Address on the Progress of the Abolition Cause; Delivered before the African Abolition Freehold Society of Boston, July 16, 1832 (Boston: Printed by Garrison & Knapp, 1832);

Thoughts on African Colonization: or, An Impartial Exhibition of the Doctrines, Principles and Purposes of the American Colonization Society (Boston: Printed & published by Garrison & Knapp, 1832);

Address Delivered in Boston, New York and Philadelphia, before the Free People of Color, in April, 1833 (New York: Printed for the free people of color, 1833);

Slavery in the United States of America. An Appeal to the Friends of Negro Emancipation, throughout Great Britain, &c. (London, 1833);

A Brief Sketch of the Trial of William Lloyd Garrison, for an Alleged Libel on Francis Todd, of Newburyport, Mass. (Boston: Printed by Garrison & Knapp, 1834);

The Maryland Scheme of Expatriation Examined. By a Friend of Liberty, anonymous (Boston: Garrison & Knapp, 1834);

An Address Delivered in Marlboro' Chapel, Boston, July 4, 1838 (Boston: Published by Isaac Knapp, 1838);

An Address Delivered at the Broadway Tabernacle, N.Y. August 1, 1838. By Request of the People of Color of That City, in Commemoration of the Complete

Emancipation of 600,000 Slaves on That Day in the British West Indies (Boston: I. Knapp, 1838);

An Address Delivered before the Old Colony Anti-Slavery Society, at South Scituate, Mass. July 4, 1839 (Boston: Dow & Jackson, printers, 1839);

Sonnets and Other Poems (Boston: O. Johnson, 1843);

American Slavery. Address on the Subject of American Slavery, and the Progress of the Cause of Freedom throughout the World. Delivered in the National Hall, Holborn, on Wednesday Evening, September 2, 1846 (London: Printed by R. Kinder, 1846?);

Letter from William Lloyd Garrison. Read at the Annual Meeting of the Pennsylvania Anti-Slavery Society (Boston: J. M. M'Kim, 1851);

Selections from the Writings and Speeches of William Lloyd Garrison (Boston: R. F. Wallcut, 1852);

Principles and Mode of Action of the American Anti-Slavery Society: A Speech (London: W. Tweedie, 1853);

No Compromise with Slavery. An Address Delivered in the Broadway Tabernacle, New York, February 14, 1854 (New York: American Anti-Slavery Society, 1854);

West India Emancipation. A Speech . . . Delivered at Abington, Mass., on the First Day of August, 1854 (Boston: American Anti-Slavery Society, 1854);

"No Fetters in the Bay State!" Speech of Wm. Lloyd Garrison, before the Committee on Federal Relations, in Support of the Petitions Asking for a Law to Prevent the Recapture of Fugitive Slaves, Thursday, Feb. 24, 1859 (Boston: R. F. Wallcut, 1859);

The New "Reign of Terror" in the Slaveholding States, for 1859-60, anonymous (New York: American Anti-Slavery Society, 1860);

No Slave Hunting in the Old Bay State: An Appeal to the People and Legislature of Massachusetts (New York: American Anti-Slavery Society, 1860);

The "Infidelity" of Abolitionism (New York: American Anti-Slavery Society, 1860);

A Fresh Catalogue of Southern Outrages upon Northern Citizens, anonymous (New York: American Anti-Slavery Society, 1860);

The Loyalty and Devotion of Colored Americans in the Revolution and War of 1812, anonymous (Boston: R. F. Wallcut, 1861);

The Abolition of Slavery the Right of the Government under the War Power, anonymous (Boston: R. F. Wallcut, 1861);

The Spirit of the South towards Northern Freemen and Soldiers Defending the American Flag against Traitors of the Deepest Dye, anonymous (Boston: R. F. Wallcut, 1861);

Southern Hatred of the American Government, the People of the North, and Free Institutions, anonymous (Boston: R. F. Wallcut, 1862);

The Abolitionists, and Their Relations to the War; a Lecture by William Lloyd Garrison, Delivered at the Cooper Institute, New York, January 14, 1862 (New York: E. D. Barker, 1862);

Fillmore and Sumner. A Letter from William Lloyd Garrison (Boston, 1874);

The Philosophy of the Single Tax Movement (New York: Sterling, 1895);

The Words of Garrison: A Centennial Selection (1805-1905) of Characteristic Sentiments from the Writings of William Lloyd Garrison; with a Biographical Sketch, List of Portraits, Bibliography and Chronology, edited by Wendell Phillips Garrison and Francis Jackson Garrison (Boston & New York: Houghton, Mifflin, 1905);

Garrison's First Anti-Slavery Address in Boston. Address at Park Street Church, Boston, July 4, 1829 (Bos-

Photograph by Mathew Brady

ton: Directors of the Old South Work, 1907);

William Lloyd Garrison on Non-resistance, together with a Personal Sketch by His Daughter, Fanny Garrison Villard, and a Tribute by Leo Tolstoi, edited by Fanny Garrison Villard (New York: The Nation Press Printing Co., 1924);

Documents of Upheaval: Selections from William Lloyd Garrison's The Liberator, 1831-1865, edited by Truman Nelson (New York: Hill & Wang, 1966);

William Lloyd Garrison, edited by George M. Fredrickson (Englewood Cliffs, N.J.: Prentice-Hall, 1968).

OTHER: *The Abolitionist; or, Record of the New-England Anti-Slavery Society,* edited by Garrison (Boston: Printed by Garrison & Knapp, 1833);

A Selection of Anti-Slavery Hymns, for the Use of the Friends of Emancipation, edited by Garrison (Boston: Garrison & Knapp, 1834);

Juvenile Poems, for the Use of Free American Children, of Every Complexion, edited by Garrison (Boston: Garrison & Knapp, 1835);

Lectures of George Thompson, with a Full Report of the Discussion between Mr. Thompson and Mr. Borthwick, the Pro-Slavery Agent, Held at the Royal Amphitheatre, Liverpool, Eng., and Which Continued for Six Evenings with Unabated Interest, Comp. from Various English Editions. Also, a Brief History of His Connection with the Anti-Slavery Cause in England, by Wm. Lloyd Garrison, edited by Garrison (Boston: I. Knapp, 1836);

George Thompson, *Lectures on British India, Delivered in the Friends' Meeting House, Manchester, England, in October, 1839,* preface by Garrison (Pawtucket, R.I.: W. & R. Adams, 1840);

Joseph Mazzini: His Life, Writings, and Political Principles, introduction by Garrison (New York: Hurd & Houghton, 1872);

Helen Eliza Garrison. A Memorial, compiled by Garrison (Cambridge, Mass.: Privately printed, 1876).

On 29 December 1865 William Lloyd Garrison brought out the last issue of the *Liberator,* the fiery abolitionist newspaper he had founded in 1831. Though his friends urged him to continue the paper, he felt that with chattel slavery dead, the *Liberator*'s work was done. In a valedictory editorial, Garrison bade farewell to his small congregation of faithful readers who had sailed with him, "against wind and tide," for thirty-five tempestuous years. He declared, with characteristic fervor, that

the struggle for freedom must go on, in the South and everywhere. But now the "beacon lights of liberty" must be kindled by a new generation of men and women.

The production of this last issue of the *Liberator* took on the aura of a sacramental rite. As Garrison wrote his final editorial, he handed it, line by line, to his assistants to be set into type. The final paragraph he typeset himself and fitted into the page form laid out on the *Liberator*'s old imposing stone. As he did, and as the page was locked up, the little group of printers gathered around, silently and sadly, to witness the end of an era.

Later, Garrison recalled the symbolism of the imposing stone. "How many days and nights have I wearily bent over it in getting ready the paper," he wrote to an old friend. "What a 'stone of stumbling' and a 'rock of offense' it was to all the enemies of emancipation." Yet, in another sense, this old stone and the sadness in the print shop that last night also symbolize the centrality of journalism to the career of William Lloyd Garrison. He is remembered today not as a great journalist but as a radical abolitionist and reformer. But his reformist philosophy was intimately connected to his character as a journalist and to his understanding of the function of journalism in a good society. The *Liberator*'s old imposing stone was not merely a "stone of stumbling" for abolition's enemies; it was an anchor, a rock of ages for Garrison. Indeed, it was the rock upon which he built his abolitionist church.

William Lloyd Garrison was born in Newburyport, Massachusetts, on 10 or 12 December 1805, the third child of Abijah and Fanny Lloyd Garrison, who had moved from Nova Scotia to this lively port at the mouth of the Merrimack River earlier that same year. The year after the birth of Lloyd (as he was called) may have been the most prosperous time in the not-very-prosperous life of Abijah Garrison, a skilled but sometimes intemperate sailing master. When sailing jobs disappeared in the Embargo of 1807, Abijah turned more frequently to liquor, much to the dismay of Fanny, a strict, strong-willed Baptist convert. One day in 1808, after the usual scenes with his wife, Abijah could stand it no more. He left Newburyport and his family, never to return to either.

The next few years were a time of deep poverty for Fanny Garrison and her young children. She tried to keep the little family together in Newburyport but could not. In 1812 she moved with James, the oldest child, to Lynn, Massachusetts, where he was apprenticed as a shoemaker. Lloyd

Garrison's birthplace in Newburyport, Massachusetts

and the baby, Marie Elizabeth, were left behind in the care of friends. Lloyd joined his mother and brother in 1814, but the shoe trade proved to be too demanding for his fragile, nine-year-old fingers. Fanny and the boys followed the shoe business to Baltimore in 1815, but neither James nor Lloyd found it to his taste. Like his father, James ran away to the sea and to the bottle, while Lloyd was sent home to Newburyport to live with family friends and to try to find his place in the world. After another false start, this time in the cabinet-making business, Garrison was finally apprenticed to learn the printing trade from Ephraim Allen, the printer/owner of the rather dull *Newburyport Herald*. On 18 October 1818, a few weeks short of his thirteenth birthday, Garrison began his career in journalism.

Many years later, Garrison remembered how awed and intimidated he had been on that first day to see how fast the compositors could set and distribute the types. But quickly he, too, became one of them; and just as quickly he grew to love the work. Mr. Allen was an appreciative master, and he rewarded Garrison's diligence and skill by appointing him shop foreman in charge of making up the pages of the paper. Like young Benjamin Franklin, Garrison, who had spent only brief periods in the primary school and grammar school in Newburyport, learned the language by setting type by day and reading the classics of English politics and poetry by night. Also like Franklin, Garrison published his first articles as anonymous letters to the editor of the paper he worked on. Mr. Allen was pleased with the writings of his mysterious correspondent, and Garrison's contributions continued for the remainder of his apprenticeship. For the young apprentice, journalism brought fulfillment and happiness, for his acceptance as a writer helped partially to wipe away his disappointment and shame that he had had so little formal schooling. "Indeed," he proudly wrote to his mother in 1823, "it is altogether a matter of surprise that I have met with such signal success, seeing I do not understand one single rule of grammar, and having a very inferior education." Like Franklin, Garrison made the type cases his primer and his university.

With a rigorous apprenticeship in writing and editing as well as printing behind him, Garrison felt ready at age twenty to take over the proprietorship of a newspaper. In the spring of 1826, only a few months past apprenticeship, Garrison bought the *Newburyport Essex Courant* with loans from Allen, his former master. He renamed the paper the *Free Press* and made it a political organ devoted to the principles of the old Federalist party.

Garrison in 1825, near the end of his apprenticeship on the Newburyport Herald *(from the original in the possession of Walter M. Merrill)*

In the *Free Press*, Garrison developed an editorial philosophy and style that were to mark his journalism throughout his career. He seemed absolutely indifferent to subscriber preferences; from the outset, he proposed to conduct the paper as he saw fit. When several disgruntled patrons canceled their subscriptions after the first issue because of the paper's strident Federalist ideology, Garrison professed to be glad to see them go. After six months of dwindling circulation, the *Free Press* folded—and Garrison blamed a pampered public that could not stand to hear the truth, that preferred flattery to reproof. Yet, despite his scorn for public opinion and his readiness to flog his readers for their follies and vices, the paper rather faithfully lived up to its name in that it freely carried information and discussion from all interested readers regardless of their point of view. This somewhat contradictory style—that is, preaching at people, yet inviting them to participate fully in the newspaper enterprise—remained a Garrison trademark. As a moralist, he was doctrinaire and dogmatic, but he believed in free inquiry. As an editor, he required complete freedom to speak the truth as he saw it, but he offered the same right to others who chose to participate in the community that the newspaper gathered around it.

After the *Free Press* failed and he was unable to find a steady position in Newburyport, Garrison moved to Boston—and it was a serendipitous move indeed. Boston in the second quarter of the nineteenth century was not only the printing and publishing capital of New England, it was the religious and reform capital of the nation. This was the beginning of a great Age of Reform, and Boston was to be its Rome. From the Beacon Street Brahmins and the Cambridge Transcendentalists to the waterfront artisans and back-street Baptists, Boston was alive with the idea of change and the ideal of progress. Out of this religious and social ferment grew the temperance movement, prison reform, dietary reform, utopian communitarianism, religious missions and Sunday schools, educational reform and free public schools, insane asylums, feminism, labor unionism, pacifism, abolitionism, and more.

The unifying spirit of this Age of Reform was perfectionism. Narrowly construed, perfectionism was an evangelical religious doctrine that rejected the pessimistic Calvinist view of human nature, declaring instead that individual sinners could themselves repudiate sin and become sanctified on earth. But the spirit of perfectionism flowed far beyond its source in evangelical Protestant Christianity.

The notion that men and women could save themselves meant also that they might act to save their world. In any age, the great impetus to reform is not the realization that man is sinful and the world flawed; that is always painfully obvious. Rather, reform grows from the belief that individuals can do something about the situation. In the 1830s, religious doctrines of perfectionism merged nicely with democratic and romantic impulses in the secular world to produce a great flood tide of reform. This flood so filled Boston that some boarding houses there catered only to reformers—and their rooms were filled.

One of these boarders was William Lloyd Garrison. His landlord, William Collier, was a temperance man and the publisher of the *National Philanthropist*, one of the first temperance newspapers in America. Garrison helped out on Collier's paper from time to time and became its editor in January 1828. Like many former Federalists who had been displaced from the political system, Garrison made the transition from political harangue to moral exhortation, filling his paper with sad tales of the evils and degradations of drink. He moved the *National Philanthropist* into other areas of moral reform as well, including a growing concern for the peace movement and the first glimmer of interest in abolition of slavery. In the exciting atmosphere of Boston in 1828, Garrison already had become something of a universal reformer.

In the summer of 1828, Garrison was invited by a group of politicians from Vermont to come to Bennington to edit the *Journal of the Times*, a paper dedicated to the reelection of President John Quincy Adams. Garrison accepted the job on the condition that he would have a free hand on the editorial helm and that he might use the paper to plump for other causes besides Adams. It quickly became apparent that the Adams campaign was the least of Garrison's concerns. The *Journal of the Times* under Garrison became a journal of reform devoted to temperance, abolition of slavery, and peace. Neither his subscribers nor his sponsors were especially pleased by the reform tack of the paper, but Garrison did not care. He operated the *Journal* on the same principle as that on which he had edited the *Free Press*. He would accept advice on every subject but one: how he should run the paper.

One of the few readers who did like the paper very much indeed lived half a country away, in Baltimore. In early 1829 he walked all the way to Bennington to offer Garrison a partnership in his antislavery newspaper, the *Genius of Universal*

Emancipation. This distant admirer was Benjamin Lundy, the man who would guide Garrison into his life's work in abolitionism.

Garrison and Lundy had met briefly the year before at Collier's boardinghouse in Boston. Lundy had come to Boston in the spring of 1828 to try to turn some of the city's religious and reform fervor toward the abolition of slavery, a cause he had been pressing nearly alone for twenty years. Lundy was a modest, self-effacing Quaker, but he had the faith, the dedication, and the courage of St. Paul. Like the rest of the country, however, Boston was not quite ready for abolitionism, even the moderate variety that Lundy preached, which called for deportation (colonization) of the freed slaves. But Garrison was ready, and Lundy's talks at Collier's set him on fire. Years later, Garrison wrote: "I feel that I owe everything, instrumentally and under God, to Benjamin Lundy." When he got the chance in 1829 to go with Lundy to Baltimore, he did not hesitate.

Baltimore must have stirred mixed emotions for Garrison. It was there that he had been so unhappy as a child, far from his home in Newburyport. It was there that his mother, whom Garrison once called "the masterpiece of womankind," had died in 1823. Though he had lived apart from her for half his childhood, Garrison had been strongly influenced by his mother and was steadfastly devoted to her memory. His independence, his courage, his deep religiosity were gifts from her. But for Garrison, Baltimore now held a bright promise, as well as the painful memory of a lost mother and a lost childhood. At age twenty-three, Garrison was to be an editor of the *Genius of Universal Emancipation*—the paper he had proclaimed in an editorial in the *National Philanthropist* as "the bravest and best attempt in the history of newspaper publications."

Garrison's relationship with Lundy was amiable and exhilarating, but the two did not always agree on principle or strategy. Garrison grew to favor immediate abolition of slavery without deportation of the freed slaves; Lundy still believed in gradual emancipation and colonization. These two principles—immediate emancipation and no colonization—became the heart of Garrison's abolitionist creed. While he did not originate these principles, no man was to be more closely identified with them. For many people, these two principles came to symbolize radical abolitionism. Though it seemed outrageous and fanatical to most Americans of the time, radical abolitionism for Garrison flowed quite easily and directly from simple religious convictions. First, slavery (man holding property in other men) was a sin, and sin must be renounced immediately, not gradually. Second, all people—whether white or black—are children of God possessed of equal rights and thus "are at liberty to choose their own dwelling place." It was as simple as that—though few besides Garrison saw the matter quite so simply in 1829.

Garrison's inevitable break with Lundy, however, had more to do with style than with ideology. While the gentle Lundy preferred to refrain from personal attacks in the *Genius*, Garrison was not so tactful. Blistering rhetoric, which he modeled after the fashion of British abolitionism, was fast becoming a Garrison trademark. By April 1830, in fact, Garrison was in prison for the criminal libel of Francis Todd, a Massachusetts slave merchant. Garrison gloried in the notoriety of his seven-week stay in the Baltimore jail. He wrote sonnets to freedom on the cell wall, and he published an indignant and self-righteous account of his martyrdom. But his absence was keenly felt at the *Genius*, which had gone bankrupt and temporarily out of publication even before Garrison went to jail. On 5 June 1830 Garrison was released from jail, after his fine was paid by New York philanthropist Arthur Tappan. Immediately, Garrison traveled north to raise money to restart the *Genius*, but he had another plan in mind as well: to begin an antislavery newspaper that would be absolutely his own. After some months of support-seeking in New England, New York, and Philadelphia, Garrison decided that the place to begin such an enterprise was in the North, and that the most auspicious place in the North was Boston.

Boston may have been an incubator of reform, but the city's embrace of Garrison was cool indeed. In October 1830, his plans for starting the *Liberator* already well under way, Garrison was unable to persuade a single church or religious society to lend him its meeting rooms for an antislavery lecture. He was forced to accept an offer of rooms from a society of freethinkers—the very same infidels and atheists he had upbraided in the *National Philanthropist* three years before. The churches would have none of Garrison's brand of radical Christianity; and their rejection hurt him deeply, for he would always believe that the abolition of slavery was the truest of Christian missions. Though his lectures in the fall of 1830 did not convert the churches, they did convert Samuel May and Samuel Sewall, two well-to-do cousins who became disciples and close friends of Garrison. With their help and the help of Isaac Knapp, an old friend from the print shops of Newburyport, Garrison put together the first issue of the *Liberator*, which appeared on New Year's Day, 1831.

The first issue of the *Liberator* was a small, four-column, four-page folio—fourteen by nine-and-a-quarter inches. To print it, Garrison and Knapp had to borrow type from another reform newspaper and set it hurriedly in the middle of the night. They struck off 400 copies that first night, many more than they had paid subscribers to receive them. Volume one, number one was a rather gray-looking paper, without cuts or ads or any but the smallest of headlines. But if the typography was dull, the words blazed with the rhetorical fire and the moral fervor that were to become synonymous with the name William Lloyd Garrison: "I am aware that many object to the severity of my language; but is there not cause for severity? I *will be* as harsh as truth, and as uncompromising as justice. On this subject, I do not wish to think, or speak, or write, with moderation. No! no! Tell a man whose house is on fire to give a moderate alarm; tell him to moderately rescue his wife from the hands of the ravisher; tell the mother to gradually extricate her babe from the fire into which it has fallen;—but urge me not to use moderation in a cause like the present. I am in earnest—I will not equivocate—I will not excuse—I will not retreat a single inch—AND I WILL BE HEARD. The apathy of the people is enough to make every statue leap from its pedestal, and to hasten the resurrection of the dead." With the 23 April 1831 issue, Garrison added a woodcut to the top of page one showing a slave auction in the heart of Washington, D.C. The paper's appearance changed little thereafter.

The first year of the *Liberator* was a physical and fiscal ordeal for Garrison and Knapp. Even after they obtained their own secondhand type and small handpress, the work still spilled into the night. They worked fourteen to sixteen hours every day but the Sabbath, collecting material, answering correspondence, setting and distributing type, and getting out the paper. Garrison said later that he scarcely had time in the early months to write editorials. Sewall, May, and a few other agents worked doggedly to drum up subscribers, but the list included only a few hundred, mostly free blacks, by the end of 1831. Both cash and credit were as short as the subscription list, and Garrison and Knapp lived on little more than stale bread and water, sleeping on cots in their little office in Merchants Hall. It was a ceaseless struggle, but Garrison relished it, for at last he was fighting the good fight in his own way. Never again would his path be lit by any lights but his own.

Though its circulation was small, the *Liberator*'s impact was surprisingly large. This was because Garrison proved to be a master manipulator of the system of editorial exchange. By the end of 1831, he was exchanging papers with more than a hundred other editors, many of them in the South. Many of these papers reprinted his editorials as examples of Yankee madness, along with their own editorials denouncing them. Then Northern papers picked up and reprinted these Southern screeds—and so the ripples widened. After Nat Turner's slave insurrection in Virginia in August 1831, Southerners seethed with rage against Garrison and his little newspaper. All over the South, grand juries, town meetings, vigilance committees, even state legislatures and governors decried Garrison's incendiary doctrines and demanded the suppression of the *Liberator*. In his tiny attic office in Boston, however, Garrison was serene. For him, this was the way life was meant to be lived. "The Liberator is causing the most extraordinary movements in the slave states among the whites, as you are doubtless already aware," he wrote to a friend. "I am constantly receiving anonymous letters, filled with abominable and bloody sentiments. These trouble me less than the wind. I never was so happy and confident in my mind as at the present time."

Garrison's confidence grew from his faith in God and in the truth. From the first issue of the *Liberator*, he proposed simply to tell the truth about slavery—God's truth. "I desire to thank God," he wrote in his famous opening statement, "that he enables me to disregard 'the fear of man which bringeth a snare,' and to speak his truth in its simplicity and power." In the second issue, he reaffirmed his "unshaken reliance in the omnipotence of truth." This would be the *Liberator*'s theme for thirty-five years.

Men who declare God's truth to hard-hearted sinners are usually called prophets, and this is indeed what Garrison thought he was. His language was harsh, he often said, because truth was harsh, and people did not want to hear it. But truth would eventually have its way. After the Nat Turner revolt, Garrison wrote with Biblical sureness: "Read the account of the insurrection in Virginia, and say whether our prophesy be not fulfilled." On another occasion he said of his "hard language": "Like the hand-writing upon the wall of the palace, it has caused the knees of the American Belshazzar to smite together in terror, and filled with dismay all who follow in his train." What Garrison called "prophesy" others called "agitation." The aboli-

Front page of the first issue of Garrison's antislavery newspaper

Woodcut of a slave auction in the heart of Washington, D.C., that was added to the Liberator's *flag in April 1831*

tionists, including Garrison, aimed to keep their unpopular message constantly before the public until at last the consciences of the people were touched. By whatever name it is called, this incessant "truth telling" was central to Garrison's understanding of the abolitionist mission and of abolitionist journalism.

Agitation was not, however, the only function, or even the chief function, of reform journalism, in Garrison's view. For Garrison, the heart of journalism was discussion—the vociferous, passionate, endless discussion of the issues that interested him. Despite his own certainty that he knew the truth and despite his unrivaled ability to proclaim it stridently, Garrison was a believer throughout his career in free discussion and untrammeled inquiry. From the beginning, he held a journalist's faith in the power of free discussion, both for the pursuit of truth and for the building of a sense of common purpose and community among reformers.

Garrison's belief that free inquiry would produce truth was essentially the standard Anglo-American faith in the marketplace of ideas, which dated back at least to John Milton's *Areopagitica* (1644). In what is perhaps his fullest statement of his philosophy of free expression, Garrison clearly had Milton in mind: "My conviction of the weakness and mutability of error is such, that the free utterance of any opinions, however contrary to my own, has long since ceased to give me any uneasiness as to the final triumph of Right. My confidence in the unconquerable energy of Truth is absolute; and therefore I ask for it, what only it requires, 'a fair field and no quarters.'" Applying this doctrine to abolitionism, Garrison believed simply that slav-

ery could not stand up to free discussion. The violent reaction of the South to the *Liberator* and other abolitionist propaganda was ample proof of this. Censorship was the South's only possible defense, for "the slave-system cannot bear investigation." Very quickly, free expression became a cause closely associated with abolitionism. Garrison made the connection simply and confidently: "Slavery and freedom of the press cannot exist together."

But Garrison had another reason for favoring open discussion and free inquiry. For Garrison, discussion was the soul of journalism. Though the *Liberator* is usually remembered for the vividness of its invective, perhaps a more striking characteristic was its devotion to reader correspondence and to the interchange of information and opinions on abolition and all the other reform questions that the paper pursued. The *Liberator* was never merely a propaganda sheet for Garrison's favorite causes; it was a forum open to the scattered individuals who viewed themselves as a community of reformers. It was a gathering together of the faithful—a kind of church service. It was, as Garrison said in his last editorial in 1865, the group's "weekly method of communicating with each other."

This aspect of the *Liberator* did not change much in its thirty-five-year run. The paper remained always the editor's personal organ, yet it also remained an open forum for reader correspondence and involvement. At his retirement in 1865, Garrison restated his belief in this dual editorial principle. "I have never consulted either the subscription list of the paper or public sentiment in printing, or omitting to print, any article touching any matter whatever." Yet he also declared that

Boston, Sept. 8, 1831.

Dear Sir:

I labor under very signal obligations to you for your disclosures, relative to my personal safety. These do not move me from my purpose the breadth of a hair. Desperate wretches exist at the south, no doubt, who would assassinate me for a sixpence. Still, I was aware of this peril when I began my advocacy of African rights. Slaveholders deem me their enemy; but my aim is simply to benefit and save them, and not to injure them. I value their bodies and souls at a high price, though I abominate their crimes. Moreover, I do not justify the slaves in their rebellion: yet I do not condemn them, and applaud similar conduct in white men. I deny the right of any people to fight for liberty, and so far am a Quaker in principle. Of all men living, however, our slaves have the best reason to assert their rights by violent measures, inasmuch as they are more oppressed than others.

My duty is plain — my path without embarrassment. I shall still continue to expose the criminality and danger of slavery, be the consequences what they may to myself. I hold my life at a cheap rate: I know it is in imminent danger: but if the assassin take it away, the Lord will raise up another and better advocate in my stead.

Again thanking you for your friendly letter, I remain, in haste,

Yours, in the best of bonds,

To La Roy Sunderland Wm Lloyd Garrison.

Letter from Garrison to fellow abolitionist La Roy Sunderland, thanking Sunderland for warning him that his life was in danger because it was believed that Garrison "had contributed in no small degree" to the Nat Turner slave rebellion in August 1831. Garrison expresses his determination to continue his abolitionist activities in spite of such threats (Courtesy of Boston Public Library).

"no journal . . . has granted such freedom in its columns to its opponents; none has so scrupulously and uniformly presented all sides of every question discussed in its pages."

Though no mortal could have been so magnanimous as Garrison remembered he was, the pages of the *Liberator*, week after week and year after year, do bear witness to the general accuracy of Garrison's claim. Of course, Garrison never held back his own views. "I will not retreat a single inch," he said in his famous opening statement; and he did not. But Garrison also fulfilled his promise to keep the *Liberator*'s columns open for free discussion. The "Communications" department was always a centerpiece of the paper, often taking all of page one and more of the four-page sheet. Indeed, in the paper's first year Garrison sometimes complained that "to accommodate our numerous correspondents we are again necessitated to exclude our own communications to the public." When tactical debates arose among abolitionists, Garrison fought ruthlessly for his own position; but he gave space to all. At such times, the *Liberator* was practically given over to publication of letters, articles, speeches, statements, and rebuttals from all points of view.

The *Liberator* carried material from true enemies as well as from opponents from within the movement. Garrison delighted in reprinting the abuse that the mainstream newspapers, from North as well as South, poured upon him and the antislavery movement. In 1834 he even started a new department of the paper called "Refuge of Oppression" to highlight these attacks and denunciations.

Of course, not all the material in the *Liberator* was controversial. From the first, the paper performed the more mundane organizational function of publicizing meetings and activities and publishing minutes and convention proceedings. The *Liberator* also carried informational, inspirational, and purely entertaining news and features. Its regular departments included children's stories, poetry, ladies' features, marriage and death notices, foreign and domestic news briefs, miscellaneous jokes and "brights," and even a few advertisements. It was, in a very real sense, a community newspaper, though its community was widely scattered. When the *Liberator* was discontinued in 1865, one long-time reader confessed to "a feeling of isolation and loneliness" at the loss of this weekly "communion with my fellow beings."

For Garrison-the-journalist as well as for Garrison-the-reformer truth and freedom were inti-mately intertwined. They were, in effect, one. The more he contemplated the physical slavery of American blacks, the more he came to abhor the moral and social slavery of all men and women. Chattel slavery became for him a compelling and universal metaphor. Individual freedom of thought and conscience, free discussion and free inquiry—what he liked to call "universal emancipation"—became his goal. For Garrison, universal emancipation was a deeply religious doctrine, as well as an intensely individualistic one. It was a radical extrapolation of the religious ideology of the founders of New England, who had sought no governor but the governor of the universe. Only when the individual is perfectly free could he be free to serve God perfectly. The mission of the *Liberator*, therefore, was the twofold mission of strident agitation and free discussion—for if to tell the truth was the virtue of the reformer, to be free was the virtue of the press.

Garrison's views on the function of reform journalism guided his approach to reform organization as he began to work in the early 1830s to build an abolitionist movement in America. Garrison was only one of several rising abolitionist spokesmen around the country in 1831, but because of the national furor over the *Liberator*, he was perhaps the most notorious; and the small group of New England reformers interested in the abolition of slavery were drawn to him. In early January 1832, after several months of debate, twelve antislavery men, including Garrison, founded the New England Anti-Slavery Society, an association based upon the two principles that slavery is a sin and that emancipation should be immediate. The number twelve was significant, they believed, because it symbolized the twelve disciples of Christ. For Garrison, this was to be a special kind of association. It was to be not merely a social or political organization but a kind of apostolic church.

The method of this association would be the same as the method of the *Liberator*: moral suasion through agitation and discussion. Agitation was mainly in the form of endless oratory, though the society did print and distribute tracts and pamphlets, including Garrison's *Thoughts on African Colonization* (1832), which opposed the idea of relocating freed slaves in Africa. The bulk of the agitation work was conducted by a handful of traveling agents who spoke in towns and villages across New England. In the beginning, Garrison and his disciples hoped to work through the churches. When that failed, they relied upon the give-and-take of face-to-face encounters with small groups of potential converts. The annual conventions of the society—called the Massachusetts Anti-Slavery Society after 1835—were extremely important to the work of building an abolitionist community. These gatherings were more like revivals than business meetings. The aim was never to plan detailed strategies and tactics; the conventions were forums for open discussion—religious meetings where the faithful gathered together to bear witness against slavery. The annual treks to Boston were pilgrimages; the pilgrims returned to their homes spiritually refreshed and reassured of their place in a communion of saints.

In May 1833 Garrison traveled to England to seek funds for a manual training school for black youths in America. He also hoped to gain the support of English abolitionists for his crusade against the ideas of gradual emancipation and colonization. While he raised no money for the school, he counted the trip a great success in building solidarity with the English antislavery movement on the principle of immediate emancipation. It was a personal triumph as well, for Garrison was accepted in England as something he was never to be in the United States: *the* leader of American abolitionism.

Garrison arrived back in New York in September just in time to participate in the founding of the New York Anti-Slavery Society. But he was not the dominant force in American abolitionism that his English friends supposed that he was, particularly outside New England. When the American Anti-Slavery Society, the first national organization devoted to immediate emancipation, was founded in December 1833, Garrison's role was more spiritual than organizational. He was not a major officer or organizer. (He was made secretary for foreign correspondence, but he resigned even this minor position within a month.) The New York and Western abolitionists distrusted his radicalism and disapproved of the harshness of his language in the *Liberator*. But Garrison's presence was felt. Most notably, he was the author of the society's "Declaration of Sentiments," which committed the group to the immediate abolition of slavery as a moral crusade and to the methods of moral suasion through agitation and discussion.

By 1835 the moral crusade of the immediate abolitionists had produced a violent backlash in both the South and the North. A mob in Charleston burned the New York mails, which were filled with antislavery propaganda published by the American Anti-Slavery Society. Southern politicians called for the extradition of Garrison, Arthur Tappan, and others to stand trial in the South for their attempts to incite slave rebellion. In the North, antislavery meetings were disrupted, and abolitionist leaders were threatened with death. In Boston on 21 October 1835, a mob broke up a meeting of the Boston Female Anti-Slavery Society and captured Garrison, who was a featured speaker. The mob led him through the streets with a rope around his waist, until Mayor Theodore Lyman intervened to save him. Garrison spent the night in jail in protective custody; and, as during his stay in the Baltimore jail in 1830, he gloried in his martyrdom.

The unity of American abolitionism in the mid-1830s was not long-lived. Garrison and his friends, following the logic of their belief in perfectionism and universal emancipation, moved gradually toward more radical and more comprehensive stands on social reform. By the late 1830s, Garrison had become an advocate of "nonresistance"—a kind of Christian anarchism which renounced any sort of coercive restraint on human freedom, including government itself. Meanwhile, the majority of American abolitionists were moving away from moral perfectionism and toward the moral relativism of practical politics and organizational work. This ideological difference was barely a crack in the movement when the American Anti-Slavery Society was formed in 1833; it grew into a chasm by 1840, splitting the movement, irreparably, into warring factions.

In May 1840 Garrison and his radical supporters from New England packed the annual convention of the American Anti-Slavery Society and gained control of the organization. The more moderate abolitionists withdrew to form the rival American and Foreign Anti-Slavery Society, to work in the growing number of state and local societies, or to help build the fledgling Liberty party. There was no united abolitionist movement after 1840. Different individuals and groups worked in different ways. At one extreme, the majority antislavery sentiment, which was not necessarily abolitionist at all, found expression in the Liberty party, the Free Soil party, and finally the Republican party. At the other extreme were the Garrisonians, who declined to compromise.

Garrison's uncompromising spirit had everything to do with his understanding of the role of the radical—and of the journalist—in society. He and his followers believed that their work was to hold forth the truth for all to see, however repugnant it might be to majority opinion. Eventually, public opinion would bend to reason. Given that great transformation in public opinion, all else would follow; without that transformation, all else would fail. The Garrisonians were not blind to practical reality. They argued, rather, that compromise would be as impractical as it would be immoral, for the movement's strength grew from its role as a beacon. People may not follow immediately or far, but they must never be allowed to forget the direction they should go. For this reason, Garrison sometimes applauded practical political work—such as the organization of the Free Soil party in 1848—even though he believed that *for him* participation in politics would be sin and a mistake. It was in precisely this way, for example, that Garrison explained the troublesome slogan "immediate emancipation": "We have never said that slavery would be overthrown by a single blow; that it ought to be, we shall always contend."

Garrison's embrace of nonresistance was probably the issue that most separated the Garrisonians from the mainstream of political abolitionism after 1840. Garrison decried the legitimacy of all human government or any other social arrangement based upon force or violence. He opposed government even to the point of declining to vote; he also became an ardent critic of organized churches and clergy. He denounced capital punishment and imprisonment for debt. He promoted the cause of international peace, encouraged utopian community ventures, and championed the individual rights of women as well as of slaves and free blacks. For example, he refused to participate in the World's Anti-Slavery Convention in London in June 1840 because women were excluded.

His opponents within the abolitionist movement charged that these causes were extraneous to the problem of freeing the slaves. Garrison replied that slavery was merely the most conspicuous manifestation of the degradation of freedom in America.

These were the themes that Garrison and the *Liberator* continued to pound out, without much change, in the 1840s and 1850s. The most important refinement of his no-government sentiment was his argument after 1842 that the U.S. Constitution was a proslavery compact—"a covenant with death and an agreement with Hell." He denounced Daniel Webster and the Compromise of 1850, and again the annual meeting of the Anti-Slavery Society (on 7 May 1850) was disrupted by an angry mob. He called on the North to secede from the union, and on 4 July 1854, in one of the most dramatic gestures of his career, he publicly burned a copy of the Constitution during a speech in Fra-

mingham, Massachusetts. For twenty years before the Civil War the *Liberator* propounded the disunionist doctrine; every issue carried a banner on page one that proclaimed: "No Union with Slaveholders."

To his opponents, Garrison was simply a reckless madman. Even some of his closest friends and associates found him increasingly difficult as the years passed by. He quarreled over political action with Frederick Douglass, the famous black abolitionist; and for ten years Garrison refused to appear on the same platform with his erstwhile colleague and friend. He denounced former associates as malignant traitors. He abandoned those who lacked the fortitude to stand firm in the place that he and God had demarcated. Yet despite his egotism and personal abrasiveness in public, Garrison remained in private the gentlest and sweetest of men. His small circle of close friends in the New England antislavery movement was more like a family than an organization, and he came to be called, with great affection, "Father Garrison." His marriage to Helen Benson in 1834 was a good one, though the early years were somewhat strained. As the decades passed, Garrison proved to be an ador-

Garrison's wife, Helen Benson Garrison, in about 1853

ing husband and a doting father. Indeed, despite his public reputation for invective, his children said that they never heard him utter a harsh word at home.

For Garrison, the Civil War was the culmination of his life's work, yet it presented him—as a pacifist as well as an abolitionist—with a fundamental crisis of principle. That Garrison would decide in favor of war and freedom, rather than peace and slavery, was presaged rather clearly by his response to John Brown's raid on the Harpers Ferry armory in 1859. Garrison opposed violence, but he believed that if anyone ever had just cause for violence it was the Southern slave. Brown's action was purely an act of self-defense against the institutionalized violence of the slavocracy. "Was John Brown justified in his attempt?," Garrison asked. "Yes, if Washington was in his. . . . I am trying him by the American standard." Garrison argued that it would be monstrous for the doctrine of nonresistance to justify disarming the oppressed but not the oppressor. Therefore, he declared, "as a peace man—an 'ultra' peace man—I am prepared to say, 'Success to every slave insurrection at the South, and in every slave country.' "

In fact, Garrison's tendency to affirm peace and pacifism as an ideal while condoning violence in practice can be traced throughout his career. It is consistent with his general view of the radical journalist, who remains an uncompromising spokesman for what *ought* to be, while not necessarily opposing the more practical fruits of his agitation. Garrison had approved the use of arms for self-defense by the Mexicans against U.S. aggression in 1846. He had praised the bravery of the abolitionist martyr Elijah Lovejoy, who took up arms to defend his printing press in Illinois in 1837. And in terms very similar to his brief for John Brown nearly three decades later, he had defended the slaves who joined Nat Turner in 1831: "In all that we have written, is there aught to justify the excesses of the slaves? No. Nevertheless, they deserve no more censure than the Greeks in destroying the Turks, or the Poles in exterminating the Russians, or our fathers in slaughtering the British. Dreadful, indeed, is the standard erected by worldly patriotism!" Thus, when the Civil War began, Garrison welcomed it as the final retribution of a just God upon American slavery.

After two decades of denouncing the Constitution and promoting Christian anarchism, the *Liberator* would seem an unlikely candidate to become a champion of Abraham Lincoln and the war policies of the Lincoln administration. But that is precisely what happened, especially after Lincoln's preliminary emancipation proclamation of September 1862. Even before the proclamation, Garrison was ebullient. "What have we to rejoice over?," he asked. "Why, I say, the war! 'What! this fratricidal war? What! this civil war? What! this treasonable dismemberment of the Union?' Yes, thank God for it all!—for it indicates the waning power of slavery and the irresistible growth of freedom, and that the day of Northern submission is past." Garrison was persuaded that this was Armageddon and that his work, therefore, was done.

In 1865 Garrison stepped down as president of the American Anti-Slavery Society, a post he had held regularly since the factional split in 1840. At the annual convention he moved that the organization be dissolved, for slavery was dead. His motion was defeated. A majority of the delegates sided with Wendell Phillips, Garrison's old friend who had come to be his chief opponent within the organization during the Civil War. Phillips believed that the end of slavery was just the first step in securing genuine civil equality for the freed slaves. Phillips and other radicals within the society feared that the South, though defeated, was unrepentant, and that only black suffrage and land redistribution would guarantee that de facto slavery would not be reimposed. Garrison disagreed. He argued that the imposition by force of civil rights and economic status would be counterproductive in the long run: "Coercion would gain nothing. In other words . . . universal suffrage will be hard to win and to hold without a general preparation of feeling and sentiment. But it will come . . . yet only by a struggle *on the part of the disfranchised*, and a growing conviction of its justice 'in the good time coming.' "

In other words, after his brief side trip into support of government suppression of a secessionist insurrection, Garrison returned to his lifelong commitment to moral suasion. The problem of the freed slaves would not be solved by force or by Constitutional amendment. The problem lay in the hearts and minds of the people. In the years after the Civil War, though he was officially retired from active duty in the abolitionist army, Garrison remained devoted to the cause of the freed slaves, especially to education and to the growth and integration of public schools. This he believed to be fundamental for the kind of grass roots social change that would be lasting and sure—change imposed not by force but by the enlightened consciences of individual men and women.

In the fourteen years after the end of the Civil War, Garrison became primarily a private person, though he did make one last pilgrimage to England and he continued to contribute articles from time to time to the *Independent* in New York. Mainly, however, Garrison passed the years tending to his wife, who had become an invalid in 1863 and died in 1876, and observing with patriarchal pleasure the marriages of children and the arrivals of grandchildren. (His daughter Helen, who married Henry Villard in 1865, was the mother of Oswald Garrison Villard, editor of the *Nation* magazine and the *New York Evening Post* for many years after 1900.)

With the suspension of the *Liberator* and his separation from Phillips and his colleagues in the American Anti-Slavery Society in 1865, Garrison's career was over. But though the 1870s was a different and less simple age than the one he knew, he continued to take an interest in a variety of reform movements, ranging from prohibition to civil rights for American Indians. Perhaps his last reform crusade was against the Chinese Exclusion Bill. In a letter to the *New York Tribune* written shortly before his death he reaffirmed the simple truths of human equality that he had been preaching since his conscience was first stirred in the 1820s: "The Chinese are our fellow-men, and are entitled to every consideration that our common humanity may justly claim. . . . Such of them as are seeking to better their condition, being among the poorer classes, by coming to these shores, we should receive with hospitality and kindness. . . . It is for them to determine what they shall eat, what they shall drink, and wherewithal they shall be clothed; to adhere to their own customs and follow their own tastes as they shall choose; to make their contracts and maintain their own rights; to worship God according to the dictates of their own consciences, or their idea of religious duty. . . . This is not a personal controversy . . . but a plea for human brotherhood."

One of Garrison's last trips before he died was to Newburyport in October 1878 to visit the office of the *Herald*, where he had begun his career in journalism exactly sixty years before. He set three of his own sonnets into type, with the same speed and skill he had so admired in the compositors he had watched that first day so long ago. The next day in Boston he spoke to the Franklin Club of New England, an association of printers. He talked of his boyhood days as an apprentice on the *Herald* and of the importance of the press in a free society. He told his fellow printers what he hoped they already knew: "If there is anything in my career that is suggestive, that may be of use to those who may hereafter come into conflict with great and

colossal wrong, it will be that by not compromising with the wrong, by speaking the truth and applying it boldly to the conscience of the people, there is no need of despairing of the final result. . . . I need not say . . . how mighty an instrumentality the press is in regard to the progress of mankind. Ours is 'the art preservative of all arts,' and it stands at the head of all. Every craft is honorable if it is useful, but the printing craft is that which takes hold of the mind and intellect and soul." Garrison died the following spring.

Throughout his life, Garrison's philosophy of journalism was as central as his perfectionism to his understanding of social reform. Both led him into a kind of love-hate relationship with public opinion. One of his favorite quotes in his early career was a line from Cicero that he used as the motto of the *Journal of the Times:* "Reason shall prevail with us more than Popular Opinion." Throughout his long career on the *Liberator* he seemed to glory in public odium. When he retired he counted the paper's small subscription list as a badge of honor. Yet he also believed that reason and popular opinion could be brought together through moral suasion and the power of the press. "We expect to conquer through the majesty of public opinion," he wrote in 1831. "Appalling as is the evil of slavery, the press is able to cope with it; and without the agency of the press, no impression can be made, no plan perfected, no victory achieved."

In short, Garrison idealized journalism as he did no other human institution. To him, journalism was the animator of social life, for it served the two great functions of social reform: agitation and discussion. Agitation—the constant reiteration of "the truth"—is the function most often associated with Garrison and the *Liberator*. But agitation was not all that Garrison brought to abolitionist journalism. Discussion—free inquiry among the members of a community of readers—seems to have been the chief work of the *Liberator* throughout its thirty-five-year life. Indeed, it might be argued that for Garrison free discussion was a substitute for government—a kind of democracy without coercion. For most of his life, Garrison opposed government in any form, including democracy, because all human governments rest upon coercion and power. But Garrison did believe in public sentiment, in moral suasion, and in voluntary association as legitimate methods for the building of moral consensus in a society of free men and women. And he believed that the press—as agitator and as forum for free discussion—could and should be the rock upon which such a free society could be built. If, for Garrison, agitation and discussion were the essence of journalism, journalism was the essence of a perfect democracy.

Letters:

The Letters of William Lloyd Garrison, edited by Walter M. Merrill and Louis Ruchames, 6 volumes (Cambridge: Harvard University Press, 1971-1981).

Biographies:

Oliver Johnson, *William Lloyd Garrison and His Times* (Boston: B. B. Russell, 1880);

Wendell Phillips Garrison and Francis Jackson Garrison, *William Lloyd Garrison, 1805-1879: The Story of his Life Told by His Children,* 4 volumes (New York: Century, 1885-1889);

Archibald H. Grimke, *William Lloyd Garrison, the Abolitionist* (New York: Funk & Wagnalls, 1891);

John Jay Chapman, *William Lloyd Garrison* (New York: Moffatt, Yard, 1913);

Ralph Korngold, *Two Friends of Man: The Story of William Lloyd Garrison and Wendell Phillips* (Boston: Little, Brown, 1950);

Russel B. Nye, *William Lloyd Garrison and the Humanitarian Reformers* (Boston: Little, Brown, 1955);

Walter M. Merrill, *Against Wind and Tide: A Biography of Wm. Lloyd Garrison* (Cambridge: Harvard University Press, 1963);

John L. Thomas, *The Liberator: William Lloyd Garrison, a Biography* (Boston: Little, Brown, 1963).

References:

Gilbert H. Barnes, *The Antislavery Impulse, 1830-1844* (New York: D. Appleton-Century, 1933);

Merton L. Dillon, "The Abolitionists: A Decade of Historiography, 1959-1969," *Journal of Southern History,* 26 (November 1969): 500-522;

Dillon, *The Abolitionists: The Growth of a Dissenting Minority* (New York: Norton, 1979);

Martin Duberman, ed., *The Antislavery Vanguard: New Essays on the Abolitionists* (Princeton: Princeton University Press, 1965);

Dwight L. Dumond, *Antislavery: The Crusade for Freedom* (Ann Arbor: University of Michigan Press, 1961), pp. 166-174;

Dumond, *Bibliography of Antislavery in America* (Ann Arbor: University of Michigan Press, 1964), p. 57;

Louis Filler, *The Crusade Against Slavery, 1830-1860* (New York: Harper, 1960);

Lawrence J. Friedman, *Gregarious Saints: Self and Community in American Abolitionism, 1830-1870* (Cambridge: Cambridge University Press, 1982), pp. 43-67;

Friedman, " 'Historical Topics Sometimes Run Dry': The State of Abolitionist Studies," *Historian,* 43 (February 1981): 177-194;

Aileen S. Kraditor, *Means and Ends in American Abolitionism: Garrison and His Critics on Strategy and Tactics, 1834-1850* (New York: Pantheon Books, 1969);

Jane H. Pease and William H. Pease, *Bound with Them in Chains: A Biographical History of the Antislavery Movement* (Westport, Conn.: Greenwood Press, 1972);

Lewis Perry, *Radical Abolitionism: Anarchy and the Government of God in Antislavery Thought* (Ithaca, N.Y.: Cornell University Press, 1973);

Perry and Michael Fellman, eds., *Antislavery Reconsidered: New Perspectives on the Abolitionists* (Baton Rouge: Louisiana State University Press, 1979);

Gerald Sorin, *Abolitionism: A New Perspective* (New York: Praeger, 1972);

James Brewer Stewart, *Holy Warriors: The Abolitionists and American Slavery* (New York: Hill & Wang, 1976);

Oswald Garrison Villard, "William Lloyd Garrison, Editor; 'The Good Old Days,' " in his *Some Newspapers and Newspaper-Men* (New York: Knopf, 1923), pp. 302-315;

Ronald G. Walters, *The Antislavery Appeal: American Abolitionism after 1830* (Baltimore: Johns Hopkins University Press, 1976).

Papers:

The principal collections of William Lloyd Garrison's papers are at Boston Public Library, Smith College, and Houghton Library, Harvard University.

William Goddard

(20 October 1740-23 December 1817)

Maurine H. Beasley
University of Maryland

MAJOR POSITIONS HELD: Publisher, *Providence (R.I.) Gazette and Country Journal* (1762-1766), *Pennsylvania Chronicle and Universal Advertiser Journal* (Philadelphia) (1767-1774), *Maryland Journal; and the Baltimore Advertiser* (Baltimore) (1773-1775, 1784-1793).

BOOKS: *The Partnership: or the History of the Rise and Progress of the Pennsylvania Chronicle, &c.* (Philadelphia: Printed by William Goddard, 1770);

Andrew Marvell's Second Address to the Inhabitants of Philadelphia (Philadelphia: Printed by William Goddard, 1773);

The Prowess of the Whig Club, and the Manœuvres of Legion (Baltimore: Printed for the author, 1777).

The printing and publishing careers of the three Goddards are so intertwined that they are best considered as a family unit. Although the attention of historians has been paid primarily to the achievements of William Goddard, recognition is also due his mother, Sarah, and his sister, Mary Katherine. Each woman achieved distinction as a printer-publisher in her own right and made it possible for William to carry on his business ventures.

Sarah and Mary Katherine Goddard represented a relatively large class of colonial Americans: women engaged in male occupations either to support themselves or to assist husbands or male relatives. Beset by a perpetual labor shortage, the colonies offered opportunities for women to run taverns, own ships, and act as blacksmiths, hunters, lawyers, shoemakers, butchers, and ferrymen. Printing and publishing were particularly attractive to women since they were carried on in shops generally attached to printers' homes. In these family enterprises, girls as well as boys learned to set type and to take part in the operations.

At least seventeen women, including the Goddards, are known to have worked as printers in colonial America, and all but one of these published a newspaper. The Goddards were unique, however, because, unlike the others, they were not widows of printers who took over their husbands' businesses. Sarah and Mary Katherine Goddard's initial motivation apparently stemmed from a desire to help William Goddard—although Mary Katherine, who never married, earned her own livelihood for decades through her business and craft skills.

Sarah Updike Goddard was the widow of a well-to-do physician when she first went into the printing business. Although the exact date of her birth is unknown, she is believed to have been born about 1700 at Cocumscussuc, Rhode Island, one of six children of Lodowick and Abigail Newton Updike, who were cousins. On both sides of the family she descended from wealthy early settlers: her mother's grandfather, Richard Smith, had purchased 30,000 acres from the Narragansett Indians; and her father's father, Gysbert Opdyck, had bought what later was named Coney Island. Her only brother, Daniel, became attorney general of the colony of Rhode Island.

The family's wealth and social position enabled Sarah Updike to gain a superior education for a woman of her day. A French tutor employed in the household taught her and her four sisters French and Latin; but only their brother studied Greek, since this was considered unsuitable for females. On 11 December 1735 she was married to Dr. Giles Goddard of Groton, Connecticut, and moved with him to New London, Connecticut, where he practiced medicine and was postmaster. The couple had four children, but only Mary Katherine and William survived to adulthood. They presumably were educated mainly by their mother, although William is thought to also have attended a local school, where he read Latin works. When Dr. Goddard died in 1757, his widow was left in comfortable circumstances.

Two years before the doctor's death, William's future career had been mapped out. He had been sent to serve as a printer's apprentice in the shop of James Parker, postmaster and printer in New

Haven. Parker, whose typography and presswork were considered among the best in the colonies, had as his silent partner Benjamin Franklin. The New Haven shop published the *Connecticut Gazette* and was managed by John Holt, later to become a leading anti-British radical. The fifteen-year-old Goddard must have made a good impression: a few months after his arrival he was dispatched on a trip through Connecticut to estimate the expenses of post offices established to handle mail for colonial forces during the French and Indian Wars.

In 1758 Parker sent Goddard to New York, where Parker also ran a larger shop that published the *New-York Weekly Post-Boy*. Here Goddard gained experience in printing almanacs and books and was exposed to the operation of the entire colonial postal system, of which Parker was comptroller under the British. After his apprenticeship ended on his twenty-first birthday in October 1761, Goddard became a journeyman printer in New York for Samuel Farley, who started the *American Chronicle* newspaper. After the Farley shop was almost destroyed by fire in July 1762, the newspaper ceased publication and Goddard moved to Providence, Rhode Island.

It was unusual for a young printer to go into business for himself without extensive experience as a journeyman, but Goddard did so. He was backed by his mother, who not only loaned him £300 with which to start but also came to Providence with Mary Katherine to assist him. Her affluence indicates that she worked for reasons other than necessity. Undoubtedly Providence appealed to the family for social, as well as commercial, reasons. Sarah Goddard had relatives there who were members of leading families and the Goddards could look forward to a pleasant reception. As the first printer in Providence, Goddard was welcomed by the city fathers, who wanted the prestige and political power of their own press to help Providence rival the neighboring city of Newport.

The first issue of the *Providence Gazette and Country Journal* appeared on 20 October 1762, containing Goddard's pledge to satisfy his readers' zest for news of the French and Indian Wars by "extensive correspondence" from abroad as well as from "settlements on this continent." Like all colonial editors, Goddard obtained his "correspondence" by clipping items from other publications. In the second issue of the weekly paper appeared an anonymous letter, possibly written by Goddard, extolling the virtues of printing, calling it "the greatest means of promoting learning that was ever invented." This indicated Goddard's intense pride

in his craft, a pride he always retained. Early issues also showed his interest in printing literary works—pirated from other publications, as was customary—and contributions from readers.

Apart from the newspaper, Goddard moved into other activities typical of colonial printers. His shop sold books and stationery, particularly the blank legal forms that provided the backbone of the early printer's trade. He published almanacs, which were best-selling items of the period; he also published a variety of pamphlets, including in 1764 one of the first against the Stamp Act, which taxed printing. Concerned like many printers over access to paper supplies, Goddard became a partner in the establishment of a paper mill. In 1764 he was named postmaster.

Little is known of the activities of Sarah and Mary Katherine Goddard during this period in Providence, although both must have been busy learning the printing and publishing business. Evidence of an active social life exists in the form of a broadside printed by William Goddard inviting ladies of the town to a "petticoat frisk" at the home of Mrs. Goddard.

In spite of the industriousness of the family, financial difficulties occurred. Goddard tried vigorously but was unable to take the colony's public printing business away from Ann Franklin—widow of Benjamin Franklin's brother James—and Samuel Hall of Newport. Naturally a contentious man, Goddard feuded with his Newport competitors, who defended the Stamp Act. Finally, on 4 May 1765, Goddard, unable to attract enough subscribers to break even, suspended publication of the *Providence Gazette*. Going to New York, he became a silent partner in the printing shop of his old employer Holt.

Goddard, however, returned to Providence frequently. He published an extra (or as he called it, "extraordinary") issue of the *Gazette* on 24 August 1765 against the Stamp Act. A month later, on 21 September, he anonymously printed, on the press of his former master Parker in Woodbridge, New Jersey, the *Constitutional Courant*, a propaganda broadside attacking the act; it created a sensation when it reached New York.

Meanwhile, the Goddard print shop in Providence continued to operate under the direction of Sarah Goddard. The "extraordinary" against the Stamp Act listed "S. and W. Goddard" as its printers and the firm turned out job printing in 1765 under the imprint "Printed by Sarah and William Goddard." Goddard returned to Providence in March 1766 to print one more issue of the *Gazette*

[APRIL, MDCCLXIII.]

Providence Gazette;
AND COUNTRY JOURNAL.

Containing the freshest Advices, *both Foreign and Domestic.*

THE [NUMB. 28.]

[Vol I.]

SATURDAY, APRIL 30, 1763.

Front page of Goddard's Providence (R.I.) newspaper, started with financial backing from his mother

against the Stamp Act, in which Sarah Goddard inserted a notice appealing for subscribers so that the paper could resume regular publication.

Unhappy with his New York undertaking, William moved to Philadelphia, leaving his mother to reorganize the Providence operation as "Sarah Goddard and Company." The company consisted of Mary Katherine; Samuel Inslee, a young New York printer; and a few apprentices. The firm continued as "Sarah Goddard and Company" from 9 August until 6 December 1766, when the imprint was changed to "Printed (in the absence of William Goddard) by Sarah Goddard and Company."

Taking over the post office and bookstore as well as doing job printing, Sarah Goddard proved herself a capable manager and successfully revived the *Gazette* on 9 August 1766. She brought the paper out each Saturday, advertising the products of her bookstore and press. Her most ambitious printing venture that year consisted of a 204-page book representing the first American publication of the letters of Lady Mary Wortley Montagu, a famous British intellectual. This publication indicates that she must have been sympathetic with efforts to elevate the status of women.

It was not easy for Sarah Goddard, then in her sixties, to publish a newspaper and run a financially troubled business. She discovered that the popular *New-England Almanack* by Benjamin West, which the Goddards were accustomed to issuing, was being sold by a Boston firm; so she resourcefully added a woodcut of the four seasons to her version of West's work and advertised it as the "true and original *New England Almanack*." Like her son, she pleaded in the *Gazette* columns for subscribers and advertisers to pay their bills, although the pleas decreased as the paper became more profitable. She also encountered labor problems, particularly after Inslee left the shop in January 1767 to take over Parker's New York paper. Eventually she took on a partner, John Carter, who joined the operation in September 1767. Subsequently the imprint became "Sarah Goddard and John Carter."

Since the Stamp Act had been repealed, the colonies were relatively calm politically during the first year that Sarah ran the *Gazette*. The columns were less passionate than before and essays, poems, translations, and other cultural material appeared. When news of the proposed Townshend Acts, levying new taxes on imports, reached Providence in the summer of 1767, however, the *Gazette* criticized them soundly. Articles attacking British policies were reprinted from Boston Patriot newspapers.

From December 1767 to March 1768, the *Ga-*

zette reprinted the "Letters from a Farmer in Pennsylvania" by John Dickinson, a lawyer. The letters had first been published in the *Pennsylvania Chronicle,* William Goddard's new newspaper in Philadelphia. The influential letters, giving a Whig view of the colonial disagreements with England, argued against taxation without representation and for a boycott of English goods. An indication of Sarah Goddard's own Whig politics comes from advice she gave her son concerning the letters. She wrote him not to allow opponents of the "Farmer" space in the *Chronicle:* "It is no small concern to me . . . to see so many abusive pieces in the *Chronicle* against the Farmer, who deserves so well of his country. Do not, I beseech you, sully all the honour you have acquired by uniting with enemies of your country. . . ."

William Goddard had begun the *Pennsylvania Chronicle and Universal Advertiser* on 26 January 1767 as the voice of the Whig party against the proprietors of the colony of Pennsylvania. His partners were Joseph Galloway and Thomas Wharton, but the trio failed to get along, leaving Goddard in a continual state of agitation. In addition to fighting privately with Galloway and Wharton, Goddard battled in print with a rival Philadelphia printer, William Bradford, in a controversy over political issues which degenerated into personal insults. In Providence, his mother, who used numerous articles from the *Chronicle,* wrote Goddard a rebuke shortly after the paper began, commenting: "I attempt to write, but [am] hardly able, for the great concern and anxious fears the sight of your late *Chronicles* gave me, to find you involved deeper and deeper in an unhappy uncomfortable situation. In your calm hours of reflecting you must see the impropriety of publishing such pieces. . . ."

William Goddard's partners persuaded him to liquidate his Providence business so that he could invest more heavily in the Philadelphia one. As part of the arrangement, they insisted that he bring his mother and sister to Philadelphia, where they promised to provide a house for the family. Sarah, who had taken over a money-losing business and made it pay, was reluctant to leave Providence; but finally, as her son expressed it, "from motives of maternal tenderness, [she] consented to leave an easy agreeable situation, and a multitude of amiable friends, and my sister agreed to accompany her." The Providence business was sold to Carter in November 1768, and the mother and daughter left for Philadelphia.

Goddard's account of the move appeared in his scathing 1770 publication *The Partnership: or the*

Front page of Goddard's Pennsylvania Chronicle, *featuring an installment of John Dickinson's anti-British "Letters from a Farmer in Pennsylvania"*

History of the Rise and Progress of the Pennsylvania Chronicle, &c. He charged that the partners failed to find a "genteel house" for the family and that they objected when he gave his mother a press so that she could print "blanks and small work" at home. So Sarah Goddard went to work in the shop along with Mary Katherine. Sarah arranged to provide William with funds in return for a one-half interest in the print shop, which she ran while he made frequent trips to collect overdue debts.

In 1769 Galloway and Wharton sold their shares of the business to Robert Towne, a journeyman printer without funds of his own, who acted as their puppet. While William Goddard continued to travel, attempting to raise money to get out of the partnership, Sarah and Mary Katherine produced the newspaper and watched out for his interests. In late December 1769 Sarah wrote William that the *Chronicle* "daily has new subscribers. . . . I shall exert myself to preserve its credit. . . . I daily mourn for your hard fate, and while I live, which cannot be long, I shall be striving to promote your interest here. . . ." A day after receiving the letter Goddard learned that his mother had died in Philadelphia on 5 January 1770.

A lengthy obituary in the *New-York Gazette* praised her for running the Providence paper, noting that "the credit of the paper was greatly promoted by her virtue, ingenuity and abilities." But the writer gave more recognition to her "uncommon attainments in literature," her "easy agreeable cheerfulness and affability," and her "sensible and edifying conversation."

After Sarah's death, Towne attempted to drive Goddard out of business; but Goddard refused to be intimidated. He made the *Chronicle* one of the most successful colonial newspapers in terms of circulation, which reached 2,500 in 1770. His book *The Partnership* provided gossipy details of his accusations against Galloway and Wharton, two of the city's most respectable figures, who set out to retaliate. Due to charges brought by Galloway, Goddard was put in jail for debt in September 1771, remaining about three weeks while his sister published the *Chronicle*. Galloway then brought charges of blackmail against Goddard, which were later dropped. But still the printer refused to silence his attacks on Galloway during Galloway's campaign for reelection to the state assembly. Despite Goddard's quarrelsome nature, he merits respect because he upheld the rights to a free press and to criticism of public officials, even when he was confronted with financial disaster.

With his Philadelphia business floundering,

Goddard decided to start afresh in Baltimore. In the spring of 1773 he purchased the printing equipment of Nicholas Hasselbach, Baltimore's first printer, who had died a few years before. Leaving his sister to run the Philadelphia shop, Goddard established the *Maryland Journal; and the Baltimore Advertiser* on 20 August 1773.

He promised that the new paper would "contain every material Piece of Intelligence, either foreign or domestic, with Accounts of the Arrival and Departure of Ships, the current Prices of Goods, the Course of Exchange, Deaths, Accidents, and Events of every Kind, that may be thought interesting to the Publick." Bearing in mind his recent experiences, he pledged that "the Freedom of the Press shall be maintained."

While Mary Katherine continued to produce the *Chronicle* like clockwork, William found it difficult to launch the *Journal* due to his frequent travels, ill health, and inadequate paper supplies. In addition, he wished to devote himself to setting up a new postal system in opposition to the official British one which he believed hampered exchange of information between the colonies. Therefore he shut down the *Chronicle* on 8 February 1774 and sent for his sister to assume management of the *Journal* with the issue of 11 February. In the spring of 1775 Goddard was again jailed in Philadelphia as a debtor but gained release after filing an equivalent of bankruptcy.

In July 1775 the Continental Congress adopted Goddard's postal system as the basis for a national postal service. Although he had hoped to gain a chief position, Goddard was appointed only to the minor post of surveyor. His sister was named postmistress of Baltimore, making her apparently the first woman to be appointed to federal office in the United States. Unhappy with his duties, Goddard attempted without success to obtain a commission as a colonel in George Washington's army. These activities kept him away from Baltimore from 1774 until 1777, when he resigned as surveyor.

Far more reliable than her erratic brother, Mary Katherine Goddard made the *Maryland Journal* one of the most vigorous voices of the American Revolution. After Goddard had been gone for a year, his name was removed from the newspaper's imprint on 10 May 1775, and Mary Katherine Goddard was listed as sole printer until 1784. In spite of paper shortages, inflation, and battles over freedom of the press, she brought out the *Journal* as regularly as she could, publishing "extraordinaries" on the Battle of Bunker Hill and the Continental Congress's call for arms. With the subscription price doubling and redoubling due to inflation, she called on subscribers to pay either in cash or in produce, including "tann'd sheepskins" which she put to use in the "complete and elegant Bookbinding Room" she added to her shop. Her paper advertised her printing services and the wares, including books and medicines, which she sold.

After Goddard's return to Baltimore, the *Journal* became embroiled in two incidents prompted by publication of items considered unpatriotic by mobs of over-zealous Patriots. One involved a misunderstanding over a letter signed "Tom Tell Truth" that urged colonists to accept a British peace proposal in 1777. It had been written by Samuel Chase, a Maryland member of the Continental Congress, who had intended it as satire; but fanatical members of the Baltimore Whig Club misunderstood the irony and demanded that the Goddards reveal the name of its "traitorous" author. Both refused, but William, unlike his calmer sister, exchanged insults with club members who tried to banish him from Baltimore. After his sister failed to persuade the authorities to protect him, Goddard made his way to Annapolis, where the governor and legislature censured the Whig Club and vindicated Goddard's right to press freedom.

Two years later the Goddards again incurred wrath when the *Journal* published a series of rhetorical questions attacking George Washington by Charles Lee, a disgraced general. This time a mob equipped with a cart and rope threatened to hang Goddard and forced him to sign a retraction, which he later repudiated. Again he appealed to Annapolis, where his rights were upheld by the legislature.

Described by her brother as an "expert and correct compositor of types," Mary Katherine Goddard gained recognition for her superior ability as a printer. During the Revolution she served as chief printer in Baltimore when the Continental Congress moved there, having been forced out of Philadelphia by the British. As a result, she ran off on her press in the winter of 1777 the first official copy of the Declaration of Independence with the names of the signers attached. Thus she scored the greatest printing coup of the period, but it was so accepted for a woman to be a printer at the time that no comment was made about her sex.

In 1781 William Goddard announced his intention of joining with Eleazer Oswald to print inexpensive editions of European books, informing the public that they would have "no Concern with any NEWS-PAPER." However, after the *Journal* be-

came a semiweekly on 14 March 1783, indicating that prosperity was returning to Baltimore following the Revolution, Goddard again involved himself in the operation, as evidenced by minor typographical changes. Finally, in January 1784, he was listed as the sole proprietor of the paper. The brother and sister each printed competing almanacs for 1784, with Goddard contending that his sister's almanac had been printed "by a certain hypocritical Character for the dirty and mean Purpose of Fraud and DECEPTION." Angry and hurt, Mary Katherine avoided her brother for the rest of her life.

After severing her connection with the newspaper, Mary Katherine hoped to continue to earn her living as postmistress. But she was removed from the position in 1789 when a new postmaster general directed that she be replaced with a man, since "more travelling might be necessary than a woman could undertake." Supported by a petition signed by 200 leading citizens, she fought unsuccessfully to keep the office, appealing personally to President Washington and to the U.S. Senate. Having managed the post office during the Revolution, when she had had to advance money out of her own pocket to pay post riders, she bitterly resented being removed when the position became a money-making one. In her last years she supported herself as a bookseller and storekeeper.

Mary Katherine Goddard died in Baltimore in 1816, leaving a small estate to her slave, Belinda Starling, whom she freed in her will. No mention of her career appeared in her obituary. Relatively little is known of her personal life and views other than what can be inferred from the columns of her newspaper. Her career testifies to her extraordinary industry and competence. A drawing of her in her 1783 almanac shows a woman with a look of determination.

At the age of forty-four, William Goddard married Abigail Angell at Cranston, Rhode Island, on 25 May 1785. He continued to publish the *Journal* until 22 February 1793, taking his brother-in-law, James Angell, as a partner in 1789 and ultimately selling out to him. Mellowing as he aged, he spent his last years in semiretirement in Johnston, Rhode Island, enjoying a tranquil domestic existence as the father of five children. In the twilight of his life, he helped with the preparation of Isaiah Thomas's *History of Printing in America* (1810) and became a member of the American Antiquarian Society founded by Thomas in 1812. Thomas praised him as an "ingenious and enterprising" printer and "capable" editor. William Goddard died in 1817.

Biography:

Ward L. Miner, *William Goddard, Newspaperman* (Durham: Duke University Press, 1962).

References:

John Eliot Alden, *Rhode Island Imprints 1727-1800* (New York: Bowker, 1949), pp. 101-141;

Charles Brigham, *Journals and Journeymen* (Philadelphia: University of Pennsylvania Press, 1950), pp. 71-79;

Nancy Fisher Chudacoff, "Woman in the News 1762-1770—Sarah Updike Goddard," *Rhode Island History*, 32 (November 1973): 99-105;

Susan Henry, "Notes Toward Liberation of Journalism History: A Study of Five Women Printers in Colonial America," Ph.D. dissertation, Syracuse University, 1976;

Eugenia A. Leonard, *The Dear-Bought Heritage* (Philadelphia: University of Pennsylvania Press, 1965), pp. 459-460;

Ellen M. Oldham, "Early Women Printers of America," *Boston Public Library Quarterly*, 10 (April-June 1958): 78-82, 150-152;

Charles Wilson Op Dyke, *The Op Dyke Genealogy* (Albany: Weed, Parsons, 1889), pp. 87-93;

Arthur M. Schlesinger, *Prelude to Independence: The Newspaper War on Britain 1764-1776* (New York: Knopf, 1958), pp. 56, 73-83, 118-122, 165;

Isaiah Thomas, *The History of Printing in America* (Worcester, Mass.: Sturtevant, 1810), pp. 157-162, 324-329;

Joseph T. Wheeler, *The Maryland Press, 1777-1790* (Baltimore: Maryland Historical Society, 1938), pp. 1-5, 11-18;

Lawrence C. Wroth, *History of Printing in Colonial Maryland* (Baltimore: Typolhetae, 1922), pp. 119-140.

Papers:

A letter of Sarah Goddard is preserved at the Providence Public Library. Copies of the Declaration of Independence printed by Mary Katherine Goddard are contained in the National Archives as well as in the Maryland Hall of Records, Annapolis, which also has her will. Other papers, including her account book and copies of her petition to retain her job as postmistress, are in the Maryland Historical Society, Baltimore. Papers pertaining to William Goddard's establishment of the postal system and the Minute Books of the Boston Committee of Correspondence are at the New York Public Library. Other material is at the Rhode Island Historical Society, the Brown University Library, and the Rhode Island State Archives, all in Providence. Files of the *Pennsylvania Chronicle* are at the Historical Society of Pennsylvania, Philadelphia; the *Providence Gazette* at the Rhode Island Historical Society, Providence; and the *Maryland Journal* at the Maryland Historical Society, Baltimore.

Horace Greeley

Daniel W. Pfaff
Pennsylvania State University

See also the Greeley entry in *DLB 3, Antebellum Writers in New York and the South.*

BIRTH: Amherst, New Hampshire, 3 February 1811.

MARRIAGE: 5 July 1836 to Mary Youngs Cheney; children: Arthur, Mary, Ida, Raphael, Gabrielle.

MAJOR POSITIONS HELD: Printer, *New-York Morning Post* (1833); founder and editor, *New-Yorker* (1834-1841), *Log Cabin* (1840-1841), *New-York Tribune* (1841-1872).

DEATH: Pleasantville, New York, 29 November 1872.

SELECTED BOOKS: *The Protection of Industry. Its Necessity and Effects* (N.p., 1842);

An Address before the Literary Societies of Hamilton College, July 23, 1844 (New York: W. H. Graham, 1844);

Protection and Free Trade, the Question Stated and Considered (New York: Greeley & McElrath, 1844);

The Tariff as It Is, Compared with the Substitute Proposed by Its Adversaries in the Bill Reported to the U.S. House of Representatives by Gen. McKay of N.C. from the Committee of Ways and Means (New York: Greeley & McElrath, 1844);

Association Discussed; or, The Socialism of the Tribune Examined. Being a Controversy between the New York Tribune and the Courier and Enquirer, by Greeley and Henry J. Raymond (New York: Harper, 1847);

Alcoholic Liquors: Their Essential Nature and Necessary Effects on the Human Constitution (New York: Brognard, 1849);

Hints toward Reforms, in Lectures, Addresses, and Other Writings (New York: Harper, 1850);

Glances at Europe: In a Series of Letters from Great Britain, France, Italy, Switzerland, &c., during the Summer of 1851. Including Notices of the Great Exhibition, or World's Fair (New York: Dewitt & Davenport, 1851);

The Crystal Palace and Its Lessons: A Lecture by Horace Greeley (New York: Dewitt & Davenport, 1852);

Why I Am a Whig: Reply to an Inquiring Friend (New York: Published at the *Tribune* office, 1852);

What the Sister Arts Teach as to Farming. An Address before the Indiana State Agricultural Society, at Its Annual Fair, Lafayette, Oct. 13, 1853 (New York: Fowlers & Wells, 1853);

A History of the Struggle for Slavery Extension or Restriction in the United States, from the Declaration of Independence to the Present Day. Mainly Compiled and Condensed from the Journals of Congress and Other Official Records, and Showing the Vote

Photograph by Mathew Brady

256

by Yeas and Nays on the Most Important Divisions in Either House (New York: Dix, Edwards, 1856);

The Tariff Question (New York, 1856);

Aunt Sally, Come Up! or, The Nigger Sale (London: Ward & Lock, 1859);

Divorce: Being a Correspondence between Horace Greeley and Robert Dale Owen (New York: R. M. Dewitt, 1860);

An Overland Journey, from New York to San Francisco, in the Summer of 1859 (New York: C. M. Saxton/Barker San Francisco: H. H. Bancroft, 1860);

The American Conflict: A History of the Great Rebellion in the United States of America, 1860-'65; Its Causes, Incidents, and Results: Intended to Exhibit Especially Its Moral and Political Phases, with the Drift and Progress of American Opinion Respecting Human Slavery from 1776 to the Close of the War for the Union, 2 volumes (Hartford, Conn.: O. D. Case/Chicago: G. & C. Sherwood, 1864-1866);

An Address on Success in Business, Delivered before the Students of Packard's Bryant & Stratton New York Business College, by Hon. Horace Greeley, at the Large Hall of the Cooper Union, Nov. 11, 1867 (New York: S. S. Packard, 1867);

Letter of Horace Greeley to Messrs. Geo. W. Blunt, John A. Kennedy, John O. Stone, Stephen Hyatt, and 30 Others, Members of the Union League Club (New York: Privately printed, 1867);

Recollections of a Busy Life (New York: J. B. Ford, 1868);

Essays Designed to Elucidate the Science of Political Economy, while Serving to Explain and Defend the Policy of Protection to Home Industry, as a System of National Cooperation for the Elevation of Labor (Philadelphia: Porter & Coates, 1869);

What I Know of Farming: A Series of Brief and Plain Expositions of Practical Agriculture as an Art Based upon Science (New York: G. W. Carleton, 1871);

Mr. Greeley's Letters from Texas and the Lower Mississippi: To Which Are Added His Address to the Farmers of Texas, and His Speech on His Return to New York, June 12, 1871 (New York: Tribune office, 1871);

Horace Greeley's Letters of Acceptance and Portland Speech (Columbus, Ohio: Nevens, printer, 1872);

The True Issues of the Presidential Campaign. Speeches of Horace Greeley during His Western Trip and at Portland, Maine. Also, Ex-President Mahan's Letters (New York, 1872);

Letter to a Politician (Brooklyn, N.Y.: Privately printed, 1877);

Greeley on Lincoln, with Mr. Greeley's Letters to Charles A. Dana and a Lady Friend; to Which are Added Reminiscences of Horace Greeley, edited by Joel Benton (New York: Baker & Taylor, 1893);

Proceedings of the First Three Republican National Conventions of 1856, 1860 and 1864; Including Proceedings of the Antecedent National Convention Held at Pittsburg, in February, 1856, as Reported by Horace Greeley (Minneapolis: C. W. Johnson, 1893).

OTHER: William Atkinson, *Principles of Political Economy; or, The Laws of the Formation of National Wealth, Developed by Means of the Christian Law of Government. Being the Substance of a Case Delivered to the Hand-Loom Weavers' Commission*, introduction by Greeley (New York: Greeley & McElrath/New Orleans: Norman, Steele, 1843);

Epes Sargent, *The Life and Public Services of Henry Clay, down to 1848*, edited and completed by Greeley (Philadelphia: Porter & Coates, 1852);

S. Margaret Fuller, *Literature and Art*, introduction by Greeley (New York: Fowlers & Wells, 1852);

Art and Industry as Represented in the Exhibition at the Crystal Palace, New York—1853-4: Showing the Progress and State of the Various Useful and Esthetic Pursuits. From the New York Tribune, edited by Greeley (New York: Redfield, 1853);

A Political Text-Book for 1860, compiled by Greeley and John F. Cleveland (New York: Tribune Association, 1860);

The Tribune Almanac for the Years 1838 to 1868, Inclusive, edited by Greeley (New York: New York Tribune, 1868);

Charles T. Congdon, ed., *Tribune Essays: Leading Articles Contributed to the New York Tribune, 1857-63*, introduction by Greeley (New York: Redfield, 1869).

Horace Greeley was the most widely known and generally revered American newspaper editor of the nineteenth century. His pulpit was the editorship of the *New-York Tribune* and the nationally circulated *Weekly Tribune*, which he founded in April and September 1841, respectively, and operated for thirty-one years until his death in 1872. Until the *Tribune*'s appearance, no single newspaper had reached as many readers in the United States. The editor's name—and the more affectionate "Uncle Horace"—were recognized everywhere.

Greeley was born on 3 February 1811 at Amherst, New Hampshire, to Zaccheus Greeley, a farmer and day laborer, and Mary Woodburn Greeley. Because the couple's first two children had died, Horace became the eldest in a family of two boys and three girls. Though sickly as a child, he helped as he was able with the never-ending farm chores such as charcoal burning and picking stones. Of the latter, he observed many years later: "Pick as closely as you may, the next ploughing turns up a fresh eruption of boulders and pebbles, from the size of a hickory-nut to that of a tea-kettle. . . . I filially love the 'Granite State,' but could well excuse the absence of sundry subdivisions of her granite." As that comment suggests, the farm was poor, and in 1820 Zack Greeley lost it and had to hide in the woods to escape debtors' prison. The family moved to Westhaven, Vermont, to eke out a bare living cutting wood and working another nearly infertile patch of ground.

Under these conditions, Greeley got little formal education, but the combination of a natural intelligence and his mother's storytelling, reading, and ballad singing from the time he was a toddler sparked the interest in ideas that was to become his life. It was said that he could read by the age of four, and as a youngster he read on his own the Bible and any other books he could get. He attended school sporadically—usually in the winter, when he was not needed to work on the farm—until he was fourteen. Beyond that, he was self-taught, a factor to which critics later attributed his tendency to promote for a while an idea that appealed to him, only to drop it in favor of another that suddenly seemed more attractive. The only direction his education had came from reading what adults, impressed with his precocity, put into his hands.

Because of his love of books, he decided at the age of eleven that he would like to become a printer; but he was turned down in his first attempt to get an apprenticeship. In 1826, when he was fifteen, he walked twelve miles to East Poultney, Vermont, where editor Amos Bliss of the *Northern Spectator* agreed to apprentice him for five years for board and forty dollars a year. The apprenticeship ended when the *Spectator* went out of business in 1830, but Greeley had learned much in his time there, both about the mechanics of typesetting and printing and the craft of rewriting and localizing copy from city papers. He sent most of the money he earned to his family, which had moved to Erie

County, Pennsylvania, to continue its meager existence by farming. Both parents had become more than moderate drinkers, which was distressing to Greeley and undoubtedly the reason for his own abstinence from liquor and lifelong advocacy of teetotalism.

After a year of poorly paid part-time job printing work in Jamestown and Lodi, New York, and in Erie, Greeley set out in 1831 at the age of twenty for New York City with about ten dollars in his pocket and the fortifying self-confidence of his experience to that point. Once there, he "began to ransack the city for work" and got a job setting a complexly annotated New Testament in agate and smaller type sizes because no one else would take such a difficult job. "My proofs on this work at first looked as though they had caught the chickenpox, and were in the worst stage of a profuse eruption," he recalled.

For the next fourteen months he held a succession of newspaper jobs with the *Evening Post*, the *Commercial Advertiser*, and the *Spirit of the Times*. At the *Spirit of the Times*, he made a fast friend of the foreman, Francis V. Story, who was about the

Greeley as a young man, engraved by J. Sartain from a daguerreotype

same age as Greeley. When the *Spirit of the Times* failed they established their own print shop, using their meager savings and borrowed money. Their first job was to print the *Morning Post*, edited and published by Dr. H. D. Shepard, a dentist. It was first issued on 1 January 1833 at two cents; it failed to attract readers even after the price was dropped to a penny. Shepard "fancied that a paper would sell, if remarkable for cheapness, though remarkable also for the absence of every other desirable quality," Greeley commented, explaining that Shepard was neither "a writer nor man of affairs" and "had no editors, no reporters worth naming, no correspondents, and no exchanges even." He could not pay the printers, who, in debt themselves, could not extend him credit. "Thus," Greeley recorded, "the first cheap-for-cash daily in New York—perhaps in the world—died when scarcely a month old." The printing firm got other jobs, however, including two publications for the state lottery—for which Greeley later was criticized by rivals—and Greeley and Story were able to survive. Their promising partnership came to an abrupt end when Story drowned while bathing in the East River on 9 July 1833.

Story was replaced in the firm, now called Greeley and Co., by his brother-in-law, Jonas Winchester. Through most of 1834, the firm printed the *Constitution*, a daily Whig campaign paper edited and published by Achilles R. Crain, with Greeley as a contributor. Though monetarily a losing proposition for the firm, since Greeley was not paid for his editorial assistance, this project helped to solidify Greeley's Whig connections. The partners entered an era of prosperity when, on 22 March 1834, with Greeley as editor and Winchester as business manager, they established the *New-Yorker*, a "weekly devoted mainly to current literature, but giving regularly a digest of all important news, including . . . election returns and other political intelligence." They operated the publication for seven and one-half years, starting with "scarcely a dozen subscribers" and building to 9,000 until the economic collapse of 1837 brought a decline.

On 5 July 1836 Greeley married Mary Youngs Cheney, a twenty-two-year-old schoolteacher from Cornwall, Connecticut, whom Greeley biographer Glyndon Van Deusen described as "a vivacious, pretty little brunette with dark curls and decided opinions." She had moved to New York in the early 1830s and met Greeley at a strictly vegetarian boardinghouse where they both ate. Greeley never had been at ease with women, and the union proved to be largely unfulfilling for both of them.

In the first five and one-half years of the marriage "Molly" Greeley had two miscarriages and two children who died at birth. Arthur ("Pickie") Greeley, their first child to survive, was the light of their lives but was overprotected to a dangerous degree, especially by his mother. Over her husband's protests, she refused to have the boy vaccinated against cholera because she distrusted conventional medicine. The boy's death of the disease at age five in 1849 deepened the underlying tension and estrangement between the parents. Though there was never any talk of divorce, to which Greeley was unalterably opposed, they spent much more time apart than together. For "Mother" Greeley, as he called her, life was a fruitless quest both in the United States and Europe for "cures" for numerous "ailments." She was usually accompanied in her travels by daughters Ida, born in 1848, and Gabrielle, born in 1857, the only children to live to adulthood. A second son, Raphael, born in 1851, died in 1857.

For Greeley, life became an equally fruitless quest for elective political office, but his disappointment was offset considerably by the fame and attention he achieved as a newspaper editor and public personage in the heyday of personal journalism in the United States. His journalistic course was the outgrowth, wrote Vernon Louis Parrington, of Greeley's having reached "two major conclusions: that agriculture and manufacturing are complementary industries, and the closer they are drawn together the better for the nation; and that a wide national economy can result only from investing the state with adequate regulatory powers. Hence his approval of [Henry] Clay's American System." Possessed of "an extremely sensitive social conscience" and "keen sympathy for those who do the work of the world," his own work, as the country entered the machine age, took him through "speculations . . . in pursuit of that remedy for domestic competition which the political economists had not provided" and a wide range of other concerns, all centered upon the betterment of mankind, particularly in the United States.

From the time he could read, politics had interested Greeley. The conservative ideas of the Whig party, grounded on the principles of thrift and industry by which he had had to make his way, had a fundamental appeal. Though not an unfailing advocate of Whig doctrine, he became a regular contributor to the *Daily Whig* newspaper in the 1830s, and that plus the success of the *New-Yorker* caught the attention of New York Whig leaders Thurlow Weed and William H. Seward, who asked

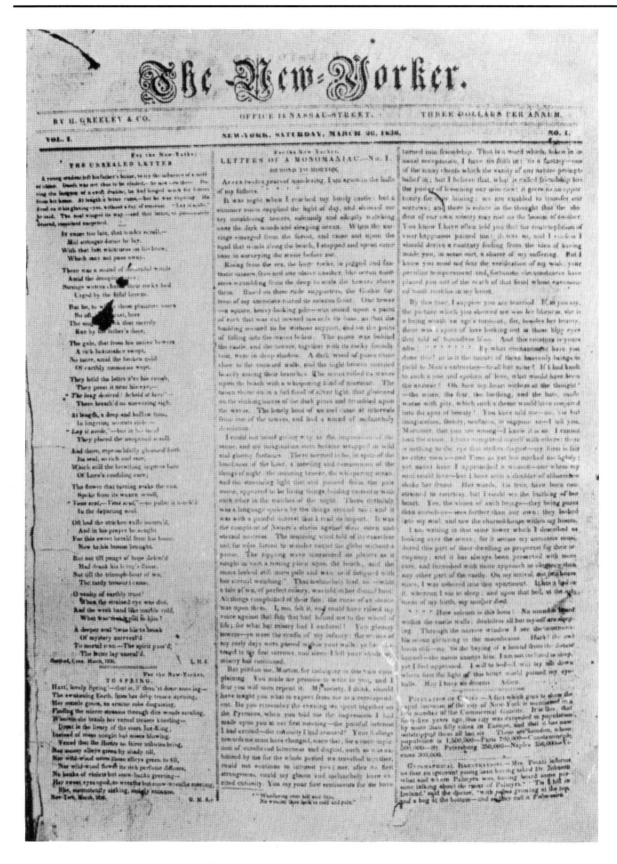

Front page of Greeley's weekly literary and political publication

Greeley's Whig political mentors, Thurlow Weed (left) and William H. Seward

him in 1838 to edit a campaign weekly which Greeley named the *Jeffersonian*. He ran it for one year, achieving a circulation of 15,000 and important influence in Seward's election as governor in 1838. This paper was followed in the 1840 campaign with the *Log Cabin*, which had an unprecedented 48,000-copy first-issue sale and reached a circulation of nearly 90,000. After the campaign, Greeley continued the *Log Cabin* as a general political weekly.

In 1841 the daily field in New York was crowded with twelve newspapers, but those of Whig persuasion—the *Courier and Enquirer, American, Express*, and *Commercial Advertiser*—sold for ten dollars a year. "A cheap paper, of the Whig school of politics, did not exist," according to James Parton, a contemporary biographer of Greeley. Greeley by then had about $1,000 in cash, printing equipment worth that much, plus a name good enough to get a $1,000 loan. It was enough to get started, and on 10 April he produced the first issue of the one-cent daily *New-York Tribune*. Within seven weeks the paper had 11,000 circulation, suggesting that Greeley had been right in gauging that reaction against the

sensationalism of the *Sun* and *Herald* would provide customers for the new paper. His conclusion was further supported when the *Sun* attacked the *Tribune* editorially and *Sun*-sponsored thugs attacked *Tribune* newsboys. On 20 September he founded the *New-York Weekly Tribune*, merging the *New Yorker* and the *Log Cabin* into it. An important factor in the *Tribune*'s survival was Greeley's formation of a partnership in July 1841 with Thomas McElrath, who had the business sense Greeley almost wholly lacked. Parton rhapsodized about this alliance: "Roll Horace Greeley and Thomas McElrath into one, and the result would be, a very respectable approximation to a Perfect man. The two, united in partnership, have been able to produce a very respectable approximation to a perfect newspaper."

Though not always echoed in later appraisals of the newspaper and its editor, Parton's statement conveys the adulation Greeley often enjoyed in his time, sparking in him a strong sense of rightness about the positions he took and undoubtedly firing his political ambitions. He was unquestionably a tireless worker, tending to all the correspondence, conferences, and supervision of the editor as well as writing an average of three columns of material each day. It was not unusual for him to take a major reporting assignment himself, as he did for a trial in Utica in late 1841, producing between four and nine columns a day about it. He also remained highly active and visible in Whig political circles; and despite his rumpled appearance, featuring a loose-fitting white "duster" and white hat (which became a kind of Greeley trademark) plus a high-pitched, grating voice, he was in demand as a speaker.

Almost always pressed for additional income because of his own carelessness in money matters and his willing support of his wife's travel and doctoring, he supplemented his income by going on a lecture tour nearly every year he edited the *Tribune*, speaking on a variety of subjects, including political economy, the right to work, land for the landless, popular education, and abstinence from alcohol. Many of these were collected in his book *Hints toward Reforms*, published in 1850. It was, he later wrote, "compactly filled with the best thought I had to offer; all designed to strengthen and diffuse sympathy with misfortune and suffering, and to promote the substantial, permanent well-being of mankind." During campaigns, of course, he often stumped for Whig candidates free of charge, but always expecting to increase his own political capital at the same time.

The popular response to Greeley had much to do with his optimistic contention that the United States of the 1840s was ripe with the promise of prosperity and growth for anyone willing to exert the effort. He looked approvingly upon reform movements of the time, particularly those for temperance and the abolition of slavery, seeing them as evidence of progress in line with his belief that God had picked the United States to demonstrate the highest success of humankind "based upon the great moral law," in Van Deusen's words, "that virtue secures happiness and vice produces misery."

Thus it was that the *Tribune* could give space for varying lengths of time to any causes or ideas that the editor found forward-looking and generally in line with his belief in an ever brighter future. He saw tariff protection, a stable currency, internal improvements, and the promotion of national self-confidence as the fundamental tenets of Whiggery; he predicted that the entire population would soon embrace them and reject the Democratic party, which he portrayed as conscienceless and evil. He was unquestionably Jeffersonian in his emphasis

Caricature of Greeley in 1846, from Yankee Doodle *magazine*

upon individual freedom, and for that reason he was open-minded to any notion that seemed egalitarian, without lingering long to consider its real merit. He was suspicious of class distinctions and of accumulations of wealth, and through the early 1840s he ran pages of material, much of it by Albert Brisbane, favorably discussing Fourierism, a French version of socialism. After Greeley and his former assistant, Henry J. Raymond of the *New York Courier and Enquirer*, debated the subject in their papers for six months in 1846-1847, however, Greeley seldom mentioned Fourierism. He looked favorably on nearly all attempts at cooperation, from communal living to labor unions. In 1849, he and McElrath, in "a desire to add practice to preaching," established the Tribune Association, by which the *Tribune* property was divided into 100 shares valued at $1,000 each. A few shares were sold to supervisory employees in the various departments, and each carried with it one vote in company decisions. In 1850 Greeley became the first president of the New York Printers' Union.

Greeley thought that women should enjoy more independence than they generally did—though he never believed that more than a tiny minority of them cared about the right to vote or about politics generally, because they were by nature suited to domestic cares. He could say of Margaret Fuller, who wrote literary criticism for the *Tribune* from 1844 to 1846, that she was "the loftiest, bravest soul that has yet irradiated the form of an American woman," but also that "noble and great as she was, a good husband and two or three bouncing babies would have emancipated her from a good deal of cant and nonsense." Still, Miss Fuller was a close friend of the Greeleys who lived with them for a time in their Turtle Bay, New York, home in the 1840s and was a frequent guest after they moved in 1853 to Chappaqua, Westchester County, about thirty-five miles from the city. She described Mrs. Greeley as a "typical Yankee schoolmistress, crazy for learning" but indifferent to housekeeping, caring for the house in "Castle Rackrent fashion."

Greeley, who farmed after a fashion on weekends at Chappaqua and near the end of his life published *What I Know of Farming* (1871), made popular the slogan "Go West, Young Man, Go West," which had been originated in 1851 by Indiana editor John Soule. The slogan reflected Gree-

The Tribune *building as it looked in Greeley's time*

Margaret Fuller, who wrote literary criticism for the New York-Tribune *and lived with Greeley and his wife at Turtle Bay, New York, in the 1840s*

ley's belief that the government should encourage homesteading by the free distribution of western lands.

His indefatigable promotion of ideas and his hopefulness won Greeley the reputation of a reformer. Van Deusen, considered his most authoritative biographer, wrote in 1953 that the reputation "was largely undeserved, for the *Tribune*'s editor was not half the reformer that he was supposed to be. There was a Greeley who yearned to build the New Jerusalem and whose sword leaped lightly to his hand, but there was also another Greeley who was calculating, conservative and full of shifts and evasions, not to mention a third Greeley who could seek refuge from reality in Utopia. The brave new world of reformer Greeley was not half so brave or new after the other Greeleys had finished tinkering with it."

There was, certainly, a manic quality about Greeley's life, leaving in the end much that could be criticized and much that could be praised. There is little dispute that the unprecedented openness of the *Tribune* advanced the conception of the press as a democratic forum for the testing of competing ideas. The paper employed more than 200 people by the 1850s and 500 by 1870, and its contributors included some of the best minds of the time. As biographer Don C. Seitz put it: "The *Tribune* office in Greeley's day harbored more real journalists than any newspaper in America ever did, except, perhaps, the *Sun,* and there the number was fewer and the talent less varied." Among these journalists was Charles A. Dana, who after fifteen years with the *Tribune,* first as city editor and then as managing editor, achieved further renown as editor of the *Sun;* Whitelaw Reid, another managing editor who eventually became the *Tribune's* owner; Henry J. Raymond, a fellow Whig activist with political ambitions who started out as a *Tribune* book reviewer, learned much about newspapering during two years as Greeley's chief assistant, became associate editor of the *Courier and Enquirer,* and in 1851 founded the *New York Times;* George Ripley, who ran the paper's sizable literary section; Solon Robinson, who established its agricultural department, a reflection of Greeley's lifelong interest in farming; and Karl Marx, who for several years interpreted the European scene from England. Seitz lists numerous others, all well known and highly regarded at the time as reporters, editors, and explorers in the realms of politics, economics, science, and the literary arts.

Greeley did not stint on expenses. By the early 1850s the *Tribune* had a dozen editors. According to Francis N. Zabriskie, "Each of these presided over a department, such as City Editor, Marine, Financial, Literary, Agricultural, Political, News Editor, Foreign and Domestic, etc., each with a more or less numerous staff. Thus the City Editor had fourteen assistants, the Marine had twelve; the telegraphic bureau had a general agent, with two subordinates (at Liverpool and Halifax) and fifty reporters in various parts of the country. There were eighteen foreign and twenty home, regular and paid, correspondents. A similar army was found connected with the publishing department," where, among other things, the *Tribune Almanac* was produced.

Van Deusen noted that "always there was pressure from the senior editor's desk for accuracy, for something fresh in the way of news, for something more to aid the paper's circulation. Send by telegraph, he told [James S.] Pike in Washington. Expense was no object when the material was fresh and interesting. Get hold of someone who had access to Congressional secrets and set him telegraphing. From the age of Eve, men had been anxious to learn what ought not to be known, and the *Trib-*

une must have some of it or be voted dull and behind the times."

Greeley's own contributions to the *Tribune* were usually produced in the evening. This is Parton's firsthand description: "The Editor-in-Chief is at his desk writing in a singular attitude, the desk on a level with his nose, and the writer sitting bolt upright. He writes rapidly, with scarcely a pause for thought, and not once in a page makes an erasure. The foolscap leaves fly from under his pen at the rate of one in fifteen minutes. He does most of the *thinking* before he begins to write, and produces matter about as fast as a swift copyist can copy. Yet he leaves nothing for the compositor to guess at, and if he makes an alteration in the proof, he is careful to do it in such a way that the printer loses no time in 'overrunning'; that is, he inserts as many words as he erases. Not infrequently he bounds up to the composing-room, and makes a correction or adds a sentence with his own hand. He is not patient under the infliction of an error; and he expects men to understand his wishes by intuition; and when they do *not,* but interpret his half-expressed orders in a way exactly contrary to his intention, a scene is likely to ensue." Of his writing, another contemporary, *Nation* editor Edwin L. Godkin, said that Greeley had "an English style which, for vigor, terseness, clearness, and simplicity, has never been surpassed, except, perhaps, by [William] Cobbett."

Assessments of Greeley's journalistic contributions are mixed. Writing in 1981, Erik S. Lunde concluded: "Greeley's policy as editor eschewed sensationalism and even reporting of sporting events at first; what was refreshing about his attitude was that he did not actively cater to his audience. He was not a Citizen Kane. Rather, he wished to establish a forum for free exchange of ideas, no matter how blatantly stated." Van Deusen's work, however, which Lunde calls "most authoritative" and "essential, well documented," offers the less frequently repeated counterpoint that

the *Tribune's* high mindedness had its limits. Quack nostrums for everything from colds to cancer flooded its advertising columns. These remedies might be good for something, Greeley averred when pressed on the subject. The paper could not distinguish between good and bad cures.... So profits triumphed over ethics, just as they did when he wrote editorial notices for pay, just as they did when he admitted paid articles to his news columns, just as they did when he cloaked sex appeal with virtue.

It was perfectly proper in Greeley's eyes to publish accounts of seductions, if proper horror was expressed over the deed. It was legitimate to notice lewd books, if so doing gave the editor an opportunity to denounce rival publishers for putting them out. It was even right to publish in lurid detail the double rape of eighteen-year-old Ann Murphy in the Broadway Cottage, provided sufficient horror was expressed and one could use the affair to assert that only Democrats ran bawdy houses in New York. . . . There had always been much in the *Tribune* that was not Sunday School, he told a friend in later years, but this was so because progress was best served by free discussion and full exposition, rather than by suppression and concealment.

Greeley was realistic enough to recognize "the fact that the public likes a certain amount of sex and crime news, and that publication of such items swells a newspaper's circulation." And despite his protestations in favor of full freedom of speech, "this did not mean that the paper always printed both sides of an argument, or even that it printed what its editor held to be the truth. Again and again his own reports of events at Washington misrepresented the situation at the capital as he actually saw it. When James Parton remarked that he could learn more about a current strike from the pages of the *Herald* than any other New York newspaper, the *Tribune*'s editor testily replied, 'Well, I don't want to encourage those lawless proceedings.' " In sum, Van Deusen found his subject a man of huge contradictions: "Doctrinaire, intensely partisan, obstinate as a pig, the *Tribune*'s editor was not one to let devotion to the truth hinder his pursuit of moral good, party gain, or spectacular news." And for it all, Greeley took full credit, writing in 1847 that "whatever is distinctive in the views or doctrines of the *Tribune* there is but *one* person responsible."

The stamp of his personality clearly deserved credit for the paper's success. In its second year, when the *Tribune*'s price was raised from one to two cents, it lost fewer than 200 of its 12,000 subscribers. Within another year circulation was 20,000 and price increases to three and then four cents did not seem to hinder circulation growth, which leveled off between 35,000 and 40,000 for the daily and about 100,000 for the weekly. There were times—especially during the Civil War—when the daily might reach 65,000 and the weekly 250,000 circulation. A semiweekly for people with regular mail service who wanted more than one paper each

week had between 15,000 and 20,000 subscribers. Greeley took a keen interest in these numbers more for the influence than for the wealth they represented. In fact, his own financial interest in the paper dwindled over the years as he sold off shares to meet one expense or another. By 1848 he had less than a third interest, and at the end of his life he held only six of the property's 100 shares.

Though he had often been in Washington on *Tribune* business, in 1848 Greeley went there as a member of Congress. As a reward for his work for Weed and Seward, he had been appointed to serve out an unexpired term in the House of Representatives. Those three months were his only term in office, though he sought reelection to Congress in 1850 and made himself available for the New York lieutenant governorship in 1854, only to be rejected by Weed and Seward in favor of his former-employee-turned-competitor, Raymond. In 1861 and 1863 he was a candidate for the U.S. Senate, both times opposed by his onetime Whig allies. He tried again for the House of Representatives in 1868 and 1870, for New York comptroller in 1869, and, capping it all, he was the Liberal Republican and Democratic candidate for president in 1872 against incumbent Republican Ulysses S. Grant. The only election he ever won was for a seat in the New York constitutional convention of 1867, where he was chairman of the suffrage committee. He had said in the *Tribune* in July 1841 that "an editor who is good for much *in* his profession will rarely seek to exchange it for an office." His lack of electoral success suggested that the voters agreed.

His inconsistencies, eccentricities, and reformist zeal were at the same time helps and handicaps to Greeley. During his brief term in the House, to much popular delight and the nearly unanimous scorn of his colleagues, he questioned members' custom of billing the government mileage costs for travel to and from their home districts based on circuitous rather than the most direct routes. He also declared congressional salaries too large and a waste of the taxpayers' money. Such righteousness could be effective in campaign oratory and *Tribune* editorials but was so uncompromising as to be detrimental in practical politics. Of the mileage episode, he later wrote: "I had expected that it would kick up some dust; but my expectations were far outrun." Similarly, his notions about the inevitable success of the American experience colored his judgment. In 1851 he made his first trip to Europe, both to see the usual tourist sights and to attend the first Exposition of All Nations' Art and Industry in London. He found some of what he saw impressive, but in the main he took note of the corruption and decay in the older countries, which fortified his belief in the new America's happy destiny. His collected letters to the *Tribune* from Europe were made available in book form as *Glances at Europe* (1851). His optimistic reflections on an 1859 trip were similarly published as *An Overland Journey, from New York to San Francisco* (1860), in which he reported on his visit to Colorado—where a town was later named for him—and his interview with Mormon prophet Brigham Young, among many other experiences.

In the years prior to the Civil War, Greeley waxed and waned on the issue of slavery; in Seitz's words, he approached "the great cause of which he was to become the chief evangel by very gradual processes." In 1854, the year of his break with his Whig mentors followed by the formation of the Republican party with Greeley in a prominent role, Congress enacted the Kansas-Nebraska Bill. The bill permitted the territories to decide the slavery issue, taking the decision away from Congress, where Greeley thought it belonged. The bill also voided the Missouri Compromise of 1820, which had prohibited slavery in the Kansas and Nebraska area. Then in 1857 came the Supreme Court's decision in the Dred Scott case, holding that slaves were property, not citizens, even if their owners took them into free territory. Greeley was outraged at these developments which threatened to so divide the country and impede its moral and material growth. He particularly hated the Dred Scott ruling, in which the Court also concluded that the Missouri Compromise had never been constitutional.

The *Tribune* was particularly vituperative on the slavery issue in 1857, at one point concluding that Northerners were superior to slaveholding Southerners because of the different systems of labor in the two sections "and their influence on intellectual activity.... It is not the habit of the slaveholder to create.... All centuries are alike to

Greeley (right) interviewing the Mormon leader Brigham Young during his Western trip in 1859, as depicted in Harper's Weekly, *3 September 1859*

him and the nineteenth is no better than the twelfth." But by 1859, Van Deusen noted, "the tone of the paper was very sensibly altered. This was probably due to the approaching Presidential contest and to a conviction that satirizing southern institutions was not likely to win the votes of southern Know Nothings and poor whites. Anxious to nationalize the Republican following, Greeley's tactics now consisted of asserting that Republicanism was essentially conservative, and of declaring earnestly that no legislative attempt would be made to interfere with the institution of slavery where it already existed. He even agreed that, if a state wanted to come into the Union with slavery, it had a perfect right to do so."

After surveying both his writing and his political activities up to the outbreak of the Civil War, Van Deusen concluded that "Greeley had not been an extremist in his attitude toward slavery and the Negro" in those years. Rather, "he had been hostile to slavery primarily because of the Slave Power's opposition to what he regarded as all-important national objectives. Therefore, his main concern had been to check the expansion of slavery. This done, he would trust to time, moral pressure, free white colonization, and the like to bring about a gradual extinction of the peculiar institution. His attitude toward the personal rights of Negroes was illustrated by what he said and did about the Negroes in New York State. There he worked for Negro suffrage, attacked social discrimination—and scolded the Negroes shrewishly because they did not see that they must work out their own salvation. He seemed to resent the drag they imposed upon social progress. His interest in them, he declared, was 'not for their own sakes only or mainly, but for the sake of the entire community.' In other words, it was primarily a national rather than a humanitarian interest."

When the war began, the *Tribune* argued that the Union must be saved, not that slavery must be destroyed. Its battle cry, "On to Richmond," which appeared in a short editorial by Charles A. Dana on 26 June 1861 and ran for a week thereafter, was thought by some to have led to the ill-advised commitment and defeat of poorly-trained Union troops in the first battle at Bull Run on 21 July 1861. Bull Run and other Union reverses and the savagery of the fighting caused Greeley to conclude that slavery was the central issue: that God was testing the people and would not save the Union unless the slaves were freed. This belief came to a head in his most famous editorial, "The Prayer of Twenty Millions," published on 20 August 1862.

"On the face of this wide earth, Mr. President, there is not one disinterested, intelligent champion of the Union cause who does not feel that all attempts to put down the rebellion, and the same time uphold its inciting cause, are preposterous and futile," Greeley wrote. "Every hour of deference to slavery is an hour of added and deepened peril to the Union." Lincoln's response that his only wish was to restore the Union—with slavery, without slavery, or part slave and part free—became one of his more frequently quoted statements. Greeley's editorial was credited with forcing the president to issue the preliminary Emancipation Proclamation in September, to be effective on 1 January 1863; in fact, Lincoln had been planning to issue the proclamation for some time before the editorial appeared.

Greeley's overall assessment of Lincoln was that he was mediocre, a tool of men and forces that he could not well understand. Accordingly, the editor was by turns encouraging and sharply critical of Lincoln's conduct of the war. With a total circulation of 287,750 reaching every corner of the country but the South, and each copy of the weekly typically serving many readers, the *Tribune* on the eve of the war was the most powerful newspaper the country had ever known, and its editor was much better able to sway public opinion than the president was. Recognizing this, Lincoln both met and corresponded with Greeley to enlist his understanding and cooperation. He even permitted Greeley in 1864 to represent him in an attempt to establish peace negotiations with the Confederates in Niagara Falls, Canada, after Greeley had informed the president that Confederate representatives "with full and complete powers for a peace" were ready to discuss terms. Lincoln, correctly, had doubted this, and the meeting produced nothing. Greeley persisted in urging peace negotiations upon Lincoln even after the Union's fortunes in battle improved, causing many to question his judgment.

Ten days after the Union victory at Gettysburg on 1-3 July 1863, the *Tribune* office was attacked by a working-class mob angered by the paper's support of the federal draft law, which permitted exemption of men between twenty and forty-five who would pay $300 into the federal treasury. Abolitionists and blacks were particular targets during four days of looting, killing, and burning throughout the city, and rioters made it clear that they would deal swiftly with Greeley if they could get him. Nevertheless, he went about his work as usual, disregarding the advice of associates that he leave the city until the rioters' passions cooled.

His proudest hour, though, came at the end of the war, when in the cause of national unity he led a campaign to free Jefferson Davis, the imprisoned former president of the Confederate States, rather than try him for treason. A trial, he argued, would reopen wounds of division that had only begun to heal and would make a martyr of Davis. Despite heavy criticism, on 13 May 1867 Greeley and four other prominent but not as widely known Northerners signed a $100,000 bond on which Davis was released. The circulation of the *Weekly Tribune* dropped by half for a time, and thousands canceled their orders for Greeley's hastily written but generally credible two-volume Civil War history, *The American Conflict* (1864-1866). He took the reaction in stride. "I was quite aware that what I did would be so represented as to alienate for a season some valued friends, and set against me the great mass of those who know little and think less," he recalled in his autobiography. But, he added, "I knew that I should outlive the hunt, and could afford to smile at the pack, even when its cry was the loudest. So I went quickly on my way; and in due time the storm gave place to a calm." Of this episode the not always sympathetic Van Deusen wrote: "No act of Greeley's entire career was more deserving of praise than his bailing of Jefferson Davis. . . . Bent upon the recreation of a united nation, he had endured scorn, contumely, the loss of money and friendships with firmness and dignity. The way was to be longer and rougher than he foresaw, but by his action he had helped to start the nation down the road to reunion. The whole episode constituted a study in courage and patriotic devotion."

More typical, however, was Greeley's reaction to the move to impeach President Andrew Johnson. Initially he was opposed on the grounds that it would divide rather than reunite the nation. But he dropped that argument as the 1868 election approached and became shrill in his call for the president's removal. He declared that Johnson's remaining in office constituted a threat of "riot, insurrection and civil war," and the *Tribune* called the president "America's most degraded son." Johnson's appraisal of Greeley had been no more complimentary. In rejecting the suggestion that Greeley be appointed postmaster general in 1866, Johnson had written that the editor was "a sublime old child" inclined "to goodness of heart so much as to produce infirmity of mind." When the Senate failed to produce the two-thirds majority necessary to remove Johnson, the *Tribune* charged that some senators had been bribed and accused Chief Justice Salmon P. Chase of improper conduct of the impeachment trial.

While it made him interesting and the *Tribune* readable, that kind of behavior did nothing to improve Greeley's political fortunes, and no doubt contributed to the decline of his newspaper's influence following the Civil War. When he was nominated for the New York governorship at the Republican convention in Syracuse in 1868 there was wild applause, but John A. Griswold got nearly all the votes on the first ballot. "By 1868 many an honest fellow had come to the conviction that, while Horace was a great man, he was scarcely fitted for the responsibilities of high office," Van Deusen wrote. "Hence it was not surprising that the delegates should cheer one way and vote another." Frequent Greeley critic Godkin captured the limits of the Greeley mystique in the *Nation:* "In public, few members of conventions have the courage to deny his fitness for any office in the country, and we verily believe that if he were proposed for the Chief Justiceship of the Supreme Court or the command of the fleet, there would be clergymen and country politicians found to maintain openly that he was equally well fitted to hear appeals in admiralty or to be an admiral himself—such are the terrors inspired by his editorial cowskin. But the minute the voting by ballot begins, the cowardly fellows repudiate him under the veil of secrecy."

Greeley was repudiated in his final try for office, as the presidential candidate of the splinter Liberal Republican party as well as the Democratic party in 1872. He had largely engineered his nomination by denunciations in the *Tribune* of the Grant administration as corrupt and unsympathetic to the South, among other failings. The reaction to his candidacy boiled with the odd mixture of currents that had churned through Greeley's life. According to Van Deusen, "A flood of congratulations poured into the *Tribune*'s office. Greeley clubs mushroomed throughout the country. There was a run on white hats in St. Louis and New Orleans." But far from all Liberal Republicans, Democrats and others disappointed by Grant's poor leadership were pleased with the prospect of Greeley as his successor. Influential editors, including Godkin and William Cullen Bryant in New York and Carl Schurz in St. Louis, were alarmed. In an editorial, "Why Mr. Greeley Should Not Be Supported for the Presidency," Bryant wrote that Greeley's candidacy had about it "a certain air of low comedy" and attacked his record during the war as "irre-

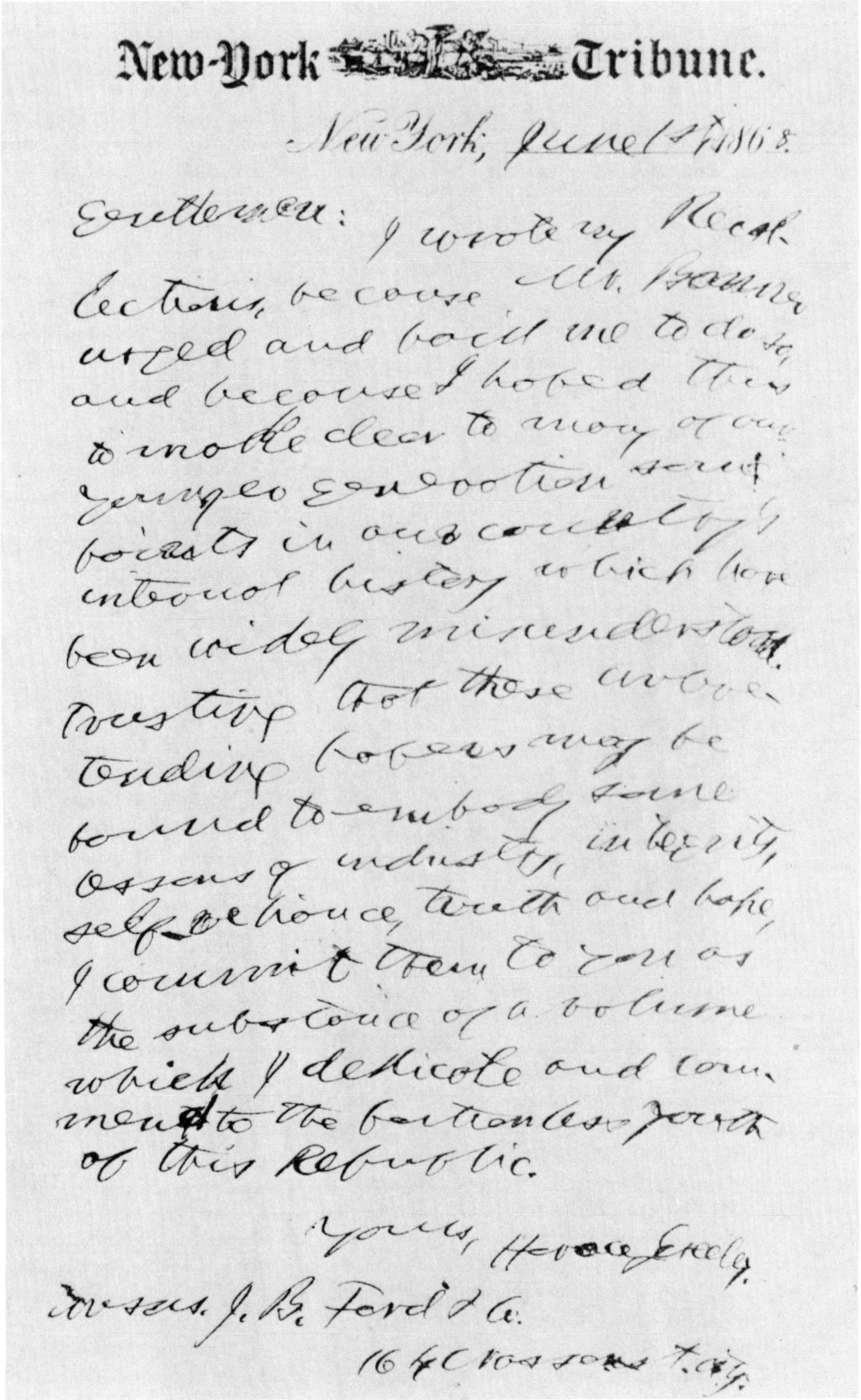

New-York Tribune.

New York, June 1st 1868.

*Gentlemen: I wrote my Recol-
lections, because Mr. Bonner
urged and paid me to do so,
and because I hoped they
to make clear to many of our
younger generation some of
points in our country's
internal history which have
been widely misunderstood.
Trusting that these unpre-
tending papers may be
found to embody some
lessons of industry, integrity,
self-reliance, truth and hope,
I commit them to you as
the substance of a volume
which I dedicate and com-
mend to the factionless youth
of this Republic.*

Yours, Horace Greeley

*Messrs. J. B. Ford & Co.
16 & Nassau st. N.Y.*

Letter from Greeley to the publisher of his autobiography, Recollections of a Busy Life

RECOLLECTIONS OF A BUSY LIFE:

INCLUDING

REMINISCENCES OF AMERICAN POLITICS
AND POLITICIANS,

FROM THE OPENING OF THE MISSOURI CONTEST TO THE
DOWNFALL OF SLAVERY;

TO WHICH ARE ADDED

MISCELLANIES:

"LITERATURE AS A VOCATION," "POETS AND POETRY," "REFORMS AND
REFORMERS," A DEFENCE OF PROTECTION, ETC., ETC.

ALSO,

A DISCUSSION WITH ROBERT DALE OWEN OF
THE LAW OF DIVORCE.

By HORACE GREELEY.

NEW YORK:
J. B. FORD & CO., PRINTING-HOUSE SQUARE.
BOSTON: H. A. BROWN & CO. CHICAGO: J. A. STODDARD & CO.
SAN FRANCISCO: FRANCIS DEWING & CO.
CINCINNATI: C. F. VENT & CO.
1868.

Title page for Greeley's autobiography

solute and cowardly, and his counsels impolitic and unwise to the last degree." Bryant concluded that a Greeley administration could only be corrupt, moving "backward and forward upon the shifting currents of expediency."

The campaign itself was conducted in this vein, with Greeley taking extraordinary abuse, including vicious cartoons by Thomas Nast that Mark Twain called "simply marvelous" in applauding Grant's "prodigious victory—for civilization and progress," a prediction that proved profoundly mistaken. Greeley's defeat, with only 43.8 percent of the vote, came just days after his wife's death on 30 October 1872, to be followed in less than a month by his own. The exact cause of his death is obscure; it was attributed by some to "brain fever." Van Deusen's conclusion was that Greeley fell into such a deep despondency in the wake of two such great losses that he "died because he had lost the

desire to live." In any case, it was a painful finish to a life during which Greeley had run all the way, faltering and stumbling at times but never giving up until the debacle of three major losses in one year. The first had been control of the *Tribune*, which he relinquished formally on 15 May to Whitelaw Reid in order to become a full-time campaigner. He had long since sold off most of his financial interest in the paper, and though he resumed the editorship after the election, Reid remained in charge. The second was his wife, to whom, despite domestic misery and their long separations, he had an intense loyalty; her death was a severe blow. The third was the presidency and with it the optimistic, if not always realistic dreams for the nation that he had so long pursued. Van Deusen's conclusion was that

> Greeley's election would probably have meant a considerable improvement in the national administration. Scandal and corruption would have had an abatement instead of an increase, as they had in Grant's second term.... And Greeley's passionate earnestness for national unity and national progress would have hastened, at least in some measure, the reconciliation of the sections.
>
> But on the other hand, Greeley's election would probably have had some unfortunate consequences.... Sobered though his natural ebullience and pugnacity might have been by the high dignity of his office, the chances are that he would have been a contentious President. If his record in public controversy meant anything, it meant that at the very least he would have fought furiously with Congress over printing and mileage and more fundamental economic policies. His objectives, so far as the South was concerned, would have been difficult of fulfillment, for he was pledged at once to clasping hands with the southern white conservatives and to protecting the Negro's political and civil rights. His humanitarian instincts would have been challenged and made mock of by a depression against which his economic philosophy would have afforded him no weapons.... His Presidency would have been a time of toil and trouble and, in all likelihood, brain fever would have claimed its victim before the end of his term.

In fact, the final farewell accorded Greeley was almost presidential in scale. Thousands filed by his coffin during the day his body lay in state in the Governor's Room of New York's City Hall. His

Four of the cartoons by Thomas Nast that attacked Greeley during the 1872 presidential campaign

funeral on 4 December 1872 at the Church of the Divine Paternity at Fifth Avenue and Forty-fourth Street began with a procession down the avenue watched by thousands. In the parade were delegations from the Lincoln Club of New York, the Typographical Society, and many other groups. Holders of the highest offices, starting with President Grant, Vice-President Schuyler Colfax, Vice-President-elect Henry Wilson, and Chief Justice Chase, were in the procession, as well as the governors of New York, New Jersey, and Connecticut and their staffs, several United States senators, and representatives of the nation's press. At the end, wrote one biographer, "there were no enemies."

Horace Greeley wrote and said much on many subjects in the course of his lifetime. When this involved taking a stand, he was unfailingly earnest in his convictions. But he was not always right or consistent, and he did not always practice what he preached. Those were his chief weaknesses. His main strengths were his industry and his caring and his belief in a better tomorrow. While those qualities, more than the negative ones, account for the success of the *Tribune*, both sides of his personality should be credited with largely establishing the American newspaper as a forum for ideas. As large a personality as he was, Greeley left something bigger than himself, though a Vermont farmer expressed surprise on hearing a year after the editor's death that the *Tribune* was still being published. "I thought Greeley was dead!" he exclaimed.

Biographies:

Lurton D. Ingersoll, *The Life of Horace Greeley, Founder of the N.Y. Tribune* (Chicago: Union, 1873);

Francis N. Zabriskie, *Horace Greeley, the Editor* (New York: Funk & Wagnalls, 1890);

James Parton, *The Life of Horace Greeley* (Boston: Houghton Mifflin, 1896);

William A. Linn, *Horace Greeley, Founder and Editor of the N.Y. Tribune* (New York: Appleton, 1903);

Don C. Seitz, *Horace Greeley: Founder of the New York Tribune* (Indianapolis: Bobbs-Merrill, 1926);

Henry Luther Stoddard, *Horace Greeley: Printer, Editor, Crusader* (New York: Putnam's, 1946);

Glyndon G. Van Deusen, *Horace Greeley: Nineteenth Century Crusader* (Philadelphia: University of Pennsylvania Press, 1953).

References:

Charles H. Brown, *William Cullen Bryant* (New York: Scribners, 1971), pp. 215-217;

Charles T. Congdon, *Reminiscences of a Journalist* (Boston: Osgood, 1880);

Charles A. Dana, "Greeley as a Journalist," in Edmund C. Stedman and Ellen M. Hutchinson, eds., *A Library of American Literature* (New York: W. E. Benjamin, 1889), VII: 78-95;

O. M. Dickerson, "Letters of Horace Greeley to Nathaniel C. Meeker," *Colorado Magazine* (March 1942): 50-62; (May 1952): 102-110;

Edwin L. Godkin, "The Week," *Nation*, 7 (16 July 1868): 42;

Erik S. Lunde, *Horace Greeley* (Boston: Twayne, 1981);

John J. Nicholay and John Hay, *Abraham Lincoln: A History*, 10 volumes (New York: Century, 1890), IX: 184-200;

Rollo Ogden, ed., *Life and Letters of Edwin Lawrence Godkin*, 2 volumes (New York & London: Macmillan, 1907), I: 298-301;

Vernon Louis Parrington, *Main Currents in American Thought*, 3 volumes (New York: Harcourt, Brace, 1927-1930), II: 247-257;

Charles Sotheran, *Horace Greeley and Other Pioneers of American Socialism* (New York: Kennerley, 1915).

Papers:

Most of Horace Greeley's papers are at the Library of Congress, Chappaqua Historical Society, New York Public Library, and the New York Historical Society. Other important collections include the Rufus W. Griswold Papers in the Boston Public Library, the Margaret Fuller Correspondence in the Harvard Library, the Salmon P. Chase Papers at the Historical Society of Pennsylvania, the Edwin D. Morgan Papers in the Albany State Library, the Mrs. H. C. Ingersoll Papers in the Library of Congress, and the Gerrit Smith Papers in the Syracuse University Library.

Duff Green

(15 August 1791-10 June 1875)

A. J. Kaul

University of Southern Mississippi

MAJOR POSITIONS HELD: Editor, *St. Louis Enquirer* (1823-1825), *United States Telegraph* (Washington, D.C.) (1825-1836), *Washington* (D.C.) *Reformer* (1837-1838), *Baltimore Pilot* (1840-1841), *New York Republic* (1844), *American Statesman* (Washington, D.C.) (1857), *People's Weekly* (1868).

BOOKS: *Prospectus of the Washington Institute: Being the Plan of a School, in Which 200 Students Will Defray the Expense of Their Education, [etc.] by Laboring in a Printing Office* (Washington, D.C.: D. Green, 1834);

The United States and England. By an American, anonymous (London, 1842);

An Argument Addressed to His Excellency, the Governor of Pennsylvania, in Support of the Bill to Incorporate the Pennsylvania Fiscal Agency (Philadelphia, 1859);

Memorial of Duff Green, President of the Sabine and Rio Grande Railroad Company, in the State of Texas, Praying Such Enlargement of the Powers and Privileges of Said Company as Will Enable Them to Extend Their Road to the Pacific, at or near Mazatlan (Washington, D.C.?, 1860);

Facts and Suggestions on the Subject of Currency and Direct Trade, Addressed to the Chamber of Commerce of Macon, Ga. (Macon, Ga.: Printed for the Chamber of Commerce, 1861);

Facts and Suggestions Relative to Finance & Currency, Addressed to the President of the Confederate States (Augusta, Ga.: J. T. Paterson & Co., printers, 1864);

Facts and Suggestions, Biographical, Historical, Financial and Political, Addressed to the People of the United States (New York: Richardson, 1866);

A Memorial and Bill Relating to Finance, National Currency, Debt, Revenue, Etc. (Memphis, Tenn.: Southwestern Publishing Co., 1869);

How to Pay Off the National Debt, Regulate the Value of Money, and Maintain Stability in the Values of Property and Labor (Philadelphia: Claxton, Remsen & Haffelfinger, 1872);

Memorial of Duff Green, of Dalton, Georgia Giving His Views on the Finances, the Exchanges of Money, *and the Products of the United States and Other Nations* (Washington, D.C.?, 1874).

Duff Green, the principal propagandist for and later the principled antagonist of Andrew Jackson, helped set the stage for the Civil War when he switched allegiance to the Great Nullifier John C. Calhoun, to states' rights, and to the Southern cause. Labeled a "firebrand of faction" and an "ambassador of slavery," Green aspired to be "the servant of the people" and "the advocate of truth and justice," forcefully arguing for independence in politics and journalism during the "Dark Ages" of the partisan press.

Green was born on 15 August 1791 near Versailles in Woodford County, Kentucky, to William and Lucy Ann Marshall Green. His mother's cou-

Duff Green

273

sin, Humphrey Marshall, had been opposed in politics by Henry Clay. "The prejudice thus created had, doubtless, its influence upon the estimate which I afterwards formed of Mr. Clay's conduct and character," Green wrote in 1866. He was sent to a neighborhood school when he was six to study grammar, arithmetic, geography, Vergil, Plutarch, and the histories of Greece, Rome, and England. Training in the classics continued at the Danville Academy, and he later taught at the Elizabethtown Academy. On his twenty-first birthday, Green was mustered into the army at Jeffersonville, Indiana, by Gen. William H. Harrison, achieving the rank of captain. He married Lucretia Maria Edwards, a sister of Gov. Ninian Edwards of Illinois, on 26 November 1813, and they had eleven children.

The entrepreneurial spirit was a driving force throughout Green's long career in politics and journalism. In 1816 he received a contract to survey public lands on the south side of the Missouri River near Boonville, Missouri. He rapidly amassed a sizable financial estate through land speculation, a profitable mercantile business in St. Louis, and contracts for carrying the mails. Green was postmaster of Chariton, Missouri, a town he founded, and established the first stage line west of the Mississippi River. In addition, he studied law, was admitted to the bar, and built a lucrative practice. He actively engaged in politics, serving as a member of the Missouri Constitutional Convention and in both houses of the state legislature.

His nearly fifty-year journalism career began in 1823 when he purchased the *St. Louis Enquirer,* which previously had been owned by Thomas Hart Benton, one of Missouri's first United States senators and a supporter of Clay. Green switched the *Enquirer*'s allegiance to Calhoun and supported Jackson for the presidency in 1824. His editorial policy pledged the *Enquirer* to serve "principles not men." "In relation to Home Politics," Green wrote on 3 January 1824, when he took control of the *Enquirer,* "our party will be the People—our favorites those men whom we believe best calculated to advance their interests. The old friends of Missouri . . . will find in the *St. Louis Enquirer,* the bold and fearless asserter of their rights and privileges. This paper will guard against the arts of faction under whatever form it may assume. . . . It is now time that the people should think for themselves, and determine who shall be supported by the republican party." Green advocated tariff reductions, economic development, and abolition of the caucus system of nominating political candidates.

During a trip between Washington, D.C., and Louisville in 1824, Green traveled with Andrew Jackson. Old Hickory urged the *Enquirer* editor to move to the nation's capital and "take charge of a paper opposed to the re-election" of John Quincy Adams. At first, Green was reluctant: "I did not consent to become the editor of a party paper in Washington." Nevertheless, he sold the *Enquirer* in 1825, moved to Washington, and bought the *United States Telegraph* from Jackson supporter John S. Meehan. Green invested $15,000 "of my own individual funds" plus about $30,000 in personal credit "to the support and circulation of the paper." En route to Washington, Green visited the Hermitage, Jackson's home in Tennessee, where Jackson told him as they parted: "Truth is mighty and will prevail."

Green insisted that his pro-Jackson agitation in the *Telegraph* was a matter of principle, not patronage: "I was not an adventurer, purchased by promises of plunder or patronage—I was a devotee, sacrificing my own private interests in the effort to maintain the rights of the people and to assert and enforce the responsibility of their public servants. . . . I acted under a sense of public duty." His polemics to prevent Adams's reelection in 1828 were aimed at "demonstrating" that the president's 1824 victory had been the result of "Bargain, Intrigue and Management." Actually, Green's animus toward Adams and the Federalists was long-standing. He believed that since as early as 1817, the Federalists had been using the emerging antislavery issue in order to impose Northern political and economic domination over the South. The antislavery issue was merely a subterfuge, Green wrote, "to array the North against the South," "to create a sectional Northern majority" that "could and would govern the North and South!" Green said that he "saw that it was no regard for the rights of the slave—no sympathy for the condition of the Negro—which stimulated their zeal, but a thirst for power, regardless of the letter or the Spirit of the Constitution, which I feared would embitter the South against the North and endanger, if not dissolve, the Union." To Green, Adams and the Federalists were antidemocratic "monarchists," opportunists who "were opposed to elective government" and the interests of "the common people, the laborers, mechanics, husbandmen and merchants."

The motto of the *United States Telegraph,* "Power is always stealing from the many to the few," aptly asserted the political convictions of Green and his newspaper. The *Telegraph*'s ardent denunciations of the Adams administration set the tone for the pro-Jackson press, incurring the wrath of the Federalist papers. The pro-Adams *National Journal* in 1827 chastised the "profligate conductors of the *Telegraph*" for establishing "a character for baseness and malignity." "Purchased and established to advance the interests of its owners at the expense of truth, and decency, and morality," the *National Journal* proclaimed, "it has found no slander too vile, no falsehood too gross, no calumny too malicious for its purpose; and the creature employed by its managers—a stranger to decency, destitute of honor, and unfortunately for society, an irresponsible agent—strikes as he is directed reckless of the consequences, well aware that being a shadow, justice has no terrors for him, and the contempt of mankind cannot reach him." Green's antagonists called the *Telegraph* the "Tel-Lie-Graph" when he claimed a 40,000 circulation. The pro-Jackson press rallied to Green's defense, willingly crediting him and the *Telegraph* with Jackson's presidential victory in 1828. "The opposition papers have long endeavored, by every species of calumny and defamation, to injure the character and destroy the influence of the *United States Telegraph*," the *Charleston Mercury* commented in 1829. "Such a course, perhaps was to have been expected of them, seeing that it was principally owing to the exertions of the *Telegraph* that the late Administration was defeated."

Historians consider Green a member of Jackson's inner circle of advisers and confidants, the "Kitchen Cabinet," although Green himself denied the connection. Nevertheless, the opposition press portrayed him as a political opportunist and usurper. The *Richmond Whig*, critical of his "unbounded influence" over Jackson in the handling of presidential appointments, asked readers: "What will you say to DUFF GREEN's being your President defacto?" The *Baltimore Patriot* castigated him as the "notorious Dictator Duff Green."

The Jackson administration rewarded Green for his editorial support with patronage contracts for government printing. Between 1829 and 1833, Green was printer to Congress and to several executive departments, earning, by his account, $50,000 a year. Government patronage notwithstanding, Green insisted that the *Telegraph* was no mouthpiece for the administration: "They mistake the relation we bear to this administration, if they suppose that we are its humble apologists; that we must seal our lips, nor venture to speak without permission of cabinet officers." Again: "It is the duty of the press to speak of public men, and at proper times to remind them of the principles which they are pledged to maintain."

Like many partisan editors of his day, Green was sometimes involved in brawls because of his inflammatory polemics against politicians and journalists. In 1828 *National Intelligencer* reporter Edward Vernon Sparhawk enraged Green by allegedly misquoting, willfully and maliciously, a *Telegraph* report of a speech on slavery. Green physically attacked Sparhawk in one of the Senate committee rooms, "wringing his nose and pulling his ears." His encounter with James Watson Webb, editor of the *New York Courier and Enquirer,* in 1830 resulted in a standoff on the steps of the Capitol. The quarrel began with Webb's support of Martin Van Buren for president in 1832. Webb traveled to Washington with the intention of horsewhipping Green before Congress, but little more than name-calling and threats came of the encounter. More serious was Green's encounter with James Blair, a congressman from South Carolina whom Green offended during the nullification controversy. Blair attacked Green on Pennsylvania Avenue on 24 December 1832, hitting him with a cane, knocking him into a gutter, and jumping on him. Green suffered a broken arm, broken collar bone, several broken ribs, and a dislocated leg; he sued Blair, who was ordered to pay a $300 fine.

The turning point in Green's political and newspaper career occurred in 1830 when an enraged Jackson broke with Vice-President Calhoun over the revelation of Calhoun's earlier criticism of Old Hickory's invasion of Florida in 1818. Green and the *Telegraph* sided with Calhoun and the Southern cause. His break with Jackson might have been predicted, since Green had supported Calhoun before supporting Jackson in 1824. The Jackson administration retaliated, replacing the *Telegraph* with Francis P. Blair's *Globe* as the party organ and, by 1833, cutting off government printing patronage.

In April 1831 Green told his readers: "The *Telegraph* never aspired to the reputation of a Government paper.... The *Telegraph* aspires to be considered the servant of the people; the advocate of truth and justice; the enemy of intrigue, corruption, and oppression; one of the organs of democracy of the country, placed as a sentinel at this post to notify them of danger." A few days earlier, smarting under the accusation that he had "deserted Jackson," Green responded: "My desire is to save him. He is on a precipice, and if he does not cast off those who have abused his confidence, his fame ... will be shipwrecked, and with it the fairest hopes of the republican party." Arguing that "truth is the best remedy in desperate cases," Green characterized himself as a martyr to its cause: "I have never intentionally deceived my readers, and to promote their interests and serve my country, have not only risked my life and impaired my health, but I have neglected a proper attention to my pecuniary affairs. Much of the profit arising from the other public printing . . . has been expended on this paper. . . ." Green remained steadfast in his conviction that "the *Telegraph* has never hoisted a false flag. . . . Let the beacon fires of principle once more be lighted up."

The breach with Jackson, according to Green, was a matter of "principles not men." His support of Jackson was based on a political covenant. As long as Jackson adhered to democratic principles, the *Telegraph* was obligated to support him; when Jackson departed from those principles, the obligation ceased. In February 1831 Green still pledged the *Telegraph* to support Jackson's reelection: "The support which the *Telegraph* gave to General Jackson was given on account of the principles and interests which it was believed that the election of Gen. Jackson would promote. . . . The *Telegraph* was pledged to support these principles." By December Green was convinced that Jackson, "surrounded by favorites" and "seduced by flatterers into a belief that his popularity controls public sentiment," was using "the patronage of Government as a prerequisite of office, instead of considering it a public trust" and was "substituting expediency for principle." When "personal devotion to an individual, instead of attachment to and maintenance of the Constitution formed the rallying word of the party," Green wrote, "then that individual no longer received our support as a candidate." On 13 February 1832 Green bitterly complained that Jackson's actions did not square with his rhetoric: "He has broken every one of his promises."

The break with Jackson complete, Green turned the *Telegraph* into a staunch defender of Southern interests, states' rights, and slavery. The *Telegraph* became a "fire-eater," opposed to abolition. "We deny that slavery, as it exists in the south, is an evil, and we intend to maintain our rights in relation to this property, at all hazard, let the interference come from what quarter it may," Green wrote in July 1833. "We know that the condition of master and servant must be, and we prefer the existing relations of society, matured by the wisdom of our fathers, to such change as the avarice, ambition, and fanaticism of Northern reformers would force upon us." The vitriol Green unleashed

in defense of slavery prompted the rival *Globe* to label the *Telegraph* a "firebrand of faction" bent on "trying to dissolve the Union." Undaunted by such criticism, the *Telegraph* under Green rapidly evolved into a virulent antiabolition newspaper.

Green founded a prototype journalism school, the Washington Institute, in 1834 to train boys to become printers. The youths would learn printing techniques in his extensive shop and would study spelling, grammar, history, languages, sciences, and philosophy. They would be paid for their work, the money to be given to them when they finished their training and were ready to set up their own shops. The Columbia Typographical Society, fearing that its members' jobs would be in jeopardy as a result of competition from institute-trained printers, officially opposed the school. Green abandoned the institute in 1835 after his printers went on strike to prevent journeymen from taking their jobs.

To counteract the "fanaticism" and "the effusions of diseased philanthropists" that he associated with the abolitionist movement, Green organized the American Literary Company in 1836. Its mission was to publish books of Southern writers, to defend slavery and states' rights, and to check the advance of abolitionist sentiments, particularly in the schools. The South Carolina legislature chartered the company with a capital stock of $250,000. The company dissolved in the face of opposition from striking typographical workers.

The most influential phase of Green's journalism career concluded in 1836 when he turned the editorship of the *United States Telegraph* over to Richard K. Cralle. The paper ceased publication on 21 February 1837, four years after the loss of the lucrative government printing patronage. For the remainder of his life, Green was involved in a wide variety of business enterprises, continued his support of Calhoun (his daughter Margaret married Calhoun's son Andrew in 1836), and engaged in pro-South politics and journalism.

After the demise of the *Telegraph*, Green in 1837 founded the *Washington Reformer*, but he abandoned the states' rights newspaper a year later. In 1840-1841 he established the *Baltimore Pilot* to support the Harrison-Tyler ticket. His first choice, Calhoun, did not have enough popular support to muster a successful candidacy. "Had you been advised by me," Green lamented in a letter to Calhoun in 1840, "you would have been at the head of the present movement and at this moment the most popular man in the United States." During the campaign, the *Pilot* took virulently anti-Catholic stands. After the Harrison-Tyler victory in 1840, support for the paper waned and the *Pilot* ceased publication in 1841.

With the death of Harrison, Tyler succeeded to the presidency and named Green an unofficial State Department messenger to England with a commission to influence public opinion concerning trade relations and slavery. His old political enemy John Quincy Adams referred to Green in a speech in 1843 as "the ambassador of slavery" at the Court of St. James's. Green wrote numerous letters to newspapers in England and France to influence relations between those countries and the United States. When he returned to the United States in 1844, Green founded the *New York Republic* for the twofold purpose of advancing relations between the United States and Europe and of supporting James K. Polk for president. After Polk's election, Green relinquished the editorship to Henry Wikoff, an assistant editor.

President Tyler sent Green to Mexico in 1844 in an attempt to acquire Texas, New Mexico, and California. The project failed and Green tried to foment a revolution that could give the United States a pretext to intervene militarily. After the Mexican War of 1846-1848, Green served as a United States agent in making payments to Mexico under the Treaty of Guadalupe Hidalgo (1848), which ceded much of the Southwest and California to the United States. Green then returned to private life to pursue his business interests in railroading and mining.

In 1857 Green published the short-lived *American Statesman* in Washington, but the paper's staunch defense of the South and its uncompromising attacks on abolitionists won little support. Green continued his advocacy of slavery and states' rights in lengthy letters to newspapers. During the Civil War, he operated ironworks for the Confederacy in Alabama and Tennessee and consulted with the Confederate leadership on matters of finance and foreign relations. With his son, Benjamin E. Green, he published in 1868 the *People's Weekly*, which contained his reminiscences and criticisms of radical Reconstruction.

In addition to organizing several business ventures to assist in the economic revitalization of the South after the war, Green wrote treatises on currency, finance, and industrial promotion. The South's war-ravaged economy could be rebuilt, he believed, by using land as the chief source of credit "to aid the development of agriculture, mining, manufactures, and commerce in the United States, and especially of the South and Western States."

Green died on 10 June 1875 at his estate, "Hopewell," near Dalton in Whitfield County, Georgia. The *Atlanta Constitution* eulogized him as "a nobleman of nature's purest mould," "a kind, amiable, sociable gentleman, of pure character and sterling integrity," and "a favorite among all who sympathized with the nullification movement," and noted that "he attained widespread celebrity and became noted as a fearless, caustic, and tireless commentator upon public men and measures."

Propagandist and practical politician, Green managed to embody many of the contradictory virtues and vices his friends and enemies imputed to him: patriot and traitor, democrat and demagogue, kind and caustic, thoughtful and impulsive, pro-Union and states' rightist. Some of the most inflammatory criticism of Green appeared in the columns of his own newspapers, especially the *United States Telegraph*. "If we know in what the freedom of the press consists," he wrote, "it is the unbiased and fearless expressions of our opinions of public men and measures, giving to others also the use of our columns for free discussions." A free and independent press that was neither a party hireling nor a slave to patronage was an article of faith with Green. His lifelong commitment was to "principles not men."

References:

Gretchen Garst Ewing, "Duff Green, Independent Editor of a Party Press," *Journalism Quarterly*, 54 (1977): 733-739;

Fletcher M. Green, "Duff Green: Industrial Promoter," *Journal of Southern History*, 2 (February 1936): 29-42;

Green, "Duff Green, Militant Journalist of the Old School," *American Historical Review*, 52 (January 1947): 247-264.

Papers:

A collection of Duff Green's letters is in the Library of Congress.

Benjamin Harris

(Birthdate unknown-circa 1720)

Lea Ann Brown
Southern Illinois University

See also the Harris entry in *DLB 42, American Writers for Children Before 1900*.

MAJOR POSITION HELD: Editor and publisher, *Publick Occurrences Both Foreign and Domestick* (Boston) (1690).

BOOKS: *The Protestant Tutor. instructing children to spel and read English and grounding them in the true Protestant Religion and discovering the errors and deceits of the Papists* (London: Printed for Benjamin Harris, 1679);

To the Honorable House of Commons Assembled in Parliament; The Case and Humble Petition of Benjamin Harris, Bookseller, Prisoner in the Kings-Bench (London, 1681);

The New England Primer (Boston: Printed by R. Pierce for Benjamin Harris, 1617-1690?; enlarged, Boston: Printed by R. Pierce for, and sold by Benjamin Harris, 1691);

Boston Almanack for the Year of Our Lord God 1692 (Boston: Printed by Benjamin Harris & John Allen, 1692);

To the Honourable House of Commons, Assembled in Parliament. The Case, and Humble Petition, of Benjamin Harris Bookseller, Lately Come from New-England (London?, 1695?);

The Holy Bible in Verse, attributed to Harris (London: Printed & sold by Benj. Harris, Senior, 1698; Boston: John Allen?, 1724).

OTHER: *Suspirium Musarum: The Sighs of the Muses. Occasion'd by the Death of His Royal Highness Prince William Duke of Glocester*, edited by Harris (London: Printed & sold by B. Harris, 1700).

Benjamin Harris presents scholars with a problem as they attempt to characterize the man given credit for publishing the first American newspaper, *Publick Occurrences Both Foreign and Domestick*, in 1690. Since very little information about his personal background is available, the facts of his life have been compiled from the evidence of his publishing career and of his other business activities. This evidence includes publication credit lines, memoirs of contemporaries, and records from legal proceedings.

Although Harris enjoys the same reputation as a champion for press freedom as his American Revolution-era counterparts, his legacy to journalists consists primarily of works he arranged to have printed and of works he personally printed. He wrote only a handful of the items he is credited with printing and selling. Therefore, his publications and the fragmentary details of his life must be objectively evaluated to determine if he really deserves praise as a crusading journalist or if the image of the defiant colonial printer, which primarily developed during the revolution and the early history of the nation, retroactively associated itself with Harris.

History's first mention of Harris occurs on the British side of the Atlantic. During 1679 Harris's Gracechurch Street print shop in London was raided. Charged with violating the printing and bookselling laws of King Charles II, he was arrested, convicted by Chief Justice Scroggs, and fined. Unable to pay the fine—John Dunton, a contemporary bookseller colleague of Harris, wrote that the fine was 500 pounds; Isaiah Thomas, a nineteenth-century historian of printing, quoted Dunton but changed the amount to five pounds—he was first confined to a pillory placed in front of his own shop, and then sentenced to a two-year prison term.

There is a discrepancy about what publication actually angered the authorities. Dunton identified *A Protestant Petition* as the offending work, but John W. Moore, another nineteenth-century historian, maintained that an item in Harris's newspaper, the

The Proteſtant CUCKOLD:

A New BALLAD.

Benjamin Harris Bookſeller.

Being a full and perfect Reſation how *B. H.* the *Proteſtant-News forger*, caught his beloved Wife *Ruth* in ill Circumſtances.

To the Tune of *Packingtons Pound* ; Or, *Timothy Daſh* the Scriveners Apprentice.

Deprendi miſerum eſt. —— Hor.

1.
Though the Town does abound ſo with Plots (and with Shams,
Yet I a true Story to you will relate;
The Godly can ſport too, and play you like Lambs,
Which does appear true by poor *Benjamin's* Fate.
There's a Judgment in't,
Which I can't chuſe but hint,
Becauſe he a Lye once from * *Crookhorn* did print:
Oh ye Tories look big, and rejoyce at this News,
For Benjamin's Wife is made free of the Stews.

D. M.'s Cure.

2.
Your Wife full of cares, and of fears, my dear *Ben,*
Durſt not lie alone in this Dangerous Age;
And finding beſides you'd no Ink in your Pen,
With a *Scrivener* ſhe thought it high time to en- (gage:
Then take't not in ſcorn,
Though you are well born,
That your Spouſe has furniſh't you with an *Ink-horn.*
Oh ye Tories look big, &c.

3.
Theſe Fines, as I take them, are things Arbitrary,
That a Subject can't lie with his Wife ev'ry Night;
Young *Stationers* beware, who hereafter ſhall marry,
That your Brides you careſs and pleaſe with all
Or to ſome young Lover, (your might:
Their wants they'l diſcover,
For long they'l not lie in *Sheets* without a *Cover.*
Oh ye Tories look big, &c.

4.
But now to the Matter of Fact we do come,
How *Benjamin* leave of the Marſhal did get,
That he with his Deareſt might then lie at home,
But th Apprentice (alas) had no notice of it:
For no ſooner were *Ben*
And his Wife laid in Den,
But the Youngſter began to *Whiſtle*, and *Hem.*
Oh ye Tories look big, &c.

5.
Madam hearing it, to the Window did creep,
To tell *Timothy* his place was ſupply'd ;
And fancying her Cuckold was laid faſt aſleep,
She told *Tim* next Night he ſhould not be deny'd:
But it was a miſtake,
For *Ben* was awake,
And ſlily reſolv'd the Appointment to break:
Oh ye Tories look big, &c.

6.
As ſoon as ſhe'd ſung her *Abi à Feneſtra,*
She ſoftly again to her warm Bed did make, (raw;
Where *Ben* much enrag'd could almoſt eat his Fleſh
But yet the cloſe Cuckold no notice would take?
Yet ſtill as he lay,
He long'd much for day, (may;
So his Wife did for next Night, as gueſs well you
Oh ye Tories look big, and rejoyce at this News,
For Benjamin's Wife is made free of the Stews.

7.
Up roſe *Ben* when 'twas day, and the Sun did up
But He, poor Cuckold, was under a Cloud; (pear,
Ruth kiſſing him, cry'd, *Wilt thou leave me, my Dear?*
Then like a true Jilt fell a weeping aloud ?
But ſhe never dreamt
That *Benjamin* meant
Her meeting the *Scrivener* ſo to prevent.
Oh ye Tories look big, &c.

8.
Juſt at the time when begins Treaſon-Fair,
And Fanatical Rebels croud *Dicks* Coffee-houſe,
Then *Timothy* did to Mis *H——* repair,
And thought himſelf ſafe as ere in Cheeſe was
For the Zealous Jade, (Mouſe ?
Ben a True Cuckold made,
And now he's no longer one in Maſquerade:
Oh ye Tories look big, &c.

9.
But the Joys of this World are all tranſitory,
And alas the Tragedy now does begin ;
For *Ben* at the door doth cry out, *Where are ye ?*
Being ſomewhat impatient till he was let in ?
Then with a huge Club,
He poor *Daſh* did Drub,
Who ſtruggled in vain that off he might Rub.
Oh ye Tories look big, &c.

10.
The Neighbours that heard the Youth murther cry,
To keep the Kings Peace, the door open did force,
Endeavouring the good man for to pacifie,
Telling him, he had taken her for better for
But think it who cou'd, (worſe :
That Horn him ſhe wou'd,
Who ſo kindly o'th' Pillory with her Husband ſtood
Oh ye Tories look big, &c.

LONDON: Printed for *Francis Smith*, 1681.

A scurrilous ballad about Harris's wife, circulated in London by his Catholic enemies during his imprisonment in King's Bench prison

279

London Post, provoked the action. It is possible that *A Protestant Petition* appeared in the *Post.*

It is in the context of Harris's first recorded encounter with official disapproval that the only mention of Mrs. Harris appears. Dunton commended the unnamed lady for standing at her husband's side during the time he was pilloried and for protecting him from the mob that gathered to mock him. His imprisonment did not compel him to abandon the newspaper business, however: one source says that he continued to edit the *Post* from his jail cell. If he did publish from behind bars, was it to prove that even jail could not silence his press or was it an economic necessity to keep his business alive?

Following his release, he returned to his print shop. In 1686 his shop was raided again; this time pamphlets linking him to seditious organizations were discovered. A warrant was issued for his arrest, but before the authorities could apprehend him, he fled to Bristol and secured passage to the American colonies.

His name first surfaces in American history in Boston. Attempts to relate him to Elizabeth Harris Glover, wife of Rev. Jose Glover who came to Cambridge in 1638 with Stephen Daye, the first colonial printer, may be correct, but more research in England is necessary. The relationship would more likely be aunt-nephew than, as Moore suggested, brother-sister, because of the difference in their ages.

His previous problems with printing officials did not persuade him to totally abandon printing even though the same king was in power and the same laws were in effect on both sides of the Atlantic. Instead of starting a newspaper, however, he and his son, Vavasour, opened a combined coffee shop and bookstore at the corner of State and Washington Streets. One source identifies the establishment as the "Coffee, Tee & Chucaletto Shop," but a copy of a 1691 almanac gives the name of the business as the "London Coffee-House." The regular clientele included one of Boston's first printers, Judge Samuel Sewall, as well as many of the city's intellectual elite. Harris's establishment was unique in Boston because he welcomed women into his shop.

Harris was one of a very small number of printers in Boston. Printers were not in demand because the city had only one printing press; the printers practiced their craft at the discretion of the local authorities. Harris began working with printing and bookselling when the license to print was in the hands of Richard Pierce. From the names

and dates imprinted on original works surviving in various archives and libraries, historians have a primary source for examining the infancy of Boston's printing industry. The imprints combined with dates from legal documents in England define the boundaries of Harris's years in the colonies: approximately 1687 to 1693.

During Harris's sojourn in Boston, his name appears singly as well as with those of Pierce and John Allen. Harris negotiated printing contracts for the same intellectual elite who patronized his shop. He arranged for Pierce to print John Tulley's 1687 almanac, and cooperated with Allen to publish a Boston almanac. The Boston almanac is noteworthy as the first colonial publication to feature color—almost all the words were printed in red. Harris's work on these almanacs apparently did not draw any comment from the authorities; the almanacs were not controversial or seditious.

Harris's most successful venture into the book publishing field, if number of reprints is a valid gauge of success, is *The New-England Primer* (1687-1690). Lines from this well-known collection of verses and prayers which Harris arranged to have printed include "Now I lay me down to sleep." The notice of its impending arrival in Boston is well documented in an advertisement from Henry Newman's *News from the Stars,* a 1691 almanac: "There is now in the Press, and will suddenly be extant, a Second Impression of the *New England Primer* enlarged, to which is added more directions for spelling the Prayer of King Edward the VI, and the Verses made by Mr. Rogers the Martyr, left as a Legacy to his Children. Sold by Benjamin Harris, at the London Coffee-House, in Boston." *News from the Stars* carried the credit "by R. Pierce for Benjamin Harris." The *Primer* probably carried the same imprint, because Pierce and Harris were still in partnership in 1690. No copy of the first edition of the *Primer* is known to exist, but the New York Public Library owns the oldest surviving volume, the 1727 Boston edition.

Although the exact date of publication is not known for the *Primer,* 25 September 1690 was the date of the single issue of *Publick Occurrences Both Foreign and Domestick.* For some reason, one copy of the publication was sent to London; it is now part of the archive collection in the London Public Office.

Harris's timing for the start of a newspaper was probably not an accident. He had been in the colonies for approximately four years and had chosen to content himself with publishing noncontroversial almanacs and spelling books. The

Numb. 1

PUBLICK
OCCURRENCES

Both *FORREIGN* and *DOMESTICK*.

Boston, Thursday *Sept.* 25th. 1690.

IT is designed, that the Country shall be furnished once a moneth (or if any Glut of Occurrences happen, oftener,) with an Account of such considerable things as have arrived unto our Notice.

In order hereunto, the Publisher will take what pains he can to obtain a Faithful Relation of all such things; and will particularly make himself beholden to such Persons in *Boston* whom he knows to have been for their own use the diligent Observers of such matters.

That which is herein proposed, is, First, That Memorable Occurrents of Divine Providence may not be neglected or forgotten, as they too often are. Secondly, That people every where may better understand the Circumstances of Publique Affairs, both abroad and at home; which may not only direct their Thoughts at all times, but at some times also to assist their Businesses and Negotiations.

Thirdly, That some thing may be done towards the Curing, or at least the Charming of that Spirit of Lying, which prevails amongst us, wherefore nothing shall be entered, but what we have reason to believe is true, repairing to the best fountains for our Information. And when there appears any material mistake in any thing that is collected, it shall be corrected in the next.

Moreover, the Publisher of these Occurrences is willing to engage, that whereas, there are many False Reports, maliciously made, and spread among us, if any well-minded person will be at the pains to trace any such false Report so far as to find out and Convict the First Raiser of it, he will in this Paper (unless just Advice be given to the contrary) expose the Name of such person, as A malicious Raiser of a false Report. It is supposed that none will dislike this Proposal, but such as intend to be guilty of so villanous a Crime.

THE Christianized *Indians* in some parts of *Plimouth*, have newly appointed a day of Thanksgiving to God for his Mercy in supplying their extream and pinching Necessities under their late want of Corn, & for His giving them now a prospect of a very *Comfortable Harvest.* Their Example may be worth Mentioning.

'Tis observed by the Husbandmen, that altho' the Withdraw of so great a strength from them, as what is in the Forces lately gone for *Canada*; made them think it almost impossible for them to get well through the Affairs of their Husbandry at this time of the year, yet the season has been so unusually favourable that they scarce find any want of the many hundreds of hands, that are gone from them; which is looked upon as a Merciful Providence.

While the barbarous *Indians* were lurking about *Chelmsford*, there were missing about the beginning of this moneth a couple of Children belonging to a man of that Town, one of them aged about eleven, the other aged about nine years, both of them supposed to be fallen into the hands of the *Indians*.

A very *Tragical Accident* happened at *Water-Town*, the beginning of this Moneth, an Old man, that was of somewhat a Silent and Morose Temper, but one that had long Enjoyed the reputation of a *Sober* and a *pious Man*, having newly buried his Wife, The Devil took advantage of the Melancholy which he thereupon fell into, his Wives discretion and industry had long been the support of his Family, and he seemed hurried with an impertinent fear that he should now come to want before he dyed, though he had very careful friends to look after him who kept a strict eye upon him, least he should do himself any harm. But one evening escaping from them into the Cow-house, they there quickly followed him found him hanging by a Rope, which they had used to tye their Calves withal, he was dead with his feet near touching the Ground.

Epidemical *Fevers* and *Agues* grow very common, in some parts of the Country, whereof, tho' many dye not, yet they are sorely unfitted for their imployments; but in some parts a more *malignant Fever* seems to prevail in such sort that it usually goes thro' a Family where it comes, and proves Mortal unto many.

The *Small-pox* which has been raging in *Boston*, after a manner very *Extraordinary* is now very much abated. It is thought that far more have been sick of it then were visited with it, when it raged so much twelve years ago, nevertheless it has not been so Mortal, The number of them that have

Front page of the only issue of the first newspaper in America

political climate, however, changed in 1689 when Sir Edmond Andros, governor of New York since 1674, was recalled to London. The commercial sector of Boston had by then taken on many of the characteristics of London's established commercial districts, but a newspaper had yet to be born. The city of 7,000—the largest city in the colonies—offered sufficient sales potential to sustain a newspaper, and the cultural and literacy levels were adequate to risk investing in this type of venture. The physical gulf of the ocean was being complemented by a mental gap as the colonists began to perceive themselves as Americans and not as Englishmen. The earlier evidence of his business acumen offers support for the conjecture that Harris took these factors, at least in part, into consideration.

Whatever the reasons, including a probable desire to return to his chosen trade, Harris compiled and issued *Publick Occurrences,* a folio of two leaves, with three printed pages and one blank page; the custom was apparently for the first reader to write a letter on the blank page and send the newspaper on to a friend. The newspaper contained local as well as foreign news; Harris intended to publish it monthly, "or if any Glut of Occurrences happen, oftener"; and it was the size of publications currently considered newspapers. Acceptance of *Publick Occurrences* as the first American newspaper requires suspending the part of the modern definition which includes a minimum of weekly publication.

Harris's articles include a speculative report that two missing children had been captured by Indians, agricultural news, an account of the suicide of a man bereaved by the recent death of his wife, and a comment on the smallpox epidemic raging in Boston at the time. Like journalists of today, he apparently believed that tragedy and fear sold newspapers. A colophon, or publisher's emblem, on page three of the publication credits Pierce with printing the sheets for Harris.

The exact reasons why the authorities ordered all copies destroyed and prohibited future issues are not recorded. Harris published the newspaper without official permission, so the authorities may simply have desired to maintain absolute control over the printers. Their reaction may also have been a response to another of Harris's articles, which discusses a skirmish between Indians who supported the English and those who supported the French.

There is no record of any repercussions from Harris's unauthorized activity beyond the prohi-

bition of future issues. If he attempted a second issue, no evidence of the publication has survived. Most likely he did not, because during 1692 and 1693 he was the official printer for Massachusetts, operating under a commission granted to him by the governor on 16 December 1692:

> *By His Excellency:—*I order Benjamin Harris to print the Acts and Laws made by the Great and General Court, or Assembly of Their Majesties' Province of Massachusetts Bay in New England, that so the people may be informed thereof.
>
> William Phips.

That the authorities would grant a commission to a man who had printed a newspaper without permission, and that the man would accept the commission from those who had silenced his press, raises significant questions about the printer's personal belief in freedom of the press. Two factors may have contributed to this chain of events. First, the smallpox epidemic apparently claimed the lives of Pierce and Pierce's wife, leaving Boston without an official printer. The officials may have commissioned Harris to quell any further attempts to work outside their jurisdiction. Second, if Harris did take economics into consideration, it made sense for him to accept the commission: his financial position was improved by the government contract.

Harris's name disappears from the *Acts and Laws* after March 1693. He apparently was superseded by Bartholomew Green, and he returned to London about this time. His son's name continues to appear on publications, indicating that the elder Harris may have left his interests in his son's hands. Harris's name is found in the proceedings of a November 1698 London Stationers' Company meeting: he was fined for failure to pay business fees. The footnote to the fine notes that his time out of the country was spent in the American colonies.

History records an unflattering picture of Harris from the time he returned to England until his death. In addition to the fine by the Stationers' Company, he drew the wrath of Dunton and of Dr. Roger Partridge. Dunton wrote angrily about being called a knave in Harris's *London Post.* He did not want praise from Harris, however: "I should have been much concerned if Ben Harris had given me a good word, for his commendation is the greatest reproach that an honest man can meet with." Dunton's memoirs contain a twenty-four-line verse which says that Dunton will forgive Harris for Har-

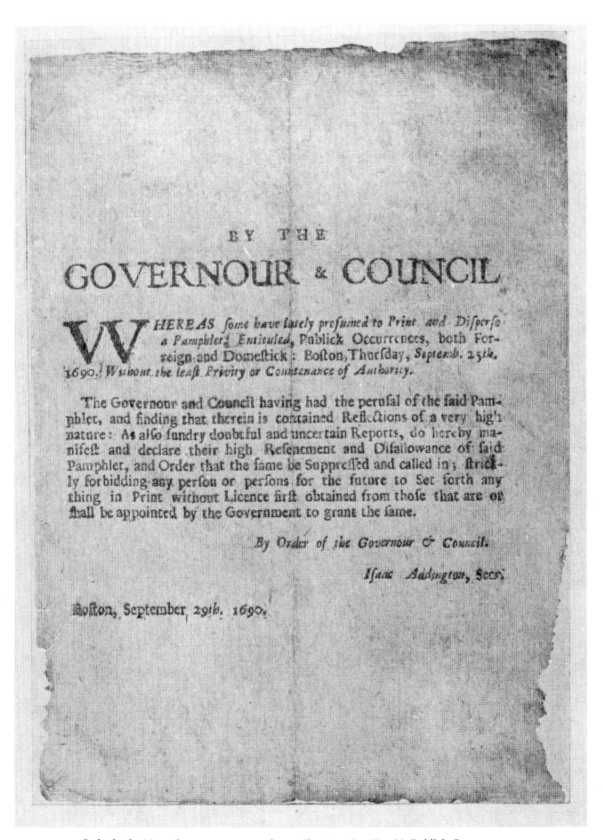

Order by the Massachusetts governor and council suppressing Harris's Publick Occurrences

To the Honourable HOUSE of COMMONS,
Affembled in PARLIAMENT. The CASE,
and Humble PETITION, of *Benjamin Harris*
Bookfeller, lately come from *New-England*.

Humbly Sheweth,

THAT your Petitioner being a *Citizen* of *London*, that formerly Liv'd in Good *Fashion* and *Repute*, hath not only been Exposed to the Indelible *Ignomy* of Standing in the *Pillory*, before his own *House*, near the *Royal-Exchange*; but also Confin'd for above two Years a Prisoner in *Execution* for Five Hundred Pound *Fine*, imposed upon him in *Hillary Term*, 1680. by the *Lord Chief-Justice* [*Scroggs*,] and the reft of the *Judges* of the Court of *King's-Bench*: And was hereby Inevitably reduced to *Ruine*, and the utmoft *Extremities* that could be imagined: And all this for no other *Crime*, or *Offence*, fo much as Alleadged againft him; fave only, that he did (in the way of his *Trade*,) caufe to be *Reprinted*, and *Sell*, a certain Book, Entituled, *An Appeal from the Country to the City, for the Prefervation of His Majefty's Perfon, Liberty, Property, and the Proteftant Religion*—

IN which *Book*, the only Words excepted againft, and charged as Criminal in the *Information* brought againft him; and upon which he receiv'd this Unparallell'd *Judgment*, are thefe, [Speaking concerning Electing of *Members* to Serve in *Parliament*] —" *We in the Countrey have done our parts in Chufing* (for the Generality) *Good* "*Members to ferve in* Parliament: *But if* (as our two laft Parliaments were) *they* " *muft be Diffolved, or Prorogued, when ever they come to* Redrefs *the Grievances of* " *the* SUBJECT, *we may be Pittyed, but not Blamed. If the Plot takes effect,* " (as in all probability it will) *our Parliaments are not then to be Condemned, for that* " *their not being fuffered to* Sit, *occafioned it.*

AND befides all thefe Hardfhips, the Year One Thoufand Six Hundred and Eighty Six, (in the Late K's. Reign,) proved more Fatal to him than all the reft, by reafon that there was Seized and Taken from him Five Thoufand of a *Book*, Entituled, *Englifh Liberties: Or, the Free-Born Subjects Inheritance*; fetting forth the *Power* and *Priviledge* of *Parliaments*, &c. And Five Hundred of another *Book*, Entituled, *The Proteftant Tutor for Children.* And befides all this, his Life was Threatned, if taken, there being Warrants at that time out againft him. And for the Prevention of what might Enfue, he, with his Wife and Children, were forced to Fly their Native Countrey, and feek a Lively-hood in *New-England* in *America*; and his Family, in coming over to *Eng'nd*, were taken *Prifoners* in *September* laft, and continue fo to this Hour in *St. Maloes.*

AND fince your Petitioner has been thus Ruin'd, and remains ftill in a Mean Condition; and that the *Parliament* in the Year 1681, were Pleafed to have your Petitioner under Nomination for *Printing* their VOTES, (tho' your Petitioner did not then Gain any thing thereby, but others went wholly away with the Profit, Sir *William Williams*, then being *Speaker*,) your Petitioner Humbly Begs, That this Honourable Houfe would take him into their Pious Confideration, fo as to Prefent him to your Honoured Speaker, that your Petitioner may be Allow'd (now) to *Print* the VOTES of this prefent *Parliament*, to Support himfelf and Family, and Pay his juft Debts.

IN which your Petitioner affures himfelf, he fhall not (becaufe Diftreft,) be poftpon'd for the Importunities of others, who enjoying Profperity, cannot pretend fo much Equity in their Requefts, though they may have Opportunites of making greater Interefts: For he is confident the Juftice of fo Wife a SENATE, will Charitably extend their Favour, not meerly to thofe that ftand Next, or are moft Importunate, but to fuch as have the moft Need of them.

YOUR poor Petitioner is not infenfible of your manifold Weighty Affairs, which much deterr'd him from Interrupting you with this his private Concern; but Hopes the difmal Circumftances he hath been under, with the afflicting Complaints of his Family, may excufe the unufual Boldnefs of it, and prevail with fo Chriftian an Affembly, to take Pitty on him and them, fo far as 'tis Juft and Reafonable.

AND your Petitioner (as in duty bound) fhall ever Pray, *For your refpective Safeties, the Bleffing of* GOD *on all your Confultations, an Hearty Agreement between the* KING *and his* Good *Subjects, the Long Life of His* MAJESTY, *the Prefervation of the* Proteftant *Religion, and our* Juft *Properties.*

Harris's petition to Parliament after his return to England from America, asking to be allowed to print the votes of that body
(The Ford Collection, New York Public Library)

ris's crimes against him only when Harris is dead. This is quite a shift from the early portion of Dunton's writings, where he described Harris as "the most ingenious and innocent companion that I had ever met with." Partridge protested that Harris and his son forged a supplement to Partridge's almanac.

Harris's only major publication during this period is *The Holy Bible in Verse* (1698). Although one of his biographers dates Harris's last publication as 1716, most historians list no credits for him after approximately 1706. Noted journalism historian Edwin Emery dismissed Harris's second period in England with the comment that Harris became associated with the distribution of patent medicines and then just faded from history.

Harris would probably have faded from history altogether except for *Publick Occurrences* and *The New-England Primer*. His motivation for involvement in both these ventures, however, as evidenced by events throughout his life, was probably economic. The story of Harris's life is just one of many which, when examined closely, forces journalists to admit that their profession has pragmatic as well as altruistic roots.

References:

Cyprian Blagden, *The Stationers' Company* (London: Allen & Unwin, 1960);

John Dunton, *The Life and Errors of John Dunton*, 2 volumes (New York: Burt Franklin, 1969);

Edwin Emery, *The Press and America*, third edition (Englewood Cliffs, N.J.: Prentice-Hall, 1972), pp. 11, 26-29;

Sidney Kobre, "The First American Newspaper: A Product of Environment," *Journalism Quarterly*, 17 (1940): 335-345;

John W. Moore, *Printers, Publishing, and Editing: 1420-1886* (New York: Burt Franklin, 1968);

Wilfred Partington, "The First American Newspaper and the *New England Primer*," *Bookman*, 76 (1933): 103-104;

Isaiah Thomas, *History of Printing in America*, 2 volumes (New York: Burt Franklin, 1964);

John T. Winterich, *Early American Books & Printing* (Boston: Houghton Mifflin, 1935);

Lawrence C. Wroth, *The Colonial Printer* (Charlottesville, Va.: Dominion Books, 1964).

John Holt

(1721-30 January 1784)

James S. Featherston
Louisiana State University

MAJOR POSITIONS HELD: Publisher, *New-York Gazette and Weekly Post-Boy* (1762-1766), *New-York Journal or General Advertiser* (1766-1782), *Independent New-York Gazette or the New-York Journal Revived* (1783-1784).

John Holt, a Virginian who became a leading colonial printer in New York, was a persuasive and influential editorial voice in the independence movement. He was an able and courageous publisher and a prolific printer who maintained high standards of workmanship. Isaiah Thomas, who is considered the father of American printing, described Holt as a "man of ardent feelings, and a high churchman, but a firm Whig, a good writer, and a warm advocate of the cause of his country." A modern historian, Edwin Emery, has termed

Holt "the most important Radical printer outside Boston" during the Revolutionary War era.

Holt was born in Williamsburg, Virginia, in 1721; his exact birthdate is not known. In 1749, he married Elizabeth Hunter; she was the sister of William Hunter, the public printer at Williamsburg and the joint postmaster general of America with Benjamin Franklin. The couple, according to biographer Layton Barnes Murphy, had two children, John Hunter Holt, who was to become the publisher of the *Virginia Gazette, or the Norfolk Intelligencer;* and Elizabeth Holt, who married Eleazer Oswald, editor of the *Philadelphia Independent Gazetteer.* (John Hunter Holt, whose press at Norfolk was seized by Virginia's Governor Dunmore in 1775, is identified by others as John Holt's son, but John Holt himself in the 26 October issue of his

New-York Journal or General Advertiser called the Norfolk printer his nephew in a footnote to a report of the press seizure.) During his early career, Holt was a merchant but failed in business. He also served as mayor of Williamsburg and was a member of the Vestry of the Bruton Parish Church. "Apparently, he was held in high esteem by the townspeople," Murphy writes. "Yet, one citizen, George Fisher, accused him of being unscrupulous and immoral. The grudge was caused by the fact Holt lodged a complaint against Fisher for selling rum to Negroes contrary to law."

After his business failure, Holt, with the help of his brother-in-law, was able to get an appointment as deputy postmaster in New Haven, Connecticut, under James Parker, a printer and postmaster of New York. Meanwhile, Benjamin Franklin, at the request of President Thomas Clap of Yale College, had set up a printing plant in New Haven, and he had planned for his nephew, Benjamin Mecom, to operate it. Mecom, however, refused, and James Parker took over the printing business. On 12 April 1755 Parker began printing the *Connecticut Gazette*, the first newspaper in that colony. On 13 December the newspaper began appearing under the imprint of James Parker and Company, with Holt as the resident partner and editor. It is believed that Holt had learned printing from his brother-in-law, Hunter.

Evidently, Holt did so well in New Haven that he was called by Parker to manage his printing business in New York. On 31 July 1760, the *New-York Gazette and Weekly Post-Boy* appeared under the imprint of James Parker and Company with Holt again as the junior partner. On 6 May 1762, Holt became the sole publisher, leasing the plant and equipment from Parker. In addition to the newspaper, Holt published books, pamphlets, handbills, broadsides, and other materials. About two-thirds of his publications were political, reflecting the interest of Holt and his readers in the struggle between the colonies and England. He also did work for the Provincial Congress of New York and printed laws, ordinances, charters, and accounts of court actions. In addition, he printed materials dealing with religion, freemasonry, economics, history, archaeology, poetry, biography, and other subjects. He sold books, ink, stationery, paper, and other supplies.

Holt openly defied the hated Stamp Act while publishing the *New-York Gazette*, and he was soon to become the favorite printer of the Sons of Liberty—although his relations with these fiery patriots apparently were strained at first. Holt had

originally intended to suspend publication of the *Gazette* rather than pay the tax, but he was persuaded to continue publishing by the Sons of Liberty. Leonard Levy, in his *Legacy of Suppression* (1960), explained: "A letter from the Sons of Liberty notified him he could best promote the cause by continuing to publish without stamps in defiance of Parliament. Holt obeyed because the letter concluded with the threat that if he refused 'depend upon it, your house, person and effects will be in imminent danger.'"

Holt then announced that he would continue to publish his newspaper on unstamped papers. He also began publishing announcements of meetings of the Sons of Liberty and other groups opposed to the Stamp Act, and from 7 November 1765 to 15 May 1766, he added these words to the heading of the *Gazette:* "The united voice of all his Majesty's free and loyal subjects in America,—Liberty and property and no stamps." Holt became an earnest, fearless, and consistent advocate of the Whig cause in a city that was largely Tory in its sympathies. He feuded editorially with James Rivington, Hugh Gaine, and other Loyalist printers. He was helped by the Sons of Liberty, who once paid more than £400 to keep him out of jail and later helped him obtain equipment and supplies for his *New York Journal*.

Holt, however, was still a poor businessman, and he soon found himself in financial difficulty. To satisfy a debt to Benjamin Franklin, he was forced to sell his house and lot at public auction. Parker also accused Holt of owing him a "considerable amount of money." Holt gave up the title of the *Gazette* for one issue because he thought that Parker was planning to publish a newspaper under that name. Clarence S. Brigham, a bibliographer and newspaper historian, explained: "Hearing that James Parker, from whom he had hired the establishment, was intending to publish a newspaper in New York, Holt gave up the title of the *Gazette*, and on May 29, 1766, called his paper 'The New York Journal, or General Advertiser,' no. 1. But learning that Parker declined publishing for the present, he resumed the old title, June 5, 1766. . . . He so continued the paper until Oct. 9, 1766. . . . Again, in view of Mr. Parker's publishing intentions, Holt, on Oct. 16, 1766, adopted a new title 'The New York Journal, or General Advertiser,' no. 1241, continuing the numbering of the *Gazette*." Holt always considered the *Journal* a continuation of the *Gazette*.

In the *Journal* Holt accused Parker of preventing delivery of his papers in New Jersey. Holt

THURSDAY, APRIL 18, 1776.

[Number 1737.]

THE NEW-YORK JOURNAL
OR, THE GENERAL ADVERTISER,

Containing the freshest ADVICES,

both FOREIGN and DOMESTIC.

PRINTED AND PUBLISHED BY JOHN HOLT, NEAR THE COFFEE-HOUSE.

Front page of Holt's pro-independence New-York Journal

resumed his printing business and also trained apprentices, as evidenced by an advertisement that appeared in the *Journal* on 17 August 1767: "Wanted, as an apprentice, by the printer of this paper, a well behaved boy who understands reading, writing, and arithmetic, and is of a reputable family. And as the advertiser has sustained great damage by the misbehavior of boys of vicious dispositions, admitted on trial, he intends for the future to take no apprentices without a fee of at least fifty pounds of New York money, and having all his clothes, found by his friends, during his apprenticeship."

Holt was forced to leave the city when the British occupied Manhattan in late August 1776. He suspended publication of the *Journal* and made a hasty retreat to New Haven, leaving most of his possessions behind. In 1777 he moved to Kingston (also known as Esopus), New York, and secured an appointment as state printer. The state gave him a press and type confiscated from Hugh Gaine, and Holt printed state documents and other materials. On 7 July 1777 he resumed publishing the *Journal* without changing the numbering. It was the first newspaper published in Ulster County, New York. The first issue of this revived newspaper carried an editorial which Charles M. Thomas cites as an excellent example of Holt's style and attitude: "After remaining for ten months past, overwhelmed and sunk, in a sea of tyrannic violence and rapine, the New York *Journal*, just emerging from the waves, faintly rears its languid head, to hail its former friends and supporters—to assure them, that unchanged in its spirit and principles, the utmost exertions of its influence as heretofore, will ever be applied, with a sacred regard to the defense of American rights and freedom, and the advancement of true religion and virtue, and the happiness of mankind."

Holt also congratulated his readers on the firmness with which they had weathered the storm and predicted ultimate success for the revolution, although he feared that it would be a long time before the enemy was driven entirely out of the country. Holt also tried to inspire confidence in the Continental currency by arguing that it was backed by sound security and was really better, in time of war, than gold and silver. Holt added that he was worried at the inflated prices of all commodities and believed that the restoration of normal prices would be of great aid in winning the war. He suggested that normal prices could be restored if each person would try to sell his goods cheaper than

those of his neighbor, rather than trying to sell them higher.

Holt continued to publish the *Journal* in Kingston until 13 October 1777; four days later, the British burned the town. Holt again fled, this time to Poughkeepsie, saving some clothing, bedding, his account books, most of his paper stock, and some type. On 11 May 1778, he resumed publishing the *Journal*, again without a gap in the numbering. He also continued to work as state printer. At times, however, his state salary was not paid on time. He also found it necessary occasionally to ask for additional state funds for paper and supplies. He was constantly in financial difficulty and was forced to advertise a barter system of payment for his customers: "And the printer, being unable to carry on his business without the necessaries of life, is obliged to fix the following prices to his work, viz.: For the newspapers 13 weeks, that is one quarter of a year (rated at three shillings per quarter), 12 pounds of fresh beef, pork, mutton, lamb, or veal, or one bushel of fresh Indian corn, or four pounds of butter, or half a cord of wood, or one hundred fifty wt. of hay, or any other article of his work, or of the necessaries of life he may want, in the like proportion." This appeal was successful, and in the 17 December 1779 issue, Holt thanked his customers for responding.

The first issue of the *Journal* published at Poughkeepsie carried an announcement that the printer was "constrained" to reduce the size of the newspaper from a sheet to a half-sheet because of his small stock of paper and his uncertainty about replenishing it. He was forced to suspend publication from 6 November 1780 to 30 July 1781 because of the scarcity of paper. He then resumed publishing the newspaper until 6 January 1782, when he again quit because of dire financial straits. He had intended to resume publication at Poughkeepsie, but the war was over before he could do so.

Because of poor business ability and the fortunes of war, Holt was almost a ruined man by the time he returned to New York. He published the first issue of his newspaper there on 22 November 1783 under the new name *Independent New-York Gazette or the New-York Journal Revived*. This was another bleak period in Holt's life. He continued to publish his newspaper and work as a state printer until his death on 30 January 1784. His widow published the newspaper for a time before selling it. It finally ceased publication on 8 March 1800.

Holt was buried on the south side of St. Paul's Chapel in New York, under a tombstone cut in letters of printing type in the form of a memorial card. The governor and other leading New York citizens attended his funeral, and he was eulogized in the *New-York Gazetteer, and Country Journal* in these words: "His country never received a wound, but his generous and sympathetic soul felt the pang. Like a genuine patriot, he devoted himself to a voluntary exile during the late war; and in several excursions of the enemy suffered very much the incendiaries of Britain, all which he bore with magnanimity. His indefatigable endeavours to serve the Whig interest, while living, justly entitled him to the veneration and esteem of every virtuous son of Columbia. . . ."

References:

Bernard Bailyn and John B. Hench, *The Press and the American Revolution* (Worcester, Mass.: American Antiquarian Society, 1980), pp. 7, 27-29, 31, 43-44, 46-49, 184, 189, 280, 286, 338-339, 354;

Clarence S. Brigham, *The History and Bibliography of American Newspapers 1690-1820*, 2 volumes (Worcester, Mass.: American Antiquarian Society, 1947), I: 635-636, 654-655;

Philip Davidson, *Propaganda and the American Revolution* (Chapel Hill: University of North Carolina Press, 1941), pp. 170-171, 229;

Edwin Emery and Michael Emery, *The Press and America: An Interpretative History of the Mass Media* (Englewood Cliffs, N.J.: Prentice-Hall, 1978), pp. 70-71, 83-84;

Sidney Kobre, *The Development of the Colonial Newspaper* (Pittsburgh: Colonial Press, 1944), pp. 134-135;

Leonard Levy, *Legacy of Suppression: Freedom of Speech and Press in Early America* (Cambridge: Belknap Press of Harvard University, 1960), p. 86;

Layton Barnes Murphy, "John Holt, Patriot Printer and Publisher," Ph.D dissertation, University of Michigan, 1965;

Victor Hugh Palsits, *John Holt: Printer and Postmaster* (New York: New York Public Library, 1920);

Arthur M. Schlesinger, *Prelude to Independence: The Newspaper War on Britain 1764-1776* (New York: Knopf, 1958), pp. 52, 53, 55-56, 69, 72-73, 77, 81, 100, 111, 114, 117, 185, 189, 191-192,194, 222, 231, 284-285, 289, 312;

Charles M. Thomas, "The Publication of Newspapers During the American Revolution," *Journalism Quarterly*, 9 (December 1932): pp. 354, 358;

Isaiah Thomas, *The History of Printing in America with a Biography of Printers and an Account of Newspapers*, edited by Marcus A. McCorison from the second edition (Barre, Mass.: Imprint Society, 1970), pp. 299, 305-306, 321, 465, 474-476, 485, 491, 494, 503-506, 515, 517, 524;

Lawrence C. Wroth, *The Colonial Printer* (Charlottesville, Va.: Dominion Books, 1964), pp. 62, 66, 132, 172.

Frank Leslie
(Henry Carter)

George Everett
University of Tennessee

BIRTH: Ipswich, Suffolk, England, 29 March 1821, to Joseph Leslie and Mary Elliston Carter.

MARRIAGES: 1841 to Sarah Ann Welham; children: Alfred, Henry, Scipio; divorced 1872. 13 July 1874 to Miriam Follin Squier.

MAJOR POSITIONS HELD: Engraver, *Illustrated London News* (1842-1848), *Gleason's Pictorial and Drawing Room Companion* (1851-1852); chief engraver, *Illustrated News* (1853); publisher, *Frank Leslie's Lady's Gazette of Fashion and Fancy Needlework*, renamed *Frank Leslie's New Family Magazine* in 1857, renamed *Frank Leslie's Monthly* in 1860, renamed *Frank Leslie's Lady's Magazine* in 1863 (1854-1880), *Frank Leslie's New York Journal of Romance* (1855-1857), *Frank Leslie's Illustrated Newspaper* (1855-1880), *Frank Leslie's Illustrirte Zeitung* (1857-1880), *Frank Leslie's Budget of Fun* (1859-1880), *Stars and Stripes* (1859-1860), *Jolly Joker* (1862-1878), *Mr. Merryman's Monthly* (1863), *Frank Leslie's Ten Cent Monthly*, renamed *Frank Leslie's New Monthly* in 1865, renamed *Frank Leslie's Pleasant Hours* in 1866 (1863-1880), *Record of Fashion* (1864-1865), *Frank Leslie's Chimney Corner* (1865-1880), *Illustracíon Americana de Frank Leslie* (1866-1870), *Frank Leslie's Children's Friend*, renamed *Frank Leslie's Boys' and Girls' Weekly* in 1866 (1866-1880), *Last Sensation*, renamed *Day's Doings* in 1870, renamed *New York Illustrated Times* in 1876 (1867-1880), *New World*, merged into *Frank Leslie's Chimney Corner* (1869), *Frank Leslie's Modenwelt* (1870-1871), *Once a Week: The Lady's Own Journal*, renamed *Frank Leslie's Lady's Journal* in 1871 (1871-1880), *Champagne* (1871), *Brickbat* (1872), *Frank Leslie's Tag für Tag*, merged into *Frank Leslie's Illustrirte Zeitung* (1873), *Frank Leslie's AmeriKanische Gartenlaube* (1873-1874), *Frank Leslie's Boys of America* (1873-1878), *Happy Home*, renamed *Young American* in 1874 (1874-1876), *Frank Leslie's Popular Monthly* (1876-1880), *Frank Leslie's Sunday Magazine* (1877-1880), *Idle Hour* (1877), *Some Other Folks* (1877), *Frank Leslie's Budget of Humorous and Sparkling Stories, Tales of Heroism,* *Adventure and Satire* (1878-1880), *Frank Leslie's Chatterbox* (1879-1880).

DEATH: New York City, 10 January 1880.

BOOKS: *Incidents of the Civil War in America* (New York: F. Leslie, 1862);
Frank Leslie's Pictorial Life of Abraham Lincoln (New York: American News Co., 1865);
Illustrated History of the National Peace Jubilee and Musical Festival. Held in Boston, June 15-19, 1869 (New York, 1869);
Frank Leslie's Historical Register of the United States Centennial Exposition, 1876, edited by Frank H. Norton (New York: Frank Leslie's Publishing House, 1877);
The American Soldier in the Civil War (New York: Bryan, Taylor, 1895).

Frank Leslie

In the annals of American journalism, the name of Frank Leslie is associated with so many firsts that he stands out as a pioneer in this field. He established the first successful illustrated news weekly, offered the first full array of specialized publications for all ages and interests, became the first journalist to use his own name as a brand name competing in the national marketplace, conducted America's first successful muckraking crusade, and staged the first self-starring media event to promote his publications. He was also the first journalist or publisher whose widow took his name and successfully extended its usefulness for many years beyond his death. It is almost as if the name were greater than the man, for Leslie was not particularly important in American intellectual, political, or literary history, so far as his originality or creativity is concerned. But above all he was an entrepreneur, and he came onto the scene at just the time when Americans seemed to realize and to accept that the businessman held the reins in the onrushing expansion of the Victorian age.

His wife's achievements were no less remarkable. Mrs. Leslie proved to be a better writer and business manager than her husband, and in the 1880s and 1890s she reveled in her exceptional role as America's empress of journalism.

Frank Leslie was born 29 March 1821 in Ipswich, some seventy miles northeast of London, as Henry Carter, the son of Joseph Leslie Carter and Mary Elliston Carter. The elder Carter was a prosperous manufacturer, and he saw to it that Henry received good schooling in addition to appropriate training in the family's glove factory. However, while he was recovering from an injury he had suffered in the school playground, the boy discovered that he liked to draw. On his way to school he passed the shop of a wood turner and observed the elaborate carvings popular at that time. These fascinated him, as did the engravings of the silversmiths he observed on the way to his father's office. He brought the three crafts of drawing, woodcarving, and engraving together in the practice of wood engraving; by the age of thirteen he had engraved an illustration of the town hall and the Ipswich coat of arms, work of a quality to amaze his elders.

His father was not pleased. Joseph Carter, a leading citizen of the mercantile class, saw the artist's life as one of improvidence and failure. When his son persisted in cluttering his room with drawings, woodblocks, and engraving tools, he sent the boy off to London to work at the glove counter of an uncle's dry goods store. The seventeen-year-old, away from close parental supervision and stimulated by the thriving artistic activity in the city, was soon spending his evenings on work to be submitted to London's many publishers.

It was customary for engravers to carve their names into woodcuts submitted for publication, but Carter wanted to conceal his work from his uncle and his father. He signed his work with the name "Frank Leslie," telling friends many years later that he got the name from a favorite novel of his boyhood. That "Leslie" was also his father's middle name was not mentioned.

In 1841, at the age of twenty, the youth began to strike out on his own. He abandoned the glove business once and for all, and encouraged by the demand for wood engravings, he married Sarah Ann Welham. Cutting himself off from prospects of family support might have been risky, but his adventure was well timed; within a year illustrated journalism would be introduced to the London market. Herbert Ingram, a successful young Nottingham publisher, had done quite well with a broadside illustrating a murder then much in the news, and had noticed that the illustrated London periodicals were selling much better than those without pictures. However, these were literary journals, with illustrations to support fiction and poems. Ingram and his brother-in-law decided to introduce a picture paper which illustrated current events, and on 14 May 1842 they produced the first issue of the *Illustrated London News*, selling 26,000 copies. Young Carter promptly submitted some of his drawings, and was soon on the new periodical's payroll. In a short time he was put in charge of the paper's engraving department.

The illustrated news weekly was a new idea, and it presented production problems unknown to the literary journals. The notion of news as a perishable commodity was familiar to many up-to-date newspapers, but it was now applied to a picture paper, meaning that each drawing and each wood engraving had to be produced on a rush basis. The new system and the young engraving foreman matured together. With six years of such experience behind him, Carter in 1848 felt that he was ready for new horizons. In his middle age he would be characterized as an energetic and enterprising man who on occasion was too eager to take on new projects before his current activities had settled into routine. The fact that he would grow restless as foreman in an expanding enterprise like the *Illustrated London News* suggests that the trait had already developed. He was destined to be an achiever.

London was a beehive of artists and engravers, and competition was so great that Carter saw limited opportunity for a young man in a hurry to reach the top. But America was another matter. One historian estimates that in 1840 there were no more than twenty wood engravers in all of America. It is true that the Americans did not yet have an illustrated news weekly, but illustrations were in high demand for the literary journals, many of which were eager to get away from the expensive metal plates to more economical woodcuts. Frank Luther Mott, the magazine historian, says that it was not uncommon for an American journal during this period to spend as much on one new plate as it did on all the literary contents of an issue.

Carter emigrated with his family in 1848, and by 1849 the New York City directory bore his listing: "Leslie, F., engraver, 98 Broadway." He was able to capitalize on the demand for his skill: an 1849 issue of *Sartain's Union Magazine* cites one of its wood engravings as having cost fifteen dollars for the artist and thirty-five dollars for the engravers Leslie and Traver, a considerable sum in 1849. But as Mott says, Leslie was "an ambitious, lively fellow," not one content to stay put in a city shop grinding out engravings. When Jenny Lind came to America for her 1850 tour, Leslie arranged with her promoter, P. T. Barnum, to illustrate the programs for her concerts, and he followed her company to various American cities and to Havana. In 1851 he joined the staff of the new picture weekly *Gleason's Pictorial Drawing Room Companion* in Boston. The new journal, a sixteen-page tabloid with eight pages of illustrations and eight pages of type, bore considerable resemblance to the *Illustrated London News*. In each issue the editors plugged the forthcoming number, telling in their best travelogue prose of the wondrous illustrations scheduled to delight the reader's eye. In the 29 May 1852 issue, for example, the work of ten artists in the coming issue is extolled, with twice as much attention given to Leslie as to any of the others: "A fine series of capital views of the great Mammoth Cave of Kentucky, taken on the spot by our artist, Mr. Leslie. These scenes embrace, first, a view of the Cave House; second, a view from the outside of the Entrance to the Cave; third, a view of the Entrance from the interior; fourth, Entrance to the Gothic Gate; fifth, the Gothic Chapel; sixth, the Star Chamber; seventh, the Bottomless Pit; and eighth, a view of the River Styx, forming a valuable

and accurate series of illustrations of this great wonder of the world."

Leslie had a full-page engraving of the *Gleason's* pressroom in the same issue in which these lines appeared. His work appears to be no finer than the dozen or so other engravings in that issue, but his is the largest; his experience with the English news weekly had trained him to produce large illustrations quickly to accompany breaking stories. At the *Illustrated London News* he had picked up (perhaps even introduced) an important technique—the assembly of large woodcuts by bolting them together. Wood engraving was a difficult and tedious process in which cross sections of Turkish boxwood were gouged out with hand tools; a full-page engraving would take a skilled engraver a week to finish. But the practice at the *Illustrated London News*, which Leslie is generally believed to have introduced to America, called for dismantling and reassembling the engraving so that several men could do the job. The square pieces of boxwood would be bolted together, and the master engraver would cut the main outlines, especially those crossing the divisions between blocks. The blocks would be separated and then distributed among assistants. The entire engraving could be finished and reassembled, ready for the printing press, within a day or two.

This system was better suited to a news weekly than to a literary journal like *Gleason's Pictorial and Drawing Room Companion*. On Thanksgiving of 1852 Leslie met with that prince of entrepreneurs, P. T. Barnum. Out of that meeting came America's first self-designed news pictorial, the *Illustrated News*. Barnum was listed as special partner, and A. E. and H. D. Beach as general partners. Leslie was put in charge of the engraving department. Within months the paper ran up a circulation estimated as high as 70,000, but there were problems. New York did not have the supply of artists available in Boston, and the machinery for pictorial printing was not fully developed. A. E. Beach (who in 1852 had sold his half interest in the *New York Sun* to his brother Moses S. Beach) had invested $20,000, and Barnum an equal amount, but more was needed to establish a news pictorial in New York. Barnum offered to double his investment if Leslie were made general manager of the whole operation, but the Beaches would not agree to the plan. The struggling *Illustrated News* was delivered into the waiting arms of the staid *Gleason's*— merged out of a promising existence after only a year on the newsstands.

Leslie did not go back to *Gleason's* as a part of

P. T. Barnum, who helped Leslie start his Illustrated News.
The paper was merged into Gleason's Pictorial and Drawing
Room Companion *after only one year*
(The Albert Davis Collection).

the package; he had other plans. After five years
in America he had saved a little money, and he was
ready to start his own publication. He saw the best
short-range prospects in the field of ladies' fashion,
and in January 1854, he brought out *Frank Leslie's
Lady's Gazette of Fashion and Fancy Needlework.* It was
a smart move; he was able to avoid the production
problems associated with a news pictorial and to
capitalize on two current phenomena: the public
craving for illustration and the picturesque hoop-
skirt dresses then coming into style. Several of the
young artists who had assisted him at the *Illustrated
News* trusted their futures to him, and his wife and
children helped in the office. The empire was
founded, and the name Frank Leslie—still not
Henry Carter's legal name—was to adorn illustrated weeklies and monthlies for the remainder
of the century.

The new journal, a twenty-five-cent monthly
of sixteen quarto pages, was an immediate success.
After a year, Leslie had enough profit to acquire a
struggling story magazine, the *New York Journal of*

Romance, which he promptly renamed *Frank Leslie's
New York Journal of Romance.* The overflow of good
material from the *Lady's Gazette,* plus the ample
artwork of Leslie's talented crew of artists and engravers, brought quick profits, and Leslie was soon
able to introduce the flagship of his flotilla of publications. The idea of a pictorial news weekly was
close to his heart, and he probably rushed into it a
bit prematurely. It was only three years since the
Illustrated News of Barnum and Beach had failed
when *Frank Leslie's Illustrated Newspaper* was first issued on 15 December 1855. But by this time Leslie
had his own steam presses and a vision of himself
dominating the pictorial field in America as the
Illustrated London News was by this time dominating
England.

Leslie's decision to introduce his new weekly
as a "newspaper" was important. To this point, his
magazines had been picture and story books. Now
he declared himself ready to portray the week's
events, presumably across the entire nation, in both
words and pictures. This meant training his artists
not only as illustrators but as reporters as well.
Many newspapers covered the week's events, but
the image in the illustrated newspaper would be
the most graphic, the most memorable. And to
many a semiliterate immigrant or unschooled laborer, the picture version would be the only version. Mott describes the new picture weekly: "It was
a small folio of sixteen pages, priced at ten cents a
number, or four dollars by the year. The contents
were highly miscellaneous. The news stories were
illustrated by large, striking pictures which were
nearly always lively and interesting and which usually followed the events they portrayed by about
two weeks—a promptitude in news illustration
never before known in America and not matched
until after the Civil War. Music, drama, the fine
arts, the turf, sports in general, army sketches, book
reviews, and serial fiction were among the earliest
departments."

In general, the new weekly emulated its cousin in London, occasionally copying English illustrations, as with Crimean War coverage. But
domestic stories sold more papers, and they were
not neglected. Whether covering the vigilante activity in San Francisco, General Walker's adventures in Nicaragua, or the unusual developments
of the three-way presidential election of 1856, *Leslie's* provided ample paragraphs and pictures. But
it was an expensive undertaking, and the under-
financed publisher had to back off a bit. Toward
the end of 1856 he hired an editor, Park Benjamin,
whom one historian has characterized as "the

father of cheap literature in the United States." Benjamin was not only a skilled literary agent but an experienced promoter and salesman. In 1857 *Leslie's* gave less and less space to current events, and increasing amounts to fiction and travel pictures. In the issue of 18 July Leslie felt called upon to apologize for the number of serial stories running simultaneously, and promised to cut the number down to one. Even so, the year provided some good news stories for illustrators: the Buchanan inauguration, the sinking of the *Central America*, and the sensational Burdell murder case.

Leslie began to feel new competitive pressure in 1857. When Harper Brothers announced plans for a new weekly to begin 3 January 1857, Leslie ran a notice in his literary column predicting graciously (and naively) that the new weekly "with the acknowledged ability, judgment and taste of the

Harpers as intellectual caterers, cannot fail to make its mark in the world of letters. It will occupy a wholly new field and not interfere at all with the Monthly or any other established journal." In the ensuing months the number of pictures in *Harper's* grew until it was running as many illustrations as *Leslie's*. Leslie's response in the issue of 5 December 1857 reflects both his ebullient self-assurance and the florid style of backbiting popular among editors at the time: "They determined to turn it into an Illustrated Paper, in order to kill us off, although they took the trouble to unnecessarily outrage the truth by assuring us in a message that theirs would not be an Illustrated Paper; that there was no rivalry against us intended. . . . We freely forgive them their feeble assault upon us and only ask that they will continue on in the way they have begun, that their journal . . . may serve . . . as a foil in its

Woodcut from Frank Leslie's Illustrated Newspaper *for 1857 depicting the sensational murder of New York dentist Harvey Burdell*

old-fogyishness to our energy and enterprise."

Harper's, however, was not to be taken lightly. It is true that the magazine jumped on the bandwagon after Leslie had paved the way, and that it was more literary journal than illustrated newspaper during the late 1850s. But by 1860 it was rivaling *Leslie's* in weekly circulation, and it was destined to outsell *Leslie's* through most of the remainder of the century. It was characteristic of Leslie that he would not foresee this. His experiences with Barnum had taught him the application of superlatives and self-acclaim, and it was much more in character for him to inaugurate new journals and extend his energies than to make a defensive response to any potential threat from competition.

Leslie shifted back from fiction to news coverage in 1858; and in the tradition of his showman mentor, he launched his first great news crusade in the issue of 8 May 1858. Preceding issues had contained few news pictures, because Leslie had his artists prowling the stables of the city's distilleries, gathering material on the "swill milk" interests. For some time cows had been fed refuse from the distilleries, and the milk from them was sold in city markets even after the poor animals had been ravaged by sores and disease. New York newspapers had attacked the abuse before, but Leslie felt that pictures, with their more emotional impact on the reader, could succeed where others had failed. He mounted a crusade in what later would be called the muckraking tradition, and the campaign was generally effective. Leslie was sued for libel by city officials involved in the scandal, and at one point was temporarily enjoined from printing any more of the drawings. Such opposition he ably turned to his advantage, presenting himself as the champion of the people, out to do battle with the moneyed interests. Some of the swill milk dealers were driven out of business, and many others were forced to clean up their operations. And of course circulation climbed, reaching 140,000 by the end of the year by Leslie's own estimate.

Frank Leslie's Illustrated Newspaper was by this time selling for six cents a copy, and its circulation rose and fell with the amount of sensational news available. After Congressman Daniel Sickles murdered District Attorney Philip Key in Washington on 27 February 1859, circulation rose for several weeks to "150,000 to 200,000," and a similar rise attended coverage of John Brown's raid, capture, trial, and execution. Leslie also recognized the value of sports as a circulation builder, and he showed remarkable enterprise, amply rewarded, in

covering the Heenan-Sayers prizefight in England. Boxing—a bloody, violent sport in the days before boxing gloves—was illegal in many places, but it was well suited to pictorial coverage, and public interest was high. Leslie sent a top artist and writer to England to witness the desperate bare-fisted struggle thirty miles from London. At the end of the fight both of Leslie's men rushed to London, where the artist's drawings were parceled among engravers hired for the task, and within twenty-four hours an extra edition of *Leslie's* was on the streets of London to amaze the locals with Yankee speed and enterprise—and, perhaps, to let the Carter family know that the boy Henry had amounted to something after all. As soon as the press run was complete the plates were hurried on board a steamer for New York, where *Leslie's* was able to publish the fight results at the same time as its competitiors, but with much more illustration and prose. The total fight edition sold 347,000 copies.

Journalistic firsts did not by any means occupy Leslie fully during these years. He was busy on other fronts as well. In 1857 he had finally changed his name, acquiring legal right to a name that was rapidly becoming valuable simply for brand identification. That year he also inaugurated a German language edition of his news weekly, giving it the name *Frank Leslie's Illustrirte Zeitung.* The paper lasted for thirty-seven years, and was the only news periodical Leslie ever started besides the picture weekly. In 1857 he sold his *Journal of Romance* and expanded the *Lady's Gazette*, renaming it *Frank Leslie's New Family Magazine.*

In 1861, with the attack on Fort Sumter, began the biggest running story in the nation's history. Among America's journalists, Leslie was perhaps best positioned to capitalize on the opportunity. Despite competition from not only *Harper's* but also a weekly 1859 newcomer, the *New York Illustrated News* (no relation to Barnum's 1853 adventure), Leslie had the most experience in pictorial coverage and the largest staff of artists and engravers. Sometime during the war his publication lost its leadership position among the pictorials, and *Harper's* usually had the edge after 1865. But at the outset, Leslie's energy and enterprise left competitors at the gate. At Fort Sumter he had an English artist (more agreeable to the Southerners than a Yankee) who provided thorough and exclusive coverage of the bombardment. Leslie assumed a strong neutral stance, and he allowed one dispatch to be datelined from "Charleston, Republic of South Carolina." He offered to buy sketches from Confederate and Union soldiers alike, and as long as a year after the war started, he offered to save back issues for his Southern subscribers. His chief competitor, Fletcher Harper, also professed neutrality, but within months was scathing the rebels as barbarians and scoundrels. Leslie's policy was more objective and certainly more responsible by twentieth-century standards of objectivity, but Harper's was more popular.

Leslie did have some bad luck: one artist lost several months' worth of sketches in the Red River campaign; another lost his work in a battle on the Rappahannock; and the toughest blow came when the experienced Henry Lovie withdrew from the war, pleading exhaustion, after an outstanding performance at Shiloh. Harper, as it happened, had no one at Shiloh, and was forced to have his New York artists concoct scenes from newspaper reports. Lovie, on the other hand, was all over the battlefield, and single-handedly provided enough sketches to permit Leslie to issue a special sixteen-page supplement on Shiloh alone. Lovie, Leslie, and Leslie's engravers formed what one historian called "the outstanding artist-publisher partnership of the war." Leslie grew to depend on Lovie too much, and when the veteran yielded to fatigue, Leslie was left without a competent artist in the West.

But he probably brought some of his problems upon himself. In the larger Harper Brothers firm, Fletcher Harper could devote full attention to the pictorial weekly while others tended to the rest of the business; but Leslie was supervising his entire stable of publications personally. He compounded the problem by starting five additional publications in the years 1861-1865. He had not the financial resources of the Harpers, and this sometimes showed. A promising fifteen-year-old artist named Thomas Nast went to work for him in 1856; Leslie later reduced his pay. On some occasions, Nast later recalled, he was not paid on time, and once the paymaster told him the reason was that Mr. Leslie had bought a yacht and the company was temporarily short of money. Nast went to the new *Illustrated News;* when that shoestring operation faltered, he returned to Leslie's employ in 1862, but the publisher again let the talented lad slip through his fingers after a few weeks. Nast would prove a priceless asset to *Harper's* for the rest of Leslie's life.

The publisher's personal life may also have contributed to some slippage in his competitive position. Leslie had first been involved with Ephraim G. Squier, archeologist and promoter of a Central

Leslie's publication office at 19 City Hall Square, shared with the New York Daily News. *Leslie moved his operations into this building in February 1860.*

American railroad, when Squier sent him some useful articles on travel and the Honduran question. Squier had also edited a Spanish language newspaper in New York. When the newspaper collapsed and the railroad venture bogged down, he cultivated his association with Leslie. When the Squiers heard in 1860 that Leslie had left his wife and was seeking a place to live, they invited him to move in with them. Soon both Squiers were involved with Leslie publications. Mrs. Squier became acting editor of the *Lady's Magazine* (formerly the *New Family Magazine*) in 1863, and was the founding editor of *Frank Leslie's Chimney Corner* in 1865. Her husband, however, had been given an especially challenging assignment, being named editor of the *Illustrated Newspaper* within months after the outbreak of the

Civil War. The appointment was announced in the issue of 21 September 1861 in a florid style which reflects the self-assurance, pomposity, pretentiousness, and insincerity of Leslie the publishing tycoon: "Owing to the largely increased circulation of his various publications . . . the Editor and Publisher of this Paper has found it necessary to make new arrangements for its conduct. . . . To this end, he has great satisfaction in announcing that he has secured the services of Hon. E. G. Squier as the future Editor of his Newspaper. Mr. Squier is too well known through his public services, and has a literary and scientific character too well established on both continents to need a word of introduction or commendation here. His name is a sufficient guarantee that the Newspaper will be conducted with vigor, independence, judgment and impartiality."

Over the next four years *Leslie's* would have up to twelve correspondents at a time covering the war, with more than eighty artists providing some 3,000 scenes of battles, bombardments, and military life. As if this were not enough to concern a little-experienced journalist, Squier's boss increasingly gave attention to Mrs. Squier. Squier retired from literary work because of "a disturbance of the eyes" and went to Peru as U.S. commissioner in May 1863; he was also observed to have begun drinking rather heavily about this time. Mrs. Squier followed him in June, but returned to New York in November while her husband remained in Peru more than a year longer. Mrs. Squier and Frank Leslie saw a great deal of each other during that time.

In sum, there were too many distractions: Leslie's unpopular policy of nonpartisanship, his selection of an inexperienced editor, his loss of key artists and their work, his diversions with his other magazines, and his tangled personal relationships all served to weaken the news weekly's position. Circulation slipped, and *Harper's* was the leading pictorial weekly by the end of the war in 1865.

At the age of forty-four Frank Leslie was hardly a has-been, and he was destined to enjoy another fifteen glorious years as a public figure. But his contributions as an innovative pictorial journalist were largely complete. His successes from that time on were as a publishing tycoon and as an expert marketer of popular culture. He entered the profitable field of children's literature in 1866 with *Frank Leslie's Boys' and Girls' Weekly*, and brought out a Spanish language version of his news weekly, *Illustración de Americana de Frank Leslie*. He also published various humor and joke magazines,

not including his name in the titles of the more earthy or risqué ones. In 1867 he launched the most lurid of his journals, the *Last Sensation*, renamed *Day's Doings* in 1870 and *New York Illustrated Times* in 1876. When the *New York Times* criticized Leslie for his gossip sheet, he replied that he failed to see why he should be condemned for illustrating the stories he copied from the *Times*'s own coverage of city police activities.

What must have been an ego-satisfying high point in Leslie's career came in 1867 when he was appointed U.S. commissioner to the Paris Universal Exhibition to judge the fine arts exhibits, receiving a gold medal from Emperor Napoleon III. With the Squiers in his entourage, Leslie proceeded grandly across the Atlantic and western Europe, sending many columns of matter to his journals to keep the American public fully informed of the affair's (and his own) importance. Leslie's sketches and Mrs. Squier's paragraphs describing the latest Paris fashions provided material much in demand in the United States, and the expedition proved so rewarding that the same threesome made a similar trip in 1870. Such expeditions were expensive, but the Leslie Publishing House had so expanded that it employed seventy wood engravers and boasted an aggregate circulation—of all its periodicals—of half a million copies a week. Leslie's personal income was about $60,000 a year.

In addition to his many periodicals, Leslie produced another type of publication which is of some journalistic interest: his pictorial histories. Examples were *Pictorial History of the Harper's Ferry Insurrection* (1859); *Frank Leslie's Pictorial History of the War of 1861* (1861-1862); *Frank Leslie's Pictorials of Union Victories* (1862); *Frank Leslie's Pictorial Life of Abraham Lincoln* (1865); *Pictorial History of the Franco-German War* (1870-1871), in German; and *Pictorial History of the Beecher-Tilton Trial* (1875). For these publications, type and woodcuts were saved from running stories and reprinted in tabloid form. This cost-saving or recycling practice was common among daily papers in that era, as they saved their best stories and pictures for reprinting in a weekly edition. The effect at *Leslie's*, however, was to provide a detailed look, in somewhat greater depth, at a significant running story, and in this sense the pictorials were like some of the special editions published by newspapers in modern times. Not being hardbound, their existence was rather ephemeral, but their impact upon students of history in that time must have been considerable.

During the early 1870s Leslie and Mrs. Squier finally obtained divorces and solemnized their

Front page of Frank Leslie's Illustrated Newspaper *for 15 May 1858*

longstanding relationship in marriage. Both were vain and energetic figures, and they spent their wedded years more in grand procession than in journalistic innovation. They built a villa at Saratoga Springs, where they entertained lavishly. At the reception for Governor Tilden, the new Mrs. Leslie appeared wearing $70,000 in jewels. They erected a pavilion to represent their company at the Centennial Exposition at Philadelphia in 1876, and Leslie completed his most ambitious publishing venture—the sumptuously illustrated *Historical Register of the United States Centennial Exposition*. Then in 1877 they set out on a much-publicized transcontinental train trip aboard a special car, the "President," a hotel on wheels which had been exhibited at the exposition. They took staff writers and artists, and a steady stream of material flowed back to New York to embellish the columns of Leslie periodicals.

Such display was more expensive than the company could afford. In 1874, the year of his second marriage, Leslie drew $70,000 in funds; but the mid-1870s were years of depression, and profits declined. The year 1879 was disastrous. Leslie had to go into a sort of partial receivership, retaining company control but yielding most profits to his debtors. He was embroiled in a court fight with his own son Henry, who took the name Frank Leslie, Jr. in order to see what profit it could bring him. Then, in late November, a fatal affliction struck—a rapidly growing tumor in the publisher's throat. He was acutely ill for no more than ten days, and these he spent valiantly getting his affairs in order. He wrote his last will on 27 December 1879, and on 10 January 1880 he died at his New York home.

On 3 January he had dictated, in the hoarse whisper to which his voice had been reduced, a document charting his company's future with his widow at the helm: "She should assume general control of the various departments of the business, as I consider no one in the country is more capable of forming correct judgment of the literary and artistic matters pertaining to the business. She has been to me a most efficient help for the last eighteen years."

Mrs. Frank Leslie inherited from her husband a country estate, a small fortune in jewels, a large business, and a mountain of debts. She also inherited a journalistic tradition of news gathering enterprise which had become increasingly dormant, but which she would revive—and with it the business—in a fairly short time.

Mrs. Frank Leslie had been born in New Orleans 5 June 1836 as Miriam Florence Follin. Her father, an unprosperous scholar of noble Huguenot ancestry, taught her five languages. The family was brought to New York, where she was further schooled in the arts, and she had a story published in James Gordon Bennett's *New York Herald* when she was scarcely fourteen. Following a brief stint as an actress, a marriage to a jewelry clerk, an annulment, and some months as a congressman's mistress, she captivated the highly literate Ephraim G. Squier. She married him in 1857, and helped him with his *Noticioso de Nueva York*. She also applied her linguistic talents to a translation of Dumas, which was published in 1858.

At the age of twenty-one the young bride already had a checkered past, but she was attractive, vivacious, intelligent, and well schooled in the social arts. There is some evidence that her parents had been taking particular pains to train her for New York society, and when the Squiers began the social whirl in the company of Frank Leslie, she was well prepared. According to *Frank Leslie's Illustrated Newspaper*, she was the belle of Abraham Lincoln's inaugural ball of 1861; she was prominently featured in the page one illustration. She was similarly displayed in the report of the presidential party of 5 February 1862 in both the *Illustrated Newspaper* and *Frank Leslie's Monthly*, as the *Lady's Gazette* had been renamed. The latter periodical in early 1863 was again renamed, this time *Frank Leslie's Ladies Magazine*, and when the editor soon after took sick leave, Mrs. Squier took over her duties. At a time when other publications were reporting the grim scenes at Vicksburg and Gettysburg, she announced that 1863 was "the year of fashions. In the course of a century there has not been a time when fashion predominated as it does now. It overrules everything." She had unusual talents in the world of fashion, plus considerable editorial ability, and in time the *Ladies Magazine* was to bring in a net annual profit of more than $39,000.

Mrs. Squier had equal interest in the field of literature, and when a new literary pictorial, *Frank Leslie's Chimney Corner*, was announced for 1865, it was her brainchild from the start. She planned it, staffed it, and defined its place. It was to be a publication not just for the ladies, but for the entire family. It was destined to be one of the mainstays among Leslie publications, lasting some twenty years.

With her multilingual talents, Mrs. Squier was an invaluable companion to Leslie in his European travels of 1867 and 1870, and to Squier in Latin America. That she may have been valuable to Leslie in nonprofessional ways was the subject of much discussion among the scandalmongers, and it was no small achievement for her to maintain her social and professional roles despite the gossips. Unfortunately, her place as editor of a women's magazine required her to voice or publish opinions on manners and morals from time to time, and her colorful past made her vulnerable to reprisal.

Following the difficult divorces of Frank Leslie and Miriam Squier in 1872 and 1873, respectively, and their much-publicized wedding in 1874, Mrs. Leslie showed new and valuable talents as head of household and entertainer of distinguished guests. She was especially effective in her role as hostess at Interlaken, Leslie's new villa between the lakes at Saratoga Springs. When any distinguished visitor came to the resort, he soon found that the Leslies would not only treat him royally at their villa and aboard their steam yacht but would also provide ample publicity and acclaim in the various Leslie publications. Receiving the most linage and the greatest number of woodcuts was Dom Pedro, the emperor of Brazil, who stayed with the Leslies before his official visit to the Centennial Exposition. Mrs. Leslie conversed with the emperor in Spanish or French as he chose, and for the benefit of the empress she demonstrated her equally fluent Italian. Miriam Leslie seemed a queenly figure with numberless talents.

When the couple set out on their highly promoted transcontinental train ride, Mrs. Leslie wrote a great amount of copy about the Indians she saw on the plains, the Palace at San Francisco, adobes and ranches at Los Angeles, the scenery at Yosemite. At Salt Lake City she capped the trip with a highly quotable interview with Brigham Young. Just before that, however, the procession had toured the mining town of Virginia City, which she described as a God-forsaken place on the side of a barren mountain, a generally lawless city whose women were "of the worst class." It was one of the few unflattering descriptions she had published in the long series of articles about the American West; for the most part, the trip, admittedly a newsmaking event staged by editors in their own self-interest, had done much to inform Eastern provincials about the rest of their country in a way that would instill pride.

The indignant editor of the *Virginia City Territorial Enterprise* did not forget Mrs. Leslie's criticisms. He felt that she was not the appropriate person to judge the character of a town's women, and he set out to judge her character in return. He got the ammunition he needed from her bitter ex-husband, E. G. Squier, and on 14 July 1878 he fired his broadside: *Territorial Enterprise Extra. Containing a Full Account of "Frank Leslie" and Wife.* The pamphlet detailed the couple's former marriages, questionable aspects of the divorce proceedings, and various other skeletons in their rather full closets. Most of the accusations were true. The Leslies had made themselves public figures, and now they were ripe for national scandal. But they were not lacking in courage, and they withstood the storm. They had become too prominent, too celebrated, to be ostracized as the result of an attack—however well aimed—from the remoteness of a Sierra mining camp.

Of the many charges made in the *Territorial Enterprise Extra,* the most difficult one to ignore was in the last section of the pamphlet, where it was averred that the Leslie empire was headed for financial collapse. For a time this seemed to be true. Leslie's debtors had already made their move to restrict his spending, and circulation was holding fairly well following declines in the mid-1870s. When Leslie suddenly fell victim to his fatal illness, half the debts had been paid and the company seemed well on the road to recovery. But when the man whose name prefaced the company's best periodical titles lay dead, the future was uncertain. Mrs. Leslie's biographer describes the crisis: "Mrs. Frank Leslie was aware that she now faced the crisis of her life. She had inherited debts and an opportunity. Her task was to pay the debts and improve the opportunity. Her success would demonstrate to an amazed nineteenth century the apparent anomaly of a woman who could do a man's work and yet remain most decidedly a woman. Instead of preaching women's rights, Mrs. Leslie proceeded to live them."

The first battles were fought in the courts, where nine lawsuits over Leslie's will and the rights to his name were successfully repelled. Next she faced her creditors, and using her jewels as security, she obtained a loan from a mysterious "Mrs. Smith" to pay off the debts. She had her name legally changed to Frank Leslie in June 1881, and there remained only one major battle: to bolster the now-slipping circulation of the Leslie periodicals. The company's standard bearer, the *Illustrated Weekly,* was especially vulnerable.

The solution came from a national tragedy, and it afforded Mrs. Leslie the opportunity to demonstrate her own ability as a journalist. On 2 July 1881 a disgruntled office seeker shot President Garfield in Washington. Hearing rumors of the shooting at about 9:30 A.M., Mrs. Leslie had two artists on the train to Washington within the hour.

Miriam Follin Squier Leslie, who legally changed her name to Frank Leslie and ran her husband's publishing empire after his death (New York Public Library)

jumped from 30,000 to 200,000, and the new "Frank Leslie" was able to write with pride: "Our illustrations of the attempted assassination and of subsequent events growing out of it have afforded the only accurate and complete pictorial history of the affair which has been given, and the enormous sales of the various editions attest very conclusively the public appreciation of the enterprise of Frank Leslie's Publishing House. We mean to hold in every respect the position and admitted lead we have long enjoyed in the illustrated journalism of the country."

She possessed not only her late husband's name, but his self-assured style as well. Even more than he, perhaps, she had demonstrated her understanding of news and its value. When Garfield finally died on a Monday evening, she ordered the presses stopped, threw away some of the issue already printed, and went to press with new pictures, finished during the night, depicting the deathbed scene. The following week, when the funeral was held in Washington and the body sent to Cleveland, she brought out the weekly one day early and sold 30,000 copies in Cleveland describing the ceremonies in Washington. The whole enterprise netted about $50,000 in profits, which she used to pay off the debt to Mrs. Smith. The Frank Leslie Publishing House was in its strongest financial position in many a year.

This prosperity enabled Mrs. Leslie to turn the news business over to her staff, and to devote more time to business, literary, and social pursuits. She wisely reduced the number of periodicals, recognizing that one periodical with 24,000 circulation was much better than a dozen periodicals with 2,000 each. At the time of the Garfield episode the company published ten periodicals with an aggregate circulation of a quarter of a million. There were 300 or 400 employees drawing a total of $32,000 a week. The company paid out $125,000 a year for manuscripts, and ranked third in the nation in consumption of ink. These were the kinds of figures the original Frank Leslie would enjoy publicizing, but his widow had a much sharper eye for the bottom line. By 1887 she had reduced the number of publications to six, with no significant loss in aggregate circulation. In 1889 she sold the aging *Illustrated Newspaper,* always costly and demanding, and gave her attention to the more profitable *Popular Monthly* and three other literary publications. The Frank Leslies were out of the newspaper business.

Having put the company on a more profitable and less demanding basis, Mrs. Leslie turned to

One was back in New York by midnight with the first round of sketches. The whole staff of the *Illustrated Newspaper* was ordered to report for work early the next morning—a Sunday. By Tuesday morning the full pictorial coverage of the shooting was on the newsstands in *Frank Leslie's Illustrated Newspaper.* On Friday an extra edition was issued, and the following Tuesday another regular edition came out with the fullest coverage yet. It was an achievement no one would have predicted. Three editions of a pictorial newspaper had been published in one week giving full coverage of a late-breaking story—and it all had been done by a woman. From that time on, her increasingly popular nickname, "the empress of journalism," seemed a title more earned than conferred.

Because of her enterprise, and because the president clung to life for two months and this provided sustained stimulus to circulation, the pictorial weekly was making money again. Circulation

lecturing and writing. She traveled and indulged a number of suitors, one of whom she married in 1891. But Willie Wilde—the brother of Oscar Wilde—was not a good husband, and the entire episode lasted only a few months. She leased the *Popular Monthly* in 1895 and essentially retired from publishing, although she had to return after three years to edit the magazine when her lessees failed to keep it going. In general she held court as the reigning queen of publishing and offered colorful opinions on a wide range of subjects. Although her own experience was relatively limited so far as breaking news coverage was concerned, she repeatedly extolled journalism as a field ripe for female conquest. She was not a feminist in the usual sense—she could effectively play her role as one of "the weaker sex" when it suited her purpose—but she was especially proud of her achievements in what was normally a man's world. She took particular delight in beginning her lectures, "Ladies and Gentlemen, I am Frank Leslie."

At the turn of the century she retired from publishing for the last time, and gave her $250,000 earnings to a financial adviser who would multiply them eightfold before she died. She lived in quiet comfort and glitter, enjoying the title she brought back from France in 1901 as the Baroness de Bazus. She died quietly at home in New York on 18 September 1914, and was buried beside Frank Leslie—and not far from E. G. Squier—in Woodlawn Cemetery. Her death was not widely noted in those days of early World War I turmoil, but she was not to be denied one last shot at the headlines. Her will disclosed that she wished to leave practically all of her $2,000,000 estate to the cause of woman suffrage. It was still a man's world, and numerous specimens came forth to contest the will and keep all that money from going to what they deemed such a useless cause. Although she had no children, her four marriages left her with many relatives who surfaced to claim part of the estate. In the end, the will held, but about half the estate was consumed in legal and administrative expenses. The remaining million was used to establish the Leslie Woman Suffrage Commission, which was instrumental in bringing the vote to women within a few years of her death.

An assessment of the Leslies' contribution to American journalism is made difficult by the fact that neither was trained at any mainstream American newspaper, and that their own *Illustrated Newspaper* was at times hard to distinguish from their other popular literature. Although they called themselves journalists, Frank Leslie's main interest was art, and Miriam Leslie's was literature. Indeed, most of the journalism histories written in the first half of the twentieth century do not mention either of the Leslies or the *Illustrated Newspaper*. Only more recently, as television and film have brought historians to see journalism in a larger sense, have the Leslies been embraced in the standard histories.

Two broad trends in twentieth-century journalism have brought new appreciation to the Leslies' pioneering efforts. One such trend is the long-term shift from alphanumeric news (words printed on paper) to nonverbal forms of news. As more and more Americans get their news from pictures rather than from prose, those who would ask how it all began increasingly go back to Frank Leslie, the man whose tombstone calls him "The Pioneer and Founder of Illustrated Journalism in America." He was indeed the first to demonstrate clearly the demand for news pictures in America.

The other modern trend which points back to the Leslies is the emphasis on marketing strategy in modern journalism. Both Frank Leslies were pioneers in the marketing of mass communication in America. Leslie had told his staff from the start, "Never shoot over the heads of the people." Like James Gordon Bennett and Ben Day, he brought new people into the news-consuming public. And he did it with a vigorous, witty style that appealed to readers. In a sense, he was a self-made popular hero.

The achievement of Mrs. Leslie is no less remarkable. She did not score as many journalistic firsts as her husband, but she proved to be an even better editor, marketer, and business manager than he was. In an era when opportunities for women were so limited, her success is more surprising, and perhaps more deserved, than his. But clearly both Leslies possessed enormous talent, and they seemed especially to complement each other. It is regrettable that they had only five years together as man and wife; had they managed to avoid their unfortunate early marriages and to begin their grand procession through the Victorian Age a bit sooner, they might well have dominated American mass media on an unprecedented scale. As each lay dying, he or she could look back on many accomplishments; but each also must have felt some terribly poignant emotions, reflecting on what might have been.

Biographies:
Madeleine B. Stern, *Purple Passage: The Life of Mrs. Frank Leslie* (Norman: University of Oklahoma Press, 1953);

Budd Leslie Gambee, Jr., *Frank Leslie and His Illustrated Newspaper, 1855-1860* (Ann Arbor: University of Michigan Department of Library Science, 1964).

References:
Louis Filler, *The Muckrakers, Crusaders for American Liberalism* (Chicago: Regnery, 1950), pp. 31, 85;

Frederic Hudson, *Journalism in the United States, from 1690 to 1872* (New York: Harper, 1873), pp. 693, 705-709;

Frank Luther Mott, *A History of American Magazines, 1850-1865* (Cambridge: Harvard University Press, 1938), pp. 31,44,130,409-415, 437-441, 452-465;

Mott, *A History of American Magazines, 1741-1850* (Cambridge: Harvard University Press, 1930), pp. 769-772;

Frank Presbrey, *The History and Development of Advertising* (Garden City: Doubleday, Doran, 1929), pp. 454, 458, 470;

Louis M. Starr, *Reporting the Civil War* (New York: Collier Books, 1962), pp. 141, 209, 210, 225;

Madeleine B. Stern, ed., *Publishers for Mass Entertainment in Nineteenth Century America* (Boston: Hall, 1980), pp. 181-189;

John Tebbel, *The Media in America* (New York: Crowell, 1974), pp. 190, 211, 235-238;

W. Fletcher Thompson Jr., *The Image of War* (New York: Thomas Yoseloff, 1959).

Sara Jane Clarke Lippincott
(Grace Greenwood)

(23 September 1823-20 April 1904)

Donna Born
Central Michigan University

MAJOR POSITIONS HELD: Editorial assistant, *National Era* (Washington, D.C.) (1850-1852); correspondent, *New York Mirror, New York Tribune, New York Times, New York Independent, Philadelphia Press* (1870-1889); columnist, *New York Independent* (1892-1904).

BOOKS: *Greenwood Leaves: A Collection of Sketches and Letters* (Boston: Ticknor, Reed & Fields, 1850);

History of My Pets (Boston: Ticknor, Reed & Fields, 1851; revised and enlarged, New York: J. B. Alden, 1885; further revised and enlarged, New York: J. W. Lovell, 1890);

Poems (Boston: Ticknor, Reed & Fields, 1851; enlarged, Boston: Ticknor, Reed & Fields, 1854);

Recollections of My Childhood, and Other Stories (Boston: Ticknor, Reed & Fields, 1852); revised as *Stories of My Childhood and Other Tales* (New York: United States Book Company, 1890);

Greenwood Leaves: A Collection of Sketches and Letters,

Second Series (Boston: Ticknor, Reed & Fields, 1854);

Haps and Mishaps of a Tour in Europe (Boston: Ticknor, Reed & Fields, 1854);

Merrie England: Travels, Descriptions, Tales and Historical Sketches (Boston: Ticknor & Fields, 1855);

A Forest Tragedy, and Other Tales (Boston: Ticknor & Fields, 1856);

Stories and Legends of Travel and History, for Children (Boston: Ticknor & Fields, 1857);

Old Wonder-eyes; and Other Stories for Children, by Lippincott and Leander K. Lippincott (New York: J. Miller, 1857);

Stories from Famous Ballads; for Children (New York: International Book Co., 1859);

Nelly, the Gipsy Girl, anonymous (New York: General Protestant Episcopal Sunday School Union & Church Book Society, 1863);

Stories of Many Lands (New York: Hurst, 1866);

Records of Five Years (Boston: Ticknor & Fields, 1867);

Stories and Sights of France and Italy (Boston: Ticknor & Fields, 1867);

Bonnie Scotland: Tales of Her History, Heroes, and Poets (Boston: J. R. Osgood, 1872);

New Life in New Lands: Notes of Travel (New York: J. B. Ford, 1872);

Heads and Tales: Studies and Stories of Pets (New York: American News Co., 1874);

Emma Abbott, Prima Donna (New York: Photo Engraving Co., printers, 1878);

Treasures from Fairy Land, by Lippincott and Rossiter W. Raymond (New York: American News Co., 1879);

Queen Victoria. Her Girlhood and Womanhood (New York: J. R. Anderson & H. S. Allen / London: S. Low, Marston, Searle & Rivington, 1883);

Some of My Pets (New York: J. B. Alden, 1884);

Stories for Home-Folks, Young and Old (New York: J. B. Alden, 1884);

Stories and Sketches (New York: Tait, 1892);

Europe: Its People and Princes.—Its Pleasures and Palaces (Philadelphia: Hubbard, n.d.).

OTHER: Eliza Greatorex, *Summer Etchings in Colorado*, introduction by Lippincott (New York: Putnam's, 1873).

Sara Lippincott, better known by her pseudonym "Grace Greenwood," was one of the earliest women newspaper correspondents; she was preceded only by Jane Swisshelm as the earliest woman Washington correspondent. Her long writing career began when she was only thirteen, with the publication of her earliest poems. In 1844, at the age of twenty-one, she began her journalism career, publishing informal letters as "Grace Greenwood." The letter genre remained the major form of her journalistic writing: for nearly sixty years, she wrote letters for various newspapers and periodicals to report her experiences and observations of Washington, Europe, and the western United States and to express her strong opinions on such issues as slavery, woman's rights, and capital punishment. Several collections of her letters were published during her lifetime.

In addition to her popular letters, her essays, stories, and sketches appeared over the years in the *Saturday Evening Post, Hearth and Home, Atlantic Monthly, Harper's New Monthly Magazine, Ladies' Home Journal, New York Times, New York Tribune*, and many other periodicals, including the English magazines *Household Words* and *All The Year Round*. She also edited one of America's first juvenile magazines, the *Little Pilgrim*. The children's stories and sketches that she wrote for the magazine were collected annually and published as gift books.

Grace Greenwood was born Sara Jane Clarke on 23 September 1823 in Pompey, New York. She was the youngest daughter of the eleven children of Thaddeus and Deborah Baker Clarke, with Puritan and New England Huguenot roots. She was the great-granddaughter of the New England theologian Jonathan Edwards. Her father was a successful physician, whose ill health forced him to an early retirement. Her mother, who was educated in the English classics, helped stimulate Sara's literary interest by reading to her.

In *Recollections of My Childhood, and Other Stories* (1852) Greenwood describes a secure and carefree childhood. A lover of nature, she played in woods and streams, rode her horse bareback (liking best to stand on the horse's back at full gallop), and "chased after rainbows." During her childhood, her family moved to Fabius, and then to Rochester, where she attended school for eight years. She wrote that she was no genius, just a "simple-hearted

Sara Jane Clarke Lippincott (Grace Greenwood) in 1879

child, that believed everything she was told." She also described herself as a good child, afraid of the "evil one," but not above playing harmless tricks or tearing her dress in a little rough play. She found great pleasure in reading, which she was most fond of doing while sitting in the apple tree near her house. She began to write when she was a young girl, and as early as 1836, her poems were published in the Rochester newspapers.

In 1842 her family moved to New Brighton, Pennsylvania; Sara joined them there the following year and began to write informal letters for George P. Morris and Nathaniel P. Willis's *New York Mirror* and *Home Journal*. The letters were signed "Grace Greenwood," and from that time on she was known as Grace, even to her friends.

Her letters were immediately popular and soon began to appear in *Godey's Lady's Book, Graham's, Sartain's, Neal's Gazette,* and the *Saturday Evening Post,* in addition to the *Mirror* and the *Home Journal.* Readers liked her strong opinions on contemporary issues, and liked the way these opinions were expressed with feminine propriety. Her lively, descriptive, and sometimes humorous letters also dealt with travel, nature, art, books, and persons she met.

In 1849 Greenwood became editor of Louis A. Godey's *Lady's Dollar Newspaper* and editorial associate of the *Lady's Book.* Godey dismissed her in 1850, however, when she offended Southern readers by writing an essay in support of abolition for the antislavery paper *National Era.*

Gamaliel Bailey, editor of the *National Era,* graciously offered her a position as his assistant on the *Era* as well as a home with his family in Washington. Greenwood accepted both offers, and she accepted, as well, a position as Washington correspondent for the *Saturday Evening Post,* for which she first wrote her "Washington Letters." Her association with the *Post* lasted until 1897.

Those early years in Washington were a time of happiness and professional growth for Greenwood. She looked back on her life with the Baileys in an article entitled "An American Salon" in the February 1890 issue of *Cosmopolitan.* She said she was proud to be associated with the *Era* because of its literary reputation as well as its commitment to abolition: it was in the *Era* that *Uncle Tom's Cabin* was first published; John G. Whittier, "our beloved prophet-poet, our laureate of freedom," was corresponding editor; and John Pierpont, Henry B. Stanton, William D. Gallagher, Bayard Taylor, and Gail Hamilton were among its writers. Greenwood was intensely interested in her new assignment to

Greenwood in 1848

cover the workings of the government for the *Era,* and she was greatly impressed with the "splendid set of men" who sat in the Senate: Daniel Webster, Henry Clay, William H. Seward, Thomas Corwin, Stephen A. Douglas, Thomas Benton, Salmon P. Chase, John P. Hale, and "he who was to undertake to make history for a new empire," Jefferson Davis. Her letters and articles from this period dealt mostly with descriptions of literary and political figures and offered little political analysis.

She enjoyed the gaiety and stimulation of the social life of Washington, where she met such "distinguished visitors" as Horace Greeley, "the great editor"; Horace Mann; Fredrika Bremer; and Dorothea Dix. But, she wrote, the "pleasantest, if not the gayest, part of . . . Washington life, . . . was spent with the Baileys and in their ever-widening social circle." It was at the Baileys' home that the Free-Soilers, of which Greenwood was a zealous member, met to give each other moral and intellectual support, "fighting the good fight against tremendous odds."

Greenwood's first book, *Greenwood Leaves,* was published in 1850. A collection of her early letters and sketches, the book became a best-seller. In the following year, *Poems,* a collection of her early verses, and *History of My Pets,* the first of her books for children, were published.

In spite of the popularity of her books, some critics found her work sentimental and overstated. Of her early, sometimes mournful verse, her brother quipped: "First the undertaker, then the minister, then Sara." Another critic complained about her profuse superlatives, saying that the word *gorgeous* "occurs on almost every page and only yields now and then to such mild adjectives as 'grand,' 'superb,' and 'delicious.' . . . Sunsets, mountains, trees, churches, paintings, music, and pyrotechnics are all 'gorgeous.' " In general, however, Greenwood's work was favorably received. John Hart noted in *Female Prose Writers of America* (1852) that Greenwood's busy life prevented her from concentrating her powers on any important work; nevertheless, her writing revealed "a noble seriousness . . . many-toned utterances of feelings, that lay deep down in the breast. . . . She has humour most rich and racy—that which springs from keenness of intellect, fullness of imagination, kindliness of temper, and playfulness of spirit." Rufus Griswold wrote in *The Female Poets of America* (1859) that she was among "the most industrious and successful of our authors, and has written with perhaps equal facility and felicity in every style. . . . All her thought is direct and honest, and her sentiment vigorous and cheerful. . . ."

Another admirer, Sarah Josepha Hale, wrote in 1855 that especially praiseworthy was Greenwood's "intenseness of feminine feeling." But it was not only "feminine feeling" that Greenwood expressed; she wrote for the cause of "feminism" as well. In a letter in the *Saturday Evening Post* in January 1850, she rather passionately defended a woman's right to a literary profession, which a few male critics had questioned: "Man is not best qualified to mark out woman's life path. . . . Woman can best judge of woman, her wants, capacities, aspirations, and powers." She praised the growing trend for women to seek independence: "Thank Heaven, woman herself is awaking to a perception of the causes which have hitherto impeded her free and perfect development. . . . She is beginning to feel, to cast off the bonds which oppress her. . . . There surely is a great truth involved in this question of 'Woman's Rights.' . . ."

In the summer of 1852, Greenwood made her first trip to Europe, where she spent eighteen months as a correspondent for the *National Era* and the *Saturday Evening Post.* She sent back interviews with famous persons such as Dickens, Thackeray, and Robert Browning, and long, descriptive meditations on art and historical places in England, France, Germany, and Italy. Of these letters, Joseph Lyman wrote in *Eminent Women of the Age* (1869): "No lady tourist from America has surpassed Greenwood in the warm tinting and gorgeous rhetoric of her descriptions, and in the vivacious interest which she felt herself, and which she conveys to others in her letters." He offers Greenwood's description of a statue of Apollo as an example of her "vigorous writing": "The indestructible glory of the lost divinity lingers about him still; and the deep, almost solemn emotion, the sigh of unutterable admiration, with which the pilgrims of art behold him now, differ little, perhaps from the hushed adoration of his early worshippers. I have never seen any work of art which I had such difficulty to realize as a mere human creation, born in an artist's struggling brain, moulded in dull clay, and from thence transferred, by the usual slow and laborious process, to marble." With such expansive prose, Greenwood's letters charmed her readers. These letters were published in 1854 in the most popular of all her books, *Haps and Mishaps of a Tour in Europe,* which remained in print for forty years. Despite its American popularity, the book was severely criticized by the *Athenaeum* of London for its sentimentality, its overstatement, and its extravagant prose, as well as for its invasion of the privacy of its English subjects.

On 17 October 1853 Greenwood married Leander K. Lippincott, a handsome and witty Philadelphian. The marriage was an unhappy one; according to the gossip of the day, Lippincott was unfaithful to Greenwood both during their courtship and after the wedding. Greenwood never discussed her marriage nor mentioned it in her writings, but one of her sentimental short stories, "Zelma's Vow," appearing in the *Atlantic* in 1859, perhaps tells of her disappointment. In the story, Zelma's lover deserts her for another woman, but Zelma keeps her grief within and turns to her art for consolation.

In 1853 Greenwood and her husband launched one of the earliest and most popular juvenile magazines in America, the *Little Pilgrim.* The stories and sketches in the magazine, written mostly by Greenwood, were intended both to entertain and to instruct. The magazine also published stories, anecdotes, letters, and puzzles written by the young readers and their parents and contributions from Greenwood's literary friends. Lippincott managed the business, and Greenwood did most of the editing. Many of the stories and sketches

Cover of the juvenile magazine published by Greenwood and her husband, Leander K. Lippincott

were collected at the end of each year and published in illustrated gift volumes, such as *A Forest Tragedy, and Other Tales* (1856), *Stories of Many Lands* (1866), *Stories and Sights of France and Italy* (1867), and *Bonnie Scotland* (1872). The magazine was very successful until it began to decline with the onset of the Civil War; it managed to remain in publication until 1875. Throughout this time, Greenwood continued writing for the *Saturday Evening Post,* and in the late 1850s, after the birth of her daughter Annie, she joined the lecture circuit for yet another source of needed income.

Although not previously considered a proper "sphere" for women, the lecture circuit proved to be a successful venture for Greenwood. She was popular and had as many engagements as she could handle. She was not part of the active reform or "Progressive" movement of the late nineteenth century, but she spoke to improve the world in various ways. She spoke in support of abolition, woman suffrage, equal pay for equal work, pacifism, the abolition of capital punishment, and improvement in prisons; she also spoke for reform in women's dress so that women could enjoy nature as freely

as men did. These topics also filled her writings, which she continued to provide to the popular periodicals.

She also gave her untiring support for the war to preserve the Union and free the slaves. For her war work—visiting army hospitals, reading and talking to the soldiers at army camps, and raising funds for medical supplies and comforts for the soldiers—President Lincoln called her "Grace Greenwood the Patriot."

In 1870 Greenwood returned to Washington and became a correspondent for the *New York Tribune,* the *New York Times,* and newspapers in Chicago, Philadelphia, and elsewhere. She also made several lecture trips through the West, visiting Pennsylvania, Ohio, Michigan, Iowa, Kansas, Utah, Nevada, and California. She was especially fond of Colorado, and she campaigned for its statehood in her Washington letters to the *New York Times.* The letters of her Western trips of 1871 and 1872 were collected and published in *New Life in New Lands* (1872). During these years, she continued to contribute stories and essays to *Hearth and Home,* the *Christian Union,* the *Ladies' Home Journal,* and other popular magazines.

From 1875 to 1877 Greenwood was in Europe with her daughter, and she sent long weekly reports of her travels to the *New York Times.* While she was away, her husband was indicted for fraud in his duties as chief clerk of the General Land Office of the Department of the Interior; he fled the country before he could be arrested. Although she never lived with him again, Greenwood always insisted that he was innocent. In 1877 she returned to Washington, and for the first time in her political reporting, she sat in the press galleries; previously, she said, she had "hovered" just outside them. Her writing had greatly improved over the years; her letters from this period are more forthrightly political and her opinions are bolder. In response to criticism of her unfeminine political "utterances," she wrote in one of her letters to the *New York Times:* "I have been roughly reminded that I was a woman, and told that I ought to be sternly remanded by public opinion to woman's proper sphere. . . . I can 'rastle' with cooking and sewing as well as any of my gentler sisters, but just at present I confess I prefer serving up a spicy hash of Southern Democratic sentiment. . . ."

In 1878 she again went to Europe, this time to continue Annie's musical education. To pay for the trip, she wrote articles for the *New York Independent* about experiences awaiting young American musicians in Europe. She also sent to the

Independent commentary on current political and literary affairs, items of interest gleaned from the French, English, and Italian newspapers, and her own observations on the events she witnessed.

Still a prolific writer, she published simultaneously in London and New York *Queen Victoria. Her Girlhood and Womanhood* (1883). Written especially for young girls, the book describes the queen in her roles as the exemplary wife and mother as well as queen. Victoria herself complimented Greenwood on the book.

In the late 1880s Greenwood and her daughter returned home, and Annie married the playwright Henry Field Winslow. Settled for the last time in Washington, Greenwood in 1892 began to write reminiscences and commentary for the *Independent*. Severe asthma forced her to move in 1900 to her daughter's home in New Rochelle, New York. She continued to write her column until a few months before she died on 20 April 1904 of acute bronchitis. She was eighty years old.

Grace Greenwood's writings were popular in their day but are no longer generally read. Her flowery and expansive writing style, her moralistic tales for children, and her romantic and sentimental stories appealed to the popular tastes and values of Victorian America, but for the most part, they lack meaning and credibility for the modern reader. Nevertheless, she made significant contributions to society through her journalistic writings, some of which are still very readable. She provided reliable descriptions of Europe at a time when Americans were eager for such information, and she helped instruct Easterners about the burgeoning, still largely unknown American West. She was one of the early women correspondents who came to Washington to cover government because of their commitment to the abolitionist cause. They also wrote about issues related to emancipation, such as nursing care for Union soldiers, rights of American Indians, universal suffrage and woman's rights, abuse of political power, and the lawmakers themselves. (In 1880, women were barred from the press galleries of Congress, not to return for almost forty years.)

In general, contemporary criticism was favorable to Greenwood's work. Joseph Lyman, with language as expansive as Greenwood's own, praised her facility in each of the forms she used during her long writing career: he called her "a letter-writer who should charm a million readers by the piquant dash and spicy flavor of her style; a delightful magazinist; a poetess, the melody and ring of whose stanzas should remind us of the most famous lyres of the world; a woman who, standing calm, graceful, and self-poised before great audiences, and thrilling them by noble and earnest words spoken in the deep gloom of national disaster, should call up rich memories of the Roman matron in her noblest form, . . . the young Corinne. . . ."

Grace Greenwood supported herself, her daughter, and even her husband for a time in a profession that offered few opportunities to women. Further, she managed that feat in Victorian America, when sentiment against women working outside the home was at its strongest. She was indeed a modern-day Corinne, a pioneer who performed with courage, intelligence, pleasure, and satisfaction to the applause of a grateful and appreciative audience.

References:

Maurine Beasley, "Pens and Petticoats: Early Women Washington Correspondents," *Journalism History,* 1 (Winter 1974-1975): 112-115;

Rufus Wilmot Griswold, *The Female Poets of America* (Philadelphia: Parry & Mcmillan, 1859), pp. 390-398;

Sarah Josepha Hale, *Woman's Record* (New York: Harper, 1855), pp. 624-629;

John Seely Hart, *Female Prose Writers of America* (Philadelphia: E. H. Butler, 1852), pp. 292-301;

Joseph Lyman, "Grace Greenwood—Mrs. Lippincott," in *Eminent Women of the Age,* edited by James Parton, et al. (New York: S. M. Betts, 1869), pp. 147-163;

Fred Lewis Pattee, *The Feminine Fifties* (Port Washington, N.Y.: Kennikat Press, 1940), pp. 276-282;

Ishbel Ross, *Ladies of the Press* (New York & London: Harper, 1936), pp. 327-329;

Elizabeth Cady Stanton, ed., *History of Woman Suffrage* (Rochester, N.Y., 1887), pp. 358-363, 828-829;

Margaret (Farrand) Thorp, *Female Persuasion* (Hamden, Conn.: Archon Books, 1971), pp. 143-178;

Barbara Welter, "Sara Jane Clarke Lippincott," in *Notable American Women 1607-1950,* edited by Edward T. James (Cambridge: Harvard University Press, 1971), pp. 407-409.

Papers:
Grace Greenwood letters may be found in the Field

Collection, Henry Huntington Library (microfilm at Princeton University Library), and the William W. Clapp and Henry W. Longfellow Papers, Houghton Library, Harvard University.

Richard Adams Locke
(22 September 1800-16 February 1871)

James Glen Stovall
University of Alabama

MAJOR POSITIONS HELD: Reporter, *New York Courier and Enquirer* (1832-1835), *New York Sun* (1835-1836); editor, *New Era* (New York) (1836-1839), *Brooklyn Eagle* (1841).

Journalism of the 1830s tilted more toward entertainment than accuracy. The journalist was expected to hold the reader's attention with florid writing, suspense-filled stories, and dramatic beginnings and endings. If the facts of a story did not make the best reading, the journalist had some license to alter them. In the 1830s, especially among members of the newly minted penny press, editors wanted readers—not reputations for truth.

That is why Richard Adams Locke is famous: he wrote one of the most fantastic and entertaining tales of the decade. He said that British astronomers, working with a large telescope in South Africa, had seen the moon as it had never been seen before. They had discovered mountains and valleys, trees and other vegetation; they had seen wildlife, animals similar to many seen on earth. And they had even seen men-like creatures moving about very much as men on earth move.

Locke had readers hanging onto every word of his stories. They clamored for more and waited impatiently for the next issue of his paper, the *New York Sun*. Readers of the paper grew in numbers and talked about the stories so much that other papers, though they were competing with the *Sun*, were forced into reprinting Locke's stories or printing summaries of them.

Obviously, not a word of what Locke wrote was true. It was merely the product of his active imagination, working in the competitive environment of New York journalism. Yet, when the truth did emerge and Locke's stories became known as the "Great Moon Hoax," Locke's reputation suffered very little. He was not dismissed from the paper and drummed out of the profession. Rather, he stayed with the *Sun* for several more years, his editors satisfied that he had brought the paper its large number of readers. When he did leave the *Sun*, he went on to work for two more publications and wrote extensively for others before dropping out of journalism entirely. Edgar Allan Poe credited him with being a fine writer and said that Locke's hoax made him give up a story idea of the same type because he did not think he could match Locke's work. Locke's escapade would have a quite different ending in the late twentieth century, of

Richard Adams Locke (Gale International Portrait Gallery)

course, but what happened to him and his moon hoax tells a great deal about the journalism of his time.

Richard Adams Locke was born in 1800 in East Brent, Somersetshire, England, a collateral descendant of the philosopher John Locke. He was the son of well-to-do parents, Richard and Anne Adams Locke, and he was educated by his mother and private tutors. His bent for writing showed up early; by the time he was eighteen, he had completed a poem of nearly 6,000 lines entitled "The Universe Restored." When he was nineteen, he went to Cambridge University, and while a student there, he contributed to several publications, including the prestigious *Imperial Magazine* and the *Bee.*

After leaving Cambridge, he started the London *Republican,* a publication with decided sympathies for the American experiment in government. The *Republican* drew only a few readers, and Locke had to abandon it. He edited a periodical devoted to science and literature called *Cornucopia* for about six months, but it, too, failed financially. He championed the cause of Catholic emancipation in the *Somersetshire Herald* for nearly two years and wrote for a number of other publications.

In 1832 Locke brought his wife, Esther Bowering Locke, whom he had married in 1826, and infant daughter Adelaide to New York, where he became a reporter for the *Courier and Enquirer.* Locke's ability and versatility as a writer had been honed by his education and experience in England, and he put it to good use in America. He covered a wide variety of stories, including the sensational murder trial of Matthias the Prophet in White Plains, New York. There he met the editor of the *New York Sun,* Benjamin Day, who recognized him as the best reporter at the trial. Day asked Locke to write a series of articles on the trial for the *Sun.* Locke did and soon found himself in trouble with the owner of the *Courier and Enquirer.* Day offered Locke twelve dollars a week to become an editorial writer for the *Sun,* an offer which Locke found generous.

Locke soon became a leading figure in New York journalism. Edgar Allan Poe described his physical appearance as having an "air of distinction." He was five feet seven inches tall and "symmetrically formed," Poe wrote: "His face is strongly pitted by the smallpox, and, perhaps from the same cause, there is a marked obliquity in the eyes; a certain calm, clear *luminousness,* however, about these latter, amply compensates for the defect, and

the forehead is truly beautiful in its intellectuality. I am acquainted with no person possessing so fine a forehead as Mr. Locke." Poe also had a great respect for Locke's ability to write. Locke's prose style, he said, is "noticeable for its concision, luminousness, completeness. . . . Everything he writes is a model in its peculiar way, serving just the purposes intended and nothing to spare."

Locke came to the *Sun* just as it was blazing a new trail in American journalism. Begun in 1833, the *Sun* was the first successful "penny paper." The "penny press" was characterized not only by its cheap price, which made it affordable to people who could never before buy a newspaper, but also by its light writing and content. Penny press editors avoided politics and other deep subjects and concentrated on human interest situations. The *Sun* placed a special emphasis on crime and police stories and by 1834 had achieved a 15,000 daily circulation, making it one of the largest-selling papers in the world.

Locke, Day, and the *Sun* were a perfect match. Locke could write the short, breezy items that Day and his readers expected. He could take situations that might appear dull to other writers and inject life into them. And he was not above pursuing an entertaining piece at the cost of accuracy.

The moon hoax saga began on 21 August 1835 with a short paragraph on the second page of the *Sun.* It quoted the Edinburgh *Courant* as saying that "some astronomical discoveries of the most wonderful description" had been made by Sir John Herschel at the Cape of Good Hope. No hint was given as to the nature of these "discoveries" until four days later. On 25 August an article credited to the supplement of the *Edinburgh Journal of Science* presented readers with a long treatise about the philosophy of man, the technical details of Sir John's telescope, and a history of the astronomer's work. The *Edinburgh Journal of Science* was also a figment of Locke's imagination. Although there had once been such a journal, it had died several years before. Like the first article, this second one gave no real indication of what was in store for the readers.

The next day, however, the picture Locke was drawing for the readers began to come into focus. The first descriptions of what the scientists had seen appeared. They included lunar vegetation, water, beaches, hills, and valleys. Later in the article, the astronomers were said to have seen animal life, including bison, goats, birds, and some sort of amphibian.

The 26 August article hooked a lot of readers—and a number of Locke's colleagues in the press. Some believed the story immediately and praised or reprinted the stories. Others expressed interested skepticism. The *Sun*'s chief rivals, the *Courier and Enquirer* and the *Journal of Commerce*, said nothing at this point. The next article continued in the vein of the previous one. It described more lakes, trees, and animals on the moon. Beavers, zebras, pheasants, and shellfish were sighted.

The article printed on Friday, 28 August, caused the greatest sensation because it described human-like creatures that the astronomers had supposedly seen. These creatures were said to be about four feet tall and covered with glossy, copper-colored hair. They also had wings resting on their backs, leading the astronomers to call them man-bats. This article brought public discussion of other matters in New York to a halt. Less than two years old at the time, the *Sun* on this date reached a circulation of nearly 20,000 (compared with 17,000 for the London *Times*). People were said to have waited until late in the afternoon for a copy of the paper, and the press ran for ten hours that day.

The moon series continued for two more days with articles describing a great building, dubbed the Temple of the Moon, and more descriptions of the man-bats. It ended by saying that the telescope the astronomers were using was ruined when it was carelessly left facing east and the reflection chamber was burned by the sun.

There is no real evidence that Locke wrote the stories intending to deceive anyone. They were simply meant to be entertainment. Yet, like Orson Welles's *War of the Worlds* radio broadcast in 1938, they were believed by many people because they were written in such an authoritative and convincing style. A group of scientists from Yale visited the *Sun* offices asking for a copy of the *Edinburgh Journal of Science*. A group of ladies in Massachusetts subscribed to a fund to send missionaries to the moon to convert the man-bats. Newspapers in London, Paris, and Glasgow reprinted the articles.

Locke was probably unprepared to deal with the attention the articles had been given and did not immediately own up to their falsity. But when a reporter for the *Journal of Commerce* sought copies of the articles so that his paper could reprint them, Locke confessed to the reporter—a good friend of his—that he had invented the story. The next day, the *Journal*, seeing a way to get back at its rival for stealing its circulation, denounced the articles as a hoax. Caught in a defensive posture, the *Sun* would neither confirm nor deny the story and advised that "every reader of the account examine it and enjoy his own opinion." In fact, the *Sun* said that it would not admit error until official word was sent from Edinburgh or from the Cape of Good Hope, where the real Herschel was working. That word eventually came, but long after the sensation had subsided.

Locke's revelation did not end the excitement that his articles had caused, nor did it greatly damage his reputation as a journalist. The articles inspired a panorama and a stage play and remained the main topic of conversation for some time afterward. With at least one notable author, the articles enhanced Locke's standing as a writer. Poe had planned to write a story about life on the moon and had actually begun it when Locke's articles appeared. Upon reading them, Poe retired his idea, believing that he could add little to what Locke had already done.

The *Sun* recognized that it had a good writer in Locke, and he was given other choice assignments—for instance, he interviewed a famous convicted murderer shortly before his execution—but Locke's tenure with the paper was to last only a year more. In the fall of 1836 he left the *Sun* to begin a new paper, the *New Era*. He attempted to do the same thing for this penny paper that he had done for the *Sun* by writing another hoax, "The Lost Manuscript of Mungo Park." No reader was fooled for a moment by this second series, and the paper died in 1839. Locke, who had become a contributor to the *New York Mirror*, then spent a short time as editor of the *Brooklyn Eagle*. His journalism career came to an end in 1841 when he got a job in the New York customhouse. He lived quietly and died at his home on Staten Island on 16 February 1871.

Locke's journalistic career was a brief one, but his talents came at the right time and place to exercise a major impact on his profession. His moon hoax articles helped establish the *New York Sun* as a successful newspaper and thus the penny press as a financially sound principle. Other cheap newspapers followed, and soon journalism was no longer the special privilege of the elite and the rich.

References:

William N. Griggs, *The Celebrated "Moon Story," Its Origins and Incidents* (New York: Bunnell & Price, 1852);

Frederick Hudson, *Journalism in the United States from 1690 to 1872* (New York: Harper, 1873), pp. 420-423;

Frank M. O'Brien, *The Story of the Sun* (New York: Doran, 1918), pp. 64-103;

Edgar Allan Poe, *The Literati* (New York: Redfield/ Boston: Mussey, 1850), pp. 120-128.

Matthew Lyon

(14 July 1749-1 August 1822)

Whitney R. Mundt
Louisiana State University

MAJOR POSITIONS HELD: Founder and editor, *Farmers' Library* (Rutland, Vt.) (1793-1794), *Fair Haven* (Vt.) *Gazette,* renamed *Farmers' Library* in 1795 (1795-1798).

In another century, on another continent, Matthew Lyon might have been called a Renaissance man. But on the frontiers of America this rough-hewn Irish immigrant was simply the man who did the work that needed to be done. He was an entrepreneur, an inventor, a soldier, a politician, and a publisher. He founded the town of Fair Haven, Vermont, and was instrumental in bringing the state of Vermont into existence. He was a U.S. Congressman from two states. More important, perhaps, he marked the ballot which made Thomas Jefferson president of the United States.

Lyon was born 14 July 1749 south of Dublin, Ireland. He attended school there, but in his early teens he was apprenticed to a printer and bookbinder in Dublin. In 1764, after a couple of years' apprenticeship, he emigrated from Ireland to America. His passage was paid to the ship's captain by a Jabez Bacon of Woodbury, Connecticut, who required Lyon, in return, to sign letters of indenture which bound him to work until the age of twenty-one. The resourceful Lyon, according to biographer Tom W. Campbell, managed to buy his freedom after working out only part of his indenture. Lyon learned that Hugh Hannah, a merchant at Litchfield, some twelve miles from Woodbury, had a pair of bulls for sale; Lyon purchased these on credit, then traded them to Bacon for his freedom. Campbell writes that "Lyon then went to Litchfield where he worked for a time for Mr. Hannah, not, however, as an indentured apprentice, but as a free young man, Hannah allowing him the

customary wages for store clerks until the forty dollars for the bulls had been worked out, and then paying him cash for his services. . . ." Afterward, Lyon occasionally alluded to the means by which he had earned his freedom in the mild oath, "By the bulls that redeemed me."

By the time he reached the age of twenty-three Lyon was a landowner in Cornwall, Connecticut, and on 23 June 1773, he married Mary Horsford. Her mother, before marrying Samuel Horsford, had been married to Daniel Allen, the uncle of Ethan Allen, shortly to become celebrated as the leader of the Green Mountain Boys. Together with Allen and a number of other adventurous souls, Lyon and his bride left Connecticut for the New Hampshire Grants, the territory which was to become Vermont. They settled in Wallingford, a few miles south of Rutland, not long before their daughter Ann was born on 20 January 1774.

The Green Mountain Boys had been organized to protect the property rights of New Hampshire Grant settlers against the claims of the colony of New York, which maintained that this land lay within its jurisdiction. But in 1775, three weeks after British troops opened fire on colonists at Lexington, the Green Mountain Boys transformed themselves from a vigilante group into a revolutionary troop. Under the command of Allen and Benedict Arnold, Lyon and other members of the troop took Fort Ticonderoga from the British on 10 May. Lyon referred to the incident many years later in a letter to Senator Armisted C. Mason of Virginia: "Eighty-five of us took from one hundred and forty British veterans, the fort Ticonderoga, which contained the artillery and warlike stores which drove the British from Boston, and aided in taking Burgoyne and Cornwallis. That fort contained when we took it more cannon, mortar pieces and other military stores than could be found in all the revolted Colonies."

Following this success, the Green Mountain Boys returned to their New Hampshire homes, and Lyon was made adjutant of his militia regiment.

On 15 April 1776 Mary Lyon gave birth to their second child James. When war was declared not long thereafter, Lyon left home to be commissioned a second lieutenant on 19 July. Perhaps he would not have been so quick to volunteer if he had known that he was soon to be accused of cowardice and dismissed from the army.

In the summer of 1776, according to historian Pliny H. White, Lyon was serving under the command of Captain John Fasset, Jr., whose troops belonged to the Northern army, led by Gen. Horatio Gates. The general assigned Fasset's men to a place called Jericho, some miles in advance of the main body of his army in what is now northern Vermont, and "exposed to the first attack of the British force under Sir Guy Carlton. The officers and men alike became uneasy at occupying so dangerous a position, without support, and though the officers were unwilling to incur the disgrace of abandoning their post, some of them did not scruple to suggest to the soldiers, that if they should mutiny and march off, the officers would be under no obligation to remain." Such an open invitation produced the expected result, and they began a retreat. Lyon was delegated to inform General Gates of the abandonment, again with the expected result. According to White, "The intelligence was received with great indignation by the whole army, and when Lyon was introduced into the presence of Gen. Gates, the rough old soldier damned him for a coward, and ordered him under arrest." Lyon argued that he had advised against the abandonment and had yielded only because he had been overruled. Nevertheless, he was court-martialed, and his sentence was to be cashiered, or discharged.

Years later, while Lyon was serving as a member of Congress, he told his side of the event in an attempt to stifle recurring references to his "wooden sword." In his version of the episode Lyon explained that his small body had been sent to occupy a point at least sixty miles in advance of the army. The men were anxious about reports of Indians in the area, and about nine o'clock that night he was awakened by the sounds of soldiers about to march off. He told them that he preferred death in battle to the dishonor of quitting his post. But "all entreaties were ineffectual," and the soldiers began to cross the river in the single canoe. As there was only one canoe, the men insisted that the officers accompany them, and Lyon "did not think it my duty to resist alone." When they had progressed to New Haven, about thirty miles south, the men offered to return to the command of the captain, and Lyon was dispatched to inform Gates, who was "enraged to the highest pitch; he swore we should all be hanged, and ordered me under arrest." According to Lyon, he proved everything at his trial with respect to his own conduct, but was included in the general sentence, along with a lieutenant who had not been present at the retreat. "The mortification of being cashiered," Lyon explained to his fellow lawmakers, "and that very undeservedly, without any other aggravation, was, I believe, quite to the extent of my power to bear. . . ."

Returning home following his discharge, Lyon found that his neighbors credited his account of the matter and restored him to his position of community leadership. In July Lyon represented Wallingford at a convention, during which he voted to form the Grant territory into a state. A constitutional convention was held, and Lyon was probably involved in writing the document that was adopted on 24 December 1777. But before that adoption, Lyon returned to military service, was promoted to captain, and took part in the operation which forced Burgoyne to surrender at Saratoga. Lyon later wrote, "I with my gun and bayonet was in many rencounters, and assisted at the taking of Burgoyne, and had the honour and pleasure of seeing his army pile their arms." In 1778 Lyon resigned his commission and returned home, where he resumed his activities as a businessman and community leader.

Sometime in 1777 Lyon had moved to Arlington, south of Wallingford. There he became clerk of the court of confiscation, which was charged with examining evidence of "treason" and with confiscating property of those adjudged guilty. Lyon purchased some of the confiscated land, possibly as a speculative investment. He also purchased proprietary rights in several townships to ungranted land which Vermont sold in order to raise revenue. Lyon sat as a member of the committee which selected the grantees. He acquired other land through tax sales conducted by the sheriff after neglect of the landowners (Tories?) to pay Vermont's first land tax. As Lyon admitted, "I had so attended to my affairs in the more advanced stages of the war, and towards its close, that I was able under the most favorable auspices to set a going a number of mills and manufactures which made me rich."

One of the townships to which he purchased the rights was located west of Rutland, near the border with New York. In 1782 Lyon went there with a work crew to construct a settlement which he called Fair Haven, and the following year he moved his family there. Mary had borne him two more children, Pamelia and Loraine, and the future must have seemed bright: the war had ended, and Lyon had founded a town in which he operated a sawmill and a gristmill. But on 29 April 1784, Mary died at thirty-two, leaving him with four children—the oldest only ten, the youngest perhaps two.

Before long Lyon married again. Beulah Chittenden Galusha, the recently widowed, twenty-year-old mother of an infant son, was the daughter of Thomas Chittenden, who had been the first governor of Vermont. Lyon had served with Chittenden in Arlington on the local committee of safety several years earlier, and probably had known his daughter then. She and her son Elijah joined Lyon and his children in Fair Haven, where he continued to develop his business interests.

In 1785 Lyon began operating a tavern and a slitting mill. Lyon's slitting mill, the only one in western Vermont, produced machine-made nails, which were very much in demand. He also produced axes, hoes, and other farm implements at his forge, as well as hollowware such as kettles and stoves. In 1790 he began operating a paper mill and is credited as the first American to use wood pulp for the manufacture of paper. (In his newspaper, the *Farmers' Library*, Lyon announced on 28 October 1794, that this issue had been printed on paper manufactured from the bark of the Basswood tree.) He did not patent his invention, proclaiming instead: "If this discovery should prove advantageous to mankind we shall be glad to bid the world—welcome to it, without the selfish reserve of an exclusive privilege or patent right."

Vermont was admitted to the Union on 4 March 1791, and Lyon, who had served the territory in various capacities for many years, began thinking about higher office. That year he entered Vermont's first congressional race. In the first balloting, Lyon received more votes than any of the other three candidates, but in the runoff he lost decisively to Israel Smith. In 1793 and 1795 Lyon lost to the same opponent, but in 1797 he emerged with a majority of votes and became one of Vermont's congressmen in the United States House of Representatives.

Shortly after his initial defeat Lyon launched a weekly newspaper in Rutland. The *Farmers' Li-*

brary appeared on 1 April 1793 with sixteen-year-old James Lyon listed as publisher, but it was clear that Matthew Lyon dictated policy and furnished the funds, as he admitted in a letter to Albert Gallatin some ten years later. It "cost me from $1,000 to $2,000 per annum for about five years to maintain a Republican press," he wrote, acknowledging that its purpose was "to break down the undue influence of the Aristo-Tory faction."

Lyon continued to publish the newspaper through 29 November of the following year, when it was sold to Judge Samuel Williams and the Reverend Samuel Williams, who altered its title to the *Rutland Herald: a Register of the Times* on 29 June 1795. Lyon had not given up his publishing aspirations, however, and he established the *Fair Haven Gazette* in 1795. No copies of this paper are known to exist, and historians rely on the statement of Pliny H. White, in his 1858 address to the Vermont Historical Society on "The Life and Services of Matthew Lyon," for evidence that the newspaper existed. White noted that the title of the newspaper was changed to the *Farmers' Library*. Under that name the newspaper was published from 27 July 1795 to 2 March 1797. It was reestablished in November and ceased publication the following year. The last issue located is dated 3 April 1798.

Although Lyon's newspapers helped to advance his political aspirations and his philosophy of government, they also served to educate and inform—satisfying Lyon's basic democratic instincts. Those instincts are also evident in the fact that Lyon established a publishing house, called Voltaire's Head, which, among other books, published the *Works of the Late Dr. Benjamin Franklin* in 1793. Another indication of Lyon's democratic instincts is his assistance in founding the Fair Haven Library Society in 1794.

Those democratic instincts did not win him universal favor in the House, where Federalist sentiment was strong. Shortly after he took his seat in 1797 he declined to join other members of Congress in a procession to the residence of President John Adams in Philadelphia; Lyon was offended by such a display of obeisance. For his pains in this matter, and his other efforts opposing elitism of various kinds, Lyon became the object of satire in the House. But the most offensive attack was in William Cobbett's Federalist *Porcupine's Gazette*, which referred to Lyon as "the beast of Vermont" and alluded to his "cowardice" in the war. Recalling the incident in which Lyon had been cashiered from the army, Cobbett referred to Lyon's "wooden sword." The phrase was picked up and repeated by members of Congress, including Roger Griswold of Connecticut. These aspersions on his courage and character led to an incident which became a cause célèbre in the fledgling nation.

As historian White relates the incident, Lyon and other members of Congress were engaged in casual conversation while the House was in recess. Lyon declared that members of the Connecticut delegation "were acting in direct opposition to the wishes and opinions of nine-tenths of their constituents, . . . and that he well knew the people of Connecticut, as he had to fight them in his own District." Griswold overheard Lyon's remarks and asked if Lyon had fought them with his wooden sword. Lyon pretended not to hear. Instead he asserted that if he were to go to Connecticut and publish a newspaper for six months he could induce the people there to recall all their representatives from Congress. Griswold allegedly responded, "When you go into Connecticut, you had better take with you your wooden sword." Lyon turned toward Griswold and spat in his face. A motion was introduced to expel Lyon from the House, but after two weeks of debate, it failed to carry. The following day, as Lyon was seated in his chair, awaiting the call to order, Griswold approached Lyon and began beating him with a walking stick. Before Lyon could disengage himself from behind his desk, Griswold had struck him several times, but Lyon managed to seize a pair of fire tongs, at which point the two were separated. A motion was introduced to expel both combatants, but this, too, failed. Caricatures to commemorate the incident appeared in the public press and still are preserved in history books.

But the worst was yet to come. Fears of war with France were growing in 1797, and Congress responded with the Naturalization Act, which increased the period of residence required to become a citizen, and the Alien Act, which gave President Adams the authority to expel foreigners by executive order. Congress also approved, on 14 July 1798, the Sedition Act, which forbade anyone to "write, print, utter or publish . . . any false, scandalous and malicious writing or writings against the government of the United States, or either house of the Congress of the United States, or the President of the United States, with intent to defame. . . ." The act made it a misdemeanor, punishable by fine and imprisonment, to criticize President Adams, who was a Federalist, but not Vice-President Thomas Jefferson, who was a Republican.

Lyon had sought to oppose the Sedition Act in a letter to the *Rutland Herald,* as his own *Farmers' Library* had temporarily ceased publication. But the editor, Williams, declined to publish it. Lyon thereupon sent the letter to the *Vermont Journal* in Windsor, where it was finally printed on 31 July 1798—after the Sedition Act had passed. In his letter Lyon explained some of his objections to the Adams administration: "As to the Executive, when I shall see the efforts of that power bent on the promotion of the comfort, the happiness, and accommodation of the people, that executive shall have my zealous and uniform support: but whenever I shall, on the part of the Executive, see every consideration of the public welfare swallowed up on a continual grasp for power, in an unbounded thirst for ridiculous pomp, foolish adulation, and selfish avarice; when I shall behold men of real merit daily turned out of office for no other cause but independency of sentiment; when I shall see men of firmness, merit, years, abilities, and experience, discarded in their applications for office, for fear they possess that independence, and men of meanness preferred for the ease with which they take up and advocate opinions, the consequence of which they know but little of—when I shall see the sacred name of religion employed as a state engine to make mankind hate and persecute one another, I shall not be their humble advocate."

In addition to using the pages of the *Vermont Journal* for his political criticism, Lyon began plans to publish a magazine as a vehicle for his views. Entitled the *Scourge of Aristocracy and Repository of Important Political Truths* and edited by Lyon's son James, the first issue appeared on 1 October 1798. In it Lyon made his political creed known and took advantage of the opportunity to strike back at his enemy Cobbett: "When every aristocratic hireling from the English Porcupine, the summit of falsehood, detraction and calumny, in Philadelphia, down to the dirty hedge-hogs and groveling animals of his race, in this and the neighboring States, are vomiting forth columns of lies, malignant abuse and deception, the Scourge will be devoted to politics, and shall commemorate the writings, essays and speeches of the ablest pens and tongues, in the Republican interest."

Two days after the appearance of the *Scourge,* a federal grand jury was convened in Rutland, and Lyon was indicted on 5 October. Three counts were specified: the first charged Lyon with seditious libel for the contents of the letter published in the *Vermont Journal;* the next two counts concerned contents of speeches Lyon had made during his congressional reelection campaign, then in prog-

Contemporary cartoon showing Lyon, with fire tongs, and Representative Roger Griswold of Connecticut, with walking stick, fighting on the floor of Congress in 1797. Griswold had made disparaging remarks about Lyon's service in the Revolutionary War, and Lyon had responded by spitting in Griswold's face. The battle depicted here took place two weeks later (The New York Historical Society).

ress. Lyon pleaded not guilty at his arraignment 6 October, and the trial was set for 8 October. His lawyers were not able to appear because of bad weather, so Lyon represented himself, arguing that the Sedition Act was unconstitutional; the judge noted that the unconstitutionality of the law was not a question for the jury to decide. Lyon argued that he had written the letter on 20 June, yet the act under which he was charged did not become law until 14 July; the judge countered that as a member of Congress Lyon knew that the act was about to be passed. Lyon maintained that his words carried no intent to defame but represented legitimate opposition to policies with which he disagreed; the judge replied that the jury must decide the question of intent from the nature of the words themselves. Lyon claimed that in any event, what he had said was true, and he asked the judge, who had dined with the president, to acknowledge that he had observed "ridiculous pomp and parade";

the judge admitted seeing only "plainness and simplicity." The jury required only an hour to bring in a verdict of guilty.

Lyon was sentenced on 9 October to serve four months in jail and to pay a $1,000 fine, plus court costs. He thus became the first victim of the Sedition Act.

Meanwhile, Lyon had been forced into a runoff in the congressional election, and he continued his campaign from his cell in the federal prison at Vergennes, Vermont. It was the first time in American history that a candidate for Congress sought election while imprisoned. In December he received a decisive margin over the other candidates, but he remained in prison until 9 February 1799. Upon his release he announced that he was on his way to Philadelphia, where Congress was in session. He thus availed himself of congressional privilege against arrest, frustrating those who were rumored to have planned his rearrest upon release from jail.

Lyon's role in that session of Congress was to be more significant than he could have envisioned or hoped. In the presidential campaign of 1800 Thomas Jefferson and Aaron Burr were the Republican nominees for the offices of president and vice-president, respectively. John Adams was the Federalist party's nominee for reelection, and C. C. Pinckney was his running mate. But the election was thrown to the House of Representatives when Jefferson and Burr each received seventy-three electoral votes for president. Adams was named on sixty-five ballots and Pinckney on sixty-four. The Constitution provided that in the event of a tie each state should have one vote and that the person with the greatest number of votes should be president; the person having the greatest number of votes after the president should be the vice-president. The Federalists threw their support to Burr because Adams had been defeated for reelection, and they regarded Burr as more pliant than Jefferson. There were sixteen states in the Union, and therefore the votes of nine states were required to elect the president. On the first ballot eight states voted for Jefferson, six for Burr, and two were divided. The two states with divided votes were Maryland, with eight representatives, and Vermont, with two. The Vermont congressman voting for Jefferson was, of course, Matthew Lyon. Jefferson was an ardent Republican who had made clear his belief that the Sedition Act was an unconstitutional abridgment of the First Amendment, and he personally had solicited contributions to pay Lyon's fine. Through thirty-five ballots the voting remained the same. But on the thirty-sixth, Vermont's other congressman, Federalist Lewis Morris, cast a blank ballot, enabling Lyon to declare the state of Vermont for Jefferson. The eight states which had voted for Jefferson previously continued to do so, and therefore Vermont became the ninth state in Jefferson's column. Lyon thus had the honor of making Thomas Jefferson president of the United States.

Lyon had had enough of the political character assassination which had become his lot in Vermont, and he resolved to move to Kentucky. He sold his property in Fair Haven and acquired 5,800 acres of land in the settlement of Eddyville, overlooking the Cumberland River in western Kentucky. In the spring of 1801 Lyon and his family, together with a number of his Vermont neighbors, made their way on flatboats from Pittsburgh down the Ohio River to the Cumberland, and thence to Eddyville. There he established a sawmill, gristmill, and papermill, as well as a shipyard and cotton-refining business. The ships he constructed were prepared under contract with the federal government, as Lyon used his political contacts to enhance his business prospects. He obtained a mail route from the postmaster general, and Jefferson appointed him commissary general for the Western army. In addition to providing food for the troops, Lyon and his sons were carrying pork, bacon lard, and venison hams to the New Orleans market. Bookselling was a lucrative sideline, and Lyon established the first printing office in Kentucky after hauling type by horseback over the Alleghenies.

But his political career was not ended. In 1802 he served a term in the Kentucky legislature, and in 1803 he was elected to Congress from his district in Kentucky. He continued to serve until 1811, when he was defeated in a bid for reelection. His business interests also suffered a reversal when a shipload of beef and pork, worth $50,000 and intended for the New Orleans market, rotted in the sun while the ship was beached on a sandbar in the Mississippi. Now beset by creditors, Lyon turned over all his business holdings to his son Chittenden, who eventually paid off all debts by supplying $28,000 from his own pocket. To raise funds Lyon petitioned Congress for a refund of the fine he had paid under the Sedition Act, which had been allowed to expire when Jefferson took office in 1801; but it was not until 1840 that Congress refunded the $1,000 fine plus $60.96 court costs to Lyon's heirs.

In 1820 Lyon sought appointment to a federal post from President James Monroe. With the approval of Congress, Monroe appointed him U.S. factor to the Cherokee Indians, and Lyon began yet another career at Spadra Bluff, on the Arkansas River in the Arkansas Territory. In 1821 he ran for the House of Representatives from the Arkansas Territory but was defeated. As U.S. factor, his job was to supervise a trading post, and in 1822 he built a flatboat, loaded it with Indian goods, and set out for New Orleans. On his return trip he brought manufactured products. It was a remarkable feat for a man of seventy-two to undertake and complete a round trip of over 3,000 miles on horseback and by boat. But it was, perhaps, too much, for he died on 1 August 1822.

Lyon was buried at Spadra Bluff, but several years later the body was removed and reinterred in Eddyville. Biographer Aleine Austin relates, without attribution, that the Cherokee Indians had preserved his body prior to burial in Arkansas, and that on the occasion of his reinterment his admirers raised the lid of the coffin to take one last look at him. "When the air touched his skin, the clear features of his face disintegrated before their astonished eyes, and blew away to the four corners of the earth."

Biographies:
Pliny H. White, *The Life & Services of Matthew Lyon* (Burlington: General Assembly of Vermont, 1858);

J. Fairfax McLaughlin, *Matthew Lyon: The Hampden of Congress* (New York: Wynkoop Hallenbeck Crawford, 1900);

Tom W. Campbell, *Two Fighters and Two Fines: Sketches of the Lives of Matthew Lyon and Andrew Jackson* (Little Rock: Pioneer Publishing, 1941);

Robert Percy Williams, *By the Bulls that Redamed Me; The Odyssey of Matthew Lyon* (New York: Exposition Press, 1972);

Aleine Austin, *Matthew Lyon: "New Man" of the Democratic Revolution, 1749-1822* (University Park: Pennsylvania State University Press, 1981).

References:
Loyal Stephen Fox, "Colonel Matthew Lyon, Biographical and Genealogical Notes," *Vermont Quarterly*, vol. 12, No. 3 (July 1944): 163-180;

Adolph O. Goldsmith, "The Roaring Lyon of Vermont," *Journalism Quarterly*, 39 (Spring 1962): 179-186;

Alvin Harlow, "Martyr for a Free Press," *American Heritage*, 6 (October 1955): 146-151;

Hudee Z. Herrick, "Matthew Lyon, the Vermont Years," M.A. thesis, University of Vermont, 1952;

William P. Kennedy, "Matthew Lyon Cast the Deciding Vote Which Elected Thomas Jefferson President in 1801," 77th Congress, 2d Session, House Document No. 825 (Washington: United States Government Printing Office, 1942);

James B. Lyon, *The Lyon Family* (Jacksonville, Fla.: By the author, 1923);

George Lucien Montagno, "Matthew Lyon, Radical Jeffersonian, 1796-1801," Ph.D. dissertation, University of California, 1954;

Elizabeth A. Roe, *Aunt Leanna: or, Early Scenes in Kentucky* (Chicago: Published for the author, 1855);

James M. Smith, *Freedom's Fetters: The Alien and Sedition Law and American Civil Liberties* (Ithaca, N.Y.: Cornell University Press, 1956), pp. 221-246.

Papers:
The Vermont Historical Society maintains a Matthew Lyon Collection; and the Manuscripts Division of the New York Public Library has a collection of Matthew Lyon Miscellaneous Papers.

Joseph Medill

Joseph P. McKerns
Southern Illinois University at Carbondale

BIRTH: Near St. John, New Brunswick, Canada, 6 April 1823, to William and Margaret Medill.

MARRIAGE: 2 September 1852 to Katharine Patrick; children: Katharine, Elinor, Josephine.

MAJOR POSITIONS HELD: Editor and publisher, *Coshocton* (Ohio) *Republican* (1850-1852), *Daily Forest City*, renamed *Cleveland Leader* in 1853 (1852-1855), *Chicago Tribune* (1855-1899).

DEATH: San Antonio, Texas, 16 March 1899.

BOOKS: *An Easy Method of Spelling the English Language Silent-Letters Omitted. Every Sound Represented, without the Aid of New Characters* (Chicago, 1867);

Payment of the Debt. A Review of the Ohio Democratic Financial New Departure. By Hon. Joseph Medill, before the Young Men's Republican Club, at Columbus, Ohio, August 31, 1871 (Chicago: Rand, McNally & Co., printers, 1871);

Illinois, by Medill and James W. Sheahan (New York: Scribners, 1880);

*Tariff Reform: A Speech Delivered before the American
    Agricultural Association, at Its Annual Meeting,
    Chicago, December 14, 1882* (Chicago, 1883);
*A Typical American. Benjamin Franklin. An Address
    Delivered before the Old-Time Printers' Association
    of Chicago, January 17, A.D. 1896* (Chicago:
    Ben Franklin Company, 1896).

Joseph Medill epitomized the best and worst
of personal journalism as editor and principal
owner of the *Chicago Tribune* between 1855 and
1899. John Tebbel said that Medill's *Tribune* "tried
lawsuits in its news columns, used everything short
of gutter language in assailing its enemies and
stopped at nothing when it advocated a cause."
Medill and the *Tribune* were synonymous for nearly
a half-century when both stood staunchly for Republicanism (particularly of the Radical kind), cap-
italism and patriotism (and therefore stridently
against labor and the various foreign ideologies associated with it, such as socialism, communism, and
anarchism), and the city of Chicago. When Medill
died in 1899 he left a financially sound and polit-

ically powerful *Chicago Tribune* as his legacy.

Joseph Meharry Medill was born on 6 April
1823 near what is now St. John, New Brunswick,
Canada. The Medill family originated in France,
where the name was probably Medille, and was
among the Huguenots expelled after the revoca-
tion of the Edict of Nantes, which had guaranteed
their freedom of worship. The family set its roots
in England, where the name changed to McDill.
Eventually, the line from which Joseph descended
settled in Northern Ireland and changed the spelling of its name to Medill; the name is pronounced
with the accent on the final syllable. Joseph's grandfather was a Belfast shipbuilder and a strict Presbyterian. A family dispute caused by his son
William's marriage to Margaret Corbett, an Episcopalian, was settled when the young couple left
for America in 1819 with a small patrimony. William Medill settled in what he thought was the state
of Maine: however, the disputed strip of land was
awarded to Canada by the Webster-Ashburton
Treaty in 1842. William and Margaret Medill's
marriage produced four sons and two daughters,
of which Joseph was the oldest son. When Medill
was nine the family moved to Stark County, Ohio,
near Massillon, and Medill completed his education
at Massillon Village Academy. *Tribune* historians
are fond of drawing comparisons between the
young Medill and the young Abraham Lincoln by
pointing out that both walked miles to obtain books
to educate themselves. Medill is said to have walked
nine miles every Saturday to Canton, Ohio, to study
Latin, logic, and natural philosophy with a clergyman; however, it is usually conceded that his formal education was meager.

At the age of twenty-one Medill began to
study law in Canton under the guidance of two local
attorneys, and he was admitted to the bar in November 1846. He set up a law practice, but business
was slow. Medill began spending time at the offices
of country newspapers in the vicinity, where he
would set type and write occasional editorials. At
one such country newspaper, the *Tuscarawas Advocate* of New Philadelphia, Medill worked with
Katharine Patrick, the daughter of the owner, who
taught Medill how to set type.

In his days as a practicing attorney and occasional journalist, Medill kept company with several soon-to-be prominent men. Among them were
Salmon P. Chase, later Lincoln's secretary of the
treasury and chief justice of the U.S. Supreme
Court; Edwin M. Stanton, future secretary of war
under Lincoln; and Henry B. Payne, a future U.S.
senator. Medill had strong political interests and

Joseph Medill

was a staunch Whig party member. In 1850 he purchased the *Coshocton* (Ohio) *Democratic Whig* and renamed the paper the *Republican,* at a time when no political party of that name existed. It was probably this event, along with Medill's later activity in the Republican party, that led some *Tribune* historians to claim that Medill gave the new party its name.

With Katharine encouraging him to pursue a journalism career, Medill moved to Cleveland and established another Whig newspaper, the *Daily Forest City,* in April 1852. On 2 September he and Katharine were married. Medill entered into a partnership with John C. Vaughan, an abolitionist from South Carolina, and shortly afterward the *Daily Forest City* was merged with Vaughan's *Free Democrat* and renamed the *Cleveland Leader.* The paper was apparently prosperous, but the party it supported, the Whigs, was doomed. Whether or not he really did name the Republican party, Medill was certainly an ardent advocate of its formation.

The *Cleveland Leader*'s call for a new party was not immediately heeded, but with the passing of the Kansas-Nebraska Act, Medill became a hero to Free-Soilers, disenchanted Whigs, and abolitionists. In the fall of 1854 Capt. J. D. Webster, one of the proprietors of the seven-year-old *Chicago Tribune,* visited Medill and offered him the position of managing editor. The *Tribune*'s dilapidated printing facilities and the owners' reluctance to invest more capital caused Medill to decline the offer. Upon his inspection visit to the *Tribune,* however, Medill was exhilarated by the bustling atmosphere of the rough and crude city of Chicago. In 1854-1855 it was no match for Cleveland, but the shrewd Medill could see that the city was on the verge of a boom. Its population had increased from 60,000 to 85,000 between 1853 and 1855. Medill learned that by the end of 1855 Illinois would have nearly 3,000 miles of railroad, including the nation's longest line, the Illinois Central, and that the city would be served by ten trunk lines and eleven branch lines; the Michigan Central Railroad boasted that it carried 3,400 immigrants into the city in a single day. Medill recognized that Chicago was a ripe newspaper market. By the spring of 1855 Medill and Vaughan decided to leave behind a prosperous *Cleveland Leader* and set out for Chicago.

In Chicago Medill was introduced to Dr. Charles H. Ray, a Democrat who had formerly edited the *Jeffersonian* in Galena, Illinois. Ray was an ardent abolitionist and an enemy of Senator Stephen Douglas. He and Medill struck a deal to enter into partnership and purchase a controlling inter-

Dr. Charles H. Ray, Medill's principal partner in the Chicago Tribune *and editor in chief of the paper from 1855 until 1863*

est in the *Chicago Tribune.* Both men abhorred the *Tribune*'s Know-Nothing editorial policy and decided to eliminate it, and both were committed to abolition and the hope for a new Republican party. Medill sold his interest in the *Cleveland Leader* to purchase a one-third interest in the *Tribune,* while Ray used his capital to acquire a one-fourth interest. Vaughan was also a partner, but he left the firm in 1857. Medill and Ray agreed that Ray would assume the title of editor in chief and have primary responsibility for the editorials while Medill took the title of managing editor with the major supervisory authority; but it was Medill's personality that made an indelible mark on the *Tribune* and Chicago during the last half of the nineteenth century. Medill was the architect of the newspaper's reputation and also became a leader among the inner circle of movers and shakers who were determined to make Chicago *the* metropolis of the nation.

Medill guided the newspaper's financial, political, and editorial course with a stern hand. He held the title of editor in chief from November when Ray left the paper, to April 1865, except for a few brief stints as the *Tribune*'s Washington correspondent. Following that period, Medill took some time to serve in public roles, including one term as mayor of Chicago; but the newspaper commanded most of his attention and dedication. He left behind no memoirs or other published works of note besides what appeared in the pages of the *Tribune*. Only once was the *Tribune* in serious financial difficulty during Medill's tenure; that was in 1858, on the heels of a depression, when for a time the *Tribune* and the *Chicago Democratic Press* operated jointly as the *Chicago Press and Tribune*. Medill arranged for loans to pay off a $65,000 debt at ten percent interest over three years; however, he surprised his creditors by reorganizing the *Tribune* and paying off the loans in twenty-one months.

Medill's philosophy was that the newspaper should be "the organ of no man, however high, no clique or ring, however influential, no faction however fanatical or demonstrative, and in all things to follow the line of common sense." Nevertheless, Medill would ignore those ideals when to do so served his interests: for example, he made his paper the major organ of the fanatical, influential Radical wing of the Republican party. And as for "common sense," it was a capitalist's common sense when it came to dealing with labor problems that often led him, through the newspaper, to support, and even recommend, inhumane retaliation against striking workers and their families.

Medill's interest in science resulted in the *Tribune* taking editorial positions on scientific issues. Medill firmly believed that all natural phenomena were caused by sunspots until he became aware of the microbe theory; then he duly attributed all natural phenomena to microbes. Once a *Tribune* correspondent filed a story on a plague devastating Egypt that was said to be caused by sunspots. When the copy reached Medill, he crossed out all references to sunspots and substituted *microbes*. Medill also campaigned for the simplification of English spelling, and for many years the *Tribune*'s news columns contained words like *infinit, favorit,* and *telegraf*. Vestiges of this campaign can be seen in the paper today in the spelling of some words such as *thru* instead of *through*.

While Medill's views on science and language can be written off as eccentric, it is impossible to dismiss his political influence through the pages of the *Tribune*. The plan to nominate and elect Lincoln as president was developed in the *Tribune*'s offices by Medill, his partners, and Republican politicians in December 1859. Frank Luther Mott said that Medill and Ray "built up the Lincoln 'boom' with

a zeal and political sagacity which placed them among the few chiefly responsible for the Illinois rail-splitter's nomination and election." Lincoln even suffered visits to the *Tribune* for strategy conferences and advice from Medill.

At the 1860 Republican convention in Chicago, Medill was in charge of seating arrangements for the state delegations; he made sure that the uncommitted delegations were seated close to the Lincoln supporters and far away from the supporters of William H. Seward. Also, Medill saw to it that Lincoln backers easily obtained tickets to the convention while the backers of other candidates had difficulty getting into the convention hall. Medill and Ray traded away cabinet and other government positions on Lincoln's behalf and often without his knowledge. After receiving the nomination, Lincoln reportedly wondered aloud to Medill and Ray if there were any important appointments left for him to make on his own.

After Lincoln's election, Medill often tried the president's patience by demanding that Lincoln "toe the line" as determined by Medill or suffer the opposition of the *Tribune*'s mighty voice. During the Civil War, the *Tribune* was uncompromising toward the South and became a spokesman for Radical Republicanism. Medill's editorials demanded a more active prosecution of the war and urged Lincoln to declare emancipation and order confiscation of Southern property. But when Lincoln issued a call for troops with an especially high quota to be drafted from Illinois, Medill balked at supporting the call and was chided by Lincoln for not living up to his belligerent bluster. Medill was also instrumental in getting several states to pass laws enabling their soldiers at the front to vote in the 1864 presidential election.

While Medill publicly pushed Lincoln to abolish slavery, his private views on race were evidently not so praiseworthy. In a letter to his brother, Maj. William H. Medill, written shortly before the latter's death at Gettysburg, Medill said: "This continent belongs to the Free American race and they are bound to have it—every inch of it, including the West Indian Islands. . . . We shall permit no nation to abuse Mexico but ourselves. . . . In future wars black and yellow men will be freely used to fight. We will not be so careful about spilling the blood of niggers."

Medill threatened to withdraw the *Tribune*'s support from Lincoln in 1864 unless the president reorganized his cabinet along Radical lines. Medill wrote to Congressman Elihu Washburne before the 1864 convention that "Lincoln has some very weak

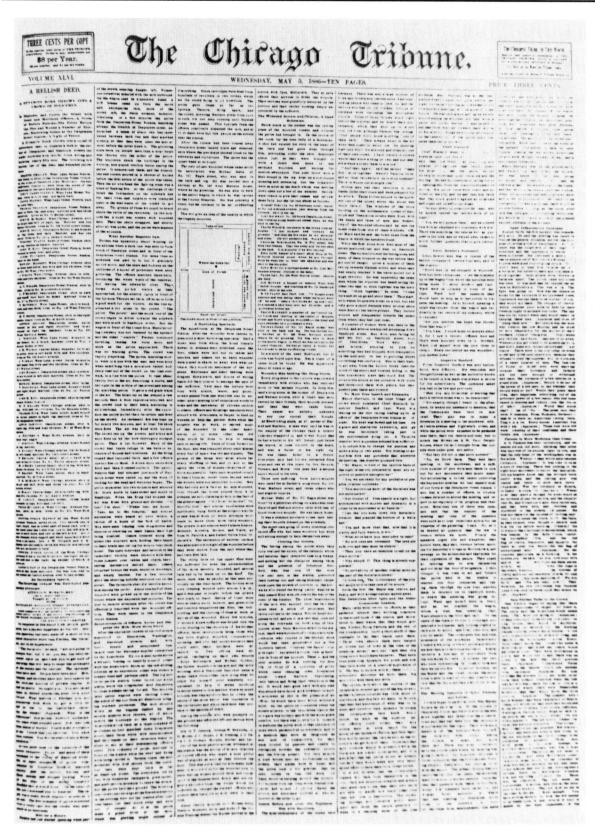

Front page of the Chicago Tribune *for 5 May 1886, carrying an account of the Haymarket Square riot in which seven policemen were killed by a bomb during a labor demonstration*

and foolish traits of character. If he had reasonable political sagacity and would cut loose from the semi-copperheads in his Cabinet and about him, if he would put live, bold, vigorous radicals in their places, no human power could prevent his renomination."

Medill and Ray often went to the front to act as their newspaper's correspondents. The war was good financially for the *Tribune:* in 1861 circulation was 18,000 but by 1864 it had increased to 40,000. It remained at that level until the 1880s, when it jumped to 80,000 during the years of labor unrest in the city.

After the war, Medill became active in public life. He served as a delegate to the state's constitutional convention in 1869 and as a member of the first Civil Service Commission in 1871. He failed in his bid for a seat in Congress when he fell twenty votes short of the Republican state party nomination. He succeeded on his next attempt at public office when the disastrous Chicago Fire of 1871 gave him a platform he rode to victory in the 1872 mayoral election.

On 10 September 1871, one month before the great fire swept through the city, a *Tribune* editorial said: "Chicago is a city of everlasting pine, shingles, sham veneers, stucco, and putty. It has miles of fire traps pleasing to the eye, looking substantial, but all sham and shingles. Walls have been run up one hundred feet high and only a single brick in thickness." But these words of warning came too late and even the stone Tribune Building was destroyed in the great fire that began on 7 October 1871 and raged for days. The *Tribune* was forced to cease publication when its building was consumed, but Medill wasted little time in obtaining alternate printing facilities. He purchased a small job printing shop at 15 Canal Street which had escaped the flames, and on 11 October the *Tribune* was back on the streets. That first postfire issue contained the famous "Cheer Up" editorial that *Tribune* historians attributed to Medill for decades afterward; but Horace White, who was editor in chief from 1865 to 1874, maintained that he was the real author. Whoever actually wrote the piece, the *Tribune* was so closely identified with Medill that Medill reaped the benefits of the fame the editorial generated. The editorial said in part: "In the midst of a calamity without parallel in the world's history, looking upon the ashes of thirty years' accumulation, the people of this once beautiful city have resolved that *Chicago shall rise again....* Let us cheer up, save what is left, and we shall come out right. The Christian world is coming to our relief. The worst is already over. In a few more days all the dangers will be past, and we can resume the battle of life with Christian faith and Western grit. Let us all cheer up." The editorial helped to inspire the city's comeback and the *Tribune* assumed leadership in supporting the reconstruction work. When Medill ran for mayor in 1872 on the "Fire-proof" ticket, he won by a landslide.

Medill's tenure as mayor, however, was nearly as disastrous as the fire that had ravaged the city. His term began on a high note of community cooperation when he came out in his inaugural speech for brick instead of pine construction and demanded a better water supply for the city. "Happily there is left which the fire cannot consume," said the mayor. "Habits of industry and self-reliance, personal integrity, business aptitude, mechanical skill, and unconquerable will . . . created what the flames devoured and these can speedily recreate more than was swept away."

While community cooperation may have been the theme of Medill's inaugural, his subsequent administration proved divisive. Medill supported prohibition and enforced it in Chicago. He also ordered that all saloons in the city close on Sundays, which for many working people was their only day of rest. Medill's strong probusiness and antilabor views further alienated those who were already alienated because of the saloon closing order and Medill's position on prohibition. Medill stood solidly on the side of the white, Anglo-Saxon, Protestant, native business class of Chicago and against the immigrant, mostly Catholic and Jewish laboring class. The immigrants' resentment toward Medill became so ugly that he announced in July 1873 that he would not seek reelection and left for Europe in August with his family. He stayed away until his term of office expired. Alderman L. L. Bond assumed the office of acting mayor upon Medill's departure. The immigrants, particularly the Germans and the Irish, formed a political coalition to support Harvey D. Colvin for mayor in 1874. Colvin was elected, and the saloons were open again on Sundays.

This episode did not mark the end of Medill's animosity toward labor and the immigrant class. When he returned from Europe in 1874 to assume complete financial and editorial control of the *Tribune,* the city was about to enter a long, divisive, and bloody period of labor conflict. Medill liked to picture himself as a "people's champion," but he invariably supported industry and business. He opposed the eight-hour workday because it would mean less profit for the industrialists and less wages for the workers. Medill denounced socialists as "communistic cranks" in the *Tribune:* "As these cranks have now adopted for their watchword increased pay or no work, let us see what that high-sounding phrase really means and what would be the result of such policy. . . . It is a thousand pities there is not some method of incarcerating them in lunatic asylums long enough for their heads to cool sufficiently to enable them to take a common sense view of things."

During the railroad strike of 1877, the Chicago Police Department decided to change its policy of firing a warning shot over the heads of strikers and instead proposed aiming low. The *Tribune* approved this plan editorially and suggested the organizing of vigilante groups to supplement the police and militia. The newspaper stated that "Chicago is too far advanced to permit her bad elements to interfere with her interests." On 23 July the *Tribune* demanded that railroad workers who refused to take wage cuts and dismissal notices

Medill and his grandchildren: Eleanor Medill Patterson, who became publisher of the Washington Times-Herald; *Joseph Medill McCormick (standing, right), who left the* Tribune *to become a U.S. senator from Illinois; Robert R. McCormick (seated, left), who became the long-time publisher of the* Tribune; *and Joseph Medill Patterson, who left the* Tribune *to found the* New York Daily News

"step out of the way. . . . If they will not step out voluntarily, they must be made to by force." The newspaper also referred to the strikers as "the scum and filth of the city." On 26 July a *Tribune* editorial declared that "capitalists would offer any sum to see the leaders . . . strung up to a telegraph pole."

Medill's *Tribune* reached the nadir of inhumanity in an 1884 editorial which suggested a solution to the problem of unemployment: "The simplest plan, probably, when one is not a member of the Humane Society, is to put arsenic in the supplies of food furnished the unemployed or the tramp. This produces death in a short time and is a warning to other tramps to keep out of the neighborhood." During the 1886 strike against McCormick Harvesting Machinery Works that culminated in the Haymarket riot, the *Tribune* stood firmly with McCormick's plant management even though it had formerly criticized the firm's business practices. In the Pullman strike of 1894, the *Tribune* bitterly fought against the strikers and even some supporters of management found it difficult to sympathize with the newspaper's stand. The *Tribune* also denounced the government for not acting more forcefully during the strike. The newspaper was nearly hysterical about the threat it perceived in the Socialist leader Eugene V. Debs, whom it branded an anarchist. Medill ordered the city editor to insert *Dictator* before every mention of Debs's name in the newspaper; the order was carried out for a time, after which the editor decided to ignore it.

During the 1890s Medill gradually transferred power in the *Tribune* to his sons-in-law Robert W. Patterson, Jr., and Robert Sanderson McCormick, the husbands of his daughters Elinor and Katharine, respectively. (Medill's third daughter, Josephine, did not marry and died in January 1892.) Nevertheless, the newspaper remained vituperative in behalf of big business and against any politician who appeared to be on the side of the workers.

Medill's legacy is the still vital and bold *Chicago Tribune* of today. Medill also was the patriarch of a genuine dynasty of American journalism. His grandsons Robert R. McCormick and Joseph M. Patterson shared the leadership of the *Tribune* until Patterson left Chicago to found the *New York Daily News.* Both McCormick and Patterson were towering figures in journalism and in American life. Medill's granddaughter, Eleanor Medill (Cissy) Patterson, was the publisher of the *Washington Times-Herald* and a force to be reckoned with in the capital. Medill's great-granddaughter Alicia Patterson

Guggenheim founded Long Island's great daily *Newsday*. Another great-granddaughter, Josephine Patterson, was a reporter for the rival *Chicago Daily News* for a time, a fact that would no doubt have caused Medill some consternation had he lived to know of it.

Medill died on 16 March 1899 in San Antonio, Texas, where he was spending the winter. It was reported that his dying words were "What is the news this morning?"

References:

Philip Kinsley, *The Chicago Tribune: Its First Hundred Years*, 5 volumes (Chicago: The Tribune Company, 1943-1946);

Joseph Logsdon, *Horace White, Nineteenth Century Liberal* (Westport, Conn.: Greenwood Press, 1971);

John Tebbel, *An American Dynasty* (Garden City: Doubleday, 1947);

Lloyd Wendt, *Chicago Tribune: The Rise of a Great American Newspaper* (Chicago: Rand McNally, 1979).

Papers:

The Medill Papers are kept in the Tribune Company Archives in Chicago.

Hezekiah Niles

(10 October 1777-2 April 1839)

Ronald Truman Farrar
University of Kentucky

MAJOR POSITIONS HELD: Editor, *Baltimore Evening Post* (1805-1811); founder and editor, *Niles' Weekly Register* (Baltimore) (1811-1835).

BOOKS: *Things as They Are; or, Federalism Turned Inside Out!! Being a Collection of Extracts from Federal Papers, &c. and Remarks upon Them, Originally Written for, and Published in the Evening Post* (Baltimore: Published at the office of the Evening Post by H. Niles, 1809);

Principles and Acts of the Revolution in America; or, An Attempt to Collect and Preserve Some of the Speeches, Orations, & Proceedings, with Sketches and Remarks on Men and Things, and Other Fugitive or Neglected Pieces, Belonging to the Revolutionary Period in the United States (Baltimore: Printed and published for the editor by W. O. Niles, 1822);

Agriculture of the United States; or, An Essay Concerning Internal Improvement & Domestic Manufactures, Shewing Their Inseperable [sic] Connection with the Business and Interests of Agriculture (N.p., 1827?);

Politics for Working Men. An Essay on Labor and Subsistence; Addressed to the Free Productive People of the U. States (Baltimore?, 1831?);

Submissions to the Convention of Agriculturalists, Manufacturers and Others, Friendly to the "American System," Assembled at New York, October 26, 1831 (New York, 1831).

OTHER: *Journal of the Proceedings of the Friends of Domestic Industry, in General Convention Met at the City of New York, October 26, 1831. Published by Order of the Convention*, edited by Niles (Baltimore, 1831).

An editor of uncommon judgment and skill, Hezekiah Niles developed his *Weekly Register* into the most authoritative political journal of the first half of the nineteenth century. Subtitled *Containing Political, Historical, Geographical, Scientifical, Statistical, Economical, and Biographical Documents, Essays and Facts: Together with Notices of the Arts and Manufactures, and a Record of the Events of the Times*, the *Weekly Register* has become as invaluable to historians in the present as it was to political figures of its own day. Through his careful, balanced selections and interpretations, Niles gained the respect of contemporary politicians of many persuasions and convincingly achieved his personal goal—to be known as "an honest chronicler." The *Weekly Reg-*

ister is particularly useful to historians because it is indexed. Niles had an index compiled and published in 1823, after the first twelve volumes had appeared; thereafter, he issued an index with the binding of each yearly volume.

Niles was born in 1777 near Chadd's Ford, Chester County, Pennsylvania, in the farmhouse of James Jefferis; his parents, Hezekiah and Mary Way Niles, had fled their home in Wilmington, Delaware, as British forces pressed toward that city. Taking refuge with other Quakers in the Jefferis household, the Niles family still found itself directly in the path of Lord Cornwallis, whose troops surged across nearby Jefferis Ford and fought the Battle of Brandywine within a month of Hezekiah's birth. His mother, the daughter of a Wilmington businessman, was a descendant of one of Pennsylvania's original settlers. His father was a carpenter and plane maker; he held local offices and developed a modestly prosperous business upon his return to Wilmington after the Revolutionary War. The elder Niles died just before Hezekiah's fourteenth birthday when he was struck on the head by a falling signpost outside his carpentry shop. Most of the father's estate was willed to the elder son, Samuel, but $3,000 went to Hezekiah. He is believed to have been educated at the Friends School in Wilmington.

In 1794, when he was seventeen, Niles was apprenticed to Benjamin Johnson, a Philadelphia printer, bookseller, and bookbinder. Given ready access to all the books in the store, young Niles began to read extensively. His interest in politics was whetted here, too; Johnson's shop, situated on Philadelphia's Market Street near what was then the federal capitol, gave him a ringside seat from which to glimpse national leaders at close hand. George Washington "often passed me in his morning walk," Niles recalled many years later in the *Register,* "and frequently seemed to give me an encouraging look, if our eyes happened to meet; to which he would sometimes add a kind nod of recognition." While still in his teens, Niles began contributing articles to the *Aurora* and other Philadelphia newspapers; these essays advocated further industrial development and the election of Thomas Jefferson, and reflected his opposition to the treaty John Jay had negotiated with England. Niles's stay in Philadelphia ended after less than three years, however; he was released from the apprenticeship when his master's business went into decline. Returning to Wilmington, Niles entered the printing business in partnership with James Adams, Jr., whose father had been the first

printer in Delaware; that venture lasted about two years. Niles, meanwhile, had come into a small fortune; on the death of his brother Samuel, Niles received the bulk of their late father's estate. With these funds he launched a partnership with Vincent Bonsal; the two men sold books and handled a number of job printing orders, including the printing of the *Delaware Gazette.* The firm lost money, notably on an ambitious book publishing effort, *The Political Writings of John Dickinson* (1801); within months Niles's fortune was wiped out and he found himself $25,000 in debt—an obligation he repaid over the years.

On 17 May 1798, a few months before his twenty-first birthday, Niles married Anne Ogden, the daughter of William Ogden, a Philadelphia tavern keeper. The Ogdens, too, were Quakers, though William Ogden had been temporarily suspended from the faith for fighting in the Revolutionary War. Hezekiah and Anne Niles had twelve children. In 1801 Niles was elected Wilmington town clerk and was later reelected for a second term; he also served two terms as assistant burgess and was prominent in state political circles.

On 12 February 1805 Niles launched a magazine in Wilmington, the *Apollo,* subtitled the *Delaware Weekly Magazine.* Containing fiction, verse, and essays, the eight-page magazine never really caught on, and Niles folded it just six months later. Shortly thereafter he left Wilmington for Baltimore to edit the *Evening Post,* a struggling four-page daily that had been started a few months before. Niles gave the paper a solid Republican political stance. His staunch support of Jeffersonian politics won him political influence, if not prosperity, during the five and a half years he edited the *Post.* A collection of his editorials defending Jefferson's foreign policy was reprinted in book form as *Things as They Are; or, Federalism Turned Inside Out!!* in 1809. However, the *Post* never attracted a large local following, and Niles, his eye on a wider audience, sold it on 10 June 1811. Within the month, Niles was circulating the prospectus for his *Weekly Register.*

Niles's vision called for a weekly sixteen-page compilation of texts of important speeches, letters, documents, and official domestic and foreign policy papers—an early-nineteenth-century counterpart to a modern day news magazine. Though the pages were small—medium octavo, or book size—Niles pledged in his prospectus to offer his readers one-fourth more reading material than was available in the largest newspapers as well as "something interesting at the present moment, and, as a book of reference, a fund of reading always at hand, a work of much probable value."

The formula worked. Niles began by giving away the *Weekly Register* to 1,500 persons whom he invited to be readers for six months before paying the five-dollar annual subscription fee. Within a month, however, he had nearly 1,900 paying subscribers. The audience was influential, and it was national in character. Within three months Niles could boast that the *Weekly Register* circulated "from Maine to Georgia, and from the Atlantic beyond the Mississippi." Regular readers included John Adams, Thomas Jefferson, Andrew Jackson, James Madison, the Marquis de Lafayette, members of Congress, foreign ambassadors, and a host of other leaders in political, diplomatic, business, and military circles. By the end of the first year the subscription list numbered more than 3,300.

A cornerstone of Niles's editorial policy was his unswerving opposition to the British. Niles frequently recalled how his own mother had been threatened at bayonet-point by a British grenadier, and he never tired of ridiculing the British crown, nobility, and other institutions. Niles believed that commerce with England siphoned away too much money from the United States, and he was outraged at the British practice of impressment—forcing American sailors into service on British craft. In one blistering editorial, Niles charged that England was "the common robber, the man-stealer, the scalper of women and children and prisoners, the incendiary and the ravisher . . . the enemy of our fathers, and our present unprincipled foe . . . the cause of every war that has afflicted the civilized world for fifty years past, the common pest of society and plague of the earth . . . the cold-calculating assassin of thirty millions of people in India, the ferocious murderer in Ireland, the minister of famine and pestilence in America . . . the most profligate and corrupt government in the universe . . . a government so polluted, so gangrened with every abomination, that it must perish of its own action, sooner or later. . . . A nation red to her armpits in the blood of innocence. . . ."

Whatever he said about the British editorially, however, Niles was able to preserve a sense of fairness and accuracy in his news columns. Indeed, Frank Luther Mott, a leading scholar in the field of journalism history, contended that *Niles' Weekly Register*'s "reputation was won at the outset by its reliable reports of fact in the events of the second war with England."

Niles opposed slavery, and was especially resolute in his denunciation of domestic slave trading.

In 1812, in one of many editorials on the matter, he wrote: "If there is any thing that ought to be supremely hated, it is the present infamous traffic that is carried on in several of the middle states, and especially in Maryland, in negroes, for the Georgia and Louisiana markets. I blush for the honor of the art of printing when I see advertisements published in the newspapers, openly avowing for the trade, and soliciting business, with the indifference of dealers in horses." However, he differed with William Lloyd Garrison and others who demanded the abolition of slavery at once. Niles favored a more gradual approach, fearing that immediate abolition would result in dissolution of the United States: "I am personally disposed to give up much," he wrote, "even of what I believe to be right in itself, to prevent the worst of all wrongs. The harmony and union of the states is a matter of the first consideration."

Niles was a Jeffersonian Republican throughout his early years, but declined to support the Republican party in the pages of the *Register*. About 1820 he declared himself to belong to no party, and later, in opposing the policies of Andrew Jackson, he identified himself as a Whig. He refused to comment on the private lives of public men, and prided himself on having ardent readers of all political persuasions. Niles did, however, enjoy close friendships with political figures—notably with Henry Clay, after whom he named one of his sons.

Niles had a deep and abiding interest in Latin America, and his *Register* carried numerous items on the region over the years. His earlier editorials, such as this one about Chile in 1825, reflected tolerance and understanding: "We must not expect that a people, so long capriciously governed and enslaved as were those of Mexico and South America should, (with the mere emancipation of themselves and their country from the dominion of royal and priestly authorities so abominable as those of Spain), suddenly enter upon and pursue that steadiness of course and liberality in all things, which distinguished those of the more enlightened, and more fortunate, colonies, which now compose the United States, wherein the principles of liberty and the rights of man, were, perhaps, quite as well understood before the revolution as since. . . . A generation, perhaps, must pass away before those who have been accustomed to see and feel power without regard to right, can be made fully sensible of what is a government of the law." In later years, however, Niles became less hopeful. His biographer, Norval Neil Luxon, characterized the shift this way: "In the quarter of a century of his editorship, Niles changed his attitude toward the South American states from eager enthusiasm, willing to overlook errors in judgment and procedure, to dispirited disillusionment, based soundly enough on a keen observation of the reasons back of the repeated revolutions in the republics."

Anne Niles died in 1824; in 1826 Niles married Sally Ann Warner of Wilmington. Eight children resulted from the second marriage.

Niles's deeply felt economic beliefs—conservative, nationalist, and protectionist—were reflected in the *Weekly Register* throughout his years as editor. More space was devoted to economic subjects than to any others, and the *Register* was, possibly, the most important source of economic information in the United States during the first third of the nineteenth century. Niles's protectionist crusade was designed to minimize what he regarded as dangerous economic reliance on Great Britain and to nurture the growth and prosperity of American business. His essays on economics were widely reprinted. In one of them, "Politics for the Working Man," he wrote: "I ask you not to vote for this man or that man, or any particular man—but this I exhort, and entreat you to do—by all that is good for the nation, by all that is beneficial for yourselves, to give your suffrages to no human being who does not stand broadly pledged, manfully and honestly 'committed,' and unquestionably devoted, to the preservation of the AMERICAN SYSTEM—the fountain of public wealth, the guarantee of private comfort—proclaiming plenty and securing peace—offering relief to the oppressed of all nations, and *establishing the independence of the United States*." His opposition to free trade placed him in a position of leadership whenever tariff policy was discussed; he was prominently involved in the protectionist conventions of 1827 at Harrisburg and 1831 at New York, and was quoted widely in the United States and abroad. On the other great economic question of that day, the Bank of the United States, Niles's views changed over time; he favored the rechartering of the bank during the Jacksonian era—though he had opposed it in 1811 as being too powerful. Summarizing the complex thought process that led to his shift in position, Niles wrote that his views had been "much softened by time and circumstances," and that he had come around to the opinion that the bank had "rendered essential services toward establishing a uniform and sound currency."

Despite his strong political views—and despite the partisanship of the press of the day—Niles confined his political editorials to issues and avoided personal attacks. Throughout his editorship, the *Register* never endorsed or opposed the election of an individual. In his prospectus, Niles had pledged that the *Register* "shall be open to all parties, temper, moderation and dignity being preserved. . . . The newspapers of the day, devoted to *party* and *partisans*, seldom dare to '*tell the truth, the whole truth, and nothing but the truth. . . .*' the dignity of the press is prostrated to the will of aspiring individuals. . . . The editor does not intend to interfere in the petty disputes between the *ins* and *outs*. . . . Its politics shall be *American*—not passive and lukewarm, but active and vigilant—not to support individuals, but to subserve the interests of the people, so far as he shall be able to discern in what their interest lies."

Niles obtained most of his material from other newspapers, domestic and foreign, and was swift and skillful in rewriting and condensing articles to fit his unique requirements. He worked long hours—at least ten each day, he observed—but thrived on the grueling schedule. Outside the office, his time was spent almost exclusively with his family. But from the very first issue, Niles came to think of the *Register*'s subscribers as family also; he frequently began editorials with a highly personalized, intimate approach: "It is now more than six months since I held a fireside conversation with my numerous readers and friends, on things of deep interest to them and myself, as joint members of the government of the United States. . . ."

One contemporary observer noted Niles's leathery face and "sharp eye with compressed lips," while another described him as "a short stout-built man, stooping as he walked, speaking in a high key, addicted to snuff but with a keen gray eye that lighted up a plain face with shrewd expression." Luxon commented that Niles's "taste for good wine and imported tobacco led his fellow editors and friends to have some good-natured fun with him while he was engaged in his editorial campaigns to educate the public to use American products."

Niles carried no advertising in the *Register*, though some advertising was permitted in the books and pamphlets compiled from the *Register*'s pages. His initial subscription rate of five dollars a year, plus postage, was maintained for thirty-seven years. He had a difficult time with collections—Mott reported that the *Register* had ten to twelve thousand dollars in subscription payments outstanding after it had been running for less than two years—yet Niles was able to earn a good living from his publication.

Noted for being one of the fastest, most efficient typesetters in the country, Niles remained keenly interested in the craft of printing throughout his life, and was frequently elected to office in the Baltimore Typographical Society. He was also active in the Masonic Order of Maryland, and was twice chosen grand high priest.

In the early 1830s Niles's health, strained by years of overwork, began to crack; frequently his columns made mention of his desire to gain some release from his strenuous responsibilities. Though he had taken his oldest son, William Ogden Niles, into the business in 1827, Niles resolutely sustained his harsh, self-imposed editorial schedule. He suffered a broken right arm in a fall on a visit to New York in 1835; the injury took months to heal and placed a serious drain on his energies. The following July a stroke caused severe paralysis to his right side. Three months later, in September 1835, Niles officially awarded his son the title of editor and publisher. Niles continued to write occasionally for the *Register*, though the paralysis on his right side required him to dictate his material. He made his will in July 1836—signing it awkwardly with his left hand—and officially retired two months later. His worsening physical condition left him in considerable pain until his death on 2 April 1839 in Wilmington.

Tributes to Niles as "the great champion of the American System" and "the consistent, faithful, and successful advocate of American industry" appeared in the country's newspapers. The *Baltimore Sun*'s editorial concluded: "Such a man is a true patriot, and as long as the United States shall preserve its independence, so long shall the name of Hezekiah Niles, the founder of *Niles' Register*, be revered, and his career shall be quoted as an example for imitation by all who desire to obtain that highest and noblest title: a good and honest man, in private life; in public, a pure disinterested patriot."

The *Register* died less than a decade later. William Ogden Niles, shortly after taking over the paper in 1835, had moved its editorial office to Washington and changed the title to *Niles' National Register*. However, he was unable to sustain the character and quality of the publication; whereas Hezekiah Niles had skillfully rewritten and interpreted newspapers and documents for the *Register*, the younger Niles often simply clipped and pasted. Far more absorbed with politics than with journalism, William Ogden Niles neglected the business affairs of the *Register* and soon found himself unable to meet his payroll. His stepmother, the administratrix of the estate, decided to offer the publication for sale. Jeremiah Hughes, a veteran of Maryland journalism and a close friend of Hezekiah Niles, bought the paper and edited it for eight and a half years until his retirement. George Beatty then moved the *Register* to Philadelphia and published it until its demise in 1848. "To the future Historian," Beatty wrote near the end of the *Register*'s existence "we commit the record, and await the judgment with full confidence."

References:

Norval Neil Luxon, *Niles' Weekly Register: News Magazine of the Nineteenth Century* (Baton Rouge: Louisiana State University Press, 1947);

Frank Luther Mott, *A History of American Magazines*, 3 volumes (Cambridge: Harvard University Press, 1938-1939), I: pp. 160, 268-270;

Mott, *American Journalism: A History: 1690-1960*, third edition (New York: Macmillan, 1962), p. 188;

John Neal, *Wandering Recollections of a Somewhat Busy Life* (Boston: Roberts, 1869), pp. 210-214.

Papers:

Letters of Hezekiah Niles are in the Hezekiah Niles Papers, the William Darlington Papers, the Henry Clay Papers, the Joseph Gales, Jr., and William Winston Seaton Papers, the Andrew Jackson Papers, the Thomas Jefferson Papers, and the James Madison Papers, all in the Library of Congress.

B. S. Osbon

(16 August 1827-6 May 1912)

A. J. Kaul
University of Southern Mississippi

MAJOR POSITIONS HELD: Reporter, *New York World* (1860-1861); naval correspondent, *New York Herald* (1861-1864); founder and editor, *Nautical Gazette* (1871-1884).

BOOKS: *Visitors' Hand Book, or, How To See the Great Eastern* (New York: Baker & Goodwin, 1860); *Handbook of the United States Navy* (New York: D. Van Nostrand, 1864).

OTHER: *Cruise of the U.S. Flagship Hartford, 1862-1863: Being a Narrative of All Her Operations Since Going into Commission, in 1862, until Her Return to New York in 1863. From the Private Journal of William C. Holton,* edited by Osbon (New York: L. W. Paine, printer, 1863).

B. S. Osbon was a "sailor of fortune" whose quest for action and adventure on the high seas took him around the world and led to a celebrated reporting career. A participant in events, he provided eyewitness accounts of important Civil War naval battles that secured his reputation as a daring reporter and the most famous naval correspondent of the war. He was imprisoned for allegedly giving information to the enemy, founded one of the first news syndicates, and established the first marine newspaper in the United States.

Bradley Sillick Osbon was born of "poor but Methodist" parents on 16 August 1827 in Rye, Westchester County, New York. A lackluster and unmanageable student, Osbon confessed to being "the worst boy in the village." His repeated delinquency chagrined his parents, especially his father, Abiathar Mann Osbon, an upright Methodist minister. He ran away from home when he was eleven to work on Hudson River canal boats; two years later he left home again, joining the crew of the *Cornelia* for a trip between New York and Liverpool, England. A "large number" of the ship's nearly 1,000 Irish immigrant passengers died of typhus on the return trip to New York. Osbon described the passage as "simply hell afloat."

Shortly after his return to New York, Osbon,

at the urging of his father, enrolled in a private school in Brooklyn to study navigation. He later joined the United States Navy and served on store-ships. Quickly tiring of such sedate service, Osbon mustered out of the navy to pursue more adventurous duty. In 1847 he sailed from New Bedford, Massachusetts, aboard a whaler that voyaged to the Arctic Ocean and Antarctica. During a layover in Hong Kong in 1851, he briefly served in the Anglo-Chinese navy, fighting pirates in the South China Sea. Osbon joined another whaling expedition, spent a winter in the Arctic, and returned to the United States in 1852 after an absence of more than five years. His stay was short: "The shore had little charm for me," he said. In 1853 he became the captain of a schooner in the Argentine navy. "I was simply a sailor of fortune, fighting for the joy of adventure." Osbon resigned from Argentine service to join the crew of a steamship as a quartermaster in 1857, ending his career in the merchant marine in 1858.

With his sailor's store of strange tales of faraway places, Osbon embarked on the lecture circuit, earning as much as $800 in three months for his entertaining stories of his adventures. "While on my lecture tour," he explained, "I was frequently asked by country editors to sit down in the office and write something about my entertainment. I was glad to do this, and little by little acquired a taste for seeing my work in public print." Osbon discovered that he had some writing ability and "surrendered all other ambition for newspaper work." He began his journalism career by contributing to many New York newspapers, "combining marine and theological subjects in a manner which the editors must have found satisfactory." His extensive sailing experience, coupled with being a minister's son, helped Osbon become "the first reporter employed by the New York *World*," which was founded on 14 June 1860 as a religious penny paper.

Osbon's reputation as a journalist was established on the *World* with his stunning eyewitness account of the siege and surrender of Fort Sumter at Charleston, South Carolina, in April 1861, to begin the Civil War. Serving as a clerk and signal officer aboard the U.S. cutter *Harriet Lane*, Osbon watched the early morning bombardment of the fort. His report to the *World*, a prototype of terse modern newswriting style, opened with a straight-forward seven-word lead paragraph: *"The ball is opened. War is inaugurated."* The nine-dollar-a-week reporter was well aware of the attack's significance. "Across the harbour the belching cannons told that the nation was rent asunder," he later wrote. "It seemed to me that the end of the world was about due." En route back to New York aboard the U.S.S. *Baltic*, Osbon interviewed the defeated Maj. Robert Anderson, Union garrison commander at Fort Sumter, and helped him polish his official report.

Osbon entered into a mistaken gentleman's agreement with Capt. Gustavus V. Fox, leader of the relief expedition to Fort Sumter, who had presented the plan for the expedition to President Lincoln. Fearing adverse criticism for the expedition's failure, Fox implored Osbon not to mention his name in the reporter's *World* accounts. Osbon agreed, thinking that it was "the proper thing to do at the time." New Yorkers reacted differently; patriotism was at fever pitch: "Everywhere were boys, running and crying war news," Osbon said. "Everywhere were knots and groups of men discussing the great event." Anderson and the expeditionary forces were hailed as heroes. Chagrined by the turn of events and his anonymity, Fox accused Osbon of taking the initiative in omitting his name from the news accounts. "Naturally, I resented this charge," Osbon said, "and told the truth." Fox was angered even more and took his revenge against Osbon several years later when he had become assistant secretary of the navy.

The *World*'s stunning reportage from Fort Sumter made a journalistic hero of Osbon and attracted the attention of Frederic Hudson, managing editor of James Gordon Bennett's *New York Herald*. Hudson offered Osbon the position of *Herald* naval editor at twenty-five dollars a week, nearly three times his *World* salary. Osbon took the job and "found the employment most congenial."

Osbon's reporting was made easier by Secretary of the Navy Gideon Welles, who gave the *Herald* reporter a roving commission to accompany naval expeditions to the South. In a letter "To All Commanding Officers," Welles said that "the Department has no objection to his acting in any staff capacity to which the commanding officer may see fit to appoint him, provided it does not interfere with the regulations of the Navy."

The navy secretary inadvertently told Osbon during an interview about a secret naval expedition being planned against Port Royal, South Carolina. While awaiting the interview in Welles's outer office, Osbon discovered maps of the Port Royal harbor. "What is uppermost in the pile is uppermost in their minds," Osbon thought. During the interview, Osbon asked Welles for a letter to the commander of the Port Royal expedition:

> "How did you know we were sending a fleet to Port Royal," Welles demanded. "Nobody but the President, Captain Dupont, General Sherman, and myself know that."
> "And me," Osbon replied.
> "Who told you?"
> "You did, Mr. Secretary, just now."

Osbon received the letter, and a warning from Welles: "If you publish or say anything concerning our plans you will be arrested and tried for court-martial. Under the regulations you can be shot."

Osbon covered the three-and-a-half-hour battle of Port Royal from the U.S. transport ship *Matanzas*. His graphic report of the 7 November 1861 engagement filled two pages of the *Herald* on 14 November: "If you can imagine the scene you can do more than I can describe," he reported. "The noise was terrific, while the bursting of the shells was as terrific as it was destructive. I counted no less than forty shells bursting at one time, and that right in the battery and in the woods where about eight hundred rebels lay. In addition to this, the Susquehanna, with her tremendous battery, aided by the Bienville, the Pawnee, and half a dozen smaller gunboats, was making the air brown with the sand, while the blue smoke of the explosion went up to make a most magnificent sight.... A moment or two elapsed—just time enough to load the guns—and again the scene was enacted afresh." In addition to his *Herald* report, Osbon, who was an artist as well as a writer, supplied *Harper's Weekly* (30 November 1861) with an illustration of the battle scene. Osbon's full red beard was largely burned off at Port Royal when the wadding from one of the artillery shells blew back into his face; otherwise, he was uninjured.

The centerpiece of Osbon's war correspondence was his coverage of Adm. David Farragut's naval expedition against New Orleans in 1862. With a letter of recommendation to Farragut from Commander David D. Porter, Farragut's foster brother, Osbon was appointed clerk on the flagship

Hartford; but when Farragut learned of Osbon's experience in naval warfare, he made Osbon fleet signal officer. "No duty could have been more congenial to my tastes or more suited to my position as correspondent," Osbon observed. "It brought me into the closest touch with the Flag Officer, and gave me the most intimate knowledge of every movement of the fleet." From the moment of his appointment, Osbon was a devoted admirer of Farragut: "He was my idol as a man, an officer and a hero from that hour."

Confederate forts south of New Orleans showered the Union naval expedition with shells and fire. "The river and its banks were one sheet of flame," Osbon reported in the *Herald* on 10 May, "and the messengers of death were moving with lightning swiftness in all directions. . . . Shot, shell, grape and cannister filled the air with deadly missiles. It was like the breaking up of a thousand worlds—crash—tear—whiz! Such another scene was never witnessed by mortal man. Steadily we steamed on, giving them shell, the forts firing rifle shot and shell, ten inch columbiads, forty-two, thirty-two and twenty-four pounder balls; and, to add to this state of affairs, thirteen steamers . . . were pouring into and around us a hailstorm of iron perfectly indescribable. Not satisfied with their firing, fire raft after fire raft was lit and set adrift to do their work of burning." A Confederate fire raft shoved into the *Hartford* set fire to the rigging, and a shell from Fort St. Philip set another fire on deck. While Osbon knelt trying to remove some shells from the flagship, Farragut scolded the reporter: "Come, Mr. Osbon, this is no time for prayer." Osbon succeeded in removing the shells and sinking the burning raft, and the reporter was praised in Farragut's official report. Osbon recalled the New Orleans battle a half century later in images undimmed by time: "Death and destruction seemed everywhere. Men's faces covered with powder—black and daubed with blood. They had become like a lot of demons in a wild inferno, working fiercely at the business of death."

In 1863 Osbon covered the last of his major Civil War naval battles, the ironclad monitor *Montauk*'s unsuccessful assault on Fort McAllister, Georgia, on the Ogeechee River. He served as clerk and signal officer on the experimental ironclad that he called a "cheesebox on a raft." According to the *Herald*'s 13 March report, the *Montauk* was struck seventy-one times and continued to fight. "The enemy was hitting us every two or three minutes," Osbon reported, "but in no wise doing the vessel any harm." Osbon was injured in the battle when a shot struck the *Montauk* pilot house: "Your correspondent was at the instant of impact on one knee writing a paragraph in his notebook. . . . It unbalanced me, and I tumbled over against the side of the narrow pilot house, when, to my surprise, I was struck by a piece of iron bolt (weighing about one pound) first on the shoulder and then on the knee." The bolt displaced his kneecap and broke two ribs.

Osbon was keenly interested in the "cheesebox" experiments, telling his *Herald* readers of their historic importance: "Europe will look upon the success of our fifteen-inch guns on shipboard as a demonstration in heavy ordnance which is second only to that of the result of improvements in ironclads over wooden ships." Osbon was covering what he would later call "the final death warrant of our wooden navies. We had loved them well, but the old order had changed. The 'wooden walls' tottered, the iron hull with its revolving turret—the 'cheesebox on a raft'—had battled its way into the world's confidence." The *Montauk* was sold at auction in 1904 and went into scrap. "I have always thought the Government should have preserved her," Osbon lamented in a nostalgic moment. "I should have done so myself had I had the means."

After the events on the Ogeechee, Osbon briefly returned to the lecture circuit, telling audiences about the *Montauk* battles and earning as much as $900 for a single lecture. In 1864 he resigned from the *Herald* and established a bureau of naval intelligence, which he claimed was "one of the first news syndicates." Osbon had received advance information about the Union attack on Wilmington, North Carolina, and offered stories of the plans to fifteen or twenty newspapers. Under his terms, the stories were not to be published until the papers received word of the actual attack. But on 19 December, five days before the attack, the *Boston Daily Advertiser* and the *Philadelphia Press* published the stories, which were reprinted in the Richmond newspapers. The "leak" proved costly to Osbon. Assistant Secretary of the Navy Gustavus Fox seized the opportunity to punish Osbon, charging him with violating the Fifty-ninth Article of War by giving information to the enemy. On 1 January 1865 Osbon was arrested at his New York City office and placed in the Capitol Prison in Washington, D.C. Osbon refused to plead guilty to the charge of furnishing the enemy with information. Relying on intervention from the president, Osbon believed he would soon be released; but during his incarceration, Lincoln was assassinated. Nevertheless, Osbon was acquitted and finally released after six months of confinement. In a letter to President Andrew Johnson in which he pleaded his innocence, Osbon bitterly complained: "My family are suffering and in actual want; my business has been broken up and ruined; my detention has been unreasonably long and severe; and my health sadly undermined by my peculiar and close incarceration." The *New York Tribune* asserted that the Osbon affair cost the government $60,000 to try an innocent man.

Osbon reestablished his news bureau "with almost the entire support of the New York City press," but his old wanderlust returned. He was involved in a one-vessel Mexican navy near Brownsville, Texas, in 1866; served as a boarding officer (a reporter who boarded vessels to gather news) for the New York Associated Press at New Orleans in 1867; and attended the Maritime Exposition at Le Havre, France, after his marriage to Eliza Balfour on 14 February 1868. While traveling in Europe, Osbon sent reports back to American newspapers. "It was not customary in those days to syndicate descriptive matter," he wrote, "so that each of my letters had to be separately written and differently constructed. Yet I did not find this a difficult undertaking, once I got going."

When he returned to the United States in 1871, Osbon invested $4,000 to found the *Nautical Gazette*, an eight-page weekly that was the first maritime journal in America. By 1873 the *Gazette* had a paid circulation of 7,000 subscribers and its size was increased to sixteen pages. He published the paper for thirteen years, selling it in 1884. For the remainder of his life, Osbon was involved in a variety of largely unsuccessful international business ventures, including steamship projects.

Osbon was eighty-four when he died at the Post-Graduate Hospital in New York City on 6 May 1912, the seventy-seventh anniversary of the founding of the *New York Herald*. Osbon's obituary in the *Herald* did not mention his spectacular Civil War naval reporting. "My husband died because he needed food and medicine," Mrs. Osbon said in the *New York World*'s obituary. "We have been existing, or trying to, on a pension of $20 a month he received from the Government." The pension was their only source of steady income. The veteran naval reporter's gold-handled presentation sword had been sold to pay for "necessities."

Adventure was the main necessity of Osbon's storybook life. Six years before his death, the aging sea captain, anchored in "a quiet harbor," still thrilled to the memories of the old days: "I voyage now in quiet and familiar waters. The compass no longer points to unknown harbours, over uncharted seas. The course is no longer marked by the flash of cutlass and the roar of guns. Like any other craft of a vanished time, I have been retired from the fiercer action of the front, trying to be content with the memories of the vanished days. Yet the smell of powder puts it all before me and makes me long sometimes for the flash and roar of battle—to feel the deck lift and rock to the thunder of heavy guns. Perhaps the old craft may be good for another voyage yet—something with just enough of the flavour of conquest and adventure to set one's pulse going and make him forget the years."

References:

J. Cutler Andrews, *The North Reports the Civil War* (Pittsburgh: University of Pittsburgh Press, 1955);

Albert Bigelow Paine, *A Sailor of Fortune: Personal Memoirs of Captain B. S. Osbon* (New York: McClure, Phillips, 1906);

Louis L. Snyder and Richard B. Morris, eds., *A Treasury of Great Reporting*, second edition (New York: Simon & Schuster, 1962), pp. 129-132.

Eleazer Oswald

(1755-30 September 1795)

Dwight L. Teeter, Jr.
University of Texas at Austin

MAJOR POSITION HELD: Publisher, *Independent Gazetteer, or, the Chronicle of Freedom* (Philadelphia) (1782-1795), *New York Journal* (1786-1787).

Perhaps because history is so often told from the winning side, standard journalism history accounts have paid little attention to the picaresque career of Eleazer Oswald. His life span of forty years included episodes as printer, soldier, publisher, duelist, coffee shop proprietor, free press theorist, fighter in the French Revolution, and unsuccessful revolutionist in Ireland. Newspapers controlled or influenced by Oswald—Philadelphia's *Independent Gazetteer, or, the Chronicle of Freedom* and the *New York Journal*—were leading voices in opposition to the adoption of the Constitution of the United States of America.

Oswald was born in 1755 in Falmouth, England, the son of a sea captain who traded with Jamaica and who disappeared when Oswald was in his early teens. At age fifteen Oswald left England for New York City, where he was apprenticed to the printer John Holt, proprietor of the *New-York Journal, or General Advertiser*. He won the affection and admiration of the Holt family, and eventually married his master's daughter, Elizabeth.

In 1775 Oswald volunteered for service with Benedict Arnold's expedition seeking to capture Crown Point and Ticonderoga. After taking a hand in the seizure of two British vessels on Lake Champlain and the unsuccessful attack on Quebec, Oswald was captured by the British. Oswald chafed at his confinement for more than a year until he was exchanged for a British prisoner of war.

Oswald returned to active duty as an artillery officer and served with distinction at the Battle of Monmouth in 1778. Oswald had been close to Benedict Arnold during the war's early years, serving for a time as his secretary during the Quebec expedition. This friendship evaporated during the late 1770s. Historian Joseph Towne Wheeler has written that Oswald was angered by Arnold's failure to return property, including Oswald's collection of French mathematical instruments. The revelation of Arnold's treason in 1780 led Oswald to express the wish that the bullet which wounded Arnold's leg during the attack on Quebec had pierced his heart instead.

Oswald clearly believed himself ill-treated in receiving inadequate promotions in military rank. His complaints were relayed to Congress after he had ended three years of meritorious, if discontented, service in 1778. The next year Congress accepted his resignation at the rank of lieutenant colonel.

After leaving the army, Oswald became a partner in the paper-making and printing business of William Goddard in Baltimore in 1779. Their *Maryland Journal* encountered rough times that year: its office was mobbed after the publication of Gen. Charles Lee's bitter article "Some Queries, Political and Military," an attack on the enormously revered Gen. George Washington. Although Goddard was compelled to sign—and later print—a disavowal of the "Queries," Oswald's response to the mob was to challenge its leader, Col. Samuel Smith, to a duel. Smith chose not to face the hot tempered Oswald on the dueling ground. Oswald's partnership with Goddard apparently ended in 1781. Perhaps believing that the mob episode had damaged his business opportunities in Baltimore, Oswald moved on to Philadelphia.

Mobs did not lie in wait for Oswald in Philadelphia, but the politics of that city were by no means calm when he published the first issue of his *Independent Gazetteer* on 13 April 1782. A ready-made enemy existed in the person of Pennsylvania's Chief Justice Thomas McKean, who was already extremely irritated over the many newspaper essays lampooning him for his love of power and his plural officeholding: from 1777 to 1783 he was simultaneously chief justice of Pennsylvania and a member of the Continental Congress from Delaware. He was to be a kind of judicial nemesis to Oswald.

Less than six months after the *Gazetteer* began publication, the newspaper published a blistering attack on the chief justice for a fine he had levied

334

against Col. Thomas Proctor. Colonel Proctor had beaten an election inspector who had had the gall to ask him to show a certificate proving that he had signed a loyalty oath. The *Gazetteer* published an item signed "A Friend to the Army" which asked of McKean: "Was ever an assault and battery punished, in this state, with the enormous fine of eighty pounds, or any sum nearly equal to it, before that of Colonel Proctor?" McKean was told that military officers deserved his respect: "They have bled freely for us, and the price of their blood has been cruelly torn from them by avarice and extortion."

Oswald was arrested and brought before McKean, who accused the printer of publishing a "seditious, scandalous and infamous libel." Oswald was released after putting up a £750 surety bond. Shortly, however, Oswald was back in custody before a furious chief justice because the 15 October 1782 *Gazetteer* had contained an abusive account of his experience: "Justice McKean and—that excrescence and superfluity of power, Judge [George] Bryan, addressed me with all the insolence and contumely of office, threatened me with the mistaken vengeance of persecuting justice,—and wished to extort [the identity of] the author of the piece in question." Oswald still refused to divulge the authorship of the item and was bailed out of jail by two friends who came up with £1,000. Oswald wrote to an old army friend, Gen. John Lamb of New York: "I am to have a public Trial . . . as a *Libeller*. The infamous English law doctrine of Libels being introduced by the more infamous Judges and Lawyers, in an American Court. O tempora; O mores!"

In his award-winning *Legacy of Suppression*, historian Leonard W. Levy wrote in 1960 that he could find no evidence that Americans had attempted to spell out, before Tunis Wortman's 1800 treatise, any systematic statement of a libertarian theory of speech and press. Levy wrote that libertarian propositions, without doubt, were "in the air at the time, but the fact is no longer susceptible to proof." He also asserted that little opposition to the concept of seditious libel could be found before the passage in 1798 of the Alien and Sedition Acts. But, as Professor Levy pointed out in his revised and expanded version of *Legacy of Suppression*—published in 1985 as *Emergence of a Free Press*—Oswald's *Independent Gazetteer* published at least one explicit attack on seditious libel as early as 1782. A correspondent calling himself "Junius Wilkes" argued in November 1782 that the Pennsylvania Constitution of 1776 justified "publications which respect the conduct of public servants; and, when

they even appear false and groundless, it is rather an inconvenience . . . a kind of *damnun absque injuria* [harm without actionable legal injury]."

In addition, Oswald's supporters desired a broader freedom than the Blackstonian variety which outlawed prepublication censorship but allowed postpublication punishment. "Junius Wilkes" contended that "the danger is precisely the same to liberty, in punishing a person *after* the performance appears to the world, as in preventing its publication in the first *instance*." The writer also complained about judges' "opportunity to create abundance of *constructive* libels; that is to raise by forced and arbitrary *construction*, publications into libels, which were never suspected to be such." Other writers, "Candid" and "Koster," urged that American courts should establish truth as a defense to a charge of libel, and "Candid" wanted to go still further: "Even mistakes in matters of fact, not proceeding from design, and malice, ought to escape punishment, because the best men, with the best intentions, may err, and too much severity towards such mistakes would render this boasted privilege [freedom of the press] a nullity."

Chief Justice McKean soon learned, early in 1783, that charging a grand jury to indict Oswald and actually getting an indictment were two quite different matters. After twice refusing to indict Oswald, the grand jury presented a memorial to McKean critical of his bringing repeated charges against the printer. When the irate chief justice would not allow the memorial to be filed with the records of his court, it was published in David Hall and William Sellers's *Pennsylvania Gazette*.

Oswald may have struggled vigorously for freedom of expression, but his concept of that freedom was limited to Oswald himself. That is, if he disagreed angrily with another's views, he believed that the dueling ground was a fine place to settle the matter. Oswald favored a bicameral legislature; a new arrival in Philadelphia, Mathew Carey, publisher of the *Pennsylvania Herald*,—who earlier had printed in Ireland and England—became linked with the Constitutionalist faction, which supported the unicameral system established by the state's constitution of 1776. Oswald published an attack on Carey and those of a like mind as "baboons of ingratitude" and jeered at the "Society of Lately Adopted Sons of Pennsylvania." Carey, later noted as a scholarly economist, responded with a poem dedicated to Oswald: *The Plagi-Scurriliad: A Hudibrastic Poem*, which pointed to undeniable similarities between some of the writings published by Oswald, on the one hand, and Britain's famed Junius Papers and John Wilkes's *New Briton,* on the other. This name-calling led to a 1786 duel in which Oswald wounded Carey in the thigh.

The *Independent Gazetteer* became an important voice opposing the adoption of a new federal constitution for the United States. Oswald's newspaper published many Anti-Federalist essays, including at least two dozen by "Centinel," Pennsylvania politician Samuel Bryan. These essays were vigorous complaints against dangers in the proposed constitution, pointing out that guarantees were lacking for freedom of speech and press, against the quartering of troops in homes, and for trial by jury in civil matters. The "Centinel" essays, as Wheeler aptly noted, should rank with the Federalist Papers in the literature of that day. Anti-Federalist complaints helped result in the adoption—to deflate opposition to the Constitution—of the Bill of Rights.

Only about fifteen of the roughly 100 newspapers published during the late 1780s expressed preponderantly Anti-Federalist views. Of these, the *Independent Gazetteer,* where Bryan's "Centinel" papers were first published, was the most important. Oswald, meanwhile, had acquired control of another newspaper through family ties. In 1786 he became a partner of his mother-in-law, Mrs. John Holt, in publishing the weekly *New York Journal.* Mrs. Holt quickly sold the *Journal* to Oswald and Andrew Brown, but Brown withdrew from the partnership in August 1786. This made Oswald one of the earliest chain publishers, with control of papers in two of the nation's largest cities.

In 1787 Oswald sold the *New York Journal* to an associate, Thomas Greenleaf. Edward Powars's *American Herald* in Boston ranked along with the *Journal* and the *Gazetteer* as the most important Anti-Federalist journals. All three publishers found that producing an Anti-Federalist newspaper was not good for business. Boycotts of these papers proved damaging. Oswald reopened William Bradford's London Coffee-House to supplement his income, and he also felt compelled to call upon his subscribers—including those who had withdrawn their subscriptions because of the *Gazetteer*'s anti-Constitution stance—to settle their accounts. Not only were there financial difficulties, but the mails were not operating well. In December 1787 "Centinel" was protesting in the *Gazetteer*'s columns that the Federalists were disrupting mail service for papers which opposed the Constitution. In February 1788 Powars complained that Boston publishers were no longer receiving exchange papers from New York. Oswald publicly blamed Fed-

eralist Postmaster General Ebenezer Hazard for the mail stoppages.

Oswald was not content to fight the Constitution—which he feared was a plot to make George Washington a king—only through his newspaper in Philadelphia and his connection with the *New York Journal.* In June 1788 James Madison commented in a letter to Washington that Oswald was in Richmond, Virginia, attempting to stir up opposition to the ratification of the Constitution in that state.

Meanwhile, in Philadelphia, Oswald's former New York partner Andrew Brown had started the *Federal Gazette* with the encouragement and support of the Federalists. A piece under the pseudonym "Obadiah Forceps" appeared in the *Gazetteer,* declaring that Brown was an embezzler and a deserter from the British army. In another issue the *Gazetteer* said that Brown was "one of the greatest *cowards, liars,* and *rascals,* the Lord ever permitted to infest Society."

This name-calling played into the Federalists' hands, for Brown brought suit for civil libel. Never content to leave bad enough alone, Oswald in the 1 July 1788 issue of the *Independent Gazetteer* discussed the pending libel case, charging that Brown was merely a tool of Oswald's old enemies, including Dr. Benjamin Rush, and noting that Dr. Rush's brother was a member of the Pennsylvania Supreme Court.

The upshot was an effort to muzzle Oswald and his newspaper through contempt of court charges. *Respublica v. Oswald* is still recognized as an important precedent in that area of law. An issue in the case was whether contempt of court could be punished without a jury trial. The attack on Oswald came through the Pennsylvania Supreme Court and his old foe Chief Justice McKean. Although Oswald was charged with attempting to subvert the course of justice through malicious publication in the *Gazetteer* of discussions of a pending case, Oswald's Anti-Federalist views—and the continuing publication of "Centinel" essays in his newspaper—doubtless contributed heavily to the bringing of the contempt charge. As Thomas R. Meehan has written, this case ultimately caused the whole issue of freedom of the press to be reviewed and the prerogative of judges to bring contempt of court charges to be examined carefully.

On 14 July 1788 Oswald was ordered to appear before the Supreme Court of Pennsylvania and was charged with contempt of court. Chief Justice McKean's anger at Oswald doubtless was fanned by Oswald's report of a Philadelphia parade celebrating the ratification of the Constitution in Pennsylvania. The *Gazetteer* published an account attributed to "Abigail Callicoe" which said that the chief justice had appeared in the parade not dressed in good Republican black but attired "all in scarlet (Like the whore of Babylon some said)." The court found Oswald guilty of contempt, and McKean fined him £10 and sentenced him to one month in prison. As Oswald was taken off to jail, his supporters gave him three cheers.

From his cell, the dauntless Oswald flailed away at McKean. The *Pennsylvania Packet* published Oswald's accusations that the chief justice's actions were "UNPRECEDENTED, ILLEGAL & UN-CONSTITUTIONAL, & WICKED & ARBI-TRARY . . . tending to pull down FREEDOM OF THE PRESS [as guaranteed by two sections of the Pennsylvania Constitution of 1776]; to abolish the immortal TRIAL BY JURY. . . ."

While Oswald was in prison his wife wrote to Benjamin Franklin, asking him to intervene. Franklin praised her wifely loyalty, but added: "It would be wise that your prudent Counsels might prevail with him to change that Conduct of his Paper by which he has made and provok'd so many Enemies."

When the Pennsylvania General Assembly convened in September 1788, Oswald took his grievances against McKean before it, demanding impeachment of the chief justice and of Justices William Augustus Atlee and Jacob Rush. After three days of hearings, Oswald's request for impeachment was defeated by the conservatives in the assembly, but not before that body had heard severe criticisms of the Supreme Court's proceedings. In 1790, two years after *Respublica v. Oswald* resulted in the printer's jail sentence, Pennsylvania's new constitution provided that juries should decide whether publications were libelous, and also made truth a defense in criminal libel cases. These provisions were so hedged with qualifications, however, that they applied only to public officials; and as the "truth" published had to be "proper for public information," they effectively eliminated truth as a defense in contempt of court cases.

Soon after the impeachment hearings in the General Assembly, Oswald again pushed his luck: he threatened to give the chief justice a thrashing. Again McKean had Oswald arrested, and the printer was brought before Supreme Court Justices Bryan, Atlee, and Rush. Five days later Justice Bryan dismissed Oswald after the printer promised to behave in a manner becoming a good citizen, especially toward Chief Justice McKean.

Oswald's experiences with courts were not always painful. In 1792 he sued the state of New York in the U.S. Supreme Court for $8,000 for public printing done by his late father-in-law. The state did not defend itself, and in 1793 the case was decided in Oswald's favor, establishing the precedent that a judgment would be passed against a state if its representatives failed to appear in court.

Oswald did not learn of the decision for some time. He had gone to England in 1792 to settle affairs connected with the death of one of his wife's relatives; but he still yearned for the soldier's life, and the French Revolution proved irresistible. As Oswald wrote to the French National Convention on 1 September 1793, "the anxiety I felt for the Success of the Revolution, determined me to defer my Return to America and to come to France and offer my Services in any manner in which I could be most usefully employed."

Oswald served as an artillery colonel at the Battle of Jemappes. Early in 1793, after taking part in a battle near Liege, Oswald was in Paris impatiently waiting for action. At that time, the French hoped that Ireland might revolt against England. Oswald, because he was an American, was thought by the French to have a certain amount of potential value as a spy, or perhaps as an agent provocateur. On 20 February 1793 Oswald set off for Ireland, asking only that he receive compensation for his expenses. He arrived in Ireland too late, as the "Volunteers had tamely suffered themselves to be disarmed by the British Soldiery." Oswald returned to France about the end of May 1793.

When he reached Paris, he found that a horse which he had bought for forty guineas had died and that the French War Department was reluctant to compensate him for the loss of the horse or to give him his back pay as a colonel. Oswald's petition to the French National Convention must have met with some success, however, for when he reappeared in America early in 1794, he disgusted pro-British citizens of New York by wearing his French uniform and a tricolored cockade.

In September 1795 Oswald was forty years old. While in New York City, he learned that a friend, Maj. Charles Tillinghast, was ill, and visited him. Oswald was stricken with yellow fever and died in New York on 30 September 1795. His death in a yellow fever epidemic was scarcely a fitting end for the printer Chief Justice McKean called a "seditious turbulent man."

This "turbulent man," however, accomplished much in his self-centered struggle for a free press. In contending for his right to criticize

McKean and the courts of Pennsylvania, Oswald wrote and published some of the earliest theoretical arguments in favor of press freedom and against the common law of seditious libel. As Oswald observed in 1778 in an angry letter to George Washington about what he perceived as his mistreatment in terms of military rank, "He that will not contend for his own rights, as an Individual, will never defend the Rights of the Community."

References:

Robert L. Brunhouse, *The Counter-Revolution in Pennsylvania 1776-1790* (Harrisburg: Pennsylvania Historical Commission, 1942);

Leonard W. Levy, *Legacy of Suppression* (Cambridge: Belknap Press of Harvard University Press, 1960); republished with a new preface as *Freedom of Speech and Press in Early American History: Legacy of Suppression* (New York: Harper Torchbooks, 1963); revised and expanded as *Emergence of a Free Press* (New York: Oxford University Press, 1985);

Jackson Turner Main, *The Antifederalists: Critics of the Constitution* (Chapel Hill: University of North Carolina Press, 1961);

Thomas R. Meehan, "The Pennsylvania Supreme Court in the Law and Politics of the Commonwealth, 1776-1790," Ph.D. dissertation, University of Wisconsin, 1960;

Dwight L. Teeter, "Decent Animadversions: Notes Toward a History of Free Press Theory," in *Newsletters to Newspapers: Eighteenth-Century Journalism*, edited by Donovan H. Bond and W. Reynolds McLeod (Morgantown: School of Journalism, West Virginia University, 1977), pp. 237-245;

Teeter, "The Printer and the Chief Justice: Seditious Libel in 1782-1783," *Journalism Quarterly*, 45 (Summer 1968): 235-242;

Joseph Towne Wheeler, "Eleazer Oswald, Lieutenant-Colonel in the Revolution, Printer in Baltimore and Philadelphia, Soldier of Fortune in the French Revolution," in *The Maryland Press 1777-1790* (Baltimore: Maryland Historical Society, 1938), pp. 19-36.

Thomas Paine

(29 January 1737-8 June 1809)

Henry T. Price
University of South Carolina

See also the Paine entry in DLB 31, *American Colonial Writers, 1735-1781*.

MAJOR POSITION HELD: Editor, *Pennsylvania Magazine* (1775).

SELECTED BOOKS: *The Case of the Officers of Excise; with Remarks on the Qualifications of Officers; and on the Numerous Evils Arising to the Revenue, from the Insufficiency of the Present Salary. Humbly Addressed to the Hon. and Right Hon. the Members of Both Houses of Parliament* (London: Privately printed, 1772; London: Printed for J. S. Jordan, 1793);

Common Sense: Addressed to the Inhabitants of America . . . (Philadelphia: Printed & sold by R. Bell, 1776; revised and enlarged edition, Philadelphia: Printed by William Bradford, 1776; expurgated edition, London: Printed for J. Almon, 1776; unexpurgated edition, Edinburgh: Sold by Charles Eliot/Sterling: Sold by William Anderson, 1776);

The American Crisis, numbers 1-4 (Philadelphia: Printed & sold by Styner & Cist, 1776-1777); number 5 (Lancaster: Printed by John Dunlap, 1778); numbers 6-7 (Philadelphia: Printed by John Dunlap, 1778); numbers 8-9 (Philadelphia: Printed by John Dunlap?, 1780); *The Crisis Extraordinary* (Philadelphia: Sold by William Harris, 1780); *The American Crisis*, numbers 10-12 (Philadelphia: Printed by John Dunlap?, 1782); number 13 (Phila-

Thomas Paine (engraving by William Sharp from 1792 portrait by George Romney)

delphia, 1783); *A Supernumerary Crisis* (Philadelphia, 1783); *A Supernumerary Crisis* [number 2] (New York, 1783); numbers 2-9, 11, and *The Crisis Extraordinary* republished in *The American Crisis, and a Letter to Sir Guy Carleton* . . . (London: Printed & sold by D. I. Eaton, 1796?);

Public Good, Being an Examination into the Claims of Virginia to the Vacant Western Territory and of the Right of the United States to the Same . . . (Philadelphia: Printed by John Dunlap, 1780; London: Printed by W. T. Sherwin, 1817);

Letter Addressed to the Abbé Raynal on the Affairs of North America . . . (Philadelphia: Printed by Melchior Steiner & sold by Robert Aitken, 1782; London: Printed for C. Dilly, 1782);

Dissertations on Government; The Affairs of the Bank; and Paper-Money (Philadelphia: Printed by Charles Cist & sold by Hall & Sellers, Robert Aitken, and William Pritchard, 1786; London: W. T. Sherman, 1817);

Rights of Man: Being an Answer to Mr. Burke's Attack on the French Revolution (London: Printed for J. Johnson, 1791; Baltimore: Printed & sold by David Graham, 1791);

Rights of Man: Part the Second (London: Printed by J. S. Jordan, 1792; New York: Printed by Hugh Gaine, 1792);

Letter Addressed to the Addressers on the Late Proclamation (London: 1792; New York: Printed by Thomas Greenleaf, 1793; Philadelphia: Printed by H. & P. Rice, 1793);

The Age of Reason: Being an Investigation of True and Fabulous Theology (Paris: Printed by Barrois, 1794; London: Sold by D. I. Eaton, 1794; New York: Printed by T. & J. Swords for J. Fellows, 1794);

Dissertation on First Principles of Government (London: Printed & sold by D. I. Eaton, 1795);

The Age of Reason: Part the Second. Being an Investigation of True and of Fabulous Theology (Paris: Printed for the author, 1795; London: Printed for H. D. Symonds, 1795; Philadelphia: Printed by Benjamin Franklin Bache for the author, 1795);

Letter to George Washington, President of the United States of America on Affairs Public and Private (Philadelphia: Printed by Benjamin Franklin Bache, 1796; London: Printed for H. D. Symonds, 1797);

The Decline and Fall of the English System of Finance (Paris: Printed by Hartley, Adlard & son/London: Reprinted for D. I. Eaton, 1796; New York: Printed by Matt & Lyon for J. Fellows, 1796);

Thomas Payne à la législature et au directoire. Ou la justice agraire opposée à la loi agraire, et aux privilèges agraire (Paris: Ragouleau, 1797); republished as *Agrarian Justice, Opposed to Agrarian Law, and to Agrarian Monopoly* . . . (London: Printed for T. Williams, 1797; Philadelphia: Printed by R. Folwell for Benjamin Franklin Bache, 1797);

A Discourse Delivered by Thomas Paine, at the Society of the Theophilanthropists, at Paris, [1797] (London: Printed & sold by T. C. Rickman, 1798);

Compact Maritime, under the Following Heads: I. Dissertation on the Law of Nations. II. On the Jacobinism of the English at Sea. III. Compact Maritime for the Protection of Neutral Commerce, and Securing the Liberty of the Seas. IV. Observations on Some Passages in the Discourse of the Judge of the English Admiralty (Washington, D.C.: Printed by Samuel Harrison Smith, 1801);

Examination of the Passages in the New Testament, Quoted from the Old and Called Prophecies Concerning Jesus Christ. To Which Is Prefixed, An Essay on Dream, Shewing by What Operations of the Mind a Dream Is Produced in Sleep, and Ap-

plying the Same to the Account of Dreams in the New Testament; with an Appendix Containing My Private Thoughts of a Future State, and Remarks on the Contradictory Doctrine in the Books of Matthew and Mark (New York: Printed for the author, 1807).

Collections: *The Writings of Thomas Paine,* edited by Moncure Daniel Conway, 4 volumes (New York: Putnam's, 1894-1896);

The Complete Writings of Thomas Paine, edited by Philip S. Foner, 2 volumes (New York: Citadel Press, 1945).

Thomas Paine, whether he be labeled journalist, propagandist, or editorialist, must be considered one of the great influentials of all time. Not only did he play an enormous role in the American Revolution, but he may have had an even greater impact on the French Revolution. Indeed, his words may have exerted considerable influence in a later crisis of his adopted land. Ever a strong critic of the institution of slavery, he often wrote that it was strange to him that the colonies should fight for freedom from England, yet deny that same precious commodity to the slaves. Abraham Lincoln said he never tired of reading Paine's work, and perhaps the words of the great writer struck home in the heart of the great emancipator.

Thomas Paine was born on 29 January 1737 in the small village of Thetford in Norfolk, England, to Joseph and Frances Cocke Pain (Paine added the *e* to his name later). Little is known of his early life, and certainly there is not much in what is known of those early years to indicate his later success as a revolutionary—nor, indeed, to explain it. The son of a middle-class Quaker father and Anglican mother, Paine as a youngster showed an occasional quirk of rebelliousness but never to the point that he could be identified as antiestablishment. He attended a grammar school in Thetford for about six years, studying a standard curriculum of English, Latin, Greek, mathematics, and classical literature and showed special skill in mathematics and poetry. Fortunately, considering his abbreviated formal education, the school was considered to be one of the best in England at that time. The earliest known written piece by Paine was an epitaph he composed at age eight to mark the death of a pet crow:

> Here lies the body of John Crow,
> Who once was high, but is now low;
> Ye brother Crows, take warning all,
> For as ye rise, so must you fall.

Paine's formal education ceased when his father brought him into the family business, corset making. At age nineteen, he went to sea aboard the privateer *King of Prussia* for about a year, then became a corset maker in London. He moved to Dover after two years and then to Sandwich, Kent, a year after that. He married Mary Lambert at Sandwich on 27 September 1759; she died less than a year later. He entered government service as an excise officer in Lincolnshire in 1761 but was dismissed in 1765 for stamping a shipment he had not actually inspected. He went back to stay-making until he was reinstated in the customs service in 1766. By this time he had provided ample evidence that he shared at least one trait with his colleague of later years, Samuel Adams: he had trouble staying with a job.

During these early years Paine was an omnivorous reader, and he continued to receive informal instruction from various scholars from his early teens to his early twenties. It is interesting to speculate on the course of American history had Paine not had the initiative to educate himself far beyond the grammar school level. Would relative ignorance have silenced his enormously influential and talented pen? Would the American Revolution have sputtered out or indeed have occurred at all without that pen?

During his second stint as an excise officer, during which he married Elizabeth Ollive in Lewes on 26 March 1771, Paine began to show his penchant for supporting the unpopular cause when he sought to organize his fellow excisemen to seek a better wage. He wrote his first important pamphlet, *The Case of the Officers of Excise,* on behalf of the cause and went to London to try to get Parliament to consider their situation in 1772-1773. Parliament declined the invitation, and the government indicated its irritation with his activities by dismissing him once again from the excise service in April 1774. This time his appeal for reinstatement fell on deaf ears. Shortly after, a grocery shop his wife had been operating ran into serious debt problems. It was only with great difficulty that Paine was able to pay off his creditors and avoid debtors' prison.

The penniless Paine and his wife separated, and Paine returned to London, where he met Benjamin Franklin. In October 1774 Paine left England for the colonies, carrying a letter of introduction from Franklin to Franklin's son-in-law in Philadelphia, Richard Bache: "The bearer, Mr. Thomas Paine, is very well recommended to me, an ingenious worthy young man. He goes to Pennsylvania with a view of settling there. I request you to give him your best advice and countenance, as he is quite a stranger there. If you put him in a way of obtaining employment as a clerk, or assistant tutor in a school, or assistant surveyor, (of all of which I think him very capable,) so that he may procure a subsistence at least, till he can make acquaintance and obtain a knowledge of the country, you will do well, and much oblige your affectionate father."

Paine's career as a journalist began shortly after his arrival in the colonies, when Bache introduced him to Robert Aitken, a well-to-do Philadelphia businessman. Aitken was trying to breathe life into a new publication, the monthly *Pennsylvania Magazine*, and hired Paine as a writer. Paine's first efforts found a ready audience in Philadelphia. Most writers of the day had considerable formal education, and their writings were generally stilted and turgid. Paine, on the other hand, wrote with the words of the common people on topics that were of interest to them. In early 1775 Aitken named Paine editor. Under Paine's direction, the magazine's circulation increased rapidly. He turned out a flood of articles on a variety of topics dear to his heart, such as science, humane treatment of animals, the abolition of slavery, woman's rights, a republican form of government, and, eventually, American independence, using a number of pseudonyms, including "Humanus," "Vox Populi," "Aesop," and "Atlanticus."

Journalists have long had the reputation of a fondness for the fruit of the vine, and Paine was no exception. Indeed, many of his enemies in later years often spoke disparagingly of him as a besotted scribbler—a charge for which there appears to be no real substantiation. Aitken, however, noted that Paine often relied on a snifter or two of brandy to help him meet and defeat deadlines, and it is known that he developed an affection for the hearty rum distilled in the colonies.

In the October 1775 issue of his magazine, five months after the Battle of Lexington, he printed an editorial titled "A Serious Thought" under the pseudonym "Humanus":

> When I reflect on the horrid cruelties exercised by Britain in [India]—How thousands perished by artificial famine—how religion and every manly principle of honor and honesty were sacrificed to luxury and pride—When I read of the wretched natives being blown away, for no other crime than because, sickened with the miserable scene, they refused to fight—When I reflect on

> these and a thousand instances of similar barbarity, I firmly believe that the Almighty, in compassion to mankind, will curtail the power of Britain.
>
> And when I reflect on the use she hath made of the discovery of this new world— that the paltry dignity of earthly kings hath been set up in preference to the great cause of the King of kings—that instead of Christian examples to the Indians, she hath basely tampered with their passions, imposed on their ignorance, and made them the tools of treachery and murder—And when to these and many other melancholy reflections I add this sad remark, that ever since the discovery of America she hath employed herself in the most horrid of all traffics, that of human flesh, unknown to the most savage nations, hath yearly (without provocation and in cold blood) ravaged the helpless shores of Africa, robbing it of its unoffending inhabitants to cultivate her stolen dominions in the West— When I reflect on these, I hesitate not for a moment to believe that the Almighty will finally separate America from Britain. Call it Independency or what you will, if it is the cause of God and humanity it will go on.
>
> And when the Almighty shall have blest us, and made us a people *dependent only upon Him*, then may our first gratitude be shown by an act of continental legislation, which shall put a stop to the importation of Negroes for sale, soften the hard fate of those already here, and in time procure their freedom.

Shortly after the publication of this piece, Paine left the *Pennsylvania Magazine* in a dispute with Aitken over pay and the editing of his work. While still editor of the magazine, Paine had composed the first of a number of tracts that would have an enormous impact on the course of the American Revolution. It is generally agreed that *Common Sense*, more than any other writing of the revolutionary period, served to coalesce the splintered views of what America was and what it could become. The pamphlet was released on 10 January 1776 and was such a success that within two months it had sold 120,000 copies. Because Paine, who was relatively unknown outside Philadelphia, published it anonymously, credit for its authorship was variously given to Benjamin Franklin, Samuel Adams, and John Adams.

Common Sense is credited with being the deciding factor in persuading many influentials, Thomas Jefferson among them, to seek independence. Its greatest impact, however, was on that audience for which it had been carefully tailored—the masses. Paine's strength as a writer and editorialist lay not in his ability to create fresh political theory but rather in his talent for presenting to the masses the thoughts of others in a language the common people could understand. Samuel Adams said that there was nothing in *Common Sense* that had not been discussed in the Continental Congress.

Until the appearance of *Common Sense*, however, no attacks had been made against King George III. Previously, the attacks had been directed at various prime ministers, Parliament, and other minions of the Crown. Apparently, this reluctance to speak ill of the king was a simple recognition that many people in the colonies were still loyal to the monarchy even if they balked at the actions taken in the name of that monarchy. In *Common Sense* Paine used the language of the people to tear down, step by step, the arguments supporting the concept of monarchy and the need for subservience by the people to any monarch.

He concluded his discourse on the evils of monarchy in general and the English monarchy in particular by saying: "In England a King hath little more to do than to make war and give away places; which, in plain terms, is to empoverish the nation and set it together by the ears. A pretty business indeed for a man to be allowed eight hundred thousand sterling a year for, and worshipped into the bargain! Of more worth is one honest man to society, and in the sight of God, than all the crowned ruffians that ever lived." Realizing that many in the colonies still regarded England as their parent country, Paine then directed his comments to deflating that notion: "But Britain is the parent country, say some. Then more shame upon her conduct. Even brutes do not devour their young, nor savages make war upon their families."

But surely there was an opportunity for reconciliation with England. Not so, said Paine. "No man was a warmer wisher for a reconciliation than myself, before the fatal nineteenth of April, 1775, but the moment the event of that day was made known, I rejected the hardened, sullen-tempered Pharaoh of England for ever; and disdain the wretch, that with the pretended title of Father of His People can unfeelingly hear of their slaughter, and composedly sleep with their blood upon his soul." But what of freedom? "O! ye that love mankind! Ye that dare oppose not only tyranny but the tyrant, stand forth! Every spot of the old world is overrun with oppression. Freedom hath been hunted round the Globe. Asia and Africa have long expelled her. Europe regards her like a stranger, and England hath given her warning to depart. O! receive the fugitive, and prepare in time an asylum for mankind."

The impact of Paine's piece on the Americans was great. On 7 June 1776 the Revolution's historian, William Gordon, reported to the Continental Congress: "Nothing could have been better timed than this performance [*Common Sense*]. . . . It has satisfied multitudes that it is their true interest immediately to cut the Gordian Knot by which the American colonies have been bound to Great Britain. . . . It has been greatly instrumental in producing a similarity of sentiment through the continent. . . ."

Paine and the Founding Fathers did not share a common motivation for their participation in the American Revolution. The Founding Fathers came for the most part from the upper socioeconomic strata of colonial society; they were doctors, lawyers, clergymen, and businessmen. Indeed, one group of historians sees protection of social and economic position as the prime reason for support of the Revolution by most of the Founding Fathers and holds that if they had been able to maintain the status quo against British pressures through nonrevolutionary means, they would have done so. It is possible that egalitarianism was not an original concern of the creators of the Revolution; even though Jefferson in the late 1760s had called for an end to slavery, he continued to own slaves himself.

One might think that the hefty sales of *Common Sense*, priced at two shillings a copy, would have introduced Paine to the pleasures of the well-to-do, but such was not the case. Instead, he gave the copyright for the piece to each of the states and donated his share of the profits to the war effort. Paine came out of the Revolutionary War as penniless as he went into it.

The opponents of independence recognized the threat posed by *Common Sense*, and in March a series of letters attacking the pamphlet appeared in the *Pennsylvania Gazette*. The letters, signed "Cato," were written by William Smith, provost of the College of Philadelphia. Paine rebutted Smith's arguments in a series of three letters to the *Pennsylvania Packet* under the pseudonym "The Forester."

In early July 1776 Paine enlisted as a private in the Pennsylvania militia. He was made an aide to Gen. Nathanael Greene of Rhode Island. It was during the long, hard winter of 1776 that he wrote the first, and best-remembered, of his *The American*

Crisis papers. If *Common Sense* changed the thinking of many colonials and made the start of the Revolution possible, then the first of the *Crisis* papers made possible its continuation. Writing beside a camp fire, Paine found the words that rekindled the spirit of a demoralized people. When the first *Crisis* paper was published in mid-December 1776, it was perhaps the bleakest period of the American Revolution. Defeat and defeatists came at the revolutionaries from all sides. Washington's ragtag army, drained by enlistment expirations and desertions and numbered at no more than 1,000 effective troops, had staggered from one near-disaster to another for the entire year. Cornwallis nagged at Washington like the hound that senses the desperation of its quarry. Had it not been for this first *Crisis* paper and the victory, two days after its issue, over the Hessians at Trenton on 25 December 1776, there is good reason to believe that the Revolution could have flickered out. Paine's essay, which so moved General Washington that he ordered it read to his troops before the attack on Trenton, has generally been credited with raising the morale of the soldiers and thereby helping to make the American victory possible. With *The Crisis* as with *Common Sense*, Paine knew his audience and wrote for it. Some passages are almost lyrical: "These are the times that try men's souls. The summer soldier and the sunshine patriot will, in this crisis, shrink from the service of his country; but he that stands it NOW, deserves the love and thanks of man and woman. Tyranny, like hell, is not easily conquered; yet we have this consolation with us, that the harder the conflict, the more glorious the triumph. What we obtain too cheap, we esteem too lightly; 'tis dearness only that gives everything its value. Heaven knows how to put a proper price on its goods; and it would be strange indeed, if so celestial an article as FREEDOM should not be highly rated." Others are coarser and more direct: "By perseverance and fortitude we have the prospect of a glorious issue; by cowardice and submission, the sad choice of a variety of evils—a ravaged country—a depopulated city—habitations without safety, and slavery without hope—our homes turned into barracks and bawdy-houses for Hessians, and a future race to provide for, whose fathers we shall doubt of. Look on this picture and weep over it! and if there remains one thoughtless wretch who believes it not, let him suffer it unlamented." The message, however, is crystal clear and impossible to misunderstand.

The war, according to Paine, was an unwanted, defensive one; the foe was evil and must bear all the guilt. He outlined graphically the rewards of victory and the penalties of defeat. His words were designed to pierce all but the hardest of hearts. They did. Sixteen *Crisis* papers appeared during the war—each written at the most necessary and effective time.

Paine reached his fortieth birthday in January 1777, and it was obvious, if not to him then certainly to his friends, that he had no future as a soldier. These friends persuaded him to leave the military and accept a position they created for him as secretary of a commission, working jointly for the Philadelphia Council of Safety and the Continental Congress, to seek a treaty with the Indians in Pennsylvania. In April of 1777 Paine, again as a result of the efforts of his friends, was named the salaried secretary of the Continental Congress's new Committee of Foreign Affairs. It was during his tenure in this post that Paine managed to embroil himself in a situation that ultimately cost him his job and earned him the enmity of many powerful people in the nascent American government. Silas Deane had been sent to France in 1776 to procure arms and ammunition for the American army. The French government, then at peace with England, did not wish to aid the Americans openly; so a dummy company was set up, headed by Caron de Beaumarchais, author of *The Barber of Seville*, to channel the materials to the rebels. Though the weapons were in fact a gift from the French and Spanish governments, the Congress was under the impression that it was purchasing them; and Deane and Beaumarchais profited handsomely on the transaction. When Congress began to get wind of what was happening, it called Deane home in March 1778 to explain his actions. When Deane arrived in Philadelphia in July without any records of his dealings, he found that Arthur Lee, his colleague in Paris, had accused him of dishonesty. Deane attacked Lee in the press. Paine, a friend of Lee, then published his "Letter to Silas Deane" in the *Pennsylvania Packet*, in which he asserted that the arms were, in fact, a gift from the French government. This public revelation caused embarrassment to the French, which in turn embarrassed the Congress. Paine was accused of revealing information to which he had access because of his official capacity. Although the pro-Deane forces lacked the power to force Paine to resign, they were able to slow Congress's deliberations on the affair. Paine, impatient as ever, resigned on 7 January 1779. Later that year he was elected clerk of the Pennsylvania Assembly.

On 4 July 1780 Paine received an honorary

The AMERICAN CRISIS.

NUMBER I.

By the Author of COMMON SENSE.

THESE are the times that try men's souls. The summer soldier and the sunshine patriot will, in this crisis, shrink from the service of his country; but he that stands it NOW, deserves the love and thanks of man and woman. Tyranny, like hell, is not easily conquered; yet we have this consolation with us, that the harder the conflict, the more glorious the triumph...

Page from the Continental Journal *(Boston) containing the first of Paine's "Crisis" papers in 1776*

Iron bridge over the River Wear near Sunderland, England, based on a design by Paine and constructed using materials from a prototype he built. The bridge was completed in 1796. Paine received no financial reward for the bridge, which no longer exists (Courtesy of Christopher Brunel).

master of arts from the University of Pennsylvania. The following year, in spite of his earlier indiscretion, he was part of a successful mission to France to procure more aid from Louis XVI.

The last of Paine's *Crisis* papers was published on 19 April 1783, exactly eight years after the firing of the shots at Lexington and Concord, and on the day that General Washington announced the end of hostilities with Great Britain.

Because he had given the profits of his writings to support the Revolution, Paine found himself in extremely uncomfortable financial circumstances at its end. In a letter to a committee of Congress he wrote: "I cannot help viewing my situation as singularly inconvenient. Trade I do not understand. Land I have none, or what is equal to none. I have exiled myself from one country without making a home of another; and I cannot help sometimes asking myself, what am I better off than a refugee, and that of the most extraordinary kind, a refugee from the country I have obliged and served, to that which can owe me no good will." Pennsylvania answered his plea with a grant of £500, New York gave him 277 acres of confiscated

Tory land near New Rochelle, and Congress finally awarded him $3,000.

Paine devoted most of his time in the late 1780s to the development of several inventions—most notably a design for an iron bridge—that had struck his interest. He took a model of the bridge with him to Paris in April 1787 in an unsuccessful attempt to secure financial backing for the project from the French Academy of Sciences and remained to witness the outbreak of the French Revolution. He then began to increasingly turn his attention to the social and political situations in England and France. The outgrowth of this concern was the appearance in March 1791 of the first part of his *Rights of Man*, a reply to Edmund Burke's reactionary *Reflections on the Revolution in France* (1790). Within months of its appearance in France, *Rights of Man* had sold two million copies. Sales in England, the other target of the treatise, were also large.

Paine left Paris in July 1791 for London, where he wrote part two of *Rights of Man* (1792). Since the second part urged revolution in Great Britain and the establishment of a republic, the British ruling class was furious with Paine. On the

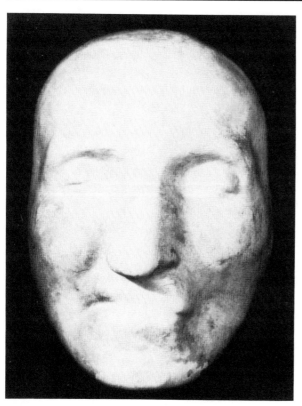

Death mask of Paine by John Wesley Jarvis, an artist with whom Paine shared lodgings for five months in 1807 (New York Historical Society, New York City)

advice of friends, Paine left England in September 1792 one step ahead of a warrant for his arrest and returned to France, where the Legislative Assembly had granted him French citizenship and the departments of Pas-de-Calais, Oise, and Puy-de-Dome had each elected him its representative to the National Convention. He was appointed vice-chairman of a special committee that was to create a new French constitution.

Paine continued to write, this time for a French audience, and devoted much of his work to an effort to save the life of the deposed king, Louis XVI. While this was going on, he was tried in absentia in England on charges of high treason, found guilty, and declared an outlaw who was to be immediately arrested should he ever again set foot on British soil. Unshaken by this turn of events, Paine continued to fight valiantly to save the doomed Louis XVI, thereby earning the implacable enmity of the radical Jacobins.

As the French Revolution, now controlled by Maximilian de Robespierre, moved inexorably toward its bloody conclusion, Paine finally came to face reality. The radicals were in power and the

Terror had begun. On 26 December 1793 Paine was once again tried in absentia, this time by the Committee of Public Safety. He was found guilty of treason and was arrested the next day and spent the next eleven months in the Luxembourg Prison. While he was confined, the first part of *The Age of Reason* was published; Paine worked on the second part in prison, and it was published in 1795. This work, in which Paine subjects many of the supernatural aspects of Christianity—including the Resurrection—to rationalistic criticism and points out contradictions in the Bible, earned him enormous hostility in England and America. Paine's position is a deistic one: he believes that a supreme being exists and created the universe after which he left it alone to operate according to inexorable natural laws. Some of the Founding Fathers, such as Franklin and Jefferson, held similar views; but they did not publish them to the world as Paine did.

It might be expected that the United States would have acted immediately to secure Paine's release, but such was not the case. The reasons for the delay remain a mystery to this day, although there is conjecture that the American minister to France, Gouverneur Morris, was reluctant to call undue attention to Paine's case lest the Committee of Public Safety decide to rid itself of a problem by adding Paine to the tens of thousands who were being sent to the guillotine. On 2 August 1794 James Monroe replaced Morris as foreign minister, and, through careful and delicate diplomacy, succeeded in gaining Paine's release on 4 November. By this time, the Terror was waning, and on 7 December 1794 the National Convention by acclamation restored Paine to his seat in that body.

Paine devoted the next several years to writing; unfortunately, he also used those years to mount a bitter attack on his old friend George Washington, who Paine felt had deserted him during his imprisonment. He finally voiced his anger in the *Letter to George Washington*, which was widely published in 1796 in the United States. In this extraordinarily virulent pamphlet, Paine lashed out at not only Washington, but also at Gouverneur Morris, John Jay, and John Adams. Such invectives as *unprincipled, selfish, treacherous,* and *hypocrite,* however, were reserved for Washington. The pamphlet shocked and dismayed hundreds of thousands of Americans and turned them against Paine. His reputation and popularity in the United States never recovered. In 1802 he returned to America.

Paine's pen was never still, and even in the last year of his life he brought discomfiture to those in high places. He died on 8 June 1809 in New

York City at the age of seventy-two. A friend of his later years, Marguerite de Bonneville, described his burial on his farm at New Rochelle: "Contemplating who it was, what man it was, that we are committing to an obscure grave on an open and disregarded bit of land, I could not help feeling most acutely. Before the earth was thrown down upon the coffin, I, placing myself at the east end of the grave, said to my son Benjamin, 'Stand you there, at the other end, as a witness for grateful America.' Looking around me, and beholding the small group of spectators, I exclaimed as the earth was tumbled into the grave, 'Oh! Mr. Paine! My son stands here as testimony of the gratitude of America, and I, for France!' "

In a bizarre epilogue, Paine's bones were disinterred in 1819 by William Cobbett, a former Tory editor who had vilified Paine in the 1790s. Having changed his own political viewpoint and come to an admiration of Paine, Cobbett decided that Paine's remains should be buried with honor in his native land; and he carried the bones back with him to England. The project of reburying Paine with a suitable monument never materialized, and after Cobbett's death the bones were lost.

Biographies:

Moncure D. Conway, *The Life of Thomas Paine* (New York & London: Putnam's, 1892);

Frank Smith, *Thomas Paine: Liberator* (New York: Stokes, 1938);

Alfred Owen Aldridge, *Man of Reason: The Life of Thomas Paine* (New York: Lippincott, 1959);

Audrey Williamson, *Thomas Paine: His Life, Work and Times* (London: Allen & Unwin, 1973);

David Freeman Hawke, *Paine* (New York: Harper & Row, 1974);

Eric Foner, *Tom Paine and Revolutionary America* (London: Oxford University Press, 1976).

References:

Philip Davidson, *Propaganda and the American Revolution 1763-1783* (Chapel Hill: University of North Carolina Press, 1941);

Samuel Edwards, *Rebel!* (New York: Praeger, 1974);

Moses C. Tyler, *The Literary History of the American Revolution*, 2 volumes (New York & London: Putnam's, 1897);

Jerome D. Wilson and William F. Ricketson, *Thomas Paine* (Boston: Twayne, 1978).

James Parker
(circa 1714-2 July 1770)

Nancy L. Roberts
University of Minnesota

MAJOR POSITIONS HELD: Publisher, *New-York Weekly Post-Boy*, renamed *New-York Gazette, Revived in the Weekly Post-Boy* in 1744; renamed *New-York Gazette; or, The Weekly Post-Boy* in 1753 (1743-1762), *Connecticut Gazette* (New Haven) (1755-1764), *Constitutional Courant* (Woodbridge, N.J.) (1765).

BOOK: *James Parker's Report of the Business of the Firm of B. Franklin & David Hall* (New York, 1766).

OTHER: *Conductor Generalis; or, The Office, Duty and Authority of Justices of the Peace, High-Sheriffs, Under-Sheriffs, Gaolers, Coroners, Constables,* *Jury-Men, and Overseers of the Poor. As also, the Office of Clerks of Assize, and of the Peace, &c. Collected out of All the books Hitherto Written on Those Subjects, whether of Common or Statute-Law. The Whole Alphabetically Digested Under the Several Titles; with a Table Directed to the Ready Finding out the Proper Matter under Those Titles. To Which Is Added, A Collection out of Sir Mathew Hales, Concerning the Descent of Lands; With Several Choice Maxims in Law, and the Office of Mayors, &c. The 2d Ed., with Large Additions,* edited by Parker (New York: Printed & sold by J. Parker, 1749).

Printer, postmaster, and journalist, James Parker established printing houses in three colonies and founded several newspapers, including the first in Connecticut, the *Connecticut Gazette,* and the first in New Jersey, the *Constitutional Courant.* In his day he was considered the equal of any printer in English North America, surpassing both William Bradford and Benjamin Franklin. Parker's far-flung printing business grew to be the most extensive of its kind, and his work was characterized by an unusual neatness and accuracy.

Parker was born about 1714 at Woodbridge, New Jersey, to Samuel Parker, a cooper, and Janet Ford Parker.

When Parker was eleven his father died. On 1 January 1727 he was apprenticed for a term of eight years to the printer William Bradford of New York. Apparently young Parker found his service difficult, because on 21 May 1733 his master offered a reward for the runaway apprentice in his *New-York Gazette,* advertising Parker as "of a fresh Complection, with short yellowish Hair." Parker eventually went to Philadelphia, where, like many promising youths, he found work at the printing establishment of Benjamin Franklin. On 26 February 1742, Franklin formed a six-year partnership with Parker "for the Carrying on the Business of Printing in the City of New-York," with Franklin supplying the press, type, and other equipment. Franklin became Parker's lifelong mentor; the pair's close friendship and trust are seen in their many letters to each other.

Meanwhile, the astute Parker no doubt noticed that Bradford's *New-York Gazette,* established in 1725 when the printer was over sixty years old, had deteriorated in appearance and content; New York clearly needed a better, more up-to-date paper. On 4 January 1743 the enterprising twenty-eight-year-old Parker founded a new paper, the third in New York, which he christened the *New-York Weekly Post-Boy.* Parker became public printer of New York, succeeding Bradford in the position on 1 December 1743. When the *Gazette* expired on 19 November 1744, Parker renamed his paper the *New-York Gazette, Revived in the Weekly Post-Boy.* It was a modest quarto at first, a larger one in 1744; in 1753 it became a small folio and in 1756 it attained the usual size of the day's newspapers. According to Frank Luther Mott in *American Journalism* (1962), Parker's paper was foremost in New York for some years, showing "a measure of independence and boldness in criticism." Certainly some of its popularity and success must be attrib-

uted to Parker's high-minded principles. The printer-journalist showed his fairness in the issue of 29 February 1748, when, after he had unwittingly published two forged letters which attacked some respectable Quakers, he wrote: "Poor Printers are often under a very unhappy dilemma, of either displeasing one Part of their Benefactors, or giving Offence to others; and sometimes get the Ill-will of both sides; It has indeed been much against my Will to print any Thing, that savour'd of Forgery, Invective, or Partyism. . . . The Press is looked on as the grand Bulwark of *Liberty Light, Truth* and Religion; and if at any Time the Innocent is attack'd unjustly, the Gospel pronounces such *Blessed;* and common Sense tells us *their Innocence will shine the more conspicuously thereby:* But on the other Hand, it often is noted that Persons are too apt to be touch'd at having any of their Faults exposed. However, if I have openly injur'd any, I am willing as openly to vindicate them, or to give them all the Satisfaction that Reason requires without being sway'd with either their high Words or low Promises. . . ."

In the autumn of 1746 Parker had become librarian of the Corporation of the City of New York. He established a system of circulation and fines, and printed a catalogue of the holdings of the library.

In 1749 Parker compiled and printed an enlarged edition of the *Conductor Generalis,* which had originally been published by Andrew Bradford in Philadelphia in 1722. This work, which summarized the duties and powers of justices of the peace, sheriffs, coroners, and other public officials, was popular among officials for many years.

Ever ambitious, in 1751 Parker established a printing office in his native Woodbridge; in January 1753 he formed a partnership with William Weyman, who managed Parker's New York office. About the same time, Parker changed the name of his paper to the *New-York Gazette; or, The Weekly Post-Boy.* From about 1753 on, Parker was greatly involved in his New Jersey plant, the first permanent one in that colony.

Parker also ventured into magazine journalism. He printed four periodicals in New York: the *Independent Reflector* (20 November 1752-22 November 1753), a weekly folio with moral and political essays edited by William Livingston; the *Occasional Reverberator* (7 September-5 October 1753), a similar experiment; the *Instructor* (6 March-8 May 1755), a quarto; and *John Englishman* (9 April-5 July 1755), another political folio.

Not only did Parker's name stand for printing

Front page of Parker's New York newspaper

and journalism in New York and New Jersey; he also extended his energies to Connecticut, where he was printer to Yale College. His first work was the printing of the laws of the college, in Latin, probably in December 1754. His old friend Franklin appointed Parker New Haven's postmaster in 1754. On 12 April 1755 Parker founded the *Connecticut Gazette*, the colony's first newspaper, in New Haven, with John Holt as manager and silent partner. Apparently Franklin had shipped the printing plant to New Haven in the fall of 1754, intending to establish either of his nephews, James Franklin or Benjamin Mecom, there; when each declined, Parker bought Franklin's equipment and assumed the task.

The first number of the *Connecticut Gazette* bore the imprint "Printed by James Parker, at the Post-Office, near the Sign of the White-Horse." The four-page weekly had two columns on each page; at first it measured about six and one-half by nine and one-half inches, later increasing to fourteen by nine and one-half inches, and it sold for "Two shillings sixpence lawful money per Quarter," postpaid. The front page of the first issue was a prospectus promising the latest news, edifying articles, and advertising space at fair rates. The first issue did not contain a great deal of news—an item from London describing the cruel murder of a woman, and another short London note that told of the equipping of several warships for the nascent French war. But the *Gazette* contained much shipping news and advertisements by merchants dealing in European and West Indies goods.

In 1756 the New York Assembly ordered Parker arrested for publishing in his *Weekly Post-Boy* some "Observations on the Circumstances and Conduct of the People in the Counties of Ulster and Orange." When Parker revealed the author's name, apologized, and paid fees, he was released. Also in 1756 Parker became comptroller and secretary of the general post offices of the British colonies.

Parker's first official printing at Woodbridge was the *Votes and Proceedings of the General Assembly of the Province of New Jersey*, probably for the session of 22 to 27 July 1756. On 26 September 1758 the New Jersey assembly made Parker public printer. Besides the usual public documents, he also printed sermons, orations, and discourses.

Parker and Weyman dissolved their New York partnership in January 1759. The following month, Parker installed his nephew, Samuel Parker, at the New York printery; the younger Parker

was in charge until Holt relieved him in the summer of 1760.

Perhaps Parker's most prominent undertaking in magazine publishing was the *New American Magazine*, printed at Woodbridge as a successor to Bradford's ill-fated *American Magazine*. Edited by Samuel Nevill under the pseudonym "Sylvanus Americanus," the octavo ran through twenty-seven numbers from January 1758 through March 1760. Like other early American magazines, it was a financial failure.

Besides public documents, newspapers, and magazines, Parker also printed works of poetry, fiction, science, history, religion, husbandry, and almanacs. In his *History of Printing in America*, Isaiah Thomas pronounced Parker "well acquainted with printing, a neat workman" who "possessed a sound judgment, and a good heart; was industrious in business, and upright in his dealings." Parker's apprentices and journeymen established impressive records in many colonies. Among them were William Goddard, first to establish a printing press in Providence, and soon after made a deputy postmaster there; and Hugh Gaine, printer of the *New York Mercury*, who worked as a journeyman in Parker's New York printery.

In his later years, Parker was deeply involved in his New Jersey affairs, enjoying the country life at Woodbridge, where he was "Captain of a Troop of Horse" and a lay reader in the Episcopalian Trinity Church. He and Holt terminated their partnership in 1762, and Holt became sole publisher of the *Weekly Post-Boy*. On 2 June 1764, Parker became judge of the Court of Common Pleas of Middlesex County, New Jersey; that year he printed a new edition of the *Conductor Generalis*.

Like many of his fellow printer-journalists, Parker detested "the fatal Black-Act" which in the spring of 1765 caused him to abandon his hopes of starting another newspaper in Burlington, New Jersey. To Franklin he wrote on 25 April 1765 that "the News of the Killing Stamp, has struck a deadly Blow to all my Hopes on that Head . . . the Cruel Stamp-Duty has filled me with fresh apprehensions, that I conceive, I shall soon drop all the Business entire." Later that year he was able to set up an independent printery in Burlington, but no newspaper ensued.

In his final years Parker suffered greatly from gout. "My Gout has held me the longest, this Time that ever I had it:—I mend now but very slow," he confided in a letter to Franklin from Burlington on 4 January 1766. As ill health curtailed his activities through the mid- and late-1760s, Parker perceived the gathering political storm: "A black Cloud seems to hang over us; but whether it will blow past, or the Thunder break in upon us all, is what he alone, who guides it, can tell," he wrote to Franklin from Woodbridge on 10 October 1765. Parker added this warning: "Poor America, is like to bleed, if the Storm blows not over:—Nay, it appears to me, that there will be an End to all government here, if it does not . . . dreadful Work is like to ensue."

Parker's Woodbridge press issued New Jersey's first newspaper on 21 September 1765. Entitled the *Constitutional Courant*, it was a protest against the Stamp Act, bearing the imprint of a fictitious publisher: "Printed by Andrew Marvel, at the Sign of the Bribe refused, on Constitution-Hill, North America." In the center of the title was the familiar Patriot illustration of a snake, cut into parts to represent the colonies, with the caption "Join or Die." According to Thomas in his *History of Printing in America*, this single-issue newspaper "contained several well-written and spirited essays against the obnoxious stamp act, which were so highly colored, that the editors of newspapers in New York, even Holt, declined to publish them. . . ." The paper sold quickly and was reprinted in New York and Boston.

"As to what relates to the *Stamp-Act,* you will doubtless hear from many Quarters, of the commotions about it," Parker wrote from Burlington to Franklin on 22 September 1765, the day after the *Constitutional Courant* appeared. "I have Reason for this once to be thankful," Parker added, "I am not a Master-Printer at New-York, or perhaps the Impetuosity of my Temper would have plunged me deep one Way or the other." However, the paper "excited some commotion in New York," according to Thomas, and government took notice; but since no one could identify the printer, no action was taken.

The *Connecticut Gazette* also began to print more and more articles on the troubles between Great Britain and the colonies. By 1764, when Parker suspended it, it had become an outspoken champion of the Patriot cause, and had begun to publicize the activities of the Sons of Liberty. The *Connecticut Gazette* was revived from 1765 to 1768 by Benjamin Mecom.

Throughout the troubled times, Parker continued to hold public office. He retained his job as comptroller and secretary of the colonial post offices, and in 1765, when the territory was divided, he managed the northern district from Woodbridge. In May 1776 Franklin secured for Parker an appointment as land waiter in the royal customs service in New York. In the fall, Parker reacquired the New York shop from Holt and resumed the old title of *New-York Gazette; or, the Weekly Post-Boy.* Holt changed the name of his paper to the *New-York Journal, or General Advertiser.*

In December 1769 Parker's printing house issued a paper addressed "To the Betrayed Inhabitants of New York," signed only by "A Son of Liberty" (Alexander McDougall). The General Assembly resolved that the paper was "a false, seditious, and infamous libel," and Parker was charged, but he died while the case was still pending.

Parker did not live to witness the culmination of the struggle that he, as a Patriot printer-journalist, had hastened. Less than five months before his death, he wrote to Franklin on 20 February 1770 that he was "so emaciated and torn by the Gout, that all the Springs of Nature fail:—I think I am drawing nigh to the Grave with a good deal of Rapidity: God only knows how soon my Course will be finished: I am desirous to resign my Will to his."

Three months later, on 10 May, in what was probably his final letter to his lifelong mentor, Parker acknowledged that " 'tis not likely I can hold long, . . .—a few Days more it will be all over with me. . . ."

Parker died while visiting a friend in Burlington on 2 July 1770 and was buried with much pomp beside his parents in the Presbyterian churchyard at Woodbridge. He was survived by his wife, Mary Ballareau Parker; a son, Samuel; and a daughter, Jane. He left one press at Burlington, one at New Haven, one at Woodbridge, and two at New York, all of which he bequeathed to his son. In an obituary in the *New York Journal* on 5 July 1770, Holt wrote that Parker "was eminent in his Profession," "possessed a sound Judgment, & extensive Knowledge," "was industrious in Business, upright in his Dealings, charitable to the Distressed," and "left a fair Character." Like his good friend Benjamin Franklin, James Parker was one of the first Americans to break a path of respectability and promise for the profession of journalism.

References:

William H. Benedict, "James Parker, the Printer, of Woodbridge," *Proceedings of the New Jersey Historical Society,* new series, 8 (July 1923): 194-199;

Charles Hopkins Clark, "Newspapers and Periodicals," in *History of Connecticut: In Monographic*

Form, volume 2 (New York: United States History Co., 1925), pp. 89-90;

George L. Clark, *A History of Connecticut: Its People and Institutions,* second edition (New York: Putnam's, 1914), pp. 311-312;

Wilberforce Eames, "The Antigua Press and Benjamin Mecom, 1748-1765," *Proceedings of the American Antiquarian Society,* new series, 38 (17 October 1928): 303-348;

Worthington C. Ford, ed., "Letters from James Parker to Benjamin Franklin," *Proceedings of the Massachusetts Historical Society,* second series, 16 (May 1902): 186-232;

Larry R. Gerlach, *Prologue to Independence: New Jersey in the Coming of the American Revolution* (New Brunswick, N.J.: Rutgers University Press, 1976);

Charles R. Hildeburn, *Sketches of Printers and Printing in Colonial New York* (New York: Dodd, Mead, 1895), pp. 34-54;

Charles H. Levermore, *The Republic of New Haven: A History of Municipal Evolution* (Port Washington, N.Y.: Kennikat Press, 1966), pp. 197-198;

Beverly McAnear, "James Parker Versus John Holt," *Proceedings of the New Jersey Historical Society,* 59 (April 1941): 77-95;

McAnear, "James Parker Versus William Weyman," *Proceedings of the New Jersey Historical Society,* 59 (1941): 1-23;

Douglas C. McMurtrie, *A History of Printing in the United States,* 2 volumes (New York: Bowker, 1936);

Jarvis Means Morse, *Connecticut Newspapers in the Eighteenth Century* (New Haven: Yale University Press, 1935);

Frank Luther Mott, *American Journalism,* third edition (New York: Macmillan, 1962), pp. 31, 39, 42n, 82n;

William Nelson, "Some New Jersey Printers and Printing in the Eighteenth Century," *Proceedings of the American Antiquarian Society,* new series, 21 (12 April 1911): 15-56;

Rollin G. Osterweis, *Three Centuries of New Haven, 1638-1938* (New Haven: Yale University Press, 1953), pp. 102-103;

Victor Hugo Paltsits, "John Holt—Printer and Postmaster: Some Facts and Documents Relating to His Career," *Bulletin of the New York Public Library,* 24 (September 1920): 483-499;

Isaiah Thomas, *The History of Printing in America (with a Biography of Printers & An Account of Newspapers),* edited by Marcus A. McCorison from the second edition (New York: Weathervane Books, 1970).

Papers:

The correspondence of James Parker and Benjamin Franklin is held by the American Philosophical Society, Philadelphia.

William Parks

(circa 1698-1 April 1750)

Roger Yarrington
University of Maryland

MAJOR POSITIONS HELD: Publisher, *Maryland Gazette* (1727-1731), *Maryland Gazette Reviv'd* (1732-1734), *Virginia Gazette* (1736-1750).

William Parks printed the first newspapers in Maryland and Virginia and was a major contributor to the early literary histories of both colonies. Lawrence Wroth, a historian of colonial printing, called him the "nurse of literature and father of journalism in Maryland and Virginia." Parks was the central figure in an early case in which truth was used as a defense against a libel charge.

He was born about 1698 in Ludlow, Shropshire, England. Isaiah Thomas said that Parks was "born and bred to printing," but it is unclear precisely what he meant or where he got the idea. He implies that Parks's father may have been a printer; however, this is at odds with Wroth, who said that Parks's own printing business, established in 1719, was the first in Ludlow.

Parks began a newspaper, the *Ludlow Post-Man, or the Weekly Journal,* in 1719; the same year he printed several books. After about two years he moved his press to Hereford. In 1723, in Reading, he began another paper, the *Reading Mercury, or Weekly Entertainer.* Thus he was the first printer in three English towns, and the publisher of the first newspapers in two of them, before he came to America.

In 1726 Parks was invited to be the public printer for Maryland by Thomas Bordley, a member of the assembly in Annapolis. The colony had been without a printer for four years. Earlier printers had included William Nuthead, who came in 1684 to St. Mary's City, Maryland, from Virginia because printing was still prohibited there; his wife Dinah, who succeeded him and thereby became the first woman printer in the colonies, and who moved the press to Annapolis; Thomas Reading; and John Peter Zenger, who started printing in Maryland in 1720 and after two years went on to New York and journalistic fame. Bordley had been responsible for having assembly debates published by Andrew

Bradford in Philadelphia in 1724. He found it difficult to accomplish the task with a printer so distant, so he took it on himself to recruit a printer, using as his authority the legislature's 1722 and 1723 resolutions to encourage the establishment of a printing press in Maryland.

Parks's proposals to the legislature to print its laws having been accepted, he was named public printer in 1726. The following year he published *A Compleat Collection of the Laws of Maryland* and began the *Maryland Gazette,* the first newspaper published south of Philadelphia and the seventh in the colonies. Wroth said that Parks, like other colonial newspaper editors, "became almost immediately an important member of the provincial society."

Parks published a typical colonial paper with relatively little local news—the assumption being, no doubt, that everyone in the little provincial capital knew all of the local news very soon. But there was great interest in news from other colonies and in foreign news. In the issue of 9 June 1730, after returning from a trip to England, Parks wrote in the *Gazette*: "I made it my particular Concern, whilst I was in England, to settle such a correspondence there; by which, upon all Occasions, I shall be furnished with the freshest intelligence, both from thence, and other Parts of Europe."

He managed to serve successfully as public printer during a period when the assembly was struggling over basic issues with the proprietor of the colony and each side was attempting to use the press. He did so primarily by conducting himself as the employee of the lower house of the assembly. For example, at the beginning of his work the lower house wanted Parks's title to be "public printer to the province"; the upper house wanted it to be "printer to his Lordship"—a reference to the proprietor of the colony. The upper house had to give in to the lower house on the question but the tactful Parks, when he printed the *Proceedings of the Assembly* in 1727, used the phrase, "Printed by William Parks, Printer to the Right Honourable the Lord Proprietor, and the Province." When he printed

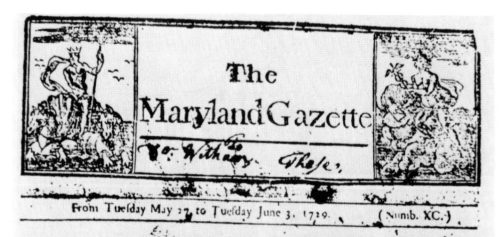

From Tuesday May 27 to Tuesday June 3, 1729.   (Numb. XC.)

Front page of Parks's Maryland Gazette, *the first newspaper published south of Philadelphia*

the *Compleat Collection of the Laws of Maryland* the same year, however, he made it clear for whom he worked. He said that the publication was "Collected and Printed by Order of the General Assembly."

He was not only a successful printer and politician but a promoter of literary development in the colony. He encouraged Maryland essayists, poets, and satirists by publishing their works regularly in the *Gazette*. He printed poetry, almanacs, and books on politics, economics, and religion. For example, in 1728 he printed *Muscipula*, a translation by a local teacher, Richard Lewis, of a satire on the Welsh by Edward Holdsworth.

In 1727 Parks had proposed to the Virginia burgesses that he print their collected laws. His proposal was accepted and in 1730 he moved to Williamsburg. His printing shop in Annapolis was maintained for another five years by his partner, Edmund Hall, and a Mr. Webb, but Williamsburg had become his home and primary business interest. His 1730 trip to England was probably to buy equipment and supplies for his Virginia printing shop.

In 1730 Parks published *Sotweed Redivivus: or the Planters Looking-Glass* for the author, "C. E., Gent." (probably Ebenezer Cooke), and *Typographica. An Ode on Printing* by John Markland, an attorney from New Kent. The latter was the first publication about printing in America; it was inscribed to William Gooch, lieutenant governor of Virginia, and praised him for encouraging printing in Virginia. Parks printed the book in Williamsburg. His 1731 publications included *The Maryland Muse* (in which appeared "The Sotweed Factor, or Voiage to Maryland," a satire on life in the colony, by Ebenezer Cooke, originally published in London in 1708); *The Virginia Miscellany*, with "new poems, essays, and translations on various subjects by several gentlemen of this country"; and *Laws of Maryland*, containing statutes enacted that year. A 15 July 1731 advertisement for *The Virginia Miscellany* in the *American Weekly Mercury* in Philadelphia said that subscriptions were being taken at Parks's house near the capitol in Williamsburg.

The *Maryland Gazette* suspended publication in 1731. In December 1732 it resumed as the *Maryland Gazette Reviv'd*, "Printed by William Parks and Edmund Hall." Publication of the Maryland paper ceased late in 1734.

The *Virginia Gazette* was initiated by Parks in 1736. It was the first newspaper in the colony. Publishing historian John Tebbel said that this was one of the best colonial papers. It reflected Parks's wide interests and great printing skills. Like Parks's

Maryland Gazette, this paper quickly became an important instrument for the dissemination of news, ideas, and the literature produced by residents of the colony.

Among Parks's many firsts was his early statement on the benefits of advertising—possibly the first such promotion published in America. In the 8 October 1736 *Virginia Gazette* he published his "Advertisement, concerning Advertisements":

> All persons who have Occasion to buy or sell Houses, Lands, Goods, or Cattle; or have Servants or Slaves Runaway; or have lost Horses, Cattle, &c. or want to give any Publick Notice; may have it advertis'd in all of these Gazettes printed in one Week, for Three Shilings, and for Two Shillings per Week for as many Weeks afterwards as they shall order, by giving or sending their Directions to the Printer hereof.
>
> And, as these Papers will circulate (as speedily as possible) not only all over This, but also the Neighboring Colonies, and will probably be read by some Thousands of People, it is very likely they may have the desir'd Effect; and it is certainly the cheapest and most effectual Method that can be taken, for Publishing any Thing of this Nature.

A Collection of All the Acts of Assembly, Now in Force in the Colony of Virginia was printed by Parks in 1737. It is considered by historians to be one of the exceptional examples of quality printing in the colonial period.

In 1737 the Maryland Assembly complained that Parks had not yet printed its 1736 acts. He printed the acts of the 1736 and 1737 sessions and then moved his entire printing establishment to Williamsburg, leaving Maryland without a printer.

On 23 September 1742 Parks advertised in Benjamin Franklin's *Pennsylvania Gazette* for a paper maker. John Conrad Sheets went from Pennsylvania to Williamsburg to help Parks set up the first paper mill south of Pennsylvania. Franklin financed the project. The mill began production in 1744 and Parks paid off Franklin with paper from the mill. Parks's two watermarks, a WP with a crown on top and a stylized Virginia coat of arms, have been found on papers in publications printed in other colonies, indicating that he produced paper in sufficient quantities to supply a number of shops in other colonies.

Parks's wide-ranging interests and industry resulted in a steady flow from his press. He printed the laws and acts of the burgesses, almanacs, man-

Front page of Parks's Virginia Gazette, *the first newspaper published in Virginia and one of the best colonial newspapers*

uals for soldiers, religious lessons, histories, and the first cookbook printed in America—*The Compleat Housewife,* first published in 1742.

The product of Parks's Williamsburg press most frequently cited as a masterwork of printing and as a valuable reference is *The History of the First Discovery and Settlement of Virginia,* by the Rev. William Stith, rector of Henrico Parish. His 340-page work was printed by Parks in 1747. Parks was taking subscriptions for it in announcements in the *Virginia Gazette* as early as 21 March 1745. Wroth calls it "the most elaborate production of its kind in the first half of the century."

Parks also was a bookbinder and, like most of his counterparts, a bookseller. His bindings improved over the years until they became superior to any produced in the colonies at the time. As John C. Oswald pointed out, Parks "operated on a considerable scale" and "deserves to rank high in any list of early American printers." Isaiah Thomas, a printer who prized quality workmanship and examined the products of virtually every early American press, gave Parks the printer's compliment: Thomas said Parks's work was "both neat and correct."

Wroth noted that Parks acquired a love of "polite letters" and gave a literary quality to his papers. He also pointed out that Parks was not only a great printer but an important citizen and as such was able to learn local news and news from other places as it became available in Williamsburg. He was a warden of Bruton Parish Church and an alderman of the town.

Thomas, in his 1810 history of printing, refers to newspaper accounts "printed more than forty years ago" of an incident when Parks was prosecuted for libel by a member of the Virginia House of Burgesses. According to Thomas, Parks got off by proving the truth of his publication. If this story is accurate, it provides an additional early instance, besides the 1735 Zenger trial, when truth was used successfully as a defense in a libel case. Although Thomas does not date the incident, it would have to have occurred between 1736, when Parks began the *Virginia Gazette,* and 1750, when he died. Thomas quotes an account from "the journals of that time":

> Some few years ago, a man was convicted of stealing sheep, at Willimsburg, in Virginia, for which crime he was prosecuted; and, on answering the demands of public justice, retired into what was called the back woods of that dominion, in order to avoid

the reproaches of his neighbors. Several years passed away; during which time he acquired considerable property, and that part of the country where he took up his residence being made a new county he was by his neighbors chosen to represent them in the house of burgesses, which then met at Williamsburg. A mischievous *libeller,* who remembered the crime formerly committed by the burgess, published an account of it in the *Gazette,* and although he did not mention the name, he clearly pointed out the transgressor, who, it seems, had defended some measures in the government that were considered as arbitrary, and who was highly offended with the freedom of the printer. The house was also displeased that one of their honorable body should be accused in a public paper of being guilty of such a base transaction.

> Parks was prosecuted for printing and publishing a *libel* against Mr. * * * * *, an honorable and worthy burgess; and many members of the honorable house would no doubt have been highly gratified, if, on that occasion, they could have introduced the Star chamber doctrine of libels, and punished Parks for daring to publish an article which, as they observed, scandalized the government by reflecting on those who are intrusted with the administration of public affairs. But Parks begged that the records of the court might be produced, which would prove the truth of the libel. This was allowed, and the records were examined, though contrary to the doctrine of some men, who would impose on the community as law, that a libel is not less a libel for being true, and that its being true is an aggravation of the offence; and, such men observe, no one must speak ill of rulers, or those who are intrusted with power or authority, be they ever so base and oppressive, and daily abuse that power. Now, mark the sequel: the prosecutor stood recorded for sheep stealing; a circumstance which he supposed time had fully obliterated, both from the records of the court, and from the minds of the people; and he withdrew, overwhelmed with disgrace, from public life, and never more ventured to obtrude himself into a conspicuous situation, or to trouble printers with prosecutions for libels. Thus, it is obvious that a free press is, of all things, the best check and restraint on wicked men and arbitrary magistrates.

The quote is not attributed to a specific paper, nor is it dated. The account may be embellished in some of its drama and moralizing, but it does indicate that Parks, who undoubtedly got along well with most authorities and was himself a citizen of some standing, did help establish the idea in America that truth should be seen not as an aggravation of libel but as a defense against it.

In 1750 Parks fell ill and died on another voyage to England. He was buried in Gosport, England. The *Virginia Gazette* was continued for a few months more and then publication ceased.

His estate was valued at £6,000 and his debts were only a little less than that. William Hunter, his journeyman printer, purchased his press and equipment from the estate for £359, a sum that indicates, along with the list of Parks's publications, that his shop was, as Wroth wrote, "one of the larger and more adequately equipped" of the period.

Wroth's careful evaluation of Parks was: "There was no printer of his day . . . Franklin excepted, whose service to typography and letters in America presents a greater claim on the interest and gratitude of posterity."

References:

Rutherfoord Goodwin, "The Williamsburg Paper Mill of William Parks, the Printer," *Papers of the Bibliographical Society of America*, 31 (1937): 1-33;

John C. Oswald, *Printing in the Americas* (New York: Gregg, 1937), pp. 94-98;

John Tebbel, *History of Book Publishing in the United States*, 4 volumes (New York: Bowker, 1972), I: 120-123;

Isaiah Thomas, *The History of Printing in America* (Barre, Mass.: Imprint Society, 1970), pp. 530-531, 552-555;

Lawrence C. Wroth, *The Colonial Printer* (Charlottesville: University Press of Virginia, 1964), pp. 179, 188, 256;

Wroth, *A History of Printing in Colonial Maryland, 1686-1776* (Baltimore, Typothetae of Baltimore, 1922), pp. 59-74;

Wroth, *William Parks, Printer and Journalist of England and Colonial America* (Richmond: The William Parks Club, 1926).

Sara Payson Willis Parton
(Fanny Fern)
(9 July 1811-10 October 1872)

Marion Marzolf
University of Michigan

MAJOR POSITION HELD: Columnist, *New York Ledger* (1856-1872).

BOOKS: *Fern Leaves from Fanny's Port-folio* (Buffalo: Derby, Orton & Mulligan, 1853; London: N. Cooke, 1853);

Little Ferns for Fanny's Little Friends (New York: Miller, Orton & Mulligan, 1854);

Fern Leaves, Second Series (New York: Miller, Orton & Mulligan, 1854);

Shadows and Sunbeams and Other Stories (London: W. S. Orr, 1854; New York: Arundel, 1881);

Ruth Hall: A Domestic Tale of the Present Time (New York: Mason, 1855);

Rose Clark (New York: Mason, 1855);

Fresh Leaves (New York: Mason, 1857);

The Play-day Book (New York: Mason, 1857);

Folly As It Flies (New York: G. W. Carleton, 1859; London: S. Low, 1868);

A New Story Book for Children (New York: Mason, 1864);

Ginger-snaps (New York: G. W. Carleton, 1870; London: S. Low, 1870);

Caper-sauce: A Volume of Chit-chat About Men, Women, and Things (New York: G. W. Carleton, 1872; London: S. Low, 1872).

One of America's first woman newspaper columnists, Sara Payson Willis, using the name Fanny Fern, wrote weekly from 1851 to 1872, primarily for the *New York Ledger.* Her columns were widely reprinted, and several of her ten books of essays were best-sellers in the United States and Great Britain. She used her pen to rise from widowed poverty and grief to independence and acclaim. A popular social critic, with a caustic wit and keen eye for injustice, she was widely respected for her attacks on sham and snobbery, her support of the virtuous and hardworking poor, and her barbed observations of upper-class life and its pretensions. Her novels are praised for their social content, and are also of interest for their heroines, who successfully deviate from the conventions to develop self-respect and independence.

Willis was one of nine children of Nathaniel and Hannah Parker Willis. She was born on 9 July 1811 in Portland, Maine, and christened Grata Payson in honor of the mother of her parents' minister, but her first name was soon changed to Sara. Shortly after her birth, the family moved to Boston, where her father established a printing business and, in 1827, founded *Youth's Companion* magazine. Two of her five brothers became successful editors of genteel magazines in New York, but they discouraged her writing efforts. She was educated in several schools, including Catharine Beecher's Hartford, Connecticut, seminary. In May 1837 she married Charles H. Eldredge, a bank cashier and son of a Boston physician. The marriage was happy and produced three daughters: Mary, born in 1839; Grace, born in 1840; and Ellen, born in 1844. In 1845 Mary died; the following year Charles died from typhoid fever. Sara was left penniless and at the mercy of her rather prosperous family, who grudgingly gave her a pittance for support, while urging her to find a way to take care of herself and her children. They encouraged her marriage to a Boston merchant, S. P. Farrington, in 1849. The marriage rapidly deteriorated, and he obtained a divorce in 1852.

After trying sewing and teaching, Willis began writing articles for the local magazines. Using the pen name "Fanny Fern," she sold the first one for fifty cents, and after 1851 her essays appeared regularly in Boston in the *Olive Branch* and the *True Flag.* The icy treatment of her Boston family was repeated by her brothers in New York. When she first began writing, she sent her brother Nathaniel some samples, asking that he help her find a market there. He replied that the city was "the most overstocked market in the country for writers" and warned her that her sketches "would do only in Boston." She "overstrained the pathetic" and her humor ran to "dreadful vulgarity sometimes," he

scolded. "I am sorry that any editor knows that a sister of mine wrote some of these which you sent me." This reply only stiffened her resolve to write, and her pen name hid her identity from her family and from others for several years.

It was not long before newspapers in New York and across the country were picking up and copying her witty, irreverent columns. This wide— but unpaid—circulation quickly established her reputation. A New York book publisher located her and brought out the first collection of her essays, *Fern Leaves from Fanny's Port-folio* (1853), which sold 80,000 copies in America and 45,000 in Great Britain in its first year. A similar book for children, *Little Ferns for Fanny's Little Friends* (1854), and *Fern Leaves, Second Series* (1854) brought her sales to 180,000 within two years and some $10,000 in royalties. This success and the encouragement of editors resulted in her moving to New York.

Among the New York editors who reprinted Fanny's articles was James Parton, then editing Nathaniel Willis's *Home Journal.* When Willis discovered that Fanny Fern was his sister, he ordered Parton to cease using her work. Parton considered this demand unjust and quit his job over the incident. Not long after, Fanny published her first novel, *Ruth Hall* (1855). On 5 January 1856 she married Parton who had achieved literary attention for his *Life of Horace Greeley* (1855). Although she continued to use her pen name, her real identity soon became widely known in the social and literary set, to the chagrin of her family and to the delight of gossips who searched for and found autobiographical material in the novel.

Ruth Hall sold over 50,000 copies in eight months, and "the flimsy dress woven about the characters revealed their identities in a scandalous manner," relates Elizabeth Bancroft Schlesinger. There were the heroine with the happy marriage, sudden widowhood, two daughters to support, and final success as a writer; the indifferent and stingy parent; the insipid and foppish brother; and the helpful publisher-mentor. The book was widely reviewed and called "banal," "shocking," "spiteful," and "in bad taste." But it was not boring. Nathaniel Hawthorne, who had been grumbling about "all these scribbling women," wrote his friend and publisher, William D. Ticknor, that he had enjoyed reading *Ruth Hall* and wanted to know about the author. "If you meet her, I wish you would let her know how much I admire her," he said. "The woman writes as if the Devil was in her; and that is the only condition under which a woman ever writes anything worth reading."

Sara Payson Willis Parton (Fanny Fern) (New York Historical Society)

Feminist literary critics of the 1960s have reappraised Fanny Fern's novel and the sensation it caused. Says Ann Douglas Wood: "There was clearly a conventional set of preconceptions as to why women should write and what kind of literature they could write, which Hawthorne disliked, and which Fanny Fern challenged and even attacked in her novel about a woman writer. *Ruth Hall* consequently gains what interest it still possesses today precisely because it is a kind of test case, questioning the validity and value of a genteel tradition in itself deserving of consideration." Hawthorne, according to Wood's argument, realized that these writing women would be his shrewd competitors in the literary market and that his work would "have no chance of success while the public taste is occupied with their trash," as he put it.

Helen Papashvily's *All the Happy Endings* (1956) makes the point that many of these women writers were widows who were forced into public display of their writing talents by the need to support themselves and their children rather than by the "unladylike desire for self-expression." Wood finds this theme explored in *Ruth Hall,* where the heroine falls into the role of bereaved widow in the first part of the book, but in the second part assumes the role of successful, business-minded, and aggressive woman "able to cast off her sentimental role as orphan, loving wife and suffering widow and move on to a bright future that is hers alone."

Ruth Hall competes with men and refuses to feel guilty about doing so, explains Wood. Her character reflects her author's own beliefs. Fanny Fern urged women with "barren and loveless lives" to find improvement and solace in writing: "Write! . . . Write! It will be a safe outlet for thoughts and feelings that maybe the nearest friend has never dreamed had place in your heart or brain . . . it is not safe for the women of 1867 to shut down so much that cries out for sympathy and expression. . . ." Women's writing, Fanny believed, would stand one day "as an accusing witness to the finer sensibility their fathers and husbands ignored or brutalized"; but more important, their writing would enable women to survive and rise out of the "dead-level" of their lives.

Rose Clark, Fanny Fern's second novel, was published in 1855. Two heroines, whose husbands have left them for different reasons, face their problems in quite contrasting ways. One continues to search for the husband she believes was faithful (he was); the other, freed by divorce, shows no interest in further romance. According to Nina Baym, the divorcée spoke for many feminists of her day—the liberated woman at that time was liberated from sex.

The 1850s and 1860s saw the rapid growth of a new market of young readers, fresh from the free common schools, who enjoyed simple and entertaining fare. Magazines and popular newspapers flourished, and with them a growing body of women writers who contributed romances, essays, and witty columns. One of the first successful popular weeklies carrying this type of reading matter was Robert Bonner's *New York Ledger,* which was founded in 1851 and soon was reaching a half-million readers. Bonner paid his authors well and attracted some of the best writing talent, which he publicized vigorously. He signed up Fanny Fern with an offer in 1856 to pay her $100 per column for a serial novel, "Fanny Ford, A Story of Everyday Life." This made her the highest-paid writer of the day, but the novel did not appear in book form until it was included in *Fresh Leaves* in 1857. She continued to write popular columns for Bonner at the rate of twenty-five dollars per column until her death.

After her three novels, Fanny gave up fiction and turned all her attention to perfecting her humorous, skeptical, and practical essays on contemporary city life. She and Parton enjoyed a busy life in New York City, although he was fonder of social events than she was. Her daughter Ellen lived with them, and in 1861 they were joined by the orphaned baby of her daughter Grace. This foursome became a close family unit until Fanny's death.

Others described Fanny as "striking" at age forty-four, "a full, commanding woman . . . who looks high, steps high, and carries her head high. She has light brown hair, florid complexion, and large, blue eyes." But Fanny's own description in "Peeps from Under a Parasol" in *Fresh Leaves* (1857) is:

> And here, by the rood, comes FANNY FERN! FANNY is a woman. For that she is not to blame; though since she first found it out, she has never ceased to deplore it. She might be prettier; she might be younger. She might be older; she might be uglier. She might be better; she might be worse. She has been both over-praised and over-abused, and those who have abused her worst, have imitated and copied her most.
>
> One thing may be said in favor of FANNY: she was NOT, thank Providence, born in the beautiful, backbiting, sanctimonious, slandering, clean, contumelious, pharisaical, phiddle-de-dee, peck-measure city— of Boston!

Her columns delighted readers of the day and her humor tempered her reformist and crusading messages, making them easier reading. She covered a wide range of topics, from accounts of her own family life and travels, to literary discussions, social conventions, customs, and politics. She was especially talented in writing about and for children. She supported women's right to vote and equal pay for women. She urged women to win independence and stand with men as equal partners. She helped found the first woman's club, Sorosis, with Jane C. Croly in New York in 1868, and was one of its first vice-presidents. But she was not content to focus her energies on woman's rights alone. As her biographer, Florence Bannard Adams, points out, "Fanny had so many wrongs to right!" She was "inspired by her deep hatred of injustice and her passionate determination to help women overcome the inequitable conditions that surrounded them, and she believed she must use all her power and influence to right these wrongs." Her defense of Walt Whitman's *Leaves of Grass* in the 10 May 1856 *Ledger* is characteristic. Many critics had attacked the strangeness of Whitman's verse and his frank references to sex, but Fanny praised his original genius and acclaimed his "strong, honest thoughts in the face of pusillanimous, toadying, republican aristocracy."

Although she was socially ignored by the literati of her day, says Schlesinger, Fanny Fern was considered one of the outstanding women of her age. The best magazines reviewed her books, of which she published a dozen. During the last six years of her life she battled cancer, but even after she lost the use of her right hand and had to have her head supported in a mechanical device, she wrote her weekly column. The week before her death, for the first time in seventeen years, she said, she had to write her editor that there would be no column. She died on 10 October 1872 and was buried in Mt. Auburn Cemetery in Cambridge, Massachusetts, with only the name "Fanny Fern" on her tombstone. Four years after her death, her daughter Ellen married Parton; they had two children. Her importance to literature comes from the influence of her perceptive, popular weekly essays and her constant encouragement to women to think for themselves and to be more self-reliant and seek wider fields of work.

Biography:
Florence Bannard Adams, *Fanny Fern or A Pair of Flaming Shoes* (West Trenton, N.J.: Hermitage Press, 1966).

References:
Nina Baym, *Woman's Fiction: A Guide to Novels by and about Women in America, 1820-1870* (Ithaca, N.Y.: Cornell University Press, 1978), pp. 251-252;

Elaine Breslaw, "Popular Pundit: Fanny Fern and the Emergence of the American Newspaper Columnist," M.A. thesis, Smith College, 1956;

James C. Derby, *Fifty Years among Authors, Books and Publishers* (New York: Carleton, 1884), pp. 208-220;

Robert P. Eckert, Jr., "Friendly, Fragrant Fanny Ferns," *Colophon*, 18 (1934);

Milton E. Flower, *James Parton, The Father of Modern Biography* (Durham, N.C.: Duke University Press, 1951);

Grace Greenwood (Sara Lippincott), "Fanny Fern—Mrs. Parton," in *Eminent Women of the Age*, edited by James Parton (Hartford, Conn.: S. M. Betts, 1868), pp. 66-84;
Life and Beauties of Fanny Fern (New York: H. Long, 1855);
Helen Papashvily, *All the Happy Endings* (New York: Harper, 1956), pp. 123-125;
James Parton, *Fanny Fern: A Memorial Volume* (New York: G. W. Carleton, 1874);
Elizabeth Bancroft Schlesinger, "Fanny Fern: Our Grandmothers' Mentor," *New York Historical Society Quarterly*, 38 (October 1954): 501-519;
Ann Douglas Wood, "The 'Scribbling Women' and Fanny Fern: Why Women Wrote," *American Quarterly*, 23 (Spring 1971): 2-24.

Papers:

A collection of letters, clippings, and an unpublished biography by Sara Parton's granddaughter, Ethel Parton, are in the Sophia Smith Collection at Smith College.

William Trotter Porter
(24 December 1809-19 July 1858)

Shirley M. Mundt
Louisiana State University

See also the Porter entry in *DLB3, Antebellum Writers in New York and the South.*

MAJOR POSITIONS HELD: Editor, *Spirit of the Times and Life in New York,* renamed *New York Spirit of the Times* in 1835 (1831-1832; 1835-1856), *American Turf Register* (1839-1844), *Porter's Spirit of the Times* (1856-1858).

WORKS: *The Big Bear of Arkansas, and Other Sketches, Illustrative of Characters and Incidents in the South and Southwest,* edited by Porter (Philadelphia: Carey & Hart, 1846);
A Quarter Race in Kentucky, and Other Sketches, Illustrative Scenes, Characters, and Incidents, Throughout "The Universal Yankee Nation," edited by Porter (Philadelphia: Carey & Hart, 1846);
Instructions to Young Sportsmen, in All That Relates to Guns and Shooting. By Lieut. Col. P. Hawker. First American, from the 9th London Ed. To Which Is Added the Hunting and Shooting of North America; with Descriptions of the Animals and Birds . . . Collated from Authentic Sources. By Wm. T. Porter, edited by Porter (Philadelphia: Lea & Blanchard, 1846).

William Trotter Porter, best known in his own

William Trotter Porter

time as a devotee of horses and horse racing, is recognized in journalism history for popularizing the American sporting magazine and for encouraging the growth of a new genre in American literature—the local color sketch, which depicted scenes, characters, and incidents illustrating life in the South and Southwest. In the *Spirit of the Times,* a sporting magazine which Porter began and which he edited for over twenty-five years, he devoted himself to giving the most thorough and up-to-date coverage of horse racing news in America, later expanding coverage to field and river sports. As interest in horse racing declined, Porter turned the *Spirit of the Times* into an outlet for humorous sketches sent to him by contributors. Exposure in the *Spirit of the Times* gave impetus to the development of the new genre. Later, Porter published in book form sketches which had appeared in his magazine.

No one in Porter's circle of friends and relatives was surprised that he should make a name for himself as editor of a publication about horses and horse racing. His grandfather Asa Porter was a wealthy New Hampshire landowner who had a passion for horses and land; and his father, Benjamin, frequently made long trips on horseback into Canada where Asa owned land given him by the British Crown. The Porters, with their fine horses and rich lands, opened their homes to the gentry of early America; as a small boy, Porter had an opportunity to meet many of his father's friends, including Daniel Webster, to whom he paid tribute years later in the *Spirit of the Times.*

Benjamin Porter set up law practice in Newbury, Vermont, in 1800 after his marriage to Martha Olcott, and was successful and well respected. But he died in 1818, when William was only eight, and, according to Francis Brinley, William's brother-in-law and biographer, left his wife and six children in "narrow circumstances and disappointed hopes." In 1821 Porter's mother bought a home in Hanover, New Hampshire, and placed the children in Moore's Indian Charity School. Connected with Dartmouth College, Moore's was originally a school for Indian youngsters, but had later been opened to other children for a small tuition fee. Studying under the dominie Archelaus F. Putnam, Porter, according to his sister, made good marks but often hid the *Compleat Angler* or a volume of Dr. Fox inside his Virgil text. His sister describes him in Brinley's biography as "generous, unselfish, modest, truthful, cheerful, always retaining the credulity and simplicity of a child," his only "loose screw" being his inability to say no and "thereby cause disappointment and perplexity to another."

Porter's dislike for Putnam's academy and his admiration for Ben Franklin, whose autobiography he read repeatedly, soon spurred him to ask his mother to let him leave school and start work in a printing office. She refused at first, but after conferring with Porter's uncles, she agreed to let him go to Andover, Massachusetts, probably in 1823, as an apprentice in the printing establishment of Flagg and Gould. In the next few years, Porter worked as a journeyman and may have taught school briefly.

In 1829 Porter went to work for the *Farmer's Herald* at St. Johnsbury, Vermont, and a year later moved to Norwich, where he was editor of the *Enquirer.*

From there Porter went to New York and worked for a few months as foreman in John T. West's printing office. But the pay was poor, and he soon left to begin his own paper. On 10 December 1831 Porter and another printer, James Howe, published their first issue of the weekly sporting paper, the *Spirit of the Times and Life in New York.* Horace Greeley, who had worked with Porter at West's, joined the staff and helped Porter for eight or nine months. Years later Greeley wrote: "My recollections of him at that period are, that he was a tall, comely youth, of about twenty-five, very urbane and kind toward those younger and less favored than himself, and a capital workman."

Early issues of the *Spirit of the Times* contained many items taken directly from English as well as American journals; police reports for New York, Philadelphia, and London; extracts from speeches; miscellaneous poems; articles on horses and sports club meetings; notes of horse races; items on game laws and hunting; and occasional stories about local occurrences. Porter modeled the paper on *Bell's Life in London* and hoped to make the *Spirit of the Times* as popular in America and abroad as that paper had become.

For a time, it looked as if Porter would not realize his dream. Between 27 October and 3 November 1832, he sold the *Spirit of the Times* to James D. Armstrong. Porter went on to edit the *New Yorker,* the *Constellation,* and the *New York Atlas Magazine,* but all were short-lived. Meanwhile, the *Spirit of the Times* was sold twice: first to Freeman Hunt and John Jay Adams, who combined it with the *Traveller* and *Porter's Family Journal,* originated by Porter's oldest brother; then to Charles J. B. Fisher. For over a year the paper ran under the cumbersome title of the *Traveler, Family Journal, Spirit of the Times and Life in New York.* Then just before 3 January 1835, Porter repurchased the copyright, changed the title to the *New York Spirit of the Times,* and started what he called a "new series."

Of himself and his early days as editor of the *Spirit of the Times,* Porter later wrote: "A mere boy, unknown and unaided, we started the project of a Sporting paper. Trammelled by circumstances, retarded by inexperience, we groped our way slowly into those Southern and Western regions of our country, where the sports we advocate were more generally appreciated and more liberally encouraged."

As the paper matured, horse racing was gaining popularity across the South and West. By 1836 sales of thoroughbreds were amounting to over a half a million dollars a year and the turf was receiving considerable attention from the wealthy and the influential. It was the perfect time for a sporting paper, and Porter, who had loved horses since boyhood and who understood the tastes of gentleman-sportsmen, capitalized on this surge of interest. He increased the size of the paper from four to eight pages and raised the price from three to five dollars per year. He solicited contributions from correspondents from all over the South and Southwest and from Canada and Europe. Among his many contributors were Alban S. Payne, whose pen name was "Nicholas Spicer"; James Oakes, who signed himself "Acorn"; George Washington Harris, "Mr. Free" and "Sugartail"; Thomas Bangs Thorpe, "The Bee Hunter"; and William P. Hawes, "Cypress, Jr."

Seven years after he began the *Spirit of the Times* Porter was able to find out firsthand the kind of reception it had among its readers in the Southern states. In 1838 he took a three-month tour through Baltimore, Wheeling, Cincinnati, Louisville, Vicksburg, Natchez, St. Francisville, and New Orleans, and wrote upon his return: "Unbounded hospitality . . . was absolutely bestowed upon us in a manner at once so elegant and so bountiful, that the mere acknowledgement of the grateful compliment fills our throat and eyes with the emotion its remembrance must ever excite."

To please his audience Porter included in the *Spirit of the Times* horse racing news of all kinds: notices of race meetings, lists of winners in races, lists of stallions, articles on the training of racehorses, tips on betting. He also included advertisements—for horse medicines, veterinarians, gunsmiths, and the like—which he thought would interest the sportsman.

Tips on trout fishing frequently appeared in the *Spirit of the Times.* Porter, himself a master of the sport, spent much of his leisure time with fellow anglers on New England trout streams. His ad-

miration for fishermen is obvious in this tribute to Daniel Webster, written in 1839: "We admire the lofty genius of the man, his giant powers of mind, his simplicity, his downright honesty. But more than all, Mr. Webster is an angler, an humble disciple of Izaak Walton. Show me the man who loves trout fishing, and I will tell you who is generous, and brave, and tenderhearted. Such a man is Mr. Webster, and as such do we love him more than we respect him for his greatness and integrity."

In March 1839 Porter purchased the *American Turf Register* from John S. Skinner. In this publication, the emphasis was on British and American sporting articles which appealed to wealthy gentleman-sportsmen, American and English racing calendars, portraits of famous turfmen, and reports of important races. In a letter written for Porter's first issue of the *American Turf Register,* Skinner wrote: "The *Spirit of the Times* may do the light skirmishing to amuse the crowd, while the more ponderous *Register* is reserved for more serious work."

In the same year Porter increased the size of the *Spirit of the Times* to twelve pages and was pleased to have seven pages of original material from thirty-three different correspondents. He also began to include costly prints of famous racehorses. With these changes, Porter was forced to raise the subscription price to ten dollars a year. It turned out to be a bad time to increase rates. The economy had not recovered substantially after the panic of 1837 and Porter's subscribers were not paying.

At the same time, however, a change was taking place in the content of the *Spirit of the Times* and in its reading audience. When Porter's brother Benjamin died in December 1840, Porter was away from the *Spirit of the Times* for a short time. He returned to find "every nook and corner of the office . . . filled with letters and communications." Porter was impressed. "We have commissions enough to employ seven men and a boy for a fortnight," he wrote. On 27 March 1841 Porter published Col. T. B. Thorpe's "Big Bear of Arkansas" in the *Spirit of the Times.* It was the beginning of what was to become known as "The Big Bear school of writing." Fortunately for Porter and for the *Spirit of the Times* the local color sketches flowed in at just the right time. The economy was forcing plantation owners and sportsmen across the country to reduce their spending. Their cutbacks in buying and racing horses had a direct effect on Porter's paper: with fewer buyers and sellers, landowners had no need for the kind of news Porter had specialized in, and with fewer races, there was little for Porter to write about. As Porter learned the local-color pieces were well liked, he turned the *Spirit of the Times* from a horse racing magazine informing wealthy landowners into a publication of rough-hewn native humor delighting the frontiersman. The switch kept the *Spirit of the Times* alive.

Nevertheless, by 1842 the subscribers owed Porter over $40,000 and his publication expenses were more than he could afford. Rather than go bankrupt, Porter sold both the *Spirit of the Times* and the *American Turf Register*. The business was taken over by John T. Richards; Porter continued as editor in chief.

Porter's own assessment of his years as owner of the *Spirit of the Times* was spelled out in an April 1843 issue. On a positive note he felt that the paper had promoted sales of thoroughbreds, thereby making horse racing a lucrative business; that it had reduced the prejudice of the Puritan North against horse racing; and that it had improved the image of American horse racing in the eyes of the British. Further, he felt that the *Spirit of the Times* had enlightened its audience on literary matters, drama, music, ballet, field sports, and even agricultural developments. But in his closing paragraphs, his discouragement was apparent: "After having thus devoted ten of the best years of our life, with all the means, the influence, the industry, and the ability we could command, we have realized—what? Why *on paper*, quite a snug little property, but, in truth, not the first red cent! With nearly Fifty Thousand Dollars due it, this journal passed on from ours into other hands, for an amount which would not command a moderate race-horse! What have we gained, then, beyond the ephemeral reputation of a newspaper writer? . . . had we the past ten years of our life to live over again, and were offered the wages of a journeyman wood-sawyer, we should certainly *hesitate* before giving up the 'wages' for the 'popularity'—the *saw* horse for the *race* horse!"

Apparently the new management was able to turn the paper's finances around. Richards dropped the subscription price of the *Spirit of the Times* to five dollars a year and in 1844 he discontinued the *American Turf Register* altogether. By 1847 the number of subscribers and the number of correspondents had increased. Although humorous sketches had appeared in very early issues of the *Spirit of the Times*, between 1840 and 1845 original local color pieces and letters from American humorists almost completely replaced the reprints of literary articles from Britain. These

sketches provided Porter with material for two collections, *The Big Bear of Arkansas, and Other Sketches* (1846) and *A Quarter Race in Kentucky* (1846).

Porter continued as editor for the *Spirit of the Times* until 1856. Then, according to Brinley, he "most unexpectedly . . . permitted his name to be associated in the publication of another weekly Sporting Journal, called 'Porter's Spirit of the Times.' Old friends and old correspondents rallied round him, and the enterprise started with flying colors; its success was unprecedented in the annals of the newspaper press, for as early as the eighth number it was backed by a circulation of 40,000 copies." The sixteen-page paper was much like the *Spirit of the Times;* many of the contributors who had sent material to Porter for the *Spirit of the Times* continued to send him articles for *Porter's Spirit of the Times*. Porter was at first in charge of sporting news and editorial policies; his partner, George Wilkes, was in charge of business matters. But as Porter's interest in the new paper lagged and his health declined, Wilkes took more control. By the time Porter died in 1858, he was contributing little more than obituaries of old friends.

By late 1859 there were three papers being published under the title *Spirit of the Times*. Richards continued to publish the original paper until 22 June 1861, when the Union discontinued mail service into the Confederate States. *Porter's Spirit of the Times*, which Abraham C. Dayton acquired from Wilkes, survived until August of that year. Wilkes, after losing a legal battle to use Porter's name, started his own paper on 10 September 1859, calling it *Wilkes' Spirit of the Times*. Both the original *Spirit of the Times* and *Porter's Spirit of the Times* tried to avoid political issues but at the same time appeal to the sporting interests of Southern readers; consequently, they were casualties of the Civil War. However, *Wilkes' Spirit of the Times* took a firm antislavery stand and thus survived the war, continuing publication until 1902.

Porter's last years were not happy. His four brothers, who had been extremely supportive over the years, had all died, the last in 1855. Porter had never married, so the loss of his brothers left him lonely and, according to Brinley, unlike his former self. In addition, he suffered frequently from severe attacks of gout, only occasionally feeling well enough to get out to the country for trout fishing. Despite his decline in health, his death came unexpectedly. On 19 July 1858 he died suddenly from congestion in his lungs, brought on by a cold.

Upon Porter's death the *New York Times* obituary noted: "*The Spirit of the Times* obtained a reputation second only to that of *Bell's Life in London.*" Porter would have been pleased. Brinley wrote: "As a turf-writer, he was without rival in this country, or even in England, where sporting literature had been cultivated for years by men of taste and education."

Porter's philosophy as an editor is best expressed in his own words: "Every editor of a newspaper should have extensive familiarity with literature; cultivated tastes, thorough knowledge of men and the world, habits of observation and great facility in giving expression to his opinions. The qualities of his heart should correspond to those of his head—he should be honest, generous and brave. . . . But into the composition of a Sporting editor should be infused, not only other ingredients but a double portion of industry, of patience, of command of temper, and of charity; verily he has need of all!"

Biography:
Francis Brinley, *Life of William T. Porter* (New York: D. Appleton, 1860).

Reference:
Norris W. Yates, *William T. Porter and the Spirit of the Times* (Baton Rouge: Louisiana State University Press, 1957).

George D. Prentice

(18 December 1802-22 January 1870)

MAJOR POSITIONS HELD: Editor, *New England Weekly Review* (1828-1830), *Louisville Daily Journal* (1830-1868).

BOOKS: *Biography of Henry Clay* (Hartford, Conn.: Hanmer, 1831; New York: J. J. Phelps, 1831);
Prenticeana; or, Wit and Humor in Paragraphs (New York: Derby & Jackson, 1860);
The Poems of George D. Prentice, edited with a biographical sketch by John J. Piatt (Cincinnati: R. Clarke, 1876).

George D. Prentice gained his journalistic fame in Kentucky: as first editor of the *Louisville Daily Journal*, putative inventor of the newspaper paragraph, wielder of pistol and bowie knife, poet and patron of the arts. He also received much blame for the Know-Nothing violence on "Bloody Monday," election day in 1855, and much credit for keeping the commonwealth in the Union during the Civil War.

But George Dennison Prentice was a genuine Yankee, born in Connecticut on 18 December 1802 and reared on the farm of his parents, Rufus and Sarah Stanton Prentice. By his own account he was something of a child prodigy. With tutoring by his mother, he was reading the Bible at age three and was enrolled in school shortly before his fourth birthday. Later he was tutored by a clergyman who

George D. Prentice (Gale International Portrait Gallery)

had studied at Yale and by his early teens knew grammar, mathematics, Latin, and Greek. Prentice taught school to earn money for college, entered

Brown University as a sophomore in 1820, and was graduated in 1823. Then he studied law, practiced briefly, and found his true vocation by writing for and editing the *Connecticut Mirror* in Hartford.

That work brought him to the attention of prominent Whigs, and he was soon editor of the *New England Weekly Review,* which was devoted to the cause of John Quincy Adams and Henry Clay. Prentice published his first issue in the fall of 1828, and, according to his obituary in the *Louisville Courier-Journal,* "His success surpassed his greatest expectations." *Harper's New Monthly Magazine* said the *Review* was "a literary weekly, which at once attracted attention from the strength and grace of its editorials." Prentice stayed at that job until the Connecticut partisans of Clay asked him to go to Kentucky to write a biography, the aim of which was to get Clay back into political office—the Senate, even the presidency.

Prentice arranged for John Greenleaf Whittier to be editor in his absence, and in the early autumn of 1830 he journeyed to Clay's home in Lexington. Not only did he tackle his primary task with such vigor that he had finished by November, he also had time to send articles back East. These were published as "Letters from a Strolling Editor to the Publisher of the N.E.W. Review." They were largely descriptions of Kentucky and the people Prentice had met and tended to be critical of political activities, particularly behavior observed at election time. The Clay book was a "campaign" biography; Henry Watterson described it as "a masterpiece of political special pleading."

The Kentucky Whigs were impressed by the Yankee and wanted a weapon to counter the Democratic blunderbuss, Shadrach Penn of the *Louisville Advertiser.* Louisville had a Whig paper, the *Focus,* but it was more literary than political and it was no match for the exuberant Penn.

Prentice's prospectus for his new paper said that it would support the Constitution and democracy and boost Henry Clay for the presidency, "steadily and without a shadow turning." The first issue of the *Louisville Daily Journal* appeared on 24 November 1830, with Prentice as editor and A. S. Buxton, former proprietor of the *Cincinnati Chronicle,* as chief financial backer and printer. Prentice wrote a friend that he had put no money into the paper but would receive half the profits. He would have other partners over the years, but the most significant would be Isham Henderson, who came aboard in 1849 and remained until the consolidation with Walter Haldeman's *Courier* in 1868.

Prentice was everything the Whigs had

wanted, for he immediately opened fire on foes far and near, especially Penn and Democrats. "Prentice, like a skilled fencer, was aggressive with his thrust of wit and satire," according to Louisville historian Josiah Stoddard Johnston, "while Penn . . . looked more to the ponderous blows of his political broadsword than to stinging paragraphs." *Harper's* said many years later that Prentice's editorials "were animated with personality, sharpened with bitterness" and that they were "a sort of intellectual cocktail." Moreover, Prentice wrote "telling squibs and pungent paragraphs, which, being something new in journalism, attracted great attention, and were widely copied. He is reputed to have been the originator in the American press of the short and pointed paragraphs now grown so popular."

Prentice found subjects—and targets—almost everywhere for his paragraphs, but his most telling were political:

> The Cincinnati representative in Congress boasts that he can "bring an argument to a p'int as quick as any other man." He can bring a quart to a pint a good deal quicker.
>
> Place confers no dignity upon such a man as the new Missouri senator. Like a balloon, the higher he rises, the smaller he looks.
>
> The editor of the ——— ——— [when he published his paragraphs in 1860 in *Prenticeana,* Prentice often chose not to use names of people or publications speaks of his "lying curled up in bed these cold mornings." This verifies what we said of him some time ago— "he lies like a dog."
>
> The "New York Express" says that unnaturalized foreigners "fill our prisons and poor-houses." Yes, and that is not the worst of it. They fill our ballot-boxes.
>
> In marriage between whites and blacks, we are by no means certain that the blacks get the best of it. Those who think black folks as good as themselves are not mistaken.
>
> Much smoking kills live men and cures dead hogs.
>
> A good way to light some cities with gas would be to set fire to their editors.
>
> Brigham Young says . . . that "the great resources of Utah are her women." It is very evident that the prophet is disposed to *husband his resources.*
>
> The "Washington Constitution" says that "our government wants nothing of Mexico but peace." Yes, but as soon as it gets one *piece,* it wants another.

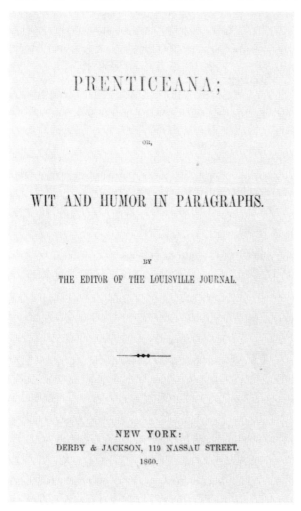

PRENTICEANA;

OR,

WIT AND HUMOR IN PARAGRAPHS.

BY

THE EDITOR OF THE LOUISVILLE JOURNAL.

NEW YORK:
DERBY & JACKSON, 119 NASSAU STREET.
1860.

*Title page for collection of Prentice's
newspaper paragraphs*

In addition to his editorial support of the Whigs, Prentice took an active part in practical politics. He was a delegate to an 1831 Whig convention in Frankfort to choose candidates.

Prentice had literary interests in addition to his political ones. He encouraged younger poets, publishing at least one poem almost every day in the *Journal.* In December 1838 he started the *Literary News Letter,* a weekly that ran for about two years. Prentice supplied much material for his literary weekly, but it also carried work by Longfellow, Irving, and Whittier, among others. Prentice wrote for other publications, too, and wrote poetry throughout his life. *Graham's* magazine carried some of his work in the early 1850s. *Harper's* alluded to his "occasional poetical effusions," but a historian closer to home declared that Prentice's blank verse work "The Closing Years" was the equal of Bryant's "Thanatopsis."

In the 1840s Prentice published the *Dollar Farmer* as a weekly supplement to the *Journal;* occasionally, the magazine appeared three times in one week. There were also campaign weeklies during election years.

Prentice also found time to report from the field, which was unusual for an editor of that period. He was in Lexington, some eighty miles from his home base, reporting on the agitation surrounding Cassius M. Clay and the suppression of his antislavery paper the *True American* in August 1845. Prentice's reports have gone largely unnoticed, but he made it a practice to cover legislative meetings and other events in Frankfort and elsewhere in the commonwealth.

Prentice was also a combatant with weapons capable of doing grave bodily harm—the pistol and the bowie knife. Prentice had early made clear that he did not subscribe to the Southern code that required dueling, but he also made clear that he was not the cowardly "Yankee schoolmaster" some of his foes expected: he could and would defend himself. Thus, according to *Harper's,* he had "at least half a dozen personal combats, in some of which he had very narrow escapes, and in two or three he was slightly wounded. He was a good marksman, and, what is more, entirely cool and intrepid in the presence of danger."

Three of his rencontres are cited most frequently, and each involved another editor. One occurred in August 1833 when George James Trotter, editor of the *Lexington Gazette,* waited for Prentice in the street; Trotter had been badly mauled by a Prentice paragraph and was made a laughingstock. Trotter fired his pistol from a distance of a few feet, and wounded Prentice in the breast. Prentice leaped on Trotter, disarmed him, threw him down, drew his bowie knife, and listened to the gathering crowd shout "Kill him!" Prentice walked away, saying he could not kill an unarmed man.

On another occasion, William E. Hughes, editor of the *Democrat,* took such umbrage at a Prentice sally that he called at the *Journal* and sent in his card. Prentice told him to wait in the street; he would load and come out. They exchanged four shots; none hit the mark, and the police stepped in.

Finally, there was Prentice's feud with R. T. Durrett, who had purchased a half-interest in the *Courier* in 1857 and served as its editor for two years. He was a Democrat; therefore he was an editorial target for Prentice. Johnston said that in one armed encounter, Prentice and Durrett fired away; neither was hit, but a bystander received a flesh wound. *Harper's* said that Prentice was angered again when, in 1858, Durrett printed in several issues that Prentice had been drunk and fallen into the river from a gangplank. Prentice called Durrett out, each fired, and each was wounded.

For the most part, however, Prentice used his pen for Whig causes and for Henry Clay, whom he admired all his life. Only in 1848 did Prentice swerve from Clay; Prentice's presidential candidate that year was Zachary Taylor. Prentice had decided as early as 1847 that Clay had no chance of being elected, although he thought Clay was the best man in the country. But Taylor was electable; as historian Betty Congleton has said, he was running on new issues, not the standard Whig issues of "the bank, the tariff, and internal improvements." Prentice believed that Taylor could command the respect and support of both Northerners and Southerners.

But the Whig party was crumbling; the old stalwarts were no longer there; Clay himself died in 1852. For many Whigs, the American, or Know-Nothing, party was the logical successor, a focus for their loyalties and enunciator of a suitable philosophy. Prentice himself supported the Know-Nothings in some respects, and thereby darkened his good name.

Prentice had claimed in his anniversary issue (26 November 1850), and subsequently, that his paper had "a circulation greater than the aggregate circulation of any three other papers in Kentucky." On 16 and 17 April 1855 he published long editorials that detailed the American party's position. His editorial on 17 April began: "Without claiming the right to speak *for* the Know-Nothing Party, we do claim the privilege of speaking *of* it and its acts and its aims . . . we have recently expressed a preference for its principles."

The American Party was a short-lived, nativist party that played on antiforeigner, anti-Catholic fears, and was vague on the most important issue of the day—slavery. Of the five daily newspapers in Louisville in 1855, only Prentice's *Journal* supported the party in the August elections. Walter N. Haldeman's *Courier* had backed the party's slate in the spring election, but Haldeman had been alienated by roughhouse tactics. Prentice, however, thought he could see the hand of the immigrant in Whig losses. He wrote on 26 July: "Foreigners made the last President, and they will continue to make Presidents in all future time, unless determined and efficient resistance be made through a harmonious organization to prevent it." The for-

eigners and Catholics had been aided, according to Prentice, by the Democratic party.

Thus the stage was set for the elections on 6 August 1855, which would thereafter be known as "Bloody Monday." In a blatantly anti-Catholic editorial, Prentice asked: "Fellow citizens, are you prepared to say that Americans shall *not* rule America?" Do your duty, he advised his readers, "by voting the American ticket." Several long editorials were devoted to the election, as were numerous single paragraphs. They were uniformly antiforeigner and anti-Catholic. "Let the foreigners keep their elbows to themselves to-day at the polls," he counseled. "There's no place for them in the ribs of the natives."

At least twenty people were killed in Louisville that day by beating, by gunshot, and by fire. The victims were Irish, German, Catholic, and Know-Nothing. The toll was probably higher; estimates run to fifty or more killed. Prentice was charged by his fellow editors, and by many others, with helping to incite the violence—even of being its chief cause. One historian, William C. Mallilieu, however, thought otherwise: "There has been too much emphasis on the part played by the famous editor of the *Louisville Journal*. He has been a scapegoat for the sins of Louisville. But, as an influential journalist and as a leader of the American-Whig party, he cannot escape all censure. His political associates and backers must also be held partly responsible for the atrocities committed by the ruffians whom they had hired to intimidate voters. Leading Democrats who encouraged or permitted the distribution of firearms to some of their followers were also culpable."

Prentice later tried to blame the Democrats (he called them "Anti-Americans") for starting the riots; this is unlikely. He fought the battle for many months, defending himself editorially against charges, countering gibes from other editors. On 10 December, four months after election day, the *Journal* said: "The editor of the Democrat may rail as long and as loudly as he pleases about the events of bloody Monday. Proof has been piled on proof that the foreigners began the massacre."

But Bloody Monday and its effects faded, and the issue became, again, slavery and Kentucky's role in the conflict. While Prentice could understand, and even support, the doctrine of states' rights, he was not in favor of being dragged into what he perceived to be someone else's fight. He knew well, and enunciated clearly, the dilemma of the border state, and he maintained his philosophy consistently up to, through, and after the Civil War.

As he explained on 2 July 1860, the Douglas and Breckinridge factions should be allowed to fight their own battles; Prentice advised his readers to vote for John Bell of Tennessee, candidate of the Constitutional Union (formerly Know-Nothing) party, "the only remaining national party in the land." He declared that Bell could carry every state in the South, "except perhaps South Carolina," because Democrats will "willingly and gladly vote for Bell, as the only hope of preventing the election of Lincoln, and putting down and crushing out the sectional organization." He urged Whigs and "Americans" to stand together. In a separate editorial quip he said that "Douglas's chance is dead, and it was too lean to have a ghost."

Prentice hammered away throughout the fall, urging election of Bell and Edward Everett, the ticket for "Union-loving men." On 31 October he pointed out that "it is of first importance that the Union men should close their ranks, mount all their sentinels, and be ready to act as the best interests of their country may demand. We shall have to contend in the Border States, with the fanaticism of the North, and the hot headed, over zealous Secessionists of the South, and upon the calmness, discretion, and moderation of the conservative masses will depend the destiny of the country." Prentice noted that the date marked the end of the campaign weekly edition of the *Journal*. It had 10,000 subscribers, he said.

The *Journal* on election day, 6 November 1860, was reminiscent of that August day five years earlier. It was loaded with urgings to frustrate the "recreants and traitors to be found on the soil of Kentucky" who were "perseveringly at work to effect the election of Lincoln, that they may have some color of excuse for precipitating a revolution." He cited the war preparations in the South and the threats of secession. "Union is our strength and safety," he counseled. And standing by itself, with a rule above and below: "God grant that Abraham Lincoln may never be our President. But why should a nation, that has calmly tolerated Van Buren and Tyler and Pierce and Buchanan in the Presidential chair, fly fiercely into fragments on account of the election of Lincoln?"

Thus the editor prepared his readers for the election of Lincoln. But, he said on 8 November, everyone should work for unity, and should guard against the disruption of the Union. In this way he began what was to be a long crusade. He carried it into January with a long account of the Knights of the Golden Circle, an organization signing up "scores if not hundreds" of young men locally—

youth who might not realize that its object was "the destruction of the Union." Prentice said that Kentucky would not bolt, but to those states that left, he said: "Depart in peace."

"Kentucky and her neighboring states may yet, if they stand firm, win the battle of the Constitution, and give our country peace," he added. The next day, 8 January, he proclaimed that Kentucky was not willing to be dragged into the conflict. On 11 January the *Journal* reported on a glorious meeting to "ratify" the Union. The meeting had been organized by the Union State Central Committee, of which Prentice was a member. The committee had been set up to unite Bell and Douglas men, promote a policy of neutrality, and keep Kentucky from being a battleground. Prentice and his allies hoped that Kentucky would stay in the Union, have the protection of the Constitution, and not play into the hands of the abolitionists.

Thus the tone of the *Journal* was decidedly pro-Union and anti-Confederacy. In the early days, especially, there was vehement denunciation of South Carolina's role and actions. Although Kentucky did not secede, the war wracked Prentice and left him broken. He was not young, and had been fighting his own wars in the *Journal* for thirty years. His beloved Union was being battered, torn apart. Worst of all, his two sons joined the Confederate forces. Even in his most troubled times, though, Prentice could retain his pungency. In the *Journal* of 1 October 1862, there appeared: "When newspaper correspondents want to tell a big lie, they generally begin with saying 'it is stated in official circles.'"

Prentice's older son, William Courtland, was fatally wounded during the battle of Augusta, Kentucky, in September 1862. In announcing the death on 2 October Prentice wrote: "He perished in the cause of the rebellion," and expressed the wish that he had fallen in the service of the Union, if he had to die. In the files of the Filson Club in Louisville there is a poem he wrote on Courtland's death; it is anguished, but resigned.

More was to come. Col. Clarence Prentice was charged with killing a soldier in Richmond, Virginia, and Prentice went to his aid, traveling through Washington and obtaining passes from both armies to pass through the lines on 28 November 1864. Clarence was acquitted on grounds of self-defense, but the father was further drained.

War's end brought little respite. Prentice was worn out and dispirited. In the spring of 1868 he sold his *Journal* stock to Isham Henderson, his partner for nearly twenty years. Henrietta Benham

Prentice, whom he had married on 18 August 1835, died. He bought a farm for Clarence a few miles from Louisville near the Ohio River, probably using proceeds from the sale of his stock and also from the sale of his big house. Soon he was no longer editor of the paper, for Henderson enticed the young, vigorous Henry Watterson from Nashville. Though Watterson had been on the Confederate side, he bore no grudges against a man of Prentice's character and leanings: they were both Union men at heart. But all of these changes came within a short period, and Prentice's life changed radically. He moved into his office and had his meals sent in. Yet he did not retreat into his shell, if Watterson is to believed; he was a contributor, and when the *Journal* and Haldeman's *Courier* combined in November 1868, the first issue mentioned pointedly that Prentice was staying on. According to Watterson, Prentice could glow with work and was lithe and active for his age. When a state press association was formed in January 1869, he was chosen its first president. In the end, though, he was a tired man, reduced to reminding his former journalistic foe and new boss, Haldeman, that he needed money. One handwritten request for forty dollars is dated (in Haldeman's hand) 25 December 1870 (an error, obviously); another mentions that Prentice needs money to tide over his son until a more advantageous time to sell crops.

Prentice died shortly after 4:00 A.M. on 22 January 1870 at Clarence's farm, to which he had gone in an open carriage to spend Christmas. The weather had been raw and Prentice had contracted influenza, which had turned into pneumonia. The journalistic outpouring was appropriate for one of the pioneers. The *Courier-Journal* ran columns on 23 January and repeated them the next day with additional stories. There was more on 25 January; then, on 2 February, Watterson addressed the state legislature, at its request. The complete eulogy was published on the following day; much of it followed the earlier material in the *Courier-Journal*. A large part of what Watterson recounted about Prentice's life probably came from Prentice himself, for just before his last trip to the farm he had given Watterson a handwritten manuscript which Watterson characterized as "an autobiographical note of the leading dates and events of his life."

In his eulogy before the legislature, Watterson declared: "From 1830 to 1861 the influence of Prentice was perhaps greater than the influence of any political writer who ever lived." He cited Prentice's personal gifts and scholarly discipline. Watterson, who had spent time in Europe before coming to Louisville, could recall that "in London . . . his fame is exceeded by that of no American newspaper writer; but the journalists of Paris, where there is still nothing but personal journalism, considered him a few years ago as the solitary journalist of genius among us." The French liked his poetry as well as his paragraphs, Watterson said. Watterson compared Prentice with William Cobbett and Horace Greeley: "He ranks with Cobbett as the greatest partisan who ever handled a public journal. He ranks with Horace Greeley as the most incisive, clear and homely writer for the people who ever vivified and illuminated the American press"; but, according to Watterson, "Greeley never had Prentice's wit, courage or accomplishments." Watterson also told how Prentice, toward the end of his life, had ceased to care for his appearance: "He let his hair and beard grow long, and was careless in his attire."

Prentice and the *Journal* put Louisville on the map because of his political leadership and brilliance as an editor, historian Johnston said, and "his literary contributions to other publications were many and varied, both in prose and verse." Other papers picked up his paragraphs, and "in many leading papers, a special department or column was maintained comprising his current sayings, entitled 'Prenticiana.' " During the Civil War, his support of the Union was so strong that Lincoln is supposed to have remarked that Prentice was worth 40,000 soldiers.

In Louisville today, there is still a statue of the editor; it sits on a pedestal before what once was the front door of the public library. It was carved from Italian marble, at Haldeman's orders, and placed above the doorway of the *Courier-Journal*'s new building in 1875. But the newspaper moved on to new quarters, and Prentice no longer had a place.

References:

Junius Henri Brown, "George D. Prentice," *Harper's New Monthly Magazine*, 50 (January 1875): 193-200;

William T. Coggeshall, *The Poets and Poetry of the West* (Columbus: Follett, Foster, 1860), pp. 121-131;

Betty C. Congleton, "Contenders for the Whig Nomination in 1848 and the Editorial Policy of George D. Prentice," *Register of the Kentucky Historical Society*, 67 (April 1969): 119-133;

Congleton, "George D. Prentice and Bloody Monday: A Reappraisal," *Register of the Kentucky Historical Society*, 63 (July 1965): 218-239;

Congleton, "George D. Prentice and his Editorial Policy in National Politics, 1830-1861," Ph.D. dissertation, University of Kentucky, 1962;

Congleton, "George D. Prentice: Nineteenth Century Southern Editor," *Register of the Kentucky Historical Society*, 65 (April 1967): 94-119;

Congleton, "The Louisville Journal: Its Origin and Early Years," *Register of the Kentucky Historical Society*, 62 (April 1964): 87-103;

Congleton, "Prentice's Biography of Henry Clay and John Greenleaf Whittier," *Filson Club Historical Quarterly*, 37 (October 1963): 325-330;

Josiah Stoddard Johnston, *Memorial History of Louis-*

ville, 2 volumes (Chicago: American Biographical Publishing Co., 1896);

William C. Mallilieu, "George D. Prentice: A Reappraisal Reappraised," *Register of the Kentucky Historical Society*, 64 (January 1966): 44-50;

James M. Prichard, "Champion of the Union: George D. Prentice and the Secession Crisis in Kentucky," *Cincinnati Historical Society Bulletin*, 39 (Summer 1981): 113-125;

Henry Watterson, *George Dennison Prentice; A Memorial Address Delivered before the Legislature of Kentucky* (Cincinnati: Clarke, 1870).

Henry Raymond

(24 January 1820-18 June 1869)

Mark Fackler
Wheaton College

MAJOR POSITIONS HELD: Chief assistant, *New-York Tribune* (1841-1843); editor, *Morning Courier and New York Enquirer* (1843-1851); editor and publisher, *New-York Daily Times*, renamed *New-York Times* in 1857 (1851-1869):

BOOKS: *Association Discussed; or, The Socialism of the Tribune Examined. Being a Controversy between the New York Tribune and the Courier and Enquirer*, by Raymond and Horace Greeley (New York: Harper, 1847);

The Relations of the American Scholar to His Country and His Times. An Address Delivered before the Associate Alumni of the University of Vermont, at Burlington, Vt., August 6, 1850 (New York: Baker & Scribner, 1850);

An Oration Pronounced before the Young Men of Westchester County, on the Completion of a Monument, Erected by Them to the Captors of Major Andre, at Tarrytown, Oct. 7, 1853 (New York: S. T. Callahan, printer, 1853);

Political Lessons of the Revolution. An Address Delivered before the Citizens of Livingston County, at Geneseo, N.Y., July 4, 1854 (New York: Baker, Godwin, printers, 1854);

A State System of Education for New York. An Address Delivered before the Literary Societies of the Rochester University, at Rochester, N.Y., July 11, 1854

(New York: Baker, Godwin, printers, 1854);

Disunion and Slavery. A Series of Letters to Hon. W. L. Yancey, of Alabama, by Henry J. Raymond, of New York (New York?, 1861?);

The Position and Duty of the Republican Party. Remarks of Hon. H. J. Raymond, at the Festival of the Republican General Committee in the City of New York, on the Celebration of Washington's Birthday, February 22d, 1862 (Albany, N.Y.: Weed, Parsons, printers, 1862);

The Rebellion and Our Foreign Relations. Remarks of Henry J. Raymond, Speaker of the Assembly on the Conduct of Our Foreign Affairs and the Action and Disposition of European Powers. In Assembly, State of New York, Mar. 5, 1862 (Albany: Weed, Parsons, 1862);

The Life of Abraham Lincoln, of Illinois, by Henry J. Raymond; and the Life of Andrew Johnson, of Tennessee. By John Savage (New York: Derby & Miller, 1864);

History of the Administration of President Lincoln; Including His Speeches, Letters, Addresses, Proclamations, and Messages. With a Preliminary Sketch of His Life (New York: Derby & Miller, 1864); enlarged as *The Life and Public Services of Abraham Lincoln* (New York: Derby & Miller, 1865; London: Stevens, 1865); republished as *Lin-*

coln, *His Life and Times,* 2 volumes (New York: Hurst, 1891);

Peace and Restoration. Speech of Hon. H. J. Raymond . . . in Reply to Hon. T. Stevens . . . Delivered in the House of Representatives, December 21, 1865 (Washington, D.C.: Printed at the Congressional Globe Office, 1865);

Restoration and the President's Policy. Speech of Hon. H. J. Raymond, of New York, on Changing the Basis of Representation, and in Reply to Hon. S. Shellabarger, of Ohio; in the House of Representatives, January 29, 1866 (Washington, D.C.: Printed at the Congressional Globe Office, 1866);

The Principles of Taxation. Speech of Hon. H. J. Raymond, of New York, on the Internal Revenue Bill, May 7, 1866 (Washington, D.C.: Printed at the Congressional Globe Office, 1866);

Constitutional Amendments. Speech of Hon. Henry J. Raymond, of New York, on the Proposed Amendment to the Constitution; Delivered in the House of Representatives, May 9, 1866 (Washington, D.C.: Printed at the Congressional Globe Office, 1866);

Restoration and the Union Party. Speech of Hon. Henry J. Raymond, of New York, on the Conditional Admission of the States Lately in Rebellion to Representation in Congress. Delivered in the House of Representatives, June 18, 1866 (New York: Baker & Godwin, printers, 1866).

PERIODICAL PUBLICATIONS: "Extracts from the Journal of Henry J. Raymond," edited by Henry W. Raymond, *Scribner's Monthly,* 19 (November 1879): 57-61; (January 1830): 419-424; (March 1880): 703-710; 20 (June 1880): 275-280.

Henry Raymond stepped into New York journalism at a time when newspapers, screaming socialism from one sector and sensationalism from another, needed the pen of an adroit political observer and a voice of reasoned moderation. Raymond's ambition, however, carried beyond the editor's desk into the political forum itself. Though he was often accused of wavering on specific legislation, Raymond's firm commitment to Republican principles eventually cost him all political influence, though he held the reigns of editorial leadership until his early death.

Henry Jarvis Raymond was born in Lima, New York, the eldest child of a farming family, and one of only three of Jarvis and Lavinia Brockway Raymond's six children to live past infancy. Ray-

Henry Raymond (photograph by Mathew Brady)

mond gave early evidence of superior intellectual skills: it is said that he could read by the age of three and deliver speeches when he was five. He enrolled at age twelve in the Genesee Wesleyan Seminary, a school of 340 boys established by the Methodist church which would later grow into Syracuse University. When Raymond finished school in 1836, his father mortgaged the farm to supplement his son's meager earnings as a country store clerk and schoolteacher in order to pay tuition at the University of Vermont at Burlington.

The university was even smaller than Raymond's prep school; only 100 students and seven faculty members met on the thirty-two-year-old campus that year. James Marsh, professor of moral philosophy who for seven years doubled as university president, became a friend and confidant of the new student. Raymond gained skill as an orator at the university; on one occasion he spoke to an audience that included the famous Whig Henry Clay, who commented, "That young man will make his mark."

While still a student at Vermont, Raymond submitted verse, book reviews, and short news items of university events to the *New-Yorker,* a literary and political news sheet edited by Horace Greeley. On several occasions Greeley printed material from his Burlington correspondent, who sometimes assumed the pen name "Fantome." In letters to Greeley, Raymond mentioned his hope for full-time employment upon his graduation, but the intemperate Greeley instead offered to sell him the entire journal—type, press, and subscribers. Wisely, Raymond judged his twenty years too few for such a risky undertaking and declined the half-serious overture.

Raymond received his degree with highest honors in 1840, in time to return to his home county to campaign for William Henry Harrison, the hero of Tippecanoe, who was running for president against incumbent Democrat Martin Van Buren. Raymond had been disappointed when the Whigs passed over Clay in favor of Harrison, but he loyally supported the party of the tariff and the national bank anyhow. The Whigs took New York by 13,000 votes in that election, much to the excitement of the twenty-year-old Raymond, for whom politics was already a passion.

Boarding a stagecoach, then a canal boat, and finally a Hudson River steamer, Raymond left rural New York to try his hand in the city. On his arrival in New York City in November 1840, he went to Greeley's Ann Street office to apply for a job. Greeley had just hired an editorial assistant, but allowed Raymond to spend as much time as he wished around the office. The arrangement turned to Raymond's advantage when the assistant abruptly left for a job in Philadelphia during a week when Greeley was also absent from the office. Raymond edited that week's *New-Yorker,* and though, due to his lack of experience, it was not a successful issue, Greeley soon thereafter awarded Raymond eight dollars a week—a salary equal to the teacher's stipend he had been offered by a school in North Carolina. Greeley assessed his new assistant as only moderately qualified, essentially ignorant of editorial judgment, and politically vagrant. Meanwhile, Raymond took delight in the variety of libraries, taverns, and theaters in New York, and supplemented Greeley's stingy salary by writing letters for out-of-state newspapers and advertising copy for patent medicines.

At this point, Raymond considered his apprenticeship to Greeley a step toward a legal or ministerial career, and he wrote to Marsh at Burlington to ask which vocation he should pursue. The liberal Marsh urged him to remain in New York and in journalism: "The press is used far less than it should be by public-spirited and enlightened

Raymond during his first years in New York (courtesy of Mrs. George T. Lambert)

men for dissipating the fogs of error which so often obscure the popular mind. In a word, we need public men devoted to the public interest and capable of guiding the public mind in the right way to right ends."

In early 1841 Greeley failed to sustain a Fourier-inspired journal called *Future,* but in April, with the approval of Whig party chief Thurlow Weed and Governor William H. Seward, Greeley launched a one-cent Whig paper, the *Tribune,* to challenge New York's powerful Democratic penny papers, the *Sun* and the *Herald,* and to celebrate and consolidate party momentum gained by Harrison's presidential victory. Though Raymond scorned Greeley's socialist ideals, both were Whig loyalists, and Raymond became the *Tribune* editor's chief assistant, still at a salary of eight dollars a week.

The young assistant showed industry and, in contrast to earlier assessments, earned praise from the editor. "Abler and stronger men I have met; a cleverer, readier, more generally efficient journalist, I never saw," Greeley later said of Raymond. Praise did not translate into a higher salary, however, and Greeley even went so far as to withhold wages during Raymond's long bout with fever that year. When he recovered, Raymond demanded and received a wage increase to twenty dollars a week, and began to study law, apparently thinking again of entering a more respected profession.

For two and a half years, Raymond learned reporting skills and editing judgment at the *Tribune*. Sent to Boston to cover Daniel Webster's famous 1842 defense of President John Tyler, whom Webster served as secretary of state despite Tyler's betrayal of the Whig platform, Raymond saw his account of the speech on the street two hours before the *Herald*'s. Months later, when Webster finally resigned his cabinet post, Raymond again beat the *Herald* with the help of a special railroad express arranged in advance. As Raymond's skill matured, Greeley more frequently placed him in charge of the entire edition, but not without stern admonition to be less "Tory" in his editorials—and to "curse Blackstone and fortune and office" and cast his future fully upon a journalistic career. Raymond obeyed, but in October 1843, the aspiring assistant had experienced enough of Greeley's stubbornness over wages. When the *Courier and Enquirer* offered Raymond an editorship at five dollars a week more than his *Tribune* salary, he left Greeley for the more conservative office of James Watson Webb's paper.

Compared to other New York papers, the *Morning Courier and New York Enquirer* was dull in appearance and content, expensive at six cents a copy, and prosperous. Merchants who wished to sell quality goods to the city's big spenders knew that the *Courier*'s 7,000 readers were a better market than the *Herald*'s 15,000 or the *Sun*'s 20,000. Plenteous advertising along with aggressive coverage of business news were *Courier* trademarks. Webb was a Whig, and so a chief editor Raymond could admire politically.

In a brief respite between jobs, Raymond married Juliette Weaver of Winooski, Vermont, on 24 October 1843. The Raymonds took up residence in a boardinghouse and Henry left for Massachusetts on his first *Courier* assignment—a speech by Daniel Webster affirming his loyalty, against hot accusations, to the Whigs.

In the 1884 campaign, Raymond stumped Genesee County for Clay against Democrat James Polk of Tennessee. Contrary to Raymond's predictions, Polk's strong stand for annexation of Texas turned the tide in his favor. A year later Raymond made an extensive trip on the Great Lakes to Chicago, where his reports told of a bustling, flat prai-

rie town of 12,000 hardworking people who seem to "have a city to create within a week." In 1846 Raymond and Greeley conducted a six-month debate in their respective papers in which Raymond criticized Fourierist socialism and Greeley defended it.

Raymond's career as a journalist was growing apace with his reputation as a skillful political operative. On his first trip to Washington, in early 1848, he covered Webster's argument before the Supreme Court in *Luther v. Borden*. On a later trip to report another Webster speech, Raymond's train ran through an open drawbridge; a broken coupling narrowly saved Raymond's car from plunging into the water. Upon hearing of the accident Webster postponed his speech for several weeks, then arranged a Senate gallery seat for the young reporter.

Elder statesman Clay seemed the logical nominee for the Whigs in 1848, but instead the party put up the Mexican War hero Gen. Zachary Taylor, a Southern slaveholder. Raymond, though disappointed, quickly fell in line, writing political statements, editing the Whig campaign magazine, and frequently speaking for the Whig ticket in New York. In the wake of Taylor's victory, several Whigs, including Webb, made trips to Washington in hope of a diplomatic appointment. With the editor away, Raymond took charge of the *Courier and Enquirer*, and continued even after Webb returned empty-handed and angry.

By the late 1840s Raymond's career and his social conservatism were well established. When soldiers called to quell a disturbance outside the Astor Place Theater shot into the mob and killed nineteen protesters, Raymond reported that despite the terrible consequences, law and order had been upheld. Raymond was present in May 1848 when representatives from six New York papers met to combine news gathering efforts. It was the beginning of the Associated Press, which Raymond would help build throughout his life.

In November 1849 Raymond was elected to the New York State Assembly, representing the city's Ninth Ward. Soon after reelection in 1850, he was made assembly speaker by the Whig majority. In addition to state politics and *Courier* duties, Raymond was named the first managing editor of the new *Harper's* magazine, a position he held for six years.

Slavery was the most important political issue in 1850, and feelings on both sides of the question were intense. Politicians who hoped to survive in such a volatile climate had to choose their words and their loyalties judiciously. Raymond aligned his position with that of Whig chief Seward, who was then serving in the U.S. Senate: no extension of slavery into western territories, no compromise on slavery's moral evil. New York Whigs were split on the problem, and Raymond knew that his position was not shared by Webb. Tension developed, and when the *Courier*'s owner, still peeved over his fallen political dreams, revised one of Raymond's editorials, the latter resigned in protest.

Raymond had met George Jones, a native of Vermont ten years his senior, at Greeley's *Tribune;* Jones had worked in the business office and since then had become a banker in Albany. As early as 1846 they had dreamed of founding a new paper to serve the half-million people of New York. Five years later, in early 1851, they determined to see their paper born if a bill then before the state assembly, which would eliminate Jones's profitable bank note business, should be passed. Fortunately for American journalism, the bill did pass and Jones was forced to seek his fortune in another field. He and another Albany bank note broker, Edward B. Wesley, each put up $20,000 to launch the new paper; Raymond was to be editor and was

George Jones, Raymond's partner in the founding of the New-York Daily Times *(courtesy of Mr. George J. Dyer)*

given twenty shares in the company, Jones and Wesley taking forty shares each. During a passage to Europe for a vacation in April 1851, Raymond wrote the prospectus for the *Daily Times,* a paper which would "endeavor to perpetuate the good, and to avoid the evil, which the past has developed, while it will strive to check all rash innovations and to defeat all schemes for destroying established and beneficent institutions. . . . It will seek to allay, rather than excite, agitation—to extend industry, temperance, and virtue. . . ." Competitors, notably the *Herald,* accused the new paper of having few plans beyond becoming a campaign sheet for Seward. Surely Raymond's vision was broader than that; but he did not intend to join the abolitionists or to promote military confrontation with the increasingly hostile Southern states. The *Times* would support Whig principles but remain independent of party and "free from bigoted devotion to narrow interests."

Within two weeks of its 18 September first edition, the *Times* boasted a circulation of 10,000. Cost of the four-page, six-column paper was one cent. Although all ads except those for abortionists or abortion medicines, or those promoting books on birth control, venereal disease, and sexual relations were invited, ad sales were low and the paper showed a loss at its first anniversary.

That early financial shortfall might have closed down the paper but for the intervention of Wesley. Jones fell ill in the fall of 1851, just as the new venture needed his acumen, and Wesley, sensing a business disaster, closed his brokerage house in Albany and moved to the *Times* office. Wesley's timely rescue gave Raymond occasion to celebrate the paper's first birthday with 24,000 "quiet, domestic, fireside conservative readers," as he described them. James Gordon Bennett could call the *Times* a "nigger penny organ," but Raymond knew his strategy: support for constitutional order; wide berth to the reformist zeal so characteristic of the *Tribune;* and Whiggish disgust, not volcanic hatred, of slavery. The paper also featured good editing, a lack of sensationalism, a large amount of news, and good foreign coverage. In 1852 Raymond doubled the size of the *Times* to eight pages and raised the price to two cents.

At the Whig convention in Baltimore in 1852, Raymond was seated as a delegate through Seward's influence. He was nearly ousted by Southern Whigs who intercepted a communiqué Raymond had written for the *Times* predicting a convention victory for Gen. Winfield Scott, the Seward favorite. Denounced for three hours in a vicious speech

Review Copyright Again.

We publish this morning a second letter of John Jay Esq. upon the general subject of an International Copyright. Mr. Jay's special object is to define more precisely than before, an opinion upon the the Author's right of property in his books; and to guard against inferences upon this point drawn from language used upon this point in his former letter. Mr. Jay holds that an Author has a right of property in his books, without regard to laws upon that subject :— while the opposite, & we think much the most general & correct opinion is, that whatever right he has in the creation of the law, he has

Manuscript page for an editorial by Raymond

by a Florida congressman, Raymond rose to his own defense, parried accusations with wit and reason, and finally saw Scott, the Mexican War hero from a Virginia plantation, nominated as the Whig candidate for president. The Northerners were less successful, however, at winning approval of their platform; the resulting soft-pedaling on slavery infuriated the radical Whigs, split the party, and gave the election to Democrat Franklin Pierce in every state but four. The New York governorship and state assembly also passed to the Democrats.

Raymond turned his vigor again to the newspaper. The *Times* could not boast the sprightly copy of the *Herald,* but for European news and special features Raymond and his editors were determined to take second place to no one. Raymond traveled to Europe in 1853 to arrange foreign correspondence and secured a series of articles by Louis Kossuth, the Hungarian revolutionary whose American tour Raymond had supported two years earlier. The *Times's* reputation for domestic coverage was heightened by long series covering the South and New York's poor. There were the inevitable arguments with competitors: in 1853, for example, Greeley accused the city's wealthy publishing houses, with whom Raymond was associated, of profiteering from their disregard of international copyright laws. Raymond argued that mass literacy required mass literature, and found the pirate-publishers guilty only of advancing American culture and providing jobs for American printers.

Raymond had decided to put politics behind him after his brief career as speaker of the assembly, but the turmoil of 1854, and perhaps his indebtedness to Thurlow Weed, produced a political opportunity he could not pass by. Early in 1854 Senator Stephen Douglas of Illinois introduced a bill approving the extension of slavery into the Nebraska Territory, repealing the Missouri Compromise of 1820. Northern Free-Soilers were shocked. At the same time, the Native American movement (Know-Nothings) and the temperance movement were agitating with such vigor that the party led by Seward, Weed, and Greeley was threatened by another split vote and Democratic avalanche. Hence, the Whig convention at Syracuse in 1854 was pivotal for the party. Greeley came desperate for nomination for governor of New York; when Weed denied his overtures, the *Tribune* editor, deeply disappointed, resigned from the alliance that since the early 1830s had shaped New York politics. The party nominated Myron Clark for governor and sought a candidate for lieutenant governor who

was neutral on prohibition and attractive to the patchwork of nativistic loyalties espoused by the Know-Nothings. Raymond seemed a good fit, and to Greeley's deeper embitterment, the younger editor received the Whig nod for lieutenant governor. Raymond campaigned little but did finally speak out against the Kansas-Nebraska Bill recently passed by Congress. In editorials Raymond condemned slavery as a moral evil, but insisted that it was a Southern issue; the North should not meddle in the local affairs of sovereign states. Clark and Raymond won that fall, but by such a narrow margin that Whig party leaders knew that their rank and file were searching for new political loyalties.

Those new loyalties were already melding into a new party in the West; and by the summer of 1855, New York Whigs were adjusting their strategy to accommodate the Republicans. Slavery was the persistent and central issue, and the Republicans opposed its extension, including the admission of new slave states below the Mason-Dixon line. The fact that most of Kansas was Southern and proslavery only strengthened Northern sentiment that popular sovereignty, however democratic in form, should not be allowed to override stronger moral principles of human rights. Whigs and Republicans met in joint convention at Syracuse in July 1855, and the following February a meeting of party officials in Pittsburgh set the stage for the first Republican national convention in Philadelphia that summer. Raymond was influential from the start. In Pittsburgh he wrote a speech calling for repeal of the Kansas-Nebraska Act and the immediate admission of Kansas as a free state. Intended for delivery to the New York delegation, the speech was unanimously adopted by the delegates as the new party's platform. Raymond helped organize New York City's first Republican rally, sharing leadership with William Cullen Bryant, Charles A. Dana, and other national figures. A true loyalist, Raymond dropped his advocacy of Seward when Weed decided that John C. Frémont would be the party's choice for president. At the same time, Raymond was obliged to relinquish hopes for a governorship or a seat in the Senate; Weed considered him too closely allied to Seward to appeal to broader Republican sentiments. The *Times* became an enthusiastic advocate during the 1856 campaign, and Raymond could take some pleasure in the fact that New York went for Frémont, elected the Republican candidate for governor, and gave the Republicans control of the legislature, despite the Democrats' national win and the prospect of a four-year Buchanan administration.

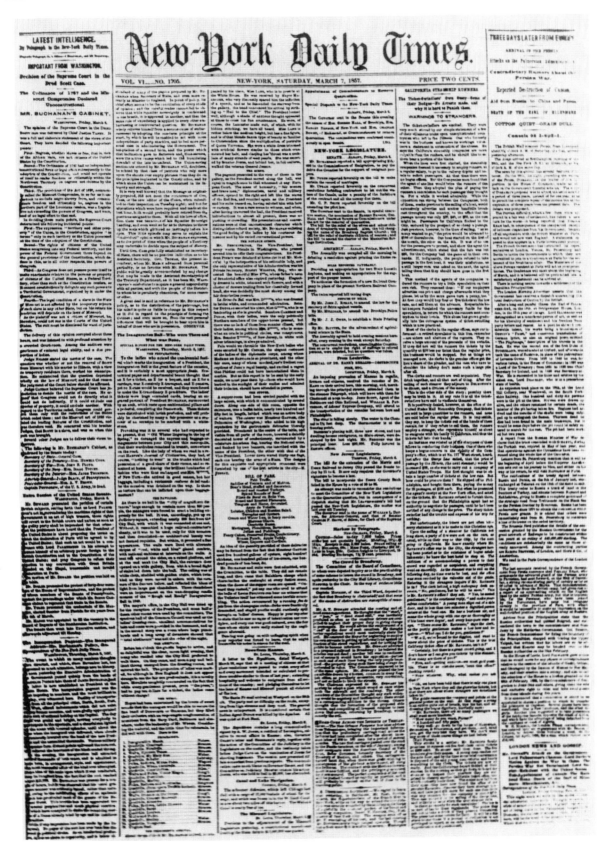

Front page of the New-York Daily Times *for 7 March 1857, featuring a report on the Dred Scott decision*

By 1857 the *Times* was a stable business in need of a suitable home, which Raymond and associates designed and built that year. Unlike the traditional dingy, back alley editorial offices Raymond had known when he arrived in New York, the new five-story Times Building at Nassau Street and Park Row was a monument fit for a national newspaper, including a reference library possibly unequaled at any other paper. Raymond was inventing the modern newspaper enterprise.

The *Times* would pass other journalistic crossroads during these years as well. In May 1857 the paper adopted a new policy of political independence. Accused by both sides of unscrupulous posturing, Raymond nonetheless announced that the paper was "hereafter entirely independent of all Political Parties—judging all events and all men upon their merits." What difficulty that principle involved was soon apparent. When his chief Washington reporter uncovered evidence of fraud in the House, Raymond was summoned to testify at hearings of a special subcommittee convened not so much to investigate the reported corruption as to discover the paper's source for the story. Raymond refused that request, insisting that "whenever any person communicates to the Editor information touching public affairs which it is important for the public to know, the confidence will be kept under all circumstances, and at any hazard." The *Times* reporter was barred from the House, though the paper's allegations were later confirmed and four House members were expelled.

Civic and family duties called for Raymond's attention during this hiatus from politics. He became a trustee of the New York Infirmary for Indigent Women and Children and assisted the founders (which included his wife) of the New York Woman's Hospital. The bonds of his marriage began to loosen in the summer of 1857 when Juliette sailed with the children to Europe, ostensibly to provide them a worthy education. Raymond spent the summer with the family overseas, returning to New York in October a leading editor and politician, but a lonely man.

Anxious to visit Europe again, Raymond found in the Franco-Austrian War of 1859 an ex-

The third home of the New-York Times, *completed in the spring of 1858. Located at the corner of Park Row and Nassau Street, the building was the first modern newspaper office.*

cuse to try front line battle reporting—and to visit his family in Paris. With his friend Judge James Forsyth and *Times* correspondent William Johnston (pen name "Malakoff"), Raymond boarded trains and mule carts to observe Napoleon III's exploits firsthand. By mid-June the French and Sardinian armies were massed outside Solferino, Italy, held by the Austrians for what was to be the decisive battle of the war. Raymond and Johnston provided American readers gruesome reports of war's brutality.

Though Raymond and Johnston were the only U.S. journalists to see the carnage, they had European competitors to beat with the story. Through Johnston's friendship with French officers and Mrs. Raymond's help in Paris, the story, composed immediately following the battle, was rushed to Paris by French couriers and placed aboard the next departing ship. Printed in the *Times* eighteen days later, the story was the first complete account to reach the United States. Raymond left Johnston with the armies, returned to Paris, gathered his family onto a steamer, and returned to New York with journalistic credits not soon forgotten.

Foreign conflict was soon replaced in the col-

Raymond's wife, Juliette Weaver Raymond, and their children in Switzerland in 1858. Mrs. Raymond is holding Aimee; standing (left to right) are Mary, Henry, and Lucy; Walter is seated in front (courtesy of Mrs. George T. Lambert).

umns of the *Times* by rumors of war between the states. In the summer of 1860 Raymond attended the Republican convention in Chicago as a Weed lieutenant firmly committed to advancing Seward as the only viable national candidate. Greeley, however, spent much of the convention arguing that Seward was far too radical to win the Southern moderates, while Joseph Medill of the *Chicago Press and Tribune* was part of a Midwest caucus grooming Abraham Lincoln. Raymond had recently been critical of the party's sectionalism, but when the national platform affirmed states' rights as a constitutional guarantee, Raymond once again embraced his old party and set to work to save a tenuous union. Following John Brown's hanging, of which he approved, Raymond said, "The union was made for all sections alike. Each must tolerate many things which it may not be able to approve in the opinions and prejudices and conduct of the other. Each must be ready to come forward in the proper spirit, waive some of its extreme demands or claims, and even something of its rights in order to preserve this Union as a whole." His was a conservative position, and when Lincoln won the party's nomination on the third ballot, Raymond swallowed his disappointment and joined the committee traveling to Springfield to inform and congratulate the winner. The *Times* was not quick to pump the Lincoln candidacy, but as the campaign progressed Raymond made his loyalty to Republican principles clear in a series of four open letters to William Yancey, a Southern secessionist who had traveled north to argue the constitutionality of disunion. The letters were published as *Disunion and Slavery* (1861?). Raymond argued against Yancey that the Constitution could not be rewritten, nor could the Union tolerate secession. Disunion meant war, he declared, though war was not his own choice. As the new year dawned, the best Raymond and other Northern moderates could hope for was that Southern moderates, especially in the border states, could be persuaded to accept Lincoln's victory as the best hope on a darkening horizon.

The following months made clear, however, that appeasement of Southern sympathies was a chimera. And Lincoln, Raymond believed, was too slow, too bogged down in making political appointments, to act on the disunion issue. In early April 1861 the *Times* published a blistering editorial calling for a national policy and accusing Lincoln of "a blindness and stolidity without a parallel in the history of intelligent statesmanship." Only days later, on 12 April the policy of Lincoln's administration was settled when Southern cannons fired on Fort Sumter. The *Times* correspondent in Charleston (who was later arrested as a spy but released) wired a terse message to New York: "War"!

With hope for peace gone, Raymond quickly took up the Northern cause, remaining with Lincoln even when more radical editors were urging a negotiated settlement.

The *Times* called upon women to meet with Mrs. Raymond to prepare bandages for the coming casualties. From this call emerged the U.S. Sanitary Commission. Raymond found it hard to stay in New York when the tempo of war was centering on Washington. Eager to be part of the action, he traveled to the capital in June and was at Bull Run to observe and record the first armed conflict. Around two o'clock on 21 July, when Gen. Irvin McDowell was claiming victory for the North, Raymond slipped into Centreville to file his dispatch. By the time he returned to the battle, however, rebel reinforcements had begun to rout the Northern volunteers, and Raymond was caught in the wild retreat to Washington. Once in the capital, he filed an update, but that story was held up by a government censor who had not yet received the commander's own report. The *Herald* beat the *Times* by two days, and Raymond's reporting reputation was tarnished by the *Times*'s early and partial account.

Raymond spent the war years traveling between New York, Albany, Washington, and the battlefields. After the long rest given the Army of the Potomac in the fall of 1861, Raymond joined many other anxious Northerners in support of Gen. George McClellan's Peninsula campaign in early 1862. He was in Virginia to observe the Battle of the Seven Days, in which Robert E. Lee pushed McClellan back to the James River and saved Richmond, and he became a kind of personal adviser to Gen. Ambrose E. Burnside during the aftermath of Fredericksburg. Raymond kept his course during the Union disasters of 1862 and 1863, while rival editors, notably Greeley, urged that hostilities end before Northern resources and manpower were exhausted. Even when Lee's troops crossed into Pennsylvania in the summer of 1863 and sent the North into panic, Raymond saw an opportunity for victory. Rational and decisive action would crush the overextended Virginians, Raymond wrote.

The draft riots that quickly followed Meade's victory at Gettysburg nearly destroyed the *Tribune*, and Raymond, unwilling to see his own investment smashed by clubs and stones, mounted Gatling guns on the roof and in the business office and issued rifles to the staff. But the draft was rescinded and the mobs returned home. The mob had abetted the Southern cause: Meade's troops had been called from Pennsylvania to restore order in New York, and Lee was able to retreat without the pressure of Northern pursuers.

As the war plodded along, the *Times* and Raymond lent more and more support to administration policies. Arbitrary arrests and the suspending of habeas corpus were "small prices to pay" for the preservation of constitutional rule, he wrote. Raymond supported Lincoln's plan to compensate slaveholders as part of the difficult transition ahead. It was a conservative scheme and fit well Raymond's prewar proclivities toward rational and brotherly relations between North and South. Raymond urged Lincoln not to issue the Emancipation Proclamation but rather to make emancipation a military tool in the hands of advancing generals. Lincoln ignored the advice.

While his paper prospered on war news—the *Times* sold for three cents in 1863 and four cents in 1864, with the presses hardly able to meet demand—Raymond was pursuing political ambitions again. He had been elected to the state assembly in 1861 and had become speaker, probably because Weed was away in Europe seeking foreign aid for the North. He worked hard for the moderate Union party, a coalition of Republicans and disenchanted Democrats who wished to put petty party differences behind them in a bold quest for a unified political front; its leaders were hopeful of isolating the radicals and building an organization to preside over postwar reconstruction. But the war was going badly, and the Union party suffered disaster in the 1862 elections. Late that year Raymond nourished hopes of replacing Preston King in the U.S. Senate, and made a pilgrimage to Albany to implore Weed's blessing. But the powerful slatemaker favored Edwin Morgan, twice New York's governor, who won the Senate seat in February 1863. Raymond wrote in his journal that he regretted having sought the nomination at all. His major political contributions that year were ideas: he argued for pressing the war to a conclusive victory; he urged reconciliation of interests with the South instead of the vengeful exaction of reparations; and he insisted that Southern members of Congress should be seated as soon as loyalty oaths could be administered in occupied territories. This was essentially Lincoln's policy as well, and both leaders faced impassioned opposition because of it.

Northern victories were scarce after Gettysburg. While bluecoats dominated the western front, in the East, where political power lay, the war was stagnating. In May 1864 Grant wasted 50,000 lives in the futile Wilderness campaign, and Lincoln, in a move no astute politician would have considered, called for 500,000 draftees from the war-weary North to fill the army's decimated ranks. Calls for peace through negotiated settlement were heard often, and Lincoln was nearly drawn into unofficial negotiations by Horace Greeley, who was roundly embarrassed when his role in the scheme became public.

Raymond approached the 1864 elections a prominent Union party figure. Considered a Weed-Seward lackey by his opponents, he was nonetheless widely admired for his rhetorical skills and for his belief in the Northern cause. The election of 1864 needed both qualities, and Raymond's talents were fully used. He wrote a campaign biography of Lincoln; drafted the party's platform, which included unconditional surrender by the South, a constitutional amendment abolishing slavery, and a railroad to the Pacific; argued persuasively for Andrew Johnson as the vice-presidential nominee; and was elected chairman of the National Union Executive Committee. This office carried with it the responsibility of raising a campaign chest; Raymond did so with all the muscle of a "machine" politician, assessing federal employees a percentage of their salary and firing those who favored the Democratic nominee, General McClellan. In October, Raymond, busy working for the national ticket, was himself nominated by the Union Central Committee for a House seat in a district controlled by the Democratic Tammany Hall. Raymond accepted with misgivings, because the Union General Committee had put up the dashing Col. Rush Hawkins for the same seat, and Raymond, unable to negotiate a truce with the inflated war hero, faced a split vote in his district.

Fortunately for the Republicans, the prosecution of the war turned in the North's favor as the election drew closer. Sherman captured Atlanta in September, making the Democratic peace platform appear to be a premature capitulation. Despite the change in the tide of war, Raymond urged a sham peace overture as a campaign ploy to assure Northern voters of Lincoln's virtuous intentions and Confederate President Jefferson Davis's intransigence. The plan involved a delegation offering peace if Davis would agree to abide by the Constitution, all "other questions"—namely, slavery—to be addressed by a popular convention. Raymond was convinced that Davis's certain refusal

would accrue political advantages for Lincoln. The president was nearly convinced, and had drafted instructions for such a delegation when his cabinet persuaded him to scrap the plan. On election night, Lincoln held an electoral vote edge of 212 to 21, though the popular vote was much closer. Raymond's margin was a narrow 464 votes, but it was enough to win his only federal office.

Raymond's support of Lincoln became even more firm as the second administration got under way. "With malice toward none, with charity for all" was Lincoln's clarion call for Reconstruction, and to these sentiments Raymond pledged his loyalty. He would hear none of the Radicals' militarism and wished that state governments and federal offices might be organized and filled by Southern voters as quickly as they pledged allegiance to the Union. For a time it appeared that Lincoln's policy of repatriation would survive his assassination, but Johnson proved to be an incompetent executive, pulling down with him the conservatives who wished to get the Union working again without exacting retribution from the rebels.

In the spring of 1865 Raymond's family left New York to resume life in Europe, the temperamental Juliette convinced that Continental schools were superior to American schools. Only seventeen-year-old Henry remained behind, and his departure to attend Yale left the family home a lifeless retreat for the tired Raymond. The Radicals who had been contained in the past now spoke forcefully again, and the Weed-Raymond team fell back on patronage to keep the New York Union convention that September under conservative control. In other Northern states the Radicals were gaining support, and when Raymond repaired to Washington for the thirty-ninth congressional session, he had not long to wait for the hardfisted "conquered province" school to assert its will.

Early in the session, which opened in December 1865, Thaddeus Stevens of Pennsylvania, the so-called dictator of the House, proposed a joint Senate-House Committee of Fifteen to screen Southern requests for representation in Congress. It was a clear ploy to block Johnson's policies, but so cleverly did Stevens present the resolution that Raymond cast his vote in favor. Raymond discovered his error only days after the committee was formed when he attempted to promote the immediate seating of a Tennessee delegation; the Tennesseans were not admitted until the following July. On 21 December Raymond made his first major speech in Congress. In the interest of "a complete restoration of the Union," he urged Congress

*Thaddeus Stevens of Pennsylvania, the "dictator" of the House
of Representatives and Raymond's archenemy
(Frederic H. Meserve Collection)*

constitutional grounds; retaliating, the Committee of Fifteen pigeonholed plans to admit the Tennesseans. Johnson's veto, however, was sustained, and Raymond joined a diminishing group in celebrating a brief presidential victory. It was to be the last such celebration.

In early March a Radical-supported Civil Rights Bill which forbade discrimination on grounds of race, came before the House. Raymond opposed the bill's imposition on state sovereignty, however much he might have applauded its principle of equal treatment under law, but on 15 March the bill passed easily. Johnson vetoed it, again citing constitutional grounds, but this time the Radicals were fully prepared to override the veto. Among New York Union-Republicans, only Raymond stood with the president; the end of political influence for both was at hand.

Raymond's opponents accused him of double-dealing, and their argument appeared cogent in June when Raymond voted—against Johnson—for the Fourteenth Amendment. His detractors labeled him "The Trimmer" for opposing the Civil Rights Bill but supporting an amendment to achieve the same purposes. Raymond countered that the latter was a constitutionally sanctioned means of winning equal treatment for blacks.

Still chairman of the National Union Executive Committee, Raymond reluctantly agreed to support the call for a national convention in August. He feared that Southern Democrats would quickly fill the gaps left by discontented Union-Republicans, and that the party would ultimately pass to Democratic control. Radical Republicans feared the same, and in a closed caucus in July Stevens engineered a resolution excommunicating any Republican who attended the Philadelphia convention. Though his influence was dissipated in committees, Raymond succeeded in keeping out the copperheads and retaining a semblance of hope for a national Republican movement. Overall, Raymond was pleased with the work of the convention, bringing it to a close with a ringing appeal to elect a Congress that would admit representatives of every state and thus complete the Union and buttress constitutional government. Raymond later estimated that the *Times* lost $100,000 in revenue and an incalculable amount of influence as a result of Philadelphia, since many readers thought the paper was swinging to the Democrats.

The Radicals charged Raymond with aligning with Democrats to defeat Unionists in Congress, and four anti-Raymond men on the national committee called a meeting in Philadelphia on 3 Sep-

to abandon the "conquered province" theory and exact of the South no more than "all just guarantees for their future loyalty to the Constitution" and proper care and protection for the "helpless and friendless freedmen." The speech was a formal challenge to Stevens, who had asserted his position that the Southern states should be treated as "conquered provinces" three days earlier.

In late January 1866 Raymond made his second address to Congress, arguing that the "conquered province" doctrine was not constitutional, that "the dead of the contending hosts sleep beneath the soil of a common country, and under one common flag." The speech was one of Raymond's best, but it fell on deaf Republican ears; Stevens called it "blasphemy." As Radical power increased, the Unionists in Congress began to capitulate, especially with Johnson and the Democrats growing closer in policy and program. In mid-February Johnson vetoed the Freedmen's Bureau Bill on

tember 1866 to elect a new chairman. Raymond responded with a call for a meeting in New York on the same day, reminding committeemen that under party rules only his call was valid. When the two meetings convened, Raymond's New York group was outnumbered seventeen to eight; he was accused in Philadelphia of abandoning Union principles and affiliating with the party's enemies, and was summarily drummed out of office. Raymond protested on procedural grounds but his defeat was confirmed by a Union state convention in Syracuse two days later. Now his only hope was at the National Union state convention in Albany. Raymond did not attend; Weed did but was ineffectual. Tammany Democrats controlled the floor, nominating the Democratic mayor of New York for governor and nominally adopting the positions set forth in Philadelphia. But the ruse did not escape Raymond. He could see that Democrats now controlled his wing of the party, and to the amazement of friend and foe alike, he swung the *Times* around to support the Radical gubernatorial candidate. Again his critics accused him of trimming, but Raymond argued that the party, not the *Times*, had changed its voice. Nevertheless, Raymond's paper now opposed the president, and more so after Johnson's drunken western tour that autumn.

Raymond returned to Washington for the second session resigned to a subordinate role in a Radical-controlled House. At the first party caucus he had to defend his right to attend against the rule banning all who had attended the Philadelphia convention. He was allowed to remain.

Raymond voted against the resolution to impeach President Johnson and opposed the Military Reconstruction Bill proposed by Stevens. Civil government, not military dictatorship, was the South's great and immediate need, he said. The bill passed the House but was substantially changed in the Senate, so that Raymond finally voted in favor of ratification. When Congress adjourned in March Raymond's political career was over. He was later nominated by Johnson as minister to Austria but the hostile Senate tabled the nomination and Raymond never received the standard reward for service to his party.

During the spring Raymond reestablished himself at the *Times*, and busy with the growth of the Associated Press, he was soon steeped again in his first profession. By summer, however, he was suffering from headaches and muscle twitches—signs of fatigue—and decided to take a holiday. With son Henry and other companions, he took passage to Europe, where he signed up foreign correspondents for the *Times* and toured Austria with his family. Back in New York in late summer, he learned that he had been named a delegate to the Republican state convention, but declined to attend—a wise decision, as it turned out, since controlling Radicals rejected all conservatives as party traitors. In the *Times*, Raymond asserted his intention to stay out of politics and invest his energy in editing the newspaper.

His voice muted, Raymond still sounded the moderate cause. He deplored the impeachment resolution passed by the House that winter, believing that it meant revolution against constitutional balances. When the Senate failed to convict, Raymond hailed the vote as a move toward saving the nation. He endorsed Grant's campaign in 1868 and even spoke for him at some rallies. He wavered from his resolution to stay out of politics when he accepted the presidency of the city's Union Republican Central Committee; but he resigned the post when it became apparent that the party's factions were not interested in reconciliation. Only a month after Grant's inauguration, the editor began to write of disillusionment born of scandal, corruption, and thievery in high places. Raymond's melancholy was eased when his family returned to New York; but it returned with his son Walter's death—the third of his children to die in infancy or youth—in February 1869. That June, following an afternoon visit to Walter's grave, Raymond stopped his carriage for the last time in front of the *Times*. Later in the evening he apparently visited Rose Eytinge, a New York actress whose friendship he had cultivated during Juliette's long residency in Europe. About midnight a carriage crew deposited Raymond—unconscious from a stroke—inside the door of his home; he died the next morning.

Raymond held thirty-four of the *Times*'s 100 shares of stock at his death. George Jones was the next largest stockholder with thirty shares. It was at first thought that Henry, Jr., about to graduate from Yale, would succeed his father, but the newspaper's three directors—Jones, Leonard Jerome, and James B. Taylor—elected John Bigelow editor. (Henry worked for a time at the *Chicago Tribune*, then bought the *Germantown* [Pennsylvania] *Telegraph*.) The *Times* was facing a battle against the corrupt Tammany machine of William Marcy (Boss) Tweed, who tried to neutralize the paper by buying control of its stock. Jones saved the *Times* from falling into Tweed's hands in 1871 when he arranged the sale of Raymond family interests to E. B. Morgan of Aurora, New York, and after a fourteen-month editorial campaign, one of the most courageous any newspaper has undertaken, Tweed was beaten, his corruptions exposed.

The *Times* remained prosperous for another decade, then began a slow decline. Republicans left the paper when Jones could not support the party nominee in 1884. Bankruptcy followed Jones's death in 1891. When Adolph Ochs bought the paper in 1896, it was losing $1,000 a day, had millions in unpaid bills, and had no hope of recovery. Ochs of course, with the help of editor in chief Charles Miller and—after 1904—managing editor Carr Van Anda, turned the *Times*'s fortunes around and made it the great "newspaper of record" that it is today. Into a marketplace of partisan and sensational journals, Raymond brought responsible news coverage without sensationalism or radical editorial biases. He had his own biases, of course, and the paper he built advocated a political posture of conservative, moderate federalism. Raymond gave readers foreign news and was a prime mover in organizing the Associated Press. He has been criticized for trying to lead two careers—politician and journalist—that are not often successfully combined. Indeed, the *Times* might have been greater

with Raymond's full-time leadership. But his personality had both sides to it, and he lived in a time when the future of the nation depended on wisdom being available in both arenas.

Biographies:

Augustus Maverick, *Henry J. Raymond and the New York Press for Thirty Years* (Hartford, Conn.: A. S. Hale, 1870);

Francis Brown, *Raymond of the Times* (New York: Norton, 1951).

References:

Meyer Berger, *The Story of the New York Times* (New York: Simon & Schuster, 1951);

Elmer Davis, *History of the New York Times* (New York: New York Times, 1921).

Papers:

Many of Raymond's letters are at the New York Public Library, the New York Historical Society, Harvard's Widener Library, Boston Public Library, and in the Abraham Lincoln Papers at the Library of Congress.

Robert Barnwell Rhett

(21 December 1800-14 September 1876)

Elizabeth Brown Dickey
University of South Carolina

MAJOR POSITION HELD: Part-owner, *Charleston (S.C.) Mercury* (1848-1865).

Robert Barnwell Rhett, sometimes called "the Father of Secession," used both oratory and the power of the press to persuade others. He advocated as early as 1832 that the South withdraw from the Union. He first distinguished himself as a politician in South Carolina and Washington, D.C. Later, his fiery editorials in the *Charleston Mercury*, one of the leading newspapers of the antebellum South, supported secession but criticized the Confederate government and the policies of President Jefferson Davis. Although Rhett aroused Southerners to secede, he assumed that the North would not fight to preserve the Union. Early in 1861 his

editorials predicted a peaceable secession.

Robert Barnwell Smith was born in Beaufort, South Carolina, the fourth son of James and Marianna Gough Smith. His ancestors included Sir John Yeamans, one of the Lords Proprietors and a governor of South Carolina; Governors Landgrave Smith and James Moore; Col. John Barnwell, who defeated the Tuscarora Indians; and Col. William Rhett, who conquered the pirates off the coast of the Carolinas.

Smith was admitted to the South Carolina Bar in 1822 and practiced law with Robert W. Barnwell in Walterboro. He began his political career in 1826 when he was elected to the South Carolina House of Representatives from St. Bartholomew's parish in what is now Colleton County. The following

Robert Barnwell Rhett (courtesy of Mr. Robert R. Lewis)

year he married Elizabeth Washington Burnet. He resigned his House seat to become South Carolina attorney general from 1832 to 1836 and was elected to Congress in 1837. That year, Smith and his five brothers changed their name to Rhett, in order to perpetuate the name of Colonel Rhett, a family hero whose lineage was dying out.

An attention getter during the first years of his congressional career, Rhett delivered sensational speeches filled with emotion. Fellow congressman and secessionist Danial Wallace wrote:

> He, from the first, made a decided impression upon the House, and was one of the few who commanded the attention of the body whenever he arose to speak, and soon established a reputation for ability and inflexible devotion to principle, which he ever after retained. He acquired, in fact, the position of a leader in the Democratic ranks of the House upon all important measures . . .
>
> In all his efforts he spoke with ability, and always with effect. Of the few members of that body who could at all times command the ear of the House, he was one. He possessed the rare faculty of ascertaining at the proper time the sense and temper of the body, and the address and ability to make both available. He had acquired, in an eminent degree, the skill and quick judgment of the parliamentarian, and knew when and

how to move and when and how to speak.

Rhett began to urge secession while he was in Congress, and he reinforced his position during a dinner in his honor in Bluffton, South Carolina, on 27 July 1844. This policy, known as the Bluffton Movement, called for states to nullify the tariff of 1842 and to take separate action if they thought national legislation to be unsuitable. Although the Bluffton Movement was short-lived, it marked the beginning of Rhett's national prominence.

In 1850 Rhett was elected to fill the remaining two years of the Senate term of George McDuffie; the seat had formerly been held by John C. Calhoun. Early in his political career Rhett had supported Calhoun, but the two became enemies after Rhett grew radical in his beliefs. Historians say that Rhett is the only South Carolinian ever to defy Calhoun without ending his political career. He valued the friendship of James Louis Petigru, "my tutor in boyhood, my friend in early manhood, my better friend in advanced life, whom neither time nor fortune, private duties nor troubles, nor the angry public contests and differences of more than 30 years, ever induced to say to me an unkind word or do an unkind deed."

In 1850 Rhett addressed the Nashville, Tennessee, convention of slaveholding states and continued his secession campaign. He told the delegates that the agricultural South and industrial North should be two countries because of cultural and economic differences. "You have tamely acquiesced until to hate and persecute the South has become a high passport to honor and power in the Union," he admonished the assembled leaders. "If Congress can legislate at all between the master and slave in a State, where can its power be stayed? It can abolish slavery in the States."

He returned to South Carolina at the end of his two-year term in the Senate in 1852 and encouraged the state to secede from the Union. In her diary of the Civil War, Mary Boykin Chestnut called Rhett "the greatest of seceders." In her biography of Rhett, Laura White wrote: "One can scarcely understand the action of the people of South Carolina in 1860 without including in his ken the remarkable activities of one man, whose eloquent and fiery preaching of the gospel of liberty and self government and of revolution to achieve these ends, beat upon their ears in season and out of season for over 30 years. . . . This propagandist was Robert Barnwell Rhett, the enfant terrible of South Carolina politics."

Rhett was devastated when his wife died in

1852 giving birth to the couple's twelfth child. Twelve years after his wife's death, he wrote his daughter Elsie Rhett Lewis, "You bear the name of her, the shadow of whose presence and love still rests upon me, and will I believe mingle with my last pulsation of life." About a year after his first wife's death, however, he married Catharine Herbert Dent of Maryland.

Robert Barnwell Rhett, Jr., said of his father: "A man of retiring disposition, amiable temper and great affection, his happiness was in his home. Self-educated in the country, and accustomed in youth to a secluded life, he was indifferent to the associations of men and was, therefore, well known only to a few. But he delighted in the society of women and children, of whom he was very fond. Morally he was one of the purest men this country has ever produced. It may truly be said of him that he never had any vices, great or small." Elsie Rhett Lewis said that her father "was six feet in height, with a rather small and beautifully shaped head, blue-gray eyes, beautiful teeth and a most charming smile and delightful laugh. In his youth he must have been very gay and full of fun, he always enjoyed a good joke very much and told one capitally. His temperament was nervous and mercurial, he was quick in movement and quick-tempered, but entirely self-controlled."

In 1861 Rhett was elected to the Confederate Provisional Congress, which organized the Confederate States of America. He quickly became disillusioned with this group when they did not elect him president of the Confederacy, although he did become a member of the Confederate Congress in Montgomery, Alabama, for a short time. He then returned to Charleston and began influencing policy and writing editorials for the *Mercury*, which the Rhett family had partially owned since the 1840s and purchased outright in 1858.

Prior to the war, the *Mercury* was an aggressive leader of the Southern states' rights press. Its editorials were read and discussed far beyond the South Carolina borders. In 1858 the paper was edited by John Heart. He and some friends, including James H. Hammond, a political rival of Rhett, had devised a scheme to purchase the *Mercury*. Because it was so heavily in debt, however, no agreements were reached and Heart's partners agreed to let Rhett, Jr., have control of the paper. They expected it to last no longer than a year. Even the Rhetts doubted its success and tried to sell the paper. When no buyers could be found, they joined forces with the antisecessionist *Charleston Standard* and backed the Democratic party.

While most of the editorials in the *Mercury* were unsigned, their content closely resembles the beliefs of Rhett, Sr. The rival *Charleston Courier* fought secession and called for moderation, but the *Mercury* took a radical viewpoint and said that the South should become a separate nation. The Rhetts believed that secession was the last chance of salvation for the South.

When South Carolina representatives voted on 20 December 1860 to secede from the Union, the *Mercury* published an "extra" edition in only five minutes. The newspaper said the day would be inscribed on the calendars of the world as an "epoch in the history of the human race."

After the war broke out with the firing on Fort Sumter on 14 April 1861, the *Mercury* supported the new nation. Through editorials, poems by subscribers, news accounts written by correspondents, and advertisements, the Rhetts tried to keep up morale. In October 1861 the paper ran this advertisement for recruits: "A great want supplied—the South must provide and supply its wants from its own resources. Now is the time to aid and support home knowledge, ability and enterprise." "Appeal to the Soldiers" is typical of the poetry printed in the *Mercury* during the war years:

Ye Gallant Hearts of kindred strain
Say, Shall I ask your gifts in vain?
The swelling breast, the flashing eye,
The maiden's startling tears reply,
No gift's enough they say, for those
Whose arms have tamed our hateful foes;
Oh, never shall the tale be told
That Southern hearts or hands withhold.
Ought the devoted warriors need,
Who march and toil and watch and bleed,
To guard their country's ancient fame
Her homes to save from sword and flame,
Her honor from pollution's breath
Her beautiful land from worse than death;
No! Let them feel, though far they roam,
They live in every heart at home.

Although he was a champion of the Southern cause, Rhett's editorials continually found fault with Confederate President Jefferson Davis, his policies, his battle plans, his cabinet members, and his followers. During each crisis of the war, Rhett's opposition grew more intense. Rhett believed Davis to be more interested in remaining in the Union than in leading a struggling new nation. On 29 October 1861 the *Mercury* said: "Our readers will remember that some time has passed since we ventured to assert that President Davis and no one else

CHARLESTON

MERCURY

EXTRA:

Passed unanimously at 1.15 o'clock, P. M. December 20th, 1860.

AN ORDINANCE

To dissolve the Union between the State of South Carolina and other States united with her under the compact entitled "The Constitution of the United States of America."

We, the People of the State of South Carolina, in Convention assembled, do declare and ordain, and it is hereby declared and ordained,

That the Ordinance adopted by us in Convention, on the twenty-third day of May, in the year of our Lord one thousand seven hundred and eighty-eight, whereby the Constitution of the United States of America was ratified, and also, all Acts and parts of Acts of the General Assembly of this State, ratifying amendments of the said Constitution, are hereby repealed; and that the union now subsisting between South Carolina and other States, under the name of "The United States of America," is hereby dissolved.

THE

UNION

IS

DISSOLVED!

Extra edition of Rhett's Charleston Mercury, *announcing the secession of South Carolina from the Union*

was responsible for the war, or rather antiwar policy of our army on the Potomac. By a strong perversion of truth, the newspaper press of the Confederate states were persisting in the charges that the Generals in command were guilty of the extraordinary and unprecedented inactivity which characterized the army. We endeavored to correct this injustice and pointed to the true source of this command policy. President Davis rejected the plan of General Beauregard to take Washington and relieve Maryland." Rhett's criticism of Davis was severe. On 4 March 1862, the paper said:

> If President Davis would give up the notion of being a Washington, Jackson and Calhoun combined and find his proper level, like Presidents Tyler and Polk, if he would surround himself in the Cabinet with strong men of the South and listen to their advice giving full scope to their sagacity and energies; and if he would leave strategy to the Commanding Generals of the Confederate armies, supplying them according to their conduct of the war, the South would very soon be redeemed from the present position of depression, difficulty and danger into which mismanagement and a great want of foresight she has been thrust.
>
> But should he subvert himself by flattery and sycophants and hug to himself the delusion of being a great and universal genius; should he assume to control and direct the whole machinery of the Government of which he is elected head—and should Congress sit in secret session aiding and abetting the Executive—whether in wisdom or in folly—while the people, whose servants they profess to be, are kept wholly in the dark as to the doings of their government, this matter will be in line for improvement.

On 13 May 1862 Rhett wrote, "The responsibility for all the blunders and inefficiences is practically, as well as constitutionally on the President." Ten days later, an editorial said, "That President Davis endangers our cause, we do not doubt . . . and if an election tomorrow was to come off for the Confederacy, we do not believe that he would get the vote of a single state in the Confederacy."

Rhett also wrote editorials damning the army, which seemed reluctant to fight. On 21 January 1862 the paper said, "For long months war has existed between the United States and the Confederate States, and so far, in its history little has been done on either side except to enlist, equip and drill troops. Preparation for invasion and preparation

for defense have occupied the two countries and their governments."

Less than a month later, the *Mercury* again questioned Davis's war policies. An editorial on 11 February said:

> But the great practical question is—how shall war be carried on, so as to reach our objective of peace and independence in the shortest time. The shorter the war, the cheaper and less bloody it must be. Our readers know our views. We have frankly expressed them. The South had, at the commencement of the war, two instruments for a speedy termination of it. The first was an active, resolute aggressive policy. Our untrained soldiery of the enemy. Whilst the motives which sustained us in battle were higher than theirs. With our ports blockaded and few manufacturers and workshops, we had little to gain and much to lose, in comparison, by delay and preparation.
>
> Promptness and vigor in a rough and ready war was our course. For this policy twelve months' volunteers were as good as ten years' volunteers. This war would not have lasted beyond the year. It could have terminated by the fall of Washington and Baltimore.

The *Mercury* also complained that newspaper reporters were not allowed to cover the proceedings of the Confederate Congress. On 21 January 1862 the paper said:

> In order that the people should govern themselves, they must know the acts of their representatives. If they do not know them, representation is a farce. Whether the representative is using their power for his own benefit rather than theirs, or as a tool of others, or an enemy, instead of a faithful agent, can only be known to the people by the publication of the proceedings of their representatives.
>
> Secrecy makes the representative a ruler of the people, without any responsibility to them and annihilates the power of the people to rule themselves. In a word, it destroys representative free government.

The *Mercury* also held members of the Confederate Congress responsible for the South's inability to win the war. On 22 May 1862 an editorial stated: "The great error of the Provensial Congress was not that it failed to support and carry out all the recommendations of the President for carrying on the war. It was not even that it did not originate measures of itself to give efficiency to the War. But its great error was in its subserviency to Executive dictation. When the President vetoed its measures to carry on the war, it succumbed and instead of overruling the Executive veto by the 2/3 vote the Constitution required, it supported the Executive veto and nullified itself and voted down its own measures. . . . It was the duty of the Congress to act independently of the Executive and to have originated and passed, despite his vetos, all the great measures the emergencies of the Confederate states required. This was the duty of the Congress, and if it had been performed in an open day, with unclosed doors, the President would have been compelled to make his administration efficient, or he would have been displaced from power. The evil effects of abdicating its constitutional power, in submission to Executive dictation, is seen in the disasters and troubles of the Confederate states."

Early in the 1860s the *Mercury* editors expected the war to be over in a few weeks because of "superior fighting men in the South, their familiarity with martial arts and the quality of leadership Southern generals could provide." Later, after the North appeared to be heading for victory, an editorial quoted a soldier's poem: "It is better for South Carolina's soil to have bodies beneath it than prisoners on top of it."

In 1863, when the South was in ruin, Rhett and the *Mercury* made an effort to build up morale. Rhett began a campaign to be elected to a new Confederate Congress. The *Mercury* pointed out the many faults of the Davis administration and said that new leadership could perhaps turn the war around. But Rhett was defeated. Laura White analyzed the election results this way: "The final, heart-breaking repudiation of the 'father of secession' had been made by his own third district. No more tragic or ironical an anticlimax could have put the period to a career punctuated from the beginning by disappointment and defeat."

Other original secessionists also lost leadership positions. In November 1863 the *Mercury* said, "Those who made this revolution do not direct it." Less than two years later, the *Mercury* was suspended just before the evacuation of Charleston. Rhett, Jr., revived it in 1866 and his father wrote an occasional editorial but the paper failed again in 1868.

Rhett suffered personally during the war. One of his sons, Lt. Robert Wood Rhett, returned from studying in Germany to enter the Confederate army and died from a wound. Another son,

Maj. Alfred Rhett, killed the commander of Fort Sumter in a duel; later, he was named commander of the fort. Rhett, Jr., an articulate and accomplished writer, believed that he should promote his father's ideas. In addition to editing the *Mercury,* he served in the South Carolina legislature during the war.

Rhett had interests in various plantations and owned slaves before the war. His plantations included Drainfield and the Oaks on the Ashepoo River in South Carolina and a rice plantation in the Altahama district of Georgia. During the Reconstruction period he rented Castle Dismal, a plantation near Eufala, Alabama. In a letter to his daughter he wrote of debts which could not be paid, crops which burned up from the heat, and a house with neither furniture nor books. Even his health failed.

His last years were spent in St. James Parish, Louisiana, where he wrote an occasional editorial for Rhett, Jr., who was now editing the *New Orleans Picayune;* he also wrote magazine articles and tutored his grandson. For some years he had suffered from cancer, and in 1875 he had four operations on his face. He described himself as "too hideous a spectacle to be seen by any but those whose love and affection can overlook my diseased deformities."

He died on 14 September 1876, and his body was brought to Charleston for burial in the family plot in Magnolia Cemetery. His grave is unmarked. After his death, the *Charleston News and Courier* called him "the paramount advocate of that secession of South Carolina which, through him, more than any other, became an accomplished fact."

Biography:
Laura A. White, *Robert Barnwell Rhett: Father of Secession* (Gloucester, Mass.: Peter Smith, 1931).

References:
Donald E. Reynolds, *Editors Make War* (Nashville: Vanderbilt University Press, 1970), pp. 58, 84-85, 147, 153, 185;

Ernest B. Segars, "A Study of the Charleston (S.C.) Mercury During Robert Barnwell Rhett, Senior's Tenure as an Editorial Writer, 1861-1863," M.A. thesis, University of South Carolina, 1972;

David Duncan Wallace, *South Carolina: A Short History* (Columbia: University of South Carolina Press, 1961), pp. 397, 403-404, 422-423, 429-432, 434, 489-490, 492, 505, 509, 511-512,

515-516, 520-523, 526, 528, 533-534, 542;
C. Vann Woodward, ed., *Mary Chestnut's Civil War*
(New Haven & London: Yale University
Press, 1981).

Papers:
Papers of Robert Barnwell Rhett, Sr., are located
at the University of North Carolina in the Southern
Historical Collection.

Thomas Ritchie
(5 November 1778-2 July 1854)

John M. Butler
Louisiana State University

MAJOR POSITIONS HELD: Editor and pub-
lisher, *Richmond* (Va.) *Enquirer* (1804-1845); editor,
Richmond Compiler (1820-1833), *Crisis* (Richmond)
(1840), *Washington* (D.C.) *Union* (1845-1851).

BOOK: *Refutation of John C. Rives's Statements Concerning the Public Printing,* anonymous (Washington, D.C., 1851?).

OTHER: Benjamin Watkins Leigh, *The Letters of
Algernon Sydney, in Defense of Civil Liberty and
against the Encroachments of Military Despotism,
Written by an Eminent Citizen of Virginia, and
First Published in the Richmond Enquirer in 1818-
19. To Which Are Added, in an Appendix, the
Remarks of Mr. Ritchie as Referred to by the Author
of "Algernon Sydney" in Page 30 of This Pamphlet*
(Richmond, Va.: T. W. White, 1830).

As the editor and publisher of the *Richmond
Enquirer* for over forty years, Thomas Ritchie was
one of the most influential journalists in the South
in the first half of the nineteenth century, and his
newspaper—established with the encouragement
of Thomas Jefferson—was one of the principal
voices of the Democratic party in the United States.
Ritchie relinquished control of the *Enquirer* to his
sons in 1845 to go to Washington to start the *Union,*
the semiofficial organ of the Polk administration.
Ritchie was born in Rappahannock, Essex
County, Virginia, on 5 November 1778. The small
village, perched high on a bluff overlooking the
Rappahannock River, was one of the many small
ports along southern rivers navigable to the small
ships of that age. Ritchie's father, Archibald Ritchie, had immigrated to America around 1740. He

Thomas Ritchie (Gale International Portrait Gallery)

was one of the numerous Scottish merchants,
clerks, and factors who sought their fortunes in the
tobacco trade of the Southern colonies. Though
there was some prejudice against them on the part
of the native-born Virginians, the Scots considered
Virginia "the land of opportunity."
By 1756 Archibald Ritchie must have been
well established, for he married into the prominent
Roane family of Essex County. His marriage to
Mary Roane meant that Ritchie's business success

had gained him acceptance into the circle of the region's leading families. Mary was the sister of Spencer Roane, later chief justice of Virginia. Mary brought with her a dowry of £500, with a promise of a similar amount upon the death of her father.

Archibald Ritchie amassed a fortune trading in imported British goods. He also bought and sold Virginia corn, wheat, and tobacco and operated a ferry on the Rappahannock River; he may have owned ships as well. He also invested heavily in land and slaves. At the time of his death in 1784, Archibald owned at least seventy-five slaves and operated a sizable plantation. He was recognized as a social equal by two of the wealthiest men in Virginia, Landon Carter and John Taylor.

Thomas Ritchie was six years old when his father died. His older brother William, twenty years old, was placed in charge of Thomas and his younger brothers John and Archibald. The decline of trade around Rappahannock following the Revolutionary War affected the Ritchie wealth, but the family remained relatively prosperous.

Ritchie was educated in the small, private grammar schools and academies which served late-eighteenth-century Virginians. He learned Latin and Greek and read the ancient classics, and many years later was still recommending this method of education to young men. He became interested in science and often wrote book reviews on scientific and technical subjects after he became editor of the *Enquirer*.

He began to read law in 1796 under the tutelage of his cousin, Judge Spencer Roane, then studied medicine in Philadelphia. Finding neither profession to his liking, he turned to teaching, and joined James Ogilvie at Ogilvie's Academy in Fredericksburg, Virginia, in 1798. During his years as a teacher Ritchie continued his program of reading and study, strengthening and enlarging his earlier education, and at this period Ogilvie's influence was prominent. Ogilvie was something of a radical; he was a follower of the English writer William Godwin, author of *Political Justice* (1793), a major statement of democratic theory.

Ogilvie stressed formal oration in his educational program and insisted that students master this art. Ritchie became an effective orator, speaking at many political gatherings in later years and devoting space in the *Enquirer* to public speeches, orations, and articles about famous orators.

Ritchie left the school in 1803 and purchased a bookstore in Richmond. In 1804, with W. W. Worsley, he purchased the holdings of the then-dead *Examiner*, formerly a power in political circles in Richmond. It had been established in December 1798 as an Anti-Federalist organ by Meriwether Jones, a prominent Richmond lawyer; the scandal-mongering James T. Callendar was a contributor and briefly editor of the paper before going over to the Federalists when President Thomas Jefferson did not appoint him postmaster. Worsley was the business and mechanical partner. The *Examiner* published its final issue on 7 January 1804, and the office burned later that month. Ritchie and Worsley purchased the "good will" of the *Examiner* and 500 subscribers. The first issue of the *Richmond Enquirer* appeared on 9 May.

The *Enquirer* was established under the auspices of President Jefferson, and was part of the plan for the creation of the Democratic party. In his first article, Ritchie said: "He fondly hopes that whenever necessity or inclination shall induce him to abandon his present pursuit, he may be able to lay his hand upon his heart and indulge the consolatory reflection that he has not dishonored the high prerogatives of the press or his own personal character."

The *Enquirer* was a four-page newspaper like most others of its time. In the first issue, Ritchie announced that the paper would appear biweekly, but supplementary half-sheets were promised for the weeks covering the sessions of Congress and the General Assembly. The subscription price was four dollars a year, payable in advance; it was soon raised to five dollars. Advertising space was sold to nonsubscribers at seventy-five cents per "square in length" for the first insertion, fifty cents for each of three subsequent insertions, and thirty-three cents for each additional insertion, "long ones in the same proportion." Rates to subscribers were fifty cents for the first insertion and thirty-three cents for each subsequent one. Ritchie announced in July 1805 that he would hold advertisements to no more than five columns to leave ample room for news. The *Enquirer* was to be maintained by official patronage and by subscriptions, which rose during the first eighteen months from 500 to 1,500.

Under Ritchie's direction, the *Enquirer* came to be called "the Democratic Bible." The initial number contained certified copies of federal laws and extracts from speeches made on the anniversary of Jefferson's election to the presidency. Without patronage it could not have survived in the Federalist atmosphere of Richmond and in competition with the well-established and popular *Gazette*, the Federalist organ. From the first, Ritchie did not disguise his purpose to speak for the Jefferson administration and his expectation of compensation for such service; on the other hand, he did not propose to become a political vassal.

Unlike most Virginians of his day, he was a disciple of Adam Smith, being well versed in the principles of the *Wealth of Nations* (1776) and those of the other great thinkers of the liberal school of political economy, Ricardo, Malthus, and Say. He was equally familiar with the writings of Voltaire, Rousseau, and Paine. With them, Ritchie believed that governments had too much power and individuals too little. He was determined that Virginia should throw off whatever relics of feudalism lingered in her society and conform her thought and legislation to the genius of republicanism. To this end he considered popular education, local reforms in the existing laws and customs, and the development of the state's natural resources indispensable prerequisites.

In the first issue of the *Enquirer* Ritchie declared: "Private character was too delicate a subject for any public print, that the editor of a public paper who prostitutes it to personal abuse or party spirit may be regarded, at least in his own sphere, almost as great an enemy to the press as the despot who would wish to paralyze its political influence altogether." He stated that the object and aim of an editor should be to excite the curiosity of the people on the great changes which are every instant taking place in the conditions of society, to make them more vigilant of the conduct of their own officers and of the administration of public affairs, to bring before them the prize productions of their countrymen on general subjects and lead them to admire and imitate the efforts of genius, to spread before them the great principles of science, to give them a "sense exquisitely keen" of those varying delights from which literature proceeds, and to encourage as much of the spirit of the party as may be necessary for the elucidation of unsettled truths without mixing with it any vulgar or personal abuse. Jefferson was so impressed with Ritchie's skill and taste as a political journalist that he once spoke of him as "culling what is good from every paper as the bee from every flower."

While Ritchie was establishing his credentials in Richmond, he married on 11 February 1807 Isabella Harminson Foushee, the daughter of Dr. William Foushee, a distinguished Richmond physician. They had twelve children. On the occasion of the birth of his fifth daughter and eighth child he wrote his brother Archibald, "What a load upon a man to do justice by such a crowd and give them all a good education. However, they must do as well as they can for themselves (the boys, of course, I mean). As to the girls, they must behave well and try to fix themselves as well as they can, or live contentedly without extravagance in their father's house."

The adoption of Virginia's general ticket law in 1800, eliminating presidential electoral districts, made necessary a greater degree of party unity and management than had existed in the past. This management was exercised by a central corresponding committee appointed early in every presidential election year by a Democratic caucus held in Richmond.

Due to the short notice sent to members of the committee, a majority of the members lived in Richmond. After 1804 the committee included Ritchie and John H. Pleasants. Through these bodies and through their constant presence and activity in Richmond, these men were able to exercise a measure of direction over the legislature and to influence or control the annual election of the governor's appointments to the executive courts. Most of their decisions were made in face-to-face meetings, which left little documentation of their actions. In time they became known as the Richmond Junto. Membership of the inner circle seems to have varied from perhaps twenty to as few as ten men, and their identities changed over the years as men died, moved away, or quarreled and withdrew.

In 1807, following the firing of the British man-of-war *Leopard* on the American frigate *Chesapeake*, Ritchie was elected secretary of the Richmond meeting to protest against the British "right of search," and when the blockade of Norfolk was threatened he became ensign of the Republican Blues, a company raised for the defense of the town. He also engaged in a brief period of service during the war of 1812.

In November 1814 Ritchie was elected public printer of Virginia by the General Assembly, a post he filled for twenty years. All the acts of the assembly of that period were printed by him.

In 1820 Claiborne W. Gooch became a partner in the *Enquirer*. Soon thereafter commenced the agitation which led to the state constitutional convention of 1829, and the proposed changes in the constitution were vigorously discussed in the *Enquirer*. On some of the most important questions a radical difference of opinion developed between Ritchie and Gooch, and this was reflected in the editorials. The result was that in 1828 Gooch retired from the management. Ritchie took John L. Cooke as a partner, with Ritchie again dictating the policy of the paper.

From 1820 to 1833 Ritchie edited the *Richmond Compiler,* a politically neutral paper devoted mainly to local and regional industrial development. So great was Ritchie's prominence in the community that no public meeting in Richmond was complete without him. Many argued that he was the power behind the throne, who dictated the course of his party.

Ritchie was tall, thin, and aristocratic, and always wore old-fashioned silk stockings and low shoes. He frequently left balls and other social gatherings to return home to write, think, and study until 3:00 A.M., then opened the office the next morning.

When President James Monroe's second term was drawing to a close in 1824, Ritchie advocated William H. Crawford for the presidency. Crawford was a Virginian and had been a supporter of Monroe's candidacy in 1816 and 1820. The election was thrown into the House when Andrew Jackson failed to obtain a majority of the electoral votes. After Henry Clay cast his influence for John Quincy Adams and later appeared as secretary of state in Adams's cabinet, Ritchie never forgave him. Thereafter Ritchie worked hard against Clay as a presidential candidate.

In the 1828 presidential election the *Enquirer* threw its whole weight in favor of General Jackson. After his election, it favored nearly all of his measures, though it never failed to express concern or dissent at any Jacksonian doctrine with which it could not agree.

Ritchie always supported state's rights; to him, this was a means to the preservation of the Union. Ritchie drew his information and inspiration chiefly from James Madison's 1799 report to the Virginia Assembly and from Edmund Pendleton's celebrated essay "The Danger Not Over," written shortly after Jefferson's first election to the presidency. The latter publication presented the evils of centralized government. Ritchie republished the essay in the *Enquirer* after Jackson's election in 1828 to serve as a warning to him. The *Enquirer* had no sympathy with the South Carolina doctrine of nullification, however, and supported Jackson in his argument against it.

For over a decade, Ritchie and his major adversary in Virginia, John Hampden Pleasants, founder of the *Virginia Whig* in 1824, battled over the issue of slavery. In 1831-1832 the two were in substantial agreement on the need to abolish slavery gradually; but they came to disagree about the issue when Ritchie started to defend the institution.

Pleasants died in 1846 in a duel with Ritchie's son, Thomas, Jr.

In 1834, after Ritchie had held the post of public printer for twenty years, the Virginia legislature was taken over by the Whigs. Ritchie was one of their earliest victims: he was removed as public printer and Samuel Shepherd elected in his place. He had been out of the office only a short time, however, when he was reelected. He held the position until 1839, when he voluntarily gave it up.

Ritchie called the first convention of editors ever held in the country; the convention met in Richmond in January 1838. He dwelt at length upon the power of the press in promoting the progress of art, extending the sphere of science, and keeping alive a spirit of vigilance over the republic. He admonished his fellow editors, each of them as poorly paid as Ritchie himself, to aim for something higher than fortune: a position of distinction and power as constructive members of society. Ritchie was a fervent advocate of better schools—even for women, a virtually unthinkable idea at that time. He also supported woman suffrage, which was still more unthinkable.

During 1840, Ritchie, while still publishing the *Enquirer,* edited a weekly paper, the *Crisis,* which dealt with educational issues. In 1843 he invited his sons William F. and Thomas, Jr., to become partners with him at the *Enquirer.* Though it had supported his candidacy in 1836, the *Enquirer* did its share to defeat Martin Van Buren in 1844 when he sought renomination for the presidency. The major concern for Ritchie was Van Buren's opposition to the annexation of Texas. Southern politicians saw the addition of Texas as a means of strengthening the South's position in the Union. Ritchie canvassed Virginia on the subject and then sent the letters, along with a personal letter from himself, to Van Buren, indicating that the state would not support Van Buren in his quest for the presidency. Van Buren returned all the material with no response. James K. Polk was nominated by the Democrats and elected. This election changed the personnel of the Democratic party; what was considered the old regime left office.

Leaving his son William as editor of the *Enquirer,* Ritchie moved to Washington in 1845, at the invitation of President Polk, to become editor of the *Washington Union.* Following the Whig victory of Harrison and Tyler in 1840, the *Globe* had ceased to be the organ of the administration, but the Whig *National Intelligencer* was not restored to the position of eminence it had enjoyed under the Madison and Monroe administrations. The *Madisonian,* which had originally been Van Buren's paper, decided to cast its lot with the Whigs. When Harrison died in 1841, however, the *Madisonian* lost its position as printer for the House of Representatives and Senate. When the Democrats came back into power with Polk in 1844, the *Globe* outfit was purchased and the *Washington Union* was issued in its place by Ritchie, then seventy years old.

In the first issue of the *Union*, dated 1 May 1845, Ritchie said of himself: "He is unalterably conscious of his deficiencies; he has much to learn; he has a new and more extensive alphabet to acquire; he has new characters to study and new duties to perform; he has scarcely twenty acquaintances in the city; but he will strive to avail himself of all the lights that he can obtain, that he may guide his new bark over the wide ocean which is spread before him. . . . " Ritchie did not, however, fare well in Washington. In the fall of 1845 he was elected printer to the House and the Senate, but soon afterwards the public printing was let out on contract. According to Frank Luther Mott, "It was in connection with the fight on Ritchie that the rule was adopted in 1846 which required the letting of the government printing to the lowest bidder. Heretofore the large sums involved in these contracts had been a reward for partisan editorial leadership in the national capital. It was a system which invited corruption, but the editors who worked under it seem to have kept relatively free of scandals. But after it was discarded, no administration organ exerted more than a tithe of the old influence. There remained some politics in the awarding of the printing, to be sure, until the establishment of the Government Printing Office in 1860; but the Washington organs never regained their power and prestige after 1846." Ritchie received the contracts again in 1849 but lost money on them. Congress appropriated $50,000 to help cover his losses.

Ritchie's advancing age and financial problems forced him to sell the *Union* in April 1851 to Andrew Jackson Donelson. The last three years of his life were divided between his home in Washington and that of a married daughter on the James River in Virginia, where he played with his grandchildren. Ritchie died in Washington on 2 July 1854, and though he never held any prominent official position, his funeral was attended by nearly all the distinguished men of the times, including the president. The pallbearers were Senators Mason and Hunter and Congressmen Bock, Caskie, and Powell, all from Virginia; Mr. Dobbin, the secretary of the navy; and W. W. Corcoran. Ritchie was buried in Hollywood, Virginia, beside his son,

Thomas, Jr., who had died earlier that year. The *Enquirer* of 24 July said of its old editor:

> Mr. Ritchie was secretary to almost all the public meetings held in Richmond during his residence there, was present at all the Legislative caucuses where Presidents and Governors and Senators were made and unmade, acted and consulted with the managers, was advised and counseled with by them, and without his knowledge and concurrence, few moves were made on the political board. . . . Mr. Ritchie was manager at all the public balls, and was the perfect gentleman in his attention to the ladies—was one of the Committee of Arrangements for all public dinners—had something to do in the preparation of the toasts—presided on these occasions with dignity and propriety—and would proclaim, when the company became a little uproarious, that "order was Heaven's first law. . . ."
>
> These civilities and duties and amusements Mr. Ritchie performed and enjoyed in his hours of relaxation; never, however, in all his pleasures, in his gayest moods, did he step beyond the bounds of temperance and moderation. But in his hours of study, or business or composition, he rarely permitted himself to be interrupted. At such times, it was his habit to retire to an upper apartment of his residence, where, in a dressing gown and slippers, free from ceremony, he could think, and cull and pour forth those lucubrations which were the mental food for thousands.

In the *Richmond Enquirer*, Ritchie edited the most famous newspaper of its era. His was one of the few newspapers which were published over more than a regional basis. During his tenure as editor, he was known as the "Napoleon of the Press." He was also given numerous other nicknames, such as "Thomas Nous Verron," "Old Nous Verron," "Momentous Crisis Ritchie," "Obita Principis Ritchie," "Father Ritchie," etc., which indicate something of his style and personality. Jackson, who belonged to the same party, called him the "greatest scoundrel in America." His prominence and influence were so great that a county in what is now West Virginia is named in his honor.

His major failing as an editor was in balancing his books. He seemed ignorant in matters of domestic and business economy. His accounts often went uncollected until they amounted to thousands of dollars, and were then frequently forgotten. He was hard put to cover the costs of his large family and his frequent entertaining, and to repay various loans from banks. Had he not been invited to Washington in 1845 to edit the *Union* he would probably have died in poverty.

Ritchie was a success because of his superior knowledge, sound judgment, genial temper, persuasive manner, and ability to work hard. Even though he presented himself as only interested in the affairs of Virginia, he was often involved in the political affairs of other states, with national figures, and in sectional interests. One of his contemporaries wrote, "If anybody ever understood the politics of the Old Dominion it was Father Ritchie, for he sounded the depths of all the abstractions of that old Commonwealth from the Resolutions of '98 to the resolutions of 1844, when a new era seemed to dawn upon the Democracy of the country." Another contemporary of Ritchie's wrote when describing his great power: "It proceeded from a knowledge on the part of the public that he was aiming with his whole soul to promote, as far as he thought right, the public interest and particularly to sustain Virginia in her highly prized principles, and to sustain her in the ascendency among the states. It strengthened the confidence felt in his disinterested devotion to these things and his freedom from selfish aspirations for himself and his friends."

Letters:

"Unpublished Letters of Thomas Ritchie," edited by W. E. Dodd, *John P. Branch Historical Papers of Randolph-Macon College*, 3 (June 1911): 199-279.

Biography:

Charles Henry Ambler, *Thomas Ritchie: A Study in Virginia Politics* (Richmond, Va.: Bell Book & Stationery Co., 1913).

References:

Harry Ammon, "The Formation of the Republican Party in Virginia, 1789-1796," *Journal of Southern History*, 19 (August 1953): 283-310;

Rex Beach, "Spencer Roane and the Richmond Junto," *William and Mary Quarterly*, second series, 22 (January 1942): 1-17;

Julian A. Chandler, *The History of Suffrage in Virginia* (Baltimore: Johns Hopkins Press, 1901), pp. 10-22;

Joseph H. Harrison, Jr., "Oligarchs and Democrats: The Richmond Junto," *Virginia Magazine of History and Biography*, 78 (April 1970): 184-198;

Amos Kendall, *Autobiography of Amos Kendall* (Boston: Lee & Shepard, 1872);

Frank Luther Mott, *American Journalism*, third edition (New York: Macmillan, 1962), pp. 188-189, 256-257;

James E. Pollard, *The Presidents and the Press* (New York: Macmillan, 1947);

William Ernest Smith, *The Francis Preston Blair Family in Politics*, 2 volumes (New York: Macmillan, 1933);

Charles T. Thrift, "Thomas Ritchie," *John P. Branch Historical Papers of Randolph-Macon College*, 1 (June 1902): 170-187;

Lyon G. Tyler, "Old Virginia Editors," *William and Mary Quarterly*, first series, 7 (July 1898): 9-17.

Papers:

The Thomas Ritchie Papers are in the Library of Congress. Other collections containing Ritchie materials include the Thomas Jefferson Papers, Library of Congress; the Coolidge Collection of Jefferson Papers, Massachusetts Historical Society; the Joseph Jones Papers, Duke University Library; and the William Wirt Papers, Southern Historical Collection, University of North Carolina.

James Rivington

(circa 1724-4 July 1802)

Michael Sewell
Texas Wesleyan College

MAJOR POSITION HELD: Editor, *Rivington's New York Gazetteer or the Connecticut, Hudson's River, New-Jersey, and Quebec Weekly Advertiser*, renamed *Rivington's New-York Loyal Gazette* in 1777, renamed *Royal Gazette* in 1777, renamed *Rivington's New-York Gazette and Universal Advertiser* in 1783 (1773-1776, 1777-1783).

BOOKS: *Catalogue of Books for Sale by James Rivington* (Philadelphia: Printed for James Rivington, 1761);

A Catalogue of Books Sold by Rivington and Brown, Booksellers and Stationers from London, at Their Stores, over against the Golden Key (Philadelphia: Heinrich Miller, 1762);

New-York, February 15, 1773. James Rivington, Bookseller, Printer, and Stationer, in New-York. Proposes to Publish a Weekly News-paper, Every Thursday, Differing Materially in Its Plan from Most Others Now Extant; He Has Been Honoured with Encouragement from The First Persons in This Country, and Now Begs Leave to Sollicit [sic] *the Public Patronage in Behalf of Rivington's New-York Gazetteer; or the Connecticut, New-Jersey, Hudson's-River and Quebec Weekly Advertiser* (New York: Printed by James Rivington, 1773);

New-York, April 27, 1775. To the Public. As Many Publications Have Appeared from My Press Which Have Given Great Offense to the Colonies. . . . (New York: Printed by James Rivington, 1775);

To the Public. Having Already Signed the Association, Recommended by the General Committee of New-York, Voluntarily and Freely;—For the Further Satisfaction of the Respectable Public, I Hereby Declare, That It Is My Unalterable Resolution Rigidly to Conform Myself to the Said Association; and I Humbly Intreat the Pardon of Those Whom I Have Offended by Any Ill Judged Publications. James Rivington, New-York, June 3, 1775 (New York: Printed by James Rivington, 1775);

The Patriot of North America, a Sketch with Explanatory Notes (New York, 1775);

James Rivington, portrait attributed to Ezra Ames after an original by Gilbert Stuart (New-York Historical Society)

The Democrat; or, Intrigues and Adventures of Jean Le Noir, Etc. (New York: Author, 1795).

James (Jemmy) Rivington, best known and most influential of the Tory editors during the American Revolution, would be notable solely for his role as a Tory spokesman, but is additionally important because of controversies that marked both his life and his reputation in history. Early in his editorship, he was an unusual guardian of freedom of the press who insisted upon balanced reports and opinion, despite Patriot displeasure with his then-strange objectivity. Yet, it was Rivington's newspaper that published the vilest and most unfounded of rumors about Patriots after the war began. The fervor of radical revolutionaries had

398

swept aside his objectivity—and his presses—as at least a minority proved to Rivington that they had little tolerance for a marketplace of words. Thus, the man who had sought objectivity in a time of opinion, who had made an effort to tell both sides, became the voice of one side. Rivington's newspaper was the principal Tory publication when British protection was at hand, and the symbol to Patriots of all that they disliked in British rule and British journalism.

Rivington was born in London around 1724, the son of Charles Rivington, a well-known book publisher and dealer, and Eleanor Pease Rivington. He and his brother John carried on the family business after their father's death in 1742. On 14 September 1752 James married Elizabeth Minshull; their only child died in infancy. In 1756 Rivington left the family firm to go into partnership with James Fletcher. Rivington and Fletcher were quite successful, publishing Tobias Smollett's *History of England* (1757-1758) for a sizable £10,000 profit; but the lure of high living, especially the racetrack at Newmarket, depleted Rivington's finances. While acquaintances thought him bankrupt, how-

Rivington in 1756, the year he left the family publishing business to go into partnership with James Fletcher, pastel portrait by Francis Cotes (New-York Historical Society)

ever, he paid all his debts and sailed to America, apparently with sufficient capital to launch a new business venture as a bookseller in Philadelphia in 1760. In 1761, in partnership with Samuel Brown, he opened a bookshop on Wall Street in New York City, followed by an art gallery in the same city in 1763. Rivington and William Miller opened a bookstore in Boston later the same year.

Rivington again lost a large sum of money through gambling, this time with the "Maryland Lottery," a land scheme that he devised. Again allegedly bankrupt, the ever-surprising and resilient Rivington quickly emerged successful in bookselling. Some biographers credit Rivington's second wife, Elizabeth Van Horne, whom he married in March 1769 after the death of his first wife, with giving impetus to his financial success. The second marriage produced two sons and a daughter.

Rivington's newspaper was established in 1773. *Rivington's New-York Gazetteer or the Connecticut, Hudson's River, New-Jersey, and Quebec Weekly Advertiser* bore a nameplate far more regional than its circulation, but the newspaper was well edited and profitable, with some fifty-five percent of its contents consisting of advertising. After a trial issue on 18 March, regular publication began on 22 April. The initial reaction to Rivington and his newspaper is typified by the praise of Isaiah Thomas in his *Massachusetts Spy*: "Few men, perhaps, were better qualified . . . to publish a newspaper." Thomas added that "no newspaper in the colonies was better printed, or more copiously furnished with foreign intelligence."

Pledging in his first issue to strive to please readers of all "Views and Inclinations," Rivington seems to have genuinely attempted to do just that. Though strongly Tory in his personal beliefs, he published countering views during an era when objectivity and balance meant little to journalists and less to readers. This impartiality might have resulted from Rivington's gentlemanly sense of fair play. Fair play was not on the minds of many Patriots, agitated by Samuel Adams and other radicals, for whom the only truth worth publishing was the truth of British injustice and iniquity.

Tests of Rivington's commitment to all views and inclinations surfaced quickly with challenges from the Sons of Liberty, a semisecret, often violent group. One of it leaders, Isaac "King" Sears, became the object of verbal attack in the *Gazetteer* of 18 August 1774. A letter signed "A Merchant of New-York" called Sears "a *tool* of the lowest order," a "*political cracker*," and "the *laughing-stock* of the whole town." Sears demanded to know the identity of the assailant. Rivington responded that he would not "deliver up any author, without his permission, and I am ready to defend the freedom of the press when attacked in my person."

As the pace of events quickened and emotions heightened for both Patriot and Tory, Rivington increasingly attacked Patriot solidarity, employing questionable as well as legitimate techniques. He printed not only news and editorial argument but satire, invective, and sneers, always with a slant against the Patriots. His writing was at best an embarrassment to the Patriots—especially when what he wrote was true; at worst, it was lies and malicious attacks. By the eve of the revolution, the Patriot Isaiah Thomas, who had praised Rivington for his qualifications as a journalist upon the founding of the *Gazetteer, referred to him as "that* JUDAS." Benjamin Edes and John Gill called Rivington "dirty" and "malicious." In turn, Rivington called Thomas's *Massachusetts Spy* the "Boston Snake of Sedition" and Edes and Gill's *Boston Gazette* "Monday's Dung Barge." The open exchange of views had turned to venom and invective.

Rivington called the New Jersey mob that hanged him in effigy on 13 April 1775 "little, flabby, piddling politicians" and "snarling curs" who were *"the very dregs of the City."* The same 20 April issue of the *Gazetteer* parodied a speech by Sears and named him "SIMPLETON SAP-SKULL." Rivington dared the mob to come and get him and, in a journalistic innovation, printed

Woodcut in Rivington's New-York Gazetteer *for 20 April 1775, depicting the editor being hanged in effigy by a Patriot mob*

an illustration of his effigy, garbed in the elegant, aristocratic attire that he himself wore.

The timing of the dare was unfortunate for Rivington, for the news of the battles of Lexington and Concord on 19 April reached New York on 23 April. A mob broke into the arsenal in New York that day and sympathies with the Patriot cause increased. Facing financial disaster as advertisers and subscribers deserted him and fearing real physical harm, Rivington made a "free and public declaration" in the *Gazetteer* on 4 May that he would henceforth act from "such principles as shall not give offence."

Rivington's promise to "not give offence" was not acceptable, or at least not accepted, in the camp of "King" Sears. On 10 May Sears and a mob descended upon the homes of the two most prominent Tories, Dr. Myles Cooper, president of Kings College, and Rivington. Rivington's printing shop and presses were wrecked but he fled to the safety of a British vessel in the harbor. Of Rivington's flight to that sanctuary, the *Pennsylvania Journal* said, "We hope the Non-exportation Agreement to Great-Britain will always except such traitors to the Liberties of America."

From the British ship on 18 May, Rivington petitioned the Second Continental Congress for pardon, professing that "however wrong and mistaken he may have been in his opinions, he has always meant honestly and openly to do his duty." The Congress referred the request to the New York Provincial Congress, which on 6 June recommended that he be allowed to continue publishing.

For a time, Rivington avoided controversy; but he soon became bolder because of the financial security of an appointment as His Majesty's printer in New York for £100 a year, and gave more and more freedom to the quills of his correspondents. Sears had fled to New Haven, Connecticut, a fugitive from justice because of his involvement in riotous acts. It was not a great enough distance to offset the acrimony between the two men, and on 20 November 1775 Sears and a Sons of Liberty mob swept into New York. The mob again wrecked Rivington's presses, and carried his type back to Connecticut.

The New York Provincial Congress protested this lawless act in a 12 December letter to Connecticut Governor Jonathan Trumbull: "We are fully aware of [Rivington's] demerits; but we earnestly wish that the glory of the present contest for Liberty may not be sullied by an attempt to restrain the Freedom of the Press." Connecticut's response, however, was that Sears was a New York citizen and not under its jurisdiction. Rivington decided to return to England, fleeing upon the British ship *Sansom* in January 1776. He did not return for over eighteen months.

The absence of Rivington's newspaper left a void of great magnitude for the Tories. Both before the fighting started and after—when Tory circulations were effectively limited to British-held territory—Rivington's newspaper was the principal inspiration for the Loyalists. It lifted the sagging hopes of the Tories when it mischievously parodied Patriot Leaders; and its news of the miseries and failures of the Patriot army must have been comforting, even when it was false.

In September 1777, Rivington returned with a new appointment as the king's printer. During his absence the Declaration of Independence had been issued and British forces had secured New York City. He renamed his newspaper the *New-York Loyal Gazette* and began publishing on 4 October. The name was changed to *Royal Gazette* on 13 December. Now engaged in a real war, the *Royal Gazette* used any means at its journalistic disposal. Rivington apparently delighted in publishing vi-

cious, unfounded rumors detrimental to Patriot leaders. George Washington satirically wrote in a letter to New York Governor George Clinton of "one of your subjects who has been a man of no small notoriety *during the whole rebellion*, and who has been so remarkably distinguished for his regard to veracity." Governor William Livingston of New Jersey voiced a similar sentiment when he wrote, "If Rivington is taken, I must have one of his ears; Governor Clinton is entitled to the other; and General Washington, if he pleases, may take his head."

After the Patriot victory at Yorktown, however, Rivington became conciliatory in tone, perhaps sensing the inevitability of British defeat. He begged the forgiveness of the Continental army and New York's civil authorities, and was permitted to remain in New York City at the war's end. He was there to report, once again objectively, Washington's farewell to his officers.

Again, however, despite the official tolerances of the authorities, Rivington was plagued by his nemesis, Sears. Sears, along with General John Lamb and Marimus Willett, visited Rivington on New Year's Eve, 1783, and forbade him to continue

Flags from Rivington's paper. The name was changed to the **Royal Gazetteer** *in 1777 to show Rivington's support for the British, who were then occupying New York City.*

to publish. The 31 December issue was Rivington's last. He lived another nineteen years, mostly in poverty and without honor, as a bookseller and stationer. His wife died in 1795 and Rivington was in debtor's prison in the spring of 1797. He died on Independence Day, 1802.

Memories of Rivington and his "lying gazette" long survived him—at least as late as the Civil War, when the editors of the *Boston Journal* rebuked the antiadministration *New York World* for "intemperate party warfare." The *Journal* editors wrote, "Rivington lives in history as well as Arnold."

Yet, a rumor also persisted, or arose later, that Rivington had been a spy for George Washington. No substantiation has been found for the rumor, which probably resulted from the difficulty of explaining why Patriots permitted so despised a Tory journalist to remain after the war without retribution. The spy theory is shallow when one considers the little Rivington could have done for the Patriots as a secret agent, as compared with the damage he did to them with his newspaper. It is more likely that Rivington received no official punishment because of respect for freedom of the press or a sense of fairness on the part of the authorities.

One will recall that the authorities twice accepted Rivington's pleas for pardon and that the New York Provincial Congress condemned the lawless, violent attacks of Sears and his mob in 1775.

Finally, it is possible that the authorities and most citizens, tired of strife and war, determined to ignore a man who could do them no further damage—a man who had been most effective and exasperating when under British protection. Stripped of that protection, he may have been viewed in terms of his personal qualities rather than his journalistic offenses. A contemporary, Ashbel Green, described Rivington as "the greatest sycophant imaginable; very little under the influence of any principle but self-interest, yet of the most courteous manner to all."

References:

John L. Lawson, "The 'Remarkable Mystery' of James Rivington, 'Spy,'" *Journalism Quarterly*, 35 (Summer 1958): 317-323, 394;

Dwight Teeter, "'King' Sears, the Mob and Freedom of the Press in New York, 1765-76," *Journalism Quarterly*, 41 (Autumn 1964): 539-544.

Anne Royall

(11 June 1769-1 October 1854)

Nickieann Fleener
University of Utah

MAJOR POSITIONS HELD: Editor/publisher, *Paul Pry* (Washington, D.C.) (1831-1836), *Huntress* (Washington, D.C.) (1836-1854).

BOOKS: *Sketches of History, Life, and Manners, in the United States. By a Traveller* (New Haven, Conn.: Printed for the author, 1826);

The Tennessean; a Novel, Founded on Facts (New Haven, Conn.: Printed for the author, 1827);

The Black Book; or, A Continuation of Travels in the United States, 3 volumes (Washington, D.C.: Printed for the author, 1828-1829);

Mrs. Royall's Pennsylvania; or, Travels Continued in the United States, 2 volumes (Washington, D.C.: Printed for the author, 1829);

Letters from Alabama on Various Subjects; to Which Is

Added, an Appendix, Containing Remarks on Sundry Members of the 20th & 21st Congress, and Other High Characters, &c. &c. at the Seat of Government (Washington, D.C., 1830);

Mrs. Royall's Southern Tour, or, Second Series of the Black Book, 3 volumes (Washington, D.C., 1830-1831).

Anne Royall's grave in Washington's Congressional Cemetery is marked by a small granite stone inscribed simply "Anne Royall, Pioneer Woman Publicist, 1769-1854." The simplicity of the marker, which was placed upon her grave nearly sixty years after her death, is in sharp contrast to both the richness of Mrs. Royall's editorial career and the abundance of legends which surround her life.

Born near Baltimore, Maryland, Anne Newport was the elder daughter of Mary and William Newport. After enduring a peripatetic childhood on the Pennsylvania frontier, Anne settled with her twice-widowed mother and younger half-brother near Sweet Springs Mountain, Virginia, where her mother was employed as a housekeeper by Major William Royall. The enthusiasm for learning of the eighteen-year-old Anne soon captured Royall's attention. A gentleman farmer, scholar, and Revolutionary War veteran, Royall opened his library to Anne and directed her studies, emphasizing history, literature, and Freemasonry. Approximately ten years later, William and Anne were married on 18 November 1794; William was in his middle fifties and Anne was twenty-eight. Her day-to-day life probably changed very little after her marriage. She studied with Royall and helped manage the plantation, a task for which Royall himself seems to have had little interest or aptitude.

Sometime around 1809, Royall visited Charleston, Virginia, to inspect land he had been investing in, sight unseen, for years. He became fond of the settlement and returned home to tell Anne of his plans to sell the plantation and move to Charleston. Mrs. Royall was pleased with the news; she later wrote that she found life in the mountains in winter almost unbearable and that she yearned to supplement her knowledge of mankind, acquired through books, with first-hand experience. However, selling the large plantation proved difficult. As time passed, Royall turned increasingly to drink and his behavior became erratic. Periods of normal behavior were punctuated by episodes in which he verbally and physically abused those around him. Mrs. Royall stayed with her husband throughout these difficult years and would never write negatively of him. Royall died on 12 December 1812 apparently from natural causes aggravated by alcoholism. Mrs. Royall inherited the bulk of his estate, including nearly 7,000 acres of land, seven slaves, and much livestock. After arranging for the plantation to be sold at auction, she left for Charleston in the spring of 1813, confident that the holdings left to her would keep her financially secure for life.

Almost immediately after reaching Charles-

ton, Mrs. Royall enthusiastically entered the business world. She invested heavily in salt, real estate, and a tavern. These investments, coupled with the expense of several lawsuits against the estate and the sale of the plantation for only a $500 promissory note, depleted her cash. Nevertheless, she remained optimistic that future income would remedy her financial difficulties. However, in June 1814, William Royall's niece, Elizabeth, and her husband, James Roane, challenged the legality of Royall's will. In part, the Roanes charged that Mrs. Royall had forged the will, had cohabitated immorally with Royall prior to their marriage, had forced him to marry her, and had ill-treated him during his life. The Roanes contended that they should inherit the estate in excess of the widow's one-third legal dower. The court denied Mrs. Royall access to any income from the estate until the case was adjudicated.

The case did not come to trial until April 1817. In the interim, Mrs. Royall lived with her niece, Anna Malvina, on income from the sale of timber from land deeded by Royall directly to Malvina prior to his death and from money earned by taking lodgers. During the trial, Mrs. Royall swore that she did not forge the will and that she never mistreated her husband; she did not deny the cohabitation charge. The jury upheld the validity of Royall's will, but the Roanes immediately appealed.

While waiting for the retrial, Mrs. Royall set out with her slave Davy to explore the newly annexed Alabama territory. Precisely why she decided to go and how she financed the horseback journey remain unclear. Shortly after she started the trip Mrs. Royall wrote the first of her "Dear Matt" letters, which would later be compiled into a book, *Letters from Alabama on Various Subjects* (1830). Matt was Mrs. Royall's young friend and legal counsel, Matthew Dunbar. Writing these letters helped Mrs. Royall realize that she had talent for interviewing, observing, and writing.

In 1819 the Roanes' appeal was heard. This time the couple triumphed, and, aside from her dower, Mrs. Royall was disinherited. The verdict unleashed a host of lawsuits against Mrs. Royall from her creditors. Virtually penniless, Mrs. Royall delegated management of her legal problems to Dunbar and went back to Alabama. Supported in part by a small stipend drawn against her dower, she spent the next eleven years in wandering about and writing down her observations of life and customs throughout the country. By 1823 she had the idea of collecting and publishing her earlier letters to Dunbar. While editing the letters Dunbar returned to her, she decided to try to make her living by travel writing. Her initial plan was to write of travels through Pennsylvania, New York, and New England, and to collect subscriptions in advance for the projected books based on those travels. In addition, with Dunbar acting as her agent, she petitioned the federal government for her pension as a Revolutionary War widow. During the early years of her travels, she also wrote her only novel, *The Tennessean* (1827) recounting the adventures of heroic American frontiersmen who undertake a journey into Mexico. The novel has never been well thought of by critics.

In spring of 1824 Mrs. Royall went to Washington, D.C., to fight personally for her pension. After a long struggle with the Pension Bureau, she was informed that only widows married prior to 1794 were eligible for benefits. She persisted in her claim and took the battle directly to Congress. Although she had the long-time support of John Quincy Adams, her claim was not allowed until 1848, and even then the sum awarded was very small.

After the initial fray with the Pension Bureau, Mrs. Royall resumed her travels. Between 1826 and 1831 she published five travel books—including the letters to Dunbar—and several multivolume works which journalism historian Madelon Schilpp described as "gems of journalism of that period of importance still to any student of social history." Although written in an undisciplined style characterized by inconsistent spelling and grammar, the books contain vivid and valuable portraits of the personalities and social customs of the times.

In her attempts to obtain funding for her travels, she came into contact with numerous individuals; the strength of her character, the vigor with which she attacked some causes and supported others, and the unusual nature of her occupation, embarked upon at such an advanced age, made her hard to forget. Because she approached newspaper editors as potential sources of funding for her travels, she became particularly well known in journalistic circles. Some editors, such as Major Mordercai M. Noah of the *Morning Courier and New York Enquirer*, spoke highly of her both in private and in print. Benjamin Day of the *New York Sun* called her the Joan of Arc of the editorial corps. Even Amos Kendall observed that although he found her "homely in person, careless in dress . . . and vulgar in manners . . . she had a tolerable education, much shrewdness, and respectable talents." Other editors disliked her. For example, Frederick Packard of the *Hampden Journal* called

her "a silly old hag" fit only for "some asylum or work house." As her visibility increased, Mrs. Royall frequently became the subject of news stories. With the publication of each book came heatedly favorable and unfavorable reviews more frequently pegged around Mrs. Royall's beliefs and personality than around the writings themselves.

In part because of her continuing battle with the Pension Bureau during these years, Mrs. Royall moved her home base to Washington, D.C., where she roomed with her close friend Sally Stack. Mrs. Royall's frequent visits to Congress, coupled with the growing attention paid to her by the press, made her known to virtually every Washington politician and bureaucrat. During her career, she met and interviewed every president from John Quincy Adams to Franklin Pierce, with Adams being a particular champion of hers.

It was in Washington that Mrs. Royall's anti-Presbyterianism resulted in her notorious trial as a common scold or public nuisance. The charges were brought after she lost her temper with a group of evangelists' children who were throwing stones through the windows of her house. As a result of her verbal outbursts, the evangelists brought obscenity charges against her in addition to the public nuisance charge. She was finally tried on the common scold charge alone in the summer of 1829. The trial generated tremendous press interest, and newspaper editors were quick to take sides. *The New York Commercial Advertiser* commended the grand jury for its courage in bringing to trial "this belligerent woman." A South Carolina editor noted that Mrs. Royall should be on trial not just for being a common scold but for being "an uncommon scold"; the phrase *uncommon scold* became a part of the Anne Royall legend. On the other side, editors like Major Noah held firm in their support. Noah expressed the hope that Mrs. Royall would be dealt with in a lenient way and the *Courier and Enquirer*'s Washington correspondent, James Gordon Bennett, sat with her throughout the proceedings. According to Royall biographer Bessie R. James, Bennett viewed the trial as an attack not just on Mrs. Royall but on press freedom in general. In spite of testimony about the goodness of her character by witnesses including Secretary of War John Easton, Mrs. Royall was found guilty. The judge spared her the public dunking the evangelists had sought, but fined her $10 and ordered a $100 bond posted to guarantee her future conduct. Two *National Intelligencer* reporters paid her fine and posted the bond. The much-publicized trial added

Front page of Royall's first "muckraking" newspaper

to Mrs. Royall's reputation as a colorful character and boosted the sales of her books.

In 1830 Mrs. Royall stopped wandering. With the help of Mrs. Stack, she collected enough money to start a newspaper in Washington. The first issue of the weekly *Paul Pry* appeared on 3 December 1831. The four-page newspaper, published in the kitchen of Mrs. Royall's Bank House residence, proclaimed itself to be an independent investigative journal. Mrs. Royall put it this way: "The welfare and happiness of our country are our politics. We shall expose all and every species of political evil and religious fraud without fear or affection." *Paul Pry* was a highly personal paper dominated by its forceful sixty-year-old editor. Written in a style which has been described as undisciplined but vivid, and containing poor punctuation, inconsistent spelling, and unconventional sentence structure, the newspaper was filled with Washington news and gossip and fulfilled its watchdog pledge. In its first issue, *Paul Pry* called for the dismissal of House of Representatives Clerk M. St. Clair Clark for abuse of privilege. The paper campaigned for the trade labor movement, for states' rights, and for President Jackson's bank policy. It exposed post office frauds and Indian land frauds. It remained staunchly anti-Presbyterian and pro-Freemason. In one major campaign, the newspaper charged that Washington's city government was largely responsible for the virulent recurring cholera epidemics in the area because it refused to improve the local sewage system and drain the swamp surrounding the city. Mrs. Royall used the columns of *Paul Pry* to praise government officials she believed to be true public servants and to bring to public attention political graft and abuse of power. *Paul Pry* generated almost equal parts of praise and criticism. One newspaper editor wrote that *Paul Pry* contained all the "scum and political filth extant." Another editor praised the paper for its "fearlessness of spirit." The wave of editorial comment prompted Mrs. Royall to observe proudly that "no paper, perhaps, has ever had so many enemies."

In part because of all its enemies, *Paul Pry* was never able to support itself completely; and with no other major source of income, Mrs. Royall found financial survival increasingly difficult. In 1836 she decided that her best strategy would be to scrap *Paul Pry* and start afresh. With the promise of a new, equally courageous investigative journal as her marketing approach, she set out for New York to gain advance subscriptions for the new paper. The journey netted enough capital for Mrs. Royall to begin her new publication. Included in

Paul Pry's final issue on 19 November 1836 was an article summarizing the accomplishments of the newspaper as a publication which had "issued a challenge for all [politicians] to remain on watch. . . ." Less than two weeks later, the first issue of the *Huntress* appeared, on 2 December 1836. In that first issue, Mrs. Royall affirmed her intention to continue the pursuit of corruption and fraud. She noted that this weekly paper would differ from *Paul Pry* only in the "introduction of amusing tales, dialogues, and essays upon general subjects." She edited the *Huntress* in this spirit for the remaining fourteen years of her life.

In spite of increasing infirmity, Mrs. Royall continued to remain personally involved with the major issues and personalities of the times. She called Samuel Morse's invention of the telegraph "a wonderful triumph of the human mind." After her first meeting with Horace Greeley, she described him as a man of "distant manners and a soft sweet voice." She called the *New Orleans Picayune* the country's best newspaper, praised its editorial independence, and reprinted George Kendall's reports from the *Picayune* on the Mexican War. She was against woman suffrage and appalled by the "immodesty" of the costume championed by Seneca Falls (New York) *Lily* editor Amelia Bloomer. Although she had once owned slaves, Mrs. Royall opposed slavery but disliked abolitionist tactics even more; she expressed concern that the abolition of slavery would end the Union. She was also antiexpansionist: she campaigned against the annexation of Oregon and aggressively condemned both Congress and land speculators for encouraging the territory's settlement.

In 1848 Mrs. Royall mourned the death of her long-time supporter John Quincy Adams. Later the same year, Congress passed a pension act under which she was granted forty dollars a month. The allowance did not make Mrs. Royall rich, but it did help insure the *Huntress*'s continued publication. As Mrs. Royall's health failed, she had to rely more heavily upon the assistance of others to keep the paper alive. Of particular importance was the work of John Henry Simmes. An orphan taken into the household fifteen years earlier, Simmes learned the printing trade on Mrs. Royall's kitchen press. Biographer James speculated that by 1854, Simmes was not only printing the paper but also writing almost all of every issue. When Simmes left the paper after his marriage in March 1854, Mrs. Royall tried to carry on without him; but publication of the *Huntress* was suspended in May. In the last issue, Mrs. Royall explained, "We are tired of

THE HUNTRESS.

EDITED AND PRINTED BY ANNE ROYALL.

Vol. 1.]   NEW SERIES.   [No. 3.

WASHINGTON, D. C., JULY 24, 1854.

CONGRESS.

HOUSE OF REPRESENTATIVES.

SPEECH OF HON. JOHN J. TAYLOR,

OF NEW YORK,

On the bill to organize the Territories of Nebraska and Kansas ; delivered in the House of Representatives, May 9, 1854.

The House being in Committee of the Whole on the State of the Union—

Mr. TAYLOR, of New York, said :

"Mr. CHAIRMAN : On a subject exciting so much interest as that now before the committee, it seems almost necessary for a representative to give his reasons for his votes. Perhaps, for another cause, I ought to say a word on this subject. It has been brought to the notice of the House by my colleague, [Mr. BENNET]— unnecessarily, as I thought, though I do not complain of it—that a respectable number of my constituents differ from me in reference to this measure. It would be pleasant, certainly, if we could agree with all our constituents, and act according to the views of them all. But as this is a thing impossible, the best course, doubtless, is for each one, unless duly instructed, to follow the dictates of his own judgment and conscience, trusting they will not lead him astray."

Mr. Taylor, like all of that name— for we believe in names—is modest, mild and unassuming in his language, and by kind persuasion he would convince any one but an idiot. But the leaders of the opposite faction do not desire conviction—they know well enough the desperate game they are playing, and are only afraid their duplicity will be discovered by their own great party, which they have been training for years past, under various names. They have no feeling against slavery ; their object is to put down the action of Congress, create discord, and delay the business of that body. See the length they go in endeavoring to persuade their poor dupes that slavery has been established in Kansas and Nebraska. They keep constantly at it—ding, dong—to provoke a civil war ; and no doubt many of their ignorant proselytes believe that Congress (who has left it to the people of these Territories) has verily established and confirmed slavery therein. They are actually bullying Congress to pass an act prohibiting slavery in Nebraska—a thing they cannot constitutionally do. Was there ever seen such glaring and empty-headed knavery ? But hear Mr. Taylor : —

"At the present day, nobody denies that a State has the entire control of the institution of slavery within her limits—that she has a constitutional right to do with it what she

Front page of last issue of Royall's second newspaper, published three months before her death

newspapers. Our printer has left us and we are not able to set type." The newspaper resumed publication in pamphlet format on 24 June 1854, but the resurrection lasted for only three issues. In the final issue on 24 July, Mrs. Royall noted that she had only "thirty-one cents in the world" and that for the first time since establishing her residency in Washington had been unable to pay her rent. She died of natural causes on 1 October 1854 at the age of eighty-five. She was laid to rest in an unmarked pauper's grave.

Though she embarked on a journalistic career late in life, Mrs. Royall contributed significantly to journalism history. As Schilpp noted, Mrs. Royall "must be recognized as one of the first, if not the very first, self-made women journalists with a national reputation." Her early travel writings make her one of America's first roving correspondents. Her perceptive, detailed reports of the customs, social issues, and personalities of her times mark her as an important social historian. Her waspish style and the overall tone of her publications led Frank Luther Mott to dub her the forerunner of the contemporary gossip columnist. The persistent independence and force of her editorial voice place her within the ranks of America's early personal journalists. And Mrs. Royall's crusading spirit, investigative zeal, and watchdog vigilance earned for her the title of "grandmother of the muckrakers."

Biographies:

Sarah Porter, *The Life and Times of Anne Royall* (Cedar Rapids, Iowa.: Torch Press, 1909);

George Stuyvesant Jackson, *Uncommon Scold* (Boston: Bruce Humphries, 1937);

Bessie Rowland James, *Anne Royall's USA* (New Brunswick, N.J.: Rutgers University Press, 1972).

References:

Heber Blankenhorn, "The Grandma of the Muckrakers," *American Mercury* (September 1927);

Maruine Beasley, "The Curious Career of Anne Royall," *Journalism History*, 3 (Winter 1976-1977): 98-102, 136;

Emily Taft Douglas, *Remember the Ladies* (New York: Putnam's, 1966), pp. 53-57, 71;

Ishbel Ross, *Ladies of the Press* (New York: Arno, 1974), pp. 27-30;

Madelon G. Schilpp and Sharon Murphy, *Great Women of the Press* (Carbondale: Southern Illinois University Press, 1983), pp. 21-26;

Irving Wallace, *Square Pegs* (New York: Knopf, 1957), pp. 243-266;

Mary O. Whitton, *These Were the Women USA 1776-1860* (New York: Hastings House, 1954), pp. 60-66;

Helen Woodward, *Bold Women* (New York: Farrar, Straus, 1953), pp. 8-23.

Benjamin Russell

(13 September 1761-4 January 1845)

Frederic B. Farrar
Temple University

MAJOR POSITIONS HELD: Editor and publisher, *Massachusetts Centinel*, renamed *Columbian Centinel* in 1790 (1784-1828).

BOOKS: *The Society of the Cincinnati* (Boston: Printed by Benjamin Russell, 1784);
An Address Delivered before the Massachusetts Charitable Mechanick Association, December 21, 1809: Being the Anniversary of the Choice of Officers, and the First Triennial Celebration of Their Publick Festival (Boston: From the press of John Eliot, jun., 1810).

Benjamin Russell

Patriot, printer, mechanic, editor, and politician, Benjamin Russell emerges as the key newspaper publisher linking eighteen-century revolutionary newspapermen such as Benjamin Franklin, Isaiah Thomas, and William Goddard with the mid-nineteenth-century journalistic giants James Gordon Bennett and Horace Greeley. There is no full-length biography of Russell, but John B. Hench has outlined in his doctoral dissertation the life of the man he calls an archetypal American "joiner." Hench analyzes the bitter newspaper rivalry in Boston between Russell's *Centinel* and Thomas Adams's *Chronicle* from 1784 until 1801. Russell's newspaper from 1784 until 1828 reveals a fiery, shrewd, innovative journalist. Russell's interest in politics and social reform parallels Greeley's, even though the explosive reform period in American life did not begin until after Russell had sold the *Centinel.*

Russell remembered all his life the thrashing that switched his career toward newspapers. On 19 April 1775, when he was thirteen, young Russell and his classmates were dismissed from school as the news arrived of the battles of Lexington and Concord. The youngsters scampered off toward the new militia army that was gathering to fight the British regulars. For three months Russell ran errands proudly for American soldiers. Shortly after the Battle of Bunker Hill, Russell's father, John Russell, a mason, came upon Benjamin, ordered him home, and emphasized the order with a whip-

ping. The young would-be soldier was immediately sent to Worcester as an apprentice to the rebel newspaperman Isaiah Thomas to learn the trade of printing on Thomas's *Massachusetts Spy*. There Russell began a lifelong friendship with Thomas and learned thoroughly the communications trade of the eighteenth century from one of its great masters.

But the patriotic Russell was not through with the army. In 1777 the apprentice had a month's duty guarding the remnants of Burgoyne's army as the British, defeated at Saratoga, trudged across Massachusetts en route to detention camps. In 1780

Russell substituted for his master in the draft and served for six months at West Point, where he witnessed the execution of Maj. John André. Before the age of twenty, Russell had firsthand experience of four key events of the American Revolution: Lexington and Concord, Bunker Hill, Saratoga, and Benedict Arnold's defection. These experiences impressed young Russell and nurtured a love of country and liberty that influenced his long newspaper career.

In 1781 Thomas released Russell from his apprenticeship. Russell remained as a journeyman in Thomas's shop until after the peace treaty was signed. While he was there, Benjamin Franklin visited Worcester and gave printing tips to Thomas's apprentices. Russell's early career followed the same pattern as Franklin's: both had little formal education; both admired their printing masters; and, both secretly submitted to newspapers anonymous, well-written articles that foretold brilliant newspaper careers. Russell, however, printed little other than the *Centinel*, while Franklin is more popularly known today for his *Poor Richard's Almanac* than for his *Pennsylvania Gazette*.

In November 1783 the young journeyman left Worcester for Boston with the ambition to publish a newspaper. He was a new husband, having married Esther Rice two months before. Esther bore three children, two boys and a girl. None of the children followed in their father's footsteps, although the daughter Abigail married James Cutler, who became a Boston printer.

In Boston, Russell teamed with William Warden to publish the *Massachusetts Centinel* on Wednesdays and Saturdays. It first appeared on 24 March 1784 with the motto, "Uninfluenced by PARTY, we aim only to be Just." The Russell and Warden print shop was "Near the State-House"; and although Russell moved his business occasionally during the next four decades, he stayed close to the capitol. Warden was considered the "seniour editor" by Russell, but he died two years after the *Centinel* was launched. Russell never took another partner; from 1786 he *was* the *Centinel*. By 1790 the *Centinel's* influence had grown far beyond the borders of Massachusetts, and the newspaper was renamed the *Columbian Centinel*. Later, it carried the notation "Benjamin Russell, Printer to the United States, for the Northern States."

Russell's *Centinel* deserved respect and fame. In the 1790s, as journalism tried to grow up, Russell acted as a responsible, modern journalist. He was among the first to consider himself an editor rather than a printer—just as, some years before, William

Goddard, who had founded the first newspapers in Providence and Baltimore, had been the first to call himself a newspaperman. In the early years of the republic, there were no news gathering services, so printers filled their columns with news copied from newspapers of other cities. Russell's *Centinel* was one of the most popular sources of news for other New England editors. Russell exchanged papers, too, but he wrote summaries of the news, bringing the stories into focus for his community. Russell was among the first to use an editorial column; this practice was imitated, and by the time Russell gave the label "Era of Good Feelings" to the Monroe administration, editorials were commonplace. Russell has been credited with being the first to use illustrations, but Benjamin Edes had had Paul Revere draw four coffins for his *Boston Gazette's* famous Boston Massacre issue in 1770. Other printers, such as Goddard, had also used illustrations; and none, including Russell, used drawings extensively. It was not until 1835 that James Gordon Bennett's *New York Herald* brought pictures, via woodcuts, to newspaper journalism.

Perhaps it is Russell's exuberant support of the Constitution that led to the impression that he introduced illustrations. As each state ratified the Constitution, Russell began illustrating the building of the federal edifice, with the states representing supporting pillars to hold up the "New Roof" that sheltered the government. This picture began in a single column of the three-column *Centinel* page, but as the eighth and ninth states reached ratification, the picture covered two columns and dominated the news page. Other newspapers used these graphics; and there is evidence that Russell's arch opponent, Thomas Adams, used the same cuts in his *Boston Independent Chronicle* and may even have used them before Russell did. Russell used some illustrations after the ratification battle, but never on a large scale. Like other eighteenth-century editors, Russell dressed up his advertising copy with drawings of spinning wheels, dental tools, ships, houses, horses, runaways, and a new invention—the umbrella.

Russell was successful because he was a good editor and a good businessman. Advertising was essential then, as it is today, for a newspaper to succeed. Hench notes that half of the 1,000 newspapers in the United States founded before 1821 died within two years. The *Centinel* lasted for forty-two years under Russell and was sold as a successful property. Only two percent of these 1,000 newspapers had a longer life than the *Centinel* or its rival, the *Independent Chronicle*. In 1785, when the *Centinel*

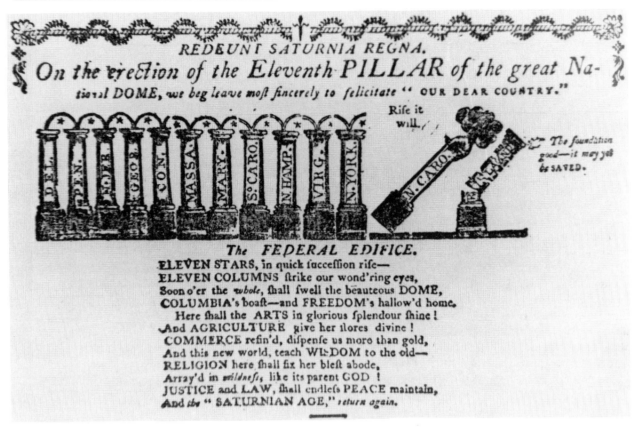

Illustration from Russell's Massachusetts Centinel *for 2 August 1788, depicting the eleven states that had ratified the Constitution as pillars supporting the "National Dome" of the "Federal Edifice." Russell was optimistic that North Carolina and Rhode Island would soon join the other states in approving the document.*

had been in business less than a year, it and the *Independent Chronicle* carried nearly seventy percent of Boston newspaper advertising, despite the fact that there were six other newspapers in the city. Russell printed many advertising supplements, as did other successful newspapermen such as John Dunlap of the *Pennsylvania Packet* in Philadelphia and Isaiah Thomas. The *Centinel's* advertising supplement of 9 June 1798 is significant because in it, Russell began to publish uniform advertising rates.

Historians say that Russell did not support the Bill of Rights; still, the *Centinel* quickly printed James Madison's proposed amendments to the Constitution. An example of Russell's historical approach to journalism was his treatment of the story of the death of his idol, George Washington. Russell did not wait to get this tragic news from another newspaper; his correspondents supplied him with important news. Such journalism, now commonplace, was unusual in 1799; and fresh news was an ingredient that made the *Centinel* readable. On the front page of the *Columbian Centinel* for Wednes-

day, 25 December 1799, Russell reprinted Washington's Farewell Address of 1796 under the heading "*The Legacy* of THE FATHER OF HIS COUNTRY." On page three, the traditional "hot news'" page of eighteenth-century American newspapers, came the news flash:

WASHINGTON IS NO MORE!

THE Editor yesterday the following letter:—
"*Alexandria, Sunday, Dec. 15, 1799.*
        "*DEAR SIR,*
        It is with extreme pain that I inform you, that Lieut. General GEORGE WASHINGTON is no more!
        "I hear his complaint was the cramp; that he was sick twenty-four hours, and died *last night* at 12 o'clock.
        "I have just returned from the house of the Physician General of the United States, Dr. CRAIK, who has not yet returned from *Mount Vernon*, which prevents my being more particular.

"All shops, &c. will be shut and no business done here to-morrow. We shall have a meeting this evening, for the purpose of making arrangements to show all the respect possible to the memory of the Saviour of our Country.—*I am, very respectfully, your obt. servt.*

"*JONATHAN SWIFT.*

"Maj. BENJAMIN RUSSELL. Boston."

Historians describe editors such as Russell as "Guardians of the Faith" and "Watchmen for the Republic" with the mission to be a "Scourge of Evil Doers." Russell took his watchdog duties seriously. As a leading Federalist editor, he defended the Washington and Adams administrations against the "lies" of Anti-Federalists; and when Thomas Jefferson was elected president, Russell really let fly. On 27 December 1800, inaccurately forecasting the results of the election, the *Centinel* said: "It is an important and consoling FACT, that it is already ascertained from the returns of electoral votes, that JOHN ADAMS has been reelected President of the United States, by a MAJORITY OF ALL THE FREE PEOPLE THEREOF. This fact ought to be proclaimed to the world, that the reputation of our country may not sink in the estimation of the wise and good of other countries;—who will regret that any policy shall impose on the United States a Chief Magistrate elected by the *influence of Negro Slaves.*— If any one doubts the facts, let him have recourse to the census of the United States—the details of which we will lay before the public."

Russell loved the Constitution, George Washington, and the Federalist party; he vilified all Anti-Federalists, especially Jefferson, and fought his opponents vigorously, receiving threats of death and bodily injury. But he was first and always a newspaperman; so, although a true Federalist, Russell followed his journalistic instinct to bring his readers the news first, be it good or bad. When the text of the Jay Treaty was leaked to the press, the *Centinel* was the first in Boston to print the text. This agreement, however, solidified the opposition to the Federalists more than any event other than the Sedition Law. When Jefferson finally was elected over Burr by the House of Representatives, Russell realized that the Federalist party was through. The party resisted valiantly for decades, until it was absorbed into the Whig and, much later, the Republican party; but the *Centinel* announced the demise first on 4 March 1801:

YESTERDAY EXPIRED
deeply regretted by MILLIONS of grateful Americans,
and by *all* GOOD MEN,
The FEDERAL ADMINISTRATION
Of the
GOVERNMENT of the *United States;*
Animated by
A WASHINGTON, an ADAMS;—a HAM-
ILTON, KNOX,
PICKERING, WOLCOTT, M'HENRY,
MARSHALL,
STODDERT and DEXTER.
AEt. 12 years.

On 23 May 1801 Russell asked: "Mr. Madison occupies apartments in the President's house at Washington. Query! Does the president of the United States keep lodgers? Or is it the intention of the Secretary of State to spunge (sic) the United States out of house rent?" The gibes continued on 12 August: "If one were to ask, *Where is the government of the United States?* It would be difficult to give a direct answer.—THE PRESIDENT, we believe, is at *Monticello;*—The *Vice-President* at *Washington;*—The *Secretary of state* some where in *Virginia;*—The *Secretary of War*, in the District of *Maine;*—The *Secretary of the Treasury* at *the seat of Government!*—The *Attorney General* at *Worcester.*— The residue, the Lord only knows where."

Russell was still attacking Jefferson as the president's second term neared its end on 6 February 1808:

"*Tanka Massa*"

The slaves of *Paramaribo*, when bleeding beneath the lashes . . . are still compelled . . . to vociferate their thanks. . . .

In this country our ideas of liberty and independence are considered so pure and so refined, that it seems impossible that our rulers should ever be guilty of any injustice towards us, and we not know it;—and knowing it—more impossible that we should even thank them for it. This would make us no better than a slave of *Paramaribo*, or one of the *little Emperor's vassals. No, no, in this, thank heaven, "we are not like other men."* Let the President of the United States bring our country into disgrace, by a conduct which shall be stamped by weakness or wickedness and mark, if the people at large will ever cry "*Tanka Massa.*—"

Russell *was* the *Centinel*, just as later in the

nineteenth century, Greeley was the *New-York Tribune* and Charles A. Dana was the *New York Sun.* Reading random *Centinel*s tells much about Russell:

> . . . *Address, delivered before the Society for promoting* AMERICAN MANUFACTURES.

> . . . Under all the disadvantages which have attended manufactures and the useful arts, it must afford the most comfortable reflection to every patriotick mind to observe their progress in the United States and particularly in Pennsylvania. For a long time after our forefathers sought an establishment in this dreary wilderness, everything necessary for their simple wants was the work of European hands. How great—how happy is the change!
> —13 October 1787

ON SLAVERY

> *If the Printer thinks the following extract of a letter, wrote to an old Sea Captain in an adjoining town, will be the means of any way, preventing that horrid inhuman trade of kidnapping an unfortunate race of human beings, he is desired to publish it, . . .*

> —*Yes, Sir, you stand accused before that* GOD *who is father of all, and who have made of one flesh all nations that dwell on earth for your conduct herein. . . .—The ghosts of these innocent blacks—which you have consigned while here on earth to slavery and misfortune—shall await around your expiring soul, . . . —Persecute no longer the children of men! . . . .*
> —21 February 1789 . . .

A FRIEND TO WOMEN

> . . . If you have good teeth—don't forget to laugh now and then.
> If you have bad ones—you must only simper.
> When you are young—sit with your face to the light.
> When you are a little advanced—sit with your back to the window.
> . . . Never touch the sore place in any one's character—for be
> assured, whoever you are, you have a sore place in your own;
> and woman is a flower that may be blasted in a moment. . . .
> If you would preserve beauty—rise early.
> If you would preserve esteem—be gentle. . . .
> —28 February 1789

WAR, WAR, WAR!!!

> . . . any party in the United States would lose its influence by advocating war. But the motive of the democrats, is to crush the federal party, amidst the din of arms, and by silencing all opposition, to render the power of our present rulers, absolute and ever lasting. . . .
> —3 November 1810

THE SLAVE TRADER

> MR. RUSSELL,—IN the following quotation from *"The West Indies,"* by MONTGOMERY, is a full-length portrait of "A Christian Broker in the trade of blood." How many of the boasted *"Friends of Liberty"* in the State of *Rhode-Island* have set for the picture, is better known there than here; and if *"the Receiver is as bad as the Thief,"* the census will shew (sic) us how many *originals* of it are to be found in the *Liberty*-loving, democratic State of *Virginia.*
> —A REAL FRIEND TO FREEDOM
> 3 November 1810

GRAND ERIE CANAL

> On Thursday the first experiment of the navigation of the Great Canal was met with the most flattering success. . . . On Saturday she took on board [at Utica] upwards of seventy persons, . . . and proceeded to Rome (16 miles) where the company was refreshed, and returned to Utica the same afternoon; performing the two passages in ten hours and 25 minutes, including stoppages amounting to two hours and 55 minutes. . . .
> 3 November 1819

The *Centinel* abounded with suggestions on temperance, education, capital punishment, food preservation, credit, government secrecy, profanity, and other reforms. One journalism historian felt that Russell's *Centinel* was "the prototype of the great American dailies as we are to see them later in the times of Greeley, Bennett, and others."

Russell held several municipal and state positions, and was president of the Printers' Mutual Protective Society. Esther Russell died before the turn of the century; Russell remarried a widow, Sarah Guest, who bore him two girls and a boy. As had been the case with his children by his first wife, none of these children entered the newspaper business. When Russell sold his *Centinel* in 1828 after forty-two years of conscientious editing, no one in the family carried on his journalism. Russell had a farewell banquet as he left the newspaper business. His old master Isaiah Thomas was invited to the dinner. The master-apprentice relationship bloomed into true affection as Thomas invited Russell to become a charter member of the American Antiquarian Society Thomas had founded in 1812.

Two years after Russell sold his newspaper, the *Centinel* was merged with the *New-England Palladium* and later with the *Gazette*, which had been the radical newspaper of the American Revolution. Finally, in 1840, the *Centinel* lost its identity forever and was absorbed into the *Boston Daily Advertiser*. Earlier, the *Advertiser* had bought Russell's chief opponent, the *Chronicle*.

Sarah Russell died at the age of sixty-one in 1837. Benjamin remained a widower until his death nearly eight years later.

Russell's personal journalism paved the way for the penny press that could inform more of the public more often. Russell was a newspaper giant and editor in an age that a leading historian has labeled "The Dark Ages of Journalism." Russell kindled a light that Greeley carried later to illuminate one goal of newspapermen: to be "a scourge to evil doers."

References:

Joseph T. Buckingham, *Specimens of Newspaper Literature*, 2 volumes (Boston: Little & Brown, 1852), II: 1-117;

John B. Hench, "The Newspaper in a Republic: Boston's 'Centinel' and 'Chronicle,' 1784-1801," Ph.D. dissertation, Clark University, 1979;

Frederick W. Hudson, *Journalism in the United States from 1690 to 1872* (New York: Harper, 1873), pp. 147, 161;

Anne Russell Marble, *From 'Prentice to Patron: The Life Story of Isaiah Thomas* (New York: Appleton, 1935);

Frank Luther Mott, *American Journalism, 1690-1960: A History*, third edition (New York: MacMillan, 1962), pp. 131-133, 153, 174;

George Henry Payne, *History of Journalism in the United States* (New York: Appleton, 1920), pp. 142-144, 169.

Papers:

Complete files of the *Centinel* are available at the American Antiquarian Society and the Library of Congress.

William Winston Seaton

(11 January 1785-16 June 1866)

Sallie A. Whelan
Louisiana State University

MAJOR POSITION HELD: Editor, *National Intelligencer* (Washington, D.C.) (1812-1864).

BOOKS: *Register of Debates in Congress*, edited by Seaton and Joseph Gales, 29 volumes (Washington, D.C.: Gales & Seaton, 1825-1837);

American State Papers: Documents, Legislative and Executive, of the Congress of the United States, edited by Seaton and Gales, 38 volumes (Washington, D.C.: Gales & Seaton, 1832-1861);

The Debates and Proceedings in the Congress of the United States, edited by Seaton and Gales, 42 volumes (Washington, D.C.: Gales & Seaton, 1834-1856).

William Winston Seaton, editor of the *National Intelligencer* for fifty-two years, was the exclusive reporter of debates in the United States Senate from 1812 until 1829; his partner, Joseph Gales, covered the House of Representatives. Seaton and Gales's coverage of the debates of Congress supply the chief record of congressional activities until

William Winston Seaton (photograph by Mathew Brady)

Congress hired its own reporters. Seaton's paper was recognized as the administration organ under Madison and Monroe.

Seaton was born on 11 January 1785 in King William County, Virginia. His parents, Augustine and Mary Winston Seaton, were members of a prominent Virginia family which had immigrated to America from Scotland in 1690. He was tutored by a man known as Ogilvie, earl of Finlater, who operated an academy in Richmond. According to his daughter, Josephine, "An absorbing delight in reading had been one of his earliest developed tastes; and in his father's solid library his opening mind was nourished on wholesome pabulum, forming the foundation of the liberal, wide-embracing culture for which he was in after life distinguished."

Seaton became editor of the *Virginia Patriot* in Richmond at age eighteen. There, he developed a close friendship with Thomas Ritchie, who later published the *Richmond Enquirer* and the *Washington Union*. Seaton then moved to Petersburg, Virginia, where he edited the *Republican*. After developing a reputation as a political editor, Seaton was asked to move to Raleigh to assist William Boylan on the *Minerva* in 1806. One year later he took over the editorship of the *North Carolina Journal*, a Republican newspaper in Halifax. There was a bitter political struggle in Halifax between the Republicans and the Federalists and Seaton was somewhat hesitant to take the position; but he was quite successful with the paper. Atlas Jones, a prominent politician of the day, called the *North Carolina Journal* the "best edited gazette in the State; more candid, more impartial, and less fermented by the spirit of party. The dignity and fairness of your editorials have a powerful influence over even prejudiced minds, and give a steadily increasing value to your journal."

Even with this success, Seaton sought more of a challenge. On 5 January 1809 he moved back to Raleigh to assist Joseph Gales, Sr., on the *Register*. While Seaton had been working in Petersburg he had made a trip to Raleigh, where he had met Gales's daughter Sarah; undoubtedly this meeting had some influence on Seaton's decision to return to Raleigh. On 30 March 1809, Sarah Gales and Seaton were married. Sarah had been schooled in the Latin and English classics and spoke fluent French and Spanish. She was an accomplished stenographer, a rare talent for a lady at that time.

In 1807 Samuel Harrison Smith had offered his newspaper, the *National Intelligencer*, for sale. Joseph Gales, Sr., was interested in the paper but did not want to move his family to Washington. He suggested that Smith, instead of selling the paper, should take Joseph Gales, Jr., as a partner. Smith eventually agreed; and in 1810 he retired, leaving Gales as sole publisher. The pressures of publishing the triweekly became too much for Gales, and he invited his brother-in-law, Seaton, to become his partner. The Seatons moved to Washington in the fall of 1812. Seaton was to hold a one-third interest in the paper.

The Seatons spent early months of the partnership meeting cabinet members and attending White House parties and dinners. In a letter to her family, Sarah told about her first dinner party at the White House:

> I would describe the dignified appearance of Mrs. Madison, but I could not do her justice. I believe that Mrs. Madison's conduct would be graced by propriety were she placed in the most adverse circumstances in life.
>
> Mr. Madison had no leisure for the ladies: every moment of his time is engrossed by the crowd of male visitors who court his notice, and after passing the first complimentary salutations, his attention is unavoid-

ably withdrawn to more important objects.

With the *Intelligencer* as the official organ of the Madison administration, the editors had little chance to express their own opinions or to criticize the government's actions. The paper was changed to a daily on 1 January 1813.

In 1813 the threat of a British invasion was growing, with British fleets stationed in the Potomac River area. By July both Gales and Seaton had volunteered for service in a District of Columbia infantry company. While one editor served, the other would return to the city to supervise the *Intelligencer*. The content of the paper suffered, as well as the size: the paper was printed on a single sheet instead of a double sheet. Friends urged the editors to devote their full attention to the paper. On 22 July Sarah wrote to her family: "Their friends think it out of reason that the paper should be neglected, and are of opinion that the proper and continual direction of the public record printed in their office is of infinitely more importance than any individual exertion they could possibly make in camp." By 27 July the threat of invasion had subsided, and Seaton and Gales returned to the *Intelligencer*.

The following year, as British troops moved closer to the city, all of the *Intelligencer*'s workmen were called to serve. The paper was forced to suspend publication until Seaton was able to convince the secretary of war to release a few of the men. On 24 August the post office was closed and no papers could be sent from the city. Seaton dismissed the workmen and rejoined the militia. By 25 August the British had set fire to most of Washington's public buildings and some private ones. Books and other valuables were taken from the *Intelligencer* office and burned in the streets, but the building itself was spared thanks to two neighborhood women who stood guard. Although some type was saved, it was said that British Admiral George Cockburn ordered all the *C*s destroyed so that the editors could not print his name.

Publication of a much smaller *Intelligencer* resumed on 31 August 1814. Because of its size, a single sheet, little news and no editorials appeared. The loss of the printing facilities, circulation lists, bookkeeping records, and correspondences set the editors back financially. Friends offered donations of as much as $30,000, but the editors refused, saying that losses would have to be replaced by the "labor of their own hands, without accepting of that gratuitous aid so generously proffered, of which, unfortunately, but too many of their fellow citizens

have much greater need than they."

By 26 September the *Intelligencer* was being published in its original size. In that issue, the editors affirmed their opposition to "the malevolence of Faction, as against the violence of the national enemy—both of which have been of late most magnanimously exerted, the one in the destruction of their property, the other in pitiful assaults on the reputation of the paper and its Editors."

The end of the War of 1812 on 24 December 1814 also brought an end to a sort of trial period for Seaton and Gales. During the war they had acted as agents of the government, not as commentators, critics, or policymakers. The "Era of Good Feeling" from 1815 to 1824 was a time for the editors to develop independence.

By 1818 Seaton and Gales owed the Bank of the United States $6,500. Although circulation of the *Intelligencer* reached 6,000 by 1823, the debts continued to mount, partly due to large sums of money owed to the editors, which they failed to collect. In a letter to James Ronaldson, who had requested payment due him, the editors wrote, "We would have paid our note long ago, would others have paid us. We have debts of 80 or an hundred thousand dollars due us."

In 1819 Seaton and Gales were awarded profitable government printing contracts, which they held for nearly ten years. These contracts kept the paper in business, but they meant that the paper was filled with congressional reports. Such reports were carried on at least two and frequently on all four pages.

The editors, both accomplished stenographers, took down the congressional proceedings in shorthand—Seaton beside the vice-president in the Senate and Gales beside the Speaker of the House. Speeches of Daniel Webster, Henry Clay, and John Calhoun were preserved through the detailed reporting. Seaton and Gales published their reports of government activities in several series of books. The *Register of Debates*, first published on 24 September 1825 and continuing until 1837, was to present a year-to-year "History of the Legislation of Government of the United States." Although the debates were not always printed verbatim, they were as accurate as possible. Also included in the *Register* were presidential messages and important executive documents. The *American State Papers*, "a Compilation of the Executive Documents, and of the Legislative Records of Congress, of date anterior to the third session of the thirteenth Congress," were published from 1832 until 1861. Reports of congressional activities

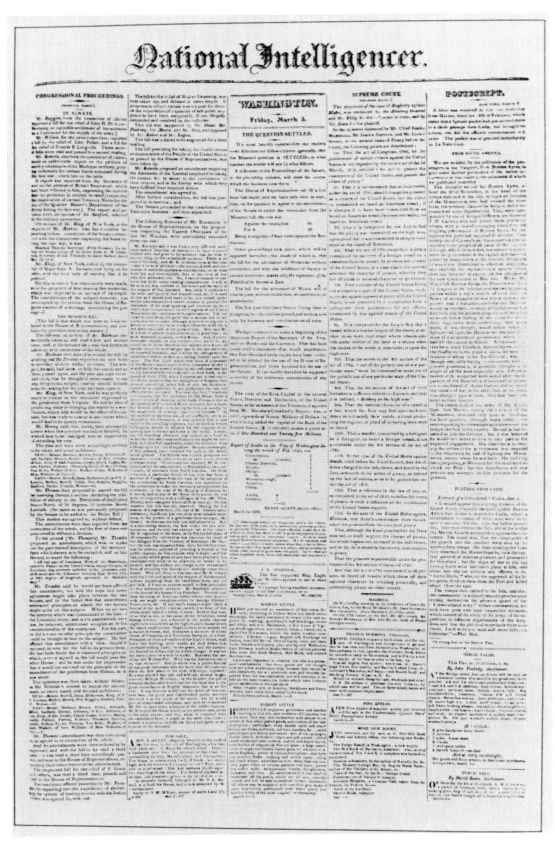

Front page of the National Intelligencer *for 3 March 1820, featuring a report on the passage of the Missouri Compromise*

were bound and published in *The Debates and Proceedings in the Congress of the United States* from 1834 until 1856. This publication was also widely known as the *Annals of Congress*. The *Intelligencer* continued to be the organ of the federal government through the Monroe administration.

Before 1824 there had been no opposition to the candidates nominated by the congressional caucus; but the editors had to choose a candidate in this election as President Monroe chose no successor. The editors selected William H. Crawford, but John Quincy Adams won the election. Relations between the editors and the new president were somewhat strained, and Adams turned to the *National Journal* as his semiofficial organ. Seaton and Gales were finally able to become friendly with the Adams administration; in 1828, when Adams and Andrew Jackson were in the running for president, the *Intelligencer* supported Adams. Seaton and Gales were strongly opposed to Jackson's political beliefs and launched attacks on him in the paper.

The editors paid dearly for these attacks when Jackson was elected. They lost the Senate printing contract in 1827 and the House contract in 1829, leaving them with only the *Intelligencer*, the *Register of Debates*, and miscellaneous printing jobs. They were still deeply in debt, but with the addition of the *American State Papers* and *The Annals of Congress*, the editors were able to stay in business during Jackson's administration.

Seaton was elected mayor of Washington in 1840 and held the position until 1850. According to his daughter, "He labored incessantly for the best interests of the community over which he was the watchful guardian, advancing with the most earnest solicitude all movements tending to its moral and intellectual progress. By his personal influence in Congress he obtained so many grants and privileges, that the results of his persuasive power became jest among the honorable members, who predicted that 'if Mr. Seaton remained mayor much longer he would bankrupt the national treasury.' " Seaton led the movement to build the Washington Monument, and was treasurer of the Smithsonian Institution after 1846.

The *Intelligencer* was once again the organ of the administration in 1841 under William Henry Harrison, but Harrison died only one month after taking office. The last time the paper served as the administration organ was under Millard Fillmore, who became president after the death of Zachary Taylor in 1850.

The editors feared the injuries the nation would suffer due to growing sectional conflicts. Although they supported the eventual abolition of slavery, they also supported the Constitution, and it allowed for slavery. They had freed their own slaves and had purchased the freedom of others, but they had done so as private individuals. They did not use the *Intelligencer* to voice their opinions on this subject. They felt that a war to prevent secession was justified but that a war to free slaves was unconstitutional.

Although the *Intelligencer* was one of the most respected Washington papers, its influence and circulation declined in the 1850s. It no longer held a monopoly on reporting the activities of Congress. Seaton and Gales favored long deliberations on a story before publication and resented the hurried reporting the telegraph encouraged. The paper was viewed by many as being behind the times. A political paper like the *Intelligencer* was no longer profitable in Washington.

In 1860 Gales died. Three years later, after fifty-three years of marriage, Seaton's wife died. On 31 December 1864 Seaton sold the *National Intelligencer*. Although he would have preferred to let the paper die, there were debts to be paid. Seaton wrote to an old friend, Boston publisher George S. Hilliard: "The parting with my old paper was painful in the extreme; but the reverses experienced from secession and the intolerance of party had reduced it to the point of extinction and no alternative was left but to see it expire or to accept the offer of some business men who thought that by withdrawing the paper from the sphere of politics and converting it into a mere news and advertising sheet they could make it pay. The country does not seem to regard it of importance to support a paper at the seat of Government which presumed to have a conscience and an independent judgment."

Seaton died on 16 June 1866 after a long and painful battle with cancer. On the day of his funeral, flags were flown at half-staff from City Hall, schools, and other public buildings. The *Intelligencer* remained in publication until 1869; historian William E. Ames, however, says that the *Intelligencer* really died in "1864 when Seaton signed his last editorial and laid down his pen."

Throughout his career, Seaton supported constitutional freedoms. He was opposed to war and tried to reason with Americans through the *Intelligencer*. Due to Seaton and Gales's detailed reporting, history has been preserved in the *Register of Debates*, *Annals of Congress*, and the *American State Papers*. After Seaton's death, a close friend wrote of him: "There is one thing in his career that ought to be emphasized, that is, his keeping the *Intelligencer* free from all personalities, not only of abuse, but partisanship." Another friend wrote of Seaton's integrity: "I was present on one occasion in his office when a man used, in vain, every argument to obtain from him the insertion of an advertisement which Mr. Seaton deemed unfitting for the pure columns of the paper. Finally an amount was offered that would have made many men waver, but Mr. Seaton's answer was this: 'Sir, there is not in the world gold enough to tempt me to insert in the *Intelligencer* one line which I should be unwilling for my wife and daughters to read.' "

References:

William E. Ames, *A History of the National Intelligencer* (Chapel Hill: University of North Carolina Press, 1972);

Josephine Seaton, *William Winston Seaton of the National Intelligencer* (Boston: James R. Osgood, 1871);

Oren Andrew Seaton, *The Seaton Family, with Genealogy and Biographies* (Topeka, Kans.: Crane, 1906).

Samuel Harrison Smith

Harry W. Stonecipher
Southern Illinois University

BIRTH: Philadelphia, 1772, to Jonathan and Susannah Bayard Smith.

EDUCATION: University of Pennsylvania, B.A., 1787; M.A., 1790.

MARRIAGE: 26 September 1800, to Margaret Bayard; children: John, Julia, Susan, Anne.

MAJOR POSITIONS HELD: Editor and publisher, *New World* (Philadelphia) (1796-1797), *Independent Gazetteer*, renamed *Universal Gazette* in 1797 (Philadelphia; moved to Washington in 1800) (1797-1810), *National Intelligencer and Washington Advertiser* (Washington, D.C.) (1800-1810).

DEATH: Washington, D.C., 1 November 1845.

BOOKS: *Prospectus for the Republication of the Monthly Review* (Philadelphia, 1794);
Philadelphia, February 20, 1796. Sir, In Compliance with the Recommendation of a Number of Gentlemen, I Have Determined to Submit to Public Patronage the Publication of a Newspaper, the Plan of Which Is Annexed. Samuel H. Smith. Proposals by Samuel H. Smith, No. 118, Chestnut Street, for Printing by Subscription, a Newspaper, to Appear Twice a Day, Called the New World, or the Morning and Evening Gazette. . . . (Philadelphia:

Printed by Samuel Harrison Smith, 1796);
Remarks on Education: Illustrating the Close Connection between Virtue and Wisdom. To Which Is Annexed, A System of Liberal Education. Which, Having Received the Premium Awarded by the American Philosophical Society, December 15th, 1797, Is Now Published by Their Order (Philadelphia: Printed for John Ormond, 1798);
History of the Last Session of Congress, Which Commenced on the Seventh of December, 1801. Taken from the National Intelligencer. . . . (Washington, D.C.: Printed by S. H. Smith for J. Conrad & Co., Philadelphia, Rapine, Conrad & Co., Washington City, [etc.], 1802);
Trial of Samuel Chase, an Associate Justice of the Supreme Court of the United States, Impeached by the House of Representatives, for High Crimes and Misdemeanors, before the Senate of the United States, by Smith and Thomas Lloyd (Washington, D.C.: Printed for Samuel H. Smith, 1805);
Oration Pronounced by Samuel H. Smith, Esquire, in the City of Washington, on Monday, the Fifth of July, 1813, by Request of a General Meeting of the Citizens, and Published at the Desire of the Committee of Arrangement (Washington, D.C.: Printed by Roger C. Weightman, 1813);
Memoir of the Life, Character, and Writings of Thomas Jefferson; Delivered in the Capitol, before the Co-

lumbian Institute, on the Sixth of January, 1827, and Published at Their Request (Washington, D.C.: S. A. Elliot, printer, 1827).

Samuel Harrison Smith, though his years as a Washington newspaper publisher were relatively brief, played an important role as a journalist and as the reporter of debates of the Congress during the first decade of the nineteenth century. Smith was only twenty-eight years old when he founded the *National Intelligencer* as a triweekly newspaper in October 1800, the year the federal government moved from Philadelphia to Washington. An ardent Republican and a friend of Thomas Jefferson, Smith was a faithful but far from servile supporter of the Jefferson administration. The *Intelligencer* during Jefferson's presidency, however, was often called the "official gazette" or the "government organ," though the paper's character clearly transcended such a limited role.

The *Intelligencer* under Smith's guidance became a valuable means of preserving a record of the congressional debates during the early Washington years. In addition, many newspapers throughout the several states relied upon Smith's reports in the *Intelligencer* for their news stories about the national government. During these years reports of the congressional debates, which were taken in shorthand by Smith, sometimes with the assistance of an associate, were also relied upon in compiling the *Annals of Congress*, later published for each session of the Congress.

The historical importance and political preeminence of the *Intelligencer* during the first decade of the nineteenth century was no doubt enhanced by the close relationship between the young publisher and Jefferson. Journalism historian James E. Pollard noted that "Jefferson was the first president to have an administration organ of his own choosing," with an editor "in whom he had great confidence and with whom he was on terms of social intimacy." Indeed, Pollard pointed out, no other president, except perhaps for Jackson, dealt with a newspaper or its editor as Jefferson dealt with the *National Intelligencer* and Smith. The publisher's wife, who had a strong social bent and a taste for politics, was also a favorite of Jefferson. Her salon became an important social center where many leading political figures of Washington gathered. The Smiths were also frequent guests at the White House during Jefferson's two terms as president.

Before he moved to Washington, Smith's entire life had been spent in Philadelphia where he was born in 1772. His father, Jonathan Smith, was a graduate of the College of New Jersey and a successful Philadelphia businessman. His mother, Susannah Bayard Smith, was the daughter of Samuel Bayard, scion of a prominent Maryland family. After his marriage, Jonathan Smith added Bayard to his legal name.

Young Samuel developed a keen interest in the early history of the Republic from his father, an ardent anti-British delegate and secretary to the Provincial Congress, a colonel in the Second Troop of the Philadelphia City Cavalry, and a strong supporter of the Articles of Confederation. In addition, the elder Smith was chief clerk of the Court of Common Pleas, was active in the Sons of Tammany, served as grand master of the Masons of Pennsylvania, was a member of the American Philosophical Society, and served as a trustee at both the College of New Jersey and the University of Pennsylvania.

Little is known of Samuel's grammar school education or his early training, but he received a bachelor of arts degree from the University of Pennsylvania in 1787. Three years later, apparently without additional formal course work, he received a master of arts degree from Pennsylvania as the result of passing the required examinations. (Smith also received an honorary master of arts in 1797 from the College of New Jersey.) Despite his educational achievement, Smith in 1790 was something less than dynamic; indeed, he was usually quiet and introspective. In physical appearance he was, according to historian William E. Ames, "a rather tall, slender person with a sparse crop of hair, small eyes, and a prominent nose. Diligence, together with a serious countenance, marked everything Smith undertook."

What Smith first undertook was to establish a printing business in Philadelphia, opening an office at 131 Chestnut Street in 1791. Three years later he proposed publishing an American edition of the *English Monthly Review*, but evidently the plans failed since no such publication resulted. He was connected, however, with the printing of the *American Universal Magazine*, a literary publication which survived for only two years. He became involved in the lively competition of Philadelphia journalism in 1796 when he began a twice-daily tabloid news sheet, the *New World*, an innovative venture in terms of the journalism of that day. The young publisher pledged to support Jefferson and the policies of the emerging Republican party, and to encourage political discussion so long as it was connected with "principles and the general good."

In the first issue on 15 August 1796, Smith warned that "party malevolence and personal resentment would be rejected." The paper was changed to a daily after two months and ceased publication a year later.

Smith's high-minded journalistic efforts faced tough competition from existing Philadelphia papers within the Republican party as well as those supporting Federalist views. The leading Republican paper in 1796 was the *Aurora*, published by Benjamin Franklin Bache, a grandson of Benjamin Franklin. Smith and Bache held widely different views on how to edit a newspaper. Bache was brash and outspoken, even attacking George Washington on occasion and calling Washington's retirement from public service a time for rejoicing. In 1797 William Cobbett, an Englishman who wrote under the pseudonym "Peter Porcupine," also appeared in Philadelphia with his *Porcupine's Gazette*, an anti-Republican newspaper. Cobbett was even more scurrilous in his criticisms of individuals than was Bache.

The competitive newspaper market in Philadelphia, however, did not deter Smith from becoming engaged once again in a journalistic venture, this time with an established Republican newspaper, the *Independent Gazetteer*. The *Gazetteer* had been founded in 1782 by Eleazer Oswald, who published it as a Saturday paper. After Oswald died, the paper was bought by Joseph Gales, Sr., a refugee journalist from England. In turn, Gales sold the *Gazetteer* to Smith in the summer of 1797. Gales, one of the first reporters to regularly cover the sessions of Congress, taught Smith to write in shorthand. To escape recurrent epidemics of yellow fever, Gales later moved to North Carolina, where he published the *Raleigh Register,* an influential Republican journal.

Smith changed the name of the paper to the *Universal Gazette* in November 1797, but he did not change its format. He continued to print government news and to publish letters bearing Latin pseudonyms, a custom in the early American press. He also wrote editorials from time to time. Though the *Gazette* supported Republican causes, Smith usually couched his opinions in moderate terms.

This effort toward political neutrality at a time of growing partisanship apparently annoyed many *Gazette* readers; it also must have been frustrating to Smith, who is known to have been strongly opposed to the Alien and Sedition Acts of 1798, the source of much of the political controversy and anti-Federalist feeling between 1798 and 1800. While Smith was convinced that Jefferson

was the man the United States needed as its next president, his reluctance to enter into political controversy prevented him from effectively defending Jefferson and fellow Republican editors against scurrilous Federalist attacks. By contrast, Bache brought both physical and legal recrimination against himself and his paper at the hands of the Federalists. When Bache died during the yellow fever epidemic in September 1798, his associate editor, William Duane, took up the bitter campaign against the Federalists.

The new publisher of the *Universal Gazette* was faced also with the problem of collecting subscriptions from readers scattered throughout a number of states. Gales had faced the same difficulty during his years as publisher of the *Gazetteer*. Confronted by such political and economic obstacles in Philadelphia, Smith began to look for other opportunities. His eyes turned naturally toward Washington, where the nation's capital was to move in 1800. If he could cover the news from the new seat of government he would be in contact with the nation's future political leaders. He also entertained thoughts of capturing a share of the public printing, a lucrative plum for any struggling publisher. Smith was contemplating marriage, and he was becoming increasingly concerned about establishing himself in a more financially rewarding position.

Smith had become engaged to Margaret Bayard, his second cousin and a daughter of John B. Bayard, a Philadelphia merchant and owner of a Maryland plantation. Bayard had been an early joiner of the Sons of Liberty and had been a colonel during the American Revolution at the battles of Brandywine, Germantown, and Princeton. He was an active Federalist, and, like Alexander Hamilton, believed that a political gentry should act as guardians of the people. Margaret, born in 1778 during the Revolution, was at age twenty-two described as "a vivacious young lady" with a dynamic personality and "rather attractive features," who "mingled graciously with people and could be counted upon as a valuable asset to almost any career." She had been indoctrinated with the Federalist political views of her father, which were in marked contrast to the Republican beliefs of her fiancé.

Indeed, the Bayards considered Smith to be a rather unsatisfactory prospective husband for their daughter. Margaret was a devout Presbyterian, while Smith, like his political mentor Jefferson, was a deist. The Bayard family was also concerned because of Smith's lack of success in Philadelphia. Margaret, as well as her brother Samuel, urged Smith to establish a newspaper in New York, where the financial prospects looked better; Samuel Bayard even expressed a willingness to provide the $12,000 to $15,000 needed to establish a paper there. Another brother, John Bayard, who had connections with a New York firm that had promised to finance the proposed Washington paper, first objected to the marriage because of the lack of adequate accommodations in Washington. As Ames noted: "Washington City in 1800 resembled an uncouth frontier settlement. The sprawling town lacked polish and culture which for years had characterized Philadelphia, the capital city of the nation during the 1790s. Lacking in the new capital were the broad avenues, tidy shops and bustling commerce to which Philadelphians were accustomed. Instead, Washington City was a jerry-built community where carpenters and joiners hurried to complete a capitol building. The White House itself was only partially completed and overlooked marshy, heavily timbered areas surrounding the capital. Roads raised clouds of dust in summer and mired carriage wheels in winter." Those objections were somehow overcome by Smith.

As it turned out, it was at the urging of Jefferson himself that the young publisher finally made the decision to follow the capital from Philadelphia to Washington. It was commonly expected that William Duane would establish the new Republican paper in Washington; but while Jefferson no doubt appreciated Duane's political services, journalism historian Frank Luther Mott believed that Jefferson "personally disliked and distrusted the *Aurora*'s type of journalism with its shrill belligerence and ready billingsgate." At any rate, Jefferson turned to Smith, who reportedly had gained his recognition in 1797 by tying for the first prize offered by the American Philosophical Society for the best essay on a system of education and a plan for free public schools. Mrs. Smith later wrote in her memoirs: "During part of the time that Mr. Jefferson was president of the Philosophical Society, Mr. Smith was the secretary. A prize offered by the society for the best system of national education was gained by Mr. Smith. The merit of this essay first attracted the notice of Mr. Jefferson to its author; the personal acquaintance that then took place led to a friendly intercourse which influenced the future destiny of my husband, as it was by Mr. Jefferson's advice that he removed to Washington and established the *National Intelligencer*. Esteem for the talents and character of the editor first won Mr. Jefferson's regard—a regard which lasted to the end of his life and was a thousand times evinced by acts of personal kindness and confidence."

Smith, without doubt, had gained the recognition of Jefferson even earlier through his pro-Republican efforts as publisher of the *New World* and the *Universal Gazette*, though his wife's memoirs fail to take note of such recognition.

In August 1800 plans for the wedding and the move to Washington took a step forward. Smith visited Washington in mid-August and rented two unfinished buildings, one for living quarters and the other to house his publishing business. In a letter to Margaret, however, he pondered whether she would really be happy in her new home because of the crudeness of the city. Smith returned to Philadelphia to seek support for his new publication, writing to top Republican leaders, including James Madison. He also ordered paper, type, and printing supplies, to be delivered in Washington by 23 September.

The couple was married on 26 September in New Brunswick, New Jersey, where Margaret's father, though retired, served as mayor, justice of the Court of Common Pleas of Somerset County, and trustee of the College of New Jersey. Following the ceremony, the couple left by carriage for Philadelphia, from where they went by stagecoach to Washington. Ames noted: "The young publisher and his wife, with much to be optimistic about, also faced great problems. The Smiths were gambling that Jefferson would become president and that his election would bring them a share of the federal printing. They were leaving the familiar surroundings in which they were reared and were moving into the uncertain but challenging society growing up around the new capital. The possibilities of success were promising but uncertain. However, if the *National Intelligencer* should fail, Smith still had the *Universal Gazette*, for he moved the subscription list to Washington City with him."

The first order of business was to establish the *Intelligencer*'s new publishing plant on New Jersey Avenue between D and E Streets, S.E., near the Capitol. Smith's debut in Washington journalism, however, was delayed a month because the boat carrying his printing equipment from Philadelphia was driven ashore in a storm. It was not until 31 October that the first issue of the *National Intelligencer and Washington Advertiser* appeared.

With the presidential election so near, the young publisher was forced to stake out an editorial position immediately. In his declaration of principles and policy in the first issue, Smith ruled out "indelicate ideas or expressions" but asserted that "the conduct of public men and tendency of public measures" would be "freely examined." He declared liberty of the press to be a "safeguard of human happiness."

The first issue of the *Intelligencer* also carried a contributed article which made an attack, however mild, on President Adams for his alleged usurpation of legislative authority in his appointment of federal judges, most of them Federalists, during his last days in office. Two letters by Adams were also printed, with appended comments by Alexander Hamilton expressing his conviction that Adams was unfit for the presidency. One historian, Culver Smith, has noted that after the pronouncements in the first issue of the *Intelligencer* no reader with any political awareness could have doubted that the editor's design to "diffuse correct information" meant support of Jefferson for president.

During the first few years Smith handled all the publishing duties except for the mechanical production of the three issues a week. He wrote the news, covered the congressional debates, chose the exchange stories, and took care of the advertising and billing. The *Universal Gazette*, which had been transferred from Philadelphia, was published as a weekly edition of the *Intelligencer*.

The *Intelligencer* was a modest four-page paper, its first and last pages devoted largely to advertising and its second page to the proceedings of Congress or other editorial matter. According to Ames:

> In a small column on the front page Smith sometimes aired his opinions on happenings in the nation's capital. The remainder of the page reported congressional proceedings and contained advertisements. Small business notices were purchased mostly by Washington City storekeepers and slave owners whose property had run away.
>
> Congressional proceedings as well as miscellaneous material, such as excerpts from current books, letters from subscribers, and lengthy political articles written by unidentified correspondents, along with clippings from other newspapers, filled page two of the *Intelligencer*. A second editorial column appeared on page three, and page four carried a variety of material. Most of the paper was devoted to congressional proceedings, but stories clipped from exchange papers were found throughout the paper.

The small type, used for both the text of stories as well as for headlines—most of them mere label heads—gave the paper a dull, gray appearance. The stories were printed in six-point type,

much smaller than that used in other papers, and the debates ran column after column with no breaks in the blocks of print. The paper's conservative makeup was consistent with its general editorial policy. Mott noted: "Politically it was not combative, and one competitor nicknamed it 'Mr. Silky Milky Smith's National Smoothing Plane.'"

In order for the *Intelligencer* to succeed as a publishing venture, Smith felt, Jefferson had to win the presidential election in November. When a tie in electoral votes occurred between Jefferson and Aaron Burr, Smith was forced to wait until mid-February, when the election issue reached the House of Representatives, before the question was resolved.

During the period between the election and the balloting in the House, the *Intelligencer* gave little indication that Smith knew about the backstage maneuvering by Federalist congressmen to swing support to Burr. By the time the issue reached the House, however, the young editor had to be aware of the political intrigue because James A. Bayard, who was Margaret's foster brother and Smith's cousin, had become a key figure in the Federalist plans.

Mrs. Smith, writing years later about the election, recounted that she and her husband waited in their parlor as the balloting began on Friday, 12 February, and continued all night. A messenger brought reports every hour, and as the time for each report grew near, Mrs. Smith wrote, "My heart would almost audibly beat and I was seized with a tremour that almost disabled me from opening the door. . . ." The balloting continued until the following Tuesday when, after thirty-six ballots, James Bayard cast a blank ballot and a number of other congressmen followed suit, giving Jefferson the victory.

During Smith's introduction to Washington journalism he apparently had suffered little annoyance from the Federalist in the White House, despite the *Intelligencer*'s support of Jefferson. Indeed, President Adams had been cordial and information had been given courteously to the young Republican editor. Smith had hoped, however, that Jefferson's election might eliminate some of the irritations produced by the Federalist-dominated Congress; but it took another election for this to occur.

In early December 1800, when the new congressional session opened in Washington, Smith prepared to report the debates and proceedings of the House of Representatives, as he had done in Philadelphia. According to Ames, "since no facilities existed in the new House chamber for reporters, or stenographers, as they were then known, Smith spoke to the Speaker of the House, Theodore Sedgwick of Massachusetts, requesting permission to place a desk inside the rail in order to better hear the debates. . . . Sedgwick, a closed-minded Federalist. . . . concluded that the dignity of the House and the convenience of members could not be preserved if such permission were granted." When the speaker's ruling was opposed by Joseph Nicholson of Maryland, a Jefferson supporter, a debate followed which resulted in a forty-five to forty-five vote, largely along party lines, with the speaker casting the deciding vote denying the request.

Smith moved to the upper gallery of the House, but his expulsion from the floor made him more determined than ever to obtain a convenient place for reporting the debates. In an editorial note in the *Intelligencer* on 14 January 1801, he vowed: "Uninfluenced by personal feeling, and guided by a *due* respect for the *Speaker,* and a sincere respect for the *People* of the United States, [the editor] will not, while he retains the power, cease, by publishing a record of truth, whatever or whomsoever it may affect, to manifest to the people, on *whose* support he relies, a spirit of dignity and moderation that frowns of power can never dismay." On the day that the note was published, however, the sergeant at arms brought a message from the speaker demanding that Smith withdraw from the gallery. The next morning Smith called on Sedgwick at his lodgings, where an interview convinced the young editor that the speaker was incompetent, and he later reported the encounter in a blistering front-page report to readers of the *Intelligencer*. For the rest of the session Smith was forced to go to the clerk of the House for information and, presumably, to publish what the clerk permitted him to copy. Other items in the *Intelligencer* may have come from representatives who were favorably disposed toward the young publisher.

"Editors throughout the country watched Smith's battle for access to the House with interest," Ames pointed out, "for already they were copying reports of congressional proceedings from the *Intelligencer*." Joseph Gales, Sr., noted that the readers of the *Raleigh Register* owed the *Intelligencer* a debt for supplying congressional bulletins. Gales pointed out that his readers could not help "considering this conduct of Mr. Sedgwick as very arbitrary, since it may deprive the people of any account at all of congressional proceedings."

In the next session of Congress, a Republican

majority took control. Smith gained readmission to the House floor, but he never considered the facilities afforded for reporting the debates entirely satisfactory during his ten years as editor of the *Intelligencer*. Smith did not try to cover the Senate during his first year in Washington. His petition filed 5 January 1802 for access to the Senate floor, however, was granted by a seventeen to nine vote. The editor told his readers that reporting Senate proceedings from the gallery, as previously required, had been impossible; the Senate vote, Smith wrote, was the opening of a new door to public information.

Smith and the *Intelligencer* also had problems with the post office. In February 1801 the editor reported that "many complaints" had been received from subscribers about irregular delivery of the *Intelligencer*. Smith put the blame squarely on the general post office, pointing out that "neglect and misconduct appear to occur in the whole extent of the line. The papers are destroyed before they reach Alexandria, Newport, Delaware, Philadelphia and New York, all of which are on the main line." Smith also engaged the assistant postmaster general in a controversy about the non-delivery issue, arguing that the Federalist administration of the mails was consciously hindering the circulation of his paper.

While Jefferson's election helped to solve Smith's problems with the executive and legislative branches, the judiciary, still dominated by Federalists, gave the Republican editor continuing difficulty. Smith's problems began in June 1801 when he published a letter criticizing the judiciary and the last minute federal judicial appointments of President Adams. The letter, signed "A Friend to Impartial Justice," maintained that Federalist judges were not administering the law impartially, as the Constitution provided. The letter argued that Adams's late judicial appointments under the Judiciary Bill of 1801 had made the courts a threat to the power of both the executive and legislative branches, and said of the judicial situation facing President Jefferson: "He found the community divided; he found the asylum of justice impure—There, where reason and truth, unagitated, and unimpaired even by suspicion, ought to preserve perpetual reign, he contemplated the dominance of political and personal prejudice, habitually employed in preparing or executing partial vengeance."

Because of the letter, the circuit court for the District of Columbia ordered the district attorney to prosecute Smith for libel. Smith regarded the

Front page of the National Intelligencer *for 13 December 1800, describing Smith's unsuccessful efforts to be allowed to report from the floor of the House of Representatives*

charge as a test of the freedom of the press guaranteed in the First Amendment. In his defense, Smith also cited the Maryland Constitution, which stated "That the liberty of the press ought to be . . . preserved." He further argued that the article was critical of a public official rather than a private person, and was directed toward the discharge of his duty, not his personal conduct. Smith contended further that the charges involved differences of opinion, and asked how it could be decided who was right or wrong in such differences. Smith also pointed out that he had not written the letter precipitating the libel action; he was therefore being tried as a printer rather than a writer. While Smith admitted that the person who wrote the letter may have been wrong in his opinions, he contended that the writer had the right to express those opinions.

The bill of indictment was returned by the grand jury marked "ignoramus," and the charges against Smith apparently were never renewed.

Another problem with which Smith was concerned during his first year in Washington had to do with the division of the printing patronage. While it is difficult to determine just how much money was involved in such patronage, one source indicates that in 1801 the printing contracts from the House alone totaled about $4,000, and that the Senate spent about half this amount. Executive printing from the departments of State, Treasury, and War for the 1794 session had totaled more than $7,000. It was a share of this printing that the publisher of the *Intelligencer* sought to bolster his new publishing venture.

While Smith was confident that he would receive some printing orders from the federal government, he knew also that he would be faced with tough competition from Duane, who also had given faithful service to Jefferson and the Republicans. Indeed, Duane had spent a great deal of time during 1801 defending himself in court as the result of his service to Republican causes. Duane had opened a printing plant in Washington, and he believed that the Republican administration ought to share the cost of his legal defense against their common political enemy—the Federalists. One way that the administration could reimburse him was through a share of the printing patronage.

By the opening session of Congress in December 1801, however, Smith had a sizable share of the government printing contracts. These included contracts for the House and the Department of State, as well as lesser contracts with other government departments. The *Intelligencer* publisher re-

ceived nearly $8,000 between 1801 and 1805 from the State Department alone; the average weekly wage for a printer during these years was $10 a week or less. The larger printing orders included pamphlet editions of the laws, often as many as 10,000 copies. Many printing orders, however, were divided among other Washington printers, including Duane. But the support which the *Aurora* publisher received proved insufficient to maintain his printing venture in Washington. With his failure as a printer, Duane also lost influence as a Republican editor, leaving Smith and his newspaper in an even stronger position. By supporting the Jefferson administration, Smith was assured a prosperous publishing business as long as the Republican party was in power.

Meanwhile, the cause which the *Intelligencer* advocated, the repeal of Adams's judiciary act, was the major issue during the congressional session that began late in 1801. Smith covered the proceedings and editorialized on the brilliance of the speeches he heard relative to the repeal. Smith's greatest contribution as a journalist was his reporting of the proceedings of the two houses of Congress during these debates. *Intelligencer* readers were supplied column after column of the debates on the judiciary bill. Papers throughout the country found the *Intelligencer* their most complete source of information on what was happening in Washington. Smith was jubilant over passage of the repeal measure on 3 March 1802, informing *Intelligencer* readers: "Hereafter we may indulge the pleasing hope that the streams of justice, unpolluted by party prejudice or passion, will flow pure."

In addition to the abolition of judgeships held by the Federalists, the other major issue during the first term of the Republican Congress was the new financial program of Secretary of the Treasury Gallatin. The secretary's main objective was to reduce the public debt without, as the Federalists proposed, using the sinking fund. Secondly, Gallatin sought to reduce taxes by reducing the spending of the War and Navy Departments, since the chance of the United States becoming involved in a European war had diminished. The editor of the *Intelligencer* informed his readers on 30 December 1801: "We are persuaded that that government is the strongest which is free from debt, and free too from taxes beyond its necessary wants."

The judiciary was again a topic of concern in the next session of Congress. One of the targets of the Republican attempt to rid the courts of Federalist domination was Supreme Court Associate

Justice Samuel Chase. Chase had angered many Republicans by his aggressive role as a circuit judge in the enforcement of the Alien and Sedition laws during the Adams administration. He incurred more hostility on 2 May 1803 with his charge to the grand jury at Baltimore, when he criticized the democratic tendencies of both the national and local governments. The *Intelligencer* reported: "This charge may be pronounced the most extraordinary that the violence of federalism has yet produced, and exhibits humiliating evidence of the unfortunate effects of disappointed ambition."

The young editor of the *Intelligencer* not only reported the impeachment trial of Justice Chase before the United States Senate, which began on 2 January 1805; he also was called upon to testify during the trial, and he later published a two-volume transcript of the trial proceedings which he and an associate had taken in shorthand. One senator, William Plumer of New Hampshire, was disappointed in Smith's performance as a witness, saying that "his nerves failed him—he stated that the sum of all he had to say was contained in an affidavit he gave last winter to the committee—& he requested and obtained liberty to read a printed copy of it which he had compared with the original." The young editor was no doubt himself disappointed when the Senate on 1 March cleared Chase of all eight counts brought against him. Smith reported in the *Intelligencer* on 5 March 1805, however, that perhaps never before "in this country, or in any other, has a tribunal of justice exhibited more honorable traits of impartiality, or dignified decorum has persevered, which reflects high honor on the Senate of the United States, and the individual who presides over their deliberation."

That presiding officer, Vice-President Burr, was involved in the next important conflict between the Jefferson administration and the federal courts. Smith, like most Republican editors, opposed Burr, and except for the praise he received in the *Intelligencer* during the Chase trial, Burr was accorded little mention in the paper. Even reports of the duel between Burr and Hamilton, in which Hamilton was killed, were not given prominent display. That all changed, however, when Burr was charged with treason by the Jefferson administration. Smith wrote in the *Intelligencer* on 13 March 1807:

> The obscurity, that has for some time enveloped the project of Aaron Burr, begins to give place to facts. From a great variety of

> information received from various quarters, we believe, it may be confidently said—
> 1. That a military plan has been formed; and
> 2. That Aaron Burr is the head of it. . . . Our decided opinion is that there ought to be no reserve on this subject. Treason and traitors are entitled to no reserve; and the people of the United States, without being unnecessarily alarmed, ought to be enabled to appreciate the danger that menaces them.

The attempts to convict Burr failed, however, and the Republicans felt even more bitter toward the judiciary, particularly Chief Justice Marshall, a longtime foe of Jefferson. Smith reported to *Intelligencer* readers on 7 September that the trial was stopped by the Federalist court to prevent truths that would have embarrassed the Federalists. Although Smith did not like the outcome of the trial, he praised the press for its calm treatment of the proceedings. In the same issue, Smith editorialized that Burr was a "dangerous person" who "deserved close watching."

The Louisiana Purchase, a major news event during Jefferson's first term of office, helped to increase the president's popularity. Smith had shared Jefferson's early misgivings about the constitutionality of the purchase, but the editor's doubts were resolved as soon as the president decided to go ahead with the purchase. In making the purchase, the Jefferson administration tried not to upset the delicate balance of power between France and England. A resumption of hostilities between those countries led Jefferson to set the nation on the policy of "millions for Defence, but not a cent for tribute."

The *Intelligencer* praised a bill appropriating money for two warships as a move which demonstrated the administration's determination "not by vain vaunting of prowess: but by actions. . . ." Smith later supported the Embargo Act, passed in December 1807, which halted American shipping with other nations. When objections were raised to the embargo—particularly in New England, where idle shops and ports all contributed to an economic depression—Smith was bewildered by the attacks on Jefferson. When the Massachusetts legislature passed a resolution calling for replacing of the embargo with naval protection for American shipping, Smith, in an uncharacteristic editorial outburst, wrote: "*Submission!* Good God! Can the idea enter into the minds of any Americans? Can it more than all enter into the minds of the sons of Massachusetts? Can they who have been rocked by their illustrious and patriotic forefathers in the cradle of revolutionary independence, . . . who risqued [sic] their property, their lives, in seventy-six, when we were weak, poor, and disunited, can these men in eighteen hundred and eight, when we are a powerful, a rich, an united people, submit to the same nation, to the same chains forged for us, and others still more galling? The idea is too monstrous. It were treason against liberty to harbor it for an instant. It would prove that commerce had made us another Carthage: and that wealth and liberty were incompatible." During the late summer of 1808, when demands for repeal of the embargo were most intense, Jefferson asked Smith for 150 replies to the petitions printed in "large good type." The embargo was repealed in 1809.

With Jefferson's retirement that year, Ames noted, Smith lost his primary reason for editing the *Intelligencer*—"the support and defense of the person he considered America's greatest living man." In 1826 he wrote in a memoir of the life of Jefferson that "if there was error in the opinion of Jefferson, it sprung from no ignoble motive. No man was more sensible to the wrongs inflicted, none more alive to the interests of his country, none more determined in his course when impelled by a clear conviction of duty."

Jefferson's retirement alone, however, did not bring about Smith's decision to sell the *Intelligencer*. His wife deplored the excessive demands the newspaper made upon her husband's energy and time; indeed, putting out the paper nearly single-handedly through the years left little time for family life. Sometimes he suspended publication for a day or two; he often discontinued the paper briefly in the summer while he took a short vacation, publishing a shortened edition for Washington readers. He once confided to his readers that he needed relief from "the laborious duties of the Editor of a public Print, and from the necessity of recruiting health, unavoidably impaired by a constant devotion to business."

As early as 1807 a notice in the *Intelligencer* had announced a desire to sell the paper, advising: "This disposition will only be made to a person of sound republican principles." When the political situation between the United States and Great Britain worsened, however, Smith reconsidered his offer to sell and instead sought additional help. An arrangement was worked out to employ Joseph Gales, Jr. Young Gales, an able stenographer, assisted in covering the congressional debates and assumed other editorial duties. On 31 August 1810

Smith finally sold the *National Intelligencer* and the weekly *Gazette* to Gales.

Two years after acquiring ownership, Gales was joined by his brother-in-law W. W. Seaton, who, like Gales, had been trained in journalism and stenography by the elder Gales in North Carolina. For half a century, Gales and Seaton's *National Intelligencer* remained a leading American newspaper. Coverage of the congressional debates continued, with one publisher sitting next to the Speaker of the House and the other beside the president of the Senate.

The *Intelligencer*'s publishing plant was destroyed by British troops during the War of 1812 while its editors were serving in the American army and taking turns going home on leave to put out the paper. The newspaper was soon back in publication, and it continued as presidential organ and government printer until the Jackson administration, when it was replaced by competitors. The *Intelligencer* remained in existence until 1869.

After Smith's retirement from publishing, the Smiths moved to their country home, "Sidney," located in northeast Washington on land that is now a part of the Catholic University of America. They had purchased the property in 1804. Even before selling the paper, Smith had become engaged in a new occupation, banking. In 1809 he was named director of the Bank of Washington, and the following year he became president. Their country life was disturbed in 1813 when President Madison appointed Smith the first commissioner of revenue for the Treasury Department, a job which necessitated a move back to the city. In 1814 Smith served a short term as Secretary of the Treasury. In 1828 he became president of the Washington Branch of the Second United States Bank, a position he held until the branch closed in 1836. In addition to his banking duties, Smith served as director of the Washington library and treasurer of the Washington Monument Society, and was a member of various education committees.

Mrs. Smith continued to be active in Washington society and was regarded as one of the capital's leading hostesses. She also wrote numerous articles which were published in *Godey's Lady's Book*, *Southern Literary Messenger*, *Peter Parley's Annual*, and *Herring and Longacre's National Portrait Gallery*, and two novels, *A Winter in Washington* (1824) and *What Is Gentility?* (1828). Neither novel has been accorded any lasting literary recognition.

The Smiths' town and country homes through the years were visited by diplomats, writers, musicians, politicians (both Federalists and Republicans), and fellow editors. The couple entertained lavishly, served rare wines, played chess and whist (a forerunner of bridge), and owned fine horses. Smith opposed nullification and advocated nationalism. He was sympathetic with workers and and the poor but, though a Republican, distrusted government by the masses. Like Jefferson, his mentor, Smith owned slaves.

Smith and Jefferson maintained their friendship, primarily through correspondence, for many years after both retired. Smith helped to negotiate the purchase of Jefferson's personal library after the Library of Congress was destroyed by the British during the War of 1812. Jefferson sold his collection of 9,000 to 10,000 volumes for $23,950. The books were finally transferred from Monticello to Washington in the summer of 1815.

Mrs. Smith died on 7 June 1844; Smith died on 1 November 1845. He was buried in Rock Creek Cemetery in Washington. Their deaths received only passing notice in the *Intelligencer,* a daily since 1813, and there was no mention of the fact that Smith had founded the newspaper.

Mott viewed the *Intelligencer* as not only the "first of the important papers in the new capital," but as "in some respects the greatest of the long line of Washington papers...." Despite Smith's closeness to Jefferson and generous share of the public printing under the Republicans, the *Intelligencer* was far less partisan than many other newspapers of the time. Perhaps the contribution of Samuel Harrison Smith to journalism is best summed up by Ames in his book-length history of the *Intelligencer:* "Smith personally contributed to the journalism of his day. During the ten years he owned and published the newspaper, he laid down the format and many of the policies the paper followed throughout its existence. He established a newspaper that supported liberal policies in a conservative manner. But as important as any of the other characteristics of the *Intelligencer* under Smith was its reputation for fairness, accuracy, and hon-

esty, a tribute to a conscientious and devoted man who established one of the important cornerstones of Washington journalism."

References:

William E. Ames, *A History of the National Intelligencer* (Chapel Hill: University of North Carolina Press, 1972);

Ames, "Samuel Harrison Smith Founds the *National Intelligencer," Journalism Quarterly,* 42 (Summer 1965): 389-396;

Constance McLaughlin Green, *Washington: Village and Capital, 1800-1878,* volume 1 (Princeton: Princeton University Press, 1962);

Frank Luther Mott, *American Journalism,* third edition (New York: Macmillan, 1962), pp. 116n, 129n, 176-178;

Mott, *Jefferson and the Press* (Baton Rouge: Louisiana State University Press, 1943);

James E. Pollard, *The Presidents and the Press* (New York: Macmillan, 1947), pp. 52-115;

Josephine Seaton, *William Winston Seaton of the National Intelligencer* (Boston: James R. Osgood, 1871);

Culver H. Smith, *The Press, Politics, and Patronage: The American Government's Use of Newspapers* (Athens: University of Georgia Press, 1977), p. 26;

Margaret Bayard Smith, *The First Forty Years of Washington Society,* edited by Gaillard Hunt (New York: Scribners, 1906);

Smith, "Washington in Jefferson's Time, from the diaries and family letters of Mrs. Samuel Harrison Smith (Margaret Bayard)," edited by Hunt, *Scribner's Magazine,* 40 (July-December 1906): 293-396.

Papers:

The Samuel Harrison Smith Papers, the Margaret Bayard Smith Diary, and the Margaret Bayard Smith Papers are in the Library of Congress, Washington, D.C.

Jane Grey Swisshelm

(6 December 1815-22 July 1884)

Kathleen L. Endres
Bowling Green State University

MAJOR POSITIONS HELD: Editor, *Pittsburgh Saturday Visiter* (1847-1857), *St. Cloud* (Minn.) *Visiter* (1858), *St. Cloud Democrat* (1858-1863), *Washington* (D.C.) *Reconstructionist* (1865-1866).

BOOKS: *Letters to Country Girls* (New York: J. C. Riker, 1853);
True Stories about Pets (Boston: Lothrop, 1879);
Half a Century (Chicago: J. G. Swisshelm, 1880).

Jane Grey Swisshelm, who opened the Capitol Hill press gallery to women, crusaded for two major reforms in her long newspaper career—abolitionism and woman's rights. A radical on abolitionism but more conservative on woman's rights, Swisshelm argued her case in a series of newspapers that she started and edited. The papers never achieved large circulations, but her editorials were reprinted in some of the more influential journals of the day, including the *New York Tribune* and the *National Era* in Washington, D.C.

Jane Grey Cannon was born in Pittsburgh on 6 December 1815 to Thomas and Mary Scott Cannon, who belonged to the Covenanter branch of the Presbyterian Church. The family moved to the nearby village of Wilkinsburg shortly after Jane was born. Thomas Cannon, a merchant, lost most of his money in the panic of 1819 and died of tuberculosis in 1823. Jane had started school at age three and continued to attend while teaching lace making to help support the family, which included an older brother and a younger sister. Influenced by her religious, abolitionist mother, a teenaged Jane Cannon spent weeks in the 1830s collecting signatures for a petition requesting Congress to abolish slavery in the District of Columbia. At the age of fourteen, she became a teacher in the village school.

On 18 November 1836 she married a farmer, James Swisshelm (pronounced *Swiz*-em). Two years later, the couple moved to Louisville, Kentucky, where James Swisshelm went into business with his brother. Jane Swisshelm's abolitionist beliefs became even more fixed and passionately held as a

result of her direct experience of the slavery system in Kentucky.

Her husband's business venture was unsuccessful, and Jane was forced to take up corset making to augment the family income. In 1839 she returned to Pennsylvania to nurse her mother in her final illness; after the mother died early the next year, Swisshelm took charge of a seminary in

430

Butler, Pennsylvania. After two years she went back to her husband, who had returned to his family's farm near Pittsburgh after his Louisville business failed. She named the farm "Swissvale."

In 1842 she started writing stories and rhymes under the pen name "Jennie Dean" for the *Dollar Newspaper* and *Neal's Saturday Gazette* of Philadelphia. Writing under her own name for the influential Pittsburgh Whig newspaper, the *Commercial Journal*, Swisshelm attacked public officials who favored slavery and argued for the right of married women to hold property. Soon such publications as the *New York Tribune, Godey's*, and the *Home Journal* began to notice her work. *Tribune* editor Horace Greeley affectionately called her "sister Jane."

Swisshelm also wrote for two Pittsburgh abolitionist newspapers, the *Spirit of Liberty* and the *Albatross*, but both had ceased publication by early 1847. Swisshelm then founded her own abolitionist paper, the *Pittsburgh Saturday Visiter* (using the spelling preferred by Dr. Samuel Johnson). The newspaper resulted from a meeting Swisshelm had with Charles Sumner, later a Republican senator from Massachusetts; George W. Julian, later a Republican senator from Indiana; and Charles Shiras, founder of the *Albatross*. Sumner, Julian, and Shiras wanted to start a radical abolitionist newspaper. Since Swisshelm had already gained a reputation for abolitionist editorials, it was decided that she would become editor and handle the weekly writing. The three men became subscribers and continued to subscribe as long as Swisshelm retained control of the newspaper.

The *Saturday Visiter* was an immediate success; the number of subscribers quickly rose to 7,000. Her readers were nationwide, even though Swisshelm refused to affiliate with any abolitionist society, fearing that she might not be able to maintain complete editorial independence. Swisshelm took a typical Free Soil-moralistic approach to the abolition of slavery: slavery was an evil and, therefore, must be destroyed wherever it existed. Swisshelm seldom stressed the economic advantages of the free labor system, a popular argument among less extreme abolitionists.

In 1850 Swisshelm went to Washington, D.C., to see the congressional debates on Henry Clay's compromise bills on slavery following the Mexican-American War. Greeley paid her five dollars per column for her Washington letters to the *Tribune*. Swisshelm felt that any compromise on the slavery question was immoral. As she wrote for Greeley, "It is very easy for you, or any other Northern gentleman to make a bow to a Southern gentleman,

and in the spirit of the 'most generous compromise,' agree that he may tear a mother from her babes and set her up on the auction block to get money to buy a race horse or gold chain, and banish her, forever, from all she has known or loved." Such emotional appeals were characteristic of Swisshelm's writing style.

While in Washington, she opened the press gallery to women, despite Vice President Millard Fillmore's argument that such an action would be unpleasant for a lady because it would attract too much attention. Despite Fillmore's misgivings, Swisshelm took her seat. She only occupied it for one day before leaving Washington, immediately after mailing an article to Greeley accusing Whig Senator Daniel Webster, a prominent figure in winning support for the Compromise of 1850, of fathering eight mulatto children. The article never appeared in the *Tribune* but it did appear in her Pittsburgh paper. The paragraph on Webster was reprinted as many as 100 times in anti-Whig and anti-Webster papers, according to Swisshelm's estimates. In 1853 she published *Letters to Country Girls*, a collection of articles from the *Visiter*.

In 1857 Swisshelm left Pittsburgh and her unhappy marriage. Taking her only child, Mary Henrietta, who had been born in 1851, she settled in St. Cloud, Minnesota, near her sister, Mrs. Henry Z. Mitchell. James Swisshelm later divorced her on grounds of desertion. In St. Cloud, she founded another newspaper, the *Visiter*, in 1858. But immediate success was not the fate of the new paper. The Democratic party leader of the county, Gen. Sylvanus Lowry, agreed to help the newcomer, provided that she editorially support President James Buchanan. Swisshelm agreed; but in her editorial of support, she argued that Buchanan promised "the entire subversion of Freedom and the planting of Slavery in every State and Territory." The editorial triggered a feud between the editor and Lowry which ended in vigilantes led by Lowry sacking her printing press and Lowry's lawyer, James C. Shepley, filing a libel suit against her for allegedly libeling Shepley's wife. Townspeople paid for the repair of the press. To resolve the libel suit, Swisshelm agreed to run a clarification of the offending article in the *Visiter*. She ran the article and discontinued the paper. The next day, she started the *St. Cloud Democrat* and reprinted the original article. Shepley soon gave up the suit.

By 1858 Swisshelm was generally aligned with the Republicans, although she attempted to disassociate herself from any political party: "I took great pains to make it understood that I belonged

Gen. Sylvanus Lowry, Democratic leader of Stearns County, Minnesota, who became Swisshelm's political enemy

to no party. . . . I was like the Israelites in the days where there was no king and 'every man did that which was right in his own eyes.' " Despite her lofty comments, she did campaign for Republican candidates in Minnesota. On at least one occasion, she joined forces with Representative Galusha P. Grow of Pennsylvania on a speaking tour; after Swisshelm had addressed a packed house, a Democratic mob burned her in effigy as the mother of the Republican party. Representative Schuyler Colfax of Indiana later confided to her that she and Senator John P. Hale of New Hampshire had "helped change the State from Democracy to the stalwart Republicanism for which it has been justly famed."

Taking a typically radical stance in 1860, Swisshelm favored the nomination of Senator William Seward of New York and Senator Salmon Chase of Ohio as the Republican candidates for the presidency and vice-presidency. Swisshelm greeted Lincoln's nomination with only a lukewarm en-

dorsement, and her opinion of him did not improve after his election. Her editorials branded him as everything from an "obstructionist" to a "pusillanimous and vacillating weakling."

With Lincoln's election, Southern states began to secede. Initially, Swisshelm recommended that the South be allowed to leave the union in peace. As she explained in her autobiography, *Half a Century* (1880), "I was in favor of not only permitting the Southern States to leave the Union, but of driving them out of it as one would drive tramps out of a drawing room. *Put* them out! and open every avenue for the escape of their slaves." But once Fort Sumter was attacked, her opinion changed. War became a necessity—a necessity to wipe slavery from the face of the earth. Such a crusade demanded that the president pursue a vigorous war policy carried out by Republican—not Democratic—generals. Lincoln's policy of appointing Democratic generals, such as George B. McClellan, to lead the Union army angered the editor, who accused the president of losing "sight of the fundamental principles of our Government, i.e. the right of the majority to rule."

In 1863 Swisshelm severed her formal management relationship with the *Democrat*, leaving the paper in the hands of her nephew. She left St. Cloud and settled in Washington, D.C. For the remainder of the war, she helped in Union hospitals, worked as a clerk in the quartermaster's office, and wrote letters on her activities and her views which were published in the *Democrat* and the *New York Tribune*.

After Lincoln's assassination, Swisshelm portrayed the slain president as a martyr. Like many other radicals of the period, she compared Lincoln to a slain Christ and blamed the South for his death. Swisshelm sided with radicals in their plans for a prolonged reconstruction of the South. When President Andrew Johnson started to follow a moderate plan, she—prompted by her radical friends, including Secretary of War Edwin Stanton—began a newspaper in Washington called the *Reconstructionist*. After the first issue, Johnson personally fired her from her job in the quartermaster's office for speaking disrespectfully of the president. In the offending editorial, she had accused the president of being "prepared before hand to serve the purposes of treason . . .; that his administration and its programme, were part and parcel of the assassination plot, we have no longer the shadow of a doubt." Soon after, the printers' union passed a resolution which forbade its members from working where the paper was printed. Her

Front page of Swisshelm's St. Cloud Visiter *for 13 May 1858, with articles and letters concerning the destruction of the paper's press by a mob*

office-residence was set on fire twice. In March 1866, the *Reconstructionist* was suspended.

Although Swisshelm was always a radical in the abolitionist movement, the editor was surprisingly moderate in her demands for woman's rights. She was more concerned with the legal rights of women than with suffrage and always argued that publicity would accomplish more for women than voting would. Because of their moderation, Swisshelm's arguments had considerable appeal and were reprinted in other newspapers throughout the nation. The editor regretted this and once complained, "Everywhere I find people much more willing to hear me on the subjects connected with *woman's* rights than on the rights of the slave. I regret this for women, as such, have few wrongs compared to those of the slave. . . ."

Swisshelm was most concerned with the rights of married women to control their own property. In the early 1840s, in Pennsylvania as in most other states, the husband controlled the wife's property, including her wages if she worked, and received custody of the children in the event of a divorce. In a series of letters published in the *Pittsburgh Daily Commercial Journal* in 1846 and 1847, Swisshelm argued that married women needed laws that would give them some control over their property. Her articles were brought to the attention of the Pennsylvania governor, who initiated reforms. The legislature in 1847 passed a bill giving wives the right to control their property without the approval of their husbands.

A popular speaker on the topic, Swisshelm petitioned the Minnesota state legislature in 1858 to include in a proposed homestead bill a protection of women's equity in homesteads. The legislature was so interested in what the editor had to say that it adjourned and reconvened so that it might hear her, because rules prohibited women from addressing the body. One minister commented on the incident, "The views of this woman are in contravention with the laws of God, and the possition [*sic*], in which he in his infinite wisdom has seen fit to place woman."

Despite such criticism, Swisshelm was seen as one of the more articulate and more moderate spokeswomen of the cause. Organizations in various states invited her to address their legislatures. At the time the Civil War broke out, Swisshelm was addressing the Massachusetts legislature on the legal disabilities of women. On a national level, Swisshelm claimed that she was asked to draft a bill which would have given women the right to make contracts and the right of custody of children in divorces. The bill was supposedly introduced in Congress.

Although she was clearly an eloquent speaker and a powerful writer on the subject, Swisshelm intentionally avoided most woman's rights conventions of the period. She had been offered the chairmanship of the Salem, Ohio, woman's rights convention, the third such meeting held in the United States, but declined. She did attend the Akron convention but was dismayed by the extremism of the participants. Despite this, suffragist Susan B. Anthony wrote Swisshelm asking for her editorial support in the cause. Swisshelm often wrote on the cause but avoided ties with any woman's rights organization.

Swisshelm died in 1884 at Swissvale, part of which she had won in 1867 in a suit against her late former husband's estate. Her active newspaper career had ended fifteen years earlier. Editors who remembered her generously overlooked her shortcomings to praise her many contributions. Those contributions were clear: she opened the congressional press gallery to women; she was a champion of the abolitionist cause; she helped establish the Republican party in Minnesota; she was an important crusader in the small—and not well-accepted—woman's rights movement; she was responsible for some legislation which gave women fundamental property rights. Yet Swisshelm had serious shortcomings. She was not an accurate reporter, as the Daniel Webster story clearly illustrates. Nor was she an original thinker in either her abolitionist or woman's rights stances. Swisshelm's strength was in distilling reform arguments of the day and then clearly and forcefully presenting them in her editorials. Her importance in both reform movements perhaps would have been greater nationally if she had chosen to cooperate with other reformers. Cooperation, conciliation, and compromise, however, were not Swisshelm's characteristics. Like other reformers of the day, she tended to be dogmatic, totally unaware of her own mistakes.

The *Nation*, four years before her death, provided perhaps the closest thing to an objective appraisal of Swisshelm's career: "She was not the first woman editor in the country but in direct participation in politics she took precedence over all journalists of her sex. She had a plain and forcible style, sufficient positiveness and impulsiveness, and did her share in fostering the anti-slavery sentiment of the North." Fifty years after her death, the *New York Times* on 27 January 1935 summarized Swisshelm's importance to women in journalism: "She was a knight crusader to whom all newspaper women should doff their hats, for she fought their battles for them long before they were born and helped to open for them the doors of the future."

Letters:

Crusader and Feminist: Letters of Jane Grey Swisshelm, edited by Arthur J. Larsen (St. Paul: Minnesota Historical Society, 1934).

References:

"An American Woman's Memoirs," *Nation* (19 August 1880): 139-140;

Celia Burleigh, "People Worth Knowing: Jane Grey Swisshelm," *Woman's Journal,* 1 (20 August 1870): 257, (27 August 1870): 265, (3 September 1870): 274;

Kathleen Endres, "Jane Grey Swisshelm: Nineteenth Century Journalist and Feminist,"

Journalism History, 2 (Winter 1975-1976): 128-131;

S. J. Fisher, "Reminiscences of Jane Grey Swisshelm," *Western Pennsylvania Historical Magazine,* 4 (July 1921): 165-174;

Frank Klement, "Jane Grey Swisshelm and Lincoln: A Feminist Fusses and Frets," *Abraham Lincoln Quarterly* (December 1950): 227-238;

Lester Burrell Shippee, "Jane Grey Swisshelm: Agitator," *Mississippi Valley Historical Review,* 7 (December 1920): 206-227;

Bertha-Monica Stearns, "Reform Periodicals and Female Reformers, 1830 to 1860," *American Historical Review,* 37 (July 1932): 678-699.

Papers:

Jane Swisshelm's papers are in the Mitchell Family Collection at the Minnesota Historical Society, St. Paul.

Isaiah Thomas

Terry Hynes
California State University, Fullerton

BIRTH: Boston, Massachusetts, 30 January 1750, to Moses and Fidelity Grant Thomas.

MARRIAGES: 25 December 1769 to Mary Dill; children: Mary Ann, Isaiah. 26 May 1779 to Mary Thomas Fowle. 10 August 1819 to Rebecca Armstrong.

MAJOR POSITIONS HELD: Printer, *Halifax* (Nova Scotia) *Gazette* (1765-1766); publisher, *Massachusetts Spy* (Boston; moved to Worcester in 1775) (1770-1786, 1788-1801); printer, *Massachusetts Spy* (1770-1776, 1778-1786, 1788-1801); copublisher, *Essex Journal* (Newburyport, Mass.) (1773-1774); publisher, *Royal American Magazine* (1774-1775), *Massachusetts Herald* (Worcester) (1783), *Worcester Magazine* (1786-1788); copublisher, *Hampshire Chronicle* (Springfield, Mass.) (1788); publisher, *Massachusetts Magazine* or *Monthly Museum of Knowledge* (1789-1793); copublisher, *New Hampshire Journal: Or, The Farmer's Weekly Museum* (Walpole) (1793-1796, 1798-1801, 1803-1807, 1808-1809),

Worcester Intelligencer; Or, Brookfield Advertiser (1794-1795), *Albany* (N.Y.) *Centinel* (1797-1798).

DEATH: Worcester, Massachusetts, 4 April 1831.

BOOKS: *An Oration: Delivered in Free Masons-Hall, Lancaster, Commonwealth of Massachusetts, on Thursday, the Twenty-fourth of June, 1779 (A. L. 5779) to the Right Worshipful Master, Worshipful Wardens and Members, &c. of Trinity Lodge* (Worcester, Mass., 1781);

A Specimen of Isaiah Thomas's Printing Types. Being as Large and Complete an Assortment as Is to Be Met with in Any One Printing-Office in America. Chiefly Manufactured by That Great Artist, William Caslon, Esq, of London (Worcester, Mass.: Printed by Isaiah Thomas, 1785);

New American Spelling Book; or, The Child's Easy Introduction to Spelling and Reading the English Tongue. To Which Is Added, an Entire New, Plain and Comprehensive English Grammar. Also, The Shorter Catechism, by the Assembly of Divines, The

Whole Adopted to the Capacities of Young Children; Rendering the Use of a Primer Unnecessary (Worcester, Mass.: Printed & sold by Isaiah Thomas, 1785);

Catalogue of Books to Be Sold by Isaiah Thomas, at His Bookstore in Worcester, Massachusetts. Consisting of Many Celebrated Authors in History, Voyages, Travels, Antiquities, Philosophy, Novels, Miscellanies, Divinity, Physick, Surgery, Anatomy, Arts, Sciences, Husbandry, Architecture, Navigation, Mathematicks, Law, Periodical Publications, Poetry, Plays, Musick, &c. &c. (Worcester, Mass.: Printed by Isaiah Thomas, 1787);

Literary Proposal. Proposal of Isaiah Thomas and Company, for Publishing by Subscription, a New Periodical Work, to Be Entitled, The Massachusetts Magazine: or Monthly Museum of Knowledge and Rational Entertainment (Boston: Printed by Isaiah Thomas, 1788);

The Only Sure Guide to the English Tongue; or, New Pronouncing Spelling Book. Upon the Same Plan as Perry's Royal Standard English Dictionary

Isaiah Thomas

(Worcester, Mass.: Printed by Isaiah Thomas, 1789);

Catalogue of Books to Be Sold by Isaiah Thomas, at His Bookstore in Worcester, Massachusetts. Consisting of History, Voyages, Travels, Geography, Antiquities, Philosophy, Novels, Miscellanies, Divinity, Physick, Surgery, Anatomy, Arts, Sciences, Husbandry, Architecture, Navigation, Mathematics, Law, Periodical Publications, Poetry, Plays, Musick, &c. &c. (Worcester, Mass.: Printed by Isaiah Thomas & Leonard Worcester, 1792);

Thomas and Andrews's Catalogue of Books, for Sale, Wholesale and Retail, at Their Book and Stationary [sic] Store, Faust's Statue, No. 45 Newbury Street. Boston. Consisting of a Very Extensive Collection of the Latest and Most Approved Authors, in Divinity, Law, Physick, Surgery, Chemistry, History, Biography, Voyages, Travels, Miscellanies, Novels, Poetry, Musick, Arts and Sciences, Philosophy, Navigation, Astronomy, Geography, Architecture, Trade and Commerce, Mathematicks, Bookkeeping, &c. &c. To All Which Large Additions Are Constantly Making (Boston: Thomas & Andrews, 1793);

The Massachusetts Compiler of Theoretical and Practical Elements of Sacred Vocal Music (Boston: Isaiah Thomas & Ebenezer T. Andrews, 1795);

Catalogue of Books to Be Sold by Thomas, Son & Thomas, at Their Bookstore, in Worcester, Massachusetts: Consisting of History, Voyages, Travels, Geography, Antiquities, Philosophy, Novels, Miscellanies, Divinity, Physic, Surgery, Anatomy, Arts, Sciences, Husbandry, Architecture, Navigation, Mathematicks, Law, Periodical Publications, Poetry, Plays, Music, &c. &c. &c. (Worcester, Mass.: Thomas, Son & Thomas, 1796);

Isaiah Thomas's Catalogue of English, Scotch, Irish and American Books for Sale, at the Worcester Bookstore. Consisting of History, Voyages, Travels, Geography, Antiquities, Philosophy, Novels, Miscellanies, Divinity, Physic, Surgery, Anatomy, Arts, Sciences, Husbandry, Architecture, Navigation, Mathematics, Law, Periodical Publications, Poetry, Plays, Music, &c &c. (Worcester, Mass.: Printed by Isaiah Thomas, 1801);

Almanack, With an Ephemeris, for the Year of Our Lord 1803 (Worcester, Mass.: Printed by Isaiah Thomas, Jun., 1802);

Eccentric Biography; or, Memoirs of Remarkable Female Characters, Ancient and Modern (Worcester, Mass.: Printed by I. Thomas, Jun., 1804);

The History of Printing in America. With a Biography of Printers, and an Account of Newspapers. To Which Is Prefixed a Concise View of the Discovery and Progress of the Art in Other Parts of the World, 2 volumes (Worcester, Mass.: From the press of Isaiah Thomas, jun. Isaac Sturtevant, printer, 1810);

An Address to the Most Worshipful Grand Lodge of Massachusetts, at the Close of the Constitutional Term of His Presiding as Grand Master (Boston: J. Eliot, Jun., 1811);

Communication from the President of the American Antiquarian Society to the Members, October 24th, 1814 (Worcester, Mass.: Printed by W. Manning, 1815);

A Catalogue of Publications in What Is Now the United States prior to the Revolution of 1775-6 (Albany, N.Y.: J. Munsell, 1874);

The Diary of Isaiah Thomas, 1805-1828, edited by Benjamin Thomas Hill, 2 volumes (Worcester, Mass.: American Antiquarian Society, 1909);

Extracts from the Diaries and Accounts of Isaiah Thomas from the Year 1782 to 1804 and His Diary for 1808, edited by Charles L. Nichols (Worcester, Mass.: American Antiquarian Society, 1916);

Three Autobiographical Fragments (Worcester, Mass.: American Antiquarian Society, 1962).

OTHER: *Laus Deo! The Worcester Collection of Sacred Harmony*, edited by Thomas (Worcester, Mass.: Printed by Isaiah Thomas, 1786);

The Perpetual Laws of the Commonwealth of Massachusetts from the Establishment of Its Constitution to the First Session of the General Court, A.D. 1788, edited by Thomas (Worcester, Mass.: Printed by Isaiah Thomas, 1788);

The Perpetual Laws of the Commonwealth of Massachusetts, from the Establishment of Its Constitution to the Second Session of the General Court, in 1798, edited by Thomas (Worcester, Mass.: Printed by Isaiah Thomas, 1799);

The Perpetual Laws of the Commonwealth of Massachusetts, from the Establishment of Its Constitution, in the Year 1780, edited by Thomas (Boston: Printed & sold by I. Thomas & E. T. Andrews, 1807).

Isaiah Thomas was one of the most important printer-publishers in America in the late eighteenth and early nineteenth centuries. His newspaper, the *Massachusetts Spy*, founded in 1770, was an important Patriot vehicle before and during the Revolutionary War. After the war, from his base in Worcester, Massachusetts, Thomas built a publishing empire extending from Maine to Georgia and inland to the Mississippi. He wrote the first history of printing in America; published in 1810, it is still a valuable source in its field. In 1812 he founded and became the first president of the American Antiquarian Society, which he endowed to carry on his work of collecting and publishing materials related to the formation of the United States.

Born on 30 January 1750 in Boston, Thomas was the youngest of five children and a member of the fifth generation of Thomases in America. His great-great-grandfather, Evan Thomas, was established as a merchant in Boston by 1640 and may have arrived in the city as early as 1632. Moses Thomas, Isaiah's father, was unsuccessful at every occupation he tried. Shortly after Isaiah's birth, Moses, according to Isaiah's later account, "left Boston with a view to provide for his family elsewhere." He went to North Carolina, where he died in 1752. Widowed and penniless, Fidelity Grant Thomas sent her three youngest children to live with friends in the country. The two oldest children, born in Hampstead, Long Island, had been left there in the care of Fidelity's relatives when she and Moses moved to Boston in the late 1740s. As was customary for women in her position, Fidelity established a small shop in Boston in order to make a living.

When Thomas was six, his mother brought him back to Boston to live with Zechariah Fowle, a printer who needed help in his shop. Some months later, on 4 June 1756, indenture papers were signed making seven-year-old Thomas an apprentice to Fowle for the next fourteen years. The agreement was a typical one of its kind: that the Fowles were to provide Isaiah with board, room, and clothing; instruct him in reading, writing and arithmetic; and teach him the art and craft of printing. Thomas's responsibilities also were typical of such agreements: "The said apprentice, his said master and mistress, well and faithfully shall serve; their secrets he shall keep close; their commandments lawful and honest everywhere he shall gladly obey; he shall do no damage to his said master, etc., or suffer it to be done by others without letting or giving seasonable notice thereof to his said master, etc.; he shall not waste the goods of his said master, etc., nor lend them unlawfully to any; at cards, dice, or any other unlawful game or games he shall not play; fornication he shall not commit; matrimony during the said term he shall not contract; taverns, alehouses or places of gaming he shall not haunt or frequent; from the service of his said master, etc., by day or night he shall not absent himself."

In later autobiographical pieces and in *The*

History of Printing, Thomas described Fowle as ignorant and indolent. Probably as a consequence, Fowle's print shop was small and ill equipped, even by the standards of the day. Thomas's assessment of his master was not wholly negative, however; he commented that Fowle was "honest in his dealings, and punctual to his engagements."

One of the earliest tasks Thomas remembered doing in Fowle's shop, even before he was formally apprenticed to the printer, was setting the type for a reprinting of "The Lawyer's Pedigree," one of the many bawdy ballads which, together with chapbooks, were the staple of Fowle's printing business. Thomas was placed on a bench eighteen inches high so that he could reach the type and, since he could not read, set the fifty-six short lines of the ballad by comparing the pieces of type with the printed copy in front of him. It took him two days to complete the task.

When Thomas was eight, Fowle printed 10,000 copies of *The New-England Primer*, one of the most enterprising jobs he undertook. Its success inspired Fowle to print an edition of the Psalter, for which he hired two journeymen printers. One of these was Samuel Draper, who became Fowle's partner in 1758 and who taught Thomas more about the printing trade than Fowle could. Fowle and Draper printed a number of sizable works in relatively large editions, including 20,000 copies of *The Youth's Instructor in the English Tongue*, a spelling book in general use at the time, and the one from which Thomas learned to spell. (Although the majority of sources credit Fowle's shop with this publication, some sources say none of the three editions of this book published in Boston between 1757 and 1762 was printed by Fowle and Draper.) After Draper left the partnership in 1761 or 1762, Fowle moved the shop to smaller quarters and returned to printing ballads.

Thomas remained with Fowle for approximately ten years without a break in service. After Draper left, Fowle seems to have paid little attention to the business and Thomas assumed more responsibility in the shop. In the early 1760s he produced his first volume: *The New Book of Knowledge, Shewing the Effects of the Planets and other Astronomical Constellations; with the Strange Events that Befall Men, Women and Children Born under Them.* During these years also, Thomas went for advice to a former printer, Gamaliel Rogers, who was then in his late fifties. Apparently Rogers inspired Thomas's interest in the history of printing by telling the young apprentice stories about early colonial printers. Thomas later wrote of him in *The*

History of Printing: "I held him in high veneration, and often recollected his instructions, which, on many occasions, proved beneficial to me." Although Thomas was clever enough to compete with other ballad printers by matching his own type-metal cuts against their woodcut illustrations, he was restless to become really competent as a printer and wanted to go to London to learn the state of the art in his craft. It was probably this desire combined with Thomas's disdain for Fowle which provoked a quarrel between master and apprentice that resulted in Thomas's breaking his indenture and sailing for Halifax, where he could get the least expensive passage to London, in late September 1765.

Instead of being merely a stop on his way to London, however, Halifax became Thomas's home for nearly six months before he sailed south again for New England. More important for his future career, it provided his first opportunity to assist in the printing of a newspaper. Almost as soon as he reached Halifax, Thomas was hired at three dollars a month by the city's only printer, Anthony Henry, who printed the province's only newspaper, the *Halifax Gazette*. The weekly paper was the official organ of the provincial government, but neither Henry nor the paper's editor, Richard Bulkeley, was very interested in its publication. Thomas made the paper more legible by using larger and cleaner type and more readable by choosing more interesting news items and including pointed editorial notes. In late 1765 and early 1766 he included much news of the opposition in other colonies to the Stamp Act and satirized the act in woodcuts. Realizing that the officials would not indefinitely tolerate being taunted in their own official journal, Henry finally fired Thomas, probably in mid-March 1766. But Henry lost the government printing anyway because the officials decided to import a printer who could keep his apprentices under better control.

After leaving Halifax, Thomas worked for about two months for printers in Portsmouth, New Hampshire: first he spent two weeks with Daniel and Robert Fowle, Zechariah's brother and nephew, respectively, who printed the *New Hampshire Gazette;* then he worked for Ezekiel Russell and Thomas Furber and helped improve their fledgling rival to the *Gazette*, the *Portsmouth Mercury and Weekly Advertiser*. Thomas later claimed that Zechariah Fowle recognized the quality of his work in the *Mercury* and invited him to return to Boston and patch up their quarrel. Thomas went back to Boston after an absence of about seven months, but within a few weeks he and Fowle were at odds again and Thomas decided to travel to London by way of printing shops in the Southern colonies.

After some misadventures on his Southern journey, including an aborted attempt to set up a print shop and newspaper in partnership with a woman in Wilmington, North Carolina, Thomas arrived in Charleston, South Carolina. After some difficulty, he obtained a position in the shop of Robert Wells, the best printer in the city. Wells had much to teach Thomas, and his bookstore provided the apprentice with a chance to broaden his knowledge. On 25 December 1769 Thomas married Mary Dill, who, he subsequently discovered, had borne an illegitimate son some years before and "had been prostituted to the purposes of more than one."

Returning to Boston in the spring of 1770, Thomas entered into a partnership of convenience with his old master, Fowle, primarily in order to make use of the latter's equipment to print a newspaper which Thomas called the *Massachusetts Spy*. While the four other newspapers then published in Boston were all weeklies, the *Spy* was to be a triweekly (with publication days of Tuesday, Thursday, and Saturday); it was also to be a quarter-sheet tabloid, a size more acceptable to the barely literate lower classes than the more common half-sheet. Sample copies of the new paper were distributed free on 17 July 1770; on 7 August the paper began regular publication. By late October Fowle agreed to sell out his interest in the shop to the more enterprising Thomas and within a few months Thomas acquired title to the shop by assuming Fowle's debts. (Fowle continued as a shopkeeper in Boston until the British military occupation in 1775, when he obtained a permit to leave the city. He then went to Portsmouth to live with his brother Daniel. He died there in 1776). After buying out Fowle, Thomas abandoned the triweekly tabloid form and switched to a semiweekly half-sheet. Within a few months he adopted the weekly, royal-sized, four-page folio format as the paper's standard, making the *Spy* the largest newspaper ever published in Boston to that time.

The prospectus of the *Spy* had contained no hint of the political firebrand the paper was to become in the cause of revolution: Thomas simply promised to provide the most recent news and advertisements to workers of moderate means. An example of Thomas's penchant for controversy occurred early in the paper's history, however, when he obtained the contract from the 1771 Harvard graduating class to print the traditional theses

which the students were prepared to defend against all comers. This contract ordinarily went to Richard Draper, publisher of the *Boston News-Letter* and a Loyalist. Clifford Shipton, one of Thomas's chief biographers, speculates that since the Whigs James Bowdoin and John Warren were members of the graduating class, the refusal of Draper may have been politically motivated. The ensuing cross fire in the pages of the *News-Letter* and the *Spy* is replete with the kind of vituperative personal attacks that were common in newspapers of the period and typical of the political party press later.

Thomas promised initially to open the pages of the *Spy* to Loyalist as well as radical points of view—the paper's motto was "Open to all Parties, but influenced by None." Within a few weeks after beginning regular publication, however, he moved decisively into the Patriot camp. Thomas later claimed that it was simply impossible for any printer-publisher to remain neutral, so he had to choose a side even though it was distasteful to him to do so. Again, however, Shipton's explanation of the situation may be more credible: when Thomas purchased Fowle's interest in the *Spy*, John Hancock assumed financial responsibility for the press, and the radicals Joseph Greenleaf and Thomas Young became regular contributors to the paper. Shipton suggests that unqualified support of the political causes of Thomas's financial and editorial allies may have been necessary to the paper's continued existence. The news columns of the *Spy* were filled with reports about the town meetings where the nonimportation and nonuse agreements were made; the work of the Committees of Correspondence, the Sons of Liberty, and other Patriot organizations; as well as addresses to the governor and his responses. The *Spy* became an outspoken advocate of independence. Much of the radical invective which originated in Thomas's paper compares negatively with the reasoned, polished style of men like Thomas Paine, however; Greenleaf's and Young's essays were often illogical rantings. The *Boston Gazette* included more well-reasoned arguments and less bombast than the *Spy* and is generally given more credit for bringing the colonists to independence.

Thomas recognized the problems caused by his business entanglements with the radicals. He sought to separate his financial affairs from the ties with Hancock, Young, and Greenleaf, and in March 1772 he explored the possibility of moving his business to Bermuda. Nothing came of the Bermuda notion, but some time between this period and the outbreak of the Revolution he was able to

Sample first issue of Thomas's Massachusetts Spy, *which was distributed free. The first regular number was issued on 7 August 1770.*

separate himself financially from the three radicals. Exactly how he achieved the break is unclear, because his papers from this period are lost. Thomas remained a radical, however, and continued to publish essays supporting the Patriot cause.

The newspaper was not the only product of Thomas's print shop during these prewar years. In 1771 he published the first of his annual almanacs, *The Massachusetts Calendar* (entitled *Thomas's New-England Almanack* beginning in 1775), which were to make his name well known throughout the country in later years. In addition to the astronomical information typically published in almanacs, Thomas included important documents, such as the Articles of Peace and the Declaration of Rights, which resulted in his almanacs being assigned a permanent value. In 1781 he published 3,000 cop-

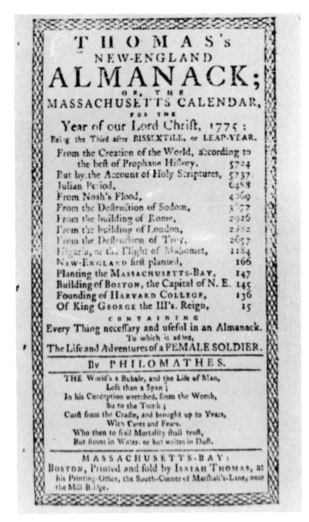

Title page for the first issue of Thomas's New-England Almanack. *Previous issues, beginning in 1771, had carried the title* The Massachusetts Calendar.

ies of the almanac; by 1797 the annual edition was 29,000 copies.

In late 1773 Thomas formed the first of the partnerships that were later to become part of his publishing empire. Some influential citizens invited Thomas to establish a newspaper in Newburyport; so he set up a former apprentice, Henry W. Tinges, to do business as his partner and publish the *Essex Journal*. Within a year, however, Tinges's mismanagement had the newspaper so deeply in debt that Thomas sold out his interest.

In February 1774 Thomas brought out the *Royal American* magazine. (This issue is dated January 1774.) Thomas said that the magazine's purpose was "to convey to posterity the labours of the learned." The *Royal American* had articles on science and history as well as lighter fare, including love stories from English magazines and a "Directory of Love" for the lovelorn; the magazine also featured engravings by Paul Revere and Paul Callender, two of the most talented men in their field. But Thomas was unable to attract much native talent, and the escalating political discord was distracting for both Thomas and his audience. Thomas edited the magazine for the first six issues, then suspended publication. When publication was resumed in September 1794, Greenleaf became editor. In March 1775 Thomas sold the magazine to Greenleaf, and it died after the outbreak of the war in April. In late 1774 Thomas was approached with a request to establish a newspaper in Worcester, a small town about forty miles west of Boston, and he prepared proposals in February 1775 for a paper to be called the *Worcester Gazette; or American Oracle of Liberty*. As a result of the outbreak of the war in April, however, Thomas moved himself and the *Spy* to Worcester instead of establishing a separate newspaper there. It is traditionally believed that Thomas's prewar publishing ventures also included printing the handbills of the Sons of Liberty after his employees had gone home for the night. It is also believed that the Patriot group met in Thomas's shop, which became known as the "sedition foundry."

Although Thomas's business thrived in the prewar years, his personal life yielded mixed results. One child was stillborn in 1770. His daughter Mary Ann was born on 27 March 1772; his son Isaiah on 5 September 1773. The rift between Thomas and his wife widened, however, and when she traveled to Newburyport with a British officer in early 1775, Thomas stopped living with her.

By early 1775 the *Spy* was a highly successful commercial as well as political venture: Thomas reported that the paper's circulation was then approximately 3,500, much of this due to its wide readership in other colonies. To maintain the intercolonial delivery of the paper, Thomas established a system of post riders—a transportation network also probably quite useful for communication among the radicals' committees of correspondence. When open warfare seemed imminent, Thomas, with the help of some Patriot friends, left Boston on the night of 16 April, sending most of his printing equipment to Worcester by wagon. Thomas himself remained near Boston and two nights later joined Paul Revere on his ride through the countryside to warn residents of the impending British attack. Early on the morning of 19 April Thomas apparently joined the militia at Lexington, an experience which yielded this overblown account in a subsequent issue of the *Spy:* "AMERICANS! forever bear in mind the BATTLE of LEXINGTON!—where British Troops, unmolested and unprovoked, wantonly, and in a most inhuman manner fired upon and killed a number of our countrymen, then robbed them of their provisions, ransacked, plundered and burnt their houses! nor could the tears of defenceless women, some of whom were in the pains of childbirth, the cries of helpless babes, nor the prayers of old age, confined to beds of sickness, appease their thirst for blood!—or divert them from their DESIGN of MURDER and ROBBERY!" On 20 April, after visiting his family in Watertown, Thomas set out on foot for Worcester, the city that was to become his home.

To reestablish the *Spy* in Worcester, Thomas had to overcome some fundamental obstacles. Type and ink, which he had formerly obtained from England, were in short supply; paper also was scarce. Initially, through the help of Hancock and Patriots on the Committee of Safety, Thomas received enough paper to resume publication of the *Spy* on 3 May, the issue containing Thomas's version of the battle of Lexington; but the lack of an adequate supply of paper continued to be a problem, and Thomas often pleaded in his newspaper for subscribers to donate rags so that he could exchange them for paper at the mill. Sometimes, due to the shortage, the newspaper was reduced to a half sheet or less.

Lack of money was perhaps the most pervasive difficulty Thomas had to deal with during the early war years. His financial situation during this time was variable. He was appointed postmaster at Worcester (the only public office he ever held) by the Provincial Congress in May 1775. When Ben-

jamin Franklin was made postmaster general by the Continental Congress, he appointed Thomas United States postmaster for Worcester in November 1775; Thomas was reappointed in succeeding years until 1802. It is not clear, however, exactly how much Thomas was paid for this position or if the payment helped him to publish the newspaper, as similar arrangements had helped postmaster-printers earlier in the eighteenth century. After he moved to Worcester, Thomas did some printing for the Provincial Congress in Watertown (he also received some paper subsidies from the congress), but it hardly paid enough to meet his debts and he was soon displaced by printers such as Benjamin Edes and John Gill of the *Boston Gazette*, whose shops were closer to the congress's headquarters. When the war broke out, the *Spy* was near the end of its subscription year, and Thomas was unable to collect $3,000 he was owed for copies of the paper already printed and delivered; without that money he could not pay his debts. Furthermore, with British-occupied Boston then out of bounds, the paper's circulation diminished to 1,500. One of Thomas's two apprentices from this period was Benjamin Russell (later publisher of the *Massachusetts Centinel*), who served six months in the Continental army as Thomas's substitute. Russell reported in later years that money was so scarce at times that Thomas and his apprentices had only bread and milk to sustain them. In March 1776 Thomas had to discontinue publication of the newspaper for about a month; when he resumed publication in April with an increased subscription price, his creditors attached the paper. From 21 June 1776 to 2 July 1778 Thomas leased the *Spy* to other printers while he traveled around the countryside to collect money owed to him, periodically returning to Worcester to check on the operation. During this period he almost established another print shop in Salem, bought and sold a farm in New Hampshire, and obtained a divorce from his wife on 27 May 1777.

After his return to Worcester in 1778, Thomas's personal and financial fortunes improved significantly. That year he brought out the first Worcester edition of his almanac. On 26 May 1779 he married his twenty-nine-year-old half-cousin, Mary Thomas Fowle, widow of Isaac Fowle (no relation to Thomas's early master). The next year he entered into a partnership in a drugstore. The *Spy* experienced a precipitous drop in circulation in 1780 from 1,200 to 271, but this seems to have been because Thomas was dropping delinquent subscribers. He purchased new type in April 1780

Front page of the first Worcester issue of the Massachusetts Spy, *with inscription by Thomas (Clifford K. Shipton,* Isaiah Thomas:
Printer, Patriot and Philanthropist, *1948)*

and was also able to obtain more adequate stocks of good paper. His combination print shop-bindery-bookstore business, with a more firmly established *Massachusetts Spy* and the regular editions of the profitable almanac, was thriving by the time the war ended in 1783. For about a month in 1783, Thomas also published an abridged edition of the *Spy* called the *Massachusetts Herald*.

By the end of the Revolutionary War, Thomas was more interested in sustaining and extending his business than he was in radical causes. The tone of the Worcester *Spy* was far more subdued than that of its Boston predecessor, although Thomas's feistiness sometimes surfaced. In 1785, for example, Massachusetts levied a tax on almanacs and newspapers; Thomas demonstrated his opposition by converting the newspaper into a weekly magazine, the *Worcester Magazine*, from April 1786 until the tax was repealed in March 1788. During Shays's Rebellion in 1786-1787, he supported the government rather than the farmers, and he published the best-selling history of the rebellion, George Richards Minot's *History of the Insurrections, in Massachusetts* (1788). During the postwar years Thomas also published the Massachusetts constitution and a collection of the state's laws, and he included important laws of the United States and information about tariffs in his almanac. Thomas also persisted for some time in referring to George Washington as "His Majesty the President" or "His Highness the President-General." During most of 1788 Thomas copublished with Ezra Weld a weekly newspaper, the *Hampshire Chronicle*, which was printed at Springfield, Massachusetts.

From 1789 until 1793 Thomas published the *Massachusetts Magazine: or Monthly Museum of Knowledge*, which included history, music, chemistry, novels, marriage announcements, death notices, and copperplate engravings. Thomas printed 800 copies of the sixty-four-page magazine. The publication ran annual deficits of up to £100 pounds, however, and Thomas sold the magazine to the editors in 1793. They continued to publish it until 1796.

The first of Thomas's major postwar partnerships was I. Thomas & Co., established in September 1788 with a combination printing office and bookstore in Boston. Initially the company had three partners, but in 1789 one dropped out and Thomas and the remaining partner, Ebenezer T. Andrews, one of Thomas's former apprentices, reorganized the firm under both their names. Thomas and Andrews became the largest printing

company in the United States and the most successful of Thomas's partnerships. In its early years the firm had five presses, compared with seven in Worcester. Its publications included spellers, hymn books, and the *Massachusetts Magazine*. By the mid-1790s the Boston firm was beginning to be more important than the parent office at Worcester. But the business relations between the two companies were somewhat confused—for example, they sent type and composing sticks back and forth between the two cities without accounting for them—s it is very difficult to sort out the operations completely. Also, since Andrews was not so skilled a craftsman as Thomas, publication costs were higher at the Boston office. This partnership lasted until August 1820, when it was terminated with some bitterness on Thomas's part because he felt that his $22,000 settlement should have been $70,000; most of Thomas's partnerships were terminated with mutual dissatisfaction, however. No complete list of Thomas's partnerships has been compiled, but at least twenty were formed, including the short-lived one with Tinges at Newburyport in 1773-1774; seven of these included Andrews as a partner. Although it is likely that Thomas, as postmaster, franked the costs of some of his business correspondence, he maintained his own messenger service between the various partnership firms because the U.S. mail service was infrequent and its parcel post facilities were expensive.

In the number of titles and copies he printed Thomas exceeded all other publishers of the colonial and early republican period. Together with his partners he published more than 900 books; Benjamin Franklin and his partners, by comparison, published approximately 800. Much of his business rested on his editions of standard British and European medical and legal texts. In addition, however, Thomas readily took risks as an innovative publisher: in 1789 he published the first novel by a native American author, *The Power of Sympathy* by William Hill Brown. (The plot of this novel closely paralleled events in the lives of two Massachusetts families, who bought most of the copies of the book to keep it out of circulation.) From Worcester Thomas published an abridgment of Richardson's *Pamela* (1794), Goldsmith's *The Vicar of Wakefield* (1795), and Rousseau's *Letters of an Italian Nun* (1796). With Andrews he published Jeremy Belknap's *American Biography* (1794), one of the earliest American biographical dictionaries; Belknap's *The Foresters* (1792); and collections of poems by Sarah Apthorp Morton and by Mercy Warren, James Otis's sister.

Perhaps the most lucrative part of Thomas's business was schoolbooks: he published the first U.S. edition of William Perry's speller, *The Only Sure Guide to the English Tongue*, in 1785. By the time he turned over management of the Worcester press to his son in 1802, Thomas had published fourteen editions of the speller for a total of 300,000 copies. He also published four editions of Perry's *Royal Standard English Dictionary* for a total of 54,000 copies. The firm of Thomas and Andrews obtained an exclusive contract to print Noah Webster's speller, grammar, and selections in Massachusetts, New Hampshire, and Rhode Island. Before the fourteen-year contract ran out in 1804, the firm published thirty editions of the speller (300,000 copies total), six editions of the grammar, and fourteen editions of the selections. Nicholas Pike's *New and Complete System of Arithmetic*, in the first Worcester edition (1795) and in subsequent revisions, was another of the schoolbook staples which brought a profit. Thomas also published Caleb Alexander's Latin and Greek grammars, considered revolutionary in their day.

In addition, Thomas was probably the most important printer of children's books in his generation. He entered the children's book field in 1779 by selling John Newbery chapbooks and the best of the English juveniles, and subsequently sold such standbys as *The History of Little Goody Two-Shoes*, *Robinson Crusoe*, and novels based on Shakespeare's plays. He started publishing children's books in 1785, published the first American edition of *Mother Goose's Melody* in 1786, and peaked with nineteen titles in 1787. Thomas listed 66 titles in 119 editions of his children's books. Ironically, he considered them to be some of the least important of his works and did not bother to deposit them in the library of the American Antiquarian Society after he founded it in 1812.

Thomas valued his Bibles far more than the children's books and he labored carefully over them. His first two Bibles, in 1786 and 1788, were for children; his first major Bible edition appeared in December 1791. Thomas's pioneering efforts in the mass production of books are reflected in his duodecimo version of the Bible, which first appeared in 1797 and which, because it was kept set in type, made a relatively low-cost Bible available to a broad audience. Almost all of the Bibles Thomas published were well received and widely circulated.

Thomas also specialized in music and medical publishing. His first major work in music, a collection of hymns he edited called *Laus Deo!*, appeared

in 1786 and was revised for subsequent editions. Thomas also brought out rival hymnals, mostly through the Boston partnership. In addition, he was the most important publisher of standard medical works in New England. In 1793 he brought out editions of William Smellie's *Set of Anatomical Tables* and Charles White's *Treatise on the Management of Pregnant and Lying in Women*, two of the most important such works of the time.

Not all of Thomas's undertakings were successful. He published a speller of his own composition in the late 1780s, but it did not sell well and was discontinued. He sometimes clashed with American writers over copyright restrictions. In the early 1790s he made several abortive efforts to expand his business into additional towns—including a seven-month venture in 1794-1795 as copublisher with Elisha Waldo of a weekly newspaper, the *Worcester Intelligencer: Or, Brookfield Advertiser*—and some of his partnerships failed.

But his successes far outweighed such failures. He continually sought new outlets for his publishing empire. In 1793, for example, he sent one of his former apprentices, David Carlisle, home to Walpole, New Hampshire, and set him up in partnership to publish the *New Hampshire Journal; Or, The Farmer's Weekly Museum;* it became a well-known newspaper, mainly because of the contributions of Joseph Dennie and Royall Tyler. Thomas was involved sporadically as a copublisher of the paper until he finally sold out his interest in 1809. Also, Thomas arranged with booksellers in other states to exchange stock in order to find a more favorable market for slow-moving items. In 1793 he built his own paper mill at Quinsigamond, near Worcester, which produced about 1,400 pounds of paper each week until Thomas sold it in 1798. At the peak of his business in the mid-1790s, Thomas employed 150 people at Worcester alone. The inventory of his Worcester printing plant and bookstore was valued at $39,679.02 in 1796. From July 1797 until October 1798 he was copublisher of the *Albany* (N.Y.) *Centinel*, a semiweekly newspaper.

In 1801 or 1802 he relinquished the management of the *Spy* and the Worcester press to his son Isaiah, Jr., but retained ownership at least of the print shop. The last book to bear Thomas's imprint was the 1802 edition of *The New-England Primer*. His fortune at the time, more than $150,000, was one of the largest in the United States. In the same year, Thomas was replaced as postmaster at Worcester by one of President Jefferson's political appointees. Thomas continued to be involved in the bookselling operations, however,

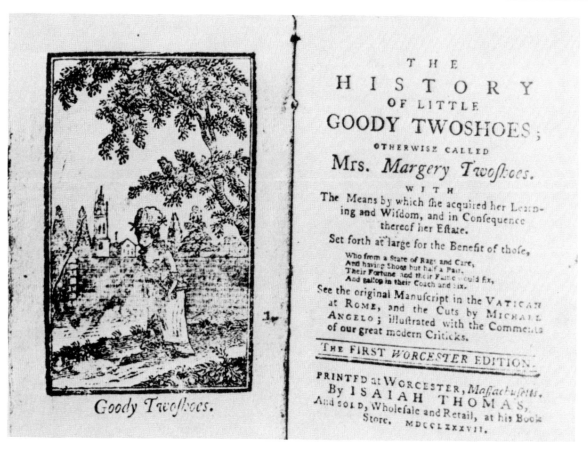

Frontispiece and title page for one of the many children's books printed by Thomas

and he even set up several partnerships between 1807 and 1813. Financial troubles with some of the partnerships kept Thomas busy during the early years of the nineteenth century. Also during these years he helped establish and was a director of the first bank in Worcester, was a partner in a Worcester tannery, and helped initiate the construction of the Boston-Worcester turnpike.

Thomas spent almost two years writing the first history of American printing, using as basic sources his own file of original newspapers, which he had begun to accumulate in the early 1790s, and his contacts with printers throughout the country. *The History of Printing in America* was published in two volumes in 1810. His main purpose was to preserve material that might otherwise be lost to posterity; he viewed his book as a collection of notes rather than a formal history and hoped that revised editions with updated material would be issued as appropriate. The American Antiquarian Society published a second edition in 1874. Partly as a consequence of the publication of his book, Thomas was elected to membership in the Massachusetts

Historical Society in 1811, the New York Historical Society in 1813, and the American Philosophical Society of Philadelphia in 1816. Dartmouth College recognized him with an honorary M.A. in 1814 and Allegheny College, Pennsylvania, awarded him an honorary LL.D. in 1818.

The learned societies of that time functioned mainly as forums for the presentation of scholarly papers, however, and Thomas saw the need for an organization that would gather and preserve sources of American history and make them available to historians. As a result of Thomas's proposals, the American Antiquarian Society was incorporated by the Massachusetts legislature in 1812 for the purpose of "the collection and preservation of the antiquities of our country, and of curious and valuable productions in art and nature [which] have a tendency to enlarge the sphere of human knowledge, aid in the progress of science, to perpetuate the history of moral and political events, and to improve and instruct posterity." Congress almost immediately made the society a depository for all government documents. In sub-

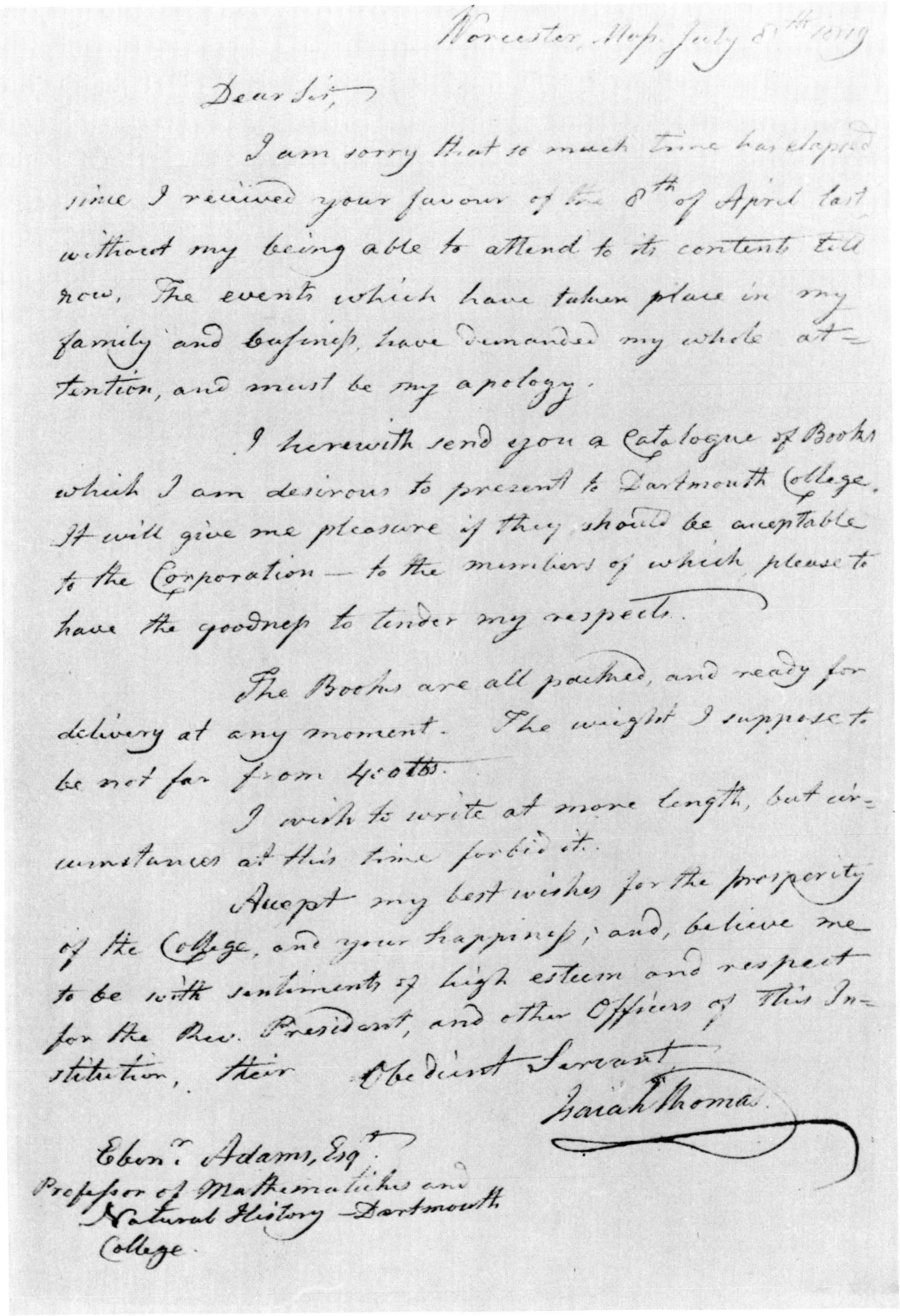

Worcester, Mass, July 5th 1819

Dear Sir,

I am sorry that so much time has elapsed since I received your favour of the 8th of April last, without my being able to attend to its contents till now. The events which have taken place in my family and business, have demanded my whole attention, and must be my apology.

I herewith send you a Catalogue of Books which I am desirous to present to Dartmouth College. It will give me pleasure if they should be acceptable to the Corporation — to the members of which, please to have the goodness to tender my respects.

The Books are all packed, and ready for delivery at any moment. The weight I suppose to be not far from 400℔.

I wish to write at more length, but circumstances at this time forbid it.

Accept my best wishes for the prosperity of the College, and your happiness; and, believe me to be with sentiments of high esteem and respect for the Rev. President, and other Officers of this Institution, their Obedient Servant

Isaiah Thomas

Ebenr Adams, Esqr
Professor of Mathematics and
Natural History Dartmouth
College.

Letter from Thomas to Professor Ebenezer Adams of Dartmouth College, concerning Thomas's donation of 470 books to the college library in 1819 (Dartmouth College Library)

sequent years, however, the society focused its attention on early American history and on printing, rather than on the broader history which Thomas envisioned. Thomas was elected president of the American Antiquarian Society at its first meeting in November 1812, and held that office until his death nineteen years later. In 1813 Thomas donated his personal library to the society to provide it with a base as a center for research. He later purchased the remains of the Mather Library and donated this to the society as well. He also donated the land and paid most of the cost for the first building of the society in Worcester, and he encouraged the society to begin its publications with a volume on American archaeology, which it published in 1820.

Thomas was an active member of many other organizations, including the fire societies of Boston and Worcester, the Boston Athenaeum (of which he was a founder), the Worcester Associate Circulating Library, the Massachusetts Humane Society, and the Auxiliary Bible Society (County of Worcester). In 1803 he organized the Society of Printers and Booksellers of Boston, later called the Faustus Association. This was a combination benevolent society and social club as well as labor union and trade association. Later, Thomas was elected an honorary member of the Philadelphia counterpart to the Faustus Association, the Typographical Society. Not only did Thomas give generously of his time and energy, but he also donated land to the city of Worcester for both a charity house and a court house. In Boston and Worcester he made bequests to fund the training of printers and the education of the children of poor printers, booksellers, and bookbinders.

Thomas was active for many years in the Order of Masons. The available evidence suggests that he joined the Massachusetts Lodge in Boston before fleeing the city in 1775. Afterwards he was active in the Lancaster Lodge near Worcester until the first Worcester Lodge was established in 1793. Thomas was selected as the First Grand Master of the Morning Star Lodge of Worcester in February 1793 and was chosen grand master in at least three subsequent years. Because of the extent of his contributions to the society, new lodges were named for him beginning in 1796. When he lived in Boston during the first decade of the nineteenth century, he was made Grand Master of the Massachusetts Lodge for four years, and for many years he traveled throughout New England on the business of the order.

Thomas's political conservatism was evident during the War of 1812: whereas he had supported mob action during the Revolution, by 1812 he believed that mobs should be punished. His humanitarianism was also evident in 1812: when British prisoners of war were confined in Worcester, he interceded for them and provided them with food. During the war he resigned from the boards of the bank and the turnpike company and helped dissolve the tannery. After the war, his bookstores in Baltimore, Albany, and Walpole failed and his fortune began to dwindle.

Thomas's second wife died in November 1818, and his son died in June 1819. In August of that year he married his second wife's sixty-two-year-old cousin and housekeeper, Rebecca Armstrong. After an apparently stormy two-and-one-half years, the couple separated in May 1822; Rebecca died in 1828. Thomas's daughter Mary Ann was divorced three times and finally returned with her son and three daughters to live with her father in Worcester. The last decade of Thomas's life was one of decreasing activity. He died at Worcester on 4 April 1831.

Biographies:

Annie Russell Marble, *From 'Prentice to Patron: The Life Story of Isaiah Thomas* (New York: Appleton-Century, 1935);

Clifford K. Shipton, *Isaiah Thomas: Printer, Patriot and Philanthropist* (Rochester, N.Y.: Leo Hart, 1948).

References:

Frank Roe Batchelder, "Isaiah Thomas, the Patriot Printer," *New England Magazine*, new series, 25 (November 1901): 284-305;

Worthington C. Ford, "The Isaiah Thomas Collection of Ballads," *Proceedings of the American Antiquarian Society*, 33 (April 1923): 34-112;

Luther Livingston, "An American Publisher of a Hundred Years Ago," *Bookman*, 11 (August 1900): 530-534;

Bruce M. Metzger, "Three Learned Printers and Their Unsung Contributions to Biblical Scholarship," *Journal of Religion*, 32 (October 1952): 254-262;

Charles Nichols, *Isaiah Thomas: Printer, Writer and Collector* (Boston: Club of Odd Volumes, 1912; New York: Burt Franklin, 1971);

Nichols, "The Portraits of Isaiah Thomas with Some Notes Upon His Descendants," *Proceedings of the American Antiquarian Society*, new series, 30 (October 1920): 251-277;

John R. Osterholm, "The Literary Career of Isaiah

Thomas, 1749-1831," Ph.D. dissertation, University of Massachusetts, 1978;

Clifford K. Shipton, "America's First Research Library," *Library Journal*, 74 (15 January 1949): 89-90;

Madeleine Stern, "Saint-Pierre in America: Joseph Nancrede and Isaiah Thomas," *Bibliographical Society of America*, 68 (July 1974): 312-325;

Benjamin Franklin Thomas, "Memoir of Isaiah Thomas," in *Transactions and Collections of the American Antiquarian Society*, 5 (Albany: Joel Munsell, 1874), pp. xvii-lxxxvii;

John T. Winterich, "Early American Books and Printing," *Publisher's Weekly*, 124 (15 July 1933): 174-176;

Hollis R. Yarrington, "Isaiah Thomas, Printer," Ph.D. dissertation, University of Maryland, 1970.

Papers:

Thomas's diaries, correspondence, business papers, imprints, newspapers, and other materials are collected in the Isaiah Thomas Papers, American Antiquarian Society, Worcester, Massachusetts.

Peter Timothy
(circa 1725-1782)

Wallace B. Eberhard
University of Georgia

MAJOR POSITIONS HELD: Editor and publisher, *South Carolina Gazette* (Charleston), renamed *Gazette of the State of South Carolina* in 1777 (1746-1780).

As printer, editor, publisher, politician, and patriot, Peter Timothy played an active and prominent role in a strategic Southern colony during a critical phase in the emergence of the United States. He literally grew up in the printing business, developed into a feisty and vigorous leader, and died—appropriately enough, some might say—in a violent storm at sea.

Timothy was one of the wave of French Huguenot refugees who came to America via Holland in the early eighteenth century. His father, Louis Timothée, arrived in Philadelphia aboard the *Britannia* on 21 September 1731 with his wife, Elizabeth, and four young children. Timothée opened a school for the teaching of French, but within the year Benjamin Franklin hired him as editor-translator for a new German-language newspaper, the *Philadelphische Zeitung*. This job, however, lasted only a few months. Timothée had been trained as a printer in Holland, and Franklin saw an opportunity to expand his network of partnerships around the young colonies. The one printer-publisher in Charles Town, South Carolina—the name was later changed to Charleston to eliminate its British tone—had died, leaving a media gap.

Franklin later wrote he sent one of his "journeymen to Charleston, South Carolina, where a printer was wanting. I furnished him with a press and letters on an agreement of partnership, by which I was to receive one-third of the profits of the business, paying one-third of the expense. He was a man of learning, and honest but ignorant in matters of account; and tho' he sometimes made me remittances, I could get no account from him, nor any satisfactory state of our partnership while he lived." But Timothée did reorganize a printing business in Charleston, and he brought out his first weekly edition of the *South Carolina Gazette* on 2 February 1734; the newspaper had been dormant since the death of the former publisher almost two years previously.

Lewis Timothy—his name now Anglicized—soon became the official printer for the colony, and aggressively sought out a variety of profitable printing arrangements. He quickly became an active member of the business community of the small but growing town at the confluence of the Cooper and Ashley Rivers. His printing office was a center of communication and commerce; as was often the custom in colonial communities, Timothy became postmaster. But he died in 1738 as the result of what was described in the *Gazette* only as an "unhappy accident" and was buried on 30 December. Left behind were six children (two had died in infancy) and a wife. The agreement between Franklin and Timothy provided for a takeover by Elizabeth Timothy in the event of her husband's death, and she was ready to meet the challenge in order to provide for her young family. The next issue of the *Gazette* appeared on 4 January 1739, carrying a notice that announced her assumption of the duties of public printer-publisher, with the hope that Charlestonians would "be kindly pleased to continue their Favours and good Offices to his poor afflicted Widow and six small Children and another hourly expected." Although the notice was signed by Mrs. Timothy, the masthead carried the notation "Printed by Peter Timothy." Elizabeth Timothy—assisted by son Peter, then about fourteen—thus became the first woman to publish a newspaper in the Southern colonies. Her reign as manager was a success. Franklin wrote later in his *Autobiography:* "The business was continued by his widow, who, being born and bred in Holland, where as I have been informed, the knowledge of accounts makes a part of female education, she not only sent me as clear a state as she could find of the transactions past, but continued to account with greatest regularity and exactness every quarter afterwards, and managed the business with such success, that she not only brought up reputably a family of children, but, at the expiration of the term, was able to purchase of me the printing-house, and establish her son in it."

The exact date when control of the *Gazette* and the printing business was turned over to Peter has not been established, but it was probably when he turned twenty-one, some time around 1746. He was obviously active in the business well before then, having been named as a participant in a libel action in 1741.

He was married on 18 December 1745 to Ann Donovan, of whom little is known. Timothy's correspondence over the years with Franklin in Philadelphia reveals that the couple had fourteen children; only four lived to maturity, including a son whom they named Benjamin Franklin. In 1748 Timothy joined with a group of seventeen young men, including merchants, planters, lawyers, a schoolteacher, a printer, a doctor, and a wigmaker, to found the Charles Town Library Society; within two years the membership was up to 130, with a fair-sized collection of books and pamphlets and a fund to support its operation. He was a member and pew holder in St. Philip's Church and became

secretary of the provincial lodge of Masons, in which he was active for many years. Until 1758, when a competing printing firm was established, he held a monopoly on official printing, and he continued to share in it thereafter.

Isaiah Thomas, founder of the American Antiquarian Society and author of the first history of American journalism, worked for another printer in Charleston in this era and described Timothy's *Gazette* thusly: "The *Gazette* was printed on a half sheet, . . . but sometimes on a whole sheet, often on a type as large as english, and at other times on long primer. The price was 15s. per quarter. In 1760 the sheet had four columns to a page and a cut of the King's arms was added to the title. Publication day was Monday, but it seldom came out on that day."

Timothy appears to have had substantial advertising, often using a good share of the front page for it, occasionally illustrating the ads with a line drawing appropriate to the item or service. He told his readers of his problems now and then, including the delay in arrival of type or paper ordered from England or Philadelphia, but most of his business difficulties were confided to Franklin in private letters; in one he apologized for not settling accounts with Franklin earlier. There were times when accounts receivable were not paid; Timothy once reported that "money comes in very slowly in Carolina, especially to me." After a four-month period during which he ran the business assisted only by a slave, he told Franklin that he had had to fire a "villainous apprentice, who might have been of vast service had he not been addicted to drink, play and scandalous company." More poignant is a comment in a 1772 letter to Franklin about his family: "My son Benjamin Franklin has just happily got through the measles and is a fine promising Boy; but as I have lost eight sons in teething, my apprehension for him will not be over until he has his Teeth."

As was the case with many Colonial printers, the *Gazette* office under both Lewis and Peter Timothy was a point for distribution of domestic mail. Peter was made provincial postmaster for South Carolina in the summer of 1756 and in 1766 he became postmaster general for the entire Southern District. These appointments put him in an exposed position during the Stamp Act crisis. In the issue of 19 October 1765 he denied that he had made an application to be the distributor of stamps in the region. The rumor was "absolutely false and void of the least foundation," he told his readers, "and I will be extremely obliged to any person for information who first raised or propagated the report." But on the following Thursday, the paper carried this notice: "Every advertisement is subject to a duty of Two Shillings each time it is inserted, which the printers are to pay weekly, it will therefore be absolutely necessary that READY MONEY be sent with ALL advertisements." This appears to be a signal that Timothy—a servant of the crown—was on the verge of complying with the act. But on the effective date of the act, 1 November 1765, his paper and its competitor suspended publication. The difficulty of trying to buck the strong Patriot sentiment was too great. Because of his position, his fortunes were at low ebb until the act was suspended. He wrote Franklin: "Find myself reduced from the most popular to the most unpopular man in this Province by taking upon me a place in the Post office at the time of the Stamp Act."

Although he had suspended his newspaper as a form of opposition, he had also opposed violent measures by the Patriots. Thus, both Loyalists and Patriots had reason to suspect him, even though he took a more aggressive Patriot role by such activities as patrolling the Charleston harbor with members of the Sons of Liberty to insure that nothing was moving among the shipping without their knowledge. In a time and place that seemed to force one into taking one side of the fence or the other, Timothy continued to show impartiality even when he had views of his own. Although he was the first in the colony to publish the proposed set of Non-Importation Agreements in 1768 in opposition to the Townshend Acts, he still allowed opponents to use the columns of his paper. He was the only Charleston printer to permit William Henry Drayton, under the pen name "Freeman," to publish a series of letters critical of the nonimportation movement. Timothy defended his action, writing that for thirty years he had published an "open press" and did not intend to change.

The *Gazette* was suspended for three lengthy intervals between 1764 and 1772. In the latter year Timothy formed a partnership with Thomas Powell, a London-trained printer, and Edward Hughes. The *Gazette* was published by Powell, Hughes and Company; Powell continued as publisher alone after Hughes's death until 1773, when Timothy became an active publisher once more. The paper continued with only occasional publishing lapses and suspensions, and on 9 April 1777, the title became *Gazette of the State of South Carolina*, instead of the *South Carolina Gazette*. Timothy's younger brother Charles joined the publishing firm during this period.

Timothy's commitment to the Patriot cause became deeper as the movement for independence grew. Although he had served the crown as office-holder and official printer, he had voiced his opposition frequently; in 1746, for instance, he had written against Governor James Glen's attempts to enforce the Sunday blue laws and was cited in grand jury presentments for his views. In the mid-1770s his actions went beyond the columns of his newspaper. In July 1774 he was elected a member of the "General Committee to correspond with the Committees of other Colonies." He was named a representative to the first provincial congress in January 1775 from the parishes of St. Philip's and St. Michael. In the same month he became secretary of the provincial congress and the Charles Town Committee. When the provincial congress formed a "Council of Safety" in 1775, he was also elected secretary of that body. He was named clerk of the second provincial congress that met in March 1776 to draw up a state constitution. Later, he served as clerk of the House of Representatives and the General Assembly.

The work of the Patriots earned the encouragement of Franklin, who wrote his support in a letter from London to Timothy, dated 7 September 1774:

> You wish me to correspond with you on public affairs. That relating to America have been and still continue in so disagreeable a situation that I cannot write upon them with pleasure. . . .
>
> Much depends on yourselves. If at the intended Congress your deputies are nearly unanimous in declaring your rights: and in resolving fairly against all Importations from here . . . you cannot fail to carry your point. This ministry must go out and give place to men of juster and more generous principles. If you divide you are lost.
>
> I believe I shall stay here another winter, and shall be glad to hear of you and yours. My love and blessing to my little name-sake. . . .

Writing to Franklin in 1777, Timothy told of his efforts on behalf of the Patriots, and his deep involvement and commitment to their cause. As secretary of the Councils of Safety he

> sat Day and Night, without a single Day's intermission continually in motion from Congress to Committee from Committee to Council to Inspection, and so on.
>
> I say, if my Friend can have an idea of the Labour I underwent in these Employ-

ments, without mentioning the incessant calls from one way or another besides, he would wonder how it was possible for one man to go thro' it all and preserve his Senses and admit it was impossible to indulge an Inclination to private Correspondence. . . . When the Consititution was framed, I was unanimously chosen Clerk of the General Assembly—I served one Session, and wrote to resign, but the Acceptance of my Resignation was refused—and when the new Assembly was chosen I was reelected, and continued in that office.

When the British began their siege of Charleston early in 1780, Timothy climbed into the steeple of St. Michael's Church to report the movements of the British fleet. When the British entered the city on 12 May, Timothy was arrested but placed on parole; he refused, however, to take the oath of allegiance to King George. Lord Cornwallis gave orders in August to seize Timothy and thirty-two other prominent citizens of the captured city. They were put on board the *Sandwich* and sent as prisoners to St. Augustine, Florida. They were not ill-treated in captivity, and in July 1781, Timothy and the other Charlestonians were put on the *Nancy* and sent to Philadelphia in a prisoner exchange. His family joined him there in December, having been sent under the "Cruel Edict of Lieut. Col. Balfour, Commandant," who decreed the exile of the families of those men "who wou'd not Sully their honour and Conscience by taking protection" offered by swearing allegiance to the king.

Timothy decided to move to Antigua, where a widowed daughter, Mrs. Frances Claudia Marchant, owned property. Timothy, Mrs. Marchant, and her child headed for the West Indies in the fall of 1782. The ship was wrecked off the Delaware capes and all aboard were lost.

At the end of the war, Timothy's widow, Ann, returned to Charleston, formed a partnership with one E. Walsh, and resurrected the *Gazette of the State of South Carolina* on 16 July 1783. She served as printer to the state and continued publishing the newspaper until her death at age sixty-five in 1792. Benjamin Franklin Timothy, educated at Princeton, took over the business and published the newspaper until 1802, when he left the printing business to become a school principal in Charleston. The *Gazette* ceased publication when Benjamin Timothy left; the last issue appeared on 20 September.

There is little disagreement among historians about Timothy's significant contributions to the revolutionary cause in his dual roles of publisher and Patriot leader. Measuring his impact on public opinion and political action is difficult, but Isaiah Thomas said that he "supported the cause of the country, and energetically opposed the measures of the British administration." In England, he was identified as "the conduit Pipe of Political matters" who was the chief offender in promoting resistance in South Carolina. Copies of his newspapers were sent to England to show "what spirit is attempted to be kept alive and inflamed." Arthur Schlesinger, Sr., singled him out as one of "certain printers [who] contributed significantly to the agitation" leading to the revolution. Frank Luther Mott said that his paper was "the strongest exponent of Patriot doctrine in the South," and Hennig Cohen said that there was agreement that "the *Gazette* was the most effective Whig newspaper" in the region.

References:

Ira L. Baker, "Elizabeth Timothy: America's First Woman Editor," *Journalism Quarterly*, 54 (Summer 1977): 280-285;

James W. Baker, "The Coming of the War for Independence and the South Carolina Press," master's thesis, University of South Carolina, 1980;

Hennig Cohen, *The South Carolina Gazette, 1732-1775* (Columbia: University of South Carolina Press, 1953);

Douglas C. McMurtrie, "The Correspondence of Peter Timothy, Printer of Charleston, with Benjamin Franklin," *South Carolina Historical and Genealogical Magazine*, 35 (October 1934): 123-129;

Frank Luther Mott, *American Journalism*, third edition (New York: Macmillan, 1962), pp. 41-42, 93;

J. Ralph Randolph, "The End of Impartiality: South-Carolina Gazette, 1763-75," *Journalism Quarterly*, 49 (Winter 1972): 702-709;

Isaiah Thomas, *The History of Printing in America*, 2 volumes (Worcester, Mass.: From the press of Isaiah Thomas, jun., Isaac Sturtevant, printer, 1810), II: 156-169;

Elizabeth Cowden Williams, "The Timothy Press," master's thesis, Drexel Institute of Technology, 1950.

Benjamin Towne

(circa 1740-8 July 1793)

Dwight L. Teeter, Jr.
University of Texas at Austin

MAJOR POSITION HELD: Publisher, *Pennsylvania Evening Post* (Philadelphia) (1775-1784).

Benjamin Towne is a seriocomic figure in the history of American journalism. His major accomplishment in a troubled life was publishing the *Pennsylvania Evening Post*, a triweekly begun in 1775 which became in 1783 the first daily newspaper in the United States. The *Evening Post* evidently moved to daily publication in a last-ditch attempt to remain in business. This desperate effort at daily journalism folded late in 1784.

Towne's career was blighted by his political side-changing, which led him to be "attainted" for treason in 1778, although the charge was later dropped. The *Evening Post* favored the American revolutionists at first, but changed political colors in 1777 when British troops occupied Philadelphia. When the troops withdrew from the city in the spring of 1778, Towne's newspaper readopted prorevolutionist sympathies.

Contrary to some accounts, Towne was not allowed to publish his newspaper undisturbed after the British troops withdrew from Philadelphia. He was harassed from time to time once the revolutionists were again in control of the city and was mobbed in 1779 by a group sympathetic to Thomas Paine, who had been attacked in the pages of the *Evening Post*. Towne discovered that in Philadelphia from 1778 to 1783, the safer course was to print only those items which supported the revolutionary order in Pennsylvania.

Towne was born in Lincolnshire, England, and learned the printing trade before coming to Pennsylvania in the 1760s. In 1769 he became a journeyman for William Goddard, publisher of the *Pennsylvania Chronicle*. Goddard had the financial support of the highly conservative political leaders Joseph Galloway and Thomas Wharton, Sr., until he angered his backers by publishing John Dickinson's "Letters from a Farmer in Pennsylvania." Dickinson, a rival politician, made the persuasive and widely republished argument that Parliament, although having the right to regulate colonial

trade, had no right to tax trade; indeed, the Farmer's Letters denied that Parliament had any authority whatsoever to tax the colonies. Galloway and Wharton then loaned £526 to Towne, making him Goddard's partner. This partnership proved unsatisfactory and was spiced by frequent squabbles between the printers. Towne left the partnership in February 1770.

For the next five years, Towne supported himself as best he could, evidently working for other Philadelphia printers and perhaps by working at times as a coppersmith. In 1774, perhaps with the backing of silent partners, he set up a printing house. A. M. Lee speculated that Towne again had the backing of Galloway and Wharton; in 1775, however, Galloway and Wharton supported the *Pennsylvania Mercury* of Enoch Story and Daniel Humphreys, so Towne's partners—if he had them—must have been other individuals.

On 24 January 1775 Towne published the first issue of his *Pennsylvania Evening Post*, Philadelphia's first evening newspaper and the fourth English language paper in the city. The *Evening Post*'s competition included William and Thomas Bradford's *Pennsylvania Journal* and the *Pennsylvania Gazette*—formerly published by Benjamin Franklin—which appeared from the printing house of William Hall, David Hall, Jr., and William Sellers. Also on the scene was John Dunlap's *Pennsylvania Packet*, which he had established in 1771 and which would become the nation's first successful daily in 1784. The newspapers competing with the *Evening Post* were all weeklies, but Towne soon changed his newspaper from weekly to triweekly publication. The *Evening Post* was published in the 12 1/2-inch by 9 1/2-inch "small quarto" format, and usually contained four pages.

More competition was on the way. On 27 January James Humphreys, Jr., began publishing the weekly *Pennsylvania Ledger;* and on 7 April Enoch Story and Daniel Humphreys—with support from Galloway and Wharton—began their *Pennsylvania Mercury*. Galloway expressed the hope that the *Mercury* would be "a free press, to recall the deluded people to their senses." On 31 December, however, the *Mercury* shop was ruined by a fire which Story asserted was set by "the infatuated populace."

By 1776 Towne's *Pennsylvania Evening Post*—along with competing Philadelphia newspapers—was embroiled in the strenuous politics accompanying the adoption of Pennsylvania's constitution of 1776. Control of Pennsylvania was wrested from the conservative legislature and a revolutionary government was formed. The Provincial Convention met from 15 July to 28 September. In addition to adopting the constitution, which was published on 10 September, the convention acted as a legislature, passing measures defining treason and forbidding sedition. The sedition law empowered any two justices of the peace to imprison "dangerous" persons for the duration of the war and forbade speech or writing which would oppose or obstruct the prosecution of the war.

Towne's newspapers published materials submitted by both supporters and opponents of the constitution. One writer praised the new frame of government for providing expanded suffrage. A writer calling himself "F," on the other hand, complained that the Provincial Convention had acted illegally by legislating; he declared that the convention was assembled only for the broader purpose of establishing the constitution. The *Evening Post* continued unhampered during the rest of 1776, even though it included comments on the constitution and the convention.

James Humphreys, Jr., of the *Pennsylvania Ledger*, however, encountered problems. His paper had been printing comments about the constitution which now seem no more or less strident than those appearing in Philadelphia's other journals. Towne appears to have played an ignoble role in helping to frighten Humphreys out of the city. On 16 November 1776 the *Evening Post* published a statement about Humphreys's *Ledger* signed by "A Tory": "I have been long anxious to see a printing press in this city subservient to the purposes of Lord and General Howe." The attack on Humphreys added, "Now it becomes all friends of arbitrary government" to assist the British. The Massachusetts newspaperman and historian Isaiah Thomas wrote that Towne published that attack using paper which Towne had borrowed from Humphreys. Humphreys then fled from Philadelphia.

The *Pennsylvania Evening Post* continued to be ostensibly loyal to the revolutionists into 1777. But in September of that year, with a British occupation force bearing down on Philadelphia, other printers

hastened to move westward to safety, hauling presses, type, and other materials in wagons. Towne stayed in the city, although he halted publication of his paper for several weeks, beginning again on 11 October. Remaining in Philadelphia, however, did not ensure a monopoly for Towne. In November, James Humphreys, Jr., returned to Philadelphia and reopened his *Pennsylvania Ledger*. And on 31 March New York printer James Robertson published what was to be the first of only twenty-five issues of the *Royal Pennsylvania Gazette*.

The *Pennsylvania Evening Post* became a solidly Tory publication, carrying proclamations by British General Howe assuring Pennsylvania men that they would be pardoned, even if they had carried arms against the British, if they would again pledge loyalty to King George.

Towne's pro-British competition soon melted away. Humphreys suspended his *Ledger* after its 23 May 1778 issue, and Robertson's *Royal Pennsylvania Gazette* was out of business after 26 May. Towne's newspaper suspended operations from 20 May to 11 June but was publishing again when the British troops left Philadelphia on 18 June.

The Pennsylvania government and the Continental Congress put Towne to work printing proclamations of the state's Supreme Executive Council and of the Congress, since his shop was the only one available while other printers were filtering slowly back into the city. But Towne's humiliation soon began. On 25 June he had the degrading experience of using his *Evening Post* to publish the Pennsylvania Supreme Executive Council's list of traitors—including the name of Benjamin Towne.

To make matters worse, the president of Princeton University, the Rev. Dr. John Witherspoon, wrote the frequently republished *Humble Confession, Declaration, Recantation, and Apology of Benjamin Towne, Printer in Philadelphia* (1778). Witherspoon ridiculed Towne for remaining in Philadelphia during the British occupation, putting excruciatingly embarrassing words in his mouth: "I turned fairly round, and printed my *Evening Post* under the protection of General Howe and his army." Witherspoon also attributed this statement to Towne: "I have been a coward since my youth, so that I cannot fight—my belly is so big I cannot run—and I am so great a lover of eating and drinking that I cannot starve."

To his further mortification, Towne's newspaper published articles in mid-1778 which demanded stringent punishment for Tories. By fall, however, Towne must have felt that the worst was over: the *Evening Post* was publishing scathing attacks on the constitution of 1776. That document, "An Associator" wrote in October, was dangerously tyrannous because it created a one-house legislature. Pennsylvania's state officials were called "weak and wicked men, who are seeking their own private emolument."

Towne pushed his luck too far in July 1779. Harsh criticisms printed in the *Evening Post* of the 1776 constitution's backers and of the famed author of *Common Sense*, Thomas Paine, endangered Towne. The *Evening Post* published a series of insulting questions under the pen name of "Cato":

> Who was an Englishman? Tom P----.
> Who was a Tory? Tom P----.
> Who was made secretary to the committee on
>   Foreign affairs? Tom P----.
> Who betrayed state affairs? Tom P----.
> Who maintains Tom P----? Nobody knows.
> Who is paid by the enemy? Nobody knows.
> Who best deserves it? Tom P----.

On 16 July Paine—using his own name—wrote a furious letter which Towne printed in the *Evening Post*. Paine demanded that Cato identify himself. That information was not forthcoming, and Cato's next article—published on 24 July—fanned the flames. Paine was excoriated for his inability to keep secrets, which had in fact led to the loss of his job as secretary to the Continental Congress's Committee on Foreign Affairs. That evening, Paine's friends in the Constitutional Society—including the painter Charles Willson Peale and Colonel John Bull—dragged Towne to their meeting. When Towne was reluctant to reveal Cato's identity, a noose was placed around his neck. Towne then identified the author as the conservative Whitehead Humphreys. The mob proceeded to Humphreys's house, and Humphreys's sister was hit in the face with a club when she answered the door. Humphreys, swinging a borrowed cane, fought his way into his dwelling and chased Peale and friends away by waving a musket out an upstairs window. Paine, meanwhile, demonstrated a limited notion of freedom of the press when he wrote in Dunlap's *Pennsylvania Packet* that the author of Cato's "infamously false" publications, "to avoid the shame and scandal of being known, tied the Printer down to such strong obligations to conceal him, that nothing but a halter noose could extort it from him."

The noose evidently encouraged timidity on Towne's part. Philadelphia, beset by food shortages and by inflation which rendered paper money of negligible value, saw serious mob violence. Towne, by 1780, was having financial difficulties. The *Evening Post* appeared irregularly, and in September, Towne was advertising for "hawkers" to sell his newspaper in the streets. Subscription sales were then the norm for newspapers, but the *Evening Post* was trying extraordinary measures to stay afloat.

In an evident last gasp to allow his paper to survive, Towne began publishing the *Evening Post* as a tiny, rather scruffy daily, appearing up to six times a week, beginning with the issue of 30 May 1783. Only twenty-six copies of the daily *Evening Post* are known to have survived; the last extant issue is dated 26 October 1784. Charles M. Thomas wrote in the *Dictionary of American Biography* that Towne himself hawked the last issue of his newspaper on the streets of Philadelphia, yelling "All the news for two coppers."

After the *Evening Post* died, Towne evidently supported himself by working as a printer. Charles Thomas noted that the firm of "Benjamin Towne & Co. (printer)" was listed in Philadelphia's city directory for 1790. Towne died at his home on Sixth Street near Arch Street on 8 July 1793. Charles Thomas suggested that the *Evening Post* failed because Towne's conduct made no permanent friends. Isaiah Thomas said, "Towne was not deficient in intellect and was a decent workman"; he was a *"bon vivant,* but he did not possess the art of accumulating and retaining wealth." Even so, Towne is remembered for publishing the nation's first daily newspaper.

References:

A. M. Lee, "First U.S. Daily '50 Years Too Early,' " *Editor & Publisher,* 66 (1934): 11, 37;

Arthur M. Schlesinger, *Prelude to Independence: the Newspaper War on Britain, 1764-1776* (New York: Knopf, 1958);

J. Paul Selsam, *The Pennsylvania Constitution of 1776* (Philadelphia: University of Pennsylvania Press/London: Oxford University Press, 1936);

Dwight L. Teeter, "Benjamin Towne: The Precarious Career of a Persistent Printer," *Pennsylvania Magazine of History and Biography,* 89 (July 1965): 316-330;

Teeter, "Legacy of Expression: Philadelphia Newspapers and Congress During the War for Independence," Ph.D. dissertation, University of Wisconsin, 1966;

Charles M. Thomas, "Benjamin Towne," *Dictionary of American Biography,* edited by Dumas Malone, volume 9 (New York: Scribners, 1936), pp. 611-612;

Isaiah Thomas, *The History of Printing in America*, edited by Marcus A. McCorison from the sec-

ond edition (New York: Weathervane Books, 1970).

James Watson Webb
(8 February 1802-7 June 1884)

Richard M. Brown

MAJOR POSITION HELD: Publisher, *New York Morning Courier*, merged to form *Morning Courier and New York Enquirer* in 1829 (1827-1861).

BOOKS: *To the Officers of the Army* (New York, 1827);

Slavery and Its Tendencies. A Letter from General J. Watson Webb to the New York Courier and Enquirer (Washington, D.C.: Buell & Blanchard, printers, 1856);

A Letter from His Excellency J. Watson Webb . . . to J. Bramley-Moore, Esq., M.P., in Reply to a Statement in the "Times" Newspaper by His Excellency W. D. Christie (Rio de Janeiro?, 1863);

A National Currency: Specie Payments. Gold and Silver. Greenbacks (New York: M. B. Brown, 1875);

Reminiscences of Gen'l Samuel B. Webb of the Revolutionary Army (New York: Globe Stationery & Printing Co., 1882).

OTHER: Sir William George Drummond Stewart, *Altowan; or, Incidents of Life and Adventure in the Rocky Mountains*, edited by Webb, 2 volumes (New York: Harper, 1846).

James Watson Webb (photograph by Mathew Brady)

One of the more colorful and combative editors of the antebellum New York press, James Watson Webb made the *Morning Courier and New York Enquirer* the leader of the commercial press, becoming one of the most influential editors in the age of personal journalism, although his political position shifted from Jacksonian to Whig to Republican. A leader in the race to be first with the news, he also led the "moral war" against the penny papers and fought numerous duels arising from his editorial activities. He became minister to Brazil following his retirement from publishing.

The eighth of nine children of Gen. Samuel Blachley Webb and Catharine Hogeboom Webb, Webb was born at Claverack, New York. His father, an aide to General Washington and commander of the Third Connecticut Regiment, was a thrice-wounded war hero and a successful speculator in land and securities. He attained national prominence as one of the founders of the Society of Cincinnati and as manager of Washington's 1789 inaugural ceremonies.

After being orphaned at the age of five, James Watson Webb grew up in the home of an aunt, Mary Hogeboom Thomas, and later in that of his sister, Maria Webb Morrell; both were well-to-do households. In 1816 Webb went to work in an elder brother's store in Cooperstown, New York, but was bored with the life of a clerk. Leaving Cooperstown in 1819 without telling his family, he went to Albany to request a military commission from Governor De Witt Clinton. Rejected, he went to Washington, where Secretary of War John C. Calhoun succumbed to his pleading and, following a written examination, commissioned him a second lieutenant. Known as "Calhoun's scrub lieutenant" because of his lack of West Point training, he spent his first two years of military duty at Governor's Island, New York. It was during this time that he met Helen Lispenard Stewart, the wealthy and socially prominent daughter of Alexander L. Stewart, a leading tycoon.

Seeking a more adventurous life, he was assigned first to Detroit and shortly after to Fort Dearborn on the present site of Chicago. Here he found much of the same monotony as at other military posts, although there were occasional times of high danger. In one incident, he crossed Illinois in the depth of winter, pursued by hostile Indians, to carry word to Fort Armstrong on the Mississippi of an impending Indian attack on Fort Snelling, Minnesota.

When the army decided to abandon Fort Dearborn in 1823, Webb took leave to return to New York and married Helen Stewart on 1 July before returning to Detroit. Although his family life was contented, Webb was restless and frustrated with the lack of opportunity for advancement. Impetuous and aggressive, he fought duels with two of his fellow officers. Finally, a quarrel with his commanding officer which threatened to result in another duel led to his resignation from the service in 1827.

When the Webbs returned to New York, his father-in-law helped Webb to become established. Webb purchased a major share in the *Morning Courier*, a new mercantile daily, and became its editor and publisher in December 1827.

Young Webb fitted well into the crude, brawling, but vital political and commercial life of New York. He made his paper a supporter of Andrew Jackson, primarily on tariff issues, although he devoted more attention to local intraparty feuding, particularly opposing his rival, Mordecai M. Noah

of the *Enquirer,* who was campaigning for sheriff. Webb was read out of the local party organization because of his breach of loyalty, but continued his support of the national party.

Webb recognized that his ambitions for journalistic success were being blocked by a ruinous competitive situation. On the advice of Noah's associate editor, James Gordon Bennett, he acquired the *Enquirer* to form the *Morning Courier and New York Enquirer,* better known as the *Courier and Enquirer,* in 1829. Combining lively and thorough political commentary with solid commercial and financial reporting, Webb's paper was growing rapidly. He had acquired as associates two of the top New York journalists, Noah and Bennett, in the merger. It was an uneasy alliance, however. From the beginning, the ambitious Bennett was maneuvering for an opportunity to undercut the new paper's political support, seeking an opportunity to establish his own party organ. His intrigues misfired, however, and although he was easily the paper's most effective political correspondent and economic analyst, Webb dismissed him. Bennett went on to found the *New York Herald.*

With advertising and subscriptions merged and growing, a new building and a new press capable of 1,300 impressions per hour were in operation by October 1829. They were outmoded in only five months and the press was replaced with one capable of 1,500 impressions hourly. Combined daily and weekly circulation neared 6,500, with frequent advertising supplements to relieve the backlog of advertising. Exceeding the combined circulation of its rivals, the *Courier and Enquirer* became the official paper for printing the state's legal notices. Gaining 500 new subscribers within a year, Webb found a third new press—a two-cylinder Napier with a 200-sheet capacity—necessary. At the same time, the size of the sheets was doubled, creating the "blanket" format. But the rapid growth did not bring Webb political or journalistic popularity, nor did it place him in a sound financial position.

Considering his editorial opinions infallible, Webb took any criticism as a personal attack and retaliated with verbal or physical abuse. In an age of newspaper vituperation, rival editors were frequently targets of his ire—particularly the editors of the *Journal of Commerce,* David Hale and Gerard Hallock, whom he denounced as pious frauds; and Col. William L. Stone of the *Commercial Advertiser,* whom he dubbed "Col. Whistle-breeches."

Much of the friction centered around Webb's success as an enterprising news gatherer, not only in local and state coverage but in Washington and foreign news as well. An expensive rivalry with the *Journal of Commerce* grew out of competition in meeting ships from Europe. In 1828 the *Courier and Enquirer* joined two other dailies to form a harbor news-boat cooperative, using rowboats to meet the ships before they docked, in order to gain possession of the newspapers in their mailbags. Webb, dissatisfied with the cooperative's performance, soon became an independent. When the *Journal of Commerce* escalated its effort by purchasing a schooner, both the *Courier and Enquirer* and the cooperative were forced into purchasing their own schooners. The cost for Webb was $3,600 for building the boat and $5,000 in annual operating costs. By 1834 the cost of independent operation had become too great and Webb rejoined the cooperative. The competition was also reflected in Webb's 1830 efforts to score beats on Washington news with an elaborate combination of pony express and steamboat to beat the mails by twenty-four hours, at a cost of $7,500 per month.

The *Courier and Enquirer*, though it was the largest and most profitable paper in New York, could not withstand Webb's lavish expenditures, which also included speculation in western land and other commodities. When the paper, one of the most strident opponents of rechartering the Second Bank of the United States, suddenly reversed its position and broke with the Jacksonians in 1832, a hue and cry arose over substantial loans by the bank's president, Nicholas Biddle, to Webb and Noah. In the ensuing investigation, Biddle was found to have bribed the *Courier and Enquirer*; but the evidence was largely circumstantial and the outcome remained controversial. The *Courier and Enquirer*, however, was now as firmly committed to the Whig party as it had been to the Jacksonians, and it turned its vitriolic war of words against its former friends.

The 1830s proved a time of turmoil and combat for Webb. In 1830 a feud with Duff Green of the *United States Telegraph* erupted into a personal confrontation when Webb went to Washington to cane his enemy. Green met him with a drawn pistol, averting the battle, but the feud continued. In 1833 Webb caned William Leggett, associate editor of William Cullen Bryant's *New York Evening Post*, after Leggett spat in his face during a chance encounter. He had three street fights with Bennett in 1836, winning the physical battles but being bested in the editorial exchanges that followed. Webb almost fought a duel with Congressman Samuel H. Gholson of Mississippi in 1837 over a revival of the

bank bribery charges. Then, in 1838, similar charges by Congressman Jonathan Cilley of Maine brought about a duel between Cilley and Webb's friend Congressman J. W. Graves of Kentucky. Cilley was killed in the affair.

Among Webb's verbal battles, the most important was that against James Fenimore Cooper. Cooper's novel *Home as Found* (1838) contained the character Steadfast Dodge, Whig editor of the *Active Enquirer*, who was seen as a parody of Webb. The *Courier and Enquirer* retaliated in a review and Cooper charged Webb with criminal libel. From February 1839 to November 1843, the matter was dragged through three libel trials and innumerable verbal skirmishes; Webb was ultimately acquitted.

Another violent confrontation took place in 1842, when charges of venality against Congressman Thomas F. Marshall of Kentucky brought a challenge. Although the duel, in which Webb was wounded, was fought in Delaware, which had no laws against dueling, Webb was indicted on an old law against leaving New York for purposes of dueling. Sentenced to two years in prison, he was pardoned when Governor William H. Seward bowed to public sentiment, including a petition with 14,000 signatures. As a condition of the pardon, however, the governor extracted a promise from Webb to forswear dueling.

Meanwhile, the *Courier and Enquirer* continued to expand in facilities, coverage, and profitability throughout the 1830s. Webb had not made any basic alterations in his six-cent paper to offset the growing influence of the penny press, simply improvements. By 1840, the *Courier and Enquirer* began to feel the pressure of competition, particularly from Bennett and the *Herald*. When Bennett engaged in a series of vulgar attacks on religion, including his own Roman Catholic church, Webb seized the opportunity to organize a "moral war" against the *Herald*. Under his leadership, the boycott injured the *Herald* but did not succeed in forcing it out of business. Instead, by 1842, Webb's own debts had mounted to the point that he took advantage of a new bankruptcy law to gain a fresh start.

Webb was able to retain control of the *Courier and Enquirer*, buying back his interest through a $57,000 mortgage on the paper. Gradually, his financial condition improved. In part, this was due to becoming the exclusive publisher of bankruptcy notices in New York City, but it was also due to the acquisition of a new associate editor, Henry J. Raymond, in 1843. Raymond, who had previously been with Horace Greeley's *New York Tribune*, was not only an excellent manager but possessed a conservative outlook which tempered Webb's impetuosity and reforming zeal. He did much to modernize the paper and broaden its interests; it became less involved in political disputes on a personal level and increased its cultural scrutiny. Raymond also brought a brightness and freshness to the paper to enable it to compete effectively with its cheaper rivals.

A politically ambitious man, Webb believed that his support of the Whigs entitled him to a reward in the form of appointment to office. Although he had become engineer in chief of New York State with the rank of major general in 1843, he was not satisfied and sought higher office. Hampered by his penchant for intraparty feuds, he nevertheless was able to gain appointment as chargé d'affaires to Austria in 1849. His first wife had died in 1848; on 9 November 1849 he married Laura Cram, and the honeymooning pair sailed for Europe, where he was to assume his new post. Then the Senate refused to confirm his appointment. Webb returned to New York to take up editorial direction of his newspaper again.

Friction was developing between Webb and Raymond on sectional issues, with Webb supporting compromise and Raymond taking an antislavery stance. In 1851 Raymond resigned to start his own paper, the *New York Times*. The split marked the beginning of a decline for the *Courier and Enquirer*. Although it remained a powerful political voice, Webb was more and more involved in the issues of states' rights and slavery, becoming a leading advocate of compromise. When the badly divided Whig party was taken over by the Republicans, Webb slowly shifted his allegiance and became a power in the new party, working to win the presidential nomination for Seward. When Lin-

coln was unexpectedly selected, Webb bowed to the choice gracefully and threw his support behind the candidate. At last it seemed that his political ambitions would be fulfilled, and he sought appointment as ambassador to either England or France.

Again in financial difficulties, he was dismayed at being offered the ambassadorship to Turkey, a low-paying post; he rejected a brigadier general's commission as inadequately salaried as well. Finally, he settled for the Brazilian mission as the best obtainable. Before his departure, faced with about $27,000 in overdue debts, he sold his declining newspaper to the *World* on 1 July 1861, and the *Courier and Enquirer* ceased to exist.

Webb proved to be a vital and effective ambassador. He got the French to promise to withdraw from Mexico, succeeded in disgracing an unfriendly British ambassador, fought against aid to Confederate privateers, protected American interests in the Paraguayan War, and settled many long-standing maritime claims. He retired in 1869 and traveled in Europe for two years before returning to a quiet life in New York.

Webb was afflicted with gout and bladder inflammation during his final years and became critically ill in the winter of 1877-1878. By the summer of 1879, however, he had recovered sufficiently to resume work on a book about his father, which was published in 1882. A final attack came on 21 May 1884. After two weeks of intense pain, he died at his New York City home on 7 June, surrounded by his family. George Andrews, a friend from his newspaper days, was also present.

Biography:

James L. Crouthamel, *James Watson Webb, A Biography* (Middletown, Conn.: Wesleyan University Press, 1969).

Noah Webster

(16 October 1758-28 May 1843)

Jo Anne Smith
University of Florida

See also the Webster entries in *DLB 1, The American Renaissance in New England; DLB 37, American Writers of the Early Republic;* and *DLB 42, American Writers for Children Before 1900.*

MAJOR POSITIONS HELD: Editor and publisher, *American Minerva* (New York), renamed *Commercial Advertiser* in 1797 (1793-1803), *Herald, A Gazette for the Country* (New York), renamed *Spectator* in 1797 (1794-1803).

SELECTED BOOKS: *A Grammatical Institute, of the English Language, Comprising, an Easy, Concise, and Systematic Method of Education, Designed for the Use of English Schools in America. In Three Parts. Part I. Containing, a New and Accurate Standard of Pronunciation* (Hartford: Printed by Hudson & Goodwin for the author, 1783);

A Grammatical Institute of the English Language, Comprising, an Easy, Concise, and Systematic Method of Education, Designed for the Use of English Schools in America. In Three Parts. Part II. Containing a Plain and Comprehensive Grammar . . . (Hartford: Printed by Hudson & Goodwin for the author, 1784);

A Grammatical Institute of the English Language; Comprising an Easy, Concise and Systematic Method of Education; Designed for the Use of Schools in America. In Three Parts. Part III: Containing the Necessary Rules of Reading and Speaking, and a Variety of Essays . . . (Hartford: Printed by Barlow & Babcock for the author, 1785);

Sketches of American Policy. Under the Following Heads: I. Theory of Government. II. Governments on the Eastern Continent. III. American States; or the Principles of the American Constitutions Contrasted with Those of European States. IV. Plan of Policy for Improving the Advantages and Perpetuating the Union of the American States (Hartford: Printed by Hudson & Goodwin, 1785);

The American Spelling Book . . . (Philadelphia: Young & M'Culloch, 1787; revised edition, Philadelphia: Published by Jacob Johnson & Co., 1804);

An American Selection of Lessons in Reading and Speaking. Calculated to Improve the Minds and Refine the Tastes of Youth. . . . Being the Third Part of A Grammatical Institute of the English Language . . . , Greatly Enlarged (Philadelphia: Printed & sold by Young & M'Culloch, 1787; revised edition, New Haven: From Sidney's Press for I. Beers & Co. and I. Cooke & Co., 1804);

An Examination into the Leading Principles of the Federal Constitution Proposed by the Late Convention Held at Philadelphia. With Answers to the Principle Objections That Have Been Raised Against the System (Philadelphia: Printed & sold by Prichard & Hall, 1787);

An Introduction to English Grammar; Being an Abridgement of the Second Part of the Grammatical Insti-

Noah Webster (courtesy of Merriam-Webster, Inc., publisher of the Merriam-Webster dictionaries)

tute (Philadelphia: Printed by W. Young, 1788);

Dissertations on the English Language; With Notes, Historical and Critical. To Which Is Added, By Way of Appendix, An Essay on a Reformed Mode of Spelling, with Dr. Franklin's Arguments on that Subject (Boston: Printed by Isaiah Thomas & Co. for the author, 1789);

Attention! or, New Thoughts on a Serious Subject; Being an Enquiry into the Excise Laws of Connecticut . . . (Hartford: Printed & sold by Hudson & Goodwin, 1789);

The Little Reader's Assistant . . . (Hartford: Printed by Elisha Babcock, 1790);

A Collection of Essays and Fugitiv Writings. On Moral, Historical, Political and Literary Subjects (Boston: Printed by I. Thomas & E. T. Andrews for the author, 1790);

The Prompter; or A Commentary on Common Sayings and Subjects, Which Are Full of Common Sense, the Best Sense in the World . . . (Hartford: Printed by Hudson & Goodwin, 1791);

Effects of Slavery, on Morals and Industry (Hartford: Printed by Hudson & Goodwin, 1793);

The Revolution in France, Considered in Respect to Its Progress and Effects (New York: Printed & published by George Bunce & Co., 1794);

A Letter to the Governors, Instructors and Trustees of the Universities, and Other Seminaries of Learning, in the United States, on the Errors of English Grammars (New York: Printed by George F. Hopkins for the author, 1798);

An Oration Pronounced before the Citizens of New-Haven on the Anniversary of the Independence of the United States, July 4th 1798 . . . (New Haven: Printed by T. & S. Green, 1798);

A Brief History of Epidemic and Pestilential Diseases; With the Principal Phenomena of the Physical World, Which Precede and Accompany Them, and Observations Deduced from the Facts Stated, 2 volumes (Hartford: Printed by Hudson & Goodwin, 1799; London: Printed for G. G. & J. Robinson, 1800);

Ten Letters to Dr. Joseph Priestly, in Answer to His Letters to the Inhabitants of Northumberland (New Haven: Printed by Read & Morse, 1800);

A Rod for the Fool's Back (New Haven?, 1800);

A Letter to General Hamilton, Occasioned by His Letter to President Adams (New York?, 1800);

Miscellaneous Papers on Political and Commercial Subjects . . . (New York: Printed by E. Belden & Co., 1802);

Elements of Useful Knowledge. Volume I. Containing a Historical and Geographical Account of the United States: For the Use of Schools (Hartford: Printed & sold by Hudson & Goodwin, 1802);

An Oration Pronounced before the Citizens of New Haven, on the Anniversary of the Declaration of Independence; July, 1802 . . . (New Haven: Printed by William W. Morse, 1802);

An Address to the Citizens of Connecticut (New Haven: Printed by J. Walter, 1803);

Elements of Useful Knowledge. Volume II. Containing a Historical and Geographical Account of the United States: For the Use of Schools (New Haven: From Sidney's Press, for the author, 1804);

Elements of Useful Knowledge. Vol. III. Containing a Historical and Geographical Account of the Empires and States in Europe, Asia and Africa, with Their Colonies. To Which Is Added, a Brief Description of New Holland, and the Principal Islands in the Pacific and Indian Oceans. For the Use of Schools (New Haven: Printed by O. Steele & Co. and published by Bronson, Walter & Co., 1806);

A Compendious Dictionary of the English Language (New Haven: From Sidney's Press, 1806);

A Dictionary of the English Language; Compiled for the Use of Common Schools in the United States (New Haven: From Sidney's Press for John & David West in Boston, Brisban & Brannan in New York, Lincoln & Gleason and Oliver D. Cooke in Hartford, and I. Cooke & Co. in New Haven, 1807);

A Philosophical and Practical Grammar of the English Language (New Haven: Printed by Oliver & Steele for Brisban & Brannan, 1807);

A Letter to Dr. David Ramsay, of Charleston, (S.C.) Respecting the Errors in Johnson's Dictionary, and Other Lexicons (New Haven: Printed by Oliver Steele & Co., 1807);

The Peculiar Doctrines of the Gospel, Explained and Defended (New York: J. Seymour, 1809);

History of Animals; Being the Fourth Volume of Elements of Useful Knowledge. For the Use of Schools, and Young Persons of Both Sexes (New Haven: Printed by Walter & Steele and published & sold by Howe & Deforest and Walter & Steele, 1812);

An Oration Pronounced before the Knox and Warren Branches of the Washington Benevolent Society, at Amherst, on the Celebration of the Anniversary of the Declaration of Independence, July 4, 1814 (Northampton: Printed by William Butler, 1814);

A Letter to the Honorable John Pickering, on the Subject of his Vocabulary; or, Collection of Words and

Phrases, Supposed to Be Peculiar to the United States of America (Boston: Printed by T. W. White and published by West & Richardson, 1817);

An Address, Delivered before the Hampshire, Franklin and Hampden Agricultural Society, at Their Annual Meeting in Northampton, Oct. 14, 1818 (Northampton: Printed by Thomas W. Shepard & Co., 1818);

A Plea for a Miserable World. I. An Address Delivered at the Laying of the Corner Stone of the Building Erecting for the Charity Institution in Amherst, Massachusetts, August 9, 1820, by Noah Webster, Esq. II. A Sermon Delivered on the Same Occasion, by Rev. Daniel A Clark, Pastor of the First Church and Society in Amherst. III. A Brief Account of the Origin of the Institution (Boston: Printed by Ezra Lincoln, 1820);

Letters to a Young Gentleman Commencing His Education: To Which is Subjoined a Brief History of the United States (New Haven: Printed by S. Convese and sold by Howe & Spalding, 1823);

An American Dictionary of the English Language . . ., 2 volumes (New Haven: Printed by Hezekiah Howe/New York: Published by S. Converse, 1828); republished as *A Dictionary of the English Language*, 12 parts (London: Printed for Black, Young & Young, 1830-1832);

The Elementary Spelling Book; Being an Improvement on the American Spelling Book (New York: Printed by A. Chandler & published by J. P. Haven & R. Lockwood, 1829);

A Dictionary of the English Language; Abridged from the American Dictionary . . . (New York: White, Gallaher & White, 1830);

Biography for the Use of Schools (New Haven: Printed by Hezekiah Howe, 1830);

An Improved Grammar of the English Language (New Haven: Published & sold by Hezekiah Howe, 1831);

History of the United States; to Which Is Prefixed a Brief Historical Account of Our English Ancestors, from the Dispersion of Babel, to Their Migration to America; and of the Conquest of South America, by the Spaniards (New Haven: Printed by Baldwin & Treadway and published by Durrie & Peck, 1832; revised edition, Cincinnati: Published by Corey, Fairbank & Webster, 1835);

Value of the Bible, and Excellence of the Christian Religion: For the Use of Families and Schools (New Haven: Published by Durrie & Peck, 1834);

A Brief View 1. Of Errors and Obscurities in the Common Version of the Scriptures; Addressed to Bible Societies, Clergymen and Other Friends of Religion.

2. Of Errors and Defects in Class-Books Used in Seminaries of Learning; Including Dictionaries and Grammars of the English, French, Greek and Latin Languages; Addressed to Instructors of Youth, and Students, with a Few Hints to Statesmen, Members of Congress, and Heads of Departments. To Which Is Added, 3. A Few Plagiarisms, Showing the Way in Which Books May Be Made, by Those Who Use Borrowed Capital (New Haven, 1834?);

Instructive and Entertaining Lessons for Youth . . . (New Haven: Published by S. Babcock and Durrie & Peck, 1835);

The Teacher; A Supplement to the Elementary Spelling Book (New Haven: Published by S. Babcock, 1836);

A Letter to the Hon. Daniel Webster, on the Political Affairs of the United States, as Marcellus (Philadelphia: Printed by J. Crissy, 1837);

Mistakes and Corrections. 1. Improprieties in the Common Version of the Scriptures; With Specimens of Amended Language in Webster's Edition of the Bible. 2. Explanations of Prepositions, in English, and Other Languages. These Constitute a Very Difficult Part of Philology. 3. Errors in English Grammars. 4. Mistakes in the Hebrew Lexicon of Gesenius, and In Some Derivations of Dr. Horwitz. 5. Errors in Butter's Scholar's Companion and in Town's Analysis. 6. Errors in Richardson's Dictionary (New Haven: Printed by B. L. Hamlen, 1837);

Appeal to Americans . . ., as Sidney (New York?, 1838?);

Observations on Language, and on the Errors of Class-Books; Addressed to the Members of the New York Lyceum. Also, Observations on Commerce, Addressed to the Members of the Mercantile Library Association, in New York (New Haven: Printed by S. Babcock, 1839);

A Manual of Useful Studies: For the Instruction of Young Persons of Both Sexes, in Families and Schools (New Haven: Printed & published by S. Babcock, 1839);

A Collection of Papers on Political, Literary and Moral Subjects (Boston: Tappan & Dennett/Philadelphia: Smith & Peck, 1843).

OTHER: *The New England Primer, "Amended and Improved . . . ,"* edited by Webster (New York: Printed by J. Patterson, 1789);

John Winthrop, A Journal of the Transactions and Occurrences in the Settlement of Massachusetts and the Other New-England, Colonies, from the Year 1630 to 1644, edited by Webster (Hartford:

Printed by Elisha Babcock, 1790);

*A Collection of Papers on the Subject of Bilious Fevers,
Prevalent in the United States for a Few Years Past,*
edited by Webster (New York: Printed by
Hopkins, Webb & Co., 1796);

*The Holy Bible, Containing the Old and New Testaments,
in the Common Version. With Amendments of the
Language by Noah Webster, LL.D.* (New Haven:
Published by Durrie & Peck, 1833).

Noah Webster's literary product—wide in its
variety, singular in its spirit—spanned more than
half a century. First producing textbooks designed
to instill patriotism in schoolchildren, later editing
periodicals that urged a young nation to shun foreign influence, and finally ignoring critics to pour
some twenty years' devoted labor into his *American
Dictionary of the English Language* (1828), Webster
made Americanism his leitmotiv. Though only a
few years of his long career were devoted to journalism, during the party press period Webster
equaled his contemporaries' editorial power while
refusing to copy their partisan extremism. But his
most enduring influence encompassed the entire
publishing field, where generations of writers and
editors were to benefit from his pioneering work
as a lexicographer and his tireless fight for improved copyright protections.

Born on 16 October 1758 in his parents' Connecticut farmhouse, Noah was the fourth of five
children of Noah Webster, Sr., and Mercy Steele
Webster. The senior Webster farmed ninety acres
in West Hartford and served as a justice of the
peace. The Webster children attended a district
school where instruction came almost entirely from
the Old Testament, a Psalter, and a spelling book.
Noah, Jr., showed such an affinity for books that
he seldom went to the fields without one and often
"rested" from his chores to read. When he was
fourteen his father permitted him to spend "half
time" being tutored for college entrance. In 1774,
a month from his sixteenth birthday, he was admitted to Yale.

The Yale of Webster's time consisted of three
drab and ill-equipped buildings known to students
as the "Brick Prison"; its acting president was considered so ineffective by Webster's class that it petitioned for his removal. Though he had a student
exemption during the American Revolution, Webster experienced some disruption of his education
when wartime austerity forced his dormitory to
close. During summers when he was home from
school, Webster sometimes joined the drills of the
militia unit commanded by his father or used his

skills as a flutist to give the troops a musical escort
through town. When British forces under General
Burgoyne crossed the Hudson, all four male Websters left Hartford with militia sent to reinforce
American troops. Before reaching Albany, however, they received triumphant word from a
mounted courier that "Burgoyne is taken!"

After this brief period of service and a bout
of smallpox, Webster returned for his final and
"best" year at Yale, where both instruction and morale had improved under a scholarly and vigorous
new president. When Webster earned his bachelor's degree in 1778, he hoped to go on to the study
of law; but the family had mortgaged the farm to
send him to school and could afford no more. His
father took him aside, gave him an eight-dollar bill,
and told him that he must now seek his own living.
Whether to sulk or, by his own account, to "med-
itate" after this news, Webster retired to his room
for three days before leaving the family home.

Like many "unconnected" young scholars of
the time, Webster turned to teaching, staying at
first in familiar territory around Hartford and New
Haven. For a time, he also read law; but the double
schedule proved too demanding and the law studies were interrupted for a year. Webster passed the
bar in April 1781 and earned a master's degree in
September. Between those dates, he had founded
his own school at Sharon, Connecticut, where he
also conducted night classes in music. He fell in
love with one of his music students, but she chose
to marry a prior suitor. At about the same time,
his writings too were rejected by an area literary
magazine. Possibly for these reasons, he abruptly
closed the school and left town. When he returned,
his students had been placed in other schools by
parents who understandably had lost confidence in
the "disappearing" schoolmaster.

Webster's next move, to Goshen, New York,
proved a major turning point. While schoolmaster
there, he started a project of burning concern to
him. He had long chafed, as both teacher and patriot, at what he considered "complete literary vas-
salage to the Mother Country" in American
schoolbooks instead of messages which would foster children's pride in their own history and native
language patterns. To provide a remedy, Webster
began work on his three-part *A Grammatical Institute, of the English Language* (1783-1785), consisting
of a speller, a grammar text, and a reader. The
spelling book, completed first, ultimately would sell
millions of copies. Young Americans from seaboard schoolrooms to frontier cabins drilled on its
"spelling words" and assimilated its patriotic hom-

ilies. Though neither of the later texts did as well, Webster's work as a textbook author greatly expanded his world. To protect his commercial interests in the works, he began the lecturing and lobbying that brought him to the attention of political leaders, honed his political interests, and led eventually to his career as a partisan journalist.

To promote copyright legislation, Webster traveled throughout the new states, supporting himself with lectures—published in 1789 as *Dissertations on the English Language*—on proposed reforms of the language. In advance of his visits, he often sent copies of his speller, along with a letter describing his goals, to influential persons. Many responded cordially. Benjamin Franklin, himself interested in reforming the alphabet and standardizing pronunciation, met and corresponded with Webster. George Washington offered introductions to "some of the first gentlemen." Soon, Webster was lecturing to, dining among, and corresponding with the nation's "best." Favorable attention further inflated Webster's already sturdy ego. He wrote his publishers that he was "making a bustle" while "diffusing useful knowledge" with his "new and laudable remarks." While on tour, Webster peppered newspapers with contributions about the Constitution, nationalism, education, and the American language. Proof that he was, indeed, "making a bustle" came when Anti-Federalist editors began printing lengthy responses that scoffed at his views and taunted him for his vanity.

Webster's fame grew; his funds did not. His costly travels merely increased his debts. From home came discouraging news that his parents' financial problems, incurred to educate him, remained unalleviated. Webster busily prepared a round of letters with entreaties for employment, vague proposals for business enterprises, and reminders to recipients of how important it was for him to find "business" in order to complete the "vast design" of his scholarly work. This time, answers were fewer and less supportive. Webster's quest for a solid means of support grew more urgent when he met and fell in love with Rebecca Greenleaf in 1787. He knew that fulfillment of the "understanding" he reached with "the lovely Becca" depended upon the wealthy Greenleaf family's acceptance of his background and belief in his future. Webster by then had acquired considerable experience as a contributor to periodicals and had observed the rise of magazines in several cities. Since there were no magazines in New York, a city which Webster regarded as the next "great commercial port in the United States," he decided to

found one. He raised the money by selling printing rights to his texts and raising contributions from friends in Connecticut.

In December Webster brought out the first issue of the *American Magazine*, which combined a digestlike collection of brief exchange items with his own essays. He announced that he would seek contributions that would "relate to this country and contain useful and curious discoveries in the history or geography of America, or ingenious remarks on the science of Government and the peculiar and interesting customs of the people in the different States." New York's first monthly was not destined for a long life, but it has won high regard from journalism historians. Frank Luther Mott, calling Webster's magazine one of the few "of any considerable importance" during the early part of the party press period, praised its "unusual variety and spirit" and the "vigorous part" it took in the dialogue on public affairs. Webster's political and intellectual passions pervaded the magazine's pages: he trumpeted support of the Constitution but called arguments for a bill of rights "declamatory nonsense"; he held that the building of a unique American history depended upon preservation of the nation's antiquities; and he called for schooling for boys and girls, rich and poor, with "morals" and nationalism as the schoolroom's most important themes.

Always a prolific penman, Webster sent a spray of letters seeking editorial contributions from members of the literary establishment. To Dr. Benjamin Rush, Webster wrote: "We want a literary intercourse, we want to be acquainted with each other, we want a mutual knowledge of the state of every part of America. . . ." To implement his goal of creating a "journal of discussion" for America, Webster carried excerpts from and reviews of many of the important writings of the time from authors representing a range of views. But the magazine, so wholly his own, not surprisingly took on his personality. That meant vigor and wit but also abrasiveness and pomposity. In consequence, Webster won followers on issues, but not enduring friends whose affection would transcend questions of "right" or "wrong." Worst of all, Webster failed to cultivate those upon whom the magazine most depended. He pilloried his own contributors, finding fault with their phrasing or accusing them of plagiarism of ideas much as though he were still a schoolmaster wielding a heavy grading pen. If an accused or abused author spoke up in his own defense, Webster responded with neither grace nor humor. Biographer Harry R. Warfel summed up

Webster's editorial style as that of a "browbeater." Even his granddaughter, the loving compiler of his notes, conceded that he lost support due to his "brashness and youth." When promised contributions remained unsent, Webster had to do more and more of the writing himself. Weary and £250 in debt, he was forced to give up the magazine in December 1788. His diary simply commented: "I have read much, written much, and tried to do much good, but with little advantage to myself. I will now leave writing and do more lucrative business."

Still delaying marriage in hope of providing Rebecca with "favorable prospects," Webster chose law as his more "lucrative business." Despite bad times, Webster hoped to build a successful practice in Hartford by capitalizing on his hometown fame. Optimistically, he told the Greenleafs that his practice and his royalties should, within a few years, allow Rebecca to "spread a decent table for her friends." But love could not wait that long. Only a month after entering practice, Webster wrote Rebecca's brother James Greenleaf to say that "no consideration" could separate him from Rebecca and that it would be "prudent and best to marry as soon as a house can be obtained and furnished," adding, "for this we depend wholly on your goodness. . . ." With Greenleaf's financial help, Webster, thirty-one, married the twenty-three-year-old Rebecca in Boston on 26 October 1789. The new bride, though devoted and supportive, knew little of frugality. She ran through James's gift of $1,000 for furniture without budgeting any of it for the kitchen or "best room." She entertained lavishly, causing one visitor, author John Trumbull, to remark of Webster, "I doubt in the present decay of business . . . whether his profits will enable him to keep up the style he sets out with. I fear he will breakfast upon *Institutes*, dine upon *Dissertations* and go to bed supperless."

By 1790, when the first of the Websters' eight children was born, Webster had long since forgone his resolve to "leave writing." By the time a second daughter was born in 1793, his pattern was set. He was again "making a bustle" with contributions to periodicals, especially with twenty-eight moralistic essays entitled "The Prompter," published anonymously in the *Hartford Courant* and in book form in 1791. While additional "loans" from James Greenleaf (one for a law library) drifted into gifts, Webster grew more involved in writing and local politics and less involved in his law practice. Again he felt at a crossroads. Halfheartedly, he said that he *could* leave writing for business or perhaps for farming but preferred to have time for his editorial pursuits.

Coincident with Webster's restlessness in 1793, Federalist leaders in New York sought a party paper to replace John Fenno's *Gazette of the United States*, which had followed the seat of national government to Philadelphia. Webster's memoirs credit James Watson with first suggesting that Webster start a New York paper to oppose the "designs" of French minister Edmond Genêt and to "maintain neutrality." Genêt had been in the United States since April. Though the avowed purpose of his visit was negotiation of a new trade treaty, Genêt had commissioned privateers to operate out of American ports and raid British ships. President Washington responded by issuing a neutrality proclamation and notifying Genêt that the privateers must leave U.S. waters. The Genêt affair intensified the already heated exchange between Federalist and Anti-Federalist newspapers. Webster, in New York in August to look into prospects for setting up in business there, stayed at a "Mr. Bradley's," where Genêt also was staying. One night he dined with the French minister's party. During the meal, Webster overheard and challenged an aide's derogatory remark about Washington and the policies of the U.S. government. According to Webster's account, Genêt then accused the officers of the American government of being "in the British interest" and of having a plan that would make America "slaves of that Kingdom." Webster reported these remarks and the exchange that followed to his old Yale classmate and friend, Oliver Wolcott, Jr., a high-ranking Federalist who later would succeed Alexander Hamilton as secretary of the treasury. At Wolcott's urging, Webster sent him an affidavit as "direct proof" of the conversation.

In the meantime, Webster met with Watson, John Jay, and Rufus King and agreed to start a progovernment New York newspaper. Backed by modest contributions from Federalist leaders, Webster entered into partnership with printer George Bunce. By 19 November, the Websters, their two little girls, and James Greenleaf and his friend Charles Lagarenne were settled in a large house Greenleaf had rented. Within a week, Webster had purchased a press and on 9 December, the first issue of the daily *American Minerva* came out. Webster announced that the *Minerva* would be the "Friend of Government, of Freedom, of Virtue and every Species of Improvement." Though the content of the *Minerva* did span many "species," its primary theme throughout Webster's editorship was the avoidance of foreign entanglements and

Front page of first issue of Webster's Federalist newspaper

the strengthening of American nationalism.

In its first month the *Minerva* had much to say about and to Genêt. It carried a series of essays by John Quincy Adams (under the pseudonym "Columbus") critical of Genét's conduct. In an apparent attempt to reassure the Frenchman and temper his recklessness, Webster addressed an open letter to Genét calling British influence in America "extremely limited and feeble" and saying that the founding of a *free Republican government* in France was the "general wish in America." Page Smith, biographer of John Adams, said that Webster had much to do with "the waning of the Frenchman's star."

Webster had many other concerns to air in the pages of the *Minerva,* and of the *Herald,* its semiweekly edition founded in 1794. Opposition to slavery was one primary theme; Webster also wrote on sanitation, research on infectious diseases, city planning, forest conservation, ways to aid the sick and poor, and many other topics. Though progovernment, Webster avoided the unrestrained name-calling characteristic of the contemporary press and showed a concern for accuracy unusual in his day. On one occasion, for example, he inquired of a source whether his translation from the French of a statement by Jefferson had "done Mr. Jefferson any injustice," promising, if so, to print a "fresh and authentic translation" so as to "set all right with the public."

Webster's faults as an editor lay not in blind partisanship but rather in long-windedness, a stiff-necked righteousness, and the acidity of his wit. He saved most of his lashing out at Anti-Federalists for his private correspondence. In one letter to Timothy Pickering, Webster called opposition editors "the *refuse,* the sweepings of the most depraved part of mankind. . . ." Webster's tense and humorless tone during the New York period no doubt reflected the many pressures he was under. He deeply *felt* the burden of being a "political spokesman." For him, political debate was not an exhilarating exchange but a deadly serious battle that should end when the most powerful verbal stroke "set things straight." Consequently, the endlessness of partisan debate exasperated him. He also believed himself "carefully watched by the partisans of France." For two years Webster produced the *Minerva* and *Herald* without editorial assistance. He labored so many hours on translations and on the crafting of his own essays that he drove himself to red-eyed exhaustion. Several times he had to suspend his reading for several days and twice he drove himself to such a "critical condition mentally and physically" that doctors doubted that he would survive.

Through it all, Webster advised readers to "be in spirit and truth *Americans*" and held that the United States should attach itself "to no foreign nation whatever." In 1795, however, when Benjamin Franklin Bache and other Anti-Federalists blasted Jay's Treaty with the British as a sellout of American rights, Webster came to the treaty's defense. Under the pseudonym "Curtius," he prepared for the *Minerva* a series of essays (two were the work of James Kent) under the title "Vindication." The *Minerva* also carried a longer series called "Defence," written by Hamilton under the pseudonym "Camillus." Mott called Webster's series "probably the most effective defense of the Jay Treaty which appeared anywhere. . . ." In a letter to James Madison, Jefferson said that he had had to stop his practice of giving fellow Anti-Federalists copies of the series for their appraisal when he found them "unable to parry the sophistry of Curtius." He then urged: "For god's sake take up your pen and give a fundamental reply to Curtius and Camillus." Jefferson's irritation and the immoderate attacks on Webster by the Anti-Federalist papers, which called him such things as a "dunghill cock of faction" and a "mortal and incurable lunatic," serve as measures of his political effectiveness.

By 1796 Webster's problems both at work and at home were being alleviated. Enough money came in from the newspapers to allow Webster to hire two assistants and turn full concentration to his editorial comments, which began running under a standing "The Minerva" flag. Household frictions that had arisen from the unhappy mixture of a serious scholar and his young family with the "boisterous and bibulous" Greenleaf and Lagarenne were solved when the Websters moved to Corlear's Hook on the East River. There Rebecca sat up nights awaiting Webster's return. Their house was in the "country" with no near neighbors and left Webster with an added "lonely half mile" to walk in an area where recent robberies had been reported. Nothing untoward occurred, however, and the family enjoyed the "pretty cottage" at Corlear's Hook. A third child, Harriet, was born there in 1797, the year the papers' names were changed to the *Commercial Advertiser* and the *Spectator.* Circulation of the papers had reached 1,700, about a third larger than the circulation of any other newspaper in the country.

Despite the relatively serene life at Corlear's Hook, Webster grew restless. He was tiring of the endless partisan debate and beginning to doubt the effectiveness of his own torrent of words. He viewed the opposition press as a "pack of scoundrels." Their practices so rankled him that decades later he continued to publish reprints of his 1794-1795 essays to give "testimony against the audacious practice of publishing misrepresentations, falsehood and calumny, for party purposes." As his taste for partisan journalism waned, Webster's deep intellectual curiosity involved him ever more deeply in the then-current controversy over how to treat victims of yellow fever. A recent epidemic had claimed many lives, including those of Benjamin Franklin Bache of the Anti-Federalist *Aurora* and John Fenno of the Federalist *Gazette of the United States*, who once had carried their partisanship to a fist-and-cane battle on the streets of Philadelphia. So intrigued was Webster with controversies over epidemic illnesses that he began making his own study of their history and causes.

In April 1798, at the age of forty, Webster decided to leave day-to-day operation of the papers in the hands of his assistants. He returned to New Haven, planning to continue to direct the "politics" of the papers while pursuing "with little interruption, my taste for science." In 1799 he completed his *Brief History of Epidemic and Pestilential Diseases*. When, during the election of 1800, internal Federalist jealousies culminated in the circulation of a Hamilton letter questioning President Adams's ability to administer due to his "extreme egotism" and "desultoriness of mind," Webster reentered the political fray. He said that Hamilton's "ambition, pride and overbearing temper" had led him into perfidy and destined him "to be the evil genius of this country." In response, Hamilton orchestrated an attack on Webster by newspapers under his influence and sought to discredit Webster's New York papers. Heaped on top of the difficulties of absentee management and the obvious decline in craftsmanship in the *Advertiser* and the *Spectator*, Hamilton's "betrayal" proved to be too much for him. Webster sought a buyer for the newspaper properties, finally disposed of them in 1803, and turned from journalism to full concentration on lexicography. Three years later, he completed his first dictionary, *A Compendious Dictionary of the English Language*.

Thanks to Webster's early labors to secure copyright protection, the sale of millions of copies of the "little blue-backed speller" now supported the Websters, giving them a life-style that was financially modest but rich in family warmth. Webster did much home teaching of his children and

joined them in musical performances. In 1806 he irately withdrew his older daughters from the neighborhood school because the superstitious schoolmistress had refused to allow them to watch a solar eclipse through the pieces of smoked glass Webster had supplied. In 1812 the Websters moved from New Haven to Amherst and entered fully into the life of the town. Webster thought Amherst so beautiful and so conducive to study that he sought to win the town a college then in process of being relocated. When that project failed, he played a substantial role in the founding of Amherst College and became president of its first board of trustees.

Webster now poured his energies into the major work of his life. It took virtually two decades, and many of his old editorial foes repeatedly scoffed at his "grandiose" undertaking. Webster persisted against both criticism and indifference. In the end, he produced a monumental achievement, the two-volume *An American Dictionary of the English Language*. The new work contained thousands more entries than had earlier dictionaries. It incorporated comparisons drawn from Webster's study of as many as twenty other languages and of the "state of the English language in England," which he traveled to England to investigate. The dictionary also included many technical terms from such fields as law and medicine. Though it abandoned earlier efforts to replace *ea* combinations with such spellings as *reeding* and *zeel*, it did set the trend for the dropping in America of the *u* from such British spellings as *colour* and *honour*. Completed in 1825, by which time the Websters had returned to New Haven, the work was published in 1828. Webster had reached seventy. His children, except for twenty-year-old Louisa, the youngest, were grown and gone from home. A ceaseless worker, Webster once again began lobbying for improvements in the copyright law and continued to give speeches and work on revision of the dictionary. He published ten books in the last decade of his life; the final one was a 373-page collection of essays, some new and some old, brought out in April 1843. In May, he contracted pleurisy. For a few days his condition appeared to improve, but on Sunday, 28 May, his lungs filled with fluid. In midevening, without signs of pain, he simply stopped breathing. Mrs. Webster and Louisa stayed on in the family home until Rebecca's death from a stroke in 1847.

For a decade before his death, as each new publication was sent to the printer. Webster had proclaimed, "now my work is done." When at last his work *was* done, it comprised a legacy astonishing in volume and of enduring quality. Webster's name is, of course, synonymous with the dictionary that is or should be at every journalist's hand. His relatively brief full-time journalistic career, though not earning him a place among America's greatest editors, stood out in its time. The *American Magazine* ranks as one of the first attempts to encourage the development of an American literary tradition. Webster's newspapers, though partisan and passionate, were not propelled by the unreasoning jets of venom that characterized many contemporary journals. He spoke clearly, forcefully, and in depth about most of the major social, political, and intellectual issues of his time, providing a meaty and lasting record for historians. Webster's *Herald* led the way in the establishment of weekly summaries to supplement daily papers; he was a leader, too, in the creation of the standing editorial column. Thus his gigantic stature as a lexicographer does not entirely overshadow his journalistic reputation as one of the best of the Federalist editors.

Biographies:

Emily Ellsworth Fowler Ford and Emily Ellsworth Ford Skeel, *Notes on the Life of Noah Webster*, 2 volumes (New York: Privately printed, 1912);

Ervin C. Shoemaker, *Noah Webster: Pioneer of Learn-*

ing (New York: Columbia University Press, 1936);

Harry R. Warfel, *Noah Webster: Schoolmaster to America* (New York: Macmillan, 1936).

References:

Frederic Hudson, *Journalism in the United States from 1690 to 1872* (Brooklyn: Haskell, 1969), pp. 188, 191, 193;

Frank Luther Mott, *American Journalism*, third edition (New York: Macmillan, 1962), pp. 133, 138, 153;

Old South Leaflets, 8 volumes (New York: Burt Franklin, 1908), VIII: 385-400;

Page Smith, *John Adams*, 2 volumes (Garden City: Doubleday, 1962), II: 805, 844, 920, 1045;

James Playsted Wood, *Magazines in the United States*, second edition (New York: Ronald Press, 1956), pp. 14, 19, 22-23, 26.

Papers:

Noah Webster's letters, newspaper clippings, and other papers are at the Robert Frost Library and Jones Library of Amherst College. The New York Public Library has other of Webster's personal papers and literary manuscripts.

George Wisner

(1812-9 September 1849)

Norman H. Sims
University of Massachusetts-Amherst

MAJOR POSITIONS HELD: Reporter, editor, and co-owner, *New York Sun* (1833-1835); editor, *Pontiac* (Mich.) *Courier* (1835-1836); editor, co-owner, *Detroit Advertiser* (1848).

BOOKS: *Address of George W. Wisner—the Whig candidate for Congress—to the people of the Third Congressional District of Michigan* (Pontiac, Mich.: Thompson's Print-Oakland Gazette Office, 1844);

Fellow Citizens of Oakland County—the Trial by Jury Is No Longer Safe (N.p., n.d.).

George Wisner played a brief but innovative role in one of the dramatic transformations of American journalism. He was a printer and editor who in 1833 became co-owner, with Benjamin Day, of the first successful penny newspaper in America, the *New York Sun*. Wisner selected the news for the *Sun* and is considered the first police reporter. His condensed reports established a model for newspaper writers. Wisner's association with the *Sun* lasted less than two years, but he made it a leader among penny newspapers. Historians credit the penny press with establishing the modern concept of news as a wide-ranging account of daily life that appeals to the masses rather than to social elites.

Wisner was born in 1812 in Springport, Cayuga County, New York, near the town of Auburn. His father, Moses Wisner, farmed about 150 acres in west central New York, not far from Syracuse. The Wisner family had immigrated to America from Switzerland around 1715. One ancestor, Henry Wisner, served in the First and Second Continental Congresses. Thomas Wisner, George's grandfather, was a lieutenant during the Revolutionary War, and Moses Wisner achieved the rank of colonel during the War of 1812.

George was the tenth of sixteen children, half of whom died before reaching the age of fourteen. He attended the local public school and read avidly in his father's ample library. At age fifteen, he entered an apprenticeship in printing with the *Cayuga Patriot*, edited by Ulysses F. Doubleday, whose son Abner later developed the game of baseball. The *Patriot*, like most newspapers of its day, was published to support a political candidate, in this case Andrew Jackson. Generally, apprenticeships lasted for five years, during which time the printer provided room and board, instruction, and a small stipend; in exchange, the apprentice cleaned the shop, ran errands, stoked the fire, and gradually learned to set type and operate the presses. Doubleday had a reputation as a demanding taskmaster, and before a year was up, young Wisner, like several apprentices before him, ran away.

Wisner went to work for the *Republican Advocate* in nearby Batavia, New York. When Doubleday advertised for the return of his apprentice, Wisner wrote to him, giving his address and challenging his former master: "You can find me here whenever you like to come. But I don't think it will be safe for you to try and force me to come back."

Wisner's belligerent attitude later brought him trouble at the *Advocate*, which was an anti-Masonic newspaper. During the 1820s the society of Free and Accepted Masons had gained considerable influence in western New York. The secret dealings of the society were exposed in 1826 by a printer named William Morgan. When Morgan mysteriously disappeared after his book was published, the state opened an investigation of the Masons. The anti-Masonic movement, which eventually became a third political party, grew with the public reaction against the society. The anti-Masonic sentiments expressed by the *Advocate* in 1828 incited a pro-Masonic mob, which gathered outside the newspaper office one day and threatened to break the presses and scatter the type. The publisher, David C. Miller, and his printers and helpers defended the office with knives and pistols. Shots were fired into the crowd and several people were injured. Wisner, who had been prominent in defending the office, was charged with attempted murder; but his attorney, William H. Seward of Auburn, a leader in the Anti-Masonic party, secured his acquittal. Nevertheless, Wisner's father felt that the incident had disgraced the family. Shortly afterward, Wisner moved to New York City.

In New York, Wisner worked on several newspapers as a compositor, or typesetter. One of these jobs was at the *Journal of Commerce*, the leading newspaper of its day. Wisner's experience in New York, and the savings he accumulated during two years of work, set the stage for his historic work at the *Sun*.

In 1833 New York City's quarter-million inhabitants were served by eleven daily newspapers with a total circulation of only about 26,500. These newspapers cost six cents a copy, but most were sold on yearly subscriptions. Politics and business, with a smattering of literature, filled their pages. The six-cent papers were expensive by the standards of the time, and carried little of interest to ordinary citizens.

Benjamin H. Day, a twenty-three-year-old printer, started the *Sun* on 3 September 1833. Penny papers had been started before—most notably the *New-York Morning Post*, with Horace Greeley as publisher, earlier the same year—but they had quickly failed. Day courageously began his newspaper in a small rented room at 222 William Street with a printing press capable of producing only 200 copies an hour. In the first issue, Day reprinted news items from out-of-town newspapers. Hoping to make the new paper appear prosperous, he ran free advertisements that he clipped from the six-cent papers. For local news, he borrowed items from the *Courier and Enquirer*, the liveliest of the six-cent papers.

When the first issue of the *Sun* hit the street, Day had two major innovations working for him: the papers cost only a penny a piece, and they could be purchased on the street from newsboys rather than by an expensive annual subscription. He could not know whether his product would catch on with the public. "Neither could he know," wrote *Sun* historian Frank M. O'Brien, "that, by this humble effort to exalt his printing business, he had driven a knife into the sclerotic heart of ancient journalism. The sixpenny papers were to laugh at this tiny intruder—to laugh and laugh, and to die."

The six-cent papers were seven or eight columns wide, were political in content, carried the same stale advertisements day in and day out, and were of little interest to ordinary people. Day's *Sun* was three columns wide, proposed to remain politically neutral, and would appeal to the growing numbers of working people and immigrants in the city.

The *Sun*'s appeal was more Wisner's doing than Day's. Before the paper was a week old, Wisner joined its small staff. In his memoirs, Day recalled that Wisner came to him "and said that if I would give him $4 a week he would get up early every morning and do these police reports." Wisner also set type and did other chores after visiting the police court, which opened at 4:00 A.M. Day offered Wisner a share of the profits should the paper become a success; Wisner used his share, and his savings, to buy half of the *Sun*. Day remembered this happening in the spring of 1834, but Wisner's name was listed on the masthead of the paper beginning on 24 October 1833. Wisner wrote the police court columns and edited the other news, while Day turned his attention to business matters such as advertising and circulation.

Wisner's police reporting brought a new style to American journalism. In terse reports, he summarized the daily parade of crimes and accidents in the police court. Previously, newspapers had rarely taken notice of the common police courts; Wisner found them a window onto the life of the city. Most of his reports dealt with drunkenness, assault, and petty thefts. He discovered human interest stories in the police office:

> Anne Jackson, does not live any where at present; but recently returned from a visit in the country. Last night she got "boozy," and was accommodated with lodgings in the watch house. Sent to the Penitentiary.

> Louisa Baldwin was found in the street with no visible means of support. The prisoner had a long tale to narrate. She said she was married to a Mr. Baldwin a year ago, and moved to the city of Washington. For five or six months, her husband treated her with all the care and tenderness of an honorable man; but after that he began to evince a coldness and indifference towards her which she could not bear. She did not disclose her anguish—but
> "Let concealment, like a worm in the bud, Feed on her damask cheek."
> About a month since, her husband married one of the prostitutes with which the capitol

is crowded during the session of Congress, and turned herself out of doors—a "lone, forsaken, and abandoned thing." She had come on from Washington with a view to search out her former friends in this city, but was unable to find them; and had wandered about all day yesterday, and was last night in search of a reputable place in which to rest her weary limbs, when the watchman brought her up. The magistrate very humanely provided for her by sending her to the alms house.

Wisner often doted over the turns of phrase he heard in police court, as when an elderly woman declared that "she felt as happy as a singed cat" or a man said that he was so drunk he "could not see a hole through a ladder."

Listing the names of persons brought into police court was another Wisner innovation; the practice brought the *Sun*, according to its own estimate, "some 25 or 30" libel suits in 1834, although few apparently reached trial. Wisner defended the practice: "As all public transactions before a public court of our city are public property, the publication of the names of the arrested parties is as much a matter of right as that of any other names in any court, city or state," he argued. In one case against the *Sun* which did reach the courts, the magistrate said that the paper had "an undoubted right to give publicity to matters taking place before the police office, and in other courts." Wisner also claimed that "a great moral reform" had resulted from the practice: he said that publication of names had caused the number of cases coming before the police on Sunday mornings to decrease by three-quarters.

Day kept the *Sun* politically independent, an innovation in itself during the age of the partisan press. The paper broke precedent by refusing to print the governor's entire message to the legislature; instead, it simply summarized the important points. In 1833 the *Sun* reported from Washington that "the proceedings of Congress, thus far, would not interest our readers." But Day could not restrain the more politically-minded Wisner, a Whig, from crusading for some special causes. The ballyhooed newspaper crusade for the public good did not develop for another sixty years, but Wisner did campaign against slavery, drinking, gambling, and prize fighting, and in favor of labor unions.

Wisner slipped small items relating to the slavery issue into the paper whenever he could. He reported cases involving runaway slaves, and on one occasion suggested that two slavecatchers should be run out of town. Day disagreed with Wisner's crusading stand, and their differences on slavery contributed to the co-owners' later split. Day said that Wisner "was a pretty smart fellow, but he and I never agreed. We split on politics. You see, I was rather Democratic in my notions. Wisner, whenever he got a chance, was always sticking in his damned little Abolition articles."

Wisner once noted that New York City had 3,048 taverns serving the 250,000 residents, which, he said, made "lots of fun" for the police reporter. Typically, Wisner treated drunks in police court with a touch of humor: "Ellen Dunham was committed for having drank too much liquor—said she did not care where she went, provided they would give her a warm place to lie down."

Wisner had first come to Day's attention in 1833 when he testified at the trial of the proprietor of a gambling house. As a reporter, he continued his campaign against the estimated 200 gambling houses in the city. He concluded that the magistrates were "wanting in energy" in enforcing the law.

Although Wisner thought that boxing was "an amusement belonging to the dark ages," he once traveled to Hoboken, New Jersey, to report a prize fight that took place in a field. The bout was fought bare-knuckled, with only thirty seconds allowed for the fighters to rest between rounds. It ended after seventy-two minutes. Wisner told readers of the *Sun:* "And this is what is called 'sports of the ring!' We can cheerfully encourage foot-races or any other humane and reasonable amusement, but the Lord deliver us from the 'ring.'"

Wisner portrayed labor unions in a positive light. He reported on the plight of women who worked up to sixteen hours a day in the garment industry, and covered a march by trade union members. In 1834 Wisner was elected secretary of the Franklin Typographical Union, an association of printers.

During an outbreak of cholera in August 1834, Wisner used investigative reporting techniques to challenge statements by the New York Board of Health. The Board of Health and the large newspapers were assuring the public that there was no epidemic of cholera, although the disease had killed 3,500 New Yorkers the previous year. Pressed by Wisner and four other reporters, the board admitted to eight deaths in two days from the disease. Instead of accepting the board's statistics, the reporters canvassed doctors and the city hospitals on their own, turning up ten deaths and eight new cases in the same period. The names and addresses of the victims were published. The *Sun* continued to point out discrepancies between its own count and the reports from the board; on 1 September 1834, for example, the *Sun* listed seventeen deaths for the previous day, while the board reported only ten.

Wisner also liked to visit interesting districts in the city and write reports on life there. One such report was written after Wisner interviewed doctors in a hospital during the cholera investigation. Another time he wrote a report on a vice district known as Five Points, and named the proprietors of its brothels, taverns, and gambling houses. Wisner apparently thought that providing a complete and accurate account of daily life required going considerably beyond the police courts. In 1834 a story began: "Reader, did you ever, just after nightfall, enter a pawnbroker's shop, and take note of the scenes that pass there? If you never did, step aside for a few minutes with us, and seat yourself here, in this obscure corner, behind the door, whence you can see what goes on without being yourself observed."

The new breed of newspaper represented by the *Sun* threatened the traditional six-cent commercial papers. Day's aggressive business practices and Wisner's breezy reporting style were rewarded by readers. In November 1834 circulation reached 10,000 copies a day. Early in 1835 the *Sun* installed a faster press and enlarged the size of its pages. By the time Wisner departed, the *Sun*'s circulation was 15,000 copies a day, by its own claim "far surpassing that of any other daily paper in the Union, and with one, perhaps two, exceptions in London, in the whole world."

Wisner's name appeared on the masthead of the *Sun* for the last time on 27 June 1835. His work at the newspaper had been tiring, including as it did gathering police news at 4:00 A.M., going out on other reporting assignments, and editing the paper. In 1835 Wisner apparently began to suffer from lung disease, and his political differences with Day resulted in quarrels. The two men parted as friends, however, with Day paying Wisner $5,000 for his share of the *Sun*. On 27 June the *Sun* notified readers: "Mr. George W. Wisner, one of the original proprietors of this paper, has voluntarily retired from the concern on account of the frailty of his health. In regard to this gentleman, it is but common justice to say that his industry, enterprise, genius and talents, have contributed largely to the present enviable heights this paper has been enabled to attain; and it is to be regretted that his health has been so seriously impaired by his constant attention to editorial duties. . . ." Richard Adams Locke took Wisner's place on the *Sun.* Locke wrote a sensational series of articles purporting to describe objects seen on the moon through a telescope. Although the articles were a hoax, they raised the *Sun's* circulation to 19,000 copies a day in 1835.

With his wife, Catharine, whom he had married in 1834, and their infant son Charles, Wisner returned to his father's farm near Auburn. In September 1835 they moved to Pontiac, Michigan, twenty-five miles north of Detroit, where Wisner began the study of law; but before long, he was back in the newspaper business. A new Whig weekly, the *Pontiac Courier,* had begun publication shortly before Wisner's arrival. Since his politics fit in well with those of the paper and his experience in journalism was far more extensive than that of anyone else in the area, Wisner became the editor of the *Courier.* In addition to general news, the paper carried political editorials on behalf of Whig issues. Wisner's easy transition from the proclaimed political neutrality of the *Sun* to the editorship of a standard partisan newspaper like the *Courier* suggests that Day was responsible for the break with partisanship at the *Sun.* In 1836 local Democrats started a rival paper to compete with the *Courier* and carry editorials favoring their cause. Wisner jousted editorially with the Democratic editor in the style typical of the times.

After a year at the *Courier,* Wisner left to work in the law office of William Draper, a leading Whig lawyer in Michigan. In 1837 he won election to the Michigan legislature. At the end of his one-year term, he was elected prosecuting attorney in Oakland County. In 1839 he opened a law partnership with Alfred Threadway. After an argument over the Masons, Wisner left to join another law partnership with his younger brother, Moses, and Rufus Hosmer. Moses Wisner later helped form the Republican party in Michigan and was elected governor in 1859.

In 1842 Wisner ran unsuccessfully for Congress; he was proposed as a candidate in 1844 but did not receive the nomination. Another son, Oscar, was born during this period. Both sons grew up to become lawyers.

The family moved to Detroit so that Wisner could edit the *Detroit Daily Advertiser,* which he purchased with two partners on 1 January 1848. But on 17 May, Wisner's law partner, Hosmer, assumed the editorial duties. Wisner had perhaps overworked himself again—in addition to editing the *Advertiser* he had taken on the job of Detroit school inspector—and his health failed. Presumably suffering from lung disease, Wisner died at age thirty-seven on 9 September 1849 at his home in Detroit.

Except for his twenty-two months at the *New York Sun,* George Wisner would have been remembered as only one of many political editors so typical of his age. But his reporting from the police office, and his attempts to cover the everyday life of New York City, made him one of the first genuine *reporters* in American newspaper history. Working at the first of the successful penny newspapers, Wisner shaped the editorial style of the *Sun,* a style that would later be imitated by the *New York Herald* and other urban newspapers. By the time Wisner died, the dull, six-cent newspapers with which the *Sun* had originally competed were mostly gone, replaced with a livelier newspaper that reported more of the commonplace events in the city.

References:

James Stanford Bradshaw, "George W. Wisner and the *New York Sun,*" *Journalism History,* 6 (Winter 1979-1980): 112, 117-121;

Frank M. O'Brien, *The Story of The Sun. New York, 1833-1918* (New York: Doran, 1918);

Michael Schudson, *Discovering the News: A Social History of American Newspapers* (New York: Basic Books, 1978);

Wm. David Sloan, "George W. Wisner: Michigan Editor and Politician," *Journalism History,* 6 (Winter 1979-1980): 113-116.

John Peter Zenger

(1697-28 July 1746)

Mary Sue F. Poole
University of South Carolina

See also the Zenger entry in *DLB 24: American Colonial Writers, 1606-1734.*

MAJOR POSITION HELD: Printer, *New-York Weekly Journal* (1733-1746).

BOOK: *A Brief Narrative of the Case and Tryal of John Peter Zenger, Printer of the New-York Weekly Journal* (New York: Printed and sold by John Peter Zenger, 1736; London: Printed for J. Wilford, 1738).

The arrest and trial of John Peter Zenger on charges of seditious libel brought about no judicial reform, for it set no legal precedent. The political factions involved won no lasting victories. But Zenger's counsel gave voice to the idea of a free and responsible press for a free and responsible people—and herein lies the greatest impact of the case on history. No longer could an oppressive administration wield the charge of libel capriciously to curb the uprisings of popular opinion. A generation later those uprisings culminated in the American Revolution; Gouverneur Morris, grandson of one of the principal players in the case, said, "The trial of Zenger in 1735 was the germ of American freedom, the morning star of that liberty which subsequently revolutionized America."

Zenger was an independent printer in New York when he was swept up in the machinations of colonial politics and charged with seditious libel. He neither wrote nor edited the articles that attacked the governor and his administration; but he did print them, and in 1735 that was crime enough. The law was clear: the greater the truth, the greater the libel; the crime against the crown was in the printing.

Zenger's involvement began with the arrival of an unpopular governor, William Cosby, in 1732. Cosby's heavy-handed administration polarized New York politicians into the court party, which was loyal to the English crown, and the popular party, which opposed Cosby's policy of governing by whim. The only newspaper extant in New York

was William Bradford's *New-York Gazette,* and since Bradford was the colony's official public printer, the court party used it to promote their views. The opposition had no such vehicle until members of the popular party approached Zenger about printing a newspaper for them.

Zenger, a German native of the Rhenish Palatinate, was born in 1697 and immigrated with his family to America in 1710. His father died en route, but Zenger, his mother, Johanna, his sister Anna Catharina, and his brother Johannes settled in New York. On 26 October 1711 the fourteen-year-old John Peter was apprenticed to William Bradford for eight years.

At the end of the apprenticeship, Zenger sought to set up his own business and eventually settled in Chestertown, Maryland, possibly with his first wife, Mary White, whom he married on 28 July 1719. Little is known of his activities in Maryland except that he petitioned the Maryland Assembly for permission to print the session laws. Although his request was approved, there is no record that he actually did the work.

Within two years Zenger was back in New York. By then a widower with a son, John, he married Anna Catharina Maulin on 11 September 1722 in the Dutch Church. Zenger was naturalized on 6 July 1723, and two months later he became a freeman of New York.

A short-lived partnership in 1725 with his former master, Bradford, produced only one book, and the next year Zenger again opened his own print shop. His work was mostly limited to political tracts and theological books written in Dutch. In 1730, however, he did publish the first arithmetic book printed in New York, Pieter Venema's *Arithmetica.*

The case that foreshadowed the First Amendment rights to a free press and free speech had its roots in a power struggle between the Morrises and the De Lanceys (also spelled Delancey and De-Lancey). Lewis Morris, a wealthy, aristocratic landowner, was chief justice of the Supreme Court. His opposition was Stephen De Lancey, a businessman with a profitable trade connection in Canada who used his position in the assembly to lobby for the merchant class. The governor, William Burnet, wanted to put an end to the sending of manufactured goods to the French in Canada because the French were using the goods in trade with the Indians and Burnet did not want the Indians so closely allied with the French. Morris led the floor fight in the assembly for the Burnet faction; he lost. In a more personal maneuver, Morris hinted to Burnet that De Lancey, a Frenchman by birth, might be holding a seat in the Assembly illegally. He lost that round, too, and when Burnet was replaced by Governor John Montgomerie in 1728, Morris no longer had entrée into the governor's office.

Montgomerie's death in 1731 set in motion the complicated chain of events that ended in Zenger's arrest and trial; Zenger himself was only peripherally involved. In the interim between Montgomerie's death and the arrival of his successor, affairs of the colony were administered by the president of the Council, Rip Van Dam. The new governor, William Cosby, arrived in New York on 1 August 1732, and produced orders from the king entitling Cosby to half of the monies Van Dam had collected.

Van Dam, figuring that Cosby had also been collecting money in the period between his appointment and his arrival, said that Cosby actually owed him £ 3,000, if all were divided equally. Cosby wanted to sue Van Dam but hesitated to do so before a jury, fearing that popular sentiment would lie with Van Dam; nor could he take the case to chancery, because he himself would have been the presiding official. Cosby made an ill-advised decision to make the Supreme Court justices Barons of the Exchequer, and he filed suit against Van Dam in this ad hoc court of equity. The justices who were to hear the case were Morris, James De Lancey—son of Stephen De Lancey—and Frederick Philipse.

Van Dam's attorneys, James Alexander and William Smith, argued that the governor did not have the authority to create the court. Morris agreed with them and refused to hear the case, an action that infuriated Cosby. The governor wrote Morris, demanding a copy of his remarks from the bench, and Morris responded by not only sending Cosby a copy but having the remarks published as well.

Without consulting the Council, Cosby removed Morris from the Supreme Court and named James De Lancey chief justice in his place. Political

battle lines were now clearly drawn between Cosby's court party and the growing popular party. Knowing that Bradford's *Gazette* could not be counted on to print their side of the conflict, Cosby's opponents determined to publish their own newspaper through Zenger's print shop. Zenger probably entered the venture for financial rather than political reasons.

In fairness to Bradford, it cannot be said that he was in total agreement with the court party. However, his position as official printer in the colony prevented him from having any control over what Cosby chose to see in print. When Cosby installed Francis Harison as editor of the *Gazette*, Bradford had no choice in the matter. Harison was not particularly bright, a condition he balanced by not being particularly ethical, either. Buranelli says of Harison, "On more than one occasion he showed a dishonesty and a stupidity so startling as to rouse wonder that anyone ever trusted him with responsibility."

Thus, on one side was the *Gazette*, edited by Harison, used by the Cosby faction, and published by Bradford, a master printer; on the other side was the *New-York Weekly Journal*, probably edited by James Alexander—although he was never identified as the editor in print—and published by Zenger, a second-rate, struggling printer with a history of business failures.

On 5 November 1733 Zenger printed the first issue of the *Journal*, "containing the freshest Advices, Foreign and Domestic." The domestic news lead that day was a first-hand report of the 29 October election in Westchester at which the sheriff, a Cosby loyalist, had contrived to insure defeat for the popular party candidate, Morris, the deposed chief justice. By tradition, in elections Quakers had been allowed to circumvent their prohibition against "swearing" an oath by "affirming." The sheriff, however, refused to let anyone vote who would not swear, thus disfranchising thirty-eight Quaker supporters of Morris. The ploy failed; Morris won even without the Quaker vote and returned to political power as a member of the assembly.

The *Journal,* a four-page folio appearing each Monday, quickly became popular; some early issues ran three editions. Alexander was something of a journalist already, having published articles in the *Gazette* before the Van Dam controversy, and he was well read in the ideas of freedom of the press. Drawing heavily on the theories and content of *Cato's Letters,* published in the *British Journal* and the *London Journal* in the early 1720s by Thomas

THE
New-York Weekly JOURNAL.

Containing the frefheft Advices, Foreign, and Domeftick.

MUNDAY April 8th, 1734.

New-Brunfwick, March 27, 1734.
Mr. *Zenger*;

I Was at a public Houfe fome Days fince in Company with fome Perfons that came from *New-York* : Moft of them complain'd of the Deadnefs of Trade : fome of them laid it to the Account of the Repeal of the *Tonnage Aĉt*, which they faid was done to gratify the Refentment of fome in *New-York* in order to diftrefs Governour *Burnet*; but which has been almoft the Ruine of that Town, by paying the *Bermudians* about *l.* 12,000 a Year to export thofe Commodities which might be carried in their own Bottoms, and the Money arifing by the Freight fpent in *New-York*. They faid, that the *Bermudians* were an induftrious frugal People, who bought no one Thing in *New-York*, but lodg'd the whole Freight Money in their own Ifland, by which Means, fince the Repeal of that Aĉt, there has been taken from *New-York* above *l.* 90,000 and all this to gratify Pique and Refentment. But this is not all ; this Money being carried away, which would otherwife have circulated in this Province and City, and have been paid to the Baker, the Brewer, the Smith, the Carpenter, the Ship-Wright, the Boat-Man, the Farmer, the Shop-Keeper, *&c.* has deadned our Trade in all its Branches, and forc'd our induftrious Poor to feek other Habitations; fo that within thefe three Years there has been above 300 Perfons have left *New-York*; the Houfes ftand empty, and there is as many Houfes as would make one whole Street with Bills upon their Doors : And this has been as great a Hurt as the Carrying away the Money, and is occafioned by it, and all degrees of Men feel it, from the Merchant down to the Carman. And (adds he) it is the induftrious Poor is the Support of any Country, and the difcouraging the poor Tradesmen is the Means of Ruining any Country. Another replies, It is the exceffive High Wages you Tradesmen take prevents your being imployed : learn to be contented with lefs Wages, we fhall be able to build, and then no need to employ *Bermudians*. Very fine, replied the firft, now the Money is gone you bid us take lefs Wages, when you have nothing to give us, and there is nothing to do. Says another, I know no Body gets Eftates with us but the Lawyers ; we are almoft come to that Pafs, that an Acre of Land can't be conveyed under half an Acre of Parchment. The Fees are not fetled by our Legiflature, & every Body takes what they pleafe ; and we find it better to bear the Difeafe than to apply for a Remedy thats worfe : I hope (faid he) our Affembly will take this Matter into Confideration ; efpecially fince our late Judge hath prov'd *no Fees are lawful but what are fettled by them.* I own a fmall Veffel, and there is a Fee for a
Lett-pafs.

Front page of Zenger's New-York Weekly Journal

Gordon and John Trenchard, Alexander kept up a steady barrage of articles on freedom of the press and responsible government. Readers also delighted in the frequent gibes at Harison, who was no match for the wit and intelligence behind the *Journal.*

By keeping Cosby's administrative blunders in the public eye, the popular party was making it increasingly difficult for the governor to maintain control of the colony. Van Dam escalated the controversy by publishing his case, detailing the unscrupulous methods Cosby had employed against him. With Zenger doing the printing, Van Dam circulated a pamphlet, *Articles of Complaint,* in New York and in London, listing thirty-four charges against Cosby.

Losing the battle of words, Cosby countered by seeking a charge of libel. On 15 January 1734 Chief Justice De Lancey charged the grand jury, saying: "The Authors are not certainly known, and yet it is an easy Matter to guess who they are, that by making Use of Mr. Van Dam's Name, have gain'd some credit among the common People, which they were not wont to have, and never thought to have deserved." The grand jury refused to return an indictment.

After the 29 September 1734 (St. Michael's Day) election ended in victory for two popular party candidates, ballads were circulated in celebration. On 15 October De Lancey again tried to obtain an indictment for libel. "You must have heard of two Scandalous Songs that are handed about, it is your Duty to enquire the Author, Printer and Publisher of them. Sometimes heavy, half-witted Men get a knack of Rhyming, but it is Time to break them of it, when they grow Abusive, Insolent, and Mischievous with it." De Lancey and Philipse ordered that, since no one could identify the author or printer, the ballads be burned before City Hall by the hangman. The grand jury again refused to return an indictment.

Meanwhile, Zenger's business was better than ever. In addition to printing the pamphlets, he enjoyed an increasing *Journal* circulation. In issue number twelve Zenger included a message to his readers: "I must acknowledge my Obligations to you to be such, that you do so plentifully supply me, that tho for some Weeks past I have used my smallest Letter, and to put as much into a Paper as was in my Power, yet I have now Supplies sufficient to fill above seven weekly Papers more. I have thought of publishing a Thursdays Journal weekly for the next Quarter."

With success, however, came accountability.

Zenger was the only person involved in the newspaper war who could not hide behind a pen name. The *Journal* was, for all practical purposes, Zenger's paper. The court party had failed twice to get grand jury indictments for libel; now the council tried another tactic. The council sent *Journal* issues 7, 47, 48, and 49 to the assembly, saying that the papers were seditious and asking for a committee from the assembly to examine them. The committee then requested the assembly to have the papers burned by the hangman. The papers were returned to the council on 2 November and three days later the sheriff delivered the council's order to the court of quarter sessions, directing the hangman to burn the four papers on 6 November. The court would not allow the order to be entered into the records. When the sheriff asked the court for compliance on 6 November, the alderman protested that the order was illegal and refused to direct the hangman to burn the papers. The sheriff then ordered his own servant to burn them; according to Zenger's own report, the event was attended by "Mr. Recorder [Harison], Jeremiah Dunbar, Esq.; and several of the Officers of the Garrison."

Zenger was arrested on Sunday, 17 November, on a council warrant "for printing and publishing several Seditious Libels dispersed throughout his Journals . . . as having in them many Things, tending to raise Factions and Tumults, among the People of this Province, inflaming their Minds with Contempt of His Majesty's Government, and greatly disturbing the Peace thereof."

With Zenger in jail, no *Journal* was printed on 18 November, but by the next week his wife had taken over the job. Zenger wrote to his subscribers in the 25 November issue that he had been denied the opportunity to communicate, either in person or in writing, until Wednesday after his arrest. "I have had since that time [his hearing on Wednesday] the Liberty of Speaking through the Hole of the Door, to my Wife and Servants by which I doubt not yo'l think me sufficiently Excused for not sending my last weeks *Journall."* Zenger's bail was set at £400, although he stated that his net worth was not more than £40, and he was held until 28 January 1735, at which time he hoped to be released. However, he was charged with printing "false, scandalous, malicious, and seditious" material in issues 13 and 23, and kept imprisoned until the trial began in April.

On 15 April Zenger's counsel, William Smith and Alexander, challenged their old adversaries De

Broadside containing two ballads in celebration of the popular party victory in the St. Michael's Day election in New York in 1734. Since neither the author nor the printer could be identified, the government ordered the ballads to be burned in front of City Hall.

Lancey and Philipse by trying to file exceptions to their commissions to the Supreme Court. De Lancey responded by disbarring Alexander and Smith. The defense was quietly handed over to Andrew Hamilton, a formidable attorney from Philadelphia, and his entry into the case was kept secret from the court until the trial began on 5 August 1735.

Hamilton's background is a mystery. Sources put his age at the time of the Zenger trial at between sixty and eighty. A Scot like Alexander, Hamilton used the surname Trent when he first came to the colonies, and it is not certain why he left Scotland. He married into a wealthy family in America, went back to England to study law at Gray's Inn, and on his return to Pennsylvania was appointed to the council and elected to the assembly. He was well known in the colonies for his legal expertise and especially for his opposition to gubernatorial meddling in the judicial system.

Neither De Lancey nor Attorney General Richard Bradley was prepared for Hamilton's response to the reading of the charges. The court's case rested solely on the point of whether or not Zenger had printed the two papers in question. Hamilton admitted that point without argument. Bradley sensed a propitious turn of events, dismissed the witnesses, and assumed a victory for the king. "For supposing they [the articles] were true, the Law says that they are not the less libellous for that; nay indeed the Law says, their being true is an Aggravation of the Crime."

Bradley had fallen into Hamilton's trap, for what Hamilton wanted was a chance to present truth as a defense against libel. Theretofore, the act of printing and publishing was enough to prove libel, but now Hamilton told Bradley, "You will have something more to do, before you make my Client a Libeller; for the words themselves must be libellous, that is false, scandalous, and seditious, or else we are not guilty."

De Lancey, of course, would not admit truth as evidence; but Hamilton had intended from the beginning to present his defense to the jury, not to the bench. Addressing the jury directly, Hamilton told them that the verdict was in reality up to them: "The [Law] supposes you to be summoned, out of the neighborhood where the Fact is Alleged to be committed; and the Reason of your being taken out of the Neighborhood is, because you are supposed to have the best Knowledge of the fact that is to be tried."

The jury found Zenger not guilty.

That night, 5 August 1735, forty citizens at-tended a dinner at the Black Horse Tavern in Hamilton's honor, and as he left the harbor the next day to return to Philadelphia several ships fired salutes. Zenger, whose name has become synonymous with freedom of the press, did not attend the dinner at the Black Horse because De Lancey did not release him from prison until the next day.

Zenger published a forty-page folio account of his case and trial, edited by James Alexander, in 1736; four editions were published in London in 1738, and one each in Lancaster, Pennsylvania, and in Boston. The pamphlet was republished in New York in 1770 when Alexander McDougall was charged with libeling the New York Assembly.

In 1737 Zenger was appointed public printer in New York and was also made public printer in New Jersey in 1738. He died 28 July 1746, survived by Anna and six children, according to his obituary notice in the 6 August *Evening Post*. He is believed to be buried in Trinity Churchyard.

Zenger's son John married in 1741 and Pieter, a son of the second marriage, married in 1751, but no records exist of their descendants; the male line of the Zenger family apparently ended when they died. There were descendants of Zenger's daughters Elizabeth and Catherine. Elizabeth married a weaver named John George Kook in 1745. Catherine, who lived to be ninety-eight, married Matthias Lane and lived in Camden, New Jersey. John Peter and Anna Zenger had three other children of whom there is no record.

As she had done during Zenger's imprisonment, Anna Zenger published the *Journal* alone until December 1748, when she turned the business over to John. The *Journal* ceased publication in 1751.

No one involved in the Zenger trial, not Hamilton or Alexander and certainly not Zenger, had any idea of the far-reaching impact the case would have. Their aim was to get Zenger out of jail and to keep publishing the *Journal*. In accomplishing that, they opened the door to a new definition of libel, they made truth a viable defense against libel charges, and they reinforced the right of a journalist to protect his sources. As historian Vincent Buranelli said, "As time passes we understand more exactly just how great a blow it would have been if Governor Cosby had been able to kill the magnificent pioneering experiment in independent journalism that the *Journal* was."

References:

James Alexander, *A Brief Narrative of the Trial of John Peter Zenger*, edited by Stanley Nider Katz

Letter from Zenger thanking Andrew Hamilton for securing his acquittal on charges of seditious libel (Livingston Rutherford,
John Peter Zenger, *1941)*

(Cambridge: Belknap Press of Harvard University Press, 1972);

John Almon, *The Trial of John Peter Zenger, of New York, Printer* (San Francisco: Sutro Branch, California State Library, Occasional Papers, English Series No. 7, 1940);

Vincent Buranelli, ed., *The Trial of Peter Zenger* (Westport, Conn.: Greenwood Press, 1975);

Livingston Rutherfurd, *John Peter Zenger* (Gloucester, Mass.: Peter Smith, 1941).

Checklist for Further Reading

Abrams, Alan E., ed. *Journalist Biographies Master Index*. Detroit: Gale Research, 1979.

Alexander, James. *A Brief Narrative of the Case and Trial of John Peter Zenger, Printer of the New York Weekly Journal*. Cambridge: Harvard University Press, 1963.

Ames, William E. "Federal Patronage and the Washington D.C. Press." *Journalism Quarterly*, 49 (Spring 1972): 22-30.

Anderson, Arlow William. *The Immigrant Takes His Stand: The Norwegian-American Press & Public Affairs, 1847-1872*. Northfield, Minn.: Norwegian-American Historical Association, 1953.

Andrews, J. Cutler. *The North Reports the Civil War*. Pittsburgh: University of Pittsurgh Press, 1955.

Andrews. *The South Reports the Civil War*. Princeton: Princeton University Press, 1970.

Armstrong, Robert D. *Nevada Printing History: A Bibliography of Imprints and Publications 1858-1880*. Reno: University of Nevada Press, 1981.

Arndt, Karl J. R., and May E. Olson. *German-American Press Research from the American Revolution to the Bicentennial*, volume 3 of *The German Language Press of the Americas*. Detroit: Gale Research, 1980.

Bailyn, Bernard, and John B. Hench. *The Press and the American Revolution*. Worcester, Mass.: American Antiquarian Society, 1980.

Bartow, Edith Merwin. *News and These United States*. New York: Funk & Wagnalls, 1952.

Baumgartner, Apollinaris W. *Catholic Journalism: A Study of Its Development in the United States, 1789-1930*. New York: Columbia University Press, 1931.

Beasley, Maurine H. *The First Women Washington Correspondents*. Washington, D.C.: George Washington University, 1976.

Beasley, and Sheila Silver. *Women in Media: A Documentary Source Book*. Washington, D.C.: Women's Institute for Freedom of the Press, 1977.

Becker, Stephen. *Comic Art in America: A Social History of the Funnies, The Political Cartoons, Magazine Humor, Sporting Cartoons, and Animated Cartoons*. New York: Simon & Schuster, 1959.

Bend, Donovan H., and Reynolds W. McLeod, eds. *Newsletters to Newspapers: Eighteenth Century Journalism*. Morgantown: West Virginia University, 1977.

Bent, Silas. *Newspaper Crusaders: A Neglected Story*. New York & London: Whittlesey House, McGraw-Hill, 1939.

Berger, Meyer. *The Story of the New York Times: The First 100 Years 1851-1951*. New York: Simon & Schuster, 1951.

Bleyer, Willard Grosvenor. *Main Currents in the History of American Journalism*. Boston: Houghton Mifflin, 1927.

Boston, Ray. "The Impact of 'Foreign Liars' on the American Press (1790-1800)." *Journalism Quarterly,* 50 (Winter 1973): 722-730.

Brantley, Rabun Lee. *Georgia Journalism of the Civil War Period.* Nashville: George Peabody College of Teachers, 1929.

Bremner, John B. *HTK: A Study in News Headlines.* Topeka, Kans.: Palidrome, 1972.

Brendon, Piers. *The Life and Death of the Press Barons.* New York: Atheneum, 1983.

Brigham, Clarence S. *History and Bibliography of American Newspapers, 1690-1820,* 2 volumes. Hamden, Conn.: Archon Books, 1962.

Brigham. *Journals and Journeymen: A Contribution to the History of Early American Newspapers.* Philadelphia: University of Pennsylvania Press, 1950.

Brucker, Herbert. *The Changing American Newspaper.* New York: Columbia University Press, 1937.

Bryan, Carter R. "Negro Journalism in America Before Emancipation." *Journalism Monographs,* no. 12 (September 1969): 1-33.

Bullock, Penelope L. *The Afro-American Periodical Press, 1839-1909.* Baton Rouge: Louisiana State University Press, 1981.

Carter, Hodding. *Their Words Were Bullets: The Southern Press in War, Reconstruction, and Peace.* Athens: University of Georgia Press, 1969.

Cater, Douglass. *The Fourth Branch of Government.* Boston: Houghton Mifflin, 1959.

Chafee, Zechariah, Jr. *Free Speech in the United States.* Cambridge: Harvard University Press, 1946.

Chafee. *Government and Mass Communications,* 2 volumes. Chicago: University of Chicago Press, 1947.

Chidsey, Donald Barr. *The Loyalists: The Story of Those Americans Who Fought Against Independence.* New York: Crown, 1973.

Collins, Jean. *She Was There: Stories of Pioneering Women Journalists.* New York: Messner, 1980.

Cook, Elizabeth C. *Literary Influences in Colonial Newspapers 1704-1750.* New York: Columbia University Press, 1912.

Covert, Cathy. " 'Passion Is Ye Prevailing Motive': the Feud Behind the Zenger Case." *Journalism Quarterly,* 50 (Spring 1973): 3-10.

Crary, Catherine S. *The Price of Loyalty: Tory Writing from the Revolutionary Era.* New York: McGraw-Hill, 1973.

Crozier, Emmet. *Yankee Reporters, 1861-65.* New York: Oxford University Press, 1956.

Cullen, Maurice R. "Middle-Class Democracy and the Press in Colonial America." *Journalism Quarterly,* 46 (Autumn 1969): 531-535.

Daniels, Jonathan. *They Will Be Heard: America's Crusading Newspaper Editors.* New York: McGraw-Hill, 1965.

Danky, James P., ed., and Maureen E. Hady, compiler. *Native American Periodicals and Newspapers 1828-1982.* Westport, Conn.: Greenwood Press, 1984.

Dann, Martin E., ed. *The Black Press: 1827-1890: The Quest for National Identity.* New York: Putnam's, 1971.

Davidson, Philip. *Propaganda and the American Revolution 1763-1783.* Chapel Hill: University of North Carolina Press, 1941.

Demaree, Albert Lowther. *The American Agricultural Press, 1819-1860.* New York: Columbia University Press, 1941.

Demeter, Richard L. *Primer, Presses and Composing Sticks: Women Printers of the Colonial Period.* Hicksville, N.Y.: Exposition Press, 1979.

Dennis, Everette E., and Melvin Dennis. "100 Years of Political Cartooning." *Journalism History,* 1 (Spring 1974): 6-10.

Detweiler, Frederick G. *The Negro Press in the United States.* Chicago: University of Chicago Press, 1922.

Dillon, Merton L. *The Abolitionists: The Growth of a Dissenting Minority.* DeKalb, Ill.: Northern Illinois University Press, 1974.

Donald, Robert. "Sunday Newspapers in the United States." *Universal Review,* 8 (September 1890): 8-89.

Drechsel, Robert E. *Newsmaking in the Trial Courts.* New York: Longman, 1983.

Dumond, Dwight L. *Southern Editorials on Secession.* New York & London: Century, 1931.

Duniway, Clyde A. *The Development of Freedom of the Press in Massachusetts.* New York & London: Longmans, Green, 1906.

Emery, Edwin. *The Story of America as Reported by Its Newspapers, 1690-1965.* New York: Simon & Schuster, 1965.

Emery, Edwin, and Michael Emery. *The Press and America: An Interpretative History of the Mass Media,* fourth edition. Englewood Cliffs, N.J.: Prentice-Hall, 1978.

Emery, Michael C., R. Smith Schuneman, and Edwin Emery, eds. *America's Front-Page News, 1690-1970.* New York: Doubleday, 1970.

Ernst, Morris L. *The First Freedom.* New York: Macmillan, 1946.

Farrar, Ronald T., and John D. Stevens, eds. *Mass Media and the National Experience.* New York: Harper & Row, 1971.

Faÿ, Bernard. *Notes on the American Press at the End of the Eighteenth Century.* New York: The Grolier Club, 1927.

Ford, Edwin H., and Edwin Emery, eds. *Highlights in the History of the American Press: A Book of Readings.* Minneapolis: University of Minnesota Press, 1954.

Forsyth, David P. *The Business Press in America.* Philadelphia: Chilton, 1964.

Frontier Press Issue, *Journalism History,* 7 (Summer 1980).

Gordon, George N. *The Communications Revolution: A History of Mass Media in the United States.* New York: Hastings House, 1977.

Gramling, Oliver. *AP: The Story of News.* New York & Toronto: Farrar & Rinehart, 1940.

Greene, Laurence. *America Goes to Press: The News of Yesterday.* Indianapolis: Bobbs-Merrill, 1936.

Gregory, Winifred, ed. *American Newspapers, 1821-1936: A Union List of Files Available in the United States and Canada.* New York: Wilson, 1937.

Hage, George S. *Newspapers on the Minnesota Frontier, 1849-1860.* St. Paul: Minnesota Historical Society, 1967.

Hagelweide, Gert, ed. *German Newspapers in Libraries and Archives: A Survey.* Düsseldorf: Droste Verlag, 1974.

Harper, Robert S. *Lincoln and the Press.* New York: McGraw-Hill, 1951.

Hart, Jim Allee. *The Developing Views on the News: Editorial Syndrome 1500-1800.* Carbondale: Southern Illinois University Press, 1970.

Hess, Stephen, and Milton Kaplan. *The Ungentlemanly Art: A History of American Political Cartoons.* New York: Macmillan, 1968.

Hester, Al, Susan Parker Hume, and Christopher Bickers. "Foreign News in Colonial North American Newspapers, 1764-1775." *Journalism Quarterly,* 57 (Spring 1980): 18-22.

Hocking, William E. *Freedom of the Press: A Framework of Principle.* Chicago: University of Chicago Press, 1947.

Hohenberg, John. *Foreign Correspondence: The Great Reporters and Their Times.* New York: Columbia University Press, 1964.

Hollis, Patricia. *The Pauper Press: A Study in Working-Class Radicalism of the 1830s.* London: Oxford University Press, 1970.

Horan, James D. *Mathew Brady: Historian with a Camera.* New York: Crown, 1955.

Horn, Maurice, and Richard E. Marshall, eds. *The World Encyclopedia of Cartoons,* 2 volumes. Detroit: Gale Research, 1980.

Hudson, Frederic. *Journalism in the United States, from 1690 to 1872.* New York: Harper, 1873.

Hughes, Helen M. *News and the Human Interest Story.* Chicago: University of Chicago Press, 1940.

Hutt, Allen. *The Changing Newspaper: Typographic Trends in Britain and America, 1622-1972.* London: Gordon Fraser, 1973.

Huxford, Gary. "The English Libertarian Tradition in the Colonial Newspaper." *Journalism Quarterly,* 45 (Winter 1968): 677-686.

Irwin, Will. *The American Newspaper,* edited by Clifford F. Weigle and David G. Clark. Ames: Iowa State University Press, 1969.

Jakes, John. *Great Women Reporters.* New York: Putnam's, 1969.

Jensen, Merrill, ed. *Tracts of the American Revolution 1763-1776.* Indianapolis: Bobbs-Merrill, 1967.

Jones, Robert W. *Journalism in the United States.* New York: Dutton, 1947.

Karolevitz, Robert F. *Newspapering in the Old West.* Seattle: Superior Publishing Company, 1965.

Katz, William A. "The Western Printer and His Publications, 1850-90." *Journalism Quarterly,* 44 (Winter 1967): 708-714.

Keller, Morton. *The Art and Politics of Thomas Nast.* New York: Oxford University Press, 1968.

Kessler, Lauren. *The Dissident Press History.* Beverly Hills, Cal.: Sage, 1984.

Klement, Frank L. *The Copperheads in the Middle West.* Chicago: University of Chicago Press, 1960.

Knight, Oliver. *Following the Indian Wars: The Story of the Newspaper Correspondents among the Indian Campaigners.* Norman: University of Oklahoma Press, 1960.

Knightley, Philip. *The First Casualty: From the Crimea to Vietnam: The War Correspondent as Hero, Propagandist, and Myth Maker.* New York: Harcourt Brace Jovanovich, 1975; revised edition, London: Quartet, 1982.

Knights, Peter R. " 'Competition' in the U.S. Daily Newspaper Industry, 1865-68." *Journalism Quarterly,* 45 (Autumn 1968): 473-480.

Kobre, Sidney. *Development of American Journalism.* Dubuque, Iowa: Brown, 1969.

Kobre. *The Development of the Colonial Newspaper.* Pittsburgh: Colonial Press, 1944.

Kobre. "The First American Newspaper: A Product of Environment." *Journalism Quarterly,* 17 (December 1940): 335-345.

Lee, Alfred McClung. *The Daily Newspaper in America: The Evolution of a Social Instrument.* New York: Macmillan, 1937.

Lee, James Melvin. *History of American Journalism.* Boston & New York: Houghton Mifflin, 1917.

Levy, Leonard W., ed. *Freedom of the Press from Zenger to Jefferson: Early American Libertarian Theories.* Indianapolis: Bobbs-Merrill, 1966.

Liston, Robert A. *The Right to Know: Censorship in America.* New York: Watts, 1973.

Lofton, John. *The Press as Guardian of the First Amendment.* Columbia: University of South Carolina Press, 1980.

Lutnick, Solomon. *The American Revolution and the British Press 1775-1783.* Columbia: University of Missouri Press, 1967.

Lyle, Jack, ed. *The Black American and the Press.* Los Angeles: Ward Ritchie, 1968.

Lyon, Peter. *The Wild, Wild West.* New York: Funk & Wagnalls, 1969.

Lyon, William H. *The Pioneer Editor in Missouri, 1808-1860.* Columbia: University of Missouri Press, 1965.

Marbut, Frederick B. *News from the Capital: The Story of Washington Reporting.* Carbondale: Southern Illinois University Press, 1971.

Marty, Martin E., John G. Deedy, Jr., and David W. Silverman. *The Religious Press in America.* New York: Holt, Rinehart & Winston, 1963.

Marzolf, Marion. *Up from the Footnote: A History of Women Journalists.* New York: Hastings House, 1977.

Mathews, Joseph J. *Reporting the Wars.* Minneapolis: University of Minnesota Press, 1957.

McLaws, Monte Burr. *Spokesman for the Kingdom: Early Mormon Journalism and the Deseret News, 1830-1898.* Provo: Brigham Young University Press, 1977.

McMurtrie, Douglas C. *The Beginnings of the American Newspaper.* Chicago: Black Cat Press, 1935.

McMurtrie. *A History of Printing in the United States.* New York: Bowker, 1936.

Meredith, Roy. *Mr. Lincoln's Camera Man, Mathew B. Brady.* New York: Scribners, 1946.

Moran, James. *Printing Presses: History and Development from the Fifteenth Century to Modern Times.* Berkeley: University of California Press, 1973.

Mott, Frank Luther. *American Journalism: A History: 1690-1960,* third edition. New York: Macmillan, 1962.

Mott, and Ralph D. Casey, eds. *Interpretations of Journalism: A Book of Readings.* New York: Crofts, 1937.

Murphy, James E., and Sharon M. Murphy. *Let My People Know: American Indian Journalism 1828-1978.* Norman: University of Oklahoma Press, 1981.

Murrell, William. *A History of American Graphic Humor,* 2 volumes. New York: Whitney Museum of American Art, 1933, 1938.

Myers, John. *Print in a Wild Land.* Garden City: Doubleday, 1967.

Nelson, Harold L., ed. *Freedom of the Press from Hamilton to the Warren Court.* Indianapolis: Bobbs-Merrill, 1967.

Nelson, and Dwight L. Teeter, Jr. *Law of Mass Communications: Freedom and Control of Print and Broadcast Media,* fourth edition. Mineola, N.Y.: Foundation Press, 1982.

Nevins, Allan. "American Journalism and Its Historical Treatment." *Journalism Quarterly,* 36 (Fall 1959): 411-412.

Nevins. *American Press Opinion, Washington to Coolidge: A Documentary Record of Editorial Leadership and Criticism, 1785-1927.* Boston: Heath, 1928.

Nevins, and Frank Weitenkamp. *A Century of Political Cartoons: Caricature in the United States from 1800 to 1900.* New York: Scribners, 1944.

North, S. N. D. *History and Present Condition of the Newspapers and Periodical Press of the United States.* Washington, D.C.: Government Printing Office, 1884.

Oak, Vishnu V. *The Negro Newspaper.* Yellow Springs, Ohio: Printed by the Antioch Press, 1948.

O'Brien, Frank M. *The Story of The Sun. New York, 1833-1918.* New York: Doran, 1918.

Ogilvie, William Edward. *Pioneer Agricultural Journalists: Brief Biographical Sketches of Some of the Early Editors in the Field of Agricultural Journalism.* Chicago: Arthur G. Leonard, 1927.

Paine, Albert Bigelow. *Th. Nast, His Period and His Pictures.* New York: Macmillan, 1904; London: Macmillan, 1904.

Paneth, Donald. *The Encyclopedia of American Journalism.* New York: Facts on File, 1983.

Park, Robert E. *The Immigrant Press and Its Control.* New York & London: Harper, 1922.

Park, Ernest W. Burgess, and Roderick D. McKenzie. *The City.* Chicago: University of Chicago Press, 1928.

Payne, George H. *History of Journalism in the United States.* New York & London: Appleton, 1920.

Penn, I. Garland. *The Afro-American Press and Its Editors.* Springfield, Mass.: Willey, 1891.

Perkins, Howard Cecil, ed. *Northern Editorials on Secession.* New York & London: D. Appleton-Century, 1942.

Pickett, Calder M. *Voices of the Past: Key Documents in the History of American Journalism.* Columbus, Ohio: Grid Publishing, 1977.

Pollard, James E. *The Presidents and the Press.* New York: Macmillan, 1947.

Presbrey, Frank. *The History and Development of Advertising.* Garden City: Doubleday, Doran, 1929.

Price, Warren C. *The Literature of Journalism: An Annotated Bibliography.* Minneapolis: University of Minnesota Press, 1959.

Price, and Calder M. Pickett. *An Annotated Journalism Bibliography 1958-1968.* Minneapolis: University of Minnesota Press, 1970.

Randolph, Ralph J. "The End of Impartiality: *South Carolina Gazette, 1763-75.*" *Journalism Quarterly*, 49 (Winter 1972): 702-709, 720.

Reynolds, Donald E. *Editors Make War: Southern Newspapers in the Secession Crisis.* Nashville, Tenn.: Vanderbilt University Press, 1970.

Rosewater, Victor. *History of Coöperative News-Gathering in the United States.* New York & London: Appleton, 1930.

Ross, Ishbel. *Ladies of the Press: The Story of Women in Journalism by an Insider.* New York & London: Harper, 1936.

Rucker, Bryce W. *The First Freedom.* Carbondale: Southern Illinois University Press, 1968.

Rutland, Robert A. *The Newsmongers: Journalism in the Life of the Nation, 1690-1972.* New York: Dial Press, 1973.

Ruud, Charles A. "Limits on the 'Freed' Press of 18th and 19th Century Europe." *Journalism Quarterly*, 56 (Autumn 1979): 521-530, 693.

Salmon, Lucy M. *The Newspaper and Authority.* New York: Oxford University Press, 1923.

Schilpp, Madelon Golden, and Sharon M. Murphy. *Great Women of the Press.* Carbondale: Southern Illinois University Press, 1983.

Schlesinger, Arthur M. *Prelude to Independence: The Newspaper War on Britain, 1764-1776.* New York: Knopf, 1958.

Schudson, Michael. *Discovering the News: A Social History of American Newspapers.* New York: Basic Books, 1978.

Schudson. *The News Media and the Democratic Process.* New York: Aspen Institute for Humanistic Studies, 1983.

Schuyler, Livingston R. *The Liberty of the Press in the American Colonies before the Revolutionary War.* New York: Thomas Whittaker, 1905.

Schwarzlose, Richard A. "Harbor News Association: The Formal Origin of the AP." *Journalism Quarterly,* 45 (Summer 1968): 253-260.

Schwarzlose. "The Nation's First Wire Service: Evidence Supporting a Footnote." *Journalism Quarterly,* 57 (Winter 1980): 555-562.

Shaw, Donald Lewis. "At the Crossroads: Change and Continuity in American Press News, 1820-1860." *Journalism History,* 8 (Summer 1981): 38-50.

Shaw. "News Bias and the Telegraph: A Study of Historical Change." *Journalism Quarterly,* 44 (Spring 1967): 3-12.

Siebert, Frederick Seaton. *Freedom of the Press in England, 1476-1776: The Rise and Decline of Government Controls.* Urbana: University of Illinois Press, 1952.

Smith, Culver H. *The Press, Politics and Patronage: The American Government's Use of Newspapers, 1789-1875.* Athens: University of Georgia Press, 1977.

Smith, James Morton. *Freedom's Fetters: The Alien and Sedition Laws and American Civil Liberties.* Ithaca, N.Y.: Cornell University Press, 1956.

Snyder, Louis L., and Richard B. Morris, eds. *A Treasury of Great Reporting: "Literature Under Pressure" from the Sixteenth Century to Our Own Time,* second edition. New York: Simon & Schuster, 1962.

Starr, Louis M. *Bohemian Brigade: Civil War Newsmen in Action.* New York: Knopf, 1954.

Stein, Meyer L. *Under Fire: The Story of American War Correspondents.* New York: Messner, 1968.

Stevens, John D. "Congressional History of the 1798 Sedition Law." *Journalism Quarterly,* 43 (Summer 1966): 247-256.

Stevens, and Hazel Dicken-Garcia. *Communication History.* Beverly Hills, Cal.: Sage, 1980.

Stewart, Donald H. *The Opposition Press of the Federalist Period.* Albany: State University of New York Press, 1969.

Stratton, Porter A. *The Territorial Press of New Mexico 1834-1912.* Albuquerque: University of New Mexico Press, 1969.

Taft, William H. *Newspapers as Tools for Historians.* Columbia, Mo.: Lucas, 1970.

Tankard, James W., Jr. "Public Opinion Polling by Newspapers in the Presidential Election Campaign of 1824." *Journalism Quarterly,* 49 (Summer 1972): 361-365.

Tebbel, John W. *The Compact History of the American Newspaper.* New York: Hawthorn, 1963.

Tebbel. *The Media in America.* New York: Thomas Y. Cromwell, 1974.

Teeter, Dwight L. " 'King' Sears, the Mob and Freedom of the Press in New York; 1765-76." *Journalism Quarterly,* 41 (Autumn 1964): 539-544.

Thomas, Isaiah. *The History of Printing in America,* second edition, 2 volumes. Albany, N.Y.: Joel Munsell, printer, 1874.

Thwaites, R. G. "The Ohio Valley Press Before the War of 1812-15." *Proceedings of the American Antiquarian Society,* new series, 19 (April 1909): 309-368.

Walett, Francis G. *Massachusetts Newspapers and the Revolutionary Crisis, 1763-1776.* Boston: Massachusetts Bicentennial Commission, 1974.

Walett. *Patriots, Loyalists, and Printers: Bicentennial Articles on the American Revolution.* Worcester, Mass.: American Antiquarian Society, 1976.

Watson, Elmo Scott. *A History of Newspaper Syndicates in the United States, 1865-1935.* Chicago, 1936.

Weeks, Lyman H. *A History of Paper-Manufacturing in the United States, 1690-1916.* New York: Lockwood Trade Journal Co., 1916.

Weisberger, Bernard A. *Reporters for the Union.* Boston: Little, Brown, 1953.

Whisenhunt, Donald W. "The Frontier Newspaper: A Guide to Society and Culture." *Journalism Quarterly,* 45 (Winter 1968): 726-728.

White, Z. L. "Western Journalism." *Harper's,* 77 (October 1888): 678-699.

Wilson, Quintus C. "Confederate Press Association: A Pioneer News Agency." *Journalism Quarterly,* 26 (June 1949): 160-166.

Wittke, Carl. *The German-Language Press in America.* Lexington: University of Kentucky Press, 1957.

Wolseley, Roland E. *The Black Press, U.S.A.* Ames: Iowa State University Press, 1971.

Wood, James Playsted. *The Story of Advertising.* New York: Roland Press, 1958.

Wroth, Lawrence C. *The Colonial Printer.* Portland, Maine: Southworth-Anthoensen Press, 1938.

Wynn Jones, Michael. *The Cartoon History of the American Revolution.* New York: Putnam's, 1975.

Contributors

S. M. W. Bass... *University of Kansas*
Maurine H. Beasley... *University of Maryland*
Margaret A. Blanchard ....*University of North Carolina at Chapel Hill*
Donna Born... *Central Michigan University*
James Boylan....................................*University of Massachusetts—Amherst*
James Stanford Bradshaw...............................*Central Michigan University*
Lea Ann Brown... *Southern Illinois University*
Richard M. Brown...................................*Chapel Hill, North Carolina*
John M. Butler ....*Louisiana State University*
Gary Coll .... *University of Wisconsin-Oshkosh*
Hazel Dicken-Garcia.. *University of Minnesota*
Elizabeth Brown Dickey.................................... *University of South Carolina*
Wallace B. Eberhard .... *University of Georgia*
Kathleen L. Endres .... *Bowling Green State University*
George Everett .... *University of Tennessee*
Mark Fackler .... *Wheaton College*
Charles A. Fair ....*Sam Houston State University*
Frederic B. Farrar ....*Temple University*
Ronald Truman Farrar...................................... *University of Kentucky*
James S. Featherston....................................*Louisiana State University*
Nickieann Fleener .... *University of Utah*
Jean Folkerts .... *Mount Vernon College*
Warren Francke ....*University of Nebraska at Omaha*
Elsie S. Hebert...*Louisiana State University*
Terry Hynes.......................................*California State University, Fullerton*
A. J. Kaul...*University of Southern Mississippi*
Michael Kirkhorn .... *University of Kentucky*
Alfred Lawrence Lorenz....................................*Loyola University in New Orleans*
Marion Marzolf ....*University of Michigan*
Joseph P. McKerns...........................*Southern Illinois University at Carbondale*
Shirley M. Mundt.....................................*Louisiana State University*
Whitney R. Mundt ....*Louisiana State University*
Sharon M. Murphy ....*Marquette University*
David Paul Nord ....*Indiana University*
Daniel W. Pfaff ....*Pennsylvania State University*
Mary Sue F. Poole .... *University of South Carolina*
Henry T. Price .... *University of South Carolina*
Nancy L. Roberts...................................... *University of Minnesota*
Jon A. Roosenraad.................................... *University of Florida*
Richard A. Schwarzlose.................................. *Northwestern University*
Michael Sewell ....*Texas Wesleyan College*
Norman H. Sims .... *University of Massachusetts—Amherst*
Wm. David Sloan..*University of Alabama*
Jeffery A. Smith .... *University of Iowa*
Jo Anne Smith... *University of Florida*
Harry W. Stonecipher........................... *Southern Illinois University*
Harry W. Stonecipher....................*Southern Illinois University at Carbondale*
James Glen Stovall..*University of Alabama*
Dwight L. Teeter, Jr. ....*University of Texas at Austin*
Sallie A. Whelan ....*Louisiana State University*
Roger Yarrington .... *University of Maryland*

Cumulative Index

Dictionary of Literary Biography, Volumes 1-43
Dictionary of Literary Biography Yearbook, 1980-1984
Dictionary of Literary Biography Documentary Series, Volumes 1-4

Cumulative Index

DLB before number: *Dictionary of Literary Biography*, Volumes 1-43
Y before number: *Dictionary of Literary Biography Yearbook*, 1980-1984
DS before number: *Dictionary of Literary Biography Documentary Series*, Volumes 1-4

C

D

G

I

J

K

L

M

N

S

T

Y

Z